**IF FOUND, please notify and arrange return to owner**. This text is an important study guide for the owner's career and/or exam preparation.

Name: _____

Address: _____

City, State, ZIP: _____

Telephone: (_____) _____ E-mail: _____

D1540430

Gleim Publications, Inc., offers five university-level study manuals:

| | |
|---|---|
| *Auditing & Systems Exam Questions and Explanations* . . . . . . . . . . . . . . | $19.95 |
| *Business Law/Legal Studies Exam Questions and Explanations* . . . . . . . . . | 19.95 |
| *Federal Tax Exam Questions and Explanations* . . . . . . . . . . . . . . . . . . | 19.95 |
| *Financial Accounting Exam Questions and Explanations* . . . . . . . . . . . . . | 19.95 |
| *Cost/Managerial Accounting Exam Questions and Explanations* . . . . . . . . . | 19.95 |

*Exam Prep Software also available @ $20 each*

The following is a list of Gleim examination review books:

| | |
|---|---|
| *CIA Review: Part I, Internal Audit's Role in Governance, Risk, and Control* . . . . . . . . . . | $29.95 |
| *CIA Review: Part II, Conducting the Internal Audit Engagement* . . . . . . . . . . | 29.95 |
| *CIA Review: Part III, Business Analysis and Information Technology.* . . . . . . . . . . | 29.95 |
| *CIA Review: Part IV, Business Management Skills* . . . . . . . . . . . . . . . . . . | 29.95 |

*CIA Test Prep* software ($49.95 per section) is also available to complement your study.

| | |
|---|---|
| *CMA/CFM Review: Part 1, Economics, Finance, and Management.* . . . . . . . . . . . . . . . | $26.95 |
| *CFM Review: Part 2CFM, Corporate Financial Management.* . . . . . . . . . . . . . . . | 26.95 |
| *CMA Review: Part 2CMA, Financial Accounting and Reporting.* . . . . . . . . . . . . . . . | 26.95 |
| *CMA/CFM Review: Part 3, Mgmt. Reporting, Analysis, and Behavioral Issues* . . . . . . . . . . | 26.95 |
| *CMA/CFM Review: Part 4, Decision Analysis, Information Systems, and Management Controls.* . . . . | 26.95 |

*CMA/CFM Test Prep* software ($44.95 per section) and *CMA/CFM Review* audios ($69.95 per section) are also available to complement your study.

| | |
|---|---|
| *CPA Review: Financial.* . . . . . . . . . . . . . . . . . . . . . . . . . . . . . . . | $39.95 |
| *CPA Review: Auditing* . . . . . . . . . . . . . . . . . . . . . . . . . . . . . . . | 39.95 |
| *CPA Review: Business* . . . . . . . . . . . . . . . . . . . . . . . . . . . . . . . | 39.95 |
| *CPA Review: Regulation* . . . . . . . . . . . . . . . . . . . . . . . . . . . . . . | 39.95 |

*CPA Test Prep* software ($49.95 per section) and *CPA Review* audios ($89.95 per section) are also available to complement your study.

| | |
|---|---|
| *EA Review: Part 1, Individuals.* . . . . . . . . . . . . . . . . . . . . . . . . . . | $29.95 |
| *EA Review: Part 2, Sole Proprietorships and Partnerships.* . . . . . . . . . . . . . . | 29.95 |
| *EA Review: Part 3, Corporations, Fiduciaries, Estate and Gift Tax, and Trusts* . . . . . . . . | 29.95 |
| *EA Review: Part 4, IRS Administration and Other Topics.* . . . . . . . . . . . . . . | 29.95 |

*EA Test Prep* software ($49.95 per section) is also available to complement your study.

Order forms are provided at the back of this book or contact us at www.gleim.com or (800) 87-GLEIM.

**Groundwood Paper and Highlighters** — This book is printed on high quality groundwood paper. It is lightweight and easy to recycle. We recommend that you purchase a highlighter specifically designed to be non-bleed-through (e.g., Avery *Glidestick*™) at your local office supply store.

## REVIEWERS AND CONTRIBUTORS

Caitlin M. Bourdon, B.A., University of Florida, is our book production coordinator. Ms. Bourdon coordinated the production staff, reviewed the manuscript, and provided production assistance throughout the project.

Kimberly Solvang Hamm, J.D., University of Washington, is our quality control editor. Ms. Hamm reviewed the manuscript, revised it for readability, and provided extensive editorial assistance.

Grady M. Irwin, J.D., is a graduate of the University of Florida College of Law, and he has taught in the University of Florida College of Business. Mr. Irwin provided substantial editorial assistance throughout the project.

Bruce S. Masingil, B.S., Florida International University, is our book production assistant. Mr. Masingil provided assistance throughout the project.

John F. Rebstock, CIA, is a graduate of the Fisher School of Accounting at the University of Florida. Mr. Rebstock reviewed portions of the manuscript.

## A PERSONAL THANKS

This manual would not have been possible without the extraordinary effort and dedication of Rachael Goodwin, Terry Hall, Jean Marzullo, and Teresa Soard, who typed the entire manuscript and all revisions; prepared the camera-ready pages; and drafted, scanned, and laid out the diagrams and illustrations in this book.

The authors also appreciate the production and editorial assistance of Matthew Carty, Katharine Cicatelli, Laura Heston, Nicolas Medina, Eloise Pinto, Chiquita Pratt, Shane Rapp, Mittal Shah, Christina Smart and Jan Strickland.

The authors also appreciate the critical reading assistance of Ben Arundel, Kendra Brewer, Jose Carrasco, Lance Mathew, Christopher North, Dhruven Parikh, Chirag Patel, Christopher Pavilonis, John Taldi, and Keith Williams.

Finally, we appreciate the encouragement, support, and tolerance of our families throughout this project.

# ELEVENTH EDITION

# CIA REVIEW

## PART III

## BUSINESS ANALYSIS AND INFORMATION TECHNOLOGY

by

**Irvin N. Gleim, Ph.D., CPA, CIA, CMA, CFM**

with the assistance of
Grady M. Irwin, J.D.

## ABOUT THE AUTHOR

Irvin N. Gleim is Professor Emeritus in the Fisher School of Accounting at the University of Florida and is a member of the American Accounting Association, Academy of Legal Studies in Business, American Institute of Certified Public Accountants, Association of Government Accountants, Florida Institute of Certified Public Accountants, The Institute of Internal Auditors, and the Institute of Management Accountants. He has had articles published in the *Journal of Accountancy, The Accounting Review,* and *The American Business Law Journal* and is author/coauthor of numerous accounting and aviation books and CPE courses.

**Gleim Publications, Inc.**
P.O. Box 12848
University Station
Gainesville, Florida 32604
(800) 87-GLEIM or (800) 874-5346
(352) 375-0772
FAX: (352) 375-6940
Internet: www.gleim.com
E-mail: admin@gleim.com

This is the first printing of the eleventh edition of *CIA Review: Part III, Business Analysis and Information Technology*. Please e-mail update@gleim.com with CIA III 11-1 included in the subject or text. You will receive our current update as a reply. Updates are available until the next edition is published.

EXAMPLE:

| | |
|---|---|
| To: | update@gleim.com |
| From: | your e-mail address |
| Subject: | CIA III 11-1 |

ISSN: 1547-8041

ISBN: 1-58194-333-4

First Printing: January 2004

## ACKNOWLEDGMENTS FOR PART III

The author is grateful for permission to reproduce the following materials copyrighted by The Institute of Internal Auditors: Certified Internal Auditor Examination Questions and Suggested Solutions, excerpts from *The Practice of Modern Internal Auditing*, *Statements of Responsibilities of Internal Auditors*, *Code of Ethics*, *Standards for the Professional Practice of Internal Auditing*, *Professional Standards Practice Releases*, and *Statements on Internal Auditing Standards*, copyright © 1980 - 1998 by The Institute of Internal Auditors, Inc.

The authors also appreciate and thank the Institute of Certified Management Accountants for permission to use questions from past CMA examination, copyright © 1982 - 1990 by the Institute of Management Accountants.

Visit our website (www.gleim.com) for the latest updates and information on all of our products.

*This publication is designed to provide accurate and authoritative information with regard to the subject matter covered. It is sold with the understanding that the publisher is not engaged in rendering legal, accounting, or other professional service.*

*If legal advice or other expert assistance is required, the services of a competent professional person should be sought.*

*(From a declaration of principles jointly adopted by a Committee of the American Bar Association and a Committee of Publishers.)*

# TABLE OF CONTENTS

# PREFACE

The purpose of this book is to help **you** prepare **yourself** to pass Part III of the CIA examination. The overriding consideration is to provide an inexpensive, effective, and easy-to-use study program. This manual

1. Defines topics tested on Part III of the CIA examination.

2. Includes all recent changes in Part III of the CIA program.

3. Explains how to optimize your grade by analyzing how the CIA exam is constructed and graded.

4. Suggests exam taking techniques to help you maximize your exam score.

5. Outlines all of the subject matter tested on Part III of the CIA exam in 10 easy-to-use study units, including all relevant authoritative pronouncements.

6. Reorganizes past exam questions according to the subunits within each of the 10 study units and presents an intuitively appealing explanation of each objective question answer.

7. Provides an opportunity for professional accountants to obtain CPE credit while preparing to pass the CIA exam. See the opposite page for more information.

Even though Gleim's four-volume *CIA Review* constitutes a complete self-study program for the CIA exam, candidates should consider enrolling in a formal review program. Local IIA chapters throughout the world have, in the past, coordinated CIA review programs and will probably continue to do so. In addition, all candidates should invest in our *CIA Test Prep* software, which is a powerful supplemental study aid to any review books or courses. Call (800) 87-GLEIM for more information.

Thank you for your interest in our materials. We deeply appreciate the thousands of letters and suggestions we have received from CIA, CMA, CFM, and CPA candidates and accounting students during the last four decades.

Please send us your suggestions, comments, and corrections concerning *CIA Review: Part III*. The last page in this book has been designed to help you note corrections and suggestions throughout your study process. It is imperative that we receive your feedback after you take the CIA exam. We pledge to continue to improve the product (with your suggestions, we hope) in the twelfth and subsequent editions.

The outline format and spacing and the question and answer formats are designed to facilitate learning, understanding, and readability. Please read the introduction of this book carefully.

To continue providing our customers with first-rate service, we request that questions about our books and software be sent to us via mail, e-mail, or fax. The appropriate staff member will give each question thorough consideration and a prompt response. Questions concerning orders, prices, shipments, or payments will be handled via telephone by our competent and courteous customer service staff.

Good Luck on the Exam,

*Irvin N. Gleim*

January 2004

# EARN CPE CREDITS WHILE STUDYING FOR THE CIA EXAM

The Gleim approach to CPE is both interactive and intense. You should be continually challenged to answer each question correctly. When you answer a question incorrectly or have difficulty, you should pursue a complete understanding by reading the answer explanation and consulting reference sources as necessary.

We offer CPE credit online that correlates with this Eleventh Edition text. Visit www.gleim.com/accounting/cpe/onlinecpe for more information.

Most of the questions in the study guide were taken from various professional examinations. Each question is revised, adapted, etc., to provide broader, up-to-date coverage of the internal auditing body of technical knowledge. In addition, publisher questions cover material added since examinations became "closed."

Finally, we ask for any supplemental comments, reactions, suggestions, etc., that you may have as you complete our CPE program. Please attach them to the online Course Evaluation or send an e-mail to cpeinfo@gleim.com.

To continue providing our customers with first-rate service, we request that questions about our books and software be sent to us via mail, e-mail, or fax. The appropriate staff member will give each question thorough consideration and a prompt response. Questions concerning orders, prices, shipments, or payments will be handled via telephone by our competent and courteous customer service staff.

Thank you for your interest, and we look forward to hearing from you.

Best Wishes in Your CPE Endeavors,

*Irvin N. Gleim*

January 2004

# PREPARING FOR AND TAKING THE CIA EXAM

## ABOUT THE CIA EXAM

### Introduction

CIA is the acronym for Certified Internal Auditor. The CIA designation is international, with the examination administered in numerous countries. The CIA exam has been administered by The Institute of Internal Auditors since 1974. The exam consists of four 3 1/2-hour parts that are given on the third Thursday and its preceding Wednesday in May and November. Each part consists of 125 four-answer multiple-choice questions.

| Part I | The Internal Audit Activity's Role in Governance, Risk, and Control | Wednesday | 8:30 - 12:00 | 3 1/2 hours |
|---|---|---|---|---|
| Part II | Conducting the Internal Audit Engagement | Wednesday | 1:30 - 5:00 | 3 1/2 hours |
| Part III | Business Analysis and Information Technology | Thursday | 8:30 - 12:00 | 3 1/2 hours |
| Part IV | Business Management Skills | Thursday | 1:30 - 5:00 | 3 1/2 hours |
| | | | | 14    hours |

Please note as you read through this introduction that CIA program rules and prices are subject to change. Please visit The IIA web site at www.theiia.org for the most up-to-date information.

**Internal Auditing**

Internal auditing is an independent, objective assurance and consulting activity designed to add value and improve an organization's operations. It helps an organization accomplish its objectives by bringing a systematic, disciplined approach to evaluate and improve the effectiveness of risk management, control, and governance processes.

Internal auditing reviews the reliability and integrity of information, compliance with policies and regulations, the safeguarding of assets, the economical and efficient use of resources, and established operational goals and objectives. Internal audits encompass financial activities and operations including systems, production, engineering, marketing, and human resources.

**The Institute of Internal Auditors (IIA)**

The IIA was organized in 1941 to develop the professional status of internal auditing. The organization's headquarters was in New York City until 1972, when it moved to Altamonte Springs, about 5 miles north of Orlando, Florida.

The IIA has an annual budget of approximately $17 million and employs a full-time staff of 100+. Presently, over 40,000 individuals have attained The Institute of Internal Auditors' CIA designation.

The IIA has chapters in more than 200 metropolitan areas and has affiliated national institutes in many countries around the world. The chapters and institutes hold regular meetings, seminars, and conferences that encourage members to network with peers, develop professional contacts, and stay informed about current issues and practices in internal auditing.

The Institute of Internal Auditors' mission is to be the primary international professional association, organized on a worldwide basis, dedicated to the promotion and development of the practice of internal auditing.

The IIA is committed to:

- Providing, on an international scale, comprehensive professional development activities, standards for the practice of internal auditing, and certification.
- Researching, disseminating, and promoting to its members and to the public throughout the world, knowledge and information concerning internal auditing, including internal control and related subjects.
- Establishing meetings worldwide in order to educate members and others as to the practice of internal auditing as it exists in various countries throughout the world.
- Bringing together internal auditors from all countries to share information and experiences in internal auditing and promoting education in the field of internal auditing.

IIA annual dues in the United States and Canada:

| | | |
|---|---|---|
| 1. | Regular members | $115 |
| 2. | Sustaining | $50 |
| 3. | Educational Member | $65 |
| 4. | Life Member | $2,100 |
| 5. | Retired Member | $30 |
| 6. | Student Member | $30 |

For non-Chapter members outside the United States, Canada, and the Caribbean nations, dues are $115. These members are also required to pay a $30 bank collection charge for drafts drawn on banks outside the U.S., Canada, and the Caribbean. Applicants, except students and sustaining members, must also pay an application fee of $25.

## CIA Board of Regents

The Board of Regents is a special committee of The Institute of Internal Auditors established to direct the certification program for internal auditors as established and/or modified by The IIA's Board of Directors.

The Board of Regents consists of at least nine regents. The regents are appointed by the Chairman of the Board of Directors to serve 3-year terms. Membership on the Board of Regents rotates, with two or three regents being appointed each year. The responsibilities of the Board of Regents include

- a. Define the common body of knowledge for the Certified Internal Auditor examination and other Institute certification examinations.
- b. Define the education, experience, character, examination, and other program requirements relating to The Institute certifications.
- c. Define continuing professional education (CPE) requirements for Institute certifications.
- d. Maintain the quality and security of examinations.
- e. Promote The Institute's certifications globally.

## IIA Certification Department

The Vice President of the Learning Center and the Certification Department staff, who are located in The IIA's Florida offices, administer the program. They undertake all of the day-to-day work with respect to the Board of Regents' responsibilities.

The chair of the Board of Regents divides the members into subcommittees. Each subcommittee is responsible for one part of the exam; i.e., each subcommittee makes the initial recommendations concerning the content and grading of its part of the examination to the Board of Regents as a whole.

## Well-Planned Evolution Rather than Abrupt Change

One of the responsibilities of The IIA Board of Regents is to continually update and enhance the sources of exam questions, which in their entirety constitute the **common body of knowledge**.

At the same time, the scope and content of the CIA exam appear to evolve so as to be predictable to CIA candidates. Addition of new topics and deletion of currently tested topics are announced at least one year in advance so candidates may plan and prepare accordingly.

Pass rates on the exam are low enough to give the examination credibility relative to the CMA and CPA exams but are high enough to encourage accounting and auditing professionals to participate in the CIA certification program. Everyone, including The IIA Board of Directors, the Board of Regents, the certification staff, CIAs, noncertified internal auditors, and the accounting/auditing profession in general, is interested in the continual upgrading and improvement of the CIA exam.

## Objectives and Content of the CIA Examination

The CIA exam tests a candidate's knowledge and ability regarding the current practice of internal auditing. It enables candidates and prospective managers to adapt to professional changes and challenges by:

- Addressing nearly all management skills.
- Focusing on the principles of management control.
- Measuring a candidate's understanding of risk management and internal controls.

The exam tests candidates' knowledge and ability with respect to the current state of the art of internal auditing practice. The **common body of knowledge**, referred to in The IIA's materials, is reflected in this edition of *CIA Review*.

---

### THE IIA'S CIA CONTENT SPECIFICATION OUTLINES

**Part I:** The Internal Audit Activity's Role in Governance, Risk, and Control

| | | |
|---|---|---|
| A. | Comply with the IIA's Attribute Standards | 20% |
| B. | Establish a risk-based plan to determine the priorities of the internal audit activity | 20% |
| C. | Understand the internal audit activity's role in organizational governance | 15% |
| D. | Perform other internal audit roles and responsibilities | 5% |
| E. | Governance, risk, and control knowledge elements | 20% |
| F. | Plan Engagements | 20% |

**Part II:** Conducting the Internal Audit Engagement

| | | |
|---|---|---|
| A. | Conduct Engagements | 30% |
| B. | Conduct Specific Engagements | 30% |
| C. | Monitor Engagement Outcomes | 10% |
| D. | Fraud Knowledge Elements | 10% |
| E. | Engagement Tools | 20% |

**Part III:** Business Analysis and Information Technology

| | | |
|---|---|---|
| A. | Business Processes | 20% |
| B. | Financial Accounting and Finance | 20% |
| C. | Managerial Accounting | 15% |
| D. | Regulatory, Legal, and Economics | 10% |
| E. | Information Technology (IT) | 35% |

**Part IV:** Business Management Skills

| | | |
|---|---|---|
| A. | Strategic Management | 25% |
| B. | Global Business Environments | 20% |
| C. | Organizational Behavior | 25% |
| D. | Management Skills | 25% |
| E. | Negotiating | 5% |

The IIA publishes Content Specification Outlines (CSOs) that outline topics covered on the CIA exam. The percentage coverage of each exam part is indicated to the right of each topic. (Note that The IIA "percentage coverage" is given in ranges, e.g., 15-25%, as presented in Appendix A. On page 4, we present the midpoint of each range to simplify and provide more relevant information to CIA candidates, e.g., 20% instead of 15-25%.) We continually adjust the content of our books and software to changes in The IIA's CSOs.

Appendix A contains the CSOs in their entirety. Remember that we have studied and restudied the CSOs in developing our *CIA Review* books and software. Accordingly, you do not need to spend time with Appendix A. Rather, it should give you confidence that Gleim's *CIA Review* is the best review source available to help you PASS the CIA exam. The CSOs refer to proficiency and awareness levels. The IIA definitions of these levels are presented below.

**Proficiency** -- Candidate is able to exhibit the competency in understanding and applying the subject matter in the workplace on a regular basis with skill and expertise.

**Awareness** -- Candidate exhibits awareness and knowledge. Candidate is able to define terms, recognize issues, and recall facts about the issues.

## Gleim Study Unit Listing

We believe our 10 study unit titles better describe the content of each part of the CIA exam. Our study unit titles and content also reflect feedback from CIA candidates. Please use the last page in this book to give us feedback after each exam. Thank you.

---

### LISTING OF GLEIM STUDY UNITS

**Part I: Internal Audit's Role in Governance, Risk, and Control**

1. Introduction to Internal Auditing
2. Charter, Independence, & Objectivity
3. Standards & Proficiency
4. Internal Audit Roles & Responsibility
5. Control I
6. Control II
7. Planning & Supervising the Engagement
8. Managing the Internal Audit Activity I
9. Managing the Internal Audit Activity II
10. Engagement Procedures

**Part II: Conducting the Internal Audit Engagement**

1. Engagement Information
2. Working Papers
3. Communicating Results and Monitoring Progress
4. Specific Engagements
5. Information Technology Audit Engagements I
6. Information Technology Audit Engagements II
7. Statistics and Sampling
8. Other Engagement Tools
9. Ethics
10. Fraud

**Part III: Business Analysis and Information Technology**

1. Business Performance
2. Managing Resources & Pricing
3. Financial Accounting -- Basic Concepts
4. Financial Accounting -- Assets, Liabilities, and Equity
5. Financial Accounting -- Special Topics
6. Finance
7. Managerial Accounting
8. Regulatory, Legal, & Economic Issues
9. Information Technology I
10. Information Technology II

**Part IV: Business Management Skills**

1. Industry Environments
2. Analytical Techniques
3. Strategic Analysis
4. Global Business Environments
5. Motivation & Communication
6. Organizational Structure & Effectiveness
7. Group Dynamics & Team Building
8. Influence & Leadership
9. Time Management
10. Negotiation

## Admission to the CIA Program

Anyone who satisfies these character, educational, and professional requirements may sit for the examination.

1. **Bachelor's degree or equivalent**. Candidates must have an undergraduate (4-year) degree or its equivalent from an accredited college-level institution.

    a.  Educational programs outside the United States and the qualifications of candidates who have completed most but not all of a degree program are evaluated by The IIA's Board of Regents to determine equivalency.

    b.  IIA affiliates have been given the authority to recommend educational and experience criteria for their countries to ensure adequate consideration of cultural and societal differences around the world. In addition, certain international professional designations (such as Chartered Accountant) may be accepted as equivalent to a bachelor's degree.

    c.  A major in accounting is not required.

2. **Character reference**. CIA candidates must exhibit high moral and professional character and must submit a character reference from a responsible person such as a CIA, supervisor, manager, or educator. The character reference must accompany the candidate's application.

3. **Work experience**. Candidates are required to have 24 months of internal auditing experience (or the equivalent) prior to receiving the CIA certificate. However, a candidate may sit for the exam before completing the work experience requirements, but (s)he will not be certified until the experience requirement is met.

    a.  An advanced academic degree beyond the bachelor's or work experience in related business professions (such as accounting, law, finance) can be substituted for one year of work experience (1-year maximum).

    b.  Equivalent work experience means experience in audit/assessment disciplines, including external auditing, quality assurance, compliance, and internal control.

    c.  Full-time college or university-level teaching in the subject matter of the examination is considered equivalent to work experience. Two years of teaching equals one year of internal auditing work experience.

    d.  Work experience must be verified by a CIA or the candidate's supervisor. An Experience Verification Form is available on The IIA web site or in the CIA brochure for use in verifying professional experience. This may accompany the candidate's application or be submitted later when criteria have been met.

If you have questions about the acceptability of your work experience, contact The IIA Certification Department at certification@theiia.org or by fax at (407) 937-1313. If you do not possess a bachelor's degree and are unsure whether your educational achievements or professional designation qualify as equivalents to a bachelor's degree, you should submit related educational/professional information with your application and include a cover letter requesting review by the Board of Regents. Include a complete description of your situation. Please submit these materials to

Certification Department
The Institute of Internal Auditors
247 Maitland Avenue
Altamonte Springs, FL 32701-4201

You will receive a response from The IIA as soon as the certification staff or the Board of Regents evaluates your request.  Applicants for equivalency may be registered for the exam pending review but should expect a separate letter regarding the outcome of the review.  Applicants who do not receive an equivalency status letter within four weeks of submission of the application and equivalency request should contact The IIA.

## How to Register and Apply for the CIA Exam

You must complete a Certified Internal Auditor Program Registration/Application Form for entrance into the CIA program.  The application form is available for download or automatic transfer at www.theiia.org.  All documents and fees must be filed to arrive at The Institute on or before March 31 for the May examination and September 30 for the November examination.  Submit the following items:

1.  A copy of your diploma, transcripts, or other proof of completion of a degree program.  This must be submitted with the application form.

2.  A Character Reference Form (also available at The IIA's web site www.theiia.org)

3.  Verification of professional work experience (can be submitted later when the criteria have been met).  Visit The IIA web site to obtain an experience verification form (www.theiia.org).

The candidate must sign the registration form agreeing to abide by The IIA Code of Ethics.  Each registrant is responsible for making timely delivery of the required fees and forms.  **The Institute cannot guarantee a candidate's right to sit for the examination if procedures are not followed.**  If sending via mail, the application should be mailed to the IIA's Atlanta address as shown on the application.

Candidates must reapply each exam cycle for any remaining parts.  A candidate may initially take one, two, three, or all four parts of the examination.  A candidate may reapply to repeat any parts failed by submitting the registration form that accompanies the grade letter by using the reapplication form on The IIA web site (www.theiia.org), or by contacting The IIA's Customer Service Center -- e-mail:  custserv@theiia.org, fax:  (407) 937-1101, or telephone:  (407) 937-1111.  The candidate must also pay the appropriate examination fee.  A candidate may take as few as one part at subsequent sittings during the two-year eligibility period.

Each person enrolled in the CIA program is responsible for providing timely written notice of any change of address to the IIA Customer Service Center.

## Eligibility Period for the Exam

A candidate has an initial eligibility period of two years (five examinations) after his/her first registration is approved.  The eligibility period is subsequently extended for two years each time a candidate sits for a part.  A candidate's eligibility will expire only if the candidate does not take a single exam part within any two-year period.  If eligibility expires, the candidate loses credit for any part or parts previously passed and must reregister for consideration as a candidate for future examinations.

## Professional Recognition Credit for Part IV

The IIA offers a Part IV Professional Recognition Credit for qualified professional certifications.  Registered candidates and new CIA candidates who have successfully completed the examination requirements for many designations are eligible to receive credit for Part IV of the CIA exam.  Please visit The IIA's website (www.theiia.org) for a complete list of certifications approved for credit.  Hence, candidates who attain the credit for Part IV and pass Parts I, II, and III satisfy the examination requirement for the CIA designation.

The CIA exam is a **nondisclosed** exam.    **Nondisclosed** means that exam questions and solutions are NOT released after each examination.  In order to keep our books and software up-to-date and relevant to CIA candidates, we request feedback on our books and software after each CIA exam.  We need to know what topics need to be added or enhanced.  Note that we are not asking for information about CIA questions, per se.  Rather, we are asking for feedback on our books and software.  This approach has been approved by The IIA.

**Special Student Examination Fee**

The registration fee is the charge for enrolling candidates in the CIA program.  The CIA examination is available to full-time students at reduced fees (half price).  For them, the member registration fee is $30 (instead of $60), plus a fee of $35 (instead of $70) per part.  Students may sit only one time for each part at this special rate.

1.    To be eligible for the reduced rate, the student must
   a.    Be a full-time student as defined by the institution in which the student is enrolled (a minimum of 12 semester hours or its equivalent for undergraduate students and 9 semester hours for graduate students).
   b.    Register for and take the CIA exam while enrolled in school.
   c.    Be enrolled as a senior in an undergraduate program or as a graduate student.

2.    In addition to the requirements above, the following items should be submitted to the Certification Department of The Institute of Internal Auditors while the student is still enrolled in school:
   a.    A Certified Internal Auditor Examination Registration/Application Form *(with school address substituted for business address)*
   b.    A completed and signed Full-Time Student Status Form in lieu of a transcript
   c.    A completed and signed Character Reference Form
   d.    Payment for the $30 registration fee and the $35 examination fee for each part

**Fees for Full-Time Educators**

Educators are invited to take the examination free of charge.  Along with the required CIA Examination Application Form, educators should include a letter attesting to their college- or university-level teaching.  These are submitted for approval of The IIA's Academic Relations Committee.  Letters must

1.    Be printed on the university's letterhead
2.    Specify the courses taught during each semester or quarter
3.    Verify that the candidate had a full-time appointment for each academic year submitted
4.    Be signed by the dean of the college of business administration

**IIA Refund and Deferral Policy**

The registration fee is neither refundable nor transferable.  The examination fee is refundable with a written request.  A $25 processing fee will be charged.  Candidates must notify The IIA in writing (via mail, fax, or e-mail) in order to make changes to their registration, such as changing examination sites, changing the examination parts being taken, deferring to sit at a later examination, or canceling the registration.  Payment of any required fees is due at the time the change is made.

Deferrals or changes may be made at no cost if written notice is received by the registration deadline (March 31 and September 30). A $25 fee will be charged for deferrals, changes, or cancelations received after the deadline. This fee increases to $70 on the Wednesday of the week before the examination.

If no written notice or deferral of cancelation is given prior to the exam and the candidate fails to appear, (s)he is classified as a no-show, and a penalty fee of $70 will be deducted from fees paid. Any remainder will be held in the candidate's account pending further instructions. Monies left in the account after a candidate's eligibility period expires are subject to forfeiture.

## CIA Exam Administration

About three weeks before the exam, candidates will receive an authorization letter with a candidate number, the exam site number and address, the date and time to report to the site, and the time the exam will begin and end (see example on the opposite page). Any errors in the authorization letter should be reported to The IIA's Certification Department at (407) 937-1323, or e-mail: certification@theiia.org. When contacting The IIA, have the candidate ID number available. If you have not received your authorization letter within two weeks before the exam or you have lost your letter, then you should contact The IIA immediately.

The following items are **required** to be admitted to the exam site:

1. Authorization letter
2. Valid photo identification

---

CIA Candidate
«Address»
«CityStateZip»
«Country»

Candidate/ID#

Dear Candidate:

This letter is your authorization to sit for the November 2004 CIA examination. You must present it along with a photo identification to gain admittance to the exam room. Arrive 30 minutes prior to start time.

Your requested language is: _____.

Your exam site is:

«SiteNo» - «SiteName»
«SiteAddr1»
«SiteAddr2»
«SiteAddr3»
«SiteCityStateZip»
«SiteCountry»

You are scheduled to take part(s):

For additional directions, contact (name and phone number of local contact).

---

## The IIA Instructions to Candidates

The IIA instructions to candidates from a recent exam are reproduced below and on the next page to give you further insight into actual exam procedures.

---

### Instructions to CIA Candidates

EXAMINATION SUPERVISORS ARE TO READ THESE INSTRUCTIONS VERBATIM TO THE CANDIDATES APPROXIMATELY FIVE MINUTES BEFORE START OF THE EXAMINATION. DO NOT EXTEMPORIZE.

(Extra copies for late arrivals, per IV.F of the "instructions.")

Do **not** open your booklet or write on the accompanying materials until instructed to do so.

As a courtesy to others, please turn off all cellular phones, beepers, etc., for the duration of the exam.

A No. 2 soft lead pencil must be used to complete the multiple-choice answer sheet. Darken only the appropriate blocks, as shown in the instructions on the multiple-choice answer sheet. **Marks outside the blocks could adversely affect the score you receive.**

At this time, please remove the white multiple-choice answer sheet and the colored control sheet from inside the exam booklet, and close the exam booklet.

On the multiple-choice answer sheet, write the exam language code (the language of your exam), exam site number and your candidate identification number in the blanks provided, and darken the appropriate boxes below each number. If your identification or ID number has fewer than 7 digits, please add any necessary zeroes to the **left** of your ID number so that the last digit of your ID number is in the space to the far right.

Locate the exam serial number on the upper left-hand corner of your exam booklet's cover, and copy this number in the space provided on the multiple-choice answer sheet.

Next, complete the control sheet, **making sure to read and sign the nondisclosure agreement**.

The specific restrictive rules that will be in effect during the examination are:

1.  No reference material, templates, or other aids may be used, except for battery- or solar-powered, nonprinting, nonprogrammable, six-function calculators with only addition, subtraction, multiplication, division, square root, and percentage functions.

2.  All answers submitted must be your own.

3.  If you must be excused from the room, notify a monitor. You will be on the honor system during your absence. Only **one** candidate may leave the room at a time.

4.  You may not talk during the examination.

5.  You may not walk about the room during the examination.

6.  No other act that appears to violate examination ethics will be permitted.

Breaking any of these rules could result in losing the privilege of sitting for this (or a future) CIA examination under Article 1 of The Institute of Internal Auditors' Code of Ethics.

You will have three and one-half hours in which to complete the examination. If you finish before the full time has elapsed, please turn in your materials and leave the room quietly.

**Your <u>examination booklet, all scratch paper and notes</u> are to be turned in with your answers.** You are not to discuss the examination with anyone.

I will announce when 30 minutes remain, when five minutes remain, and when time has expired. Please do **not** ask me or the other proctors to interpret any questions, as we are not permitted to discuss the content of the examination.

-- (continued) --

CANDIDATES WHO HAVE CONCERNS REGARDING EXAM QUESTIONS or the testing experience should submit their comments by fax (+1-407-937-1313) or by e-mail to certification@theiia.org. These comments must be received within 96 hours of completion of the exam so that they will be available to the Board of Regents for review before grading begins. Comments on exam questions must identify the general content of the question and briefly outline any perceived flaw. Candidate input will be gratefully acknowledged and considered in the evaluation of the exam and the testing program. If you prefer, I can collect specific comments and forward them to The IIA Certification Department.

Before beginning work on the exam, read carefully all the instructions on the exam booklet's cover and opening page.

Upon opening your exam booklet, check the page numbers to ensure no pages are missing. After the last question (Question #80), the phrase "End of Part" should appear.

Are there any questions?

You may now open your exam booklet and begin work.

## Grading the CIA Exam and Grade Reporting

The examination proctors return the CIA examinations to The IIA offices by registered mail, Federal Express, or other means to guarantee the safety and security of the examination. The week following the examination, the exams are received and checked against shipping control lists prepared by the proctors. Individual candidate numbers are checked on each answer sheet of every candidate's exam. The highest priority is given to assuring that no candidate papers are misplaced or lost.

The grading process includes both a review of the suggested responses before the exam is given and a post-exam review of all questions that perform poorly in terms of difficulty and reliability. After this review, the Board may choose to accept more than one response as correct on certain questions that did not perform as well as expected.

The multiple-choice question answer sheets are graded using an optical scanner, and all irregularities are researched. If the difficulty of an exam part is higher than expected, a difficulty adjustment may be added to all candidates' scores before exam results are finalized. Statistical information from pre-tested questions is used to maintain comparable difficulty from one CIA exam to the next. Because the exact number of questions required to pass the exam may be slightly different from one exam to another, all raw scores are converted onto a reporting scale of 250 to 750 points, in order to ensure a common standard. A scaled score of 600 points or higher is required to pass the CIA exam. (A scaled score of 600 would be the equivalent of achieving 75 percent correct on an exam of appropriate difficulty.)

Examination results are mailed by July 15 for May exams and January 15 for November exams. If you earn a passing score, you are notified of passing and no specific grade is released. If you earn a score below the passing mark, it is reported to you along with a brief analysis of your exam performance by topic so you can see how much additional effort is required (see sample grade release letter on the next page). Plan on receiving good news soon!

DATE

CIA CANDIDATE
ADDRESS
CITYSTATEZIP
COUNTRY

Dear NAME:                                                    I.D. No.  #####

Thank you for taking the November 2003 Certified Internal Auditor examination.  Your results are listed below.  CIA exam scores are now reported on a scale of 250 to 750 points (see insert), and a scaled score of 600 points or higher is required for successful completion of each part of the exam.  No scores are released for parts passed.

| PART I | PART II | PART III | PART IV* |
|---|---|---|---|
| PREVIOUSLY PASSED | PREVIOUSLY PASSED | 485 | PASSED |

*If you have now passed Parts I, II, and III and plan to apply for Professional Recognition Credit for Part IV, please provide the necessary documents and payment by DATE in order to ensure prompt processing of your request.  Instructions and a list of approved certifications are available on The IIA's web site (www.theiia.org) under Certifications/CIA.

***All scores are considered final.***  In order to help guide your future study, an analysis of the strengths and weaknesses of your exam performance is provided below for any part on which you received a non-passing score.  The analysis includes (1) the main topic areas for the exam part (see IIA web site for detailed outline), (2) the percentage of questions tested in each topic area, and (3) an assessment of improvement needed based on your performance on the November 2003 exam.

**Performance Assessment For Part III**

Business Processes (15-25%):  You need a moderate amount of improvement in this area.

Financial Accounting and Finance (15-25%):  You performed competently in this area but should review it during study.

Managerial Accounting (10-20%):  You performed competently in this area but should review it during study.

Regulatory, Legal, and Economics (5-15%):  You performed competently in this area but should review it during study.

Information Technology (IT) (30-40%):  You need a large amount of improvement in this area.

We wish you the best in your pursuit of the Certified Internal Auditor designation.

The IIA Certification Department

## Maintaining Your CIA Designation

After certification, CIAs are required to maintain and update their knowledge and skills.  Practicing CIAs must complete and report 80 hours of Continuing Professional Education (CPE) every two years.  Every February, CIAs who are required to report in the current year will receive reporting forms and instructions from The IIA.  Completed forms should be filed with The IIA by May 31 of the required reporting year.  Each July, participants in the current year's CPE program will receive a status report acknowledging acceptance of the number of hours reported.  Even-numbered certificates report in even years and odd-numbered certificates in odd years.

## PREPARING TO PASS THE CIA EXAM

### Control: How To

You have to be in control to be successful during exam preparation and execution. Control can also contribute greatly to your personal and other professional goals. The objective is to be confident that the best possible performance is being generated. Control is a process whereby you

1. Develop expectations, standards, budgets, and plans.
2. Undertake activity, production, study, and learning.
3. Measure the activity, production, output, and knowledge.
4. Compare actual activity with expected and budgeted activity.
5. Modify the activity, behavior, or study to better achieve the desired outcome.
6. Revise expectations and standards in light of actual experience.
7. Continue the process or restart the process in the future.

Every day you rely on control systems implicitly. For example, when you groom your hair, you use a control system. You have expectations about the desired appearance of your hair and the time required to style it. You monitor your progress and make adjustments as appropriate. The control process, however, is applicable to all of your endeavors, both professional and personal. You should refine your personal control processes specifically toward passing the CIA exam.

In this book, we suggest explicit control systems for

1. Preparing to take the CIA exam
2. Studying an individual Gleim study unit
3. Answering individual multiple-choice questions

Most endeavors will improve with explicit control. This is particularly true of the CIA examination.

1. Develop an explicit control system over your study process.

2. Practice your question answering techniques (and develop control) as you prepare solutions to recent CIA questions during your study program.

3. Prepare a detailed plan of steps you will take at the CIA exam.

### How Many Parts to Take

The CIA examination consists of four parts; however, according to The IIA, you may choose to take only one part at each sitting.

Our recommendation is to take and pass all four parts the first time. Some candidates, however, will not be able to follow this approach for a variety of reasons. Parts I and II cover internal auditing subject matter, whereas Part III, Business Analysis and Information Technology, and Part IV, Business Management Skills, cover a wide variety of material. Thus, most candidates planning to sit for only two parts of the initial exam will choose Parts I and II because of the efficiencies involved. Part III is the least related to traditional accounting. Part IV tests material more familiar to accounting majors.

Candidates have an initial eligibility period of 2 years from the first exam after their registration is approved. In addition, each time a candidate sits for an exam part, the candidate's eligibility period is extended 2 years from the date of the last exam part taken. A candidate's eligibility expires only if the candidate does not take a single exam part within any 2-year period. If a candidate's eligibility expires, the candidate loses credit for any part or parts passed and must submit a new CIA Exam Application Form and appropriate fees in order to take future examinations.

## Study Plan, Time Budget, and Calendar

Complete one *CIA Review* study unit at a time. Initially, budget 3 to 4 hours per study unit (1 to 2 hours studying the outline and 1 to 2 minutes each on all the multiple-choice questions). Depending on your background, you may need significantly more time to prepare.

| | |
|---|---:|
| This Introduction | 2 |
| 10 study units at 3.5 hours each | 35 |
| General review | 3 |
| Total Hours | 40 |

Each week you should evaluate your progress and review your preparation plans for the time remaining prior to the exam. Use a calendar to note the exam dates and the weeks to go before the exam. Marking a calendar will facilitate your planning. Review your commitments, e.g., out-of-town assignments, personal responsibilities, etc., and note them on your calendar to assist you in keeping to your schedule.

## How to Study a Study Unit (books only*)

1. Gain an overview of the study unit -- familiarity with the topic, number of pages of outline, number of multiple-choice questions -- and estimate the time you will invest.

2. Answer five to ten multiple-choice questions. Choose one or two questions from each subunit.

3. The purpose of answering multiple-choice questions before working through the study outline is to understand the standards to which you will be held. This will motivate you to concentrate on the study outline.

4. Work through the study outline. Learn and understand the concepts. Remember, you are aiming toward the analysis, synthesis, and evaluation levels of knowledge, not rote memorization. Study the outlines with the objective of being able to explain the subject matter to third parties.

* We recommend using *CIA Test Prep* software as discussed on the next page. It will give you a definite advantage.

5. After you are comfortable with the study outlines, apply your multiple-choice question answering technique (see page 17) to answer all of the multiple-choice questions by marking the correct answer before consulting the answer and answer explanation. It is essential to mark your answer choice before looking at the answer. Use the bookmark at the back of each Gleim *CIA Review* book to cover the answers.

6. Develop a 75%+ proficiency level within each study unit. You will achieve this proficiency level by studying the outlines and answering multiple-choice questions.

Learning from questions you answer incorrectly is very important. Each question you answer incorrectly is an opportunity to avoid missing actual test questions on your CIA exam. Thus, you should carefully study the answer explanations provided until you understand why the original answer you chose is wrong, as well as why the correct answer indicated is correct. This study technique may prove to be the difference between passing and failing for many CIA candidates.

You **must** determine why you answered questions incorrectly and learn how to avoid the same error in the future.  Reasons for missing questions include:

    a.   Misreading the requirement (stem)
    b.   Failing to understand what is required
    c.   Making a math error
    d.   Applying the wrong rule or concept
    e.   Being distracted by one or more of the answers
    f.   Incorrectly eliminating answers from consideration
    g.   Lacking any knowledge of the topic tested
    h.   Employing bad intuition (Why?) when guessing

7.    Gleim *CIA Test Prep* software will significantly benefit your study efforts, especially when using the 20-question test routine discussed next.

## Adding CIA Test Prep Software

Using *CIA Test Prep* really works!  The software forces you to commit to your answer choice before looking at answer explanations.  It also keeps track of your time and the results of your effort.  Each study session and each test session are kept in the performance history and are viewable in either a table or a graphical format.

Each Test Prep disk covers a different part of the CIA exam, includes over 1,000 questions, and contains a Windows™ version of the program.  All questions have been updated to reflect the current subject matter.

Read and study the following six steps regarding how to use the software with the books. Using *CIA Test Prep* will greatly facilitate your study and success on the CIA exam!  DO NOT neglect diagnosing the reasons for answering questions incorrectly; i.e., learn from your mistakes while studying so you avoid making mistakes on the CIA exam.

---

Avoid studying Gleim questions to learn the correct answers.  Use Gleim questions to help you learn how to answer CIA questions under exam conditions.  Expect the unexpected and be prepared to deal with the unexpected.  Always take one 20-question test in test mode *before* studying the material in each study unit.  These test sessions will allow you to practice answering questions you have not seen before.  Become an educated guesser when you encounter questions in doubt; you will outperform the inexperienced exam taker.

---

The best way to prepare to PASS:

**1** In test mode, answer a 20-question test from each study unit before studying the study unit.

**2** Study the knowledge transfer outline for the study unit in your Gleim book.

**3** Take two or three 20-question tests in test mode after studying knowledge transfer outlines.

**4** After EACH test session, immediately switch to study mode and select questions "missed on last session" so you can reanswer these questions AND analyze why you answered each question incorrectly.

**5** Continue the process until you approach a 75% proficiency level.

**6** Modify the process to suit your individual learning process.

It is imperative that you complete at least one or two study units a week so you can review your progress and realize how attainable a comprehensive CIA review program is when using Gleim books and software. Remember to get ahead of your schedule to give yourself confidence.

> After you complete each 20-question test, ALWAYS do a study session of questions you missed. FOCUS on why you selected the incorrect answer, NOT the correct answer. You want to learn from your mistakes during study so you avoid mistakes on the exam.

## If You Failed One or More Parts

The pass rate on each part of the CIA exam averages about 45%. Thus, you may not pass all parts attempted. If you failed one or more parts, you should retake them the next time the CIA exam is offered.

1. Once you have put the reaction to the bad news behind you, you should regroup and begin implementing the suggestions in this introduction. The Gleim system really works! Avoid thinking "I knew that" or "I don't have to study that again." What you knew and how you took the exam last time did NOT work. Develop new and improved perspectives.

2. Avoid failure on the next exam by **identifying**, **correcting**, and **understanding** your mistakes as you practice answering multiple-choice questions during your study sessions. Use *CIA Test Prep* software as described above. This methodology applies to all CIA candidates. Understand your mistakes while you study so you can avoid mistakes on the exam.

As you practice answering multiple-choice questions under exam conditions, it is imperative that you restudy each question you answer incorrectly.

**Multiple-Choice Question Answering Technique**

The following suggestions are to assist you in maximizing your score on each part of the CIA exam. Remember, knowing how to take the exam and how to answer individual questions is as important as studying/reviewing the subject matter tested on the exam.

1. **Budget your time**. We make this point with emphasis. Just as you would fill up your gas tank prior to reaching empty, so too should you finish your exam before time expires.

   a. You will have 210 minutes to answer 125 multiple-choice questions.

   b. As you work through individual multiple-choice items, monitor your time. Your goal is to answer all of the items and achieve the maximum score possible.

2. **Answer the items in numerical order**.

   a. Do **not** agonize over any one item. Stay within your time budget.

   b. Mark any items you are unsure of with a big "?" and return to them later if time allows.

   c. Plan on going back to all questions marked with a "?."

   d. Never leave a multiple-choice item unanswered on your answer sheet. Your score is based on the number of correct responses. You will not be penalized for guessing incorrectly.

3. **For each multiple-choice item:**

   a. **Cover up the answer choices** with your hand or a piece of scratch paper. Do not allow the answer choices to affect your reading of the item stem.

      1) If four answer choices are presented, three of them are incorrect. These incorrect answers are called **distractors**. Often, distractors are written to appear correct at first glance until further analysis.

      2) In computational items, distractors are often the result of making common mistakes.

   b. **Read the item** stem carefully (the part of the question that precedes the answer choices) to determine the precise requirement.

      1) You may wish to underline or circle key language or data used in the stem.

      2) Focusing on what is required enables you to ignore extraneous information and to proceed directly to determining the correct answer.

         a) Be especially careful to note when the requirement is an **exception**; e.g., "Which of the following is **not** an indication of fraud?"

   c. **Determine the correct answer** before looking at the answer choices.

      1) By adhering to these steps, you know what is required and which are the relevant facts.

      2) However, some multiple-choice items are structured so that the answer cannot be determined from the stem alone.

   d.   **Read the answer choices** carefully.

      1)   Even if answer (A) appears to be the correct choice, review the remaining answer choices. You may discover that answer (B), (C), or (D) is a better choice.

      2)   Treat each answer choice as a true-false question. Consider marking a "T" or an "F" next to each answer choice as you analyze it.

   e.   **Select the best answer**. Circle the most likely or best answer choice on the question booklet. If you are uncertain, guess intelligently to improve on your 25% chance of getting the correct answer.

      1)   For many of the multiple-choice questions, two answer choices can be eliminated with minimal effort. Eliminating them can reduce the risk of random guessing and increase your chances of success.

4.   After completing your first pass through all 125 questions, return to the questions that you marked with a "?."

5.   While answering questions, make sure you are within your time budget so you will have enough time to transfer your answers in an unhurried manner. Do not wait until the very end of the exam session to transfer answers because you may run out of time.

6.   After you have answered all 125 questions, **transfer your answers to the objective answer sheet**.

   a.   Double-check that you have transferred the answers correctly; e.g., recheck every fifth or tenth answer from your question booklet to your answer sheet to ensure that you have not fallen out of sequence.

## If You Don't Know the Answer

Guess, but make it an educated guess, which means select the best possible answer. First, rule out answers that you feel are obviously incorrect. Second, speculate on The IIA's purpose and/or the rationale behind the question. These steps may lead you to the correct answer. Third, select the best answer, or guess between equally appealing answers. Mark the question with a "?" in case you have time to return to it for further analysis. However, unless you made an obvious mistake or computational error, try to avoid changing answers at the last minute. Your first guess is usually the most intuitive.

If you cannot make an educated guess, read the item and each answer and pick the best or most intuitive answer. Never leave a question unanswered.

Do **not** look at the previous answer to try to detect an answer. The answers are random, but it is possible to have four or more consecutive questions with the same answer letter, e.g., answer B.

**NOTE:** Do not waste time beyond the amount budgeted. Move ahead and stay on or ahead of schedule.

# TAKING THE CIA EXAM

## CIA Examination Preparation Checklist

1. **Register** for the exam program (see pages 6 and 7) by March 31 for the May exam dates or September 30 for the November exam dates.

2. **Apply** to take the desired parts on the same application form (for the initial registration and application), or file the reapplication form.

   a. As soon as your examination location is confirmed by The IIA, make travel and lodging reservations.

3. Acquire your study materials. Rely on *CIA Review* and *CIA Test Prep* as your primary study source.

4. Plan your study program.

5. Locate a suitable place to study.

6. Implement your study program.

7. Periodically review, reassess, and revise your study program as needed.

8. Recognize that an orderly, controlled study program builds confidence, reduces anxiety, and produces success!

9. **Pass the examination!**

## Exam Psychology

Plan ahead for the exam and systematically prepare for it. Go to the exam and give it your best. Neither you nor anyone else can expect more. If you have undertaken a systematic preparation program, you will do well.

Maintain a positive attitude and do not become depressed if you encounter difficulties before or during the exam. An optimist will usually do better than an equally well-prepared pessimist. Remember, you are not in a position to be objective about your results during the exam. Many well-prepared examination candidates have been pleasantly surprised by their scores. Indeed, you should be confident because you are competing with many less-qualified persons who have not prepared as well as you. Optimism and a fighting spirit are worth points on every exam, and fear or depression tends to impair performance.

## Logistical and Health Concerns

As soon as The IIA notifies you of your examination site, find suitable quarters at a hotel within walking distance of both the exam site and restaurants, if possible.  Try to avoid being dependent on a car, parking spaces, etc., during the exam.

Some CIA examination sites are on university campuses.  Begin by calling the student union to inquire about accommodations.  Call the university's general number and ask for room reservations at the student union.  If rooms are not available at the student union, ask for the office in charge of meetings, which should be able to recommend a convenient hotel.

Even if the exam is being given within driving distance of your home, consider staying by yourself at a hotel on Tuesday and Wednesday evenings to be assured of avoiding distractions.  The hotel should be quiet and have a comfortable bed and desk suitable for study.  If possible, stay at a hotel with recreational facilities that you normally use, e.g., a pool, exercise room, etc.

Plan to arrive at your hotel early Tuesday.  To avoid any surprises, visit the examination site Tuesday afternoon or evening (remember, starting time is 8:30 a.m. Wednesday).  Make sure you know where it is and how to get there.  Decide where you want to sit so you have everything settled before Wednesday morning.  You should locate the restroom to avoid confusion if you need to use it during the exam.  Also, check on the availability of vending machines close to the exam room (for a quick soda, coffee, snack, etc., during the exam).

On Tuesday and Wednesday evenings, confine your study to a brief review of the major points covered in the next day's exam sessions.  Concentrate on the sideheadings and key terms in *CIA Review*.  For most CIA candidates, the best advice is to relax the evening before and to get a good night's rest.  Sleep disturbance is less likely if you follow your normal routines.  However, individual tastes vary, and you should do what you know has led to exam success in the past.

Proper exercise, diet, and rest during the weeks before the exam are very important.  High energy levels, reduced tension, and a positive attitude are among the benefits.  A good aerobic fitness program, a nutritious and well-balanced diet, and a regular sleep pattern will promote your long-term emotional and physical well-being as well as contribute significantly to a favorable exam result.  Of course, the use of health-undermining substances should be avoided.

## Pencils, Calculators, and Other Materials

The IIA specifically requires a No. 2 or soft-lead pencil for the multiple-choice answer sheet because it has a machine-gradable format.  Nonprinting, nonprogrammable, battery- or solar-powered, six-function hand-held calculators are permitted during the CIA exam.  You must supply your own pencils and calculator.

Although the instructions to proctors indicate that no food or beverages are allowed in the exam room, you should probably bring a thermos that you can take outside (if the proctors do not relent) to have a quick cup of tea, coffee, etc. Alternatively, there may be vending machines near the examination room.

## Examination Tactics

1.  Arrive at the site in time to have a margin of safety. Remember to bring your authorization letter and photo ID. Check in and select a seat. One advantage of being early is that you will have your choice of seats.

2.  Dressing for exam success means emphasizing comfort, not appearance. Be prepared to adjust for changes in temperature, e.g., remove a sweater or put on a coat. Do not bring notes, this text, other books, etc., to the exam. You will only make yourself nervous and confused by trying to cram during the last 5 minutes before the exam. Books are not allowed in the exam room anyway. You should, however, bring an adequate supply of authorized items, e.g., pencils, erasers, a timepiece, and an appropriate calculator (nonprinting, nonprogrammable, battery- or solar-powered, six-function hand-held).

3.  Use a clear plastic bag to carry your exam supplies. A larger size is more appropriate for storing pencils, an eraser, a calculator, breath mints, chewing gum, candy, etc.

4.  Read the exam instructions carefully.

5.  Answer the 125 questions in chronological order, circle the correct (or best guess) answer to each question. You can and should write in your exam booklet. Mark questions that you are leaving for later or you wish to review with big question marks.

6.  You have 210 minutes (3.5 hours) to answer 125 questions. If you allocate 1.4 minutes per question, you will use only 175 minutes, leaving 35 minutes to review your answers and transfer your answers to the machine readable answer sheet. If you pace yourself during the exam, you will have adequate time to complete each part.

7.  After you worked through all 125 questions, you should return to the questions you have marked with question marks and select the best answer.

8.  After you have answered all 125 questions, review each question carefully. If you made an obvious mistake, e.g., misread the question, make the correction. DO NOT, however, begin changing answers and second guessing yourself. Your first answer to each question should be based on the systematic question answering technique that you have practiced throughout your preparation program.

9.  As a final step, transfer all of your answers from your exam booklet to your machine readable answer sheet carefully and deliberately. Darken the correct answer with a number 2 pencil. Recheck your sequence; the question number in your exam booklet should correspond with the question number on your answer sheet (a sure way to fail is to transfer your answers incorrectly).

10. Do not discuss the examination and your solutions with other candidates at the noon breaks or on Wednesday evening. This will only make you nervous and reduce your confidence. Obviously such discussions cannot affect your grade. Remember that you are as competent as other candidates and were well-prepared for the exam.

11. As soon as you complete the exam, we would like you to e-mail, fax, or write to us with your comments on our books and software. We are particularly interested in which topics need to be added or expanded. We are NOT asking about specific CIA questions. Rather, we are asking for feedback on our books and software. Use the last two pages in each Gleim book to send us your comments. This approach is approved by The IIA.

# STUDY UNIT ONE
# BUSINESS PERFORMANCE

(29 pages of outline)

This study unit addresses the analysis of performance by business organizations. A pervasive consideration is the pursuit of **quality** in all aspects of the organization's activities. The importance of quality management has been recognized by the **International Organization for Standardization**, which has issued quality assurance standards. Also crucial to successful business performance is effective planning. The aspect of planning covered in this study unit is **forecasting**, including a variety of mostly quantitative forecasting models. The study unit continues with **project management**, a topic of growing importance to all types of organizations in a technology-based society. The next subunit describes **business process reengineering** and its implications, concluding with an approach to the persistent problem of bottleneck management.

## 1.1 QUALITY CONSIDERATIONS

1.  The emergence of the **total quality management (TQM)** concept is one of the most significant developments in recent years. TQM recognizes that quality improvement can increase revenues and decrease costs significantly.

    a.  **Quality** is difficult to define, and any single definition will have weaknesses. Consequently, multiple perspectives should be maintained: attributes of the product (performance, serviceability, durability, etc.), customer satisfaction, conformity with manufacturing specifications, and value (relation of quality and price).

        1)  One of the dimensions of quality is **conformance**, or how well a product and its components meet applicable standards. The traditional view is that conforming products are those with characteristics that lie within an acceptable specified range of values that includes a target value. This view also regards a certain percentage of defective (nonconforming) units as acceptable.

            a)  The traditional view was superseded by the **zero-defects (goalpost conformance)** approach which seeks to eliminate all nonconforming output.

            b)  An extension of this approach is the **robust quality (absolute quality conformance)** concept. Its goal is to reach the target value in every case because hidden quality costs occur when output varies from the target even though the units are within specifications.

2. TQM treats the pursuit of quality as a **basic organizational function**, which is as important as production or marketing.

   a. TQM is the continuous pursuit of quality in every aspect of organizational activities through

      1) A philosophy of doing it right the first time,
      2) Employee training and empowerment,
      3) Promotion of teamwork,
      4) Improvement of processes, and
      5) Attention to satisfaction of customers, both internal and external.

         a) TQM emphasizes the **supplier's relationship with the customer**, identifies customer needs, and recognizes that everyone in a process is at some time a customer or supplier of someone else, either within or without the organization.

         b) Thus, TQM begins with external customer requirements, identifies internal customer-supplier relationships and requirements, and establishes requirements for external suppliers.

            i) Companies tend to be vertically organized, but TQM requires strong **horizontal linkages**.

3. The **management of quality** is not limited to quality management staff, engineers, and production personnel.

   a. The role of internal auditors may include not only evaluating but also assisting in designing and operating quality information, measurement, and reporting systems.

      1) In particular, they can contribute to problem solutions through measuring and reporting quality costs.

4. **Implementation of TQM** cannot be accomplished by application of a formula, and the process is lengthy and difficult. The following phases are typical:

   a. Establishing an executive-level quality council of senior managers with strong involvement by the CEO
   b. Providing quality training programs for senior managers
   c. Conducting a **quality audit** to identify improvement opportunities and identify strengths and weaknesses compared with competitors
   d. Preparing a **gap analysis** to ascertain what is necessary to bridge the gap between the company and its competitors and to establish a database for the development of the strategic quality improvement plan
   e. Developing strategic quality improvement plans for the short and long term
   f. Conducting employee communication and training programs
   g. Establishing quality teams, which ensure that goods and services conform to specifications
   h. Creating a measurement system and setting goals
   i. Revising compensation, appraisal, and recognition systems
   j. Reviewing and revising the entire effort periodically

5. Various management **processes, tools, and measures** should be adopted.

     a. **Policy deployment** is the systematic planning of corporate objectives and the detailed ways in which organizational subunits will approach the accomplishment of their related goals. The purpose is **goal congruence**.

     b. **Quality function deployment** ensures that customer requirements are translated into design requirements at each step in product development. It is an umbrella concept most useful in an environment in which the **Plan-Do-Check-Act (PDCA) Cycle** (the Deming Wheel) is used at all levels.

         1) PDCA is a "management by fact" or scientific method approach to continuous improvement. PDCA creates a **process-centered environment** because it involves studying the current process, collecting and analyzing data to identify causes of problems, planning for improvement, and deciding how to measure improvement (**Plan**).

         2) The plan is then implemented on a small scale if possible (**Do**).

         3) The next step is to determine what happened (**Check**).

         4) If the experiment was successful, the plan is fully implemented (**Act**).

         5) The cycle is then repeated using what was learned from the preceding cycle.

     c. **Kaizen** is the Japanese word for the continuous pursuit of improvement in every aspect of organizational operations.

         1) For example, a budget prepared on the kaizen principle projects costs based on future improvements. The possibility of such improvements must be determined, and the cost of implementation and the savings must be estimated.

     d. **Employee involvement** means training and empowering employees to harness their creativity for problem solving. Quality control circles are used to obtain input from employees and to locate the best perspective on problem solving.

     e. **Suppliers' management** is the careful selection of suppliers and the cultivation of long-term relationships based on the consistent ability to meet mutual expectations.

     f. **Competitive benchmarking** "involves continuously evaluating the practices of best-in-class organizations and adapting company processes to incorporate the best of these practices."

     g. **Quality training** familiarizes all employees with the means for preventing, detecting, and eliminating nonquality. The educational processes are tailored to the appropriate groups.

     h. **Reward and recognition** for quality improvement should be group oriented. They should be based on quality measures.

     i. **Customer retention** is a vitally important measure of service quality because loyal customers spend more, refer new customers, and are less costly to service.

     j. Statistical and other **quantitative methods** are used to identify quality problems.

6. The **costs of quality** must be assessed in terms of relative costs and benefits. Thus, an organization should attempt to minimize its total cost of quality. Moreover, nonquantitative factors must also be considered. For example, an emphasis on quality improves competitiveness, enhances employee expertise, and generates goodwill.

     a. **Conformance costs** include costs of prevention and costs of appraisal, which are financial measures of internal performance.

         1) **Prevention** attempts to avoid defective output. These costs include preventive maintenance, employee training, review of equipment design, and evaluation of suppliers.

         2) **Appraisal** embraces such activities as statistical quality control programs, inspection, and testing.

b.   **Nonconformance costs** include costs of internal failure (a financial measure of internal performance) and external failure costs (a financial measure of customer satisfaction).

    1)   **Internal failure** costs occur when defective products are detected before shipment. Examples are scrap, rework, tooling changes, and downtime.

    2)   The costs of **external failure**, e.g., warranty costs, product liability costs, and loss of customer goodwill, arise when problems occur after shipment.

    3)   **Environmental costs** are also external failure costs, e.g., fines for nonadherence to environmental law and loss of customer goodwill.

c.   **Quality cost indices** may be calculated to measure the cost of maintaining a given level of quality, for example, total quality costs divided by direct labor costs.

d.   Examples of **nonfinancial measures of internal performance** are manufacturing cycle efficiency (value-added production time ÷ manufacturing cycle time), ratio of good output to total output, defects per product line, the half-life method (time required to reduce the defect ratio by 50%), and new product development time.

e.   Examples of **nonfinancial measures of customer satisfaction** are percentage of defective goods shipped, customer complaints, customer response time, on-time deliveries, survey data, and market share.

7.   **Quality and productivity** do not necessarily have an inverse relationship. The optimal level of quality costs traditionally has been deemed to occur where the conformance cost curve intercepts the nonconformance cost curve, which corresponds to the minimum point on the total cost curve. Thus, beyond some point, incurrence of prevention and appraisal costs is not cost beneficial.

a.   However, the **robust quality** view is that this relationship does not always hold. Improving quality and reducing costs in each category may be possible if the most efficient prevention methods are applied.

    1)   For example, selection of a supplier meeting high quality standards regarding defect rates and delivery times may drive down not only failure costs but also the prevention and appraisal costs incurred when supplier performance was less reliable.

8.   **Management of time** is related to TQM.

a.   **Product development time** is a crucial factor in the competitive equation. A company that is first in the market with a new product has obvious advantages.

    1)   Reducing development time is also important because **product life cycles** are becoming shorter.

    2)   Companies need to respond quickly and flexibly to new technology, changes in consumer tastes, and competitive challenges.

b.   One financial measure of product development is **breakeven time**, which is the time from management approval of the project to the time when the cumulative present value of its cash inflows equals the cumulative present value of the investment cash outflows.

    1)   The most popular method of determining breakeven time calculates the time required for the present value of the cumulative cash flows to equal zero.

        a)   An alternative that results in a longer breakeven time is to consider the time required for the present value of the cumulative cash inflows to equal the present value of all the expected future cash outflows.

c. **Customer-response time** is the delay from placement of an order to delivery of the good or service. Response time is a function of **time drivers**. A change in a time driver causes a change in the time required for an activity. Such changes reflect uncertainty about arrivals of customers in the queue and bottlenecks (points at which capacity is reached or exceeded).

　　1) Response time consists of **order receipt time** (delay between the customer's placement of an order and its receipt by the production facility), **manufacturing lead or cycle** time (delay from the order's receipt by the production facility to its completion), and **order delivery time**.

　　2) Manufacturing lead or cycle (throughput) time equals **order waiting time** plus **manufacturing time**.

　　3) **Queuing (waiting-line) theory** is a group of mathematical models for systems involving waiting lines. The objective of queuing theory is to minimize the total cost of the system, including both service and waiting costs, for a given rate of arrivals. Mathematical solutions are available for simple systems having unscheduled random arrivals. For other systems, simulation must be used to find a solution.

9. **Benchmarking** is a tool used in the implementation of a total quality management approach. The following outline describes techniques for improving the effectiveness of benchmarking, which is a means of helping organizations with productivity management and business process analysis.

a. Benchmarking is a **continuous evaluation** of the practices of the **best organizations** in their class and the adaptation of processes to reflect the best of these practices. It entails analysis and measurement of key outputs against those of the best organizations. This procedure also involves identifying the underlying key actions and causes that contribute to the performance difference.

　　1) Benchmarking is an ongoing process that entails quantitative and qualitative measurement of the difference between the performance of an activity and the performance by the best in the world. The benchmark organization need not be a competitor.

b. The first phase in the benchmarking process is to **select and prioritize benchmarking projects**.

　　1) An organization must understand its critical success factors and business environment to identify **key business processes and drivers** and to develop parameters defining what processes to benchmark. The criteria for selecting what to benchmark relate to the reasons for the existence of a process and its importance to the entity's mission, values, and strategy. These reasons relate in large part to satisfaction of end users or customer needs.

c. The next phase is to **organize benchmarking teams**. A team organization is appropriate because it permits an equitable division of labor, participation by those responsible for implementing changes, and inclusion of a variety of functional expertise and work experience.

　　1) Team members should have knowledge of the function to be benchmarked, respected positions in the organization, good communication skills, teaming skills, motivation to innovate and to support cross-functional problem solving, and project management skills.

d.  The benchmarking team must thoroughly **investigate and document the organization's** internal processes.  The organization should be seen as a series of processes, not as a fixed structure.  A **process** is a network of related and independent activities joined by their outputs.  One way to determine the primary characteristics of a process is to trace the path a request for a product or service takes through the organization.

  1)  The benchmarking team must also develop a **family of measures** that are true indicators of process performance and a process taxonomy, that is, a set of process elements, measures, and phrases that describes the process to be benchmarked.

e.  Researching and **identifying best-in-class performance** is often the most difficult phase.  The critical steps are setting up databases, choosing information-gathering methods (internal sources, external public domain sources, and original research are the possible approaches), formatting questionnaires (lists of questions prepared in advance), and selecting benchmarking partners.

f.  The **data analysis** phase entails identifying performance gaps, understanding the reasons they exist, and prioritizing the key activities that will facilitate the behavioral and process changes needed to implement the benchmarking study's recommendations.  Sophisticated statistical and other methods may be needed when the study involves many variables, testing of assumptions, or presentation of quantified results.

g.  **Leadership** is most important in the implementation phase of the benchmarking process because the team must be able to justify its recommendations.  Moreover, the process improvement teams must manage the implementation of approved changes.

10. A managerial performance evaluation method that embraces quality among other factors is the **balanced scorecard** approach.  Multiple measures permit a determination as to whether a manager is achieving certain objectives at the expense of others that may be equally or more important.  For example, an improvement in operating results at the expense of new product development would be apparent using this approach.

a.  The scorecard is a **goal congruence** tool that informs managers about the nonfinancial factors that top management believes to be important.

b.  As mentioned previously, measures may be financial or nonfinancial, internal or external, and short term or long term.

c.  The factors in the scorecard vary with the firm and its choice of strategy (product differentiation, cost leadership, etc.).  A typical scorecard includes measures in four categories:

  1)  Profitability
  2)  Customer satisfaction
  3)  Innovation
  4)  Efficiency, quality, and time

11. Stop and review!  You have completed the outline for this subunit.  Study multiple-choice questions 1 through 28 beginning on page 52.

## 1.2 ISO FRAMEWORK

1. In 1987, the International Organization for Standardization (ISO) introduced **ISO 9000**, a series of standards designed to provide **quality assurance**. The ISO rules specify that its standards be periodically revised every 5 years in light of technological and market developments.

    a. The **revised quality management system standards** (ISO 9000:2000 series) were launched in December of the year 2000. For specific and up-to-date information, see the ISO website (www.iso.ch).

    b. Although compliance with the standards is voluntary, many firms throughout the world have adopted them either for competitive reasons or out of fear that adoption will soon become a requirement to sell in international markets. Quality is considered to be synonymous with ISO 9000 registration.

2. ISO 9000 is a set of generic standards for establishing and maintaining a quality system within a company, but standards say nothing about the quality of the end product. The marketplace makes this determination.

    a. The objective is to ensure consistent quality (even though that quality may be poor). The important thing is consistency.

3. The ISO 9000 series, as revised in 2000, is actually a set of three standards.

    a. ISO 9000:2000, *Quality Management Systems - Fundamentals and Vocabulary*, describes the definitions used in the ISO 9000 standards.

    b. ISO 9001:2000, *Quality Management Systems - Requirements*, is the standard that provides a model for quality assurance programs. The old standards, ISO 9001, 9002, and 9003, have been integrated into this new standard.

    c. ISO 9004:2000, *Quality Management Systems - Guidelines for Performance Improvements*, provides guidance for continual improvement of a quality management system.

4. Some companies are obtaining ISO 9000 certification because of fear that the **European Union** will require compliance with the standards in an attempt to restrict imports.

    a. The standards are not yet mandatory except among regulated products (for which health and safety are concerns) such as medical devices, telecommunications equipment, and gas appliances.

    b. Some customers demand that suppliers register.

    c. Many American companies see registration as a key to remaining competitive. ISO registration makes customers more comfortable with suppliers' products and services.

    d. Although market pressure is the main driving force, many companies implementing the standards uncover internal process and quality improvements as a result. ISO 9000 forces companies to share information and understand who internal customers and users are.

5. The major milestone is organizing a **quality management system (QMS)**.

    a. Typical items included in the QMS are

        1) The company quality policy

        2) The company quality manual, which documents how the company's quality system complies with the requirements of the standards

        3) The organization structure

4) Common company-wide procedures

5) Each department's mission and responsibilities

6) Each department's quality plans, operating controls, and training plan

b. One success factor is how well employees have been educated as to the firm's quality standards.

c. The first clause under the standards relates to management commitment, which is demonstrated by the amount of resources dedicated to quality.

6. Another important requirement is an ISO 9000 **internal audit system**. Internal audits assure that the company is complying with the documented QMS procedures and ISO 9000 standards.

7. A **registrar**, or external auditor, must be selected. Registrars are usually specialists within certain Standard Industrial Classification (SIC) codes.

a. Following an on-site visit, the registrar, if convinced that a quality system conforms to the selected standard, issues a certificate describing the scope of the registration. Registration is usually granted for a 3-year period.

b. Some companies have preliminary audits by official registrars.

c. All employees are subject to being audited. They must have the ability to "say what they do" and to demonstrate that they "do what they say."

8. The ISO has also promulgated a set of environmental standards known as **ISO 14000**. These standards are comparable in purpose to ISO 9000 but concern **environmental quality** systems. Although they have not been as widely adopted as the ISO 9000 standards, they may someday become a necessity for conducting business in international markets.

a. ISO 14000 establishes internationally recognized standards that will diminish barriers to trade and make it easier to do business across borders, both for importers and for exporters.

b. Some companies feel that adherence to ISO 14000 standards will reduce monitoring and inspection by regulatory agencies.

c. A survey of managers found that failure to obtain ISO 14000 certification could constitute a potential nontariff trade barrier because customers around the world will require such certification.

d. At present, the main benefit of instituting ISO 14000 standards is internal; companies learn how well their environmental management system operates relative to those of other companies.

e. Some companies have decided to try for ISO 14000 certification because they found that ISO 9000 was such a beneficial program.

f. Some European countries already have environmental systems standards in place, and how these single-country standards will mesh with ISO 14000 is not clear. However, individual countries' standards are typically more strict than the ISO 14000 standards.

g. There is some concern that regulators might try to use voluntary ISO audits or self-audits as a basis for punitive action. To allay these fears in the U.S., the Environmental Protection Agency has issued new audit guidelines that are intended to avoid such self-incrimination.

9. Stop and review! You have completed the outline for this subunit. Study multiple-choice questions 29 through 32 beginning on page 61.

## 1.3 FORECASTING

1.  Forecasts are the basis for business plans, including budgets. They attempt to answer questions about the outcomes of events (e.g., the effect of a war involving a producer of oil on the oil market), the timing of events (e.g., when will unemployment fall), or the future value of a statistic (e.g., sales). In addition to intuition (informed judgment), many quantitative methods are useful in projecting the future from past experience.

    a.  Examples of forecasts include sales projections, inventory demand, cash flow, and future capital needs.

        1)  Most models are used in the forecasting process. They are used to make decisions that optimize future results.

        2)  The reliability of the forecast should be determined before using it. No objective method can determine the reliability of judgmental forecasts. When quantitative methods are used, however, measurement of reliability is usually possible, e.g., by calculating the standard error of the estimate.

2.  **Correlation analysis** is used to measure the strength of the linear relationship between two or more variables. Correlation between two variables can be seen by plotting their values on a single graph to form a scatter diagram. If the points tend to form a straight line, correlation is high. If they form a random pattern, there is little correlation. Correlation measures only linear relationships.

    a.  If the points form a curve, several possibilities exist.

        1)  A linear relationship (a straight line) may be used to approximate a portion of the curve.

        2)  A linear relationship exists between some other function of the independent variable x (e.g., log x) and the dependent variable y.

        3)  No relationship exists.

    b.  In standard notation, the coefficient of correlation is r; the coefficient of determination is $r^2$.

    c.  The **coefficient of correlation** measures the relative strength of the linear relationship. It has the following properties:

        1)  The magnitude of r is independent of the scales of measurement of x and y.

        2)  $-1.0 \leq r \leq 1.0$

            a)  A value of −1.0 indicates a perfectly inverse linear relationship between x and y.

            b)  A value of zero indicates no linear relationship between x and y.

            c)  A value of +1.0 indicates a direct relationship between x and y.

d.  **Scatter diagrams** may be used to demonstrate correlations. Each observation creates a dot that pairs the x and y values. The collinearity and slope of these observations are related to the coefficient of correlation by the above-stated rules.

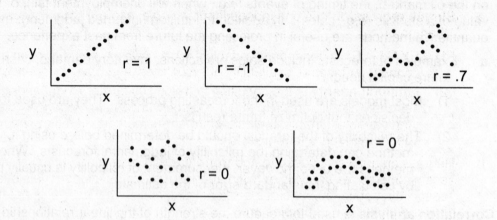

e.  The **coefficient of determination ($r^2$)**, or the coefficient of correlation squared, may be interpreted as the proportion of the total variation in y that is explained or accounted for by the regression equation.

1)  It is approximately equal to 1 minus the quotient of the unexplained variation divided by the total variation when the sample is large. The following is the formula:

$$r^2 = 1 - \frac{\sum (y_i - \hat{y})^2}{\sum (y_i - \overline{y})^2}$$

If:    $r^2$ = the coefficient of determination
    $\sum$ = summation
    $y_i$ = an actual data point
    $\hat{y}$ = a point on the regression line calculated from the sample linear regression equation
    $\overline{y}$ = the mean of the observed data points

2)  EXAMPLE: The assertion that new car sales are a function of disposable income with a coefficient of correlation of .8 is equivalent to stating that 64% ($.8^2$) of the variation of new car sales (from average new car sales) can be explained by the variation in disposable income (from average disposable income).

3)  Because $r^2$ increases as the number of independent variables increases, regardless of whether the additional variables are actually correlated with the dependent variable, $r^2$ may be adjusted (reduced) to allow for this effect. If k is the number of independent variables and n is the number of observations, the formula for adjusted $r^2$ is

$$r^2 - \frac{(k - 1)}{(n - k)} \times (1 - r^2)$$

3. **Regression (least squares) analysis** extends correlation to find an equation for the linear relationship among variables. The behavior of the dependent variable is explained in terms of one or more independent variables. Thus, regression analysis determines functional relationships among quantitative variables.

    a. **Simple regression** has one independent variable, and **multiple regression** has more than one.

        1) EXAMPLE: A dependent variable such as sales is dependent on advertising, consumer income, availability of substitutes, and other independent variables.

        2) **Multicollinearity** is the condition in which two or more independent variables are strongly correlated. The effect is greater uncertainty regarding the coefficient of the variables; that is, their standard errors increase. Multicollinearity is a concern in multiple regression.

    b. Regression analysis is used to find **trend lines in business data** such as sales or costs (time series analysis or trend analysis) and to develop models based on the association of variables (cross-sectional analysis, a method that is not time related as is trend analysis). Examples are

        1) Trend in product sales
        2) Trend in overhead as a percentage of sales
        3) Relationship of direct labor hours to variable overhead
        4) Relationship of direct material usage to accounts payable

    c. Some reasonable basis should exist for expecting the variables to be related.

        1) If they are obviously independent, any association found by regression is mere coincidence.

        2) Regression does not determine causality, however. Although x and y move together, the apparent relationship may be caused by some other factor.

            a) EXAMPLE: A strong correlation exists between car-wash sales volume and sunny weather, but sales volume does not cause sunny weather.

        3) The statistical relationships revealed by regression and correlation analysis are valid **only** for the range of the data in the sample.

    d. The **simple regression equation** is

$$y = a + bx + e$$

        If:  y = the dependent variable
             a = the y-axis intercept (the fixed cost in cost functions)
             b = the slope of the regression line (the variable portion of the total cost in cost functions)
             x = the independent variable
             e = the error term

        1) **Assumptions of the model** are that

            a) For each value of x, there is a distribution of values of y. The means of these distributions form a straight line. Hence, x and y are linearly related.

            b) The error term (e) is normally distributed with a mean or expected value equal to zero.

                i) The y-intercept (a) and the slope of the regression line (b) also have normal distributions.

c)   Errors in successive observations are statistically independent.

   i)   Thus, the estimators are unbiased.

   ii)  **Autocorrelation (serial correlation)** occurs when the observations are not independent; in other words, later observations may be dependent on earlier ones.

d)   The distribution of y around the regression line is constant for different values of x.

   i)   Thus, the observations are characterized by **homoscedasticity** or **constant variance**. The deviation of points from the regression line does not vary significantly with a change in the size of the independent variable.

   • **Heteroscedasticity** is the condition in which the variance of the error term is not constant.

   ii)  Graphically, the model is represented by a series of normal distributions (subpopulations of y) around the regression line. As noted above, these subpopulations have the same variance.

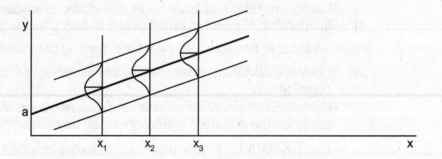

e.   From linear algebra, the **equation for a straight line** may be stated as follows:

$$y = a + bx$$

If:   a = the y-axis intercept
      b = the slope of the line

1)   Regression analysis uses the **method of least squares**, which minimizes the sum of the squares of the vertical distance between each observation point and the regression line.

2)  EXAMPLE:  Observations are collected on advertising expenditures and annual sales for a firm.

| Sales ($000,000s) | Advertising ($000s) |
|:---:|:---:|
| 28 | 71 |
| 14 | 31 |
| 19 | 50 |
| 21 | 60 |
| 16 | 35 |

a)  According to the regression equation that results from using least squares computations, expected sales equal 4.2 plus .31 times the advertising expenditure.

$$y = 4.2 + .31(x)$$

b)  The observations are graphed as follows:

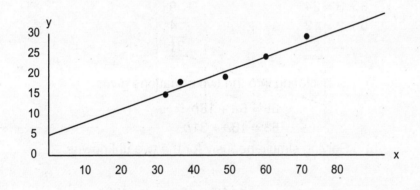

f.  Regression analysis is particularly valuable for **budgeting** and cost accounting purposes.  For instance, it is almost a necessity for computing the fixed and variable portions of mixed costs for flexible budgeting.

g.  The following **equations** can be used to determine the equation for the least squares regression line (the equation for the line is in the form of y = a + bx):

$$\sum y = na + b\left(\sum x\right)$$

$$\sum xy = a\left(\sum x\right) + b\left(\sum x^2\right)$$

1)    EXAMPLE: The use of the two equations can be illustrated with the following data based on a set of six paired observations (n = 6):

| y | x |
|---|---|
| $ 6 | 2 |
| 7 | 3 |
| 5 | 2 |
| 4 | 1 |
| 8 | 3 |
| 6 | 2 |
| $\Sigma y = \$36$ | $\Sigma x = 13$ |

| $\Sigma xy$ | $\Sigma x^2$ |
|---|---|
| 6 × 2 = 12 | 4 |
| 7 × 3 = 21 | 9 |
| 5 × 2 = 10 | 4 |
| 4 × 1 = 4 | 1 |
| 8 × 3 = 24 | 9 |
| 6 × 2 = 12 | 4 |
| 83 | 31 |

a)    Substituting into the two equations gives

$$36 = 6a + 13b$$
$$83 = 13a + 31b$$

b)    Solving simultaneously for the two unknowns,

$$1116 = 186a + 403b$$
$$\underline{1079 = 169a + 403b}$$
$$37 = 17a$$

c)    Thus, a = 2.176. Solving for b in the second original equation gives

$$83 = 13(2.176) + 31b$$
$$83 = 28.288 + 31b$$
$$31b = 54.712$$
$$b = 1.765$$

d)    Hence, future costs can be predicted by using the following equation:

$$y = \$2.176 + \$1.765x$$

e) Alternative formulas that are ordinarily simpler to use are given below:

   i) The slope may be expressed as

$$b = \frac{n\Sigma\, xy - \Sigma\, x \Sigma\, y}{n\Sigma\, x^2 - (\Sigma\, x)^2}$$

   ii) The value of the y-intercept may be expressed as

$$a = \bar{y} - b(\bar{x})$$

h. The statistical significance of the **slope of the regression line** is important because, if its true value is zero, changes in the independent variable have no effect on the dependent variable.

   1) Because the distribution of b is normal, the t-distribution may be used to determine whether b is significantly different from zero, i.e., whether one can reject the null hypothesis that b equals zero.

      a) One approach is to divide b by the standard error of the estimate of b. (The formula is not given here. The standard error is usually provided in the computer output.) If the result exceeds the critical value of t determinable from a standard table, the conclusion is that b is not zero. For example, this critical value is 2.0 for a sample of 60, 58 degrees of freedom (60 – 2 parameters of a and b estimated), and a 95% confidence level.

      b) Another approach is to construct a precision interval (b ± t multiplied by the standard error of the estimate of b). If the interval does not contain zero, the null hypothesis may be rejected.

         i) The value of t is the critical value for the given sample size, degrees of freedom, and confidence level used in the first approach.

i. **Discriminant analysis** is a variation of regression analysis in which independent variables are categorical; i.e., each observation is assigned a category.

   1) EXAMPLES:

      a) High, medium, low
      b) Good, bad
      c) Male, female

j. A **scattergraph** is a diagram of a set of paired observations. This method entails drawing a line to approximate the relationship suggested by the data.

   1) The scattergraph method suffers from being reliant on the judgment of the person visualizing the line.

   2) Once the line has been drawn, the equation of the line can be determined from any two points on the line.

k.   The **high-low method** is used to generate a regression line by basing the equation on only the highest and lowest of a series of observations.

1)   EXAMPLE: A regression equation covering electricity costs could be developed by using only the high-cost month and the low-cost month. If costs were $400 in April when production was 800 machine hours and $600 in September when production was 1,300 hours, the equation would be determined as follows:

| | | | | |
|---|---|---|---|---|
| High month | $600 | for | 1,300 | hours |
| Low month | 400 | for | 800 | hours |
| Increase | $200 | | 500 | hours |

Because costs increased $200 for 500 additional hours, the variable cost is $.40 per machine hour. For the low month, the total variable portion of that monthly cost is $320 ($.40 × 800 hours). Given that the total cost is $400 and $320 is variable, the remaining $80 must be a fixed cost. The regression equation is y = 80 + .4x.

2)   The major criticism of the high-low method is that the high and low points may be abnormalities not representative of normal events.

4.   **Time series** or **trend analysis** relies on past experience. Changes in the value of a variable (e.g., unit sales of a product) over time may have several possible components.

a.   In time series analysis, the dependent variable is regressed on time (the independent variable).

b.   The **secular trend** is the long-term change that occurs in a series. It is represented by a straight line or curve on a graph.

c.   **Seasonal variations** are common in many businesses. A variety of analysis methods includes seasonal variations in a forecasting model, but most methods make use of a seasonal index.

d.   **Cyclical fluctuations** are variations in the level of activity in business periods. Although some of these fluctuations are beyond the control of the firm, they need to be considered in forecasting. They are usually incorporated as index numbers.

e.   **Irregular** or **random variables** are any variations not included in the categories above. Business can be affected by random happenings (e.g., weather, strikes, fires, etc.).

f.   The **percentage-of-sales** method is the most widely used for sales forecasting. It adjusts the current level of sales by a specified percentage increase or decrease. This method is a form of trend analysis that is convenient and easy to apply and intuitively appealing to managers. It is also useful for developing **pro forma financial statements** by estimating items that vary directly with sales as percentages of expected sales.

1)   This method is based on the assumptions that most items directly correlate with sales and that the current levels of all assets are optimal for the current sales level.

5.   **Exponential smoothing** is a technique used to level or smooth variations encountered in a forecast. This technique also adapts the forecast to changes as they occur.

a.   The simplest form of smoothing is the moving average, in which each forecast is based on a fixed number of prior observations. Exponential smoothing is similar to the moving average.

b.   Exponential means that greater weight is placed on the most recent data, with the weights of all data falling off exponentially as the data age. The selection of alpha ($\alpha$), the smoothing factor, is important because a high alpha places more weight on recent data.

c.  The equation for the forecast (F) for period t + 1 is

$$F_{t+1} = \alpha(x_t) + (1 - \alpha)F_t$$

If:  $x_t$ = the observation for period t
t = the most recent period
$\alpha$ = the smoothing factor ($0 \le \alpha \le 1$)
$F_t$ = the forecast for period t

1)  This method weights the observation for period t by $\alpha$ and the forecast for period t by ($1 - \alpha$).

6.  **Learning curves** reflect the increased rate at which people perform tasks as they gain experience.  The time required to perform a given task becomes progressively shorter, but this technique is applicable only to the early stages of production or of any new task.

a.  Ordinarily, the curve is expressed as a percentage of reduced time to complete a task for each doubling of cumulative production.  Research has shown learning curve percentages to be between 60% and 80%.  In other words, the time required is reduced by 20% to 40% each time cumulative production is doubled, with 20% being common.

1)  One common assumption made in a learning curve model is that the **cumulative average time per unit** is reduced by a certain percentage each time production doubles.

a)  The alternative assumption is that **incremental unit time** (time to produce the last unit) is reduced when production doubles.

2)  EXAMPLE:  An 80% learning curve would result in the following performance for the lots shown, when run in sequence (top to bottom).

| Cumulative Number of Tasks | Cumulative Average Time per Unit |
|---|---|
| 100 | 3.0 |
| 200 | 2.4 (3.0 × 80%) |
| 400 | 1.92 (2.4 × 80%) |
| 800 | 1.536 (1.92 × 80%) |
| 1,600 | 1.228 (1.536 × 80%) |

b.  **Graphical presentation**

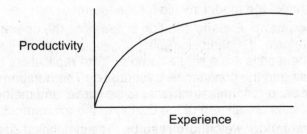

c.    If the average time for 100 units in the example on the previous page were 3 minutes per unit, the total time would be 300 minutes. At an average time of 2.4 minutes for 200 units, the total time would be 480 minutes. In other words, the additional 100 units required only 180 minutes (480 – 300), or 1.8 minutes per unit.

7.    **Simulation** is a technique for experimenting with logical and mathematical models using a computer.

a.    Despite the power of mathematics, many problems cannot be solved by known analytical methods because of the behavior of the variables and the complexity of their interactions, e.g.,

1)    Corporate planning models
2)    Financial planning models
3)    New product marketing models
4)    Queuing system simulations
5)    Inventory control simulations

b.    **Experimentation** is neither new nor uncommon in business. Building a mockup of a new automobile, having one department try out new accounting procedures, and test-marketing a new product are all forms of experimentation. In effect, experimentation is organized trial and error using a model of the real world to obtain information prior to full implementation.

c.    **Models** can be classified as either physical or abstract.

1)    Physical models include automobile mockups, airplane models used for wind-tunnel tests, and breadboard models of electronic circuits.

2)    Abstract models may be pictorial (architectural plans), verbal (a proposed procedure), or logical-mathematical. Experimentation with logical-mathematical models can involve many time-consuming calculations. Computers have eliminated much of this costly drudgery and have led to the growing interest in simulation for management.

d.    The **simulation procedure** has five steps.

1)    **Define the objectives**. The objectives serve as guidelines for all that follows. The objectives may be to aid in the understanding of an existing system (e.g., an inventory system with rising costs) or to explore alternatives (e.g., the effect of investments on the firm's financial structure). A third type of objective is estimating the behavior of some new system such as a production line.

2)    **Formulate the model**. The variables to be included, their individual behavior, and their interrelationships must be defined in precise logical-mathematical terms. The objectives of the simulation serve as guidelines in deciding which factors are relevant.

3)    **Validate the model**. Some assurance is needed that the results of the experiment will be realistic. This assurance requires validation of the model -- often using historical data. If the model gives results equivalent to what actually happened, the model is historically valid. Some risk remains, however, that changes could make the model invalid for the future.

4)    **Design the experiment**. Experimentation is sampling the operation of a system. For example, if a particular policy is simulated on an inventory model for two years, the results are a single sample. With replication, the sample size can be increased and the confidence level raised. The number of runs to be made, length of each run, measurements to be made, and methods for analyzing the results are all part of the design of the experiment.

5)    **Conduct the simulation -- evaluate results**. The simulation should be conducted with care. The results are analyzed using appropriate statistical methods.

e. The **Monte Carlo technique** is often used in simulation to generate the individual values for a random variable. A random number generator is used to produce numbers with a uniform probability distribution (equal likelihoods of occurrence). The second step is to transform these numbers into values consistent with the desired distribution.

  1) The performance of a quantitative model may be investigated by randomly selecting values for each of the variables in the model (based on the probability distribution of each variable) and then calculating the value of the solution. If this process is performed a large number of times, the distribution of results from the model will be obtained.

  2) EXAMPLE: A new marketing model includes a factor for a competitor's introduction of a similar product within 1 year. Management estimates a 50% chance that this event will happen. For each simulation, this factor must be determined, perhaps by flipping a coin, or by putting two numbers in a hat and selecting one number. Random numbers between 0 and 1 could be generated. Numbers under .5 would signify introduction of a similar product; numbers over .5 would indicate the nonoccurrence of this event.

f. The advantages of simulation are as follows:

  1) Time can be compressed. A corporate planning model can show the results of a policy for 5 years into the future, using only minutes of computer time.

  2) Alternative policies can be explored. With simulations, managers can ask what-if questions to explore possible policies, providing management with a powerful new planning tool.

  3) Complex systems can be analyzed. In many cases, simulation is the only possible quantitative method for analyzing a complex system such as a production or inventory system, or the entire firm.

g. The limitations of simulation are as follows:

  1) Cost. Simulation models can be costly to develop. They can be justified only if the information to be obtained is worth more than the costs to develop the model and carry out the experiment.

  2) Risk of error. A simulation results in a prediction of how an actual system would behave. As in forecasting, the prediction may be in error.

h. **Sensitivity Analysis**. After a problem has been formulated into any mathematical model, it may be subjected to sensitivity analysis.

  1) A trial-and-error method may be adopted in which the sensitivity of the solution to changes in any given variable or parameter is calculated.

    a) The risk of the project being simulated may also be estimated.

    b) The best project may be one that is least sensitive to changes in probabilistic (uncertain) inputs.

  2) In **linear programming** problems, sensitivity is the range within which a constraint value, such as a cost coefficient or any other variable, may be changed without changing the optimal solution. Shadow price is the synonym for sensitivity in that context.

8.    The **term structure of interest rates** is useful in forecasting interest rate changes.  It is the relationship between yield to maturity and time to maturity.  It is important to corporate treasurers, who must decide whether to borrow by issuing short- or long-term debt, and to investors, who must decide whether to buy short- or long-term bonds.  The term structure is graphically depicted by a yield curve.

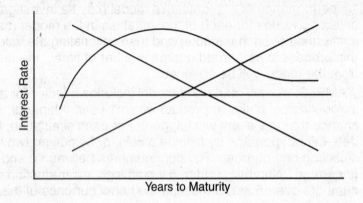

a.    The graph above illustrates four common yield curves.  In most years, long-term rates have been higher than short-term rates, so the yield curve is usually upward sloping.

b.    When plotting a yield curve, the default risk of instruments, their taxability, their callability, and any sinking fund provisions are held constant.

c.    The following are the major theories explaining the slopes of the yield curve:

1)    The **liquidity preference theory** is based on **interest rate risk**, which is the risk of loss associated with a change in bond prices caused by a change in interest rates.  For a given change in rates, the price change will be greater the longer the term of the security.  Other things being equal, short-term securities (and a lower interest rate) may be preferred by investors because their greater liquidity protects against a loss resulting from a change in interest rates.  Thus, investors accept lower yields on short-term securities.  A complementary effect is the tendency of debtors to borrow long-term (and pay a higher interest rate) to match the maturities of investments and assets.  Also, long-term borrowing avoids the expense of turning the debt over frequently.  Hence, debtors are willing to pay a higher rate for long-term funds.  The preferences of lenders and debtors cause short-term rates to be lower than long-term rates.  This theory implies that, under normal conditions, a positive maturity risk premium exists that increases with years to maturity, causing the yield curve to be upward-sloping.

2) **Expectations theory** is based on the belief that a long-term interest rate is an average of future expected short-term interest rates. Future inflation is incorporated into this relationship. For this reason, the yield curve will slope upward if future rates are expected to rise, slope downward if interest rates are anticipated to fall, and remain flat if investors think the rate is stable. Under the pure expectations theory, the maturity risk premium, the default risk premium, and the liquidity premium are all zero.

    a) EXAMPLE: The following are the computed yields to maturity of 1-year, 2-year, and 3-year bonds:

| Years to Maturity | Yield to Maturity |
|:---:|:---:|
| 1 | 5% |
| 2 | 8% |
| 3 | 10% |

        i) Given this yield curve structure, the market's expectations for future interest rates can be estimated by calculating the geometric ratios of the yields to maturity.

$$Year\ 2: \quad \frac{(1.08)^2}{(1.05)} - 1 = 0.1109 = 11\%$$

$$Year\ 3: \quad \frac{(1.10)^3}{(1.08)^2} - 1 = 0.1411 = 14\%$$

        ii) This example clearly shows how long-term rates are created by a series of expected short-term rates.

3) The **market segmentation theory** assumes that each borrower and lender has a preferred maturity. For example, a bank may prefer short-term investments because its deposit liabilities require security of principal, whereas an insurer may prefer to purchase long-term debt to be certain of a given level of income. Given strong maturity preferences, the slope of the yield curve under the market segmentation theory depends on the supply of funds and the demand therefor in the long-term and short-term markets. Thus, the yield curve could be either flat, upward sloping, or downward sloping. An upward-sloping yield curve occurs when there is a large supply of short-term funds relative to demand but a shortage of long-term funds. A downward-sloping curve indicates strong demand for funds in the short-term market compared with the long-term market. A flat curve indicates a balance between the short-term and long-term markets.

d. A downward-sloping term structure implies that the market expects short-run inflation to be higher than long-run inflation.

e. An upward-sloping term structure implies that the market expects long-run inflation to be higher than short-run inflation.

9.   A variant of intuitive forecasting is **scenario analysis** (scenario planning). This technique involves developing formal written descriptions of equally likely future alternatives (usually two to four). It is a qualitative procedure (that may reflect some quantitative input) reflecting an understanding that future events involve many variables not susceptible to quantification.

   a.   A **longitudinal scenario** concerns how future conditions will develop from current conditions.

   b.   The more common **cross-sectional scenario** describes a future state at a certain moment in time.

   c.   Scenario analysis is a long-range forecasting method (often 5 years or more) that is based on **multiple forecasts**. For example, scenarios may be written about how very favorable, normal, or unfavorable economic conditions will affect a particular market, product, or industry.

      1)   This strategic planning method is beneficial because it **avoids surprise**.

10.  Well-designed **surveys** using questionnaires or interviews are often used to determine customer preferences, attitudes, and tastes. They also may be used to gather opinions from experts.

11.  Stop and review! You have completed the outline for this subunit. Study multiple-choice questions 33 through 76 beginning on page 62.

## 1.4 PROJECT MANAGEMENT TECHNIQUES

1.   Project management techniques are designed to aid the planning and control of large-scale projects having many interrelated activities.

   a.   A **project** is a temporary undertaking with specified objectives that often involves a cross-functional team and working outside customary organizational lines. Hence, interpersonal skills are at a premium in project management because a manager may not have line authority over some team members.

   b.   The **project life cycle** consists of

      1)   **Conceptualization** (setting overall objectives, budgets, and schedules)
      2)   **Planning** (obtaining resources, assigning duties, and coordinating activities)
      3)   **Execution** (monitoring, correcting, meeting expectations, and finishing the project within time and budgetary limits)

         a)   The largest amount of resources are used during this stage.

      4)   **Termination** (turning the project over to the user and redistributing project resources)

   c.   **Project management software** is available. Among other things, it should

      1)   Specify and schedule required activities.
      2)   Provide sensitivity analysis of the effects of changes in plans.
      3)   Calculate a project's critical path.
      4)   Establish priorities.
      5)   Be able to modify or merge plans.
      6)   Manage all types of project resources.
      7)   Monitor progress, including adherence to time budgets for activities.

d. Example applications

1) Building construction
2) Research and development projects
3) New product planning
4) Feasibility studies
5) Audit studies
6) Movie production
7) Conversion to a new computer information system

2. Three of the more common scheduling techniques are Gantt or bar charts, PERT, and CPM. These techniques are suitable for any project having a target completion date and single start. **Gantt charts** or **bar charts** are simple to construct and use. To develop a Gantt chart, divide the project into logical subprojects called activities or tasks. Estimate the start and completion times for each activity. Prepare a bar chart showing each activity as a horizontal bar along a time scale.

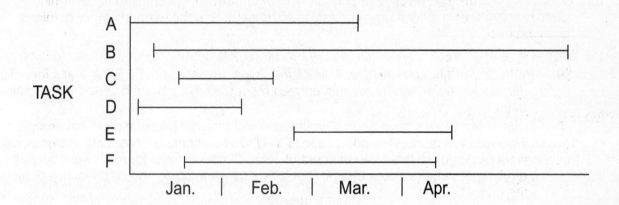

a. The major advantage of the Gantt chart is its simplicity. It forces the planner to think ahead and define logical activities. As the project progresses, actual completion times can be compared with planned times. Furthermore, the technique requires no special tools or mathematics and can be used on small projects as well as large ones.

b. The major disadvantage is that interrelationships among activities are not shown. Several special methods have been developed to show these on a Gantt chart, but they are feasible only for simple relationships.

3. **Program Evaluation and Review Technique (PERT)** was developed to aid managers in controlling large-scale, complex projects. PERT diagrams are free-form networks showing each activity as a line between events. A sequence of lines shows interrelationships among activities. PERT diagrams are more complex than Gantt charts, but they have the advantages of incorporating probabilistic time estimates and identifying the critical path.

a. **Events** are discrete moments in time representing the start or finish of an activity. They consume no resources.

b. **Activities** are tasks to be accomplished. They consume resources (including time) and have a duration over time.

c.  The **network diagram** is formed by

1)  The lines (activities) connected from left to right in the necessary sequence of their accomplishment. They can be marked with time lengths.

2)  Circles representing events and numbered for identification

d.  The **critical path** is the longest path in time through the network. It is critical because, if any activity on the critical path takes longer than expected, the entire project will be delayed. Every network has at least one critical path. Some have more than one.

1)  The **mean completion time** for the critical path is the sum of the means of the activity times.

2)  The **standard deviation of the completion time** for the critical path is the square root of the sum of the variances (squares of the standard deviations) of the activity times.

a)  EXAMPLE: If the critical path has two activities, and the standard deviations of the completion times are 3 and 4, the standard deviation for the critical path is

$$\sqrt{3^2 + 4^2} = 5$$

e.  Paths that are not critical have **slack time**. One advantage of PERT is that it identifies this slack time, which represents unused resources that can be diverted to the critical path.

f.  Several techniques have been developed to include cost information in the analyses. This variation of PERT is often called **PERT-Cost**. It entails combining activities into work packages to facilitate cost control. By estimating costs for each work package, a manager can develop a budget that indicates when costs should be incurred during the project.

g.  **Activity times** can be expressed probabilistically. Computer programs are available to make the calculations and find critical paths.

h.  PERT analysis includes probabilistic estimates of activity completion times. **Three time estimates** are made – optimistic, most likely, and pessimistic.

1)  The time estimates for an activity are assumed to approximate a beta probability distribution. In contrast with the normal distribution, this distribution has finite endpoints (the optimistic and pessimistic estimates) and is unimodal; that is, it has only one mode (the most likely time).

2)  PERT approximates the mean of the beta distribution by dividing the sum of the optimistic time, the pessimistic time, and four times the most likely time (the mode) by six.

3)  The **standard deviation** is approximated by dividing the difference between the pessimistic and optimistic times by six. The basis for the latter approximation is that various probability distributions have tails that lie about plus or minus three standard deviations from the mean. For example, 99.9% of observations in the normal distribution are expected to lie within this range.

i.  EXAMPLE: If an activity can be completed in 6 days (optimistic time), 10 days (most likely time), or 20 days (pessimistic time), the expected duration is 11 days {[6 + (4 × 10) + 20] ÷ 6}.

1)  Thus, the most likely time is weighted the most heavily.

2)  The standard deviation is 2.33 [(20 − 6) ÷ 6].

j.  EXAMPLE:

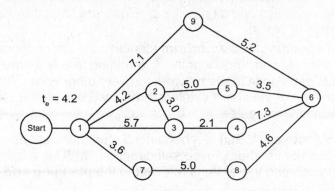

1)  For the network above, the following are the paths and path times:

| Path | Time (hours) |
| --- | --- |
| Start-1-9-6 | 16.5 |
| Start-1-2-5-6 | 16.9 |
| Start-1-2-3-4-6 | 20.8 |
| Start-1-3-4-6 | 19.3 |
| Start-1-7-8-6 | 17.4 |

2)  Path Start-1-2-3-4-6 is the critical path because it has the longest time.

k.  In the example above, path 1-3 takes only 5.7 hours, whereas the critical path events (1-2-3) take 7.2 hours.  The slack time represented by path 1-3 is thus 7.2 – 5.7, or 1.5.  People assigned to path 1-3 have an extra 1.5 hours to help elsewhere.

4.  The **critical path method (CPM)** was developed independently of PERT and is widely used in the construction industry.  CPM may be thought of as a subset of PERT.  Like PERT, it is a network technique.  Unlike PERT, it uses deterministic time and cost estimates.  Its advantages include cost estimates plus the concept of "crash" efforts and costs.

a.  Activity times are estimated for normal effort and crash effort.  **Crash time** is the time to complete an activity assuming that all available resources were devoted to the task (overtime, extra crew, etc.).

b.  Activity costs are also estimated for normal and crash efforts.

c.  These estimates allow the project manager to estimate the costs of completing the project if some of the activities are completed on a crash basis.

d.  The **network diagram** is constructed in the same manner as PERT diagrams.  Once the diagram is constructed, the critical paths are found for normal and crash times. More than one critical path may exist for each diagram.

e.  **Crashing the network** means finding the minimum cost for completing the project in minimum time.

f.  CPM computer programs allow updating of the solution as work proceeds.

5.  **Network models** are used to solve managerial problems pertaining to project scheduling, information systems design, and transportation systems design.  Networks consisting of nodes and arcs may be created to represent in graphic form problems related to transportation, assignment, and transshipment.  The shortest-route, minimal spanning tree, and maximal flow problems are other applications of network models.

a.  A **shortest-route algorithm** minimizes total travel time from one site to each of the other sites in a transportation system.

b.    The **maximal flow algorithm** maximizes throughput in networks with distinct entry (source node) and exit (sink node) points. Examples of applications are highway transportation systems and oil pipelines. Flows are limited by capacities of the arcs (e.g., highways or pipes).

c.    The **minimal spanning tree algorithm** identifies the set of connecting branches having the shortest combined length. A spanning tree is a group of branches (arcs) that connects each node in the network to every other node. An example problem is the determination of the shortest telecommunications linkage among users at remote sites and a central computer.

6.    **Management by objectives (MBO)** is a behavioral, communications-oriented, responsibility approach to management and employee self direction. MBO is a comprehensive management approach and therefore is relevant to the **planning and control** of projects.

a.    MBO is based on the Theory Y philosophy that employees

1)    Want to work hard if they know what is expected.
2)    Like to understand what their jobs actually entail.
3)    Are capable of self-direction and self-motivation.

b.    MBO requires

1)    Senior management participation and commitment to the program. These managers must

a)    Determine the overall direction and objectives for the organization.
b)    Communicate these effectively in operational or measurable terms.
c)    Coordinate subordinates' objectives with overall objectives.
d)    Follow up at the end of the MBO cycle period to reward performance and review problems.

2)    Integration of the objectives for all subunits into a compatible, balanced system directed toward accomplishment of the overall objectives.

3)    Provisions for regular periodic reporting of performance toward attainment of the objectives.

4)    Free and honest communications between supervisor and subordinate.

5)    A commitment to a Theory Y philosophy on the part of supervisors.

6)    An organizational climate that encourages mutual trust and respect.

c.    **Steps necessary to implement an MBO program** include establishing objectives and action plans (the planning steps) and periodic review and final appraisal (the control steps).

1)    Each subordinate should define his/her job objectives and the specific actions (s)he would like to take over the next time period to help reach those job objectives.

2)    The subordinate's objectives and activities should be reviewed within the context of the objectives at higher levels.

3)    When the subordinate's objectives are at odds with upper-level objectives, a **coaching session** is necessary.

a)    This process frequently represents the acid test of MBO because the supervisor must avoid dictating the subordinate's objectives if the spirit of participation is to be preserved.

          b)    If the subordinate's objectives are deemed by the supervisor to be inappropriate, and the subordinate cannot be **coached** out of them, the supervisor can either

              i)    Let the subordinate learn by failing in doing the job his/her way, or
              ii)   Overrule on this particular issue.

          c)    A commitment to Theory Y, trust in subordinates, and the supervisor's job security (the confidence to allow subordinates still more latitude) will play important roles.

          d)    The clearer the definition of job and organizational objectives and the greater the degree of trust and communication between supervisor and subordinate, the easier it is to avoid these dilemmas in implementing MBO.

    4)    The supervisor and subordinate should mutually set and agree on a realistic action plan that can be accomplished by the end of the period.

    5)    Flexibility should be maintained during the period to accommodate unforeseen changes. Thus, after developing objectives and action plans, the third step in the MBO cycle is **periodic review**.

          a)    At regular intervals, objectives should be reconsidered to determine whether they are appropriate in the light of changed circumstances. Otherwise, progress toward achievement of the established objectives should be evaluated and feedback provided.

    6)    At the end of the MBO cycle, the supervisor and subordinate should meet for a **final performance appraisal**. They should review the results, analyze and discuss differences, and use the discussion for learning and performance feedback (not as correction or discipline).

    7)    The MBO cycle should then be repeated.

7.    Stop and review! You have completed the outline for this subunit. Study multiple-choice questions 77 through 87 beginning on page 77.

## 1.5 BUSINESS PROCESS ANALYSIS

1.    One approach to business process analysis is **reengineering** (also called **business process reengineering**). It entails process innovation and core process redesign. Instead of improving existing procedures, it finds new ways of doing things.

    a.    The emphasis is on simplification and elimination of nonvalue-adding activities. Thus, reengineering is not continuous improvement, it is not simply downsizing or modifying an existing system, and it should be reserved for the most important processes.

        1)    In the modern highly competitive business environment, an organization may need to adapt quickly and radically to change. Thus, reengineering is usually a cross-departmental process of innovation requiring substantial investment in information technology and retraining. Successful reengineering may bring dramatic improvements in customer service and the speed with which new products are introduced.

        2)    Reengineering may be contrasted with **automation**, or the computerization of existing manual methods; **rationalization**, or the streamlining of procedures to make automation more efficient; and a **paradigm shift**, or a complete change in the very nature of the business.

b.   One well-known tool useful in reengineering is **work measurement**, a process that involves analysis of activities. The nature and extent of a task, the procedures needed for its execution, and the efficiency with which it is carried out are determined by work measurement.

1)   This technique is appropriate when management takes an **engineered-cost** approach to control. Such an approach is indicated when the workload is divisible into control-factor units, for example, accounting entries made, lines of text word processed, or number of packages shipped. In work measurement, the cost of a control-factor unit is treated as a variable cost for budgeting purposes.

2)   One method used for work measurement is **micromotion study**, which requires videotaping the performance of a job, e.g., assembly-line activities.

3)   Another method is **work sampling**, a technique that involves making numerous random observations of an activity to determine what steps it normally requires.

c.   Reengineering and TQM techniques eliminate many traditional **controls**. They exploit modern technology to improve productivity and decrease the number of clerical workers. Thus, the emphasis is on developing controls that are automated and self-correcting and require minimal human intervention.

1)   The emphasis therefore shifts to monitoring internal control so management can determine when an operation may be out of control and corrective action is needed.

a)   Most reengineering and TQM techniques also assume that humans will be motivated to work actively in improving operations when they are full participants in the process.

2)   **Monitoring** assesses the quality of internal control over time. Management considers whether internal control is properly designed and operating as intended and modifies it to reflect changing conditions. Monitoring may be in the form of separate, periodic evaluations or of ongoing monitoring.

a)   Ongoing monitoring occurs as part of routine operations. It includes management and supervisory review, comparisons, reconciliations, and other actions by personnel as part of their regular activities.

2.   When a production process consists of interdependent operations, for example, when one part must be manufactured before another operation can continue, **bottlenecks** result in idle time. Thus, the items waiting in line to be processed and the items waiting for the output of the bottleneck are idle.

a.   The **theory of constraints (TOC)** is a short-term approach to managing bottlenecks (binding constraints) in production and distribution processes. Its basic principle is that short-term profit maximization requires maximizing the contribution margin of the binding constraint (the throughput contribution). However, TOC analysis defines all costs as fixed in the short-term except direct materials costs. Accordingly, the **throughput contribution** equals sales dollars minus direct materials costs, which include materials handling costs as well as raw materials and purchased components. This approach is a type of **supervariable costing** because only direct materials costs are inventoried.

1)   The objective of TOC analysis is to **maximize throughput contribution** and to **minimize investments** (defined as materials costs of all inventories, plus R&D costs, plus fixed assets) and other operating costs (defined as all operating costs other than direct materials costs necessary to earn the throughput contribution).

2) TOC analysis **identifies the bottleneck operation** that determines the throughput contribution (the operation with large inventories waiting to be processed).

   a) The bottleneck operation establishes the processing schedule for nonbottleneck operations. Hence, nonbottleneck production should not be allowed to exceed what can be processed by the bottleneck operation.

   b) In the longer-term, actions should be undertaken to improve the capacity of the bottleneck operation so that the increase in the throughput contribution exceeds the additional costs.

   c) Production flow is managed using a **drum-buffer-rope (DBR)** system. The **drum** (or drummer providing the beat to which a production process marches) is the bottleneck operation or binding constraint. The **buffer** is a minimal amount of work-in-process input to the drum that is maintained to ensure that it is always in operation. The **rope** is the sequence of activities preceding and including the bottleneck operation that must be coordinated to avoid inventory buildup. Analysis of the rope includes consideration of lead times.

3) The **optimal strategy** to avoid bottleneck problems is to redesign processes, apply improved technology, redesign products to make them easier to manufacture, or, possibly, to eliminate some products that are difficult to manufacture. **Value engineering** is useful for this purpose because it explicitly balances product cost and the needs of potential customers (product functions).

4) To summarize, the steps in a **TOC analysis** include

   a) Determining the bottleneck operation or binding constraint, that is, the one that restricts output to less than the amount demanded.

   b) Discovering the best use of the bottleneck operation, for example, by choosing the optimal product mix or by enhancing product flow through minimizing setups, ascertaining the appropriate lot size, improving the quality of units produced, and focusing on the throughput contribution instead of efficiency.

   c) Using the DBR system to manage production through the bottleneck operation.

   d) Increasing the bottleneck operation's capacity after the foregoing procedures are complete, provided that the throughput contribution exceeds the cost.

   e) Redesigning the process or product(s) for greater flexibility and faster throughput.

5) A **TOC report** should present relevant performance measures, for example, of throughput contribution, elimination of bottlenecks, reduction of average lead times, and number of unfilled orders.

6) TOC analysis complements **activity-based costing (ABC)** because it has a short-term materials-related perspective on product profitability. ABC has a long-term perspective with a focus on all product costs, including driver analysis and unit costing as a basis for strategic pricing and product mix decisions. Moreover, TOC analysis, unlike ABC, addresses the issues of resource constraints and operational capacity. Also unlike ABC, it can ascertain the optimal product mix in the short run.

3. Stop and review! You have completed the outline for this subunit. Study multiple-choice questions 88 through 90 beginning on page 81.

## QUESTIONS

### 1.1 Quality Considerations

Questions 1 and 2 are based on the following information. The management and employees of a large household goods moving company decided to adopt total quality management (TQM) and continuous improvement (CI). They believed that, if their company became nationally known as adhering to TQM and CI, one result would be an increase in the company's profits and market share.

**1.** The primary reason for adopting TQM was to achieve

  A. Greater customer satisfaction.

  B. Reduced delivery time.

  C. Reduced delivery charges.

  D. Greater employee participation.

Answer (A) is correct. *(CIA, adapted)*
**REQUIRED:** The primary reason for adopting TQM.
**DISCUSSION:** TQM is an integrated system that anticipates, meets, and exceeds customers' needs, wants, and expectations.
Answer (B) is incorrect because reduced delivery time is one of many potential activities that need improvement. Answer (C) is incorrect because reduced delivery charges is one of many potential activities that need improvement. Answer (D) is incorrect because increased employee participation is necessary to achieve TQM, but it is not the primary purpose for establishing the program.

**2.** Quality is achieved more economically if the company focuses on

  A. Appraisal costs.

  B. Prevention costs.

  C. Internal failure costs.

  D. External failure costs.

Answer (B) is correct. *(CIA, adapted)*
**REQUIRED:** The necessary focus for achieving quality more economically.
**DISCUSSION:** Prevention attempts to avoid defective output. Prevention costs include preventive maintenance, employee training, review of equipment design, and evaluation of suppliers. Prevention is less costly than detection and correction of defective output.

**3.** A traditional quality control process in manufacturing consists of mass inspection of goods only at the end of a production process. A major deficiency of the traditional control process is that

  A. It is expensive to do the inspections at the end of the process.

  B. It is not possible to rework defective items.

  C. It is not 100% effective.

  D. It does not focus on improving the entire production process.

Answer (D) is correct. *(CIA, adapted)*
**REQUIRED:** The major deficiency of a traditional quality control process.
**DISCUSSION:** The process used to produce the goods is not thoroughly reviewed and evaluated for efficiency and effectiveness. Preventing defects and increasing efficiency by improving the production process raises quality standards and decreases costs.
Answer (A) is incorrect because other quality control processes can also be expensive. Answer (B) is incorrect because reworking defective items may be possible although costly. Answer (C) is incorrect because no quality control system will be 100% effective.

**4.** Under a total quality management (TQM) approach

  A. Measurement occurs throughout the process, and errors are caught and corrected at the source.

  B. Quality control is performed by highly trained inspectors at the end of the production process.

  C. Upper management assumes the primary responsibility for the quality of the products and services.

  D. A large number of suppliers are used in order to obtain the lowest possible prices.

Answer (A) is correct. *(CIA, adapted)*
**REQUIRED:** The true statement about total quality management.
**DISCUSSION:** Total quality management emphasizes quality as a basic organizational function. TQM is the continuous pursuit of quality in every aspect of organizational activities. One of the basic tenets of TQM is doing it right the first time. Thus, errors should be caught and corrected at the source.
Answer (B) is incorrect because total quality management emphasizes discovering errors throughout the process, not inspection of finished goods. Answer (C) is incorrect because all members of the organization assume responsibility for quality of the products and services. Answer (D) is incorrect because the total quality management philosophy recommends limiting the number of suppliers to create a strong relationship.

**5.** Which of the following is a characteristic of total quality management (TQM)?

    A. Management by objectives.

    B. On-the-job training by other workers.

    C. Quality by final inspection.

    D. Education and self-improvement.

**Answer (D) is correct.** *(CIA, adapted)*
**REQUIRED:** The characteristic of TQM.
**DISCUSSION:** According to management theorist W. Edwards Deming's well-known 14 points, education and self-improvement are essential. Knowledge is opportunity. Hence, continuous improvement should be everyone's primary career objective.
Answer (A) is incorrect because one of the 14 points recommends elimination of numerical quotas. MBO causes aggressive pursuit of numerical quotas. Answer (B) is incorrect because informal learning from coworkers serves to entrench bad work habits. One of the 14 points stresses proper training of everyone. Answer (C) is incorrect because another of the 14 points states that quality by final inspection is unnecessary if quality is built in from the start.

**6.** In which of the following organizational structures does total quality management (TQM) work best?

    A. Hierarchal.

    B. Teams of people from the same specialty.

    C. Teams of people from different specialties.

    D. Specialists working individually.

**Answer (C) is correct.** *(CIA, adapted)*
**REQUIRED:** The structure in which TQM works best.
**DISCUSSION:** TQM advocates replacement of the traditional hierarchal structure with teams of people from different specialities. This change follows from TQM's emphasis on empowering employees and teamwork. Employees should have proper training, necessary information, and the best tools; be fully engaged in the decision process; and receive fair compensation. If such empowered employees are assembled in teams of individuals with the required skills, TQM theorists believe they will be more effective than people performing their tasks separately in a rigid structure.
Answer (A) is incorrect because hierarchal organization stifles TQM. Answer (B) is incorrect because TQM works best with teams of people from different specialties. Answer (D) is incorrect because teamwork is essential for TQM.

**7.** The most important component of quality control is

    A. Ensuring goods and services conform to the design specifications.

    B. Satisfying upper management.

    C. Conforming with ISO-9000 specifications.

    D. Determining the appropriate timing of inspections.

**Answer (A) is correct.** *(CIA, adapted)*
**REQUIRED:** The most important component of quality control.
**DISCUSSION:** The intent of quality control is to ensure that goods and services conform to the design specifications. Whether the focus is on feedforward, feedback, or concurrent control, the emphasis is on ensuring product or service conformity.
Answer (B) is incorrect because quality control is geared towards satisfying the customer, not upper management. Answer (C) is incorrect because ensuring the conformance with ISO-9000 specifications is a component of a compliance audit, not quality control. Answer (D) is incorrect because determining the appropriate timing of inspections is only one step towards approaching quality control. Consequently, it is not the primary component of the quality control function.

**8.** The cost of scrap, rework, and tooling changes in a product quality cost system is categorized as a(n)

    A. Training cost.

    B. External failure cost.

    C. Internal failure cost.

    D. Prevention cost.

**Answer (C) is correct.** *(CMA, adapted)*
**REQUIRED:** The categorization of the cost of scrap, rework, and tooling changes in a product quality cost system.
**DISCUSSION:** According to SMA 4-R, internal failure costs are incurred when detection of defective products occurs before shipment. Examples of internal failure costs are scrap, rework, tooling changes, and downtime.
Answer (A) is incorrect because training costs are prevention costs. Answer (B) is incorrect because the costs of external failure, such as warranty expense, product liability, and customer ill will, arise when problems are discovered after products have been shipped. Answer (D) is incorrect because prevention costs are incurred to avoid defective output. Examples include preventive maintenance, employee training, review of equipment design, and evaluation of suppliers.

**9.** The four categories of costs associated with product quality costs are

    A.  External failure, internal failure, prevention, and carrying.

    B.  External failure, internal failure, prevention, and appraisal.

    C.  External failure, internal failure, training, and appraisal.

    D.  Warranty, product liability, training, and appraisal.

Answer (B) is correct.  *(CMA, adapted)*
**REQUIRED:** The categories of product quality costs.
**DISCUSSION:** SMA 4R lists four categories of quality costs: prevention, appraisal, internal failure, and external failure (lost opportunity).  Costs of prevention include attempts to avoid defective output, including employee training, review of equipment design, preventive maintenance, and evaluation of suppliers.  Appraisal costs include quality control programs, inspection, and testing.  Internal failure costs are incurred when detection of defective products occurs before shipment, including scrap, rework, tooling changes, and downtime.  External failure costs are incurred after the product has been shipped, including the costs associated with warranties, product liability, and customer ill will.
Answer (A) is incorrect because carrying cost is not one of the elements of quality costs.  Answer (C) is incorrect because training costs are not a category of quality costs.  Answer (D) is incorrect because warranty, product liability, and training are not cost categories identified by SMA 4R.

**10.** The cost of statistical quality control in a product quality cost system is categorized as a(n)

    A.  Internal failure cost.

    B.  Training cost.

    C.  External failure cost.

    D.  Appraisal cost.

Answer (D) is correct.  *(CMA, adapted)*
**REQUIRED:** The cost category that includes statistical quality control.
**DISCUSSION:** SMA 4R lists four categories of quality costs: prevention, appraisal, internal failure, and external failure (lost opportunity).  Appraisal costs include quality control programs, inspection, and testing.  However, some authorities regard statistical quality and process control as preventive activities because they not only detect faulty work but also allow for adjustment of processes to avoid future defects.
Answer (A) is incorrect because internal failure costs arise after poor quality has been found; statistical quality control is designed to detect quality problems.  Answer (B) is incorrect because statistical quality control is not a training cost.  Answer (C) is incorrect because external failure costs are incurred after the product has been shipped, including the costs associated with warranties, product liability, and customer ill will.

**11.** Listed below are selected line items from the cost-of-quality report for Watson Products for last month.

| Category | Amount |
| --- | --- |
| Rework | $   725 |
| Equipment maintenance | 1,154 |
| Product testing | 786 |
| Product repair | 695 |

What is Watson's total prevention and appraisal cost for last month?

    A.  $786

    B.  $1,154

    C.  $1,940

    D.  $2,665

Answer (C) is correct.  *(CMA, adapted)*
**REQUIRED:** The total prevention and appraisal costs.
**DISCUSSION:** According to SMA 4R, the costs of prevention and appraisal are conformance costs that serve as financial measures of internal performance.  Prevention costs are incurred to prevent defective output.  These costs include preventive maintenance, employee training, review of equipment design, and evaluation of suppliers.  Appraisal costs are incurred to detect nonconforming output.  They embrace such activities as statistical quality control programs, inspection, and testing.  The equipment maintenance cost of $1,154 is a prevention cost.  The product testing cost of $786 is an appraisal cost.  Their sum is $1,940.
Answer (A) is incorrect because $786 is the appraisal cost.  Answer (B) is incorrect because $1,154 is the prevention cost.  Answer (D) is incorrect because $2,665 includes rework, an internal failure cost.

**12.** All of the following would generally be included in a cost-of-quality report except

A. Warranty claims.

B. Design engineering.

C. Supplier evaluations.

D. Lost contribution margin.

Answer (D) is correct. *(CMA, adapted)*
**REQUIRED:** The item that does not normally appear in a cost-of-quality report.
**DISCUSSION:** A cost-of-quality report includes most costs related to quality, including the costs of external failure, internal failure, prevention, and appraisal. Lost contribution margins from poor product quality are external failure costs that normally do not appear on a cost-of-quality report because they are opportunity costs. Opportunity costs are not usually recorded by the accounting system, thereby understating the costs of poor quality. Lost contribution margins from reduced sales, market share, and sales prices are external failure costs that are also not usually included in a cost-of-quality report.
Answer (A) is incorrect because the costs of warranty claims are readily measurable external failure costs captured by the accounting system. Answer (B) is incorrect because the cost of design engineering is a prevention cost that is usually included in cost-of-quality reports. Answer (C) is incorrect because the cost of supplier evaluations is a prevention cost that is usually included in cost-of-quality reports.

**13.** Conformance is how well a product and its components meet applicable standards. According to the robust quality concept,

A. A certain percentage of defective units is acceptable.

B. Units are acceptable if their characteristics lie within an acceptable range of values.

C. The goal is for all units to be within specifications.

D. Every unit should reach a target value.

Answer (D) is correct. *(Publisher)*
**REQUIRED:** The true statement about robust quality.
**DISCUSSION:** Conformance is how well a product and its components meet applicable standards. The traditional view is that conforming products are those with characteristics that lie within an acceptable specified range of values that includes a target value. This view also regarded a certain percentage of defective (nonconforming) units as acceptable. The traditional view was superseded by the zero-defects approach that sought to eliminate all nonconforming output. An extension of this approach is the robust quality concept. Its goal is to reach the target value in every case. The reason is that hidden quality costs occur when output varies from the target even though the units are within specifications.
Answer (A) is incorrect because the traditional view of quality treats a certain number of defective units as acceptable. Answer (B) is incorrect because the traditional view of quality deems that a unit is acceptable if it is within a range of specified values. Answer (C) is incorrect because the robust quality concept is an extension of the zero-defects approach. The goal of robust quality is in every case to reach a target value, not merely a range of acceptable values.

**14.** The Plan-Do-Check-Act (PDCA) Cycle is a quality tool devised by W.E. Deming. It is best described as

A. A "management by fact" approach to continuous improvement.

B. An ongoing evaluation of the practices of best-in-class organizations.

C. The translation of customer requirements into design requirements.

D. The responsibility of every employee, work group, department, or supplier to inspect the work.

Answer (A) is correct. *(Publisher)*
**REQUIRED:** The best description of PDCA.
**DISCUSSION:** PDCA is a "management by fact" or scientific method approach to continuous improvement. PDCA creates a process-centered environment because it involves studying the current process, collecting and analyzing data to identify causes of problems, planning for improvement, and deciding how to measure improvement (Plan). The plan is then implemented on a small scale if possible (Do). The next step is to determine what happened (Check). If the experiment was successful, the plan is fully implemented (Act). The cycle is then repeated using what was learned from the preceding cycle.
Answer (B) is incorrect because competitive benchmarking is an ongoing evaluation of the practices of best-in-class organizations. Answer (C) is incorrect because quality deployment is the translation of customer requirements into design requirements. Answer (D) is incorrect because the "quality at the source" concept emphasizes the responsibility of every employee, work group, department, or supplier to inspect the work.

**15.** Which of the following quality costs are nonconformance costs?

    A. Systems development costs.

    B. Costs of inspecting in-process items.

    C. Environmental costs.

    D. Costs of quality circles.

Answer (C) is correct.  *(Publisher)*
    **REQUIRED:** The nonconformance costs.
    **DISCUSSION:** Nonconformance costs include internal and external failure costs. External failure costs include environmental costs, e.g., fines for violations of environmental laws and loss of customer goodwill.
    Answer (A) is incorrect because systems development costs are prevention (conformance) costs. Answer (B) is incorrect because costs of inspecting in-process items are appraisal (conformance) costs. Answer (D) is incorrect because costs of quality circles are prevention (conformance) costs.

**16.** Quality costing is similar in service and manufacturing organizations. Nevertheless, the differences between these organizations have certain implications for quality management. Thus,

    A. Direct labor costs are usually a higher percentage of total costs in manufacturing organizations.

    B. External failure costs are relatively greater in service organizations.

    C. Quality improvements resulting in more efficient use of labor time are more likely to be accepted by employees in service organizations.

    D. Poor service is less likely to result in loss of customers than a faulty product.

Answer (B) is correct.  *(Publisher)*
    **REQUIRED:** The true statement distinguishing quality considerations in service and manufacturing organizations.
    **DISCUSSION:** External failure costs arise when problems occur after delivery. They occur because products or services are nonconforming or otherwise do not satisfy customers. External failure costs in service enterprises are even more important than in manufacturing environments. Faulty goods sometimes may be reworked or replaced to a customer's satisfaction, but poor service tends to result in a loss of customers.
    Answer (A) is incorrect because direct labor costs are usually a higher percentage of total costs in service organizations. Answer (C) is incorrect because service activities are usually more labor intensive than in modern manufacturing environments. Thus, more efficient labor usage is more likely to be viewed as a threat to employee job security in service organizations. Answer (D) is incorrect because the badwill resulting from poor service may be even more likely than a defective product to result in loss of customers.

**17.** According to the robust quality concept,

    A. The minimum point on the total quality cost curve occurs when conformance cost per unit equals nonconformance cost per unit.

    B. Improving quality requires tradeoffs among categories of quality costs.

    C. Beyond some point, incurrence of prevention and appraisal costs is not cost beneficial.

    D. Costs in all categories of quality costs may be reduced while improving quality.

Answer (D) is correct.  *(Publisher)*
    **REQUIRED:** The robust quality view about quality costs.
    **DISCUSSION:** The optimal level of quality costs traditionally has been deemed to occur where the conformance cost curve intercepts the nonconformance cost curve, which corresponds to the minimum point on the total cost curve. Thus, beyond some point, incurrence of prevention and appraisal costs is not cost beneficial. However, the modern robust quality view is that this relationship does not always hold. Improving quality and reducing costs in each category may be possible if the most efficient prevention methods are applied. For example, selection of a supplier meeting high quality standards regarding defect rates and delivery times may drive down not only failure costs but also the prevention and appraisal costs incurred when supplier performance was less reliable.
    Conformance costs do not necessarily have to continue to increase to obtain additional reductions in nonconformance costs.

**18.** When evaluating projects, breakeven time is best described as

A. Annual fixed costs ÷ monthly contribution margin.

B. Project investment ÷ annual net cash inflows.

C. The point at which cumulative cash inflows on a project equal total cash outflows.

D. The point at which discounted cumulative cash inflows on a project equal discounted total cash outflows.

Answer (D) is correct. *(CMA, adapted)*
**REQUIRED:** The definition of breakeven time.
**DISCUSSION:** Breakeven time evaluates the rapidity of new product development. The usual calculation determines the period beginning with project approval that is required for the discounted cumulative cash inflows to equal the discounted cumulative cash outflows. However, it may also be calculated as the point at which discounted cumulative cash inflows on a project equal discounted total cash outflows. The concept is similar to the payback period, but it is more sophisticated because it incorporates the time value of money. It also differs from the payback method because the period covered begins at the outset of a project, not when the initial cash outflow occurs.
Answer (A) is incorrect because it is related to breakeven point, not breakeven time. Answer (B) is incorrect because the payback period equals investment divided by annual undiscounted net cash inflows. Answer (C) is incorrect because the payback period is the period required for total undiscounted cash inflows to equal total undiscounted cash outflows.

**19.** Management of a company is attempting to build a reputation as a world-class manufacturer of quality products. Which of the following measures would not be used by the firm to measure quality?

A. The percentage of shipments returned by customers because of poor quality.

B. The number of parts shipped per day.

C. The number of defective parts per million.

D. The percentage of products passing quality tests the first time.

Answer (B) is correct. *(CIA, adapted)*
**REQUIRED:** The measure not used for quality measurement.
**DISCUSSION:** The number of parts shipped per day would most likely be used as a measure of the effectiveness and efficiency of shipping procedures, not the quality of the product. This measure does not consider how many of the parts are defective.
Answer (A) is incorrect because the percentage of shipments returned measures quality by the number of defective units. Answer (C) is incorrect because the number of defective parts per million measures quality by the number of defective units. Answer (D) is incorrect because the percentage of products passing quality tests the first time measures quality by the number of nondefective products.

**20.** In year 2, a manufacturing company instituted a total quality management (TQM) program producing the following report:

Summary Cost of Quality Report (000s)

| | Year 1 | Year 2 | % Change |
|---|---|---|---|
| Prevention costs | $ 200 | $ 300 | +50 |
| Appraisal costs | 210 | 315 | +50 |
| Internal failure costs | 190 | 114 | −40 |
| External failure costs | 1,200 | 621 | −48 |
| Total quality costs | $1,800 | $1,350 | −25 |

On the basis of this report, which one of the following statements is most likely true?

A. An increase in conformance costs resulted in a higher quality product and therefore resulted in a decrease in nonconformance costs.

B. An increase in inspection costs was solely responsible for the decrease in quality costs.

C. Quality costs such as scrap and rework decreased by 48%.

D. Quality costs such as returns and repairs under warranty decreased by 40%.

Answer (A) is correct. *(CMA, adapted)*
**REQUIRED:** The true statement about a report prepared by a company using a TQM program.
**DISCUSSION:** TQM emphasizes the supplier's relationship with the customer, and recognizes that everyone in a process is at some time a customer or supplier of someone else, either within or outside the organization. The costs of quality include costs of conformance and costs of nonconformance. Costs of conformance include prevention costs and appraisal (inspection) costs. Nonconformance costs are composed of internal failure costs and external failure costs, such as lost opportunity. Conformance costs (prevention and appraisal) increased substantially, whereas the nonconformance costs (internal and external failure) decreased. Hence, the increase in conformance costs resulted in a higher quality product.
Answer (B) is incorrect because prevention costs also increased substantially, which could also have led to higher quality products. Answer (C) is incorrect because scrap and rework are internal failure costs, which decreased by 40%. Answer (D) is incorrect because returns and repairs are external failure costs, which decreased by 48%.

**21.** Quality cost indices are often used to measure and analyze the cost of maintaining a given level of quality. One example of a quality cost index, which uses a direct labor base, is computed as

$$Quality\ cost\ index = \frac{Total\ quality\ costs}{Direct\ labor\ costs} \times 100$$

The following quality cost data were collected for May and June:

|                      | May      | June      |
|----------------------|----------|-----------|
| Prevention costs     | $ 4,000  | $  5,000  |
| Appraisal costs      | 6,000    | 5,000     |
| Internal failure costs | 12,000 | 15,000    |
| External failure costs | 14,000 | 11,000    |
| Direct labor costs   | 90,000   | 100,000   |

Based upon these cost data, the quality cost index

A. Decreased 4 points from May to June.

B. Was unchanged from May to June.

C. Increased 10 points from May to June.

D. Decreased 10 points from May to June.

Answer (A) is correct.  *(CIA, adapted)*
**REQUIRED:** The change, if any, in the quality cost index.
**DISCUSSION:** The index for May was 40% [($4,000 + $6,000 + $12,000 + $14,000) ÷ $90,000], and the index for June was 36% [($5,000 + $5,000 + $15,000 + $11,000) ÷ $100,000].
Answer (B) is incorrect because the index decreased.
Answer (C) is incorrect because the increase in prevention costs was 10% of the increase in labor costs. Answer (D) is incorrect because the decrease in appraisal costs was 10% of the increase in labor costs.

**22.** Tocon Company produces two components: A-1 and A-2. The unit throughput contribution margins for A-1 and A-2 are $150 and $300, respectively. Each component must proceed through two processes: Operation 1 and Operation 2. The capacity of Operation 1 is 180 machine hours, with A-1 and A-2 requiring 1 hour and 3 hours, respectively. Furthermore, Tocon can sell only 45 units of A-1 and 100 units of A-2. However, Tocon is considering expanding Operation 1's capacity by 90 machine hours at a cost of $80 per hour. Assuming that Operation 2 has sufficient capacity to handle any additional output from Operation 1, Tocon should produce

|     | Units of A-1 | Units of A-2 |
|-----|--------------|--------------|
| A.  | 180          | 0            |
| B.  | 45           | 100          |
| C.  | 45           | 75           |
| D.  | 0            | 60           |

Answer (C) is correct.  *(Publisher)*
**REQUIRED:** The optimal product mix given expanded capacity.
**DISCUSSION:** A-1's throughput contribution margin per unit of the scarce resource (the internal binding constraint) is $150 ($150 UCM ÷ 1 machining hour). A-2's throughput contribution margin per unit of the scarce resource is $100 ($300 UCM ÷ 3 machine hours). Consequently, Tocon should produce as much A-1 as it can sell (45 units). If Tocon adds 90 machine hours to increase the capacity of Operation 1 to 270 hours (180 + 90), it cannot produce additional units of A-1 because the external binding constraint has not been relaxed. However, it can produce additional units of A-2. Given that the UCM per machine hour of A-2 is $100 and that the cost is $80 per hour, adding capacity to Operation 1 is profitable. Thus, Tocon should use 45 machine hours to produce 45 units of A-1. The remaining 225 machine hours (270 - 45) should be used to produce 75 units (225 ÷ 3 hours) of A-2. The latter amount is within the external binding constraint.
Answer (A) is incorrect because Tocon can sell only 45 units of A-1. Answer (B) is incorrect because Tocon can produce only 75 units of A-2 if it produces 45 units of the more profitable A-1. Answer (D) is incorrect because Tocon should produce as much of A-1 as it can sell.

Questions 23 and 24 are based on the following information.

Wolk Corporation is a highly automated manufacturing firm. The vice president of finance has decided that traditional standards are inappropriate for performance measures in an automated environment. Labor is insignificant in terms of the total cost of production and tends to be fixed, material quality is considered more important than minimizing material cost, and customer satisfaction is the number one priority. As a result, delivery performance measures have been chosen to evaluate performance.

The following information is considered typical of the time involved to complete orders:

- Wait time:
  - From order being placed to start of production — 10.0 days
  - From start of production to completion — 5.0 days
- Inspection time — 1.5 days
- Process time — 3.0 days
- Move time — 2.5 days

**23.** What is the manufacturing cycle efficiency for this order?

- A. 25.0%.
- B. 13.6%.
- C. 37.5%.
- D. 69.2%.

Answer (A) is correct. *(CMA, adapted)*
**REQUIRED:** The manufacturing cycle efficiency statistic.
**DISCUSSION:** Manufacturing cycle efficiency is defined as the quotient of the time required for value-added production divided by total manufacturing lead time. For this order, the total lead time is 12 days (5.0 + 1.5 + 3.0 + 2.5), and the manufacturing cycle efficiency is 25% (3 days of processing ÷ 12).

Answer (B) is incorrect because 13.6% includes the 10 days prior to production in the denominator, a period not included in the calculation of manufacturing cycle efficiency. Answer (C) is incorrect because inspection time and move time should be included in the denominator. Answer (D) is incorrect because the calculation involves dividing the 3 days of processing time by the total of 12 days to complete production.

**24.** What is the delivery cycle time for this order?

- A. 7 days.
- B. 12 days.
- C. 15 days.
- D. 22 days.

Answer (D) is correct. *(CMA, adapted)*
**REQUIRED:** The delivery cycle time for the order.
**DISCUSSION:** The delivery cycle time is defined as the entire time from receipt of the order until delivery of the order. This period equals 22 days (10.0 + 5.0 + 1.5 + 3.0 + 2.5)

Answer (A) is incorrect because 7 days excludes the wait time. Answer (B) is incorrect because 12 days ignores the 10 days of the waiting period prior to the start of production. Answer (C) is incorrect because 15 days incorporates the wait time but not the production periods.

Questions 25 and 26 are based on the following information. This information is relevant to a theory of constraints (TOC) analysis. A manufacturer that can sell all of its output produces its sole product using three operations. Each unit sells for $120, and direct materials costing $48 per unit are added at the start of the first operation. Other variable costs are immaterial. The following annual cost and capacity information is available concerning those operations:

| | Operation 1 | Operation 2 | Operation 3 |
|---|---|---|---|
| Total capacity per year | 200,000 units | 150,000 units | 180,000 units |
| Total output per year | 150,000 units | 150,000 units | 150,000 units |
| Fixed cost of operations (not including direct materials) | $1,200,000 | $1,800,000 | $2,250,000 |

**25.** Assume that additional workers are hired for the bottleneck operation to expedite setups and materials handling. The cost of the additional workers is $50,000 per year. As a result, the annual output of the bottleneck operation will increase by 500 units. The change in operating income attributable to the increase in workers is

A. $50,000

B. $36,000

C. $(14,000)

D. $(20,000)

Answer (C) is correct. *(Publisher)*
**REQUIRED:** The change in operating income.
**DISCUSSION:** Operation 2 is the bottleneck because it is functioning at its capacity. The incremental annual throughput contribution (revenues – direct materials costs) from adding workers to Operation 2 is $36,000 [500 units × ($120 unit price – $48 DM per unit)]. Because the cost of the additional workers is $50,000, the change in operating income is $(14,000).
Answer (A) is incorrect because $50,000 is the incremental cost. Answer (B) is incorrect because $36,000 is the incremental throughput contribution. Answer (D) is incorrect because $(20,000) is based on the assumption that an additional $12 per unit of fixed costs will be applied.

**26.** Assume that X Company offers to perform the Operation 2 function on 1,000 units at a unit price of $40, excluding direct materials cost. Which of these mutually exclusive offers is acceptable?

A. X but not Y.

B. Y but not X.

C. X or Y.

D. Neither offer should be accepted.

Answer (A) is correct. *(Publisher)*
**REQUIRED:** The acceptable offer(s), if any.
**DISCUSSION:** X's offer should be accepted because its cost is $40,000 (1,000 units × $40), but the increase in throughput contribution is $72,000 [1,000 units × ($120 unit price – $48 DM per unit)]. X's offer effectively increases the capacity of the bottleneck operation. Y's offer should be rejected because it will result in the incurrence of additional costs with no increase in throughput contribution, given that Operation 2 is already producing at its 150,000-unit capacity.

**27.** Which of the following statements regarding benchmarking is false?

A. Benchmarking involves continuously evaluating the practices of best-in-class organization and adapting company processes to incorporate the best of these practices.

B. Benchmarking, in practice, usually involves a company's formation of benchmarking teams.

C. Benchmarking is an ongoing process that entails quantitative and qualitative measurement of the difference between the company's performance of an activity and the performance by the best in the world or the best in the industry.

D. The benchmarking organization against which a firm is comparing itself must be a direct competitor.

Answer (D) is correct. *(Publisher)*
**REQUIRED:** The false statement about benchmarking.
**DISCUSSION:** Benchmarking is an ongoing process that entails quantitative and qualitative measurement of the difference between the company's performance of an activity and the performance by a best-in-class organization. The benchmarking organization against which a firm is comparing itself need not be a direct competitor. The important consideration is that the benchmarking organization be an outstanding performer in its industry.

**28.** An example of an internal nonfinancial benchmark is

A. The labor rate of comparably skilled employees at a major competitor's plant.

B. The average actual cost per pound of a specific product at the company's most efficient plant.

C. A $50,000 limit on the cost of employee training programs at each of the company's plants.

D. The percentage of customer orders delivered on time at the company's most efficient plant.

Answer (D) is correct. *(CIA, adapted)*
**REQUIRED:** The internal nonfinancial benchmark.
**DISCUSSION:** Benchmarking is a continuous evaluation of the practices of the best organizations in their class and the adaptation of processes to reflect the best of these practices. It entails analysis and measurement of key outputs against those of the best organizations. This procedure also involves identifying the underlying key actions and causes that contribute to the performance difference. The percentage of orders delivered on time at the company's most efficient plant is an example of an internal nonfinancial benchmark.
Answer (A) is incorrect because the labor rate of a competitor is a financial benchmark. Answer (B) is incorrect because the cost per pound of a product at the company's most efficient plant is a financial benchmark. Answer (C) is incorrect because the cost of a training program is a financial benchmark.

## 1.2 ISO Framework

**29.** According to ISO 9000 standards, which of the following is false in regard to registrars?

A. Most employees are subject to being audited.

B. Companies may have preliminary audits by registrars.

C. Employees must be able to competently describe their jobs and demonstrate that they are performing properly.

D. Upon satisfactory completion of an on-site visit, a registrar may issue a certificate describing the scope of the registration, which is valid for 3 years.

Answer (A) is correct. *(Publisher)*
**REQUIRED:** The false statement with regard to registrars.
**DISCUSSION:** During an on-site visit, the registrar has the right to audit all employees if he or she decides to do so. Each employee must have the ability to explain their jobs and show that they are capable of performing properly.
Answer (B) is incorrect because some companies have preliminary audits by registrars to prepare for the official audit. Answer (C) is incorrect because employees must be able to "say what they do" and demonstrate that they "do what they say." Answer (D) is incorrect because a registrar who is convinced that a quality system conforms to the selected standard issues a certificate describing the scope of the registration. The registration is usually valid for a 3-year period.

**30.** Which of the following is not true about the advantages of adopting ISO 9000 standards?

A. Adoption of ISO 9000 standards may allow the company to sell products in foreign markets.

B. ISO registration makes customers more comfortable with the supplier's products and services.

C. ISO 9000 allows companies to understand who internal customers and users are without sharing private information.

D. ISO registration may help companies discover internal process and quality improvements.

Answer (C) is correct. *(Publisher)*
**REQUIRED:** The advantages of ISO 9000 registration.
**DISCUSSION:** Market pressure is usually the main driving force for companies that adopt ISO 9000 standards. However, many of the companies that register uncover internal process and quality improvement as a result. ISO 9000 forces companies to share information, which leads to a better understanding of who internal customers and users are.
Answer (A) is incorrect because many foreign countries are beginning to require adoption of ISO 9000 standards as a prerequisite for a company to sell products or services in that country. Answer (B) is incorrect because many companies view ISO registration as a key to remaining competitive. ISO registration allows customers to be more comfortable with suppliers' products and services. Answer (D) is incorrect because many companies that implement ISO 9000 standards uncover internal process and quality improvements.

**31.** Why have many European Union countries not adopted ISO 14000 standards?

    A. Adhering to ISO 14000 standards will not reduce monitoring and inspection by regulatory agencies.

    B. Individual European Union countries' standards are typically more strict than ISO 14000 standards.

    C. Regulators are permitted to use voluntary audits as a basis for punitive action.

    D. ISO 14000 standards will not make it easier to do business across borders.

Answer (B) is correct. *(Publisher)*
**REQUIRED:** The reason many European Union countries have not adopted ISO 14000 standards.
**DISCUSSION:** Many European countries already have environmental systems in place, and many individual countries' standards are typically more strict than the ISO 14000 standards.
    Answer (A) is incorrect because adhering to ISO 14000 standards does not guarantee less monitoring or inspection by regulatory agencies. Answer (C) is incorrect because many countries in the European Union have adopted measures similar to the ones in the US to prevent self-incrimination during voluntary ISO audits. Answer (D) is incorrect because ISO 14000 establishes internationally recognized standards that are intended to diminish trade barriers and make it easier to do business across borders.

**32.** Which of the following is not required when ISO 9000 standards are adopted?

    A. Organization of a quality management system.

    B. Creation of an internal audit system.

    C. Consistent high quality products.

    D. On-site inspections by a registrar.

Answer (C) is correct. *(Publisher)*
**REQUIRED:** ISO 9000 requirements.
**DISCUSSION:** ISO 9000 is a set of generic standards for establishing and maintaining a quality system within a company. The standards provide no basis for judging the quality of the end product. The marketplace will make this determination on its own. The objective of ISO 9000 standards is to ensure consistent quality, even if the quality is poor.
    Answer (A) is incorrect because one of the most important steps to adhering to ISO 9000 standards is to organize a QMS. A QMS explains the company's quality control and management's commitment to quality. Answer (B) is incorrect because internal audits assure that the company is complying with the documented QMS procedures and ISO 9000 standards. Answer (D) is incorrect because a registrar must ensure that the company's quality control system conforms to the selected standard.

## 1.3 Forecasting

**33.** What coefficient of correlation results from the following data?

| X | Y |
| --- | --- |
| 1 | 10 |
| 2 | 8 |
| 3 | 6 |
| 4 | 4 |
| 5 | 2 |

    A. 0

    B. −1

    C. +1

    D. Cannot be determined from the data given.

Answer (B) is correct. *(CIA, adapted)*
**REQUIRED:** The coefficient of correlation.
**DISCUSSION:** The coefficient of correlation (in standard notation, r) measures the strength of the linear relationship. The magnitude of r is independent of the scales of measurement of X and Y. Its range is −1.0 to 1.0. A value of −1.0 indicates a perfectly inverse linear relationship between X and Y. A value of zero indicates no linear relationship between X and Y. A value of +1.0 indicates a perfectly direct relationship between X and Y. As X increases by 1, Y consistently decreases by 2. Hence, a perfectly inverse relationship exists, and r must be equal to −1.0.
    Answer (A) is incorrect because a perfect negative correlation exists. Answer (C) is incorrect because an inverse, not a direct, relationship exists. Answer (D) is incorrect because a linear relationship exists between X and Y.

**34.** In regression analysis, which of the following correlation coefficients represents the strongest relationship between the independent and dependent variables?

    A. 1.03

    B. −.02

    C. −.89

    D. .75

Answer (C) is correct. *(CIA, adapted)*
**REQUIRED:** The correlation coefficient with the strongest relationship between independent and dependent variables.
**DISCUSSION:** Because the range of values is between −1.0 and 1.0, −.89 suggests a very strong inverse relationship between the independent and dependent variables. A value of −1.0 signifies a perfect inverse relationship, and a value of 1.0 signifies a perfect direct relationship.
    Answer (A) is incorrect because 1.03 is an impossible value. Answer (B) is incorrect because −.02 is a very weak correlation coefficient. Answer (D) is incorrect because .75 is .25 from the maximum value, whereas −.89 is .11 from the minimum value.

**35.** The internal auditor of a bank has developed a multiple regression model which has been used for a number of years to estimate the amount of interest income from commercial loans. During the current year, the auditor applies the model and discovers that the $r^2$ value has decreased dramatically, but the model otherwise seems to be working okay. Which of the following conclusions are justified by the change?

A. Changing to a cross-sectional regression analysis should cause $r^2$ to increase.

B. Regression analysis is no longer an appropriate technique to estimate interest income.

C. Some new factors, not included in the model, are causing interest income to change.

D. A linear regression analysis would increase the model's reliability.

Answer (C) is correct. *(CIA, adapted)*
**REQUIRED:** The implication of the decrease in $r^2$.
**DISCUSSION:** The coefficient of determination ($r^2$) is the amount of variation in the dependent variable (interest income) that is explained by the independent variables. In this case, less of the change in interest income is explained by the model. Thus, some other factor must be causing interest income to change. This change merits audit investigation.
Answer (A) is incorrect because cross-sectional regression analysis is inappropriate. The auditor is trying to estimate changes in a single account balance over time. Answer (B) is incorrect because regression analysis may still be the most appropriate methodology to estimate interest income, but the auditor should first understand the factors that may be causing $r^2$ to decrease. The reason may be a systematic error in the account balance. Answer (D) is incorrect because linear regression models are simpler models, but the auditor should be searching for a systematic error in the account balance or applying a more complex model.

Questions 36 through 39 are based on the following information.

In preparing the annual profit plan for the coming year, Wilkens Company wants to determine the cost behavior pattern of the maintenance costs. Wilkens has decided to use linear regression by employing the equation $y = a + bx$ for maintenance costs. The prior year's data regarding maintenance hours and costs, and the results of the regression analysis, are given below and in the opposite column.

| | | Hours of Activity | Maintenance Costs |
|---|---|---|---|
| Average cost per hour | $9.00 | | |
| a | 684.65 | January | 480 | $ 4,200 |
| b | 7.2884 | February | 320 | 3,000 |
| Standard error of a | 49.515 | March | 400 | 3,600 |
| Standard error of b | .12126 | April | 300 | 2,820 |
| Standard error of the estimate | 34.469 | May | 500 | 4,350 |
| $r^2$ | .99724 | June | 310 | 2,960 |

| | Hours of Activity | Maintenance Costs |
|---|---|---|
| January | 480 | $ 4,200 |
| February | 320 | 3,000 |
| March | 400 | 3,600 |
| April | 300 | 2,820 |
| May | 500 | 4,350 |
| June | 310 | 2,960 |
| July | 320 | 3,030 |
| August | 520 | 4,470 |
| September | 490 | 4,260 |
| October | 470 | 4,050 |
| November | 350 | 3,300 |
| December | 340 | 3,160 |
| Sum | 4,800 | $43,200 |
| Average | 400 | $ 3,600 |

Regression data:

| | |
|---|---|
| Average cost per hour | $9.00 |
| a | 684.65 |
| b | 7.2884 |
| Standard error of a | 49.515 |
| Standard error of b | .12126 |
| Standard error of the estimate | 34.469 |
| $r^2$ | .99724 |

**36.** In the standard regression equation $y = a + bx$, the letter $b$ is best described as a(n)

A. Independent variable.

B. Dependent variable.

C. Constant coefficient.

D. Variable coefficient.

Answer (D) is correct. *(CMA, adapted)*
**REQUIRED:** The meaning of the letter $b$ in the standard regression equation.
**DISCUSSION:** In the standard regression equation, $b$ represents the variable coefficient. For example, in a cost determination regression, $y$ equals total costs, $b$ is the variable cost per unit, $x$ is the number of units produced, and $a$ is fixed cost.
Answer (A) is incorrect because $x$ is the independent variable. Answer (B) is incorrect because the dependent variable is $y$. Answer (C) is incorrect because the constant coefficient is $a$.

**37.** The letter $x$ in the standard regression equation is best described as a(n)

A. Independent variable.

B. Dependent variable.

C. Constant coefficient.

D. Coefficient of determination.

Answer (A) is correct. *(CMA, adapted)*
**REQUIRED:** The meaning of the letter $x$ in the standard regression equation.
**DISCUSSION:** The letter $x$ in the standard regression equation is the independent variable. For example, in a regression to determine the total cost of production, $x$ equals units produced.
Answer (B) is incorrect because the dependent variable is $y$. Answer (C) is incorrect because the constant coefficient is $a$. Answer (D) is incorrect because $r^2$ is the coefficient of determination.

**38.** Refer to the information preceding question 36. Based upon the data derived from the regression analysis, 420 maintenance hours in a month would mean the maintenance costs (rounded to the nearest dollar) would be budgeted at

   A. $3,780

   B. $3,600

   C. $3,790

   D. $3,746

Answer (D) is correct. *(CMA, adapted)*
**REQUIRED:** The budgeted maintenance costs given the activity level.
**DISCUSSION:** Substituting the given data into the regression equation results in a budgeted cost of $3,746 (rounded to the nearest dollar).

$$y = a + bx$$
$$y = 684.65 + 7.2884(420)$$
$$y = \$3,746$$

**39.** Refer to the information preceding question 36. The percentage of the total variance that can be explained by the regression equation is

   A. 99.724%

   B. 69.613%

   C. 80.982%

   D. 99.862%

Answer (A) is correct. *(CMA, adapted)*
**REQUIRED:** The percentage of the total variance that can be explained by the regression equation.
**DISCUSSION:** The coefficient of determination ($r^2$) measures the percentage of the total variance in cost that can be explained by the regression equation. If the coefficient of determination is .99724, 99.724% of the variance is explained by the regression equation. Thus, the values in the regression equation explain virtually the entire amount of total cost.

**40.** A division uses a regression in which monthly advertising expenditures are used to predict monthly product sales (both in millions of dollars). The results show a regression coefficient for the independent variable equal to 0.8. This coefficient value indicates that

   A. The average monthly advertising expenditure in the sample is $800,000.

   B. When monthly advertising is at its average level, product sales will be $800,000.

   C. On average, every additional dollar of advertising results in $.80 of additional sales.

   D. Advertising is not a good predictor of sales because the coefficient is so small.

Answer (C) is correct. *(CIA, adapted)*
**REQUIRED:** The significance of the regression coefficient for the independent variable.
**DISCUSSION:** The regression coefficient represents the change in the dependent variable corresponding to a unit change in the independent variable. Thus, it is the slope of the regression line.
Answer (A) is incorrect because a regression coefficient is unrelated to the means of the variables. Answer (B) is incorrect because to predict a specific value of sales, the value of the independent variable is multiplied by the coefficient. The product is then added to the y-intercept value. Answer (D) is incorrect because the absolute size of the coefficient bears no necessary relationship to the importance of the variable.

**41.** An internal auditor for a large automotive parts retailer wishes to perform a risk analysis and wants to use an appropriate statistical tool to help identify stores that would be out of line compared to the majority of stores. The most appropriate statistical tool to use is

   A. Linear time series analysis.

   B. Cross-sectional regression analysis.

   C. Cross tabulations with chi-square analysis of significance.

   D. Time series multiple regression analysis to identify changes in individual stores over time.

Answer (B) is correct. *(CIA, adapted)*
**REQUIRED:** The best statistical tool for identifying stores that deviate from the majority.
**DISCUSSION:** Time series data pertain to a given entity over a number of prior time periods. Cross-sectional data, however, pertain to different entities for a given time period or at a given time. Thus, cross-sectional regression analysis is the most appropriate statistical tool because it compares attributes of all stores' operating statistics at one moment in time.
Answer (A) is incorrect because linear time series analysis is inapplicable. It is a simple model that compares data for an individual store over time. Answer (C) is incorrect because cross tabulations have to be built on a model of expectations. Unless the model is built, the analysis is not useful. Answer (D) is incorrect because the objective is to compare stores at one moment in time. Multiple regression time series analysis compares the performance of an individual store over a period of time.

**42.** Violation of which assumption underlying regression analysis is prevalent in time series analysis?

    A. Variance of error term is constant.

    B. Error terms are independent.

    C. Distribution of error terms is normal.

    D. Expected value of error term equals zero.

Answer (B) is correct. *(Publisher)*
    **REQUIRED:** The assumption frequently violated in time series analysis.
    **DISCUSSION:** Time series analysis is a regression model in which the independent variable is time. In time series analysis, the value of the next time period is frequently dependent on the value of the time period before that. Hence, the error terms are usually correlated or dependent on the prior period; i.e., they are characterized by autocorrelation (serial correlation).
    Answer (A) is incorrect because constant variance of the error term is usually met. Answer (C) is incorrect because normal distribution of the error term is usually met. Answer (D) is incorrect because an expected value of the error term equal to zero is usually met.

**43.** The moving-average method of forecasting

    A. Is a cross-sectional forecasting method.

    B. Regresses the variable of interest on a related variable to develop a forecast.

    C. Derives final forecasts by adjusting the initial forecast based on the smoothing constant.

    D. Includes each new observation in the average as it becomes available and discards the oldest observation.

Answer (D) is correct. *(CIA, adapted)*
    **REQUIRED:** The item that best describes the moving-average method of forecasting.
    **DISCUSSION:** The simple moving-average method is a smoothing technique that uses the experience of the past N periods (through time period t) to forecast a value for the next period. Thus, the average includes each new observation and discards the oldest observation. The forecast formula for the next period (for time period t+1) is the sum of the last N observations divided by N.
    Answer (A) is incorrect because cross-sectional regression analysis examines relationships among large amounts of data (e.g., many or different production methods or locations) at a particular moment in time. Answer (B) is incorrect because regression analysis relates the forecast to changes in particular variables. Answer (C) is incorrect because, under exponential smoothing, each forecast equals the sum of the last observation times the smoothing constant, plus the last forecast times one minus the constant.

**44.** As part of a risk analysis, an auditor wishes to forecast the percentage growth in next month's sales for a particular plant using the past 30 months' sales results. Significant changes in the organization affecting sales volumes were made within the last 9 months. The most effective analysis technique to use would be

    A. Unweighted moving average.

    B. Exponential smoothing.

    C. Queuing theory.

    D. Linear regression analysis.

Answer (B) is correct. *(CIA, adapted)*
    **REQUIRED:** The most effective analysis technique to forecast the percentage growth in next month's sales.
    **DISCUSSION:** Under exponential smoothing, each forecast equals the sum of the last observation times the smoothing constant, plus the last forecast times one minus the constant. Thus, exponential means that greater weight is placed on the most recent data, with the weights of all data falling off exponentially as the data age. This feature is important because of the organizational changes that affected sales volume.
    Answer (A) is incorrect because an unweighted average will not give more importance to more recent data. Answer (C) is incorrect because queuing theory is used to minimize the cost of waiting lines. Answer (D) is incorrect because linear regression analysis determines the equation for the relationship among variables. It does not give more importance to more recent data.

---

Questions 45 and 46 are based on the following information.

Moss Point Manufacturing recently completed and sold an order of 50 units that had costs as shown in the next column.

The company has now been requested to prepare a bid for 150 units of the same product.

| | |
|---|---:|
| Direct materials | $ 1,500 |
| Direct labor (1,000 hours × $8.50) | 8,500 |
| Variable overhead (1,000 hours × $4.00)* | 4,000 |
| Fixed overhead ** | 1,400 |
| | $15,400 |

\* Applied on the basis of direct labor hours
\*\* Applied at the rate of 10% of variable cost

---

**45.** If an 80% learning curve is applicable, Moss Point's total cost on this order would be estimated at

   A.  $26,400

   B.  $32,000

   C.  $38,000

   D.  $41,800

Answer (A) is correct. *(CMA, adapted)*
**REQUIRED:** The total cost of a new order given a learning curve percentage.
**DISCUSSION:** Assuming that the cumulative average-time model applies, an 80% learning curve means that the cumulative average time per unit (and labor cost, given a constant labor rate) declines by 20% when unit output doubles in the early stages of production. The first lot size was 50 units, which was produced at a total cost of $15,400 ($1,500 for materials and $13,900 for labor and overhead). Materials costs are strictly variable and should remain proportional to production. The labor ($8,500) and variable overhead ($4,000) costs (labor-related), however, will be affected by the learning curve. The average cost per lot for labor and variable overhead after 100 units have been produced should be 80% of the costs of the first lot of 50 units. Thus, the average labor and variable overhead cost per 50-unit lot will be $10,000 (80% × $12,500). If production doubles again (to a total production of 200 units or four lots of 50 each), the cumulative average cost for labor and variable overhead will be $8,000 per lot (80% × $10,000). Given four lots of 50 each, at an average cost of $8,000 per lot, the total cost for labor and variable overhead must be $32,000. Adding $6,000 for raw materials ($1,500 per 50-unit lot) gives a total variable cost of $38,000 for 200 units. Fixed overhead is 10% of total variable cost, so total cost is $41,800. The total cost for the last 150 units is $26,400 ($41,800 – $15,400).
Answer (B) is incorrect because $32,000 is the total cost for labor and variable overhead for 200 units. Answer (C) is incorrect because $38,000 is the total variable cost for 200 units. Answer (D) is incorrect because $41,800 is the total cost for 200 units.

---

**46.** If Moss Point had experienced a 70% learning curve, the bid for the 150 units would

   A.  Show a 30% reduction in the total direct labor hours required with no learning curve.

   B.  Include increased fixed overhead costs.

   C.  Be 10% lower than the total bid at an 80% learning curve.

   D.  Include 6.40 direct labor hours per unit at $8.50 per hour.

Answer (D) is correct. *(CMA, adapted)*
**REQUIRED:** The true statement about the bid for an incremental 150 units given a 70% learning curve effect.
**DISCUSSION:** The sum of the direct labor hours for the initial lot of 50 units was 1,000. A second lot of 50 would reduce the cumulative hours per lot to 700 (70% × 1,000). A doubling to four lots would reduce the cumulative hours per lot to 490 (70% × 700). Thus, for an output of 200 units, the total hours worked would be 1,960 (4 × 490). Subtracting the 1,000 hours required for the first 50 units from the 1,960-hour total gives 960 hours for the last 150 units. Dividing 960 hours by 150 units produces a per-unit time of 6.4 hours.
Answer (A) is incorrect because, with no learning curve effect, estimated total hours would be 4,000 instead of 1,960, a change of more than 50%. Answer (B) is incorrect because fixed costs applied per lot would decline because they are based on labor hours, which are declining. Answer (C) is incorrect because, with no learning curve effect, estimated total hours would be 4,000 instead of 1,960, a change of more than 50%.

**47.** The average labor cost per unit for the first batch produced by a new process is $120. The cumulative average labor cost after the second batch is $72 per product. Using a batch size of 100 and assuming the learning curve continues, the total labor cost of four batches will be

A. $4,320

B. $10,368

C. $2,592

D. $17,280

Answer (D) is correct. *(CMA, adapted)*
**REQUIRED:** The total labor cost assuming the learning curve continues.
**DISCUSSION:** The learning curve reflects the increased rate at which people perform tasks as they gain experience. The time required to perform a given task becomes progressively shorter. Ordinarily, the curve is expressed in a percentage of reduced time to complete a task for each doubling of cumulative production. One common assumption in a learning curve model is that the cumulative average time (and labor cost) per unit is reduced by a certain percentage each time production doubles. Given a $120 cost per unit for the first 100 units and a $72 cost per unit when cumulative production doubled to 200 units, the learning curve percentage must be 60% ($72 ÷ $120). If production is again doubled to 400 units (four batches), the average unit labor cost should be $43.20 (60% × $72). Hence, total labor cost for 400 units is estimated to be $17,280 (400 × $43.20).
Answer (A) is incorrect because $4,320 equals the cost of the items in the fourth batch. Answer (B) is incorrect because $10,368 is based on the assumption that the cumulative average unit labor cost is reduced by the learning curve percentage with each batch, not each doubling of output. Answer (C) is incorrect because $2,592 represents the labor cost of 100 units at the unit rate expected after another doubling of production to eight batches.

**48.** A company is simulating the actions of a government agency in which 50% of the time a recall of a product is required, 40% of the time only notification of the buyer about a potential defect is required, and 10% of the time no action on its part is required. Random numbers of 1 to 100 are being used. An appropriate assignment of random numbers for the recall category would be

A. 1-40

B. 40-90

C. 61-100

D. 11-60

Answer (D) is correct. *(CMA, adapted)*
**REQUIRED:** The appropriate random numbers to be assigned to an alternative possibility.
**DISCUSSION:** Given a 50% chance of a recall, 50 different numbers should be assigned to that alternative. This answer is the only alternative with 50 numbers (11-60).
Answer (A) is incorrect because 1-40 is an appropriate assignment of random numbers for the notification category. Answer (B) is incorrect because 40-90 includes 51 numbers. Answer (C) is incorrect because 61-100 is an appropriate assignment of random numbers for the notification category.

**49.** Quick Response Plumbing (QRP), a wholesale distributor, supplies plumbing contractors and retailers throughout the Northeast on a next-day delivery basis. QRP has a centrally located warehouse to accept receipts of plumbing supplies. The warehouse has a single dock to accept and unload railroad freight cars during the night. It takes 5 hours to unload each freight car. QRP's prior records indicate that the number of freight cars that arrive in the course of a night range from zero to five or more, with no indicated pattern of arrivals. If more than two freight cars arrive on the same night, some freight must be held until the next day for unloading. QRP wants to estimate the wait time when more than two freight cars arrive in the same night. The appropriate technique to analyze the arrival of freight cars is

A. Integer programming.

B. Linear programming.

C. Monte Carlo simulation.

D. Regression analysis.

Answer (C) is correct. *(CMA, adapted)*
**REQUIRED:** The appropriate technique to analyze the arrival of freight cars given no indicated pattern of arrivals.
**DISCUSSION:** The Monte Carlo simulation method is often used to generate the individual values for a random variable. The performance of a quantitative model under uncertainty may be investigated by randomly selecting values for each variable in the model (based on the probability distribution of each variable) and then calculating the value of the solution. If this process is performed many times, the distribution of results from the model will be obtained.
Answer (A) is incorrect because integer programming is a variation of linear programming that concerns problems in which some variables are not continuous. Integer programming problems are also known as discrete models because the variables take on discrete, noncontinuous values. Answer (B) is incorrect because linear programming is a technique used to maximize a revenue or profit function, or minimize a cost function, subject to constraints such as limited resources or minimum (or maximum) levels of production time. Answer (D) is incorrect because regression analysis is used to find an equation for the linear relationships among variables.

**50.** Through the use of decision models, managers thoroughly analyze many alternatives and decide on the best alternative for the company. Often the actual results achieved from a particular decision are not what was expected when the decision was made. In addition, an alternative that was not selected would have actually been the best decision for the company. The appropriate technique to analyze the alternatives by using expected inputs and altering them before a decision is made is

A. Expected value analysis.

B. Linear programming.

C. Program Evaluation Review Technique (PERT).

D. Sensitivity analysis.

Answer (D) is correct. *(CMA, adapted)*
**REQUIRED:** The technique that involves altering expected inputs during the decision process.
**DISCUSSION:** Sensitivity modeling can be used to determine the outcome of a variety of decisions. A trial-and-error method may be adopted, usually in a computer model, to calculate the sensitivity of the solution (variability of outcomes) to changes in a variable.
Answer (A) is incorrect because expected value analysis is used to determine an anticipated return or cost based upon probabilities of events and their related outcomes. Answer (B) is incorrect because linear programming optimizes a function given certain constraints. Answer (C) is incorrect because PERT is a network technique used to plan and control large projects.

**51.** Which one of the following items would most likely not be incorporated into the calculation of a division's investment base when using the residual income approach for performance measurement and evaluation?

A. Fixed assets employed in division operations.

B. Land being held by the division as a site for a new plant.

C. Division inventories when division management exercises control over the inventory levels.

D. Division accounts payable when division management exercises control over the amount of short-term credit used.

Answer (B) is correct. *(CMA, adapted)*
**REQUIRED:** The item most likely not incorporated into the calculation of a division's investment base.
**DISCUSSION:** An evaluation of an investment center is based upon the return on the investment base. These assets include plant and equipment, inventories, and receivables. Most likely, however, an asset, such as land, that is being held by the division as a site for a new plant would not be included in the investment base because it is not currently being used in operations. Total assets in use rather than total assets available is preferable when the investment center has been forced to carry idle assets.
Answer (A) is incorrect because fixed operating assets are controlled by the division manager and contribute to profits. Answer (C) is incorrect because inventories are operating assets that contribute to profits and are controlled by the division manager. Answer (D) is incorrect because the level of accounts payable is an operating decision that should be considered in the evaluation of the division manager.

**52.** Which denominator used in the return on investment (ROI) formula is criticized because it combines the effects of operating decisions made at one organizational level with financing decisions made at another organizational level?

A. Total assets employed.

B. Equity.

C. Working capital plus other assets.

D. Total assets available.

Answer (B) is correct. *(CMA, adapted)*
**REQUIRED:** The ROI denominator.
**DISCUSSION:** ROI equals income divided by invested capital. The denominator may be defined in various ways, e.g., total assets available, assets employed, working capital plus other assets, and equity. If equity (total assets − total liabilities) is chosen, a portion of long-term liabilities must be allocated to the investment center to determine the manager's resource base. One problem with this definition of the resource base is that, although it has the advantage of emphasizing return to owners, it reflects decisions at different levels of the entity: short-term liabilities incurred by the responsibility center (operating decisions) and long-term liabilities controlled at the corporate level (long-term financing decisions).
Answer (A) is incorrect because it reflects an assumption that the subunit manager does not influence the resource base (denominator of the ROI calculation). Answer (C) is incorrect because working capital plus other assets reflects the assumption that the manager controls short-term credit. However, no corporate-level decision to allocate long-term liabilities to subunits is necessary. Answer (D) is incorrect because it reflects an assumption that the subunit manager does not influence the resource base (denominator of the ROI calculation).

**53.** Listed below is selected financial information for the Western Division of the Hinzel Company for last year.

| Account | Amount (thousands) |
|---|---|
| Average working capital | $ 625 |
| General and administrative expenses | 75 |
| Net sales | 4,000 |
| Average plant and equipment | 1,775 |
| Cost of goods sold | 3,525 |

If Hinzel treats the Western Division as an investment center for performance measurement purposes, what is the before-tax return on investment (ROI) for last year?

A. 34.78%

B. 22.54%

C. 19.79%

D. 16.67%

Answer (D) is correct. *(CMA, adapted)*
REQUIRED: The before-tax ROI for an investment center.
DISCUSSION: An investment center is responsible for revenues, expenses, and invested capital. Given average plant and equipment of $1,775 and average working capital of $625, the net investment is $2,400. Before-tax profit is $400 ($4,000 sales – $3,525 cost of goods sold – $75 general expenses). If before-tax ROI equals before-tax profit divided by net investment, the answer is 16.67% ($400 ÷ $2,400).
Answer (A) is incorrect because 34.78% results from subtracting working capital from plant and equipment in calculating the net investment. Answer (B) is incorrect because 22.54% fails to include average working capital in the total for the net investment. Answer (C) is incorrect because 19.79% results from not subtracting general and administrative expenses in the calculation of before-tax profit.

**54.** Residual income is a better measure for performance evaluation of an investment center manager than return on investment because

A. The problems associated with measuring the asset base are eliminated.

B. Desirable investment decisions will not be neglected by high-return divisions.

C. Only the gross book value of assets needs to be calculated.

D. The arguments about the implicit cost of interest are eliminated.

Answer (B) is correct. *(CMA, adapted)*
REQUIRED: The reason residual income is a better measure of performance evaluation than return on investment.
DISCUSSION: Residual income is the excess of the amount of the ROI over a targeted amount equal to an imputed interest charge on invested capital. The advantage of using residual income rather than percentage ROI is that the former emphasizes maximizing a dollar amount instead of a percentage. Managers of divisions with a high ROI are encouraged to accept projects with returns exceeding the cost of capital even if those projects reduce the department's ROI.
Answer (A) is incorrect because this method uses the same asset base. Answer (C) is incorrect because this method uses the same asset base. Answer (D) is incorrect because use of the residual income method requires a knowledge of the cost of capital; thus, arguments about the implicit cost of interest may escalate with use of the residual income method.

**55.** James Webb is the general manager of the Industrial Product Division, and his performance is measured using the residual income method. Webb is reviewing the following forecasted information for his division for next year:

| Category | Amount (thousands) |
|---|---|
| Working capital | $ 1,800 |
| Revenue | 30,000 |
| Plant and equipment | 17,200 |

If the imputed interest charge is 15% and Webb wants to achieve a residual income target of $2,000,000, what will costs have to be in order to achieve the target?

A. $9,000,000

B. $10,800,000

C. $25,150,000

D. $25,690,000

Answer (C) is correct. *(CMA, adapted)*
REQUIRED: The maximum costs consistent with meeting a residual income target.
DISCUSSION: Residual income is the excess of the amount of the ROI over a targeted amount equal to an imputed interest charge on invested capital. If a manager has $19,000,000 of invested capital ($17,200,000 of plant and equipment + $1,800,000 of working capital), a 15% imputed interest charge equals $2,850,000. Adding $2,000,000 of residual income to the imputed interest results in a target profit of $4,850,000. This profit can be achieved if costs are $25,150,000 ($30,000,000 revenue – $4,850,000 profit).
Answer (A) is incorrect because this level of cost would result in a residual income greater than $2,000,000. Answer (B) is incorrect because this level of cost would result in a residual income greater than $2,000,000. Answer (D) is incorrect because $25,690,000 results from subtracting working capital from plant and equipment in determining invested capital.

**56.** REB Service Co. is a computer service center. For the month of May, REB had the following operating statistics:

| | |
|---|---|
| Sales | $450,000 |
| Operating income | 25,000 |
| Net profit after taxes | 8,000 |
| Total assets | 500,000 |
| Shareholders' equity | 200,000 |
| Cost of capital | 6% |

Based on the above information, which one of the following statements is true? REB has a

A. Return on investment of 4%.

B. Residual income of $(5,000).

C. Return on investment of 1.6%.

D. Residual income of $(22,000).

Answer (B) is correct.  *(CMA, adapted)*
**REQUIRED:** The true statement about the company's performance.
**DISCUSSION:** Return on investment is commonly calculated by dividing pretax income by total assets available. Residual income is the excess of the return on investment over a targeted amount equal to an imputed interest charge on invested capital. The rate used is ordinarily the weighted-average cost of capital. Some companies measure managerial performance in terms of the amount of residual income rather than the percentage return on investment. Because REB has assets of $500,000 and a cost of capital of 6%, it must earn $30,000 on those assets to cover the cost of capital. Given that operating income was only $25,000, it had a negative residual income of $5,000.
Answer (A) is incorrect because, although the firm's return on equity investment was 4%, its return on all funds invested was 5% ($25,000 pretax operating income ÷ $500,000). Answer (C) is incorrect because ROI is commonly based on before-tax income. Answer (D) is incorrect because $(22,000) equals the difference between net profit after taxes and targeted income.

**57.** Managerial performance may be measured in many ways. For example, an internal nonfinancial measure is

A. Market share.

B. Delivery performance.

C. Customer satisfaction.

D. Manufacturing lead time.

Answer (D) is correct.  *(Publisher)*
**REQUIRED:** The internal nonfinancial measure.
**DISCUSSION:** Feedback regarding managerial performance may take the form of financial and nonfinancial measures that may be internally or externally generated. Moreover, different measures have a long-term or short-term emphasis. Examples of internal nonfinancial measures are product quality, new product development time, and manufacturing lead time (cycle time).
Answer (A) is incorrect because market share is an external nonfinancial measure. Answer (B) is incorrect because delivery performance is an external nonfinancial measure. Answer (C) is incorrect because customer satisfaction is an external nonfinancial measure.

**58.** Many forms of performance feedback are based on accounting information. For example, a divisional manager may be evaluated based on return on investment (income ÷ investment). One step in the process of developing a performance measure based on accounting information is to determine the basis for stating the measure in terms of dollars. Thus, if ROI is the chosen measure, and investment is defined as total assets, comparability issues are most likely to arise when the attribute used to calculate total assets is

A. Current cost.

B. Current disposal price.

C. Historical cost.

D. Present value.

Answer (C) is correct.  *(Publisher)*
**REQUIRED:** The attribute most likely to create comparability problems.
**DISCUSSION:** Historical cost creates comparability issues because returns on significantly depreciated assets may be higher than those on newer assets that have been acquired using inflated dollars. Thus, otherwise similarly situated managers may report different operating results. Moreover, managers may be reluctant to replace aging assets.
Answer (A) is incorrect because current cost is an attempt to remedy the theoretical deficiencies of historical cost by presenting more accurate balance sheet values. Answer (B) is incorrect because current disposal price is an attempt to remedy the theoretical deficiencies of historical cost by presenting more accurate balance sheet values. Answer (D) is incorrect because present value is an attempt to remedy the theoretical deficiencies of historical cost by presenting more accurate balance sheet values.

**59.** An organization's managerial decision-making model for capital budgeting is based on the net present value of discounted cash flows. The same organization's managerial performance evaluation model is based on annual divisional return on investment. Which of the following is true?

A. Divisional managers are likely to maximize the measures in the decision-making model.

B. Divisional managers are likely to maximize the measures in the performance evaluation model.

C. The manager has an incentive to accept a project with a positive net present value that initially has a negative effect on net income.

D. The use of models with different criteria promotes goal congruence.

Answer (B) is correct. *(Publisher)*
**REQUIRED:** The true statement about use of different models for decision making and managerial evaluation.
**DISCUSSION:** Effective management control requires performance measurement and feedback. This process affects allocation of resources to organizational subunits. It also affects decisions about managers' compensation, advancement, and future assignments. Furthermore, evaluating their performance serves to motivate managers to optimize the measures in the performance evaluation model. However, that model may be inconsistent with the organization's model for managerial decision making.
Answer (A) is incorrect because self-interest provides an incentive to maximize the measures used in performance evaluation. Answer (C) is incorrect because a manager evaluated on the basis of annual ROI has an interest in maximizing short-term net income, not long-term NPV. Answer (D) is incorrect because the models should be synchronized so that the goals of the organization and the manager are congruent.

**60.** Which of the following criteria would be most useful to a sales department manager in evaluating the performance of the manager's customer-service group?

A. The customer is always right.

B. Customer complaints should be processed promptly.

C. Employees should maintain a positive attitude when dealing with customers.

D. All customer inquiries should be answered within 7 days of receipt.

Answer (D) is correct. *(CIA, adapted)*
**REQUIRED:** The criterion most useful for evaluating a customer-service group.
**DISCUSSION:** A criterion that requires all customer inquiries to be answered within 7 days of receipt permits accurate measurement of performance. The quantitative and specific nature of the appraisal using this standard avoids the vagueness, subjectivity, and personal bias that may afflict other forms of personnel evaluations.
Answer (A) is incorrect because customer orientation is difficult to quantify. Answer (B) is incorrect because the standard specified is vague. Answer (C) is incorrect because no measure of a positive attitude has been specified for the employee.

**61.** Using the balanced scorecard approach, an organization evaluates managerial performance based on

A. A single ultimate measure of operating results, such as residual income.

B. Multiple financial and nonfinancial measures.

C. Multiple nonfinancial measures only.

D. Multiple financial measures only.

Answer (B) is correct. *(Publisher)*
**REQUIRED:** The nature of the balanced scorecard approach.
**DISCUSSION:** The trend in managerial performance evaluation is the balanced scorecard approach. Multiple measures of performance permit a determination as to whether a manager is achieving certain objectives at the expense of others that may be equally or more important. These measures may be financial or nonfinancial and usually include items in four categories: profitability; customer satisfaction; innovation; and efficiency, quality, and time.
Answer (A) is incorrect because the balanced scorecard approach uses multiple measures. Answer (C) is incorrect because the balanced scorecard approach includes financial measures. Answer (D) is incorrect because the balanced scorecard approach includes nonfinancial measures.

**62.** Focusing on customers, promoting innovation, learning new philosophies, driving out fear, and providing extensive training are all elements of a major change in organizations. These elements are aimed primarily at

A. Copying leading organizations to better compete with them.

B. Focusing on the total quality of products and services.

C. Being efficient and effective at the same time, in order to indirectly affect profits.

D. Managing costs of products and services better, in order to become the low-cost provider.

Answer (B) is correct.  *(CIA, adapted)*
    **REQUIRED:** The purpose of focusing on customers, promoting innovation, learning new philosophies, driving out fear, and providing extensive training.
    **DISCUSSION:** TQM is a comprehensive approach to quality. It treats the pursuit of quality as a basic organizational function that is as important as production or marketing. TQM is the continuous pursuit of quality in every aspect of organizational activities through a philosophy of doing it right the first time, employee training and empowerment, promotion of teamwork, improvement of processes, and attention to satisfaction of customers, both internal and external. TQM emphasizes the supplier's relationship with the customer, identifies customer needs, and recognizes that everyone in a process is at some time a customer or supplier of someone else, either within or without the organization.
    Answer (A) is incorrect because competitive benchmarking is just one tool for implementing TQM. Answer (C) is incorrect because TQM's primary focus is not profitability. Answer (D) is incorrect because TQM's primary focus is not cost reduction.

Questions 63 and 64 are based on the following information. The management and employees of a large household goods moving company decided to adopt total quality management (TQM) and continuous improvement (CI). They believed that, if their company became nationally known as adhering to TQM and CI, one result would be an increase in the company's profits and market share.

**63.** The primary reason for adopting TQM was to achieve

A. Greater customer satisfaction.

B. Reduced delivery time.

C. Reduced delivery charges.

D. Greater employee participation.

Answer (A) is correct.  *(CIA, adapted)*
    **REQUIRED:** The primary reason for adopting TQM.
    **DISCUSSION:** TQM is an integrated system that anticipates, meets, and exceeds customers' needs, wants, and expectations.
    Answer (B) is incorrect because reduced delivery time is one of many potential activities that need improvement. Answer (C) is incorrect because reduced delivery charges is one of many potential activities that need improvement. Answer (D) is incorrect because increased employee participation is necessary to achieve TQM, but it is not the primary purpose for establishing the program.

**64.** Quality is achieved more economically if the company focuses on

A. Appraisal costs.

B. Prevention costs.

C. Internal failure costs.

D. External failure costs.

Answer (B) is correct.  *(CIA, adapted)*
    **REQUIRED:** The necessary focus for achieving quality more economically.
    **DISCUSSION:** Prevention attempts to avoid defective output. Prevention costs include preventive maintenance, employee training, review of equipment design, and evaluation of suppliers. Prevention is less costly than detection and correction of defective output.

**65.** Total quality management in a manufacturing environment is best exemplified by

A. Identifying and reworking production defects before sale.

B. Designing the product to minimize defects.

C. Performing inspections to isolate defects as early as possible.

D. Making machine adjustments periodically to reduce defects.

Answer (B) is correct.  *(CIA, adapted)*
    **REQUIRED:** The activity characteristic of TQM.
    **DISCUSSION:** Total quality management emphasizes quality as a basic organizational function. TQM is the continuous pursuit of quality in every aspect of organizational activities. One of the basic tenets of TQM is doing it right the first time. Thus, errors should be caught and corrected at the source, and quality should be built in (designed in) from the start.

**66.** One of the main reasons that implementation of a total quality management program works better through the use of teams is

A. Teams are more efficient and help an organization reduce its staffing.

B. Employee motivation is always higher for team members than for individual contributors.

C. Teams are a natural vehicle for sharing ideas, which leads to process improvement.

D. The use of teams eliminates the need for supervision, thereby allowing a company to reduce staffing.

Answer (C) is correct. *(CIA, adapted)*
**REQUIRED:** The reason that implementation of a TQM program works better through the use of teams.
**DISCUSSION:** TQM promotes teamwork by modifying or eliminating traditional (and rigid) vertical hierarchies and instead forming flexible groups of specialists. Quality circles, cross-functional teams, and self-managed teams are typical formats. Teams are an excellent vehicle for encouraging the sharing of ideas and removing process improvement obstacles.
Answer (A) is incorrect because teams are often inefficient and costly. Answer (B) is incorrect because high motivation does not directly affect the process improvement that is the key to quality improvement. Answer (D) is incorrect because the use of teams with less supervision and reduced staffing may be by-products of TQM, but they are not ultimate objectives.

**67.** A traditional quality control process in manufacturing consists of mass inspection of goods only at the end of a production process. A major deficiency of the traditional control process is that

A. It is expensive to do the inspections at the end of the process.

B. It is not possible to rework defective items.

C. It is not 100% effective.

D. It does not focus on improving the entire production process.

Answer (D) is correct. *(CIA, adapted)*
**REQUIRED:** The major deficiency of a traditional quality control process.
**DISCUSSION:** The process used to produce the goods is not thoroughly reviewed and evaluated for efficiency and effectiveness. Preventing defects and increasing efficiency by improving the production process raises quality standards and decreases costs.
Answer (A) is incorrect because other quality control processes can also be expensive. Answer (B) is incorrect because reworking defective items may be possible although costly. Answer (C) is incorrect because no quality control system will be 100% effective.

**68.** Under a total quality management (TQM) approach

A. Measurement occurs throughout the process, and errors are caught and corrected at the source.

B. Quality control is performed by highly trained inspectors at the end of the production process.

C. Upper management assumes the primary responsibility for the quality of the products and services.

D. A large number of suppliers are used in order to obtain the lowest possible prices.

Answer (A) is correct. *(CIA, adapted)*
**REQUIRED:** The true statement about total quality management.
**DISCUSSION:** Total quality management emphasizes quality as a basic organizational function. TQM is the continuous pursuit of quality in every aspect of organizational activities. One of the basic tenets of TQM is doing it right the first time. Thus, errors should be caught and corrected at the source.
Answer (B) is incorrect because total quality management emphasizes discovering errors throughout the process, not inspection of finished goods. Answer (C) is incorrect because all members of the organization assume responsibility for quality of the products and services. Answer (D) is incorrect because the total quality management philosophy recommends limiting the number of suppliers to create a strong relationship.

**69.** Which of the following is a key to successful total quality management?

A. Training quality inspectors.

B. Focusing intensely on the customer.

C. Creating appropriate hierarchies to increase efficiency.

D. Establishing a well-defined quality standard, then focusing on meeting it.

Answer (B) is correct. *(CIA, adapted)*
**REQUIRED:** The key to successful total quality management.
**DISCUSSION:** TQM emphasizes satisfaction of customers, both internal and external. TQM considers the supplier's relationship with the customer, identifies customer needs, and recognizes that everyone in a process is at some time a customer or supplier of someone else, either within or without the organization. Thus, TQM begins with external customer requirements, identifies internal customer-supplier relationships and requirements, and establishes requirements for external suppliers.
Answer (A) is incorrect because total quality management (TQM) de-emphasizes specialized quality inspectors.
Answer (C) is incorrect because centralization often needs to be reduced to implement a TQM process. Answer (D) is incorrect because TQM involves continuous improvement; once a standard is reached, continuous improvement requires its constant reevaluation.

**70.** Which of the following is a characteristic of total quality management (TQM)?

    A.  Management by objectives.

    B.  On-the-job training by other workers.

    C.  Quality by final inspection.

    D.  Education and self-improvement.

Answer (D) is correct.  *(CIA, adapted)*
    **REQUIRED:**  The characteristic of TQM.
    **DISCUSSION:**  According to management theorist W. Edwards Deming's well-known 14 points, education and self-improvement are essential.  Knowledge is opportunity.  Hence, continuous improvement should be everyone's primary career objective.
    Answer (A) is incorrect because one of the 14 points recommends elimination of numerical quotas.  MBO causes aggressive pursuit of numerical quotas.  Answer (B) is incorrect because informal learning from coworkers serves to entrench bad work habits.  One of the 14 points stresses proper training of everyone.  Answer (C) is incorrect because another of the 14 points states that quality by final inspection is unnecessary if quality is built in from the start.

**71.** In which of the following organizational structures does total quality management (TQM) work best?

    A.  Hierarchal.

    B.  Teams of people from the same specialty.

    C.  Teams of people from different specialties.

    D.  Specialists working individually.

Answer (C) is correct.  *(CIA, adapted)*
    **REQUIRED:**  The structure in which TQM works best.
    **DISCUSSION:**  TQM advocates replacement of the traditional hierarchal structure with teams of people from different specialities.  This change follows from TQM's emphasis on empowering employees and teamwork.  Employees should have proper training, necessary information, and the best tools; be fully engaged in the decision process; and receive fair compensation.  If such empowered employees are assembled in teams of individuals with the required skills, TQM theorists believe they will be more effective than people performing their tasks separately in a rigid structure.
    Answer (A) is incorrect because hierarchal organization stifles TQM.  Answer (B) is incorrect because TQM works best with teams of people from different specialties.  Answer (D) is incorrect because teamwork is essential for TQM.

**72.** One of the main reasons total quality management (TQM) can be used as a strategic weapon is that

    A.  The cumulative improvement from a company's TQM efforts cannot readily be copied by competitors.

    B.  Introducing new products can lure customers away from competitors.

    C.  Reduced costs associated with better quality can support higher shareholder dividends.

    D.  TQM provides a comprehensive planning process for a business.

Answer (A) is correct.  *(CIA, adapted)*
    **REQUIRED:**  The reason TQM can be used as a strategic weapon.
    **DISCUSSION:**  TQM is a comprehensive approach to quality.  It treats the pursuit of quality as a basic organizational function that is as important as production or marketing.  Because TQM affects every aspect of the organization's activities, it permeates the organizational culture.  Thus, the cumulative effect of TQM's continuous improvement process can attract and hold customers and cannot be duplicated by competitors.
    Answer (B) is incorrect because new products can be quickly copied by competitors and therefore do not provide a sustained competitive advantage.  Answer (C) is incorrect because TQM does not focus solely on cost reduction.  Answer (D) is incorrect because TQM is only one tool of strategic management.

**73.** Faced with 3 years of steadily decreasing profits despite increased sales and a growing economy, which of the following is the healthiest course of action for a chief executive officer to take?

    A. Set a turnaround goal of significantly increasing profits within 2 months. Set clear short-term objectives for each operating unit that, together, should produce the turnaround.

    B. Reduce staff by 10% in every unit.

    C. Classify all job functions as either (a) adding value in the eyes of the customer (such as production and sales) or (b) not adding value in the eyes of the customer (such as accounting and human resources). Reduce staff in the non-value-adding functions by 20%.

    D. Implement a plan to encourage innovation at all levels. Use early retirement and reemployment programs to trim staff size.

Answer (D) is correct. *(CIA, adapted)*
    **REQUIRED:** The healthiest course of action given decreasing profits despite increasing sales.
    **DISCUSSION:** Organizational decline has been found to have the following characteristics: greater centralization, lack of long-term planning, reduced innovation, scapegoating, resistance to change, high turnover of competent leaders, low morale, nonprioritized downsizing, and conflict. Reversing these characteristics is the key to reversing organizational decline, for example, by encouraging innovation in all aspects of the organization's activities and by redeploying personnel.
    Answer (A) is incorrect because this response illustrates two of the characteristics of organizational decline: increased centralization of decision making and lack of long-term planning. The exclusive emphasis on short-term results is likely to be counterproductive. Answer (B) is incorrect because another characteristic of organizational decline is nonprioritized downsizing. By itself, downsizing rarely turns a company around. Answer (C) is incorrect because reducing staff disproportionately in control functions could have disastrous consequences.

**74.** The International Organization for Standardization has developed standards for ring networks that include fault management, configuration management, accounting management, security management, and performance monitoring. Which of the following controls is included in the performance-monitoring standards?

    A. Reporting the failure of network fiber-optic lines.

    B. Recording unauthorized access violations.

    C. Compiling statistics on the number of times that application software is used.

    D. Allocating network costs to system users of the network.

Answer (C) is correct. *(CIA, adapted)*
    **REQUIRED:** The controls included in performance-monitoring standards.
    **DISCUSSION:** The International Organization for Standards consists of standards organizations from more than 75 countries. Its performance-monitoring standards pertain to management's ongoing assessment of the quality of performance over time. Recording software usage is a performance-monitoring control concerned with the extent and efficiency of network software use.
    Answer (A) is incorrect because the failure of network fiber-optic lines is a fault management control. Answer (B) is incorrect because recording unauthorized access violations is a security management control. Answer (D) is incorrect because allocating network costs to system users of the network is an accounting management control.

Questions 75 and 76 are based on the following information. Listed below are costs of quality that a manufacturing company has incurred throughout its operations. The company plans to prepare a report that classifies these costs into the following four categories: preventive costs, appraisal costs, internal failure costs, and external failure costs.

| Cost Items | Amount |
| --- | --- |
| Design reviews | $275,000 |
| Finished goods returned due to failure | 55,000 |
| Freight on replacement finished goods | 27,000 |
| Labor inspection during manufacturing | 75,000 |
| Labor inspection of raw materials | 32,000 |
| Manufacturing product-testing labor | 63,000 |
| Manufacturing rework labor and overhead | 150,000 |
| Materials used in warranty repairs | 68,000 |
| Process engineering | 180,000 |
| Product-liability claims | 145,000 |
| Product-testing equipment | 35,000 |
| Repairs to equipment due to breakdowns | 22,000 |
| Scheduled equipment maintenance | 90,000 |
| Scrap material | 125,000 |
| Training of manufacturing workers | 156,000 |

**75.** The costs of quality that are incurred in detecting units of product that do not conform to product specifications are referred to as

A. Preventive costs.

B. Appraisal costs.

C. Internal failure costs.

D. External failure costs.

Answer (B) is correct. *(CIA, adapted)*
REQUIRED: The costs of quality that are incurred in detecting units of product that do not conform to product specifications.
DISCUSSION: The categories of quality costs include conformance costs (prevention and appraisal) and nonconformance costs (internal failure and external failure). Appraisal costs embrace such activities as statistical quality control programs, inspection, and testing. Thus, the cost of detecting nonconforming products is an appraisal cost.
Answer (A) is incorrect because prevention attempts to avoid defective output, e.g., by employee training, review of equipment design, preventive maintenance, and evaluation of suppliers. Answer (C) is incorrect because internal failure costs are incurred when detection of defective products occurs before shipment, including scrap, rework, tooling changes, and downtime. Answer (D) is incorrect because external failure costs are incurred after the product has been shipped, including the costs associated with warranties, product liability, and loss of customer goodwill.

**76.** The dollar amount of the costs of quality classified as preventive costs for the manufacturing firm would be

A. $643,000

B. $701,000

C. $736,000

D. $768,000

Answer (B) is correct. *(CIA, adapted)*
REQUIRED: The preventive costs.
DISCUSSION: Prevention attempts to avoid defective output, e.g., by employee training, review of equipment design, preventive maintenance, and evaluation of suppliers. Accordingly, the preventive costs equal $701,000 ($275,000 design reviews + $180,000 process engineering + $90,000 scheduled maintenance + $156,000 training).
Answer (A) is incorrect because $643,000 omits scheduled equipment maintenance and includes labor inspection of raw materials (an appraisal cost). Answer (C) is incorrect because $736,000 includes the cost of product testing equipment (an appraisal cost). Answer (D) is incorrect because $768,000 includes the cost of product testing equipment and labor inspection of raw materials. Both costs are appraisal costs.

### 1.4 Project Management Techniques

**77.** When using PERT (Program Evaluation Review Technique), the expected time for an activity when given an optimistic time (A), a pessimistic time (B), and a most likely time (m) is calculated by which one of the following formulas?

    A. $(b - a) \div 2$

    B. $(a + b) \div 2$

    C. $(a + 4m + b) \div 6$

    D. $(4abm) \div 6$

Answer (C) is correct. *(CMA, adapted)*
    **REQUIRED:** The formula for calculating the expected time for an activity when using PERT.
    **DISCUSSION:** PERT was developed to aid managers in controlling large, complex projects. PERT analysis includes probabilistic estimates of activity completion times. Three time estimates are made: optimistic, most likely, and pessimistic. The time estimates for an activity are assumed to approximate a beta probability distribution. PERT approximates the mean of the beta distribution by dividing the sum of the optimistic time, the pessimistic time, and four times the most likely time by six.
    Answer (A) is incorrect because the most likely time estimate should be included in the formula. Answer (B) is incorrect because the most likely time estimate should be included in the formula. Answer (D) is incorrect because all time estimates are not weighted equally.

**78.** The process of adding resources to shorten selected activity times on the critical path in project scheduling is called

    A. Crashing.

    B. The Delphi technique.

    C. Material-requirements planning.

    D. A branch-and-bound solution.

Answer (A) is correct. *(CIA, adapted)*
    **REQUIRED:** The process of adding resources to shorten selected activity times on the critical path.
    **DISCUSSION:** When making a cost-time trade-off, the first activity to be crashed (have its completion time accelerated) is one on the critical path. To select an activity on another path would not reduce the total time of completion. The activity chosen should have a completion time that can be accelerated at the lowest possible cost per unit of time saved.
    Answer (B) is incorrect because the Delphi technique is a qualitative forecasting approach. Answer (C) is incorrect because material-requirements planning is an inventory model. Answer (D) is incorrect because a branch-and-bound solution is an integer programming solution.

**79.** California Building Corporation uses the critical path method to monitor construction jobs. The company is currently 2 weeks behind schedule on Job #181, which is subject to a $10,500-per-week completion penalty. Path A-B-C-F-G-H-I has a normal completion time of 20 weeks, and critical path A-D-E-F-G-H-I has a normal completion time of 22 weeks. The following activities can be crashed:

| Activities | Cost to Crash 1 Week | Cost to Crash 2 Weeks |
|---|---|---|
| BC | $ 8,000 | $15,000 |
| DE | 10,000 | 19,600 |
| EF | 8,800 | 19,500 |

California Building desires to reduce the normal completion time of Job #181 and, at the same time, report the highest possible income for the year. California Building should crash

    A. Activity BC 1 week and activity EF 1 week.

    B. Activity BC 2 weeks.

    C. Activity EF 2 weeks.

    D. Activity DE 1 week and activity EF 1 week.

Answer (D) is correct. *(CMA, adapted)*
    **REQUIRED:** The activity that should be crashed (speeded up at additional cost) to maximize income.
    **DISCUSSION:** Activities that are to be crashed in a CPM problem should be ones that are on the critical (longest) path. Thus, activity BC should not be selected because it is not on the critical path. To finish activity BC 2 weeks early would not reduce the total time to complete the project. Therefore, the only feasible choices are DE and EF on the critical path. The total cost to crash DE and EF for 1 week each is $18,800 ($10,000 + $8,800), which is less than the cost to crash either activity for 2 weeks. Thus, DE and EF should be crashed for 1 week each because the total cost is less than the $21,000 ($10,500 × 2) 2-week delay penalty.
    Answer (A) is incorrect because BC is not on the critical path. Answer (B) is incorrect because BC is not on the critical path. Answer (C) is incorrect because the cost of crashing EF 2 weeks is $19,500, which is greater than the total cost to crash DE and EF for 1 week each.

**80.** In a PERT network, the optimistic time for a particular activity is 9 weeks, and the pessimistic time is 21 weeks. Which one of the following is the best estimate of the standard deviation for the activity?

A. 2

B. 6

C. 9

D. 12

Answer (A) is correct.  *(CMA, adapted)*

**REQUIRED:** The standard deviation for the completion time of a PERT project given an optimistic time and a pessimistic time.

**DISCUSSION:** PERT analysis includes probabilistic estimates of activity completion times. Three time estimates are made: optimistic, most likely, and pessimistic. The time estimates for an activity are assumed to approximate a beta probability distribution. In contrast to the normal distribution, this distribution has finite endpoints (the optimistic and pessimistic estimates) and is unimodal; that is, it has only one mode (the most likely time). PERT approximates the mean of the beta distribution by dividing the sum of the optimistic time, the pessimistic time, and four times the most likely time (the mode) by six. The standard deviation is approximated by dividing the difference between the pessimistic and optimistic times by six. The basis for the latter approximation is that various probability distributions have tails that lie about plus or minus three standard deviations from the mean. For example, 99.9% of observations in the normal distribution are expected to lie within this range. Accordingly, if the pessimistic and optimistic times are 21 and 9 weeks, respectively, the standard deviation is 2 weeks (12 ÷ 6).

Answer (B) is incorrect because 6 is the approximate number of standard deviations between the tails of the normal distribution. Answer (C) is incorrect because 9 weeks is the pessimistic estimate. Answer (D) is incorrect because 12 weeks is the difference between the optimistic and the pessimistic estimates.

**81.** A PERT network has only two activities on its critical path. These activities have standard deviations of 6 and 8, respectively. The standard deviation of the project completion time is

A. 7

B. 10

C. 14

D. 48

Answer (B) is correct.  *(CMA, adapted)*

**REQUIRED:** The standard deviation of the project completion time given the standard deviations of the activity times on the critical path.

**DISCUSSION:** The mean time for the critical path is simply the sum of the means of the activity times. However, the standard deviation equals the square root of the sum of the variances (squares of the standard deviations) of the times for activities on the critical path. The standard deviation of the project completion time (time for the critical path) is therefore the square root of 100 ($6^2 + 8^2$), or 10.

Answer (A) is incorrect because 7 is the average standard deviation. Answer (C) is incorrect because 14 is the sum of the standard deviations. Answer (D) is incorrect because 48 is the product of the standard deviations.

Questions 82 and 83 are based on the following information. The PERT network diagram and the corresponding activity cost chart for a manufacturing project at Networks, Inc. are presented below. The numbers in the diagram are the expected times (in days) to perform each activity in the project.

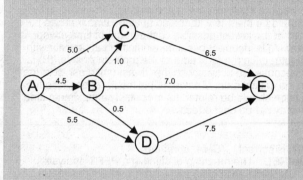

| Activity | Normal Cost | Crash Time | Crash Cost |
|---|---|---|---|
| AB | $3,000 | 3.50 days | $4,000 |
| AC | 5,000 | 4.50 | 5,250 |
| AD | 4,000 | 4.00 | 4,750 |
| BE | 6,000 | 5.00 | 7,000 |
| CE | 8,000 | 5.00 | 9,200 |
| DE | 6,000 | 6.50 | 6,750 |
| BC | 2,500 | .50 | 3,500 |
| BD | 2,000 | .25 | 2,500 |

**82.** The expected time of the critical path is

A. 12.0 days.

B. 13.0 days.

C. 11.5 days.

D. 11.0 days.

Answer (B) is correct. *(CMA, adapted)*
REQUIRED: The expected time of the critical path.
DISCUSSION: The critical path is the longest path. The longest path in the diagram is A-D-E, which requires 13 days (5.5 + 7.5) based on expected times.

**83.** In order to keep costs at a minimum and decrease the completion time by 1 1/2 days, Networks, Inc. should crash activity(ies)

A. AD and AB.

B. DE.

C. AD.

D. AB and CE.

Answer (A) is correct. *(CMA, adapted)*
REQUIRED: The activity(ies) that can be crashed by a specified number of days at the least cost.
DISCUSSION: The critical (longest) path is A-D-E, which has an expected time of 13 days (see preceding question). However, to decrease the project's completion time by 1.5 days, paths A-B-C-E (4.5 + 1.0 + 6.5 = 12 days) and A-B-D-E (4.5 + .5 + 7.5 = 12.5 days) as well as A-D-E must also be shortened. Hence, A-D-E must be reduced by 1.5 days, A-B-C-E by .5 day, and A-B-D-E by 1.0 day. The only way to decrease A-D-E by 1.5 days is to crash activity AD (5.5 expective time − 4.0 crash time = 1.5 days). Crashing DE results in a 1.0-day saving (7.5 − 6.5) only. Crashing AB is the efficient way to reduce both A-B-C-E and A-B-D-E by the desired amount of time because it is part of both paths. The incremental cost of crashing AB is $1,000 ($4,000 crash cost − $3,000 normal cost) to shorten the completion time by 1.0 day (4.5 − 3.5). The alternatives for decreasing both A-B-C-E and A-B-D-E are more costly.
    Answer (B) is incorrect because crashing activity DE saves only 1.0 day (7.5 − 6.5) on the critical path and does not reduce the time needed for A-B-C-E. Answer (C) is incorrect because crashing AD does not reduce the time necessary to complete A-B-C-E or A-B-D-E. Answer (D) is incorrect because AB and CE are not on the critical path.

**84.** When making a cost-time trade-off in PERT analysis, the first activity that should be crashed is the activity

   A. With the largest amount of slack.

   B. With the lowest unit crash cost.

   C. On the critical path with the maximum possible time reduction.

   D. On the critical path with the lowest unit crash cost.

Answer (D) is correct.  *(CMA, adapted)*
  **REQUIRED:** The first activity that should be crashed when making a cost-time trade-off in PERT analysis.
  **DISCUSSION:** When making a cost-time trade-off, the first activity to be crashed (have its completion time accelerated) is one on the critical path. To select an activity on another path would not reduce the total time of completion. The initial activity chosen should be the one with the completion time that can be accelerated at the lowest possible cost per unit of time saved.
  Answer (A) is incorrect because eliminating an activity with slack will not reduce the total time of the project. Answer (B) is incorrect because the activity with the lowest unit crash cost may not be on the critical path. Answer (C) is incorrect because the time reduction should be related to its cost. The maximum time reduction may not be cost effective.

**85.** In PERT, slack is the

   A. Uncertainty associated with time estimates.

   B. Difference between the latest starting time and earliest finishing time.

   C. Path that has the largest amount of time associated with it.

   D. Number of days an activity can be delayed without forcing a delay for the entire project.

Answer (D) is correct.  *(CMA, adapted)*
  **REQUIRED:** The meaning of slack in a PERT analysis.
  **DISCUSSION:** PERT diagrams are free-form networks showing each activity in a large project as a line between events. The critical path is the longest path in time through the network. That path is critical in that, if any activity on the critical path takes longer than expected, the entire project will be delayed. Paths that are not critical have slack time. Slack is the number of days an activity can be delayed without forcing a delay for the entire project.
  Answer (A) is incorrect because uncertainty is reflected in the use of probabilistic estimates of completion times. Answer (B) is incorrect because the difference between the latest starting time and earliest finishing time is irrelevant. Answer (C) is incorrect because the path with the largest amount of time associated with it is the critical path.

**86.** The network below describes the interrelationships of several activities necessary to complete a project. The arrows represent the activities. The numbers between the arrows indicate the number of months to complete each activity.

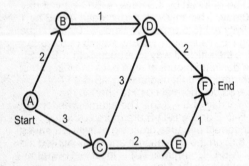

The shortest time to complete the project is

   A. 5 months.

   B. 6 months.

   C. 8 months.

   D. 14 months.

Answer (C) is correct.  *(CIA, adapted)*
  **REQUIRED:** The shortest time to complete the project.
  **DISCUSSION:** The longest, or critical, path in the network from node (A) to node (F) is path A-C-D-F. All other paths are shorter than path A-C-D-F, so the activities along those paths can be completed before the activities along path A-C-D-F. Thus, the shortest time to complete the project is 8 months (3 + 3 + 2).
  Answer (A) is incorrect because the project cannot be completed in less than 8 months. Answer (B) is incorrect because the project cannot be completed in less than 8 months. Answer (D) is incorrect because no path through the network requires 14 months.

**87.** A shortest-route algorithm is used in network models to

A. Identify bottlenecks in a network and hence identify the longest path.

B. Minimize total travel time from one site to each of the other sites in a transportation system.

C. Maximize throughput in networks with distinct entry (source node) and exit (sink node) points.

D. Identify the set of connecting branches having the shortest combined length.

Answer (B) is correct.  *(CIA, adapted)*
**REQUIRED:** The purpose of a shortest-route algorithm used in network models.
**DISCUSSION:** Network models are used to solve managerial problems pertaining to project scheduling, information systems design, and transportation systems design.  Networks consisting of nodes and arcs may be created to represent in graphic form problems related to transportation, assignment, and transshipment.  The shortest-route, minimal spanning tree, and maximal flow problems are other applications of network models.  A shortest-route algorithm minimizes total travel time from one site to each of the other sites in a transportation system.
Answer (A) is incorrect because the critical path method (CPM) is intended to identify bottlenecks in a network and hence identify the longest path.  Answer (C) is incorrect because the maximal flow algorithm maximizes throughput in networks with distinct entry (source node) and exit (sink node) points.  Examples of applications are highway transportation systems and oil pipelines.  Flows are limited by capacities of the arcs (e.g., highways or pipes).  Answer (D) is incorrect because the minimal spanning tree algorithm identifies the set of connecting branches having the shortest combined length.  A spanning tree is a group of branches (arcs) that connects each node in the network to every other node.  An example problem is the determination of the shortest telecommunications linkage among users at remote sites and a central computer.

## 1.5 Business Process Analysis

**88.** Reengineering is the thorough analysis, fundamental rethinking, and complete redesign of essential business processes.  The intended result is a dramatic improvement in service, quality, speed, and cost.  An internal auditor's involvement in reengineering should include all of the following except

A. Determining whether the process has senior management's support.

B. Recommending areas for consideration.

C. Developing audit plans for the new system.

D. Directing the implementation of the redesigned process.

Answer (D) is correct.  *(CIA, adapted)*
**REQUIRED:** The item not included in an internal auditor's involvement in reengineering.
**DISCUSSION:** Internal auditors should not become directly involved in the implementation of the redesign process.  This involvement would impair their independence and objectivity.  Staff assignments of internal auditors should be rotated periodically whenever it is practicable to do so.

**89.** Monitoring is an important component of internal control.  Which of the following items would not be an example of monitoring?

A. Management regularly compares divisional performance with budgets for the division.

B. Data processing management regularly generates exception reports for unusual transactions or volumes of transactions and follows up with investigation as to causes.

C. Data processing management regularly reconciles batch control totals for items processed with batch controls for items submitted.

D. Management has asked internal auditing to perform regular audits of the controls over cash processing.

Answer (C) is correct.  *(CIA, adapted)*
**REQUIRED:** The item not an example of monitoring.
**DISCUSSION:** Monitoring assesses the quality of internal control over time.  Management considers whether internal control is properly designed and operating as intended and modifies it to reflect changing conditions.  Monitoring may be in the form of separate, periodic evaluations or of ongoing monitoring.  Ongoing monitoring occurs as part of routine operations.  It includes management and supervisory review, comparisons, reconciliations, and other actions by personnel as part of their regular activities.  However, reconciling batch control totals is a processing control.
Answer (A) is incorrect because budgetary comparison is a typical example of a monitoring control.  Answer (B) is incorrect because investigation of exceptions is a monitoring control used by lower-level management to determine when their operations may be out of control.  Answer (D) is incorrect because internal auditing is a form of monitoring.  It serves to evaluate management's other controls.

**90.** Which of the following is a short-term approach to managing bottlenecks or binding constraints in production and distribution processes?

A. Theory of constraints.

B. Reengineering.

C. Rationalization.

D. Micromotion study.

Answer (A) is correct.    *(Publisher)*
**REQUIRED:** The term that is a short-term approach to managing bottlenecks.
**DISCUSSION:** The theory of constraints (TOC) is a short-term approach to managing bottlenecks (binding constraints) in production and distribution processes.  Its basic principle is that short-term profit maximization requires maximizing the contribution margin of the binding constraint (the throughput contribution).
Answer (B) is incorrect because reengineering an approach to business process analysis that entails process innovation and core process redesign.  Instead of improving existing procedures, it finds new ways of doing things.  Answer (C) is incorrect because rationalization is yet another approach to business process analysis.  It is the streamlining of procedures to make automation more efficient.  Answer (D) is incorrect because a micromotion study is a method used for work management, and it requires videotaping the performance of a job.

Use Gleim's *CIA Test Prep* for interactive testing with over 2,000 additional multiple-choice questions!

# STUDY UNIT TWO
# MANAGING RESOURCES AND PRICING

(26 pages of outline)

This study unit continues the treatment of business processes that began in the first study unit. The first subunit concerns the management of resources in the supply chain, particularly inventory. The second subunit addresses the objectives and factors that influence the pricing of the organization's products and services. The last subunit covers the management of the human capital of the organization.

## 2.1 INVENTORY AND SUPPLY CHAIN MANAGEMENT

1.  Inventory management concerns the effective and efficient acquisition, use, and distribution of inventory.

    a.  An organization carries inventories because of the difficulty in predicting the amount, timing, and location of supply and demand. Thus, one purpose of **inventory control** is to determine the optimal level of inventory necessary to minimize costs.

    b.  Although traditional inventory management **minimizes inventory** and the related holding costs, many companies use inventory as a hedge against inflation as well as a guarantee of future availability.

    c.  Inventory carrying costs are sometimes transferred to **suppliers or customers**.

        1)  If a manufacturer knows exactly when materials are needed, orders can be placed so that materials arrive no earlier than when actually needed.

            a)  This practice relies on a supplier who takes the responsibility for storing the needed inventory and shipping it to arrive on time.

            b)  Suppliers are more willing to provide this service when they have many competitors.

        2)  Customers sometimes carry large quantities of inventory when given special quantity discounts or extended credit terms.

        3)  If customers are willing to accept long lead times, inventory can be manufactured to order to avoid storing large quantities.

        4)  Although these measures can reduce inventory carrying costs, additional costs might be incurred by adopting them. Shortage (stockout) costs may be incurred when an item is out of stock. These include the lost contribution margin on sales, customer ill will, and production interruptions.

    d.  **Order costs** include all costs associated with preparing a purchase order.

    e.  **Carrying costs** include rent, insurance, taxes, security, depreciation, and opportunity cost (i.e., the cost incurred by investing in inventory rather than making an income-earning investment). Carrying costs may also include a charge for spoilage of perishable items or for obsolescence.

    f.  **Inventory policies** should consider the types of costs and any limitations the firm may have, such as storage space.

        1)  Constraints may also be imposed by suppliers.
        2)  The cost of maintaining inventory records should also be considered.

g.  **Reorder points, safety stock, stockout cost**

1)  The cost of holding safety stock and the cost of stockouts should be minimized.

   a)  Safety stock is the amount of extra stock that is kept to guard against stockouts. It is the inventory level at the time of reordering minus the expected usage while the new goods are in transit.

   b)  Stockout costs are lost sales, lost production, customer dissatisfaction, etc.

   c)  The problem may be diagrammed as follows:

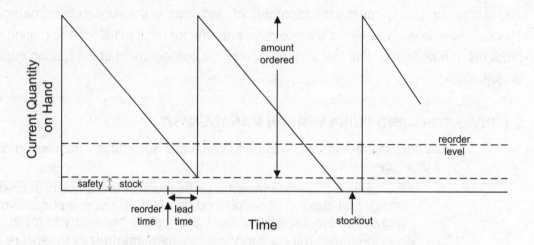

   i)  The economic order quantity (EOQ) determines order size.

   ii)  The reorder point is the intersection of the reorder level and the downward-sloping total inventory line that allows sufficient lead time for an order to be placed and received.

2.  **Purchasing** is the inventory management function that concerns the acquisition process. It encompasses choice of suppliers, contract negotiation, the decision whether to purchase centrally or locally, and value analysis.

   a.  The process is initiated by **purchase requisitions** issued by the production control function. Purchase requisitions ultimately result from make-or-buy decisions made when production processes were designed. For a retailer, the purchase decision is the same as the decision about what to sell.

   b.  The **choice of suppliers** depends on price, quality, delivery performance, shipping costs, credit terms, and service.

   1)  Purchasers with a **competitive orientation** and considerable economic power may be able to extract very favorable terms from suppliers.

   2)  Purchasers with a **cooperative orientation** adopt a longer-term approach. The purchaser and the supplier are viewed as committed to a partnership involving joint efforts to improve quality. This orientation includes the purchaser's willingness to help develop the supplier's managerial, technical, and productive capacities. Thus, it tends to result in minimizing the number of suppliers.

   c.  **Ordering** may be a complicated task when a onetime, expensive purchase is made. It may also be as simple as a phone call or a computer message. Indeed, organizations increasingly are linked with vendors by **electronic data interchange (EDI)**. EDI permits the transmission via computer of purchase orders, invoices, and payments, thereby reducing reorder times, inventories, and document-handling costs.

d. **Tracking purchases** involves following up to anticipate any deviations from delivery times, quantities, and quality. Tracking may prevent production interruptions.

e. The **receiving function** verifies the time of delivery, the quality and quantity received, and the price. It also notifies purchasing, the subunit that requested the delivery, inventory control, and accounting.

f. **Negotiation of contracts** depends on the nature of the item to be purchased. For a customized item, the organization may use competitive bidding, with the contract awarded to the lowest and best bidder; it may negotiate with a **sole-source supplier** to reduce purchasing lead time; or it may order through a supplier catalog.

    1) When purchased items are standardized and in high demand, the organization may also preselect a sole-source supplier to which orders will be sent as needed. Given great enough demand, the purchaser and supplier may even agree to a long-term contract with some terms left open. A **blanket contract** covers numerous items, and an **open-ended contract** permits terms to be added or the period of the agreement to be extended.

g. Large organizations must decide whether to **buy centrally or locally**. Buying centrally increases the organization's bargaining power and allows it to exploit the expertise of corporate-level specialists. The latter consideration is important given the trend toward purchasing items abroad. Centralized buying is facilitated by developments in information technology.

    1) Buying locally is indicated when items are unique to decentralized subunits, when a just-in-time (JIT) system is in place, and when longer lead times are to be avoided.

h. Purchasing shares responsibility for **value analysis** with the production and engineering functions. Value analysis determines the purpose of an item, whether that purpose is necessary, whether a less costly standard item can be found that serves the same purpose, and whether the item can be simplified or its specifications changed to reduce the cost. Thus, value analysis is performed by teams of specialists to ascertain how the performance of an item that is either produced or purchased can be improved or its cost decreased.

3. **Economic Order Quantity (EOQ)**

a. **Inventory models** are quantitative models designed to control inventory costs by determining the optimal time to place an order (or begin production) and the optimal order quantity (production run).

    1) The timing of an order can be periodic (placing an order every X days) or perpetual (placing an order whenever the inventory declines to X units).

       a) **Periodic order systems** place minimal emphasis on record keeping. However, a risk of substantial overstock or understock may arise unless inventories are checked for assurance that the model is still appropriate.

       b) **Perpetual systems** detect an inventory decline to the reorder point by entering every withdrawal on a perpetual record that shows the balance.

          i) An alternative is to use the **two-bin method** for physical storage. In this system, the reorder level amount is stored separately from the balance of the items. When the stock clerk removes the last item from the balance bin, an order should be placed. The reorder level bin is then used until the order is received.

       c) Physical inventories should be taken to reconcile records and verify models in either a periodic or a perpetual system.

b.   The **basic EOQ model** minimizes the sum of ordering (setup) costs and carrying costs.

1)   The following are the characteristics of this model:

a)   Demand is known and uniform throughout the period.

b)   The fixed costs of ordering are eliminated when the total cost equation is differentiated to arrive at the EOQ.

c)   Cost per order (setup) and unit carrying cost are constant.

i)   Thus, the model is based on variable costs.

d)   Full replenishment occurs instantly when the last item is used, stockout costs are zero, and no safety stock is held.

2)   The EOQ is the square root of twice the periodic demand multiplied by the order (setup) cost, divided by the periodic unit carrying cost.

$$X = \sqrt{\frac{2aD}{k}}$$

If: X = EOQ
$a$ = variable cost per order (setup)
D = periodic demand in units
k = unit periodic carrying cost

3)   EXAMPLE: If periodic demand is uniform at 1,000 units, the cost to place an order is $4, and the cost to carry one unit in inventory for a period is $2, the EOQ is 63.25 units.

$$EOQ = \sqrt{\frac{2(\$4)(1,000)}{\$2}} = 63.25 \text{ units}$$

4)   The **average level of inventory** for this model will be one-half of the EOQ. The formula shows that the EOQ varies directly with demand and order (setup) costs, but inversely with carrying costs. Thus, if demand quadruples, the EOQ will only double.

5)   The EOQ is a **periodic model**. The number of orders (production runs) per period is given by the periodic demand divided by the EOQ.

6) The EOQ results from **differentiating** the total cost with regard to order (production) quantity. It is the minimum point on the total cost curve. It also corresponds to the intersection of the variable carrying cost and the variable ordering cost curves. The fundamental EOQ model is based on variable costs. As explained previously, order (setup) cost and unit carrying cost are variable, and fixed costs are eliminated when the total cost equation is differentiated.

$$c = \left(\frac{D}{x}\right)a + \frac{xk}{2} + F$$

If: c = total cost
x = EOQ
a = variable cost per order (setup)
D = periodic demand in units
k = unit periodic carrying cost
F = fixed costs

$$dc/dx = \frac{-Da}{x^2} + \frac{k}{2}$$

Setting dc/dx = 0 at minimum total cost,

$$\frac{-Da}{x^2} + \frac{k}{2} = 0$$

$$\frac{k}{2} = \frac{Da}{x^2}$$

$$x^2 = \frac{2Da}{k}$$

$$X = \sqrt{\frac{2aD}{k}}$$

c. Variations of the EOQ model are numerous.

1) The **effects of quantity discounts** can be considered by using trial and error. The EOQ is found as shown on the previous page, and, if it is below the discount level, the total cost equals the sum of the purchase cost plus annual carrying and order costs. Next, the minimum order quantity needed to obtain the discount is considered, and total cost is found for this level. This process is repeated for multiple levels of discount. The optimal order quantity is the one giving the lowest periodic total cost.

2) **Lead time** is accounted for by simply placing orders in advance. If back ordering is acceptable to customers, it can also be incorporated into the model.

3) The **limitations of the EOQ model** are its restrictive assumptions, especially that of constant demand. But it can be combined with probability concepts to form an effective perpetual system.

     d.  **Probabilistic models** have been developed for the situation in which demand is random yet has a known distribution.

         1)  In a perpetual system, the possibility of running out of stock exists only during the reorder period, the time between placing and receiving the order. The reorder point is found by using the probability distribution for demand during the period.

            a)  The order quantity is found by using the basic EOQ model and average demand.

            b)  If stockout costs are known, an optimal reorder point can be found.

                i)  If these costs are unknown, management can select a service level or probability of being in stock that can be used to find the reorder point.

     e.  Among the **limitations of inventory models for control** are that they are restricted to one item at a time and that they consider each item of equal importance.

         1)  If a firm has 10,000 line items, 10,000 calculations would have to be made. Computer programs are available to perform the computations, but they still need periodic review.

         2)  The importance of items can vary from essential to immaterial. The priority of an item needs to be considered in establishing controls.

         3)  A third limitation is that demand is often more variable than expected. Seasonal variations, as well as unexpected changes, can be provided for by including a forecasting model to estimate the demand to be used in the inventory model.

4.  **The ABC system** is a simple inventory management technique.

     a.  This method controls inventories by dividing items into three groups.

         1)  **Group A** -- high-dollar-value items, which account for a small portion (perhaps 10%) of the total inventory usage

         2)  **Group B** -- medium-dollar-value items, which may account for about 20% of the total inventory items

         3)  **Group C** -- low-dollar-value items, which account for the remaining 70% of sales or usage

     b.  The ABC system permits the proper **degree of managerial control** to be exercised over each group. The level of control reflects cost-benefit concerns.

         1)  Group A items are reviewed on a regular basis.

         2)  Group B items may not need review as often as group A items, but may need review more often than group C items.

         3)  For group C, extensive use of models and records is not cost effective. It is cheaper to order large quantities infrequently.

5.  **Materials requirements planning (MRP)** is an integrated computer-based information system designed to plan and control raw materials used in a production setting. MRP is characterized as a **push-through system** because production is activated by forecasts of demand, not actual customer needs.

     a.  MRP is also a **dependent-demand system**. It assumes that the forecasted demand for materials is typically dependent upon some other factor, which can be programmed into the computer, e.g., the demand for the completed product.

     b.  The timing of deliveries is vital to avoid production delays.

c.   EXAMPLE:  An auto manufacturer need only tell a computer how many autos of each type are to be manufactured.  The MRP system determines how many of every component part will be needed.  The computer will generate a complete list of every part and component needed.

d.   MRP, in effect, creates schedules of when items of inventory will be needed in the production departments.  If parts are not in stock, the computer will automatically generate a purchase order on the proper date (considering lead times) so that deliveries will arrive on time.

6.   Modern inventory control favors the **just-in-time (JIT)** model.  Companies have traditionally built parts and components for subsequent operations on a preset schedule.  Such a schedule provides a cushion of inventory so that the next operation will always have parts to work with -- a **just-in-case method**.

a.   In contrast, JIT limits output to the demand of the subsequent operation.  **Reductions in inventory levels** result in less money invested in idle assets; reduction of storage space requirements; and lower inventory taxes, pilferage, and obsolescence risks.

1)   High inventory levels often mask **production problems** because defective parts can be overlooked when plenty of good parts are available.  If only enough parts are made for the subsequent operation, however, any defects will immediately halt production.

2)   The focus of **quality control** under JIT shifts from the discovery of defective parts to the prevention of quality problems, so **zero machine breakdowns** (achieved through preventive maintenance) and **zero defects** are ultimate goals.  Higher quality and lower inventory go together.

b.   JIT is a reaction to the **trends** of global competition and rapid technological progress that have resulted in shorter product life-cycles and greater consumer demand for product diversity.

1)   **Goals**.  Higher productivity, reduced order costs as well as carrying costs, faster and cheaper setups, shorter manufacturing cycle times, better due date performance, improved quality, and more flexible processes are goals of JIT methods.  The ultimate objectives are increased competitiveness and higher profits.

c.   JIT systems are based on a **manufacturing philosophy** popularized by the Japanese that combines purchasing, production, and inventory control.  Minimization of inventory is a goal because many inventory-related activities are viewed as **nonvalue-added**.  Indeed, carrying inventory is regarded as a symptom of correctable problems, such as poor quality, long cycle times, and lack of coordination with suppliers.

d.   However, JIT also encompasses changes in the **production process** itself.  JIT is a **pull system**; items are pulled through production by current demand, not pushed through by anticipated demand.  Thus, one operation produces only what is needed by the next operation, and components and raw materials arrive just in time to be used.  To implement this approach and to eliminate waste of materials, labor, factory space, and machine usage, the factory is reorganized to permit what is often called **lean production**.

1)   Plant layout in a JIT-lean production environment is not arranged by functional department or process but by **manufacturing cells**.  Cells are sets of machines, often grouped in semicircles, that produce a given product or product type.

a)   Each worker in a cell must be able to operate all machines and, possibly, to perform support tasks, such as setup activities, preventive maintenance, movement of work-in-process within the cell, and quality inspection.

       b)   In a pull system, workers might often be idle if they were not multiskilled. Hence, central support departments are reduced or eliminated, space is saved, fewer and smaller factories may be required, and materials and tools are brought close to the point of use. Manufacturing cycle time and setup time are also reduced. As a result, on-time delivery performance and response to changes in markets are enhanced, and production of customized goods in small lots becomes feasible.

       c)   A cellular organization requires workers to operate as effective teams, so **employee empowerment** is crucial in a JIT-lean production system. Greater participation by employees is needed to achieve continuous improvement and zero defects goals. They may have the power to stop production to correct a problem, be consulted about changes in processes, or become involved in hiring co-workers. Thus, managers in such a system usually play more of a facilitating than a support role.

  e.   The Japanese term **kanban** and JIT have often been confused. JIT is the total system of purchasing, production, and inventory control. Kanban is one of the many elements in the JIT system as it is used in Japan. Kanban means **ticket**. Tickets (also described as cards or markers) control the flow of production or parts so that they are produced or obtained in the needed amounts at the needed times.

       1)   A basic kanban system includes a **withdrawal kanban** that states the quantity that a later process should withdraw from its predecessor and a **production kanban** that states the output of the preceding process. A **vendor kanban** tells a vendor what, how much, where, and when to deliver.

       2)   Many companies have not been comfortable with controlling production using tickets on the production floor. Computerized information systems have been used for many years, and these companies have been reluctant to give up their computers in favor of the essentially manual kanban system. Instead, they have integrated their existing systems, which are complex computerized planning systems, with the JIT system.

  f.   Another feature of the lower inventory levels in a JIT system is elimination of the need for several traditional **internal controls**. Frequent receipt of deliveries from suppliers often means less need for a sophisticated inventory control system and for control personnel.

       1)   JIT also may eliminate central receiving areas, hard copy receiving reports, and storage areas. A central warehouse is not needed because deliveries are made by suppliers directly to the area of production.

       2)   The quality of parts provided by suppliers is verified by use of statistical controls rather than inspection of incoming goods. Storage, counting, and inspecting are eliminated in an effort to perform only value-adding work.

  g.   In a JIT system, the dependability of **suppliers** is crucial. Organizations that adopt JIT systems therefore develop close relationships with a few carefully chosen suppliers who are extensively involved in the buyer's processes.

       1)   Long-term contracts are typically negotiated to reduce order costs. Indeed, some major retailers have agreed to **continuous replenishment** arrangements whereby a supplier with superior demand forecasting ability essentially tells the buyer when and how much to reorder.

       2)   Buyer-supplier relationships are further facilitated by **electronic data interchange (EDI)**, a technology that allows the supplier access to the buyer's online inventory management system. Thus, electronic messages replace paper documents (purchase orders and sales invoices), and the production schedules and deliveries of the parties can be more readily coordinated.

h.  A concept closely related to JIT is **continuous replenishment of products (CRP)**. In a CRP system, such as Wal-Mart's, inventory management is the supplier's responsibility. When customers pay for goods at checkout, **point-of-sale (POS) devices** note bar codes and send automatic purchase orders to a central computer. The orders from all stores are then collected and retransmitted to the supplier. Thus, purchases are adjusted to demand with great speed.

7.  Modern manufacturing environments impose control and improve quality through **automation**, whether involving one piece of equipment, a cell, or an integrated plant.

   a.  An example of the use of automation and advanced technologies is a **flexible manufacturing system (FMS)**, which consists of computer-controlled machinery that performs many different programmed functions. By eliminating machine setup time, strengthening control, and automating handling processes, an FMS permits the efficient production of small numbers of different products by the same machines. A company can therefore more accurately match output with consumer tastes and avoid long production runs of identical goods.

      1) An FMS consists of two or more computer-controlled machines linked by automated handling devices such as robots and transport systems.

8.  **Computer-aided design and manufacturing (CAD-CAM)** models and predicts the outcomes of alternative product decisions.

   a.  CAD-CAM is essentially a system that combines storage and retrieval of drawings and parts attributes, computer graphics for drawing and display, data acquisition and control, and mathematical modeling and control.

   b.  The database created in the design phase (CAD) can be used to produce a bill of materials for the manufacturing phase (CAM). CAM can use CAD drawings and information to give specific instructions to individual machines.

   c.  CAD-CAM helps engineers examine more options, conduct sophisticated simulations and tests, and make themselves more effective.

      1) Product value and quality are improved.
      2) The need for physical prototypes is reduced.

   d.  CAD-CAM systems are usually expensive, high-risk, high-payback investments.

9.  A **computer-integrated manufacturing (CIM)** system involves designing products using computer-aided design (CAD), testing the design using computer-aided engineering (CAE), manufacturing products using computer-aided manufacturing (CAM), and integrating all components with a computerized information system.

   a.  CIM entails a holistic approach to manufacturing in which design is translated into product by centralized processing and robotics. The concept also includes materials handling. The advantages of CIM include flexibility, integration, and synergism.

      1) **Flexibility** is a key advantage. A traditional manufacturing system might become disrupted from an emergency change, but CIM will reschedule everything in the plant when a priority requirement is inserted into the system. The areas of flexibility include

         a) Varying production volumes during a period
         b) Handling new parts added to a product
         c) Changing the proportion of parts being produced
         d) Adjusting to engineering changes of a product
         e) Adapting the sequence in which parts come to the machinery

    f) Adapting to changes in materials

    g) Rerouting parts as needed because of machine breakdowns or other production delays

    h) Allowing for defects in materials

  2) CIM integrates all production machinery using one computer system.

  3) **Benefits** of CIM include improved product quality (less rework), better customer service, faster response to market changes, greater product variety, lower production costs, and shorter product development times.

  4) **JIT** is sometimes adopted prior to CIM because JIT simplifies production processes and provides a better understanding of actual production flow, which are essential factors for CIM success.

  5) The flexibility offered by CIM is almost a necessity for **JIT suppliers**. For example, a company that provides JIT deliveries to automobile plants cannot adapt to changing customer production schedules with a manual system unless a high inventory level is maintained.

  6) The emphasis is on **materials control** rather than the direct labor control that is dominant in most cost systems.

  7) CIM is an addition to, not a substitute for, other types of manufacturing concepts such as JIT. In other words, JIT should already be in place for CIM to work most effectively.

10. **Manufacturing resource planning (MRP-II)** is a closed-loop computerized manufacturing system that integrates all facets of a manufacturing business, including production, sales, inventories, schedules, and cash flows.

 a. The same system is used for both financial reporting and management of operations (both use the same transactions and numbers).

 b. MRP-II uses a **master production schedule (MPS)**, which is a statement of the anticipated manufacturing schedule for selected items for selected periods.

  1) MRP also uses the MPS. Thus, MRP is a component of an MRP-II system.

11. **Enterprise resource planning (ERP)** is the latest phase in the development of computerized systems for managing organizational resources. ERP is intended to integrate enterprise-wide information systems. ERP connects all organizational operations (personnel, the financial accounting system, production, marketing, distribution, etc.) and also connects the organization with its suppliers and customers.

12. **Supply-chain management**. The relationship of an organization with its suppliers has already been described in the sections on purchasing and JIT. This section concentrates on the distribution element of the supply chain.

 a. The **supply chain** consists of flows from sources of raw materials, components, finished goods, services, or information through intermediaries to ultimate consumers.

  1) These flows and the related activities may occur across the functions in an organization's **value chain** (R&D, design, production, marketing, distribution, and customer service). These flows and the related activities also may occur across separate organizations.

  2) The activities in the supply chain, wherever they occur, should be integrated and coordinated for optimal cost management.

    a) For example, an organization may help its suppliers to improve their processes, with mutual cost, efficiency, time, and quality improvements.

3) Sharing of information and coordination among the organizations in the supply chain can avoid the **bullwhip or whiplash effect** on inventories. This phenomenon begins when retailers face uncertain demand from consumers caused by randomness in buying habits. However, the variability of retailers' orders to manufacturers is affected by factors in addition to consumer demand. In turn, manufacturers' orders to suppliers may reflect a still greater variability because those orders depend on factors in addition to retailer demand.

    a) **Causes.** The bullwhip effect, that is, a cascade of demand variability throughout the supply chain, may be caused by

        i) Difficulties of predicting demand and derived demand at each link in the supply chain

        ii) The need to purchase or manufacture goods in cost-efficient batches

        iii) Changes in price that may encourage purchases in anticipation of future increases

        iv) Shortages that may lead to rationing by suppliers or manufacturers and hoarding by manufacturers or retailers

4) Sharing of information about sales, inventory, pricing, advertising campaigns, and sales forecasts by all functions and organizations in the supply chain moderates demand uncertainty for all parties. The desired results are

    a) Minimization of inventories held by suppliers, manufacturers, and retailers
    b) Avoidance of stockouts
    c) Fewer rush orders
    d) Production as needed by retailers

5) Supply-chain inventory management faces certain **difficulties**, for example,

    a) Incompatibility of the information systems of the parties
    b) Refusal of some parties to share information, possibly because of security concerns
    c) Devoting insufficient resources to the task
    d) Fear that others will not meet their obligations

b. **Distribution** is the transfer of goods (and, in other contexts, services and information) from producers to customers or from distribution centers to merchandisers. Thus, distribution manages outflows, and purchasing manages inflows. Among the interrelated issues involved in distribution are selection of distribution channels, inventory placement, means of transportation, shipment schedules, routes, and carriers.

c. A **distribution channel** is a series of interdependent marketing institutions that facilitate the transfer of a product from producer to ultimate consumer or industrial user. A distribution channel creates place, time, and possession utility by bringing sellers and buyers together.

1) **Intermediaries** include merchant middlemen, agents, brokers, consignees, and facilitating intermediaries.

    a) **Merchant middlemen** are intermediaries who buy the goods outright and necessarily take title to them. They include merchant wholesalers and most retailers.

    b) An **agent** represents a principal in negotiating purchases, sales, or both, but does not take title to the goods.

    c) A **broker** serves as a go-between. Unlike an agent, a broker ordinarily does not maintain a relationship with a particular buyer or seller. A broker also does not assume title risks.

d)    A **consignee** merely sells the consignor's goods for a fee.  Title remains with the consignor until the goods are sold and title passes to the buyer.

e)    **Facilitating intermediaries** are persons or firms outside the channel that perform some services (inventory control, financial services, risk management, information services, promotions) more effectively and efficiently than the channel members.

2)    **Channel structure**.  Conventional distribution systems consist of one or more independent producers, wholesalers, and retailers, each of which is a separate profit-maximizing business.  The profit objective of each independent channel member may result in actions that are not profit maximizing for the system as a whole, and the system offers no means for defining roles and controlling channel conflict.

a)    In vertical distribution systems, producers, wholesalers, and retailers act as a unified system.  Channel conflict is managed through common ownership, contractual relationships, or administration by one or a few dominant channel members.

b)    Horizontal distribution systems consist of two or more companies at one level of the channel working together to exploit new opportunities, such as the introduction of ATMs in supermarkets.  The joint nature of horizontal distribution efforts is the tool for managing channel conflict.

c)    In a multichannel system, a single firm sets up two or more channels to reach one or more customer segments.  Because such a system is managed by a single firm, channel conflicts can be evaluated and managed internally.

d.    **Inventory placement** concerns the location of finished goods.

1)    **Forward placement** puts inventory close to final customers at a distribution center (warehouse), wholesaler, or retailer.  This option minimizes transportation costs and delivery times.

2)    **Backward placement** involves keeping inventory at a factory or maintaining no inventory at all.  This option is indicated when products are customized or when regional demand fluctuates unpredictably.  Centralizing the inventory helps to smooth the effects of changes in regional demand.

e.    The five types of transportation are aircraft, railroad, highway, pipeline, and water.

1)    Transportation by **aircraft** is the fastest but most expensive.  Moreover, facilities are limited, and considerable rehandling is needed.

2)    **Rail** is a cheap method of transporting large amounts of freight, but delivery times are slow and may vary substantially.  Rehandling is also necessary.

3)    Transporting freight by **highway** is a flexible method because virtually all destinations in the U.S. can be reached via truck.  Furthermore, shipment is relatively fast, no rehandling is required, and rates are lower than rail for small amounts and short distances.

4)    **Pipelines** are available only for gases, liquids, and solids in the form of slurry.  Operating costs are low and no packaging is needed, but not all geographic areas are served.

5)    **Water-based carriers** serve only limited areas, but capacity is high and unit cost low.

f.    Scheduling movements of freight is a complex process that balances purchasing, production, customer response times, shipping costs, and selection of routes and carriers.

g.   The management of distribution can be facilitated by **distribution resource planning (DRP)**, a methodology with procedures similar to those of MRP-II. Instead of expected demand, DRP begins with gross requirements forecasted at the retail level. It also needs to determine inventory levels, lead times, and a distribution structure.

   1)   The usual DRP system responds to the **pull of orders** by retailers for replenishment of their stock.

   2)   An alternative is a **push system**. The supplying location considers orders from all ordering locations and inventory availability. Thus, it improves inventory allocation by considering the total system's needs.

13.   Stop and review! You have completed the outline for this subunit. Study multiple-choice questions 1 through 16 beginning on page 109.

## 2.2 PRICING

1.   **Pricing Objectives**

   a.   Profit maximization. Classical economic theory assumes all firms always select the price that results in the highest profit.

   b.   Target margin maximization. This objective is stated as a percentage ratio of profits to sales.

   c.   Volume-oriented objectives set prices to meet target sales volumes or market shares.

   d.   Image-oriented objectives set prices to enhance the consumer's perception of the firm's merchandise mix.

   e.   Stabilization objectives set prices to maintain a stable relationship between the firm's prices and the industry leader's prices.

2.   **Price-Setting Factors**

   a.   Supply of and demand for products and services are determined by customers' impact on demand, the actions of competitors, and costs.

   b.   **Internal factors**

   1)   Marketing objectives may include survival, current profit maximization, market-share leadership, or product-quality leadership.

   2)   Marketing-mix strategy

   3)   All relevant costs (variable, fixed, and total costs) in the value chain from R&D to customer service affect the amount of a product that the company is willing to supply. Thus, the lower costs are in relation to a given price, the greater the amount supplied.

   4)   Organizational locus of pricing decisions

   5)   Capacity

   a)   For example, under **peak-load pricing**, prices vary directly with capacity usage. Thus, when idle capacity is available, that is, when demand falls, the price of a product or service tends to be higher given a peak-load pricing approach.

c.  **External factors**

1)  The market: supply and demand

a)  The type of market (pure competition, monopolistic competition, oligopolistic competition, or pure monopoly) affects the price. For example, a monopolist is usually able to charge a higher price because it has no competitors. However, a company selling a relatively undifferentiated product in a highly competitive market may have no control over price.

b)  Customer perceptions of price and value

c)  The price-demand relationship

i)  The **demand curve for normal goods** is ordinarily downward sloping to the right (quantity demanded increases as the price decreases).

ii)  However, over some intermediate range of prices, the reaction to a price increase for **prestige goods** is an increase, not a decrease, in the quantity demanded. Within this range, the demand curve is upward sloping. The reason is that consumers interpret the higher price to indicate a better or more desirable product. Above some price level, the relation between price and quantity demanded will again become negatively sloped.

d)  **Price elasticity of demand**. If demand is price elastic (inelastic), the ratio of the percentage change in quantity demanded to the percentage change in price is greater (less) than 1.0. For example, if customer demand is price elastic, a price increase will result in the reduction of the seller's total revenue.

2)  Competitors' products, costs, prices, and amounts supplied

d.  The **time dimension** for price setting is important. Whether the decision is for the short-term (generally, less than 1 year) or the long-term determines which costs are relevant and whether prices are set to achieve tactical goals or to earn a targeted return on investment. For example, short-term fixed costs may be variable in the long-term, and short-term prices may be raised (lowered) when customer demand is strong (weak).

1)  From the long-term perspective, maintaining price stability may be preferable to responding to short-term fluctuations in demand. A policy of predictable prices is desirable when the company desires to cultivate long-term customer relationships. This policy is only feasible, however, when the company can predict its long-term costs.

3.  **General Pricing Approaches**

a.  **Cost-based pricing** involves setting a price that will recover the value chain costs and provide the desired return on investment.

b.  **Market-based pricing** involves basing prices on the product's perceived value and competitors' actions rather than on the seller's cost. Nonprice variables in the marketing mix augment the perceived value. For example, a cup of coffee may have a higher price at an expensive restaurant than at a fast-food outlet. Market-based pricing is typical when there are many competitors and the product is undifferentiated, as in many commodities markets, e.g., agricultural products or natural gas.

c.  **Competition-based pricing**

1)  Going-rate pricing bases price largely on competitors' prices.

2)  Sealed-bid pricing bases price on a company's perception of its competitors' prices.

d.   **New product pricing**

1)   Price skimming is the practice of setting an introductory price relatively high to attract buyers who are not concerned about price and to recover research and development costs.

2)   Penetration pricing is the practice of setting an introductory price relatively low to gain deep market penetration quickly.

e.   **Pricing by intermediaries**

1)   Using markups tied closely to the price paid for a product

2)   Using markdowns -- a reduction in the original price set on a product

f.   **Price adjustments**

1)   **Geographical pricing**

a)   FOB-origin pricing charges each customer its actual freight costs.

b)   A seller that uses uniform delivered pricing charges the same price, inclusive of shipping, to all customers regardless of their location.

i)   Thus, both nearby and distant customers are charged the same amount.  This policy is easy to administer, permits the company to advertise one price nationwide, and facilitates marketing to faraway customers.

c)   Zone pricing sets differential freight charges for customers on the basis of their location.  Customers are not charged actual average freight costs.

d)   Basing-point pricing charges each customer the freight costs incurred from a specified city to the destination regardless of the actual point of origin of the shipment.

e)   A seller that uses freight-absorption pricing absorbs all or part of the actual freight charges.  Customers are not charged actual delivery costs.

2)   **Discounts and allowances**

a)   Cash discounts encourage prompt payment, improve cash flows, and avoid bad debts.

b)   Quantity discounts encourage large volume purchases.

c)   Trade (functional) discounts are offered to other members of the marketing channel for performing certain services, such as selling.

d)   Seasonal discounts are offered for sales out of season.  They help smooth production.

e)   Allowances (e.g., trade-in and promotional allowances) reduce list prices.

3)   **Discriminatory pricing** adjusts for differences among customers, the forms of a product, or locations.

4)   **Psychological pricing** is based on consumer psychology.  For example, consumers who cannot judge quality may assume higher prices correlate with higher quality.

5)   Promotional pricing temporarily reduces prices below list or even cost to stimulate sales.

6)   Value pricing entails redesigning products to improve quality without raising prices or offering the same quality at lower prices.

7)   International pricing adjusts prices to local conditions.

g.   **Product-mix pricing**

1)   Product-line pricing sets price steps among the products in the line based on costs, consumer perceptions, and competitors' prices.

2)   Optional-product pricing requires the firm to choose which products to offer as accessories and which as standard features of a main product.

3)   Captive-product pricing involves products that must be used with a main product, such as razor blades with a razor. Often the main product is relatively cheap, but the captive products have high markups.

4)   By-product pricing usually sets prices at any amount in excess of storing and delivering by-products. Such prices allow the seller to reduce the costs and therefore the prices of the main products.

5)   Product-bundle pricing entails selling combinations of products at a price lower than the combined prices of the individual items. This strategy promotes sales of items consumers might not otherwise buy if the price is low enough. An example is season tickets for sports events.

h.   Certain pricing tactics may be illegal. For example, in the U.S., pricing products below cost to destroy competitors (**predatory pricing**) is illegal.

1)   The U.S. Supreme Court has held that a price is predatory if it is below an appropriate measure of costs and the seller has a reasonable prospect of recovering its losses in the future through higher prices or greater market share.

2)   **Price discrimination** among customers also may be illegal. In the U.S., the **Robinson-Patman Act** makes such pricing illegal if it has the effect of lessening competition, although price discrimination may be permissible if the competitive situation requires it and if costs of serving some customers are lower. The Robinson-Patman Act applies to manufacturers, not service entities.

3)   Another improper form of pricing is **collusive pricing**. Companies may not conspire to restrict output and set artificially high prices. Such behavior violates antitrust laws.

4)   Still another inappropriate pricing tactic is selling below cost in other countries (**dumping**), which may trigger retaliatory tariffs and other sanctions.

4.   **Cost-based pricing** begins with a cost determination followed by setting a price that will recover the value chain costs and provide the desired return on investment. When an industry is characterized by significant product differentiation, e.g., automobiles, cost-based and market-based pricing approaches are combined.

a.   A **cost-plus price** equals the cost plus a markup. Cost may be defined in many ways. Most companies use either absorption manufacturing cost or total cost when calculating the price. Variable costs may be used as the basis for cost, but then fixed costs must be covered by the markup.

1)   Following are four commonly used cost-plus pricing formulas:

a)   $Price = Total\ cost + (Total\ cost \times Markup\ percentage)$

b)   $Price = Absorption\ manufacturing\ cost + (Absorption\ manufacturing\ cost \times Markup\ percentage)$

c)
$$Price = \begin{array}{c} Variable \\ manufacturing \\ cost \end{array} + \left( \begin{array}{c} Variable \\ manufacturing \\ cost \end{array} \times Markup\ percentage \right)$$

d)
$$Price = \begin{array}{c} Total \\ variable \\ cost \end{array} + \left( \begin{array}{c} Total \\ variable \\ cost \end{array} \times Markup\ percentage \right)$$

2) The costs of unused capacity in production facilities, distribution channels, marketing organizations, etc., are ordinarily not assignable to products or services on a cause-and-effect basis, so their inclusion in overhead rates may distort pricing decisions. Including the fixed costs of unused capacity in a cost-based price results in higher prices and in what is known as the **downward (black hole) demand spiral**.

   a) As higher prices depress demand, unused capacity costs increase, the fixed costs included in prices increase, and demand will continue to spiral downward. One way to avoid this problem is not to assign unused capacity costs to products or services. The result should be better operating decisions and better evaluation of managerial performance.

5. A **target price** is the expected market price for a product or service, given the company's knowledge of its consumers' perceptions of value and competitors' responses.

   a. The company's contacts with its customers and its market research studies provide information about consumers' perceptions of value.

   b. The company must also gain information about competitors' potential responses by learning about their technological expertise, products, costs, and financial positions. This information may be obtained from competitors' customers, suppliers, employees, and financial reports. Reverse engineering of their products is also possible.

   c. Subtracting the unit target operating income determines the long-term unit **target cost**. Relevant costs are all future value-chain costs whether variable or fixed.

      1) Because it may be lower than the full cost of the product, the target cost may not be achievable unless the company adopts comprehensive cost-reduction measures.

      2) The Japanese concept of **Kaizen** is relevant to target costing. A policy of seeking continuous improvement in all phases of company activities facilitates cost reduction, often through numerous minor changes.

      3) **Value engineering** is a means of reaching targeted cost levels. It is a systematic approach to assessing all aspects of the **value chain** cost buildup for a product: R&D, design of products, design of processes, production, marketing, distribution, and customer service. The purpose is to minimize costs without sacrificing customer satisfaction.

         a) Value engineering requires identifying value-added and nonvalue-added costs. **Value-added costs** are costs of activities that cannot be eliminated without reducing the quality, responsiveness, or quantity of the output required by a customer or the organization.

         b) Value engineering also requires distinguishing between cost incurrence and locked-in costs. **Cost incurrence** is the actual use of resources, whereas **locked-in** (designed-in) costs will result in use of resources in the future as a result of past decisions. Traditional cost accounting focuses on budget comparisons, but value engineering emphasizes controlling costs at the design stage before they are locked in.

6.   The **product life cycle** begins with R&D, proceeds through the introduction and growth stages, continues into the product's mature stage, and finally ends with the harvest or decline stage and the final provision of customer support. **Life-cycle costing** is sometimes used as a basis for cost planning and product pricing. Life-cycle costing estimates a product's revenues and expenses over its expected life cycle. The result is to highlight upstream and downstream costs in the cost planning process that often receive insufficient attention. Emphasis is on the need to price products to cover all costs, not just production costs.

   a.   A concept related to life-cycle cost that is relevant to pricing is **whole-life cost**, which equals life-cycle costs plus after-purchase costs (operating, support, repair, and disposal) incurred by customers. Reduction of whole-life costs is a strong competitive weapon. Customers may pay a premium for a product with low after-purchase costs.

7.   Stop and review! You have completed the outline for this subunit. Study multiple-choice questions 17 through 26 beginning on page 115.

## 2.3 MANAGING HUMAN RESOURCES

1.   Managing human resources means acquiring, retaining, and developing employees. These functions should be consistent with the strategy and structure of the organization. The essential activities include

   a.   Developing a **human resource strategy**. Such a strategy at its broadest is a systems approach that treats employees and future employees as **human capital**, that is, as intangible assets whose fullest potential should be developed.

   b.   Recruitment and selection.

   c.   Evaluation of performance.

   d.   Training and development.

2.   Research indicates that a **people-centered** human resource strategy improves employee retention and profits. Jeffrey Pfeffer (see Kreitner, *Management*, 9th ed., page 357) suggests the following practices:

   a.   A job security policy

   b.   Stringent hiring procedures

   c.   Employee empowerment (e.g., use of self-managed teams)

   d.   Basing compensation on performance

   e.   Comprehensive training

   f.   Reduction of status differences

   g.   Information sharing

3.   **Human resource planning** consists of forecasting future employment requirements. It includes the hiring, training, and monitoring of employees. Planning includes scanning the external environment to understand the area's labor supply, workforce composition, and work patterns. Companies often perform such analysis before building a new plant in a new geographic area, but regular analyses at established locations is sometimes overlooked. Companies must forecast future employee needs to insure adequate resources when needed. Labor resources are not always as mobile as raw materials.

4.   **Job analysis** is the first step. It entails interviewing superior employees about the way they accomplish their tasks, analyzing work flows, and studying the methods used to achieve work-unit objectives.

   a.   Has the nature of the job changed? If so, the job description should be rewritten.

   b.   If the job's nature remains the same, the job specifications should be written from the job description and sent to personnel to be advertised.

  c. A **job description**, based on job analysis, should list basic duties.  For higher-level positions, reporting relationships may also be included.

    1) EXAMPLE:  For an accounting clerk, the job description might include

      a) Preparing payroll checks
      b) Maintaining inventory ledgers
      c) Preparing invoices

  d. **Job specifications**, based on the job description, should list the abilities needed by a person hired for that job.

    1) EXAMPLE:  The job specifications for an accounting clerk might list

      a) 10-key facility
      b) Typing ability at a specified number of correct words per minute
      c) Experience in a similar position for a specified number of years
      d) Bondable
      e) Education to a specified level and, perhaps, in specified types of courses

    2) For other jobs, other factors may be pertinent:

      a) Physical characteristics, e.g., strength, stamina
      b) Personal characteristics, e.g., personality, communication skills

    3) Some sources include job specifications within the definition of job description.

5. **Recruitment**

  a. Sources of personnel

    1) Advertising in media (e.g., newspapers and employer or other Internet sites)
    2) Referrals (networking)
    3) Walk-ins
    4) Internal job posting and computerized staff inventories of existing employees
    5) Targeted recruiting sources, e.g., colleges and universities
    6) Temporary placement and part-time employees
    7) Employment agencies and executive headhunters

  b. Governmental constraints and restrictions on recruiting (examples from U.S. law)

    1) **Title VII of the 1964 Civil Rights Act** prohibits discrimination on the basis of race, color, religion, sex, or national origin.  It applies to private employers of 15 or more persons, unions, employment agencies, joint labor-management committees controlling apprenticeships or training programs, state and local governments, and educational institutions.

      a) Discrimination is permissible on the basis of a **bona fide occupational qualification**; e.g., clergy can be selected on the basis of religious faith.

      b) The **Equal Employment Opportunity Commission** has the right to bring discrimination suits against employers in federal courts.

    2) The **Age Discrimination in Employment Act of 1967** prohibits discrimination on the basis of age (as amended in 1978).  This act applies to the 40 and older age group.

3) Certain rules pertaining to discrimination against people with disabilities are provided by the **Vocational Rehabilitation Act**, which requires employers with federal contracts to take affirmative action to employ and advance qualified individuals.

   a) The **Americans with Disabilities Act (AD of 1990)** expands the Civil Rights Act of 1964 and the Vocational Rehabilitation Act to include protection from employment discrimination with respect to hiring, promotion, and termination. Employers are required by the ADA to make **reasonable accommodation** for applicants or employees with disabilities.

4) Governmental reviews evaluate compliance with employment law by checking

   a) Sources of employees recruited for each job category
   b) Advertising
   c) Estimates of employees needed for coming year
   d) Statistics on number of applicants processed by sex, race, etc., for each job category and level

5) The following cannot be done in recruiting interviews:

   a) Make notation of sex
   b) Ask marital status (may ask after hiring for insurance purposes)
   c) Ask for number of children (may ask after hiring for insurance purposes)
   d) Ask for height and weight
   e) Ask for criminal record (only for security clearance)
   f) Ask type of military discharge
   g) Ask age

6) Summary of compliance criteria

   a) Does the employment practice have an unequal impact on the groups covered by law?
   b) Is the practice justified by job-related (bona fide occupational qualification) requirements or is it otherwise legally defensible as necessary to the organization?

7) The modern trend, reinforced not only by legal requirements but by the need for fresh viewpoints, is to **recruit for diversity**.

   a) In this context, diversity may be defined to include not only legally protected categories but also other differences such as background and personality. Genuine diversity is an absence of any form of intolerance and the creation of a heterogeneous culture.
   b) Moreover, recruiting for diversity must be accompanied by an emphasis on **retention**.

6. Using **temporary or part-time workers** gives management the flexibility to adjust quickly to changing market conditions.

   a. Such workers can often be paid lower salaries and given fewer benefits than full-time workers.
   b. Disadvantages of hiring temporary or part-time workers include the lack of long-term benefits to the company from training programs and less employee loyalty to the firm.

   c.  These workers can improve the morale of permanent employees, however, by relieving overtime pressures or by performing the more tedious and less desirable tasks.

      1)  On the other hand, they may reduce the morale of permanent employees who might desire more overtime work or who might believe that their jobs are threatened.

   d.  **Leasing** employees has a variety of administrative benefits because the lessor prepares payrolls, pays the employees, files tax returns, etc. (S)he also assumes liability for unemployment claims.

      1)  However, the behavioral disadvantages of directly hiring temporary or part-time workers also apply to employee leasing.

7.  **Employee Selection**. Requirements should come from job specifications developed from each job description and include education; experience; physical characteristics, e.g., strength and stamina; and personal characteristics, e.g., personality, confidence, and skills.

   a.  All requirements, including selection tests, must be based on their relationship to the ability to perform successfully in a specific job category.

   b.  According to Del J. Still (see Kreitner, pp. 359-360), the **selection process** involves

      1)  Preparation by developing job descriptions and job specifications and writing interview questions
      2)  Reviewing those questions for fairness and conformity with the law
      3)  Organizing by defining the roles and methods of interviewers
      4)  Collecting information from applicants
      5)  Evaluating
      6)  Meeting to discuss information about applicants
      7)  Deciding whether to offer employment

   c.  **Interviewing** is the most frequently used selection method. Because of the weaknesses of the unstructured interview (i.e., its susceptibility to cultural and other forms of bias), the **structured interview** is preferable. It consists of written questions related to the job that have standard answers. The interview is conducted, and the questions are created and scored by a committee, so as to minimize bias. Types of questions address

      1)  Job situations
      2)  Job-related knowledge
      3)  Simulation of job activity
      4)  Employee requirements

8.  **Applicant Testing**. Testing applicants for jobs with quantifiable output (e.g., jobs requiring clerical skills or manual dexterity) is easier than testing for positions with a less tangible work product (e.g., public relations director or human resource manager).

   a.  All tests must be validated in each organization and for minority and nonminority groups before they can be predictive of successful performance.
   b.  Tests must be given to all applicants for the same job category.
   c.  It is not easy or inexpensive to validate a test.
   d.  Test validity is the capacity to measure accurately what it was designed to measure.
   e.  Test reliability is the ability of a test to obtain the same scores in repeated administrations, regardless of validity.
   f.  Lie detector tests, drug tests, DNA screening, AIDS tests, and personality tests are significant and controversial matters.

9. **Orientation** is the introduction to the workplace and one of the most common types of training. The employees receive their first formal information about

   a. Overall organizational objectives
   b. Overall organizational chart, i.e., the pecking order
   c. Benefits, e.g.,

      1) Retirement plan
      2) Attendance regulations
      3) Vacation and sick leave

   d. Organizational procedures, e.g.,

      1) Grievance procedures
      2) Safety rules (e.g., fire drills, etc.)

10. **Training and Development**

    a. **Training** consists of organizational programs to prepare employees to perform currently assigned tasks (e.g., on-the-job training or formal off-site programs).

       1) On-the-job or experiential training, for example, by job rotation, apprenticeships, and mentoring arrangements, is usually less costly than off-the-job training but may disrupt the workplace and result in increased errors. It is suited to acquisition of technical skills.

       2) Off-the-job training, for example, in classroom lectures, film study, and simulations, is well suited to development of problem solving and interpersonal abilities and to teaching of complex skills.

       3) Computer-based training is expected to become more common.

    b. **Development** includes organizational programs to prepare people to perform future tasks and acquire new skills.

       1) The focus is mostly on management and organizational development to develop human relations skills. Management coaching and mentoring enhance the development process.

    c. Training has been defined to encompass training and development. Kreitner (p. 373) defines it broadly as "using guided experience to change employee behavior or attitude."

    d. The **evaluation and appraisal** process helps identify training and development needs. Individual strengths and weaknesses should be noted to permit identification of training and development opportunities. Also, jobs and markets change, leading to a need for workers with different skills. Organizations seem to thrive when workers value lifelong learning.

       1) Viewing performance evaluation as a training and developmental process, as well as an evaluative process, can foster a culture in which evaluation is sought out.

       2) A **training needs assessment** should be conducted to determine what training is relevant to employees' jobs, to determine what training will improve performance, to determine whether training will make a difference, to distinguish training needs from organizational problems, and to link improved job performance with the organization's objectives and bottom line.

       3) **Self assessment** by employees is another means of identifying training and development needs, but this usually yields shorter term training needs and often has more to do with employees' personal career goals than strategic business needs. Thus, many companies use self assessment only as a supplement to other approaches.

    e.    Training and development programs are successful when they achieve the greatest retention (learning) of skills and knowledge that are transferred to the job. The following is a paradigm for the process of learning skills or facts:

        1)   Establishing objectives
        2)   Modeling the skills or making a meaningful presentation of facts
        3)   Practice
        4)   Feedback

## 11. Evaluation

    a.    An important aspect of management is the evaluation of employees.

        1)   Evaluations are important to the employee, the employer, and the organization as a whole.

        2)   Evaluations provide an opportunity for growth of the employee and, when done properly, can be instrumental in the prevention of future disputes.

            a)   Documentation must be complete, accurate, and consistent.

            b)   Employees should be notified of appraisals and given an opportunity to discuss them.

            c)   Different techniques are necessary to accommodate different employee performance levels.

    b.    **Purposes of evaluation**

        1)   Uses performance criteria to identify necessary job-related abilities
        2)   Uses performance goals to help employees direct their energies toward the organization's expectations without constant supervision
        3)   Uses performance outcomes to promote employee satisfaction by acknowledging when jobs are completed and done well
        4)   Distinguishes effective from ineffective job performance
        5)   Helps the employer and the organization develop employee strengths and identify weaknesses
        6)   Helps in setting base pay levels

    c.    **Problems of evaluation**

        1)   Design of an appraisal system can be faulty if the

            a)   Criteria for evaluations are poor or inappropriate.
            b)   Technique is cumbersome or not understood by users.
            c)   Criteria focus on wrong attributes causing emphasis on wrong things (e.g., personal appearance rather than job accomplishments).
            d)   Senior management does not lend support.

        2)   Evaluation-based problems

            a)   **Halo effect**. A manager's judgment on one positive trait affects rating on other traits. The converse of the halo effect is the **horn effect**. It occurs when the manager allows one negative trait to influence the evaluation of other traits.

            b)   **Central tendency**. All personnel are rated within the same narrow range; e.g., "All my people are good." In a sense, this means all employees are rated as being average. The **forced normal distribution method** essentially results in central tendency because most employees must be rated average.

            c)   **Recency effect**. Most recent behavior overshadows overall performance.

    d)    **Differing standards**.  Some managers have stricter standards than others, making cross-departmental comparisons difficult.

    e)    **Personal bias**.  Traits may not reflect actual job performance, so appraisal can be biased by the degree to which the manager likes the subordinate.

    f)    **Leniency error** occurs when a manager fails to give a negative evaluation because of fear of damaging a good working relationship with a worker.

    g)    **Contrast error** is the tendency to rate people relative to other people, rather than according to performance standards.  If most employees are mediocre, a person performing at what might be only an average level is rated as "outstanding."  That same person might be rated as "poor" in another department where most workers perform at an above-average level.  Although at times it may be appropriate to compare people, the normal rating process should compare a worker's performance with job requirements, not with the performance of others.

    h)    Traits like dependability or industriousness may have very little to do with the job expected of an employee and are too subjective to be measured.

    i)    Trait scales tend to equate subjectively both pertinent and nonperformance traits (e.g., quality of work and appearance may receive equal points toward total appraisal score on many scales).

    j)    The once-a-year process tends to affect the usefulness and accuracy of any job-related information.

    k)    According to **attribution theory**, people attempt to determine whether observed behavior is internally or externally caused.

        i)    Behavior that is unusual for a particular individual is perceived to be externally caused.  If it is not unusual, causation is ordinarily perceived to be internal.

        ii)    If everyone in similar circumstances behaves in a certain way, causation is believed to be external.  Otherwise, causation is deemed to be internal.

        iii)    However, biases may distort attributions.

- **Fundamental attribution error** is a bias in judgments about the behavior of other people.  This bias is a tendency to overestimate internal factors and underestimate external factors.
- **Self-serving bias** is the tendency to attribute one's successes to internal factors (e.g., diligence and talent) and failures to external factors (e.g., bad luck).

    d.    **Major types of appraisals**

    1)    **Rating scales** for personal traits have many of the weaknesses discussed previously.

    2)    **Management by objectives (MBO)** is a participative process in which supervisors and subordinates mutually establish objectives.  A rating is based on achievement of the objectives.

    3)    The **critical incident technique** provides a list of critical aspects of the job that the evaluator uses to rate employee performance.  Critical incidents (both superior and inferior performance) should be documented by supervisors when they occur.

    4)    **Behaviorally anchored rating scales (BARS)** contain descriptions of good and bad performance.  They are developed through job analysis for a number of specific job-related behaviors and then used for evaluation of employees.

     5) A supervisor may write a **narrative** (essay) to describe employee performance. This technique is time consuming and may challenge supervisors with poor writing skills.

     6) A **weighted checklist** consists of randomly ordered items that describe specific employee behaviors. The relative weights are unknown to the supervisor.

     7) **Rankings** of coworkers may be made by supervisors based on specific job-related behaviors. However, they tend to cause resentment and do not quantify the differences among those compared.

e. **Characteristics of effective evaluation systems**

     1) Relevant. Criteria should be reliable and valid. They should relate to employee functions, that is, to activities over which the employees exert control.

     2) Unbiased. Systems should be based on performance of the job, not on unrelated personal characteristics.

     3) Significant. Systems should focus on the important part of the job rather than whatever is convenient to evaluate. This avoids misdirection or confusion of employee effort.

     4) Practical. Systems should be as objective, easy to use, clearly understood, and efficient as possible.

f. **Criteria for effective appraisal**

     1) Employees must understand the appraisal.
     2) They must believe that the appraisal is fair.
     3) They must believe that it is important to them and their jobs.

g. A manager can make appraisals easier and more effective by being involved in employee affairs.

     1) Spending a little time with each employee each day and offering praise as well as constructive criticism facilitates acceptance of appraisals.

h. A **360° performance appraisal** is a multirater model for employee assessment in the age of teamwork. It is based on giving workers feedback from peers, customers, supervisors, and subordinates. Feedback is typically provided anonymously.

     1) Appraisal is subjective, and popularity is sometimes more important than performance.

     2) Evaluations do not include copies of the employee's job description or performance goals.

i. **Team ratings** are necessary for any organization that uses teamwork as a part of the work process. Team ratings can be handled in much the same way as individual performance appraisals, but many firms argue that a different method is needed when evaluating teamwork. Thus, team ratings are often conducted by someone other than management, such as the teams themselves or customers.

     1) The first step is to define excellence in team performance. This definition is made available to the team members in the form of a **team agreement**, which determines how the team operates. Without a definition of good performance, a team's performance cannot be evaluated.

     2) Teams are jointly accountable for their work. Thus, if any member of the team fails, the other members must ask how they could have helped.

     3) A good team rating system should separate feedback sessions from salary reviews. People may not be candid if they think that their responses will affect the compensation of teammates.

     4) Team evaluations should be conducted in a "safe" environment, which means with managers not present. Often a neutral facilitator will lead the discussions.

12. **Compensation and benefits** are extrinsic rewards to employees. They should satisfy individual needs, encourage positive expectations, be equitable, and be related to performance. Compensation and benefits take many forms, each with its own advantages and disadvantages. Cost and ease of administration are also considerations. Regardless of the other factors, market competitiveness is a requirement for pay and benefit policies.

13. **Human Resource Planning**

   a. A **human resource audit** evaluates compliance with laws and regulations, determines whether operations are efficient, and considers the company's recruitment and salary and benefit programs.

   b. It is a thorough analysis of the human capital of the organization that permits

   1) Scheduling of training to develop experienced staff as needed
   2) Appropriate promotion decisions
   3) Analysis of staffing needs

   c. Information should be compiled about employees' education, experience, work histories, and compensation histories.

   d. Human resource or human asset accounting attempts to measure the value, and the changes in value, of the organization's investment in human capital.

14. **Downsizing** results from organizational decline, changes in the business cycle, or business combinations. The objectives are cost reduction, improved efficiency, and higher profits.

   a. These purposes are often not achieved because many companies follow cycles of hiring, firing, and rehiring that do not yield the expected benefits to offset the harm to terminated employees, the loss of morale of the survivors, and the damage to communities.

   b. Downsizing also tends to have a disproportionate effect on women and members of minorities, who tend to be the last hired and first fired.

   c. The more enlightened view is that employees are not readily disposable commodities but rather valuable resources who should be terminated only as a last resort. This view seeks alternatives to involuntary termination.

   1) Redeployment involves retraining or transferring employees.
   2) Voluntary retirement programs offer accelerated retirement benefits, severance allowances, or other compensation.
   3) Employees may be shifted to lower-level positions.
   4) All employees may be asked to accept reduced hours or pay.
   5) Outplacement assists laid-off employees in finding new jobs.
   6) Federal law requires companies with 100 or more employees to give 60 days' notice of facilities' closings or layoffs.

15. Stop and review! You have completed the outline for this subunit. Study multiple-choice questions 27 through 41 beginning on page 118.

## QUESTIONS

### 2.1 Inventory and Supply Chain Management

1. When the economic order quantity (EOQ) decision model is employed, the <List A> are being offset or balanced by the <List B>.

| | List A | List B |
|---|---|---|
| A. | Ordering costs | Carrying costs |
| B. | Purchase costs | Carrying costs |
| C. | Purchase costs | Quality costs |
| D. | Ordering costs | Stockout costs |

Answer (A) is correct. *(CIA, adapted)*
**REQUIRED:** The true statement about cost relationships in the EOQ.
**DISCUSSION:** The objective of the EOQ model is to find an optimal order quantity that balances carrying and ordering costs. Only variable costs should be considered. The EOQ is the point where the ordering cost and carrying cost curves intersect. It corresponds to the minimum point on the total inventory cost curve.
Answer (B) is incorrect because purchase costs are not directly incorporated into the EOQ model. Answer (C) is incorrect because neither purchase costs nor quality costs are incorporated into the EOQ model. Answer (D) is incorrect because stockout costs are not directly incorporated into the EOQ model.

---

Questions 2 and 3 are based on the following information.

Candman Company is a wholesale distributor of candy. The company leases space in a public warehouse and is charged according to the square feet occupied. Candman has decided to employ the economic order quantity (EOQ) method to determine the optimum number of cases of candy to order.

The company placed 2,400 orders the last year. Data for the high-activity month, the low-activity month, and the year for the purchasing and warehouse operations appear in the next column.

The annual charges for the warehouse totaled $12,750 last year. In addition, the annual insurance and property taxes on the candy stored in the warehouse amounted to $1,500 and $2,250, respectively. The average monthly inventory last year was $75,000.

Long-term capital investments are expected to earn 12% after income taxes. Candman is subject to an effective income tax rate of 40%.

| | High-Activity Month (160 Orders) | Low-Activity Month (100 Orders) | Annual Costs |
|---|---|---|---|
| Purchasing Dept. | | | |
| Manager | $ 1,600 | $1,600 | $ 23,400 |
| Clerks | 1,750 | 1,250 | 18,000 |
| Supplies | 400 | 260 | 3,500 |
| Warehouse | | | |
| Supervisor | 1,550 | 1,550 | 18,600 |
| Rcvg. clerks | 2,200 | 1,700 | 20,500 |
| Ship. clerks | 2,800 | 2,500 | 31,200 |
| Totals | $10,300 | $8,860 | $115,200 |

---

2. The incremental cost of placing an order that would be used in the EOQ model is

A. $48

B. $35

C. $24

D. $19

Answer (D) is correct. *(CMA, adapted)*
**REQUIRED:** The order cost used in the EOQ model.
**DISCUSSION:** The incremental cost of additional orders equals the variable costs incurred in purchasing and receiving inventory (but not costs associated with shipping). Using the high-low method of analysis, these variable costs can be computed by determining the apparent variable costs for the two given levels of activity. For 160 orders, the relevant costs with a variable element include purchasing clerks, $1,750; supplies, $400; and receiving clerks, $2,200. The total is $4,350. For 100 orders, these costs are $1,250, $260, and $1,700, respectively, for a total of $3,210. As the number of orders increased by 60, the costs increased by $1,140. Consequently, the variable or incremental costs per order must have been $19 ($1,140 ÷ 60 orders).
Answer (A) is incorrect because $48 equals total annual cost divided by total orders from the previous year. Answer (B) is incorrect because $35 equals total annual cost minus the costs associated with the shipping clerks, divided by total orders from the previous year. Answer (C) is incorrect because $24 includes the costs associated with shipping.

**3.** Refer to the information preceding question 2. The annual carrying cost, stated as a percentage, that would be used in the EOQ model is

A.  42%

B.  37%

C.  34%

D.  22%

Answer (A) is correct.  *(CMA, adapted)*
**REQUIRED:** The percentage annual carrying cost used in the EOQ model.
**DISCUSSION:** The annual carrying costs are $12,750 for the warehouse, $1,500 for insurance, and $2,250 for property taxes. These costs total $16,500. In addition, the company desires a 12% after-tax return on investments. Because the tax rate is 40%, the 12% after-tax return equals a 20% before-tax return (12% ÷ 60%). A 20% return on the $75,000 average investment in inventory is $15,000. Hence, the total carrying cost is $31,500 ($16,500 + $15,000). This amount is 42% of the $75,000 investment in inventory.
Answer (B) is incorrect because 37% does not consider insurance and property taxes. Answer (C) is incorrect because 34% is based on a 12% before-tax return. Answer (D) is incorrect because 22% equals carrying costs other than return on investment divided by average inventory.

**4.** The calculation of an economic order quantity (EOQ) considers

A.  The purchasing manager's salary.

B.  A corporate charge for advertising expenses.

C.  The shipping costs to deliver the product to the customer.

D.  Capital costs.

Answer (D) is correct.  *(CMA, adapted)*
**REQUIRED:** The true statement about the calculation of the economic order quantity.
**DISCUSSION:** The determination of the economic order quantity balances the variable costs of ordering and carrying inventory. Factors in the equation include the cost of placing an order, unit carrying cost, and annual demand in units. Carrying costs include storage costs, handling costs, insurance, property taxes, obsolescence, and the opportunity cost of investing capital in inventory. Thus, the return on capital that is forgone when it is invested in inventory should be considered.
Answer (A) is incorrect because the purchasing manager's salary is a fixed cost. The EOQ model includes variable costs only. Answer (B) is incorrect because advertising is not an ordering or carrying cost. Answer (C) is incorrect because the cost of shipping to customers is a selling expense.

**5.** A characteristic of the basic economic order quantity (EOQ) model is that it

A.  Is relatively insensitive to error.

B.  Should not be used when carrying costs are large in relation to procurement costs.

C.  Is used when product demand, lead-time, and ordering costs are uncertain.

D.  Should not be used in conjunction with computerized perpetual inventory systems.

Answer (A) is correct.  *(CMA, adapted)*
**REQUIRED:** The characteristic of the basic EOQ model.
**DISCUSSION:** The basic EOQ model equals the square root of the quotient of (1) the product of twice the demand times the cost per order, (2) divided by the periodic carrying cost. Hence, the model is relatively insensitive to error. A given percentage error in a value results in a lower percentage change in the EOQ.
Answer (B) is incorrect because the EOQ model can be used regardless of the relationship between carrying and holding costs. Answer (C) is incorrect because product demand and ordering costs must be known with some certainty. Answer (D) is incorrect because an EOQ model can be used with any type of system.

**6.** Companies that adopt just-in-time purchasing systems often experience

A.  An increase in carrying costs.

B.  A reduction in the number of suppliers.

C.  A greater need for inspection of goods as the goods arrive.

D.  Less need for linkage with a **vendor's** computerized order entry system.

Answer (B) is correct.  *(CMA, adapted)*
**REQUIRED:** The true statement about companies that adopt just-in-time (JIT) purchasing systems.
**DISCUSSION:** The objective of JIT is to reduce carrying costs by eliminating inventories and increasing the deliveries made by suppliers. Ideally, shipments of raw materials are received just in time to be incorporated into the manufacturing process. The focus of quality control under JIT is the prevention of quality problems. Quality control is shifted to the supplier. JIT companies typically do not inspect incoming goods; the assumption is that receipts are of perfect quality. Suppliers are limited to those who guarantee perfect quality and prompt delivery.
Answer (A) is incorrect because carrying costs typically decline in JIT companies. Less inventory is on hand.
Answer (C) is incorrect because in a JIT system, materials are delivered directly to the production line ready for insertion in the finished product. Answer (D) is incorrect because the need for communication with the vendor is greater. Orders and deliveries must be made on short notice, sometimes several times a day.

**7.** A manufacturing company is attempting to implement a just-in-time (JIT) purchase policy system by negotiating with its primary suppliers to accept long-term purchase orders which result in more frequent deliveries of smaller quantities of raw materials. If the JIT purchase policy is successful in reducing the total inventory costs of the manufacturing company, which of the following combinations of cost changes would be most likely to occur?

|  | Cost Category to Increase | Cost Category to Decrease |
|---|---|---|
| A. | Purchasing costs | Stockout costs |
| B. | Purchasing costs | Quality costs |
| C. | Quality costs | Ordering costs |
| D. | Stockout costs | Carrying costs |

Answer (D) is correct. *(CIA, adapted)*
**REQUIRED:** The combination of cost changes.
**DISCUSSION:** The objective of a JIT system is to reduce carrying costs by eliminating inventories and increasing the deliveries made by suppliers. Ideally, shipments are received just in time to be incorporated into the manufacturing process. This system increases the risk of stockout costs because the inventory buffer is reduced or eliminated.
Answer (A) is incorrect because the supplier may seek a concession on the selling price that will raise purchasing costs, but the manufacturing company's stockout costs will increase. Answer (B) is incorrect because the cost of quality is not necessarily affected by a JIT system. Answer (C) is incorrect because fewer purchase orders are processed by the manufacturer, so the ordering costs are likely to decrease. However, the cost of quality is not necessarily affected by a JIT system.

**8.** Arnold Enterprises uses the EOQ model for inventory control. The company has an annual demand of 50,000 units for part number 191 and has computed an optimal lot size of 6,250 units. Per-unit carrying costs and stockout costs are $13 and $3, respectively. The following data have been gathered in an attempt to determine an appropriate safety stock level:

| Units Short Because of Excess Demand During the Lead Time Period | Number of Times Short in the Last 40 Reorder Cycles |
|---|---|
| 200 | 6 |
| 300 | 12 |
| 400 | 6 |

The annual cost of establishing a 200-unit safety stock is expected to be

A. $2,600

B. $4,040

C. $4,260

D. $5,200

Answer (B) is correct. *(CMA, adapted)*
**REQUIRED:** The cost of establishing safety stock.
**DISCUSSION:** The annual cost consists of the carrying cost of the 200 units of safety stock at $13 each, or $2,600, plus the stockout costs incurred when 200 units are insufficient. The stockout cost per unit is $3. The excess demand has been 100 units (300 – 200) greater than the proposed safety stock 30% of the time (12 ÷ 40). The cost per stockout was $300 ($3 × 100). Demand has exceeded the safety stock by 200 units (400 – 200) 15% of the time (6 ÷ 40). The cost per stockout was $600 ($3 × 200). Given 30% and 15% probabilities of $300 and $600 stockout costs, respectively, the expected stockout cost for a 200-unit safety stock is $180 per inventory cycle [(30% × $300) + (15% × $600)]. Given 8 cycles (50,000 units ÷ 6,250 EOQ), the annual cost of a 200-unit safety stock is therefore $4,040 [$2,600 + (8 × $180)].
Answer (A) is incorrect because $2,600 is the annual carrying cost of 200 units of safety stock. Answer (C) is incorrect because $4,260 is the annual cost of establishing a 300-unit safety stock. Answer (D) is incorrect because $5,200 is the annual cost of establishing a 400-unit safety stock.

Questions 9 through 11 are based on the following information.  The diagram presented represents the economic order quantity (EOQ) model.

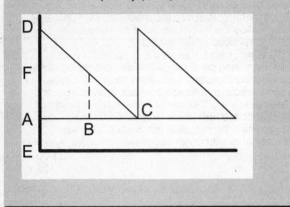

**9.** Which line segment represents the reorder lead time?

A.  AB.

B.  AE.

C.  AF.

D.  BC.

Answer (D) is correct.  *(CMA, adapted)*
    **REQUIRED:**  The line segment representing the reorder lead time.
    **DISCUSSION:**  The quantity of inventory on hand is represented by the y axis and time by the x axis.  The reorder lead time is represented by the line segment BC.
    Answer (A) is incorrect because AB is the time between receipt of the last order and the placing of the next order.  Answer (B) is incorrect because AE is the safety stock.  Answer (C) is incorrect because AF represents the quantity of inventory that will be used during the reorder lead time.

**10.** Which line segment identifies the quantity of safety stock maintained?

A.  AB.

B.  AE.

C.  AC.

D.  BC.

Answer (B) is correct.  *(CMA, adapted)*
    **REQUIRED:**  The line segment representing the quantity of safety stock maintained.
    **DISCUSSION:**  Quantities of inventory are shown along the y axis.  Safety stock is represented by the line AE.
    Answer (A) is incorrect because AB is the time between the receipt of the last order and the placing of the next order.  Answer (C) is incorrect because AC is the time to consume the EOQ.  Answer (D) is incorrect because BC is the reorder lead time.

**11.** Which line segment represents the length of time to consume the total quantity of materials ordered?

A.  DE.

B.  BC.

C.  AC.

D.  AE.

Answer (C) is correct.  *(CMA, adapted)*
    **REQUIRED:**  The line representing the time to consume all the materials ordered.
    **DISCUSSION:**  Time is shown along the x axis.  The line segment AC depicts the time to consume an entire order (to reduce the inventory to the safety stock).
    Answer (A) is incorrect because DE represents the total inventory on hand just after an order has been received.  Answer (B) is incorrect because BC is the reorder lead time.  Answer (D) is incorrect because AE is the safety stock.

**12.** Each stockout of a product sold by A.W. Inn Co. costs $1,750 per occurrence. The carrying cost per unit of inventory is $5 per year, and the company orders 1,500 units of product 24 times a year at a cost of $100 per order. The probability of a stockout at various levels of safety stock is

| Units of Safety Stock | Probability of a Stockout |
|---|---|
| 0 | .50 |
| 100 | .30 |
| 200 | .14 |
| 300 | .05 |
| 400 | .01 |

The optimal safety stock level for the company is

A. 0 units.

B. 100 units.

C. 300 units.

D. 400 units.

Answer (D) is correct. *(CMA, adapted)*
  **REQUIRED:** The optimal level of safety stock.
  **DISCUSSION:** The total expected cost of safety stock equals the sum of the expected annual stockout cost and the expected annual carrying cost. Annual expected stockout cost equals the cost per occurrence ($1,750), times the probability of a stockout per cycle, times the number of cycles (24). Annual expected carrying cost of a safety stock equals the unit carrying cost ($5) times the number of units. Hence, a safety stock of 400 units has the lowest total expected cost.

| Units Held | Carrying Cost | Expected Stockout Cost Per Cycle | Expected Stockout Cost for 24 Cycles | Total Expected Cost |
|---|---|---|---|---|
| 0 | $ 0 | $875.00 | $21,000 | $21,000 |
| 100 | 500 | 525.00 | 12,600 | 13,100 |
| 200 | 1,000 | 245.00 | 5,880 | 6,880 |
| 300 | 1,500 | 87.50 | 2,100 | 3,600 |
| 400 | 2,000 | 17.50 | 420 | 2,420 |

  Answer (A) is incorrect because a safety stock of 0 units has a total expected cost of $21,000. Answer (B) is incorrect because a safety stock of 100 units has a total expected cost of $13,100. Answer (C) is incorrect because a safety stock of 300 units has a total expected cost of $3,600.

Questions 13 and 14 are based on the following information. The Huron Corporation purchases 60,000 headbands per year. The average purchase lead time is 20 working days. Maximum lead time is 27 working days. The corporation works 240 days per year.

**13.** Huron Corporation should carry safety stock of

A. 5,000 units.

B. 6,750 units.

C. 1,750 units.

D. 250 units.

Answer (C) is correct. *(CMA, adapted)*
  **REQUIRED:** The amount of safety stock to be carried.
  **DISCUSSION:** Safety stock is defined as the amount of extra stock that is kept to guard against stockouts. It is the inventory level at the reorder point minus the expected usage during the lead time. Daily usage is 250 units (60,000 per year ÷ 240 days). Given a maximum lead time of 27 days and a normal lead time of 20 days, a safety stock for 7 days (27 – 20) should be maintained. Hence, safety stock is 1,750 units (7 × 250 units).
  Answer (A) is incorrect because 5,000 units represents the quantity expected to be sold during the normal lead time. Answer (B) is incorrect because 6,750 units includes not only the safety stock but also the units expected to be sold during the normal lead time. Answer (D) is incorrect because 250 units is 1 day's sales.

**14.** Huron Corporation should reorder headbands when the quantity in inventory reaches

A. 5,000 units.

B. 6,750 units.

C. 1,750 units.

D. 5,250 units.

Answer (B) is correct. *(CMA, adapted)*
  **REQUIRED:** The reorder point in units.
  **DISCUSSION:** The reorder point is the quantity on hand when an order is placed. With a 20-day normal lead time, a 7-day safety stock, and usage of 250 units per day, an order should be placed when 27 days of inventory are on hand, a total of 6,750 units (27 × 250).
  Answer (A) is incorrect because 5,000 units does not allow for safety stock. Answer (C) is incorrect because 1,750 units covers only safety stock. Answer (D) is incorrect because 5,250 units includes only 1 day of safety stock.

Questions 15 and 16 are based on the following information. Ryerson Computer Furniture Inc. (RCF) manufactures a line of office computer chairs. The annual demand for the chairs is estimated to be 5,000 units. The annual cost to hold one unit in inventory is $10 per year, and the cost to initiate a production run is $1,000. There are no computer chairs on hand, and RCF has scheduled four equal production runs of computer chairs for the coming year, the first of which is to be run immediately. RCF has 250 business days per year, sales occur uniformly throughout the year, and production start-up is within one day. RCF is considering using the following formula for determining the economic order quantity (EOQ):

$$EOQ = \sqrt{\frac{2AD}{K}}$$

If:  A = cost to initiate a production run per purchase order
     D = annual unit demand
     K = cost of carrying one unit per year

**15.** The number of production runs per year of computer chairs that would minimize the sum of carrying and setup costs for the coming year is

A. 1

B. 2

C. 4

D. 5

Answer (D) is correct.  *(CMA, adapted)*
**REQUIRED:** The number of production runs that minimizes the sum of setup and carrying costs.
**DISCUSSION:** The EOQ minimizes the sum of carrying and setup costs. The EOQ is the amount at which carrying costs are equal to setup costs. Thus, plugging the data into the EOQ formula results in the following:

$$EOQ = \sqrt{\frac{2(\$1,000)(5,000)}{\$10}} = 1,000 \text{ units}$$

Thus, if each lot consists of 1,000 units, five production runs per year are needed to meet the 5,000-unit demand. At this level, setup costs will total $5,000 (5 × $1,000). Carrying costs will also equal $5,000 ($10 per unit carrying cost × average inventory of 500 units). Accordingly, total costs are minimized at $10,000.
Answer (A) is incorrect because a single production run indicates an EOQ of 5,000 units. The carrying costs of $25,000 [$10 × ($5,000 ÷ 2)] would exceed the $1,000 of setup costs. Answer (B) is incorrect because two production runs correspond to an EOQ of 2,500 units and an average inventory of 1,250 units. The resulting $12,500 of carrying costs would exceed the $2,000 of setup costs. Answer (C) is incorrect because four production runs correspond to an EOQ of 1,250 units and an average inventory of 625 units. The resulting $6,250 of carrying costs would exceed the $4,000 of setup costs.

**16.** If RCF does not maintain a safety stock, the estimated total carrying costs for the computer chairs for the coming year based on their current schedule is

A. $4,000

B. $5,000

C. $6,250

D. $12,500

Answer (C) is correct.  *(CMA, adapted)*
**REQUIRED:** The estimated total annual carrying costs assuming no safety stock is held.
**DISCUSSION:** Given four production runs and an annual demand of 5,000 units, each production run must generate 1,250 units. Inventory will total 1,250 units at the completion of each run but will decline to zero just prior to the next run. Thus, the average inventory is 625 units (1,250 ÷ 2), and the total carrying cost is $6,250 ($10 × 625 units).
Answer (A) is incorrect because the cost of maintaining an average inventory of 625 units is $6,250. Answer (B) is incorrect because $5,000 is based upon an EOQ of 1,000 units and an average inventory of 500 units. Answer (D) is incorrect because $12,500 is based on the maximum inventory level.

## 2.2 Pricing

**17.** Which one of the graphs depicts the demand curve for prestige goods?

A.

B.

C.

D.

Answer (C) is correct. *(CIA, adapted)*
**REQUIRED:** The graph depicting the demand curve for prestige goods.
**DISCUSSION:** Over some intermediate range of prices, the reaction to a price increase for prestige goods is an increase, not a decrease, in the quantity demanded. Within this range, the demand curve is upward sloping. The reason is that consumers interpret the higher price to indicate a better or more desirable product. Above some price level, the relation between price and quantity demanded will again become negatively sloped.
Answer (A) is incorrect because this graph describes the familiar, negatively sloped relation between price charged and the resulting demand level for normal goods. Answer (B) is incorrect because the demand curve can be linear or curvilinear. Answer (D) is incorrect because this demand curve has the same basic shape as the demand curve for prestige goods, but it bends the wrong way. As prices increase, quantity demanded first falls and then rises in this graph.

**18.** Buyer-based pricing involves

A. Adding a standard markup to the cost of the product.

B. Determining the price at which the product will earn a target profit.

C. Basing prices on the product's perceived value.

D. Basing prices on competitors' prices.

Answer (C) is correct. *(CIA, adapted)*
**REQUIRED:** The definition of buyer-based pricing.
**DISCUSSION:** Buyer-based pricing involves basing prices on the product's perceived value rather than on the seller's cost. Nonprice variables in the marketing mix augment the perceived value. For example, a cup of coffee may have a higher price at an expensive restaurant than at a fast-food outlet.
Answer (A) is incorrect because adding a standard markup to the cost of the product is cost-plus pricing. Answer (B) is incorrect because determining the price at which the product will earn a target profit is target profit pricing. Answer (D) is incorrect because basing prices on competitors' prices is going-rate pricing.

**19.** Market-skimming pricing strategies could be appropriate when

- A. No buyers want the product at a high price.
- B. The costs of producing a small volume are low.
- C. Competitors can easily enter the market.
- D. The product is of poor quality.

Answer (B) is correct. *(CIA, adapted)*
**REQUIRED:** The circumstances under which market-skimming pricing strategies are appropriate.
**DISCUSSION:** Market-skimming pricing is used when a new product is introduced at the highest price possible given the benefits of the product. For market skimming to work, the product must appear to be worth its price, the costs of producing a small volume cannot be so high that they eliminate the advantage of charging more, and competitors cannot enter the market and undercut the price.
Answer (A) is incorrect because, if no buyers want the product at a high price, this marketing strategy is inappropriate. Answer (C) is incorrect because, if competitors can easily enter the market, they can undercut the price. Answer (D) is incorrect because the product quality and image must support a high price.

**20.** Which of the following pricing policies involves the selling company setting freight charges to customers at the actual average freight cost?

- A. Freight absorption pricing.
- B. Uniform delivered pricing.
- C. Zone pricing.
- D. FOB-origin pricing.

Answer (B) is correct. *(CIA, adapted)*
**REQUIRED:** The pricing policy that results in setting freight charges at actual average cost.
**DISCUSSION:** In uniform delivered pricing, the company charges the same price, inclusive of shipping costs, to all customers regardless of their location. This price is the company's average actual freight cost. Thus, both nearby and distant customers are charged the same amount. This policy is easy to administer, permits the company to advertise one price nationwide, and facilitates marketing to faraway customers.
Answer (A) is incorrect because, in freight absorption pricing, the selling company absorbs all or part of the actual freight charges. Customers are not charged actual delivery costs. Answer (C) is incorrect because, in zone pricing, differential freight charges are set for customers on the basis of their location. Customers are not charged actual average freight costs. Answer (D) is incorrect because, in FOB-origin pricing, each customer pays its actual freight costs.

**21.** Which of the following price adjustment strategies is designed to stabilize production for the selling firm?

- A. Cash discounts.
- B. Quantity discounts.
- C. Functional discounts.
- D. Seasonal discounts.

Answer (D) is correct. *(CIA, adapted)*
**REQUIRED:** The price adjustment strategy intended to stabilize production.
**DISCUSSION:** Seasonal discounts are designed to smooth production by the selling firm. For example, a ski manufacturer offers seasonal discounts to retailers in the spring and summer to encourage early ordering.
Answer (A) is incorrect because cash discounts encourage prompt payment. Answer (B) is incorrect because quantity discounts encourage large volume purchases. Answer (C) is incorrect because functional or trade discounts are provided to channel members in return for the performance of certain functions, such as selling, storing, and record keeping.

**22.** In which product-mix pricing strategy is it appropriate for the seller to accept any price that exceeds the storage and delivery costs for the product?

A. By-product pricing.

B. Optional-product pricing.

C. Captive-product pricing.

D. Product-bundle pricing.

Answer (A) is correct. *(CIA, adapted)*
**REQUIRED:** The pricing strategy that accepts any price greater than storage and delivery costs.
**DISCUSSION:** A by-product is a product of relatively minor importance generated during the production of one or more other products. Its production entails no additional costs. Any amount received above the storage and delivery costs for a by-product allows the seller to reduce the main product's price to make it more competitive.
Answer (B) is incorrect because optional products are offered for sale along with the main product. They are unlikely to have a zero production cost, so the seller must receive a price above their storage and delivery costs. Answer (C) is incorrect because captive products must be used along with the main product, such as film for use with a camera. Sellers often make their profits on the captive products rather than on the main product, which is sold at a low price. The captive products therefore will be priced well above the storage and delivery costs. Answer (D) is incorrect because product bundles are combinations of products sold together at a reduced price, such as season tickets for a theater. Products are bundled to promote the sale of certain items that consumers might not otherwise purchase. The combined price of the bundle must be low enough to encourage consumers to buy the bundle but must recover production costs and provide some profit for the seller, so the price must exceed storage and delivery costs.

**23.** Several surveys point out that most managers use full product costs, including unit fixed costs and unit variable costs, in developing cost-based pricing. Which one of the following is least associated with cost-based pricing?

A. Price stability.

B. Price justification.

C. Target pricing.

D. Fixed-cost recovery.

Answer (C) is correct. *(CMA, adapted)*
**REQUIRED:** The concept least associated with cost-based pricing.
**DISCUSSION:** A target price is the expected market price of a product, given the company's knowledge of its customers and competitors. Hence, under target pricing, the sales price is known before the product is developed. Subtracting the unit target profit margin determines the long-term unit target cost. If cost-cutting measures do not permit the product to be made at or below the target cost, it will be abandoned.
Answer (A) is incorrect because full-cost pricing promotes price stability. It limits the ability to cut prices. Answer (B) is incorrect because full-cost pricing provides evidence that the company is not violating antitrust laws against predatory pricing. Answer (D) is incorrect because full-cost pricing has the advantage of recovering the full long-term costs of the product. In the long term, all costs are relevant.

**24.** If a U.S. manufacturer's price in the U.S. market is below an appropriate measure of costs and the seller has a reasonable prospect of recovering the resulting loss in the future through higher prices or a greater market share, the seller has engaged in

A. Collusive pricing.

B. Dumping.

C. Predatory pricing.

D. Price discrimination.

Answer (C) is correct. *(Publisher)*
**REQUIRED:** The pricing strategy characterized by charging a price that is below an appropriate measure of costs when the seller reasonably expects to recover the loss through higher prices or a greater market share.
**DISCUSSION:** Predatory pricing is intentionally pricing below cost to eliminate competition and reduce supply. Federal statutes and many state laws prohibit the practice. The U.S. Supreme Court has held that pricing is predatory when two conditions are met: (1) the seller's price is below "an appropriate measure of its costs," and (2) it has a reasonable prospect of recovering the resulting loss through higher prices or greater market share.
Answer (A) is incorrect because collusive pricing involves a conspiracy to set higher prices. Answer (B) is incorrect because dumping is defined under U.S. law as sale by a non-U.S. company in the U.S. market of a product below its market value in the country where it was produced. Such sale is illegal if it threatens material injury to a U.S. industry. Answer (D) is incorrect because price discrimination entails charging different prices to different customers for essentially the same product if the effect is to lessen competition substantially; to tend to create a monopoly; or to injure, destroy, or prevent competition.

**25.** Fulford Company applies the target pricing and costing approach. The following information about costs and revenues of Fulford's product are available for the year just ended:

| | |
|---|---|
| Unit sales | 60,000 |
| Unit selling price | $        400 |
| Cost of goods sold | 13,200,000 |
| Value-chain operating costs excluding production | 7,920,000 |

Fulford plans to increase unit sales to 80,000 by reducing the product's unit price to $320. If Fulford desires a unit target operating income of 12%, by what amount must it reduce the full cost per unit?

A. $32.00

B. $38.40

C. $70.40

D. $80.00

Answer (C) is correct. *(Publisher)*
REQUIRED: The necessary reduction in the full cost per unit.
DISCUSSION: Unit target operating income is $38.40 (12% × $320 unit target price). Hence, the unit target full cost is $281.60 ($320 – $38.40). The current full cost per unit is $352.00 [($13,200,000 CGS + $7,920,000 other value chain operating costs) ÷ 60,000 units sold], so the necessary reduction in the full cost per unit is $70.40 ($352.00 – $281.60).
Answer (A) is incorrect because $32.00 equals the current full cost per unit minus the new unit target price. Answer (B) is incorrect because $38.40 is the unit target operating income. Answer (D) is incorrect because $80.00 equals the change in the unit price.

**26.** A company's product has an expected 4-year life cycle from research, development, and design through its withdrawal from the market. Budgeted costs are

| | |
|---|---|
| Upstream costs (R&D, design) | $2,000,000 |
| Manufacturing costs | 3,000,000 |
| Downstream costs (marketing, distribution, customer service) | 1,200,000 |
| After-purchase costs | 1,000,000 |

The company plans to produce 200,000 units and price the product at 125% of the whole-life unit cost. Thus, the budgeted unit selling price is

A. $15

B. $31

C. $36

D. $45

Answer (D) is correct. *(Publisher)*
REQUIRED: The unit selling price.
DISCUSSION: Whole-life costs include after-purchase costs (operating, support, repair, and disposal) incurred by customers as well as life-cycle costs (R&D, design, manufacturing, marketing, distribution, and research). Hence, the budgeted unit whole-life cost is $36 [($2,000,000 + $3,000,000 + $1,200,000 + $1,000,000) ÷ 200,000 units], and the budgeted unit selling price is $45 (125% × $36).
Answer (A) is incorrect because $15 is the budgeted unit manufacturing cost. Answer (B) is incorrect because $31 is the budgeted unit life-cycle cost. Answer (C) is incorrect because $36 is the budgeted unit whole-life cost.

## 2.3 Managing Human Resources

**27.** The protected group under the Age Discrimination in Employment Act of 1967, as amended, is defined as anyone in which age group?

A. 35 through 60.

B. 40 through 75.

C. 40 and older.

D. 45 and older.

Answer (C) is correct. *(CMA, adapted)*
REQUIRED: The protected age group under the Age Discrimination in Employment Act.
DISCUSSION: The Age Discrimination in Employment Act is designed to protect individuals aged 40 and older from employment discrimination. The act has been amended to eliminate the mandatory retirement age. However, certain managerial employees are not protected by this amendment.

**28.** Evaluating performance is not done to

A. Determine the amount of nondiscriminatory benefits that each employee deserves.

B. Assess the available human resources of the firm.

C. Motivate the employees.

D. Determine which employees deserve salary increases.

Answer (A) is correct. *(Publisher)*
**REQUIRED:** The statement that is not a purpose of performance evaluations.
**DISCUSSION:** There are many reasons for evaluating performance. Evaluations reinforce accomplishments, help in assessing employee strengths and weaknesses, provide motivation, assist in employee development, permit the organization to assess its human resource needs, and serve as a basis for wage increases. Nondiscriminatory benefits are given to everyone in the organization in equal amounts regardless of title, pay, or achievement of objectives.

**29.** When a manager generalizes from the evaluation of one or a few traits to the employee's total performance, (s)he has made

A. A judgmental evaluation.

B. An evaluation subject to the halo effect.

C. A projection.

D. An objective evaluation.

Answer (B) is correct. *(Publisher)*
**REQUIRED:** The type of evaluation that generalizes from an evaluation of a few of an employee's traits.
**DISCUSSION:** The halo effect occurs when the appraiser judges one or a few employee traits and carries over this judgment to the evaluation of the employee's other traits. The halo effect can be positive or negative.
Answer (A) is incorrect because a judgmental evaluation is based on nonverifiable, subjective criteria. Answer (C) is incorrect because projection is the process of attributing one's own traits to another person. Answer (D) is incorrect because an objective evaluation uses verifiable, often quantitative criteria.

**30.** A manager discovers by chance that a newly hired employee has strong beliefs that are very different from the manager's and from those of most of the other employees. The manager's best course of action would be to

A. Facilitate the reassignment of the new hire as quickly as possible before this situation becomes disruptive.

B. Ask the rest of the team for their reaction and act according to the group consensus.

C. Take no action unless the new hire's behavior is likely to cause harm to the organization.

D. Try to counsel the new hire into more reasonable beliefs.

Answer (C) is correct. *(CIA, adapted)*
**REQUIRED:** The manager's best course of action when a new employee has strong beliefs that are very different from the manager's beliefs.
**DISCUSSION:** The only legitimate grounds on which the supervisor may take action is the employee's behavior. Personal beliefs, such as those on religious and political matters, cannot be the basis of personnel actions. Discrimination on the basis of personal beliefs could expose the organization to legal action.

**31.** A company allows each of its departments to develop its own system for evaluating performance. Linda Ward, the personnel director, should communicate appraisal information to a new employee by

A. Presenting anything that is pertinent to the listener's situation.

B. Providing an overview of all systems within the company.

C. Describing how her own performance is evaluated.

D. Discussing each department's evaluation system in detail.

Answer (A) is correct. *(Publisher)*
**REQUIRED:** The best method of discussing performance evaluations with a new employee.
**DISCUSSION:** The personnel director should tailor the discussion to the listener by describing how the employee's department evaluates performance and what is expected of him/her. The director should also obtain feedback from the employee to determine if everything is clearly understood. Discussing information that is irrelevant to the new employee's appraisal information would confuse the new employee.

**32.** A disadvantage of separating performance evaluations from wage-increase decisions is that

A. Not enough emphasis is placed on short-run performance.

B. Financial rewards may lose their motivational effect.

C. Employees may not be motivated by good appraisals.

D. The employee's performance evaluation does not consider the financial status of the company overall.

Answer (C) is correct.  *(Publisher)*
**REQUIRED:** The disadvantage of separating performance appraisals from wage increases.
**DISCUSSION:** The employee may not be motivated immediately by a good appraisal because of the delay in receipt of any monetary reward. The evaluation may also not be taken as seriously by the employee if compensation is not correlated with performance.
Answer (A) is incorrect because an advantage of separating appraisals from wage increases is that more emphasis is placed on long-term objectives and goals. Answer (B) is incorrect because this separation does not deprive money of its motivational power, but it does emphasize other rewards, such as feelings of achievement and the recognition of superiors. Answer (D) is incorrect because an advantage of separating performance evaluations from wage-increase decisions is that the employee's good performance can be separated from the overall company's bad financial performance.

**33.** A company that wishes to improve its rate of retention of its experienced employees might

A. Abolish its hire-from-within policy.

B. Improve its fringe benefit package.

C. Initiate job simplification programs.

D. Set a mandatory retirement age.

Answer (B) is correct.  *(Publisher)*
**REQUIRED:** The way to improve employee retention.
**DISCUSSION:** Fringe benefits (e.g., pensions and profit-sharing plans) may be contingent on duration of employment. Accordingly, they motivate employees to remain with the company.
Answer (A) is incorrect because reduced opportunity for advancement may motivate employees to find jobs elsewhere. Answer (C) is incorrect because job simplification may result in boredom, lessened job satisfaction, and a higher turnover rate. Answer (D) is incorrect because abolition of a mandatory retirement age would be more appropriate.

**34.** A company that formerly paid certain management employees on a salary plus commission basis decided to compensate a test group solely with commissions. Performance of these employees declined. The most likely explanation for this result is that

A. The employee received special attention.

B. Compensation was a motivational factor.

C. Compensation was not a hygiene factor.

D. Increased concerns about security made the employees risk averse.

Answer (D) is correct.  *(Publisher)*
**REQUIRED:** The most likely reason for the performance decline.
**DISCUSSION:** A straight salary with commissions rewarded increased efforts while providing greater security and a reduction in anxiety. Satisfaction of the need for security may have permitted the employees to adopt promising and profitable but more risky strategies. Since people concerned about security needs tend to be risk averse, the change in compensation method probably caused the performance decline.
Answer (A) is incorrect because the famous Hawthorne studies suggest that the employees' knowledge of their special status would improve their output. Answer (B) is incorrect because Herzberg defines a motivational factor as one whose absence will not diminish performance but whose presence will be a motivator. Answer (C) is incorrect because a performance decline followed a reduction in the security of compensation; hence, money was probably a hygiene (maintenance) factor according to Herzberg's two-factor theory of motivation.

**35.** The human resource department of an organization observed that accounting staff turnover was unusually high. Exit interviews indicated that the accounting department work schedule was highly restrictive for accountants who had young children. To improve the retention of skilled employees in the accounting department, the best solution would be to

A. Implement a program of job rotation within the accounting department.

B. Promote job enlargement for the positions experiencing the greatest turnover.

C. Provide job sharing and flextime opportunities for accounting department employees.

D. Enrich the jobs of accounting department employees.

Answer (C) is correct. *(CIA, adapted)*
**REQUIRED:** The best way to improve employee retention.
**DISCUSSION:** Job sharing and flextime allow employees to adjust their work schedules and hours to better achieve personal objectives. These programs can increase worker loyalty and motivation.
Answer (A) is incorrect because job rotation would not adequately address the scheduling issue. Answer (B) is incorrect because job enlargement would not adequately address the scheduling issue. Answer (D) is incorrect because job enrichment would not adequately address the scheduling issue.

**36.** The factor that would not contribute to retention of experienced employees would be

A. Initiation of job enrichment programs.

B. Adherence to federal regulations regarding sex discrimination in paying and promoting workers.

C. Paying new employees more than older ones.

D. Adoption of flextime rules.

Answer (C) is correct. *(Publisher)*
**REQUIRED:** The factor not contributing to employee retention.
**DISCUSSION:** When old employees discover that newcomers are being hired at higher salaries, the group hired first will be unhappy, feeling that their greater experience should warrant greater reward. In the short run, the newcomers will be satisfied. But it is possible that next year's newcomers will be hired at still higher salaries, contributing to the overall dissatisfaction. Thus, such a policy will provide incentives for experienced workers to leave the company.
Answer (A) is incorrect because a more intrinsically satisfying job will improve the retention rate. Answer (B) is incorrect because employees subject to discrimination may be strongly motivated to find other jobs. Answer (D) is incorrect because greater freedom in determining his/her hours may enable a worker to remain with the company when other responsibilities (e.g., child care) might have compelled him/her to leave.

**37.** The value of retaining employees is determined by

A. Human asset accounting.

B. Financial accounting.

C. Cost accounting.

D. Human resource planning.

Answer (A) is correct. *(Publisher)*
**REQUIRED:** The method used to determine the value of retaining employees.
**DISCUSSION:** Human resource or human asset accounting attempts to measure the value, and the changes in value, of the organization's investment in human assets. Although this "asset" is enormously valuable (sometimes estimated at two or three times the annual payroll), it is not shown in balance sheets or accounted for in earnings statements. One experimental measurement approach is a sort of "present value" of human resources. Another is a "cost" approach, with dollar investments (training, customer goodwill, etc.) offset by reductions (e.g., retirement).
Answer (B) is incorrect because this traditional accounting method does not value the organization's human assets. Answer (C) is incorrect because this traditional accounting method does not value the organization's human assets. Answer (D) is incorrect because it merely audits the skills of the current employees and forecasts needs.

**38.** An employee with a good background and years of experience earns a salary at the top of his/her range. Under the company's compensation program, the employee must earn a promotion in order to increase his/her salary above the usual annual increase. Which of the following is most likely to be an effect on his/her behavior?

A. The employee may refuse new duties or tasks.

B. The employee may become less productive.

C. The employee may not be motivated to improve performance.

D. The employee may seek a position with another company.

Answer (D) is correct. *(Publisher)*
**REQUIRED:** The effect on the employee's behavior of the limitation on possible rewards.
**DISCUSSION:** When an employee can earn a desired salary increase only through a promotion, (s)he is likely to be motivated to perform better. If this does not result in a promotion, (s)he will probably look for another job.

**39.** A company's compensation program does not allow for salary increases based on above-average performance after an employee reaches the top of a position's salary range. It also pays some employees higher salaries because of their educational qualifications. This company could improve the program by

A. Allowing each manager to set up his/her own system of salary increases.

B. Providing only monetary compensation.

C. Developing a system that equates years of experience with education.

D. Decreasing the annual percentage increase in each salary range.

Answer (C) is correct. *(Publisher)*
**REQUIRED:** The improvement in the described compensation program.
**DISCUSSION:** A company with a compensation program that stops rewarding above-average performance at the top of each salary range and rewards education with higher compensation could improve the system in several ways. These include starting a bonus program for above-average performance, refusing to hire a person at the top of a salary range unless (s)he will be promoted quickly, and equating experience and education so that employees are treated fairly.
Answer (A) is incorrect because the company should administer a uniform system of salary increases. Answer (B) is incorrect because the company could improve its system if it provided other compensation, such as assisting with an employee's tuition or recognizing an employee who has given many years of service. Answer (D) is incorrect because the company would please all employees by increasing this percentage.

**40.** Which of the following methods of employee evaluation is best used in a situation where employees are heavily involved in teamwork?

A. 360-degree performance appraisal.

B. Attribution method.

C. Critical incident technique.

D. Behaviorally anchored rating scales (BARS).

Answer (A) is correct. *(Publisher)*
**REQUIRED:** The type of employee evaluation that is best in a teamwork environment.
**DISCUSSION:** The 360-degree performance appraisal is a model for employee assessment in the age of teamwork. It is based on giving workers feedback from peers, customers, supervisors, and those who work for the employee. Feedback is typically provided anonymously and is usually subjective.
Answer (B) is incorrect because this is a nonsense term. Answer (C) is incorrect because the critical incident technique is based on having a list of critical aspects of a job against which to compare the employee's performance; it would usually not be effective in a team situation. Answer (D) is incorrect because BARS is based on specific job-related behaviors.

**41.** If a supervisor fails to give an employee a negative evaluation because of fear of damaging a good working relationship, this is known as the

A. Leniency error.

B. Recency effect.

C. Halo effect.

D. Contrast error.

Answer (A) is correct. *(Publisher)*
**REQUIRED:** The term referring to the avoidance of giving a negative evaluation because of fear of damaging a good working relationship.
**DISCUSSION:** A leniency error is when a manager fails to give a negative evaluation because of fear of damaging a good working relationship with an employee.
Answer (B) is incorrect because the recency effect means that the employee's most recent behavior overshadows overall performance. Answer (C) is incorrect because the halo effect means the manager's judgment on one positive trait affects the rating on other traits. Answer (D) is incorrect because a contrast error is the tendency to rate people relative to other people, without consideration of performance standards.

---

Use Gleim's *CIA Test Prep* for interactive testing with over 2,000 additional multiple-choice questions!

# STUDY UNIT THREE
# FINANCIAL ACCOUNTING -- BASIC CONCEPTS

(18 pages of outline)

Financial accounting provides the information reported in a complete set of financial statements. The balance sheet presents financial position and the income statement presents performance. The other two basic financial statements are the statement of cash flows and the statement of changes in equity. Financial statements may be prepared for any entity, e.g., a business, school, government, or fraternal organization. Because the CIA examination is international in scope, this study unit outlines the international sources of the body of knowledge regarding financial statement preparation for business enterprises and the underlying financial accounting theory. It also covers the procedural aspects of financial reporting. U.S. GAAP will not be tested.

Study Units 3 through 5 cover International Accounting Standards (IAS). The IASs and related Interpretations were issued by the predecessor to the current standard setter, the International Accounting Standards Board. They will be effective until amended or superseded by pronouncements of the Board. Its standards are called International Financial Reporting Standards (IFRSs).

The following is a list of current Standards:

**IAS 1**  Presentation of Financial Statements
**IAS 2**  Inventories
**IAS 3**  Superseded
**IAS 4**  Withdrawn
**IAS 5**  Superseded
**IAS 6**  Superseded
**IAS 7**  Cash Flow Statements
**IAS 8**  Net Profit or Loss for the Period, Fundamental Errors and Changes in Accounting Policies
**IAS 9**  Superseded
**IAS 10**  Events after the Balance Sheet Date
**IAS 11**  Construction Contracts
**IAS 12**  Income Taxes
**IAS 13**  Superseded
**IAS 14**  Segment Reporting
**IAS 15**  Information Reflecting the Effects of Changing Prices
**IAS 16**  Property, Plant and Equipment
**IAS 17**  Accounting for Leases
**IAS 18**  Revenue
**IAS 19**  Employee Benefits
**IAS 20**  Accounting for Government Grants and Disclosure of Government Assistance
**IAS 21**  The Effects of Changes in Foreign Exchange Rates
**IAS 22**  Business Combinations
**IAS 23**  Borrowing Costs

**IAS 24**  Related Party Disclosures
**IAS 25**  Superseded
**IAS 26**  Accounting and Reporting by Retirement Benefit Plans
**IAS 27**  Consolidated Financial Statements and Accounting for Investments in Subsidiaries
**IAS 28**  Accounting for Investments in Associates
**IAS 29**  Financial Reporting in Hyperinflationary Economies
**IAS 30**  Disclosures in the Financial Statements of Banks and Similar Financial Institutions
**IAS 31**  Financial Reporting of Interests in Joint Ventures
**IAS 32**  Financial Instruments: Disclosures and Presentation
**IAS 33**  Earnings per Share
**IAS 34**  Interim Financial Reporting
**IAS 35**  Discontinuing Operations
**IAS 36**  Impairment of Assets
**IAS 37**  Provisions, Contingent Liabilities and Contingent Assets
**IAS 38**  Intangible Assets
**IAS 39**  Financial Instruments: Recognition and Measurement
**IAS 40**  Investment Property
**IAS 41**  Agriculture
**IFRS 1**  First-time Adoption of International Financial Reporting Standards (effective January 1, 2004)

In keeping with the way in which the IASs present information, we have omitted all currency symbols. In some situations, this treatment may seem awkward for candidates accustomed to seeing items presented with monetary units indicated. Be prepared for exam questions that may or may not include monetary units.

## 3.1 FRAMEWORK FOR THE PREPARATION AND PRESENTATION OF FINANCIAL STATEMENTS

1. **Objective of Financial Statements**

   a. Business enterprises should provide information about financial position, performance, and changes in financial position that is helpful to many users in making economic decisions. However, these statements do not provide all necessary information.

   b. Financial statements should show the results of management's stewardship or its accountability for assets.

   c. Users need to evaluate the ability of the enterprise to generate cash and the timing and certainty of its generation.

   d. An enterprise's financial position is determined by its economic resources, financial structure, liquidity and solvency, and adaptability.

   e. Information about performance and its variability helps to predict changes in the resources the enterprise may control, how effectively it will use additional resources, and its capacity to generate cash from existing resources.

   f. Information about changes in financial position is useful in assessing financing, investing, and operating activities. For this purpose, funds may be defined in different ways.

   g. Information about financial position is primarily provided in a balance sheet. Information about performance is primarily provided in an income statement. Information about changes in financial position is provided in a separate statement, such as a cash flow statement or a funds flow statement.

   h. The components of financial statements interrelate because they present different aspects of the same transactions and other events.

2. The principal **qualitative characteristics** of information in financial statements are understandability, relevance, reliability, and comparability.

   a. Information should be readily **understandable** by reasonably knowledgeable and diligent users, but relevant information should not be excluded because of its complexity.

   b. **Relevance**. Useful information is relevant to user decision making. Information has relevance if users are able to predict the outcome of future events or confirm or correct their prior expectations.

      1) **Materiality** is a threshold or cut-off point. The issue is whether a given item or error is large enough so that its omission or misstatement will influence users.

   c. **Reliability**. Information is reliable if it is free of material error and bias and users can depend upon it to represent faithfully the economic transactions or events it purports to represent or could reasonably be expected to represent.

      1) **Substance over form**. To be **representationally faithful**, transactions and other events must be accounted for in accordance with their substance and economic reality, not their legal form.

      2) **Neutrality**. Reliable information must be free of bias intended to produce a predetermined result or induce certain behavior.

      3) **Prudence** is a reaction to the uncertainty arising from estimates. It includes a degree of caution in the exercise of judgment. Such prudence does not condone introducing bias into the financial statements through deliberate understatement of assets and income or overstatement of liabilities and expenses.

      4) **Completeness**. Reliable information is complete within the limits of materiality and cost.

    d.  **Comparability**. Financial statements must be comparable for the same entity over time. They should also be comparable among different entities.

        1)  Thus, measurement and display should be consistent throughout an entity over time and for different entities.

        2)  Compliance with IASs, including disclosure of accounting policies, promotes comparability.

        3)  Financial statements should report information for preceding periods.

    e.  **Constraints on Relevant and Reliable Information**.

        1)  **Timeliness**. Management needs to balance reliability and timeliness because undue delay may cause a loss of relevance. The primary criterion for determining this balance is how best to serve the needs of economic decision makers.

        2)  **Balance between Benefit and Cost**. This balance is a pervasive constraint that requires a judgment as to whether the benefits of information exceed its cost. The judgment may be difficult because, for example, costs are not necessarily borne by the users who reap the benefits.

        3)  **Balance among Qualitative Characteristics**. Professional judgment is needed to determine the appropriate tradeoffs that will achieve the objective of financial statements.

        4)  **True and Fair View**. Applying the qualitative characteristics and appropriate accounting standards should result in financial statements that reflect a true and fair view, or fair presentation, of financial position, performance, and changes in financial position.

3.  **Elements of Financial Statements**

    a.  The elements are classes of transactions and other events classified based on their economic characteristics. The following directly relate to the measurement of **financial position** in the balance sheet:

        1)  **Assets** are resources "controlled by the enterprise as a result of past events and from which future economic benefits are expected to flow to the enterprise."

            a)  The benefit is the potential for a direct or indirect contribution to the inflow of cash in the future.

            b)  Neither legal ownership nor legal control is essential to the existence of an asset.

        2)  **Liabilities** are current obligations "of the enterprise arising from past events, the settlement of which is expected to result in an outflow from the enterprise of resources embodying economic benefits."

            a)  The obligation is current and should be distinguished from a future commitment. However, the obligation need not be legally enforceable.

            b)  A liability arises from a past transaction or event, for example, a sale of goods that results in a liability for a future rebate to a customer.

            c)  A liability substantially measured by means of estimation is sometimes called a **provision**, for example, for warranty claims or pension obligations. In some countries, a provision is not treated as a liability, but the definition in the Framework is broader.

3) "**Equity** is the residual interest in the assets of the enterprise after deducting all its liabilities."

    a) This definition applies regardless of the enterprise's form of organization.

    b) Equity may be further classified, for example, into contributions of funds by owners, retained earnings, reserves for appropriations of retained earnings, and reserves for capital maintenance adjustments.

       i) Reserves may be required by law to give creditors protection from losses. Other reserves may be created when national tax law provides tax advantages for transfers to these revenues. These transfers are not expenses.

b. The following elements directly relate to measurement of **performance** in the income statement:

1) **Income** is defined as "increases in economic benefits during the accounting period in the form of inflows or enhancements of assets or decreases of liabilities that result in increases in equity, other than those relating to contributions from equity participants." Income includes revenues and gains. Thus, revenues and gains are not treated as separate elements.

    a) Revenues occur in the course of ordinary activities.

    b) Gains meet the definition of income but may or may not occur in the course of ordinary activities. For example, gains may result from the sale of noncurrent assets.

       i) Gains may be unrealized.

       ii) Gains are usually reported separately.

2) **Expenses** are defined as "decreases in economic benefits during the accounting period in the form of outflows or depletions of assets or incurrences of liabilities that result in decreases in equity, other than those relating to distributions to equity participants." Expenses include losses. Thus, losses are not treated as separate elements.

    a) Expenses include items arising in the course of ordinary activities.

    b) Losses meet the definition of expenses but may or may not occur in the course of ordinary activities. For example, losses may result from the sale of noncurrent assets or from natural disasters.

       i) Losses may be unrealized.

       ii) Losses are usually reported separately and often net of related income.

c. **Capital maintenance adjustments** are changes in equity resulting from revaluing or restating assets or liabilities, but these changes are not income statement items under certain concepts of capital maintenance. Capital maintenance may be financial or physical.

1) **Financial capital maintenance** results in profit only if the financial amount of net assets at period-end exceeds the financial amount of net assets at the period's beginning, after excluding distributions to, or contributions from, owners. The measurement may be in nominal units of money or in units of constant purchasing power.

2) **Physical capital maintenance** results in profit only if the physical productive capacity of the entity (or the equivalent resources or funds) at period-end exceeds the physical productive capacity at the period's beginning, after excluding distributions to, or contributions from, owners. The current cost measurement basis must be used.

> 3) Thus, profit is earned only when inflows of assets exceed the amounts needed to maintain capital, that is, when income exceeds expenses, including any appropriate capital maintenance adjustments.

4. **Recognition of Elements of Financial Statements**

   a. **Recognition** is the incorporation in the balance sheet or income statement totals of an item depicted in words and as a monetary amount that satisfies both the definition of an element and the recognition criteria. Disclosure of accounting policies used or in the notes or explanatory matter is not a satisfactory alternative to recognition of such an item.

   b. **Criteria**. Recognition of an element should occur if the following criteria are met:

      1) Any future economic benefit associated with the item will probably flow to or from the enterprise.

         a) Probability is the degree of uncertainty regarding the future flow of economic benefits.

      2) The cost or value of the item is measurable with reliability.

         a) Reliability is not impaired if reasonable estimates of cost or value are used.

   c. Recognition of income occurs concurrently with recognition of increases in assets or decreases in liabilities.

      1) The usual procedures for income recognition, such as that revenue be earned, reflect the recognition criteria, that is, reliable measurement and a sufficient probability. Thus, income is recognized when an increase in future economic benefits associated with an increase in an asset or a decrease in a liability has arisen that can be reliably measured.

   d. Recognition of expenses occurs concurrently with recognition of increases in liabilities or decreases in assets.

      1) Expenses are recognized if the costs are directly associated with the earning of particular income items. This process is often called **matching**. Matching is simultaneous or combined recognition of the revenues and expenses that result directly and jointly from the same transactions or other events.

      2) Expenses are also recognized when they are broadly or indirectly associated with income. In these cases, a **systematic and rational allocation** procedure, such as depreciation or amortization, is used.

      3) **Immediate recognition** of expenses is appropriate when an expenditure results in no future economic benefit or when that benefit does not qualify or ceases to qualify as an asset.

5. **Measurement** is the determination of the amounts at which the elements are to be recognized. Different measurement bases are used.

   a. **Historical cost** is the most common basis. Assets are recorded at the cash paid or the fair value of other assets given. Liabilities are recorded at the amount of proceeds received or, in some cases, at the amount of cash expected to be paid to satisfy the obligation.

   b. **Current cost**. Assets are recorded at the amount of cash to be paid if the same or an equivalent asset were currently obtained. Liabilities are recorded at the undiscounted amount of cash needed for current settlement.

    c.   **Realizable (settlement) value**. Assets are recorded at the amount of cash currently obtainable by sale in an orderly disposal. Liabilities are recorded at the undiscounted amount of cash expected to be paid for settlement in the normal course of business.

    d.   **Present value**. Assets (liabilities) are recorded at the discounted value of the future net cash inflows (outflows) that are expected to be generated (required for settlement) in the normal course of business.

6.   Stop and review! You have completed the outline for this subunit. Study multiple-choice questions 1 through 9 beginning on page 141.

## 3.2 ACCRUAL ACCOUNTING

1.   Under **cash-basis accounting**, income is recognized when cash is received.

    a.   Expense is recognized when paid.

    b.   Cash-basis accounting is subject to manipulation by arranging payments or receipts before or after the end of an accounting period.

    c.   The cash basis cannot properly reflect transactions in which cash payments or receipts relate to several financial reporting periods.

2.   To overcome the problems of cash-basis accounting, **accrual-basis accounting** is used. If an item is within the definition of an element of financial statements and meets the criteria for recognition and measurement, accrual accounting procedures will apply to it. Accrual accounting recognizes the financial effects of transactions and other events in the periods when they occur and records and reports them in the periods to which they relate.

    a.   Accordingly, accrual accounting considers not only cash transactions but also noncash exchanges of goods or services, credit transactions, nonreciprocal transfers, price changes, changes in form of assets or liabilities, etc.

    b.   Most accounting transactions are recorded when cash is paid or received (or a specific commitment to pay or receive cash is made or received).

        1)   As a result, **adjusting entries** are made at the end of a period to ensure proper income and expense recognition for that period.

            a)   **Reversing entries** are then made at the beginning of the next period.

        2)   When an item of income or expense has met the recognition criteria but the cash has not been received or paid, the income or expense must be accrued. **Accruals** anticipate future cash flows and entail recognition of assets or liabilities and the related liabilities, assets, revenues, expenses, gains, or losses. Sales or purchases on account, interest, and taxes are common accruals.

            a)   Accruals of income are made when the recognition criteria are met prior to receipt of payment (debit a receivable; credit income).

            b)   Accruals of expense are recorded when expense has been incurred but not paid (debit expense; credit a payable).

            c)   Accrual entries may be reversed at the beginning of the next period.

3)  When cash has been received or paid but the receipt or payment has not met the recognition criteria for income or expense, the item must be deferred. **Deferrals** concern past cash flows and result in recognition of liabilities (for receipts) and assets (for payments), with deferral of the related income and expense items. The deferral ends when the obligation is satisfied or the future economic benefit is used up. Prepaid insurance and unearned subscriptions are typical deferrals.

   a)  Deferrals of expense occur when expenses have been prepaid.

      i)  If the expense account was debited at the time cash was paid, the adjusting entry is to debit prepaid expense and to credit expense.

      ii)  If the asset account (prepaid expense) was debited, the adjusting entry is to debit expense and credit prepaid expense.

   b)  Deferrals of income occur when income has been received in advance.

      i)  If the income account was credited at the time cash was received, the adjusting entry is to debit income and to credit unearned income.

      ii)  If the liability account (unearned income) was credited, the adjusting entry is to debit unearned income and to credit income.

3.  Financial statements are the output of the accrual **accounting cycle**. The order of steps in the accounting cycle is as follows: identification and measurement of transactions and other events required to be recognized, journalization, posting from the journals to the ledgers, the development of a trial balance, adjustments to produce an adjusted trial balance, statement presentation, closing, taking a post-closing trial balance (optional), and making reversing entries (optional).

4.  Stop and review! You have completed the outline for this subunit. Study multiple-choice questions 10 through 16 beginning on page 144.

## 3.3 REVENUE RECOGNITION

1.  As defined in the Framework, revenue is income arising in the ordinary course of an enterprise's activities. The timing of recognition is the principal issue in accounting for revenue.

   a.  Recognition occurs when the flow of future economic benefits to the enterprise is probable, and such benefits are reliably measurable.

2.  **IAS 18**, *Revenue*, is the pronouncement with the widest applicability to revenue recognition. It concerns revenue resulting from sales of goods, rendering of services, and others' use of enterprise assets that provides returns of interest, royalties, and dividends.

   a.  Goods include not only items produced for sale but also merchandise, land, and other property held for resale.

   b.  Services involve "the performance by the enterprise of a contractually agreed task over an agreed period."

   c.  Other IASs apply to certain other revenues, for example, those from leases, equity-based investments, and changes in fair value of financial assets and liabilities.

3.  IAS 18 defines **revenue** as "the gross inflow of economic benefits during the period arising in the course of the ordinary activities of an enterprise when the inflows result in increases in equity, other than increases relating to contributions from 'participants.'"

   a.  Thus, amounts collected on behalf of a principal or otherwise on behalf of third parties, such as sales or value-added taxes, are not revenue.

4.   **Measurement**. Revenue is measured at the fair value of the consideration received or receivable by the enterprise, which is ordinarily determined by the agreement of the parties to the transaction and after due allowance for trade discounts and volume rebates.

  a.   **Fair value** is defined as "the amount for which an asset could be exchanged, or a liability settled, between knowledgeable, willing parties in an arm's-length transaction."

  b.   When the cash inflow is deferred, the fair value may be less than the nominal amounts of cash received or receivable, for example, when the seller accepts a note with a below-market rate.

   1)   **Imputed interest**. If the transaction is effectively a financing arrangement, future receipts are discounted at an imputed rate to determine the fair value. This rate is the more clearly determinable of either the prevailing rate for a similar instrument given the issuer's credit standing or the rate that discounts the nominal amount to the cash sales price.

    a)   The difference between the nominal consideration and the fair value is interest revenue.

  c.   An exchange is not deemed to result in revenue when the goods or services involved are of a similar nature or value.

   1)   In an exchange of dissimilar goods or services, revenue is generated that is measured at the fair value received (or given up) and adjusted for any cash transferred.

5.   The recognition criteria may need to be applied separately to different parts of a transaction, as when a sale of goods also provides for subsequent servicing.

  a.   The recognition criteria may also need to be applied to two or more transactions, as when a sale of goods occurs at the same time as a separate agreement by the seller to repurchase.

6.   **Sales of Goods**

  a.   Revenue is recognized when five conditions are met:

   1)   The enterprise has transferred the significant risks and rewards of ownership.

    a)   This transfer usually occurs with the passage of title or possession.

    b)   Retention of significant risks of ownership may occur in many ways, for example, when a sale is contingent upon resale, when the buyer may rescind for a reason stated in the contract and the probability of return is uncertain, or when the seller is obligated for unsatisfactory performance beyond the normal warranty.

    c)   Mere retention of legal title does not preclude revenue recognition.

   2)   The enterprise has neither continuing managerial involvement to an extent associated with ownership nor effective control over the goods.

   3)   The amount can be reliably measured.

   4)   It is probable that the economic benefits will flow to the enterprise.

    a)   In some cases, this criterion may be met only when the consideration is received or when an uncertainty is eliminated.

     i)   If an uncertainty arises regarding the collectibility of recognized revenue, the amount involved is recognized as an expense, not as an adjustment of revenue. This principle applies to revenue from services, interest, royalties, and dividends, as well as sales of goods.

          5)    Transaction costs can be reliably measured.

               a)    Revenues and expenses related to the same transaction or other event should be matched. But if expenses cannot be reliably measured, revenues are not recognized, and any consideration already received is recorded as a liability.

7. **Rendering of Services**

    a.    If the outcome of a services transaction can be reliably estimated, revenue is recognized based on the **stage of completion**. The outcome can be reliably estimated when four conditions are met:

          1)    Revenue can be reliably measured.
          2)    It is probable that the economic benefits will flow to the enterprise.
          3)    The stage of completion can be reliably measured.

               a)    Recognition based on the stage of completion is also known as the percentage-of-completion method. Construction contracts are accounted for in this manner.

          4)    The costs incurred and the costs to complete can be reliably measured.

    b.    Reliable estimates ordinarily are possible pursuant to an agreement among the parties that stipulates the enforceable rights of each party, the consideration, and the terms of settlement.

          1)    An effective internal financial budgeting and reporting system is also needed.
          2)    Revisions of estimates as services are performed, are customary, and do not necessarily indicate that reliable measurement of revenue is not feasible.

    c.    The stage of completion of services should be estimated using the method that results in a reliable measurement of the particular transaction, for example, surveys of work performed, services performed to date divided by total services, or costs incurred to date divided by total costs.

          1)    Progress payments and advances are not necessarily correlated with the services performed.

    d.    In practice, if the number of acts to be performed over a defined period cannot be determined, the straight-line method of revenue recognition is used barring evidence that another method is more representative of the stage of completion.

    e.    If the outcome of a services transaction cannot be reliably estimated, recognized revenue equals recognized recoverable expenses.

8. **Interest, Royalties, and Dividends**

    a.    These amounts result from the use by others of enterprise assets. Revenue from these sources is recognized if two conditions are met:

          1)    It is probable that the economic benefits will flow to the enterprise.
          2)    Revenue can be reliably measured.

    b.    **Interest** is recognized on a time proportion basis that considers the asset's effective yield.

          1)    An asset's **effective yield** is the discount rate used to equate the future cash receipts the asset will generate with its initial carrying amount.

               a)    Interest revenue includes amortization of discount or premium on a debt security.

          2)    Only interest accrued after acquisition of an interest-bearing investment is recognized as revenue.

c.    **Royalties**, for example, fees for use of patents, copyrights, or software, are recognized pursuant to the relevant agreement on the accrual basis.  Royalties accrue according to the relevant agreement unless, based on the substance of that agreement, another systematic and rational basis is more appropriate.

d.    **Dividends** are recognized when the shareholder has the right to be paid.  Dividends from pre-acquisition net profit are a recovery of the cost of the equity securities.  However, dividends are revenue unless they clearly represent such a recovery.

9.    IAS 18 provides for **disclosures** that include accounting policies related to revenue recognition, such as the method for determining the stage of completion.  It also provides for disclosure of the amounts of the significant categories of revenue for the period and the amount of revenue from exchanges included in each significant category.

10.    Stop and review!  You have completed the outline for this subunit.  Study multiple-choice questions 17 through 24 beginning on page 146.

## 3.4 FINANCIAL STATEMENTS

1.    **IAS 1**, *Presentation of Financial Statements*, defines financial statements as "a structured financial representation of the financial position of, and the transactions undertaken by, an enterprise."  The governing body of an enterprise is responsible for the statements.

2.    A **complete set of financial statements** includes a balance sheet, an income statement, a statement of changes in equity, a cash flow statement, notes, and a presentation of accounting policies.

a.    The statement of changes in equity shows either all such changes or all changes except those from capital transactions with, or distributions to, owners.

3.    **Pervasive Issues**

a.    Financial position, financial performance, and cash flows should be fairly presented, and properly applying IASs almost always results in **fair presentation**.

1)    Compliance with IASs should be disclosed provided all requirements of relevant pronouncements are met.

2)    The notes and disclosure of accounting policies cannot be used to compensate for inappropriate accounting.

3)    In rare cases, compliance with an IAS may be misleading, and departure from the IAS is permitted if it is necessary for a fair presentation and full disclosure is made.

b.    **Accounting policies** are specific bases, conventions, rules, and practices adopted to prepare and present financial statements.  They should be selected and applied to meet all requirements of IASs and interpretations.  Absent such a requirement, management must use its judgment in developing policies that provide relevant and reliable information.

1)    Management's judgment may be guided by IASs concerning similar issues, the IASC Framework, previous comments of other standard setters, and industry practices.

c.    Financial statements are prepared on a **going concern** basis unless management, based on an assessment of information for at least the next 12 months, expects to liquidate the enterprise or cease trading.

1)    Disclosure should be made of material uncertainties relating to circumstances that may create significant doubt about the enterprise's ability to continue.

d.    The **accrual basis** should be used to prepare all financial statements except the cash flow statement.

e.   **Consistency** of presentation and classification, including consistent application of accounting policies, should be retained unless a change in presentation is indicated by

1)   A significant change in operations or by a review of the financial statement preparation

2)   An IAS or Interpretation

f.   **Material** items are separately presented, and immaterial amounts are **aggregated** with similar amounts.

g.   **Offsetting** of assets and liabilities ordinarily is not allowed unless required or permitted by an IAS or unless gains, losses, and expenses from similar transactions or events are immaterial.

h.   **Comparative information** ordinarily should be disclosed regarding the previous period for all numerical information in the financial statements.

1)   Comparative, descriptive, or narrative information should also be presented if it is relevant to understanding the current statements.

2)   An amendment of the presentation or classification of financial statement items requires reclassification of comparative amounts unless such reclassification is impracticable.

4.   **Structure and Content**

a.   Financial statements, and components of financial statements, should be **identified** clearly. Furthermore, the following should be prominently displayed:

1)   Identification of the reporting enterprise
2)   Whether the statements are for one enterprise or a group
3)   The balance sheet date or the period covered
4)   The currency used
5)   The precision of the amounts reported

b.   Financial statements are **reported annually** or more frequently. If the balance sheet date changes, however, annual statements may cover a different period.

1)   The reason for the nonannual reporting period and the lack of comparability of comparative amounts should be disclosed.

c.   Reporting should be **timely**. Thus, financial statements should be issued within 6 months of the balance sheet date.

d.   **Balance Sheet**

1)   Whether to present separate classifications on the balance sheet of **current and noncurrent** assets and liabilities should be determined based on the nature of operations. If this distinction is not made, assets and liabilities are presented in order of liquidity. In either case, however, amounts expected to be recovered or settled in more than 12 months should be disclosed.

a)   **Current assets** are expected to be realized, or are held for sale or consumption, in the normal course of the operating cycle. Assets are also current if they are unrestricted cash or cash equivalents or are held for trading purposes or for the short term and are expected to be realized within 12 months.

i)   All other assets are **noncurrent**, including long-term tangible, intangible, operating, and financial assets.

       ii)    The **operating cycle** extends from the acquisition of materials entering into a process to realization in cash or an instrument readily convertible to cash.

- Inventories and trade receivables that enter into the normal operating cycle are current even though they are expected to be realized in more than 12 months.
- Marketable securities are current only if they are expected to be realized within 12 months.

   b)   **Current liabilities** are expected to be settled in the normal course of the operating cycle or are due to be settled within 12 months.

       i)    All other liabilities are **noncurrent**, including long-term financing for working capital that is not due within 12 months.

       ii)    Certain liabilities, such as trade payables and capital accruals for various operating costs, are part of working capital, and are deemed to be current even if they are due to be settled in more than 12 months. Other liabilities, such as the current portion of long-term debt, are not settled as part of the current operating cycle but are classified as current because they are due within 12 months.

2)   Exclusive of requirements by other IASs or of any additional items required for a fair presentation, the **minimum presentation** on the face of the balance sheet includes the following (but no particular order or format is prescribed):

   a)   Property, plant, and equipment
   b)   Intangible assets
   c)   Financial assets [other than d), f), and g)]
   d)   Equity-based investments
   e)   Inventories
   f)   Trade and other receivables
   g)   Cash and cash equivalents
   h)   Trade and other payables
   i)   Income tax liabilities and assets
   j)   Provisions
   k)   Noncurrent interest-bearing liabilities
   l)   Minority interest
   m)   Issued capital and reserves

3)   Additional items should be separately presented based on judgments about the nature, liquidity, and materiality of assets (e.g., separate reporting of goodwill and assets arising from development expenditures); function of the items within the enterprise; and the amounts, nature, and timing of liabilities.

4)   Further disclosures should be made on the face of the balance sheet or in the notes. These subclassifications of line items should be appropriate to the enterprise's operations.

   a)   Related party receivables and payables should be separately disclosed.

   b)   The enterprise should disclose shares authorized, issued, fully paid, or not paid; par value (or that there is none); a reconciliation of shares outstanding at the beginning and end of the period; rights of, and restrictions on, shares; shares held by the enterprise itself or its subsidiaries and associates; shares reserved under option and sales contracts; reserves of equity; dividends proposed or declared; and unrecognized cumulative preference dividends.

e.  **Income Statement**

1)  Exclusive of requirements by other IASs or of any additional items required for a fair presentation, the **minimum presentation** on the face of the income statement includes the following:

    a)  Revenue
    b)  Results of operating activities
    c)  Finance costs
    d)  Share of profits and losses of associates and joint ventures accounted for under the equity method
    e)  Tax expense
    f)  Profit or loss from ordinary activities
    g)  Extraordinary items
    h)  Minority interest
    i)  Net profit or loss

2)  To explain the elements of performance, additional line items and amended descriptions and ordering of items may be needed. The materiality, nature, and functions of income and expenses are relevant to these judgments.

3)  An **analysis of expenses** based on their nature or function preferably should be presented on the face of the income statement. However, it may also be presented in the notes.

    a)  The **nature-of-expense method** aggregates items based on their nature, for example, depreciation, wages, cost of materials, or advertising.

    b)  The **cost-of-sales method** requires allocating costs to functions, that is, cost of sales, distribution, or administration.

    c)  The method chosen depends on which results in the fairest presentation. If the cost-of-sales method is used, additional disclosures about the nature of expenses is required.

4)  Dividends per share, declared or proposed, should be disclosed on the face of the income statement or in the notes.

5)  The determination of **net profit or loss** includes all recognized items of income and expense unless an IAS allows or requires their exclusion.

6)  Net profit or loss includes **profit or loss from ordinary activities** and extraordinary items. Both are disclosed on the face of the income statement.

    a)  **Extraordinary items** result from events or transactions that are clearly different from ordinary activities and are not expected to recur frequently and regularly. Examples are an expropriation of assets or a natural disaster.

    b)  Each extraordinary item is separately disclosed. However, a total may be disclosed on the income statement if the nature and amount of each item are disclosed in the notes.

    c)  The nature and amounts of some items included in profit or loss from ordinary activities are separately disclosed if their size, nature, or incidence make them relevant to explaining enterprise performance. This disclosure is usually in the notes. Examples are writedowns of inventory or plant assets, disposals of plant assets, disposals of long-term investments, restructuring of the enterprise, and litigation settlements.

7) A **discontinuing operation (DO)** is part of an enterprise that is being disposed of in accordance with a single plan. It constitutes a separate major line of business or geographical operating area that is distinct for operational and reporting purposes. Furthermore, a DO is a **restructuring** for which a **provision** may be recognized.

   a) The **initial disclosure event (IDE)** is the earlier of entry into a binding agreement to sell substantially all of the DO's assets or the approval and announcement by the enterprise's governing body of a detailed, formal plan of discontinuance.

   b) The **recognition and measurement** principles in other IASs apply to the reporting of a DO.

   c) Disclosures about a DO should be included in the financial statements beginning with the period of the IDE, including descriptions of the DO, the business or geographical segment in which it is reported, and the IDE; the timing of completion of the DO; the carrying amounts of total assets and liabilities to be disposed of; revenues, expenses, and pre-tax profit or loss from ordinary activities of the DO; income tax expense relating thereto; and net operating, investing, and financing cash flows of the DO.

   d) If an IDE occurs after the reporting period but before the financial statements are authorized to be issued, the disclosures described above should be made.

   e) If an enterprise disposes of assets or settles liabilities of a DO or reaches a binding agreement to do so, it must disclose on the face of the financial statements the pre-tax gain or loss and related income tax expense for any gain or loss recognized on the disposal or settlement.

      i) Net selling prices (minus disposal costs) of net assets subject to binding sales agreements, timing of the cash flows, and the carrying amount of the net assets are also disclosed (in the notes or on the face of the statements).

8) Disclosures are presented separately for each DO and are updated for subsequent changes in cash flows until the DO is substantially completed or abandoned.

9) Disclosures about a DO may be presented in the notes or on the face of the statements except as indicated in 7)e) above. However, a DO should not be presented as an extraordinary item.

10) **Comparative information** in statements prepared after the IDE should be restated to segregate continuing and discontinuing items.

11) An IDE may indicate the need to recognize or reverse an **impairment loss**. Thus, the recoverable amount (higher of the net selling price or value in use) should be estimated for each asset or the asset's cash-generating unit (which may be the DO if it is disposed of in its entirety). Negotiations with potential purchases or conclusion of a binding sale agreement.

f. **Statement of Changes in Equity**

   1) A separate component of the financial statements should present

      a) Net profit or loss.

      b) Items of income, expense, gain, or loss recognized directly in equity and the total of such items.

         i) Combining a) and b) gives total gains and losses from the enterprise's activities.

ii) Examples of such items are revaluation surplus for property, plant, and equipment (under the allowed alternative treatment); gains and losses on available-for-sale financial assets (an optional treatment); and certain foreign currency exchange differences.

c) The cumulative effect of changes in accounting policy and the correction of fundamental errors determined under the benchmark treatments (adjustments of the opening balance of retained earnings).

2) This statement or the notes should present

a) Capital transactions with, and distributions to, owners.

b) Beginning and ending balances of accumulated profit or loss (retained earnings) and the movements during the period.

c) A reconciliation of the beginning and ending balances of each class of equity capital, share premium, and reserve, with separate disclosure of each movement.

g. **Cash Flow Statement**

1) A cash flow statement is presented for each period for which financial statements are presented because users need to assess the enterprise's ability to generate cash and cash equivalents.

a) **Cash equivalents** are short-term, highly liquid investments readily convertible to known amounts of cash. Their risk of changes in value is insignificant. Usually, only investments with short maturities, e.g., 3 months or less, qualify.

2) Cash flows are classified and separately disclosed as from operating, investing, or financing activities.

3) **Operating activities** are the principal revenue-producing activities of the enterprise. They also include any other activities that are not investing or financing activities. Examples are

a) Cash inflows from sales of goods and services, royalties, fees, commissions, refunds of taxes, and contracts held for dealing or trading.

i) Securities and loans held for dealing or trading are similar to inventory. Thus, the related cash flows are deemed to be from operating activities.

b) Cash outflows to suppliers, employees, and governments.

4) **Investing activities** include acquiring, or disposing of, long-term assets and other investments that are not cash equivalents. Examples are

a) Cash inflows from sales and cash outflows from purchases of property, plant, and equipment; intangibles; other long-term assets; equity or debt of other enterprises; and interests in joint ventures.

b) Cash inflows from repayments of advances and loans made to others and from futures, forward, option, and swap contracts.

c) Cash outflows from advances and loans made to others and from futures, forward, option, and swap contracts.

5) **Financing activities** result from changes in equity capital and borrowing. Examples are

    a) Cash inflows from issuing equity instruments and long- or short-term debt.

    b) Cash outflows from purchases and redemptions of the enterprise's own shares and from repayments of debt, including a lessee's payments that reduce the liability arising from a finance lease.

6) **Cash flows from operating activities** are reported using the direct method or the indirect method.

    a) The **direct method** discloses major classes of gross cash flows. It is the preferable (but not required) method because it provides more information than the indirect method. This information may be obtained from the accounting records or by adjusting sales, cost of sales, and other income statement items for

        i) Changes in inventories and in operating receivables and payables.
        ii) Other noncash items.
        iii) Investing or financing cash flows.

    b) The **indirect method** adjusts net profit or loss for noncash transactions, deferrals or accruals of past or future operating cash flows, and income or expense related to investing or financing cash flows. The result is net cash flow from (used by) operating activities.

        i) The adjustments are similar to those for the direct method.

7) Major classes of gross **cash flows from investing and financing activities** are reported separately.

8) Cash flows may be reported on a **net basis** if they are on behalf of customers and reflect customers' activities, for example, demand deposit transactions of a bank or funds held by a brokerage for its clients.

    a) Cash flows also may be reported on a net basis if the turnover of items is quick, amounts are large, and maturities are short, for example, principal amounts for credit card debt, purchases and sales of investments, and other short-term borrowings.

    b) A **financial institution** may report certain cash flows on a net basis:

        i) Acceptances and repayments of deposits with fixed maturities
        ii) Deposit transactions with other institutions
        iii) Advances and loans made to, and repaid by, customers

9) A **transaction in a foreign currency** is recorded using the exchange rate at the date of the cash flow.

    a) **Translation** of a foreign subsidiary's cash flows is also at current rates.

    b) However, **IAS 21**, *The Effects of Changes in Foreign Exchange Rates*, permits use of a weighted-average rate that approximates the actual rate for recording foreign currency transactions and for translation purposes.

        i) The effects of exchange rate fluctuations on cash and cash equivalents is separately reported as a reconciling item after operating, investing, and financing activities.

10) A cash flow from an **extraordinary item** is classified as operating, investing, or financing and disclosed separately.

11) Cash flows from **interest and dividends** should be separately disclosed and consistently classified as operating, investing, or financing.

   a) Total interest paid is disclosed whether it was expensed or capitalized.

   b) A financial institution customarily classifies interest paid or received and dividends received as operating items, but other enterprises have not reached a consensus on their treatment. Interest paid may be on operating or financing cash flow. Interest and dividends received may be operating or investing cash flows.

   c) Dividends paid are operating or financing cash flows.

12) A cash flow associated with **income taxes** is separately disclosed. It is classified as an operating item unless specifically and practicably identified with investing or financing activities.

13) If the equity or cost method is used to account for an investment in an associate or a subsidiary, cash flow reporting is limited to cash flows between the investor and the investee.

   a) If proportionate consolidation is used to report a **joint venture**, a proportionate share of the jointly controlled entity's cash flows are included in the consolidated cash flow statement. If the equity method is used, the cash flows reported are those related to the investment and other transactions between the enterprise and the jointly controlled entity.

14) Aggregate cash flows from **acquisitions and disposals of business units** are separately disclosed and classified as investing items.

15) **Noncash investing and financing transactions** are not reported in the cash flow statement but are disclosed elsewhere in the financial statements in a manner that conveys all relevant information. Examples are acquisition of a business unit by issuing equity instruments, a finance lease, and the conversion of debt to equity.

16) The policy for determining the **components of cash and cash equivalents** should be disclosed.

   a) The amounts in the cash flow statement and the balance sheet should be reconciled.

h. **Notes to the Financial Statements**

1) Notes describe the basis of preparation and the significant policies applied, make disclosures required by IASs, and provide additional information needed for a fair presentation.

   a) Notes are presented systematically, and each statement is cross-referenced to any related information in the notes.

   b) When presented in normal order, the notes include a statement of compliance with IASs followed by a statement of the measurement basis(es) and accounting policies applied, supporting information for financial statement items, and other disclosures (e.g., contingencies, commitments, and other financial disclosures).

i. **Interim Financial Reporting**

1) An **interim period** is shorter than a full year. An **interim financial report** contains either a complete set of financial statements or a set of condensed financial statements.

2) The **minimum content** of an interim financial report includes condensed versions of the balance sheet, income statement, statement of changes in equity, and cash flow statement. It also includes selected notes.

3) If the interim report includes a complete set of statements, they should meet the requirements for annual statements. If condensed statements are published, they should include the headings and subtotals in the annual statements.

   a) Other line items or notes are included if necessary to prevent the interim report from being misleading.

   b) Basic and diluted earnings per share (EPS) are presented on the face of the income statement.

   c) The notes should contain information about use of accounting policies and computational methods, the seasonality of operations, unusual items, changes in estimates, debt and equity transactions, dividends, segment data, material subsequent events, changes in the enterprise's composition, and changes in contingencies.

4) The interim report should contain a comparative balance sheet as of the end of the prior year, a cumulative income statement for the year to date, comparative income statements for the prior-year interim period and year to date, a cumulative statement of equity for the year to date and a comparative statement for the prior year-to-date period, and a cumulative statement of cash flows for the year to date and a comparative statement for the prior year-to-date period.

5) **Materiality** is determined in relation to the interim data.

6) If an estimate in an interim report changes significantly in the final interim period, but no interim report is published for that period, disclosures should be made in the notes to the annual statements.

7) The same **accounting policies** should be applied in interim and annual statements.

   a) Frequency of measurement should not affect annual results, so interim measurements are made on a year-to-date basis. Thus, if an item is recognized and measured in an earlier interim period and the estimate changes in a later interim period, the earlier estimate is adjusted in the later interim report.

8) Revenues received and costs incurred unevenly over the year should not be anticipated or deferred at the end of an interim period unless such treatment is appropriate at year-end.

9) Interim reports ordinarily require a greater use of estimates than annual reports.

5.  Stop and review! You have completed the outline for this subunit. Study multiple-choice questions 25 through 45 beginning on page 149.

## QUESTIONS

### 3.1 Framework for the Preparation and Presentation of Financial Statements

**1.** The measurement basis most often used to report a long-term payable representing a commitment to pay money at a determinable future date is

- A. Historical cost.
- B. Current cost.
- C. Net realizable value.
- D. Present value of future cash flows.

Answer (D) is correct. *(CIA, adapted)*
**REQUIRED:** The measurement basis most often used to report a long-term payable representing a commitment to pay money at a determinable future date.
**DISCUSSION:** The measurement basis most commonly adopted by enterprises in preparing their financial statements is historical cost. However, it is usually combined with other measurement bases (attributes). The attribute used to measure a long-term receivable or payable is the present or discounted value of its future cash flows.
Answer (A) is incorrect because historical cost is used to measure property, plant, and equipment and most inventories. Answer (B) is incorrect because some inventories are measured at current (replacement) cost. Answer (C) is incorrect because short-term receivables and some inventories are reported at net realizable value.

**2.** In December year 1, catalogs were printed for use in a special promotion in January year 2. The catalogs were delivered by the printer on December 13, year 1, with an invoice for 70,000 attached. Payment was made in January year 2. The 70,000 should be reported as a deferred cost at the December 31, year 1 balance sheet date because of the

- A. Matching principle.
- B. Revenue recognition principle.
- C. Reliability principle.
- D. Cost principle.

Answer (A) is correct. *(CIA, adapted)*
**REQUIRED:** The principle dictating that costs be deferred.
**DISCUSSION:** Matching is the simultaneous or combined recognition of revenues and expenses resulting directly and jointly from the same transactions or other events. Expenses should be associated with the revenues that they help to create. Because the catalogs are still on hand at the balance sheet date, they will not contribute to an inflow of economic benefits until the next period. Hence, the cost should be deferred and matched with the revenues of the following period.
Answer (B) is incorrect because the revenue recognition principle determines the period in which revenue is recognized. Answer (C) is incorrect because reliable information is free of error and bias and is representationally faithful. Answer (D) is incorrect because the cost principle states that cost is the usual basis for recording most assets and liabilities.

**3.** Because of inexact estimates of the service life and the residual value of a plant asset, a fully depreciated asset was sold in 2004 at a material gain. This gain most likely should be reported

- A. In the other revenues and gains section of the 2004 income statement.
- B. As part of sales revenue on the 2004 income statement.
- C. In the extraordinary item section of the 2004 income statement.
- D. As an adjustment to prior periods' depreciation on the statement of changes in equity.

Answer (A) is correct. *(CIA, adapted)*
**REQUIRED:** The reporting of a material gain.
**DISCUSSION:** Income includes revenue and gains. Their essential nature is the same, and they are not treated as separate financial statement elements. Revenues occur in the course of ordinary activities. Gains may or may not occur in the course of ordinary activities. For example, gains may occur from the sale of noncurrent assets. Thus, the gain on the sale of a plant asset is not an operating item and should be classified in an income statement with separate operating and nonoperating sections in the other revenues and gains section.
Answer (B) is incorrect because the asset sold was not stock in trade. Answer (C) is incorrect because the transaction does not meet the criteria of an extraordinary item, which results from an event or transaction that is clearly different from ordinary activities and is not expected to recur frequently and regularly. Answer (D) is incorrect because the transaction is not the correction of a fundamental error in the financial statements of a prior period.

**4.** Assume that employees confessed to a 500,000 inventory theft but are not able to make restitution. How should this material fraud be shown in the company's financial statements?

A. Classified as a loss and shown as a separate line item in the income statement.

B. Initially classified as an accounts receivable because the employees are responsible for the goods. Because they cannot pay, the loss would be recognized as a write-off of accounts receivable.

C. Included in cost of goods sold because the goods are not on hand, losses on inventory shrinkage are ordinary, and it would cause the least amount of attention.

D. Recorded directly to retained earnings because it is not an income-producing item.

Answer (A) is correct. *(CIA, adapted)*
**REQUIRED:** The reporting of an inventory theft.
**DISCUSSION:** Expenses include losses. Their essential nature is the same, and they are not treated as separate financial statement elements. Losses may or may not occur in the course of ordinary activities. For example, they may result from nonreciprocal transactions (e.g., theft), reciprocal transactions (e.g., a sale of plant assets), or from holding assets or liabilities. Losses are typically displayed separately.
Answer (B) is incorrect because no restitution will be made. Thus, recording the item as a receivable, then writing it off, is not consistent with the substance of the event. Answer (C) is incorrect because, although some inventory shrinkage is expected in the normal course of processing, fraud is abnormal. Hence, the item should be recorded as a loss. Answer (D) is incorrect because losses are included in the determination of net profit or loss.

**5.** The assets of a liquidating enterprise should be shown on the balance sheet at their

A. Undepreciated historical cost.

B. Fair market value.

C. Realizable value.

D. Current cost.

Answer (C) is correct. *(CIA, adapted)*
**REQUIRED:** The valuation of the assets.
**DISCUSSION:** When liquidation is imminent, and the going concern assumption is no longer valid, the most appropriate valuation method for assets is realizable value, which is the amount of cash currently obtainable by sale in an orderly disposal.
Answer (A) is incorrect because a going concern should report assets at their undepreciated historical cost. When liquidation appears imminent, historical cost is inappropriate for balance sheet reporting. Answer (B) is incorrect because an enterprise facing liquidation is expected to dispose of its assets in a "forced" or "distressed" sale and is unlikely to realize the fair value amount. The net realizable value of the assets is the appropriate amount for reporting purposes. Answer (D) is incorrect because current cost is only appropriate when the going concern assumption is applicable and the effects of changing prices are to be measured and reported in the financial statements.

**6.** An objective of financial reporting is

A. Providing information useful to investors, creditors, donors, and other users for decision making.

B. Assessing the adequacy of internal control.

C. Evaluating management results compared with standards.

D. Providing information on compliance with established procedures.

Answer (A) is correct. *(CIA, adapted)*
**REQUIRED:** The objective of financial reporting.
**DISCUSSION:** The objectives of financial reporting are concerned with the underlying goals and purposes of accounting. They are to provide information that (1) is useful to those making investment and credit decisions, assuming that those individuals have a reasonable understanding of business and economic activities; (2) is helpful to current and potential investors and creditors and other users in assessing the amount, timing, and uncertainty of future cash flows; and (3) discloses economic resources, claims to those resources, and the changes therein.
Answer (B) is incorrect because assessing the adequacy of internal control is a function of internal auditing, not financial reporting. Answer (C) is incorrect because evaluating management results compared with standards is a function of internal auditing, not financial reporting. Answer (D) is incorrect because providing information on compliance with established procedures is a function of internal auditing, not financial reporting.

**7.** An enterprise with total assets of 100,000,000 and net profit of 9,000,000 purchases staplers with an estimated life of 10 years for 1,000. In connection with the purchase, the company debits miscellaneous expense. This scenario is most closely associated with which of the following concepts or principles?

    A. Materiality and going concern.

    B. Relevance and neutrality.

    C. Reliability and comparability.

    D. Materiality and the balance between cost and benefit.

**Answer (D) is correct.** *(CIA, adapted)*
    **REQUIRED:** The concepts or principles most closely associated with the choice of an accounting method.
    **DISCUSSION:** In principle, wasting assets should be capitalized and depreciated. However, the effect on the financial statements of expensing rather than capitalizing and depreciating the staplers is clearly not material given that they cost 1,000 and the enterprise has total assets of 100,000,000. The choice of treatment is not large enough to influence the decisions of financial statement users. The balance between benefit and cost is a pervasive constraint, not a qualitative characteristic. The benefits should exceed the cost of information. Specifically, the cost of producing the information about depreciation expense over 10 years for the staplers probably is higher than the benefits of the information for decision making. Thus, the expedient procedure of expensing the 1,000 should be followed.
    Answer (A) is incorrect because the going-concern principle relates to circumstances in which there is doubt as to the viability of the enterprise. Answer (B) is incorrect because relevance and reliability are two of the principal qualitative characteristics of information in financial statements. Information is relevant if it permits users to predict the outcome of future events or confirm or correct their prior expectations. Reliability provides assurance that the information is reasonably free from error and bias and represents what it purports to represent. Thus, reliable information must be neutral, that is, free from error and bias. Answer (C) is incorrect because comparability is a principal qualitative characteristic. Financial statements must be comparable for the same enterprise over time and also among different enterprises. Information is relevant if it permits users to predict the outcome of future events or confirm or correct their prior expectations.

**8.** In recording transactions, which of the following best describes the relation between expenses and losses?

    A. Losses are extraordinary charges to income, whereas expenses are ordinary charges to income.

    B. Losses are material items, whereas expenses are immaterial items.

    C. Losses are expenses that may or may not arise in the course of ordinary activities.

    D. Expenses can always be prevented, whereas losses can never be prevented.

**Answer (C) is correct.** *(CIA, adapted)*
    **REQUIRED:** The best description of the distinction between expense accounts and loss accounts.
    **DISCUSSION:** Expenses are defined as "decreases in economic benefits during the accounting period in the form of outflows or depletions of assets or incurrences of liabilities that result in decreases in equity, other than those relating to distributions to equity participants." Expenses include losses. Thus, losses are not treated as separate elements. Expenses include items arising in the course of ordinary activities. Losses meet the definition of expenses but may or may not occur in the course of ordinary activities. For example, losses may result from the sale of noncurrent assets or from natural disasters.
    Answer (A) is incorrect because not all losses are extraordinary items. Answer (B) is incorrect because losses may be immaterial, and most expenses are material. Answer (D) is incorrect because some expenses cannot be prevented, or at least not in the short run. Some losses can be prevented.

**9.** To comply with the matching principle, the cost of labor services of an employee who participates in the manufacturing of a product normally should be charged to the income statement in the period in which the

    A. Work is performed.

    B. Employee is paid.

    C. Product is completed.

    D. Product is sold.

**Answer (D) is correct.** *(CIA, adapted)*
    **REQUIRED:** The period when the cost of direct labor should be charged to income.
    **DISCUSSION:** Recognition of expenses occurs concurrently with recognition of increases in liabilities or decreases in assets. Expenses are recognized if the costs are directly associated with the earning of particular income items. This process is often called matching. Matching is simultaneous or combined recognition of the revenues and expenses that result directly and jointly from the same transactions or other events. This direct relationship is exemplified by the sale of a product. This transaction results in revenue (sales revenue) for receipt of cash or a receivable, the recognition of an expense (cost of sales) for the sacrifice of the product to a customer, and a decrease in inventory. The direct labor cost of manufacturing the product is absorbed by the finished goods inventory and is not recognized until sale.

## 3.2 Accrual Accounting

**10.** A service enterprise keeps its accounting records on a cash basis. During the recent year, the enterprise collected 600,000 from customers. The following information is also available:

|  | Beginning of Year | End of Year |
|---|---|---|
| Accounts receivable | 120,000 | 180,000 |
| Unearned revenue | 0 | |

What was the amount of service revenue for the year on an accrual basis?

A. 525,000

B. 555,000

C. 645,000

D. 675,000

Answer (C) is correct. *(CIA, adapted)*
**REQUIRED:** The amount of service revenue for the year on an accrual basis.
**DISCUSSION:** The amount of service revenue for the year on an accrual basis equals 645,000 (600,000 cash collected – 15,000 unearned revenue + 60,000 increase in accounts receivable).
Answer (A) is incorrect because 525,000 deducts rather than adds the 60,000 increase in receivables. Answer (B) is incorrect because 555,000 deducts the increase in receivables and adds the increase in unearned revenue. Answer (D) is incorrect because 675,000 adds the 15,000 increase in unearned revenue.

---

Questions 11 through 13 are based on the following information.

An enterprise is in the equipment rental business. Part of its unadjusted trial balance at December 31, 2004, is as follows:

| | |
|---|---|
| Cash | 17,400 |
| Prepaid insurance | 3,600 |
| Property, plant, and equipment | 180,000 |
| Accumulated depreciation | 32,000 |
| Accounts payable | 12,000 |
| Share capital | 60,000 |
| Retained earnings | 38,000 |
| Rental revenue | 171,000 |
| Salaries and wages expense | 80,000 |
| Utilities expense | 14,000 |

On October 1, 2004, the enterprise paid 18,000 to renew its only insurance policy for a 3-year period beginning on that date. This transaction has not been recorded.

Salaries and wages of 1,700 have been incurred but not paid as of December 31, 2004.

At December 31, 2004, the balance per bank statement was 12,000. Outstanding checks amounted to 6,900. Interest of 40 was credited to the enterprise's account by the bank during December, but has not yet been entered on the books.

---

**11.** What amounts should be reported for prepaid insurance and insurance expense in the annual financial statements prepared at December 31, 2004?

| | Prepaid Insurance | Insurance Expense |
|---|---|---|
| A. | 16,500 | 1,500 |
| B. | 16,500 | 5,100 |
| C. | 18,000 | 3,600 |
| D. | 20,100 | 1,500 |

Answer (B) is correct. *(CIA, adapted)*
**REQUIRED:** The prepaid insurance and insurance expense.
**DISCUSSION:** The insurance policy in effect at the beginning of the year expired and was renewed during the year. Hence, the entire 3,600 beginning balance in the prepaid insurance account should be expensed. The amount of the prepayment on the new policy to be expensed is 1,500 [3 months elapsed × (18,000 ÷ 36-month duration of the policy)]. The debit balance in prepaid insurance at year-end is therefore 16,500 (18,000 – 1,500), and total insurance expense is 5,100 (3,600 + 1,500).
Answer (A) is incorrect because the existing balance in the prepaid insurance account should be expensed. Answer (C) is incorrect because insurance expense should be recognized for the last 3 months of the year. Answer (D) is incorrect because prepaid insurance should be credited and insurance expense debited for 3,600.

**12.** The required adjusting entry at December 31, 2004 related to salaries and wages is

A. Salaries & wages expense    1,700
    Income summary          1,700

B. Salaries & wages payable    1,700
    Salaries & wages expense      1,700

C. Salaries & wages expense    1,700
    Salaries & wages payable      1,700

D. Income summary    1,700
    Salaries & wages payable      1,700

Answer (C) is correct. *(CIA, adapted)*
    **REQUIRED:** The adjusting entry for salaries and wages.
    **DISCUSSION:** An expense incurred but not yet paid is an accrued expense. The adjusting entry to record an accrued expense of 1,700 for unpaid salaries and wages is to debit an expense account and credit a liability account.
    Answer (A) is incorrect because the income summary account is used for closing entries, not adjusting entries. Answer (B) is incorrect because the entry shown is a reversing entry that could be made at the beginning of the subsequent period. Answer (D) is incorrect because the debit should be to an expense account.

**13.** The journal entry required to close the utilities expense account is

A. Utilities expense    14,000
    Income summary        14,000

B. Income summary    14,000
    Utilities expense        14,000

C. Rental revenue    14,000
    Utilities expense        14,000

D. Utilities expense    14,000
    Retained earnings        14,000

Answer (B) is correct. *(CIA, adapted)*
    **REQUIRED:** The journal entry required.
    **DISCUSSION:** All income statement account balances are closed either to a summary account (such as income summary or revenue and expense summary) or to retained earnings. The normal balance of an expense account is a debit; therefore, an expense account is credited in a closing entry.
    Answer (A) is incorrect because an expense account should be credited in a closing entry, and the income summary account should be debited. Answer (C) is incorrect because an expense account should not be closed to a revenue account. Such offsetting is not good practice. Answer (D) is incorrect because an expense account should be credited in a closing entry.

**14.** The correct order of the following steps of the accounting cycle is

A. Posting, closing, adjusting, reversing.

B. Posting, adjusting, closing, reversing.

C. Posting, reversing, adjusting, closing.

D. Adjusting, posting, closing, reversing.

Answer (B) is correct. *(CIA, adapted)*
    **REQUIRED:** The proper sequence of steps in the accounting cycle.
    **DISCUSSION:** The order of the steps in the accounting cycle is identification and measurement of transactions and other events required to be recognized, journalization, posting from the journals to the ledgers, the development of a trial balance, adjustments to produce an adjusted trial balance, statement presentation, closing, taking a postclosing trial balance (optional), and making reversing entries (optional).
    Answer (A) is incorrect because adjusting entries are made prior to closing. Answer (C) is incorrect because reversing entries are made after adjustments and closing entries. Answer (D) is incorrect because posting is done prior to adjusting.

**15.** An enterprise has made all necessary adjusting entries and is now closing its accounts for the period. Dividends of 30,000 were declared and distributed during the year. The entry to close the dividends account would be

A. Retained earnings    30,000
    Dividends        30,000

B. Dividends    30,000
    Retained earnings       30,000

C. Income summary    30,000
    Dividends        30,000

D. Dividends    30,000
    Income summary       30,000

Answer (A) is correct. *(CIA, adapted)*
    **REQUIRED:** The entry to close the dividends account.
    **DISCUSSION:** Assuming an account entitled "dividends" or "dividends declared" is debited when dividends payable is credited on the declaration date, it must be closed at the end of the period. The balance in this account is closed directly to retained earnings. The effect of declaring and paying dividends is to reduce retained earnings, so the entry is a debit to retained earnings and a credit to dividends.
    Answer (B) is incorrect because the closing entry should credit dividends and debit retained earnings. Answer (C) is incorrect because dividends is closed directly to retained earnings. Answer (D) is incorrect because dividends is closed directly to retained earnings by a credit.

**16.** Which of the following statements is the best description of reversing entries?

    A.  The recording of reversing entries is a mandatory step in the accounting cycle.

    B.  Reversing entries are made at the end of the next accounting period, after recording regular transactions of the period.

    C.  Reversing entries are identical to the adjusting entries made in the previous period.

    D.  Reversing entries are the exact opposite of the adjustments made in the previous period.

Answer (D) is correct. *(CIA, adapted)*
**REQUIRED:** The best description of reversing entries.
**DISCUSSION:** Reversing entries are made at the beginning of a period to reverse the effects of adjusting entries made at the end of the preceding period. They are optional entries made for the sake of convenience in recording the transactions of the period. In order for reversing entries to reverse the prior adjustments, they must be the exact opposite of the adjustments made in the previous period.
Answer (A) is incorrect because reversing entries are optional. Answer (B) is incorrect because reversing entries are made at the beginning of the next accounting period. Answer (C) is incorrect because reversing entries are the exact opposite of the adjustments made in the previous period.

## 3.3 Revenue Recognition

**17.** The practice of recording advance payments from customers as a liability is an example of applying the

    A.  Going concern assumption.

    B.  Monetary unit assumption.

    C.  Historical cost principle.

    D.  Revenue recognition principle.

Answer (D) is correct. *(CIA, adapted)*
**REQUIRED:** The assumption or principle justifying recording advance receipts as liabilities.
**DISCUSSION:** Recognition of revenue occurs when the flow of future economic benefits to the enterprise is probable and such benefits are reliably measurable. Recording advance payments as a liability reflects a determination that the receipt of future economic benefits is not sufficiently certain to merit revenue recognition, given that the enterprise has not yet performed its obligations.
Answer (A) is incorrect because the going concern assumption is that the business will have an indefinite life. Answer (B) is incorrect because the monetary unit assumption is that money is the common denominator by which economic activity is conducted and that the monetary unit provides an appropriate basis for accounting measurement and analysis. Answer (C) is incorrect because the historical cost principle reflects the practice that many assets and liabilities are accounted for and reported on the basis of acquisition price.

**18.** An enterprise sells a durable good to a customer on January 1, 2003, and the customer is automatically given a 1-year warranty. The customer also buys an extended warranty package, extending the coverage for an additional 2 years to the end of 2005. At the time of the original sale, the company expects warranty costs to be incurred evenly over the life of the warranty contracts. The customer has only one warranty claim during the 3-year period, and the claim occurs during 2004. The company will recognize income from the sale of the extended warranty

    A.  On January 1, 2003.

    B.  In years 2004 and 2005.

    C.  At the time of the claim in 2004.

    D.  December 31, 2005, when the warranty expires.

Answer (B) is correct. *(CIA, adapted)*
**REQUIRED:** The recognition of revenue from the sale of an extended warranty.
**DISCUSSION:** Because warranty costs are expected to be incurred evenly over the life of the warranty contracts, the income should be recognized on the straight-line basis over the life of the extended warranty contract.
Answer (A) is incorrect because the recognition of income from the sale of the extended warranty is deferred until the extended warranty period begins. Answer (C) is incorrect because the income should be recognized evenly over the life of the contract. It is not related to the timing of the claims. Answer (D) is incorrect because income is recognized over the life of the warranty, not at expiration.

**19.** An enterprise had cash receipts from sales of 175,000 during 2004, of which 30,000 was unearned at the end of 2004. At the end of 2003, the company had 40,000 of unearned revenue, all of which was earned in 2004. The company's sales revenue for 2004 would be

   A.  145,000

   B.  165,000

   C.  175,000

   D.  185,000

Answer (D) is correct. *(CIA, adapted)*
**REQUIRED:** The sales revenue for 2004.
**DISCUSSION:** The sales revenue earned in 2004 equals 2004 cash receipts, minus any receipts in 2004 for which the revenue has not yet been earned, plus the revenue earned from cash receipts in 2003, or 185,000 (175,000 − 30,000 + 40,000).
  Answer (A) is incorrect because 145,000 equals 2004 revenue from 2004 sales. Answer (B) is incorrect because 165,000 adds, rather than subtracts, the 2004 unearned revenue and subtracts, rather than adds, the 2003 receipts for which revenue was earned in 2004. Answer (C) is incorrect because 175,000 equals the cash receipts for 2004.

**20.** ABC operates a catering service that specializes in business luncheons for large corporations. ABC requires customers to place their orders 2 weeks in advance of the scheduled events. ABC bills its customers on the tenth day of the month following the date of service and requires that payment be made within 30 days of the billing date. Conceptually, ABC should recognize revenue from its catering services at the date when a

   A.  Customer places an order.

   B.  Luncheon is served.

   C.  Billing is mailed.

   D.  Customer's payment is received.

Answer (B) is correct. *(CIA, adapted)*
**REQUIRED:** The moment when revenue should be recognized.
**DISCUSSION:** Income, which includes revenue and gains, should not be recognized until an increase in future economic benefits related to an increase in an asset or a decrease in a liability is sufficiently certain and can be measured reliably. The most common time at which these two conditions are met is when the product or merchandise is delivered or services are rendered to customers. Thus, the enterprise has substantially accomplished what it must do to be entitled to future economic benefits when it serves the luncheon. It should then accrue a receivable and revenue.
  Answer (A) is incorrect because the certainty and measurability criteria are not met when the customer places an order. Answer (C) is incorrect because the date for billing is a matter of administrative procedure and convenience. The revenue should be recognized at the date the service was performed. Answer (D) is incorrect because the revenue should be recognized at the point of performance of the service. To wait until the receivable is collected is to ignore the accrual basis of accounting, which is identified in the Framework for the Preparation and Presentation of Financial Statements as an underlying assumption of financial accounting.

**21.** If sales are accounted for using the installment method, which of the following is(are) only recognized in proportion to the cash collected on the sales during the period?

   A.  Sales.

   B.  Sales and cost of sales.

   C.  Sales and cost of sales and selling expenses.

   D.  Sales and cost of sales and administrative expenses.

Answer (B) is correct. *(CIA, adapted)*
**REQUIRED:** The item(s) recognized only in proportion to cash collected under the installment method.
**DISCUSSION:** Under the installment method, the gross profit on sales (sales − cost of sales) is not recognized until cash is collected. The proportion of cash collected on the sales during the accounting period determines the proportion of the gross profit on those sales that is recognized during the period. Hence, both sales and cost of sales are deferred.
  Answer (A) is incorrect because sales and cost of sales are recognized in proportion to cash collections. Answer (C) is incorrect because only the gross profit is deferred on sales for which cash has not yet been collected. Answer (D) is incorrect because only the gross profit is deferred on sales for which cash has not yet been collected.

**22.** Using the cost-recovery method of revenue recognition, profit on an installment sale is recognized

   A.  On the date of the installment sale.

   B.  In proportion to the cash collections.

   C.  After cash collections equal to the cost of goods sold have been received.

   D.  On the date the final cash collection is received.

Answer (C) is correct. *(CIA, adapted)*
**REQUIRED:** The timing of revenue recognition using the cost-recovery method.
**DISCUSSION:** Under the cost-recovery method, no revenue is recognized until cash payments by the buyer exceed the seller's cost of the merchandise sold. This method is appropriate when collection of the revenue is very uncertain.
  Answer (A) is incorrect because the accrual basis recognizes revenue on the date of the installment sale. Answer (B) is incorrect because the installment basis recognizes revenue in proportion to the cash collections. Answer (D) is incorrect because, after the cash collections equal the cost of sales, revenue is to be recognized for any further collections.

**23.** On February 1, year 1 a computer software firm agrees to program a software package. Twelve payments of 10,000 on the first of each month are to be made, with the first payment March 1, year 1. The software is accepted by the client June 1, year 2. How much year 1 revenue should be recognized?

A.  0

B.  100,000

C.  110,000

D.  120,000

Answer (A) is correct.  *(CIA, adapted)*
**REQUIRED:**  The revenue recognized in the year in which payments begin if delivery occurs in the next period.
**DISCUSSION:**  Recognition of an element of financial statements (e.g., income, which includes revenue and gains) requires that two criteria be met.  It must be probable that any future economic benefit associated with the item will flow to or from the enterprise, and the cost or value of the item must be measurable with reliability.  The usual procedures for income recognition, e.g., that income be earned, reflect these criteria.  Thus, income is recognized when an increase in future economic benefits is associated with an increase in an asset or a decrease in a liability.  However, the enterprise has not substantially completed what it must do to be entitled to the benefits represented by the advance payment, and the receipt of future economic benefits is not sufficiently certain to merit income recognition.  Accordingly, a liability should be recognized because the entity has a current obligation arising from a past event that will require an outflow of economic benefits, that is, to deliver the software or to refund the customer's money.  Thus, a liability for 100,000 and revenue of 0 should be recognized for year 1.
NOTE:  This analysis assumes that the sale of the software is a sale either of goods or of services for which the appropriate conditions have not been met.  Under IAS 18, *Revenue Recognition*, revenue is recognized for a sale of goods when the enterprise has transferred the significant risks and rewards of ownership, the enterprise has neither continuing managerial involvement to an extent associated with ownership nor effective control over the goods, the amount can be reliably measured, it is probable that the economic benefits will flow to the enterprise, and transaction costs can be reliably measured.  For a sale of services, revenue is recognized when revenue can be reliably measured, it is probable that the economic benefits will flow to the enterprise, the stage of completion can be reliably measured, and the costs incurred and the costs to complete can be reliably measured.

**24.** A building contractor has a fixed-price contract to construct a large building.  It is estimated that the building will take 2 years to complete.  Progress billings will be sent to the customer at quarterly intervals.  Which of the following describes the preferable point for revenue recognition for this contract if the outcome of the contract can be estimated reliably?

A.  After the contract is signed.

B.  As progress is made toward completion of the contract.

C.  As cash is received.

D.  When the contract is completed.

Answer (B) is correct.  *(CIA, adapted)*
**REQUIRED:**  The moment when revenue should be recognized.
**DISCUSSION:**  Under the percentage-of-completion method, revenues and expenses are recognized based on the stage of completion at the balance sheet date if the outcome of the contract can be estimated reliably.  For a fixed-price contract, the outcome can be estimated reliably if (1) total revenue can be measured reliably, (2) it is probable that the economic benefits of the contract will flow to the enterprise, (3) contract costs to complete and stage of completion can be measured reliably, and (4) contract costs can be clearly identified and measured reliably so that actual and estimated costs can be compared.
Answer (A) is incorrect because revenue is not recognized until progress has been made toward completion.  Answer (C) is incorrect because the cash basis is inappropriate.  An accrual method, that is, the percentage-of-completion method, should be used.  Answer (D) is incorrect because the completed-contract method is not a permissible method.

## 3.4 Financial Statements

**25.** The major distinction between the multiple-step and single-step income statement formats is the separation of

A. Operating and nonoperating data.

B. Income tax expense and administrative expenses.

C. Cost of goods sold expense and administrative expenses.

D. The effect on income taxes of extraordinary items and the effect on income taxes of profit or loss from ordinary activities.

Answer (A) is correct. *(CIA, adapted)*
**REQUIRED:** The major distinction between the multiple-step and single-step income statement formats.
**DISCUSSION:** The IASs do not require a particular income statement format, although, at a minimum, certain line items must be presented, including one for the results of operating activities. The single-step income statement provides one grouping for income items and one for expense items. The "single step" is the one subtraction necessary to arrive at net profit or loss. The multiple-step income statement matches operating income and expenses separately from nonoperating items.
Answer (B) is incorrect because both formats separate income tax expense and administrative expenses. Answer (C) is incorrect because both formats separate cost of goods sold expense and administrative expenses. Answer (D) is incorrect because intraperiod income tax allocation procedures must be applied to both formats.

**26.** At January 1, year 1, a sole proprietorship's assets totaled 210,000, and its liabilities amounted to 120,000. During year 1, owner investments amounted to 72,000, and owner withdrawals totaled 75,000. At December 31, year 1, assets totaled 270,000, and liabilities amounted to 171,000. The amount of net profit for year 1 was

A. 0

B. 6,000

C. 9,000

D. 12,000

Answer (D) is correct. *(CIA, adapted)*
**REQUIRED:** The amount of net profit or loss.
**DISCUSSION:** Net profit or loss may be derived using the basic accounting equation (assets = liabilities + equity). Equity at 1/1/year 1 was 90,000 (210,000 of assets – 120,000 of liabilities). Equity at 12/31/year 1 was 99,000 (270,000 – 171,000). Because owner transactions decreased net assets by 3,000 (72,000 investment – 75,000 withdrawals), net profit must have been 12,000 [99,000 – (90,000 – 3,000)].
Answer (A) is incorrect because the enterprise did have a net profit. Answer (B) is incorrect because 6,000 mistakenly deducts the 72,000 and adds the 75,000. Answer (C) is incorrect because 9,000 is the difference between beginning and ending equity without taking into consideration the capital transactions with, and distributions to, the owner.

**27.** An enterprise has a 50% gross margin, general and administrative expenses of 50, interest expense of 20, and net profit of 10 for the year just ended. If the corporate tax rate is 50%, the level of sales for the year just ended was

A. 90

B. 135

C. 150

D. 180

Answer (D) is correct. *(CIA, adapted)*
**REQUIRED:** The sales for the year.
**DISCUSSION:** Net profit equals sales minus cost of sales, G&A expenses, interest, and tax. Given a 50% tax rate, profit before tax must have been 20 [10 net profit ÷ (1.0 – .5 tax rate)]. Accordingly, profit before interest and tax must have been 40 (20 profit before tax + 20 interest), and the gross margin (sales – cost of sales) must have been 90 (40 profit before interest and tax + 50 G&A expenses). If the gross margin is 50% of sales, sales equals 180 (90 gross margin ÷ .5).
Answer (A) is incorrect because 90 is the gross margin. Answer (B) is incorrect because 135 is 150% of the gross margin. Answer (C) is incorrect because 150 assumes profit before tax equals 50% of net profit.

**28.** Which combination below explains the impact of credit card interest incurred and paid during the period on (1) equity on the balance sheet and (2) the statement of cash flows?

| | (1)<br>Effect on Equity<br>on Balance Sheet | (2)<br>Reflected on<br>Statement of<br>Cash Flows as a(n) |
|---|---|---|
| A. | Decrease | Investing outflow |
| B. | Decrease | Operating or financing outflow |
| C. | No effect | Financing or investing outflow |
| D. | No effect | Operating outflow |

Answer (B) is correct. *(CIA, adapted)*
**REQUIRED:** The effect of interest paid on the balance sheet and cash flow statement.
**DISCUSSION:** Interest incurred is classified as interest expense on the income statement, which in turn reduces equity on the balance sheet by reducing retained earnings. According to IAS 7, cash payments for interest made by an enterprise that is not a financial institution may be classified on the statement of cash flows as an outflow of cash from operating or financing activities.
Answer (A) is incorrect because interest payments are classified as an operating or financing outflow on the statement of cash flows. Answer (C) is incorrect because credit card interest charges reduce equity. Answer (D) is incorrect because credit card interest charges reduce equity.

Questions 29 through 32 are based on the following information. Balance sheets on December 31, year 1 and December 31, year 2 are presented below:

|  | Dec 31, year 1 | Dec. 31, year 2 |
|---|---|---|
| Assets: | | |
| Cash | 50,000 | 60,000 |
| Accounts receivable | 95,000 | 89,000 |
| Allowance for uncollectible accounts | (4,000) | (3,000) |
| Inventory | 120,000 | 140,000 |
| Property, plant, and equipment | 295,000 | 340,000 |
| Accumulated depreciation | (102,000) | (119,000) |
| Total Assets | 454,000 | 507,000 |

| Liabilities and Equity: | | |
|---|---|---|
| Trade accounts payable | 62,000 | 49,000 |
| Interest payable | 8,000 | 11,000 |
| Bonds payable | 200,000 | 200,000 |
| Unamortized bond discount | (15,000) | (10,000) |
| Equity | 199,000 | 257,000 |
| Total Liabilities and Equity | 454,000 | 507,000 |

Additional information for the year 1:

1. Cash payments to suppliers of merchandise were 180,000.
2. Sales revenue was 338,000.
3. 3,000 of accounts receivable was written off.
4. Equipment was acquired for 65,000.
5. Depreciation expense was 30,000.
6. Interest expense was 20,000.

**29.** Cost of goods sold in year 2 was

A. 147,000

B. 160,000

C. 167,000

D. 180,000

Answer (A) is correct.   (CIA, adapted)
REQUIRED: The cost of goods sold.
DISCUSSION: Cost of goods sold equals beginning inventory, plus purchases, minus ending inventory. To determine cost of goods sold, purchases must be calculated. Purchases equal 167,000 (49,000 ending accounts payable + 180,000 payments to suppliers – 62,000 beginning accounts payable). Thus, cost of goods sold equals 147,000 (120,000 beginning inventory + 167,000 purchases – 140,000 ending inventory).
Answer (B) is incorrect because 160,000 results from assuming that 180,000 of cash payments to suppliers equaled purchases. Answer (C) is incorrect because 167,000 equals purchases. Answer (D) is incorrect because 180,000 is the amount of cash payments to suppliers.

**30.** Cash collections from customers in year 2 were

A. 341,000

B. 338,000

C. 344,000

D. 335,000

Answer (A) is correct.   (CIA, adapted)
REQUIRED: The cash collections from customers.
DISCUSSION: Cash collections from customers equals beginning accounts receivable, plus sales revenue, minus accounts written off, minus ending accounts receivable. In year 2, cash collections from customers were 341,000 (95,000 + 338,000 – 3,000 – 89,000).
Answer (B) is incorrect because 338,000 is the sales revenue for the year. Answer (C) is incorrect because 344,000 includes the 3,000 of accounts written off. Answer (D) is incorrect because 335,000 is sales revenue minus accounts written off.

**31.** The carrying amount (cost minus accumulated depreciation) of property, plant, and equipment disposed of in year 2 was

A. 7,000

B. 17,000

C. 20,000

D. 32,000

Answer (A) is correct.   (CIA, adapted)
REQUIRED: The carrying amount of property, plant, and equipment disposed of.
DISCUSSION: The cost of PPE disposed of is 20,000 (295,000 beginning PPE + 65,000 acquisitions – 340,000 ending PPE). The accumulated depreciation is 13,000 (102,000 beginning accumulated depreciation + 30,000 depreciation expense – 119,000 ending accumulated depreciation). Thus, the carrying amount of PPE disposed of is 7,000 (20,000 cost of PPE – 13,000 accumulated depreciation).
Answer (B) is incorrect because 17,000 is the difference between ending and beginning accumulated depreciation. Answer (C) is incorrect because 20,000 is the cost of the PPE disposed. Answer (D) is incorrect because 32,000 results from using the change in the PPE account without acquisitions minus the accumulated depreciation.

**32.** Cash interest payments in year 2 were

    A.  8,000

    B.  12,000

    C.  20,000

    D.  25,000

Answer (B) is correct. *(CIA, adapted)*
    **REQUIRED:** The cash interest payments.
    **DISCUSSION:** The interest payable credited in year 1 was 15,000 (20,000 interest expense – 5,000 amortized bond discount). Thus, the cash interest payment was 12,000 (8,000 beginning interest payable + 15,000 interest payable credited in year 1 – 11,000 ending interest payable).
    Answer (A) is incorrect because 8,000 is the beginning interest payable. Answer (C) is incorrect because 20,000 is the interest expense for year 1. Answer (D) is incorrect because 25,000 is the interest expense plus the amortized discount.

**33.** A reader of a statement of cash flows wishes to analyze the major classes of gross cash receipts and gross cash payments from operating activities. Which methods of reporting cash flows from operating activities will supply that information?

    A.  Both the direct and indirect methods.

    B.  Only the direct method.

    C.  Only the indirect method.

    D.  Neither method.

Answer (B) is correct. *(CIA, adapted)*
    **REQUIRED:** The method of reporting the major classes of gross cash flows from operating activities.
    **DISCUSSION:** The statement of cash flows may report cash flows from operating activities in either an indirect or a direct format. The direct format reports the major classes of operating cash receipts and cash payments as gross amounts. The indirect presentation adjusts net profit or loss to the same amount of net cash from operating activities that would be determined in accordance with the direct method. To arrive at this amount, the indirect method adjusts net profit or loss for the effects of noncash transactions, deferrals or accruals of past or future operating cash flows, and income or expense related to financing or investing activities.
    Answer (A) is incorrect because only the direct method supplies information about major classes of gross cash receipts and payments related to operating activities. Answer (C) is incorrect because the direct method, rather than the indirect method, supplies information about major classes of gross cash receipts and payments related to operating activities. Answer (D) is incorrect because the direct method reports major classes of gross cash receipts and payments from operating activities.

**34.** In the statement of cash flows, the payment of cash dividends appears in the <List A> activities section as a <List B> of cash.

| | List A | List B |
|---|---|---|
| A. | Operating or investing | Source |
| B. | Operating or financing | Use |
| C. | Investing or financing | Use |
| D. | Investing | Source |

Answer (B) is correct. *(CIA, adapted)*
    **REQUIRED:** The treatment of cash dividends in a statement of cash flows.
    **DISCUSSION:** According to IAS 7, dividends paid may be treated as a cash outflow from financing activities because they are a cost of obtaining resources from owners. However, they may also be treated as operating items to help determine the enterprise's ability to pay dividends from operating cash flows.

**35.** The comparative balance sheet for an enterprise that had net profit of 150,000 for the year ended December 31, 2004, and paid 125,000 of dividends during 2004 is as follows:

|  | 12/31/04 | 12/31/03 |
|---|---|---|
| Cash | 150,000 | 180,000 |
| Accounts receivable | 200,000 | 220,000 |
| Total assets | 350,000 | 400,000 |
| Payables | 80,000 | 160,000 |
| Share capital | 130,000 | 125,000 |
| Retained earnings | 140,000 | 115,000 |
| Total | 350,000 | 400,000 |

If dividends paid are treated as a cost of obtaining financial resources, the amount of net cash from operating activities during 2004 was

A. 70,000

B. 90,000

C. 150,000

D. 210,000

Answer (B) is correct.  *(CIA, adapted)*
**REQUIRED:** The amount of net cash from operating activities during 2004.
**DISCUSSION:** Net profit is adjusted to determine the net cash from operations. The payment of cash dividends is regarded as a cash flow from a financing activity. Hence, it is not a reconciling item. However, the decrease in accounts receivable (220,000 – 200,000 = 20,000) during the period represents a cash inflow (collections of pre-2004 receivables) not reflected in 2004 net profit. Moreover, the decrease in payables (160,000 – 80,000 = 80,000) indicates a cash outflow (payment of pre-2004 liabilities) that also is not reflected in 2004 net income. Accordingly, net cash from operations was 90,000 (150,000 + 20,000 – 80,000).
Answer (A) is incorrect because 70,000 fails to add to net profit the reduction in accounts receivable. Answer (C) is incorrect because 150,000 is net profit. Answer (D) is incorrect because 210,000 subtracts the reduction in receivables and adds the reduction in payables.

**36.** In the determination of cost of goods sold, <List A> must be <List B> cash payments for goods along with other adjustments.

|  | List A | List B |
|---|---|---|
| A. | An increase in accounts payable | Added to |
| B. | A decrease in accounts payable | Added to |
| C. | An increase in inventory | Added to |
| D. | A decrease in inventory | Subtracted from |

Answer (A) is correct.  *(CIA, adapted)*
**REQUIRED:** The calculation of cost of goods sold.
**DISCUSSION:** To convert from the cash basis (cash payments) to the accrual basis (cost of goods sold), an increase in accounts payable must be added to cash payments for goods to determine net purchases. Net purchases is then adjusted for the change in inventory to determine cost of goods sold.
Answer (B) is incorrect because a decrease in accounts payable must be subtracted from, not added to, cash payments. Answer (C) is incorrect because an increase in inventory must be subtracted from, not added to, cash payments to calculate cost of goods sold. Answer (D) is incorrect because a decrease in inventory must be added to, not subtracted from, cash payments to calculate cost of goods sold.

**37.** A corporation reported salaries expense of 190,000 for December of the current year. The following data are from its records:

|  | Dec. 31 | Nov. 30 |
|---|---|---|
| Prepaid salaries | 46,000 | 40,000 |
| Salaries payable | 170,000 | 140,000 |

The amount of cash payments for salaries during December of the current year was

A. 154,000

B. 166,000

C. 214,000

D. 226,000

Answer (B) is correct.  *(CIA, adapted)*
**REQUIRED:** The amount of cash payments for salaries during December of the current year.
**DISCUSSION:** An increase in prepaid salaries indicates that salaries expense is less than the cash paid for salaries. An increase in salaries payable indicates that salaries expense is more than the cash paid for salaries. Thus, the amount of cash payments for salaries was 166,000 (190,000 salaries expense + 6,000 increase in prepaid salaries – 30,000 increase in salaries payable).
Answer (A) is incorrect because 154,000 subtracts the 6,000 increase in prepaid salaries instead of adding it. Answer (C) is incorrect because 214,000 subtracts the increase in prepaid salaries instead of adding it and adds the 30,000 increase in salaries payable instead of subtracting it. Answer (D) is incorrect because 226,000 adds the 30,000 increase in salaries payable instead of subtracting it.

**38.** In reconciling net profit on an accrual basis to net cash from operating activities, what adjustment is needed to net profit because of (1) an increase during the period in prepaid expenses and (2) the periodic amortization of premium on bonds payable?

|   | (1)<br>Increase in<br>Prepaid Expenses | (2)<br>Amortization of Premium<br>on Bonds Payable |
|---|---|---|
| A. | Add | Add |
| B. | Add | Deduct |
| C. | Deduct | Add |
| D. | Deduct | Deduct |

Answer (D) is correct. *(CIA, adapted)*
**REQUIRED:** The adjustments to reconcile accrual-basis net profit to net cash from operating activities.
**DISCUSSION:** An increase in prepaid expenses indicates that cash outlays for expenses exceeded the related expense incurred; thus, net profit exceeded net cash from operating activities, and a deduction is needed in the reconciliation. Also, the amortization of premium on bonds payable causes a reduction of interest expense but does not increase cash; therefore, net profit exceeds net cash from operating activities, and a deduction is needed in the reconciliation.
Answer (A) is incorrect because the increase in prepaid expenses requires a deduction from net profit in the reconciliation. Answer (B) is incorrect because the increase in prepaid expenses requires a deduction from net profit in the reconciliation. Answer (C) is incorrect because amortization of premium on bonds payable requires a deduction from net profit in the reconciliation.

**39.** An enterprise has publicly announced a detailed, formal plan to dispose in its entirety of a component of the enterprise that represents a separate major line of business that is distinct operationally and financially. Which of the following is the proper treatment of the disclosures that should be made after the announcement?

A. As part of continuing operations.

B. As a discontinuing operation.

C. As an extraordinary item.

D. As a prior-period item.

Answer (B) is correct. *(CIA, adapted)*
**REQUIRED:** The reporting of the disposal of a component of an enterprise.
**DISCUSSION:** A discontinuing operation (DO) is a separate major line of business or geographical operating area that is distinct for operational and reporting purposes. Furthermore, it is a component that the enterprise is disposing of under a single plan. The initial disclosure event (IDE) is the earlier of entry into a binding agreement to sell substantially all of the DO's assets or the approval and announcement by the enterprise's governing body of a detailed, formal plan of discontinuance. Disclosures about a DO should be included in the financial statements beginning with the period of the IDE.
Answer (A) is incorrect because the component is to be terminated (discontinued). Answer (C) is incorrect because discontinuing operations are not extraordinary items. They are not clearly distinct from ordinary activities. Answer (D) is incorrect because disclosures begin with the period of the IDE.

**40.** Assuming all of the following involve material amounts, which is most likely to be classified as an extraordinary item in the income statement?

A. A loss because of an expropriation of assets by a foreign government.

B. A loss because of adjustments of accruals on long-term contracts.

C. A gain because of the disposal of assets associated with a discontinuing operation of a business.

D. A loss because of a lawsuit that resulted from charges of patent infringement. The company had unsuccessfully defended a similar suit 5 years ago.

Answer (A) is correct. *(CIA, adapted)*
**REQUIRED:** The item most likely to be properly classified as an extraordinary item.
**DISCUSSION:** Net profit or loss includes profit or loss from ordinary activities and extraordinary items. Both are disclosed on the face of the income statement. Extraordinary items result from events or transactions that are clearly different from ordinary activities and are not expected to recur frequently and regularly. Examples are an expropriation of assets or a natural disaster. Each extraordinary item is separately disclosed. However, a total may be disclosed on the income statement if the nature and amount of each item are disclosed in the notes.

**41.** An enterprise changes its method of accounting for depreciation during the current year because it believes that the result will be a more appropriate presentation in the financial statements. In its income statement for the year, how should the enterprise report the adjustment resulting from the change in accounting policy if the alternative treatment allowed by the IASs is used?

A. Not disclosed in the financial statements.

B. Reported as an adjustment to beginning retained earnings.

C. Disclosed as a separate type of depreciation expense, directly following depreciation expense for the current year.

D. Included in the determination of net profit or loss for the current period.

Answer (D) is correct. *(CIA, adapted)*
**REQUIRED:** The treatment of a change in depreciation methods.
**DISCUSSION:** Under IAS 8, *Net Profit or Loss for the Period, Fundamental Errors, and Changes in Accounting Policies*, the benchmark treatment provides that a change in accounting policy should be applied retrospectively unless any resulting adjustment that relates to prior periods is not reasonably determinable. If the adjustment to the opening balance of retained earnings cannot be reasonably determined, the change in accounting policy should be applied prospectively. Given that the benchmark treatment is not indicated, the allowed alternative treatment, that is, a cumulative-effect adjustment included in the determination of current net profit or loss, is permissible unless the amount to be included in current net profit or loss is not reasonably determinable. In that case, the allowed alternative treatment provides for the change in accounting policy to be applied prospectively. In the current period, a change in depreciation methods is reported by a cumulative-effect adjustment under the allowed alternative treatment. Pro forma comparative information also should be presented if practicable.
Answer (A) is incorrect because changes in accounting policies must be disclosed in the financial statements for the period. Answer (B) is incorrect because the benchmark treatment reports an adjustment to beginning retained earnings. Answer (C) is incorrect because the cumulative effect on net profit or loss should be reported.

**42.** Which of the following is a unique reporting problem associated with the determination of the results of operations for an interim period?

A. Advertising and similar costs expensed in one interim period may benefit other interim periods in the same annual period.

B. Cost of goods sold for an interim period reflects only the amount of product cost applicable to sales revenue recognized in the interim period.

C. Depreciation for an interim period represents an estimate.

D. An extraordinary loss occurring in the second quarter must be prorate d over the last three interim periods of the year.

Answer (A) is correct. *(CIA, adapted)*
**REQUIRED:** The unique reporting problem associated with determining interim results of operations.
**DISCUSSION:** Costs and expenses other than product costs should be either charged to income in interim periods as incurred or allocated among interim periods based upon the benefits received. Accordingly, costs such as advertising should be deferred in an interim period if the benefits extend beyond that period; otherwise, they should be expensed as incurred. But such a determination is difficult, and deferral raises the additional issue of how the deferred costs should be allocated among quarters. Thus, many companies expense the costs as incurred even though they may benefit other interim periods in the same annual period.
Answer (B) is incorrect because the only product costs appropriate to expense in an interim period are the ones related to the revenue transactions recognized in the same interim period. Answer (C) is incorrect because the annual depreciation amount is an estimate. The depreciation amount for an interim period is simply a pro rata amount of the annual estimate. Answer (D) is incorrect because an extraordinary item is to be reported in the interim period in which it occurs rather than allocated to multiple interim periods. This approach is consistent with the way extraordinary items are handled on an annual basis.

**43.** An extraordinary gain occurs in the second fiscal quarter. How should the gain be accounted for?

A. Recognized in full in the second quarter.

B. Recognized equally over the second, third, and fourth quarters.

C. Recognized only in the annual financial statements.

D. Recognized equally in each quarter, by restating the first quarter.

Answer (A) is correct. *(CIA, adapted)*
**REQUIRED:** The accounting treatment in interim statements of an extraordinary gain.
**DISCUSSION:** Extraordinary items result from events or transactions that are clearly different from ordinary activities and are not expected to recur frequently and regularly. Examples are an expropriation of assets or a natural disaster. Extraordinary items should be disclosed separately and included in the determination of net profit for the interim period in which they occur. Gains and losses similar to those that would not be deferred at year-end should not be deferred to later interim periods of the same year. Hence, the extraordinary gain should not be prorated.

**44.** A newly acquired plant asset is to be depreciated over its useful life. The rationale for this process is the

A. Economic entity assumption.

B. Monetary unit assumption.

C. Materiality assumption.

D. Going concern assumption.

Answer (D) is correct. *(CIA, adapted)*
**REQUIRED:** The rationale for depreciation.
**DISCUSSION:** A basic feature of financial accounting is that the enterprise is assumed to be a going concern in the absence of evidence to the contrary. The going concern concept is based on the empirical observation that many enterprises have an indefinite life. The reporting entity is assumed to have a life long enough to fulfill its objectives and commitments and therefore to depreciate wasting assets over their useful lives.
Answer (A) is incorrect because the economic entity assumption provides that economic activity can be identified with a particular unit of accountability. Answer (B) is incorrect because the monetary unit assumption provides that all transactions and events can be measured in terms of a common denominator, for instance, the dollar. Answer (C) is incorrect because the materiality assumption simply implies that items of insignificant value may be expensed rather than capitalized and depreciated or amortized. The difference in treatment is not large enough to influence users if the item is not material.

**45.** The following data were extracted from the financial statements of a company for the year ended December 31, 2004.

| | |
|---|---:|
| Net profit | 70,000 |
| Depreciation expense | 14,000 |
| Amortization of intangibles | 1,000 |
| Decrease in accounts receivable | 2,000 |
| Increase in inventories | 9,000 |
| Increase in accounts payable | 4,000 |
| Increase in plant assets | 47,000 |
| Increase in share capital | 31,000 |
| Decrease in short-term notes payable | 55,000 |

There were no disposals of plant assets during the year. Based on the above, a statement of cash flows will report a net increase in cash of

A. 11,000

B. 17,000

C. 54,000

D. 69,000

Answer (A) is correct. *(CIA, adapted)*
**REQUIRED:** The net increase in cash during 2004 as reported on the statement of cash flows.
**DISCUSSION:** Depreciation and amortization are noncash expenses and are added to net profit. A decrease in receivables indicates that cash collections exceed sales on an accrual basis, so it is added to net profit. To account for the difference between cost of goods sold (a deduction from net profit) and cash paid to suppliers, a two-step adjustment of net profit is necessary. The difference between CGS and purchases is the change in inventory. The difference between purchases and the amount paid to suppliers is the change in accounts payable. Accordingly, the conversion of CGS to cash paid to suppliers requires deducting the inventory increase and adding the accounts payable increase. An increase in plant assets indicates an acquisition of plant assets, causing a decrease in cash, so it is deducted. An increase in share capital represents a cash inflow and is added to net profit. A decrease in short-term notes payable is deducted from net profit because it reflects a cash outflow. Thus, cash increased by 11,000 (70,000 net profit + 14,000 + 1,000 + 2,000 – 9,000 + 4,000 – 47,000 + 31,000 – 55,000).
Answer (B) is incorrect because 17,000 results from subtracting the amortization and the decrease in receivables and adding the increase in inventories. Answer (C) is incorrect because 54,000 results from adjusting net profit for the increase in plant assets and the increase in share capital only. Answer (D) is incorrect because 69,000 results from failing to make the adjustments for receivables, inventories, notes payable, and accounts payable.

Use Gleim's *CIA Test Prep* for interactive testing with over 2,000 additional multiple-choice questions!

# STUDY UNIT FOUR
# FINANCIAL ACCOUNTING -- ASSETS, LIABILITIES, AND EQUITY

(31 pages of outline)

Study Unit 4 is the second of three study units devoted to financial accounting. **Assets** are resources controlled by an enterprise as a result of past events and from which future economic benefits are expected to flow to the enterprise. The essence of assets is that, singly or in concert, they can be controlled by the entity so that they contribute to the generation of future net cash inflows. However, many common characteristics of assets are not shared by all assets. Thus, assets need not be acquired at a cost, tangible, legally enforceable, or exchangeable.

**Liabilities** are present obligations arising from past events that are expected to be settled by outflows of resources embodying economic benefits.

The **equity** of an enterprise is the residual interest in the assets of the enterprise that remains after deducting its liabilities. It is affected not only by the enterprise's operations but also by transactions with shareholders, such as capital contributions and dividends.

**NOTE:** In keeping with the way in which the IASs present information, we have omitted all currency symbols. In some situations, this treatment may seem awkward for candidates accustomed to seeing items presented with monetary units indicated. Be prepared for exam questions that may or may not include monetary units.

## 4.1 RECEIVABLES

1. According to **IAS 39**, *Financial Instruments: Recognition and Measurement*, financial assets include receivables originated by the enterprise, that is, created by providing money, goods, or services directly to a debtor. Receivables originated by the enterprise that are of short duration and have no stated interest rate (e.g., trade receivables, also called accounts receivable) are usually measured at the original invoice amount. They are recognized when the risks and rewards of ownership are transferred to the buyer in a sale of goods or when services are performed.

   a. The **net method** records receivables net of the applicable sales discount. If the payment is not received during the discount period, an interest income account, such as sales discounts forfeited, is credited at the end of the discount period or when the payment is received.

   b. The **gross method** accounts for receivables at their face value. If a discount is taken, a sales discount is recorded and classified as an offset to sales in the income statement to yield net sales.

2.    **Bad Debts**

a.    All financial assets are subject to review for impairment at the balance sheet date. If it is probable that all amounts due cannot be collected, the recoverable amount should be estimated, and the impairment or bad debt loss should be included in the periodic net profit or loss.

1)    The loss is measured by the difference between the carrying amount and the present value of future cash flows discounted at the instrument's original effective interest rate, but the cash flows of short-term receivables ordinarily are not discounted. The carrying amount of the asset is reduced directly or by use of an allowance account to the estimated recoverable amount (realizable value).

a)    A reversal up to the amount of the writedown may be recognized in net profit or loss in a subsequent period if it is objectively related to an event after the writedown.

b.    The **allowance method** records the impairment or bad debt loss systematically, usually as a percentage of either sales or the level of accounts receivable on an annual basis.

1)    The credit is to an allowance contra to accounts receivable.

2)    As accounts receivable are written off, they are charged to the allowance. The write-off has no effect on working capital or total assets because the asset and the allowance are reduced by equal amounts.

3)    If the impairment or bad debt loss is a percentage of sales, the impairment is considered a function of sales on account. This approach is income-statement oriented.

4)    If the allowance is adjusted to reflect a percentage of accounts receivable, the impairment is a function of both sales and collections. This approach is balance-sheet oriented.

5)    A common method of estimating the impairment or bad debt loss is an analysis of accounts receivable known as an **aging schedule**. Stratifying the receivables according to the time they have been outstanding permits the use of different percentages for each category. The result should be a more accurate estimate of the recoverable amount than if a single rate is used.

3.    **Other Revenue Recognition Methods Applicable to Receivables**

a.    The **installment method** recognizes profit on a sale when cash is collected rather than when the sale occurs. This method is used only when collection of the sales price is not reasonably assured.

1)    Both revenues and cost of sales are recognized in the period of sale, but the gross profit is deferred to the periods in which cash is collected.

2)    Special deferred gross profit and installment receivable accounts must be established for each year because the gross profit rate usually changes yearly.

b.    The **cost-recovery method** may be used when receivables are collected over an extended period, considerable doubt exists as to collectibility, and a reasonable estimate of the loss cannot be made. Profit is recognized only after collections exceed cost. Subsequent receipts are treated entirely as revenues.

4. **Accounts Receivable – Disposition**

   a. **Pledging**. A pledge (a general assignment) is the use of receivables as collateral (security) for a loan. The borrower agrees to use collections to repay the loan. Upon default, the lender can sell the receivables to recover the loan proceeds.

      1) A pledge is a relatively informal arrangement not reflected in the accounts, but disclosure in the notes should be made. The loan is recorded in the normal way.

   b. **Assignment**. An assignment (a specific assignment) is a more formal borrowing arrangement in which the receivables are used as security. The assignor (borrower) signs a promissory note and financing agreement, and specific receivables serve as collateral. The assignee (lender) reduces its risk by accepting only accounts with a high probability of collection.

      1) Occasionally, the debtors are notified to make payments to the assignee, but most assignments are not on a notification basis.

      2) The loan is at a specified percentage of the face value of the collateral, and interest and service fees are charged to the assignor.

      3) Assigned accounts should be segregated from other accounts (debit accounts receivable assigned, credit accounts receivable), and a liability should be recognized. If the creditor may sell or repledge the collateral, it should recognize an asset and a liability.

   c. An enterprise recognizes a financial asset only when it becomes a party to the contractual provisions of the instrument. An enterprise derecognizes a financial asset (or a portion thereof) when it loses control of the contractual rights the asset represents.

      1) **Control** is lost when the enterprise realizes the rights to the benefits of the contract, the rights expire, or the enterprise surrenders the rights. Moreover, whether loss of control has occurred depends on the positions of both the transferor and the transferee.

      2) Control is not lost, for example, if the entity may reacquire the asset (unless it is readily obtainable in the market or the price is fair value) or when the transferor is entitled and obligated to repurchase or redeem at a price giving the transferee a lender's return.

      3) Control ordinarily is lost when the transferee may obtain the benefits of the asset, for example, if the transferee may freely sell or pledge the full fair value of the asset.

      4) After derecognition, periodic net profit or loss will include the difference between the carrying amount transferred and the proceeds, plus or minus any prior adjustment reflecting the fair value of the asset that had been reported in equity. If a new financial asset is created or a new financial liability is assumed, the calculation is adjusted for the fair value of the asset or liability.

      5) If part of a financial asset is transferred, the carrying amount is allocated based on relative fair values at the date of sale. A gain or loss is recognized based on the proceeds of the part sold.

      6) **Transfers of receivables with recourse**. When the conditions above are met, the transfer of receivables with recourse is accounted for as a sale, with the proceeds of the sale reduced by the fair value of the recourse obligation (a new financial liability).

d.  **Factoring arrangements** discount receivables on a nonrecourse, notification basis. The receivables are sold outright, usually to a transferee (the factor) that assumes the full risk of collection, even in the event of a loss. When the conditions for loss of control are met, a factoring arrangement is accounted for as a sale of financial assets.

1)  The transferor receives money that can be immediately reinvested into new inventories. It can offset the fee charged by the factor by eliminating its bad debts, credit department, and accounts receivable staff.

2)  The factor usually receives a high financing fee plus a fee for performing the collection. Furthermore, the factor can often operate more efficiently than its clients because of the specialized nature of its services.

3)  EXAMPLE: Assume a factor charges a 2% fee plus an interest rate of 18% on all monies advanced to the company. Monthly sales are 100,000, and the factor advances 90% of the receivables submitted after deducting the 2% fee and the interest. Credit terms are net 60 days. What is the cost to the transferor of this arrangement?

| | |
|---|---:|
| Amount of receivables submitted | 100,000 |
| Minus: 10% reserve | (10,000) |
| Minus: 2% factor's fee | (2,000) |
| Amount accruing to the transferor | 88,000 |
| Minus: 18% interest for 60 days (on 88,000) | (2,640) |
| Amount to be received immediately | 85,360 |

The transferor will also receive the 10,000 reserve at the end of the 60-day period if it has not been absorbed by sales returns and allowances. Thus, the total cost to factor the sales for the month is 4,640 (2,000 factor fee + interest of 2,640). Assuming that the factor has approved the customers' credit in advance, the seller will not absorb any bad debts.

a)  The journal entry to record the preceding transaction is

| | | |
|---|---:|---:|
| Cash | 85,360 | |
| Equity in factored receivables | 10,000 | |
| Factor fee expense | 2,000 | |
| Prepaid interest | 2,640 | |
| Accounts receivable | | 100,000 |

5.  **Notes Receivable**. When a note receivable is **discounted** (usually at a bank), the holder is borrowing the maturity amount (principal + interest at maturity) of the note. The bank usually collects the maturity amount from the maker of the note.

a.  Thus, the steps to discount a note receivable are to

1)  Compute the maturity amount.

2)  Compute the interest on the loan from the bank (the bank's interest rate times the maturity value of the note).

3)  Subtract the bank's interest charges from the maturity amount to determine the loan proceeds.

b.  The entries to record the transaction are

| | |
|---|---|
| Cash | (amount received from the bank) |
| Interest expense or revenue | (the difference dr or cr) |
| Notes receivable | (carrying amount) |

    c.    The transaction also may require recognition of a new financial liability. If the maker dishonors the note, the bank will collect from the person or entity that discounted the note.

    d.    When computing yearly interest, the day the note is received, made, etc., is not included, but the last day of the note is counted.

        1)    EXAMPLE: A 30-day note dated January 17 matures on February 16. There are 14 days (31 – 17) left in January, and 16 days must be counted in February for a 30-day note. Accordingly, the maturity date is February 16.

    e.    Notes receivable should be recorded at their present value. Thus, noninterest-bearing notes and notes bearing interest rates other than the market rate should be revalued to their present value.

    f.    EXAMPLE: A 10-year note has a maturity amount of 10,000 and pays 10% annually. Its present value is 5,813 when issued if the current market rate of interest is 20% at issuance. Interest is due at the end of each period, and the principal is due in full at the end of 10 years. The present value of the maturity amount equals 10,000 times the present value factor for an amount of 1 at a rate of 20% for 10 periods. This factor is .162. The present value of the 10 interest payments of 1,000 each (10% × 10,000) equals 1,000 times the present value factor for an ordinary annuity of 1 at a rate of 20% for 10 periods. This factor is 4.192. The sum of these present values equals the present value of the note.

$$10,000 \times 0.162 = 1,620$$
$$1,000 \times 4.193 = 4,193$$
$$\text{Present value} \quad \underline{5,813}$$

        1)    When the note is received, it should be recorded at 5,813.

        2)    The value of the note is not changed for subsequent interest rate changes.

        3)    The discount (10,000 – 5,813) is amortized over the 10-year life by the interest method.

6.    Stop and review! You have completed the outline for this subunit. Study multiple-choice questions 1 through 11 beginning on page 187.

## 4.2 INVENTORY

1.    **IAS 2**, *Inventories*, applies to historical cost inventories other than those for work in progress under a construction contract; financial instruments; agricultural and forest products, minerals, and agriculture produce measured at net realizable value; and biological assets related to agricultural activity.

2.    **Inventories** are assets consisting of items held for sale in the ordinary course of business, work in progress, or materials or supplies to be used in production or in the rendition of services.

    a.    Inventories include goods purchased and held for resale, land or other property held for resale, finished goods and work in progress of a manufacturer, materials and supplies, and costs of services for which the related revenues have not been recognized.

3.    Inventories are measured at the **lower of cost or net realizable value**.

a.    **Cost** encompasses all costs of purchase (after subtraction of such items as trade discounts) and conversion and other costs of bringing inventories to their current location and condition, such as taxes, transport, and handling.

b.    **Conversion costs** include direct costs, e.g., **direct labor**, and systematically allocated fixed and variable production overheads. **Fixed overheads** are indirect costs that are relatively uncorrelated with production volume, e.g., depreciation, maintenance, and administration. **Variable overheads** are indirect costs that are nearly directly correlated with production volume, e.g., indirect materials and labor.

1)    Fixed overheads are allocated based on **normal capacity**, an expected average use of facilities under normal conditions. Unallocated overheads are expensed, and, if production is unusually high, fixed overhead per unit is decreased to avoid measurement above cost. Variable overheads are allocated based on actual use.

2)    If **joint products** or main product and a **by-product** are produced simultaneously, joint conversion costs are allocated on a rational and consistent basis, for example, relative sales values at the time of separate identification or at the time of completion. If a by-product is immaterial, it may be measured at net realizable value and subtracted from the cost of the main product.

c.    **Other costs** of bringing inventories to their current cost and location may include nonproduction overheads or design costs for specially made goods.

1)    Costs expensed as incurred include abnormal waste of materials and labor, storage costs, selling costs, and certain administrative overheads.

d.    Cost for a **service provider** principally includes the costs of personnel who are directly involved in the provision of services and the relevant overheads.

e.    If they approximate cost, **standard costs** may be used. They are based on normal levels of labor, materials, efficiency, and use of capacity. The **retail method** also may be used if the results approximate cost.

f.    **Net realizable value (NRV)** equals estimated selling price in the ordinary course of business minus estimated completion and selling costs. If the cost of inventories is not recoverable, for example, because of increases in completion or selling costs, obsolescence, or decreases in selling prices, they are written down to NRV.

1)    Writedowns are usually on a per-item basis, but sometimes writedowns for groups of similar or related items, such as a product line, may be proper. For a service provider, writedowns may be proper for each service for which costs are accumulated and a separate price is charged.

2)    Materials are not written down if the finished goods will be sold for an amount at least equal to cost. Otherwise, materials may be written down.

3)    NRV is assessed each period. Accordingly, inventory may be written up to the lower of cost or the revised NRV.

4.    Inventory sold is expensed when the related revenue is recognized.

a.    Losses and writedowns to NRV are expensed when they occur.

b.    A reversal of a writedown to NRV because of an increase in NRV reduces the amount of inventories expensed in the period of the reversal.

5. Inventory quantities are usually determined by either physical counts at the end of reporting periods or perpetual records. However, goods not physically on hand may properly be included in inventory. For example, goods out on consignment are effectively part of the inventory.

   a. Moreover, whether goods recently purchased or sold and currently in transit are properly included in inventory may be a function of the shipping terms in the relevant contract.

      1) The term **FOB shipping point** means that title passes to the buyer at the time and place of shipment.

      2) The term **FOB destination** means that title passes when tender of delivery of the goods is made at the destination.

   b. **Periodic Inventory Systems**. In a periodic system, a purchases account is used and the beginning inventory remains unchanged during the accounting period.

      1) Cost of goods sold (calculated at year-end only) equals goods available for sale (beginning inventory + purchases) minus ending inventory.

      2) Ending inventory is determined by a physical count at year-end.

      3) At year-end, the beginning inventory and purchases accounts are closed to cost of goods sold, and the ending inventory account is opened; this becomes the beginning inventory account in the next period.

   c. **Perpetual Inventory Systems**. In a perpetual system, purchases are directly recorded in the inventory account. Cost of goods sold is debited and inventory is credited as the goods are sold.

      1) A manufacturer usually maintains separate materials, work-in-progress, and finished goods accounts. The transfer to finished goods reflects completion of production.

      2) A physical inventory count at least once a year is usually necessary, although some entities use statistical sampling and other procedures to make estimates.

         a) An **inventory over-and-short account** is debited and inventory credited if the physical count is less than the perpetual balance, or vice versa. This inventory correction account is closed to income summary at the end of the period.

      3) A modified perpetual system may be used to record quantities only.

      4) No adjusting or closing entries are needed, except to the over-and-short account.

6. **Cost Formulas**. **Specific identification** should be used to assign the costs of items that are not usually interchangeable and of goods and services segregated for specific projects.

   a. The **benchmark treatment** is to account for the costs of inventories not assigned using specific identification by using the first-in, first-out (FIFO) method or the weighted-average method.

   b. The **allowed alternative treatment** is to account for the costs of inventories not assigned using specific identification by using the last-in, first-out (LIFO) method.

7.   **Descriptions of Inventory Cost Formulas**

a.   The **first-in, first-out (FIFO) method** considers the first goods purchased to be the first goods sold. Accordingly, ending inventory consists of the latest purchases. Cost of goods sold consists of goods purchased at the beginning of the current period and in prior periods.

   1)   The valuation will be the same regardless of whether the inventory is valued at the end of the period (a periodic system) or on a perpetual basis.

b.   The **weighted-average method** divides the total cost of beginning inventory and all purchases by the sum of the number of units in beginning inventory plus those purchased to obtain a weighted-average unit cost.

   1)   The **moving-average method** calculates a weighted average to date that can be used only with perpetual inventory records in which inventory values are also included. After each purchase, a new weighted-average unit cost is computed for the merchandise then on hand.

c.   The **last-in, first-out (LIFO) method** considers the most recent purchases to be sold first. Accordingly, ending inventory is priced at the cost of beginning inventory and the earliest purchases if inventory increases.

   1)   If perpetual records include cost data, the results under LIFO periodic may differ from those under LIFO perpetual depending on when sales were made. Thus, if a sale were made on the first day of the period, it would be made out of beginning inventory under a LIFO perpetual system.

d.   The **retail method** converts ending inventory at retail to cost. The advantage is that a physical inventory can be taken at retail and then converted to cost. The cost ratio used to convert retail to cost depends upon the flow assumption used. If a **weighted-average** flow is assumed, the cost ratio should be goods available at cost over goods available at retail. If a **FIFO** assumption is used, the cost ratio should be cost of purchases over purchases at retail. If a **LIFO** flow assumption is used, the cost of ending inventory depends on the cost of beginning inventory. If ending inventory is less than beginning inventory, the cost ratio should be cost of beginning inventory over beginning inventory at retail. Any increase (stated at retail) should be valued at the ratio of cost of purchases over purchases at retail.

   The **lower-of-cost-or-NRV** concept may be applied to the retail method. In this approach, markups are added to beginning inventory and purchases at retail to obtain goods available at retail. Markdowns are not subtracted. The result is a higher denominator in the cost-retail ratio and a lower ending inventory.

   1)   EXAMPLE:

| | At Cost | At Retail |
|---|---|---|
| Beginning inventory | 90,000 | 130,000 |
| Purchases | 330,000 | 460,000 |
| Markups | | 10,000 |
| Markdowns | | 40,000 |
| Sales | | 480,000 |

   2)   Ending inventory at retail is 80,000 (130,000 + 460,000 + 10,000 – 40,000 – 480,000).

   3)   The cost-retail ratio, assuming a weighted-average flow, is 420 ÷ 560. Markups and markdowns are included in goods available at retail.

   4)   The cost-retail ratio, assuming a FIFO flow, is 330 ÷ 430 if all markups and markdowns are applied to goods purchased this period. Under FIFO, all ending inventory is deemed to be from current-period purchases.

        5) The cost-retail ratio, assuming LIFO flow, is 90 ÷ 130 because ending inventory of 80,000 retail is less than beginning inventory of 130,000. If inventory had increased, the increment would be valued using a cost-retail ratio of 330 ÷ 430.

        6) The cost-retail ratio, assuming a weighted-average flow and a lower-of-cost-or-NRV approach, is 420 ÷ 600 because markups, not markdowns, are included in the calculation of the percentage. This method is typically used if LIFO is not used.

   e. The **gross profit method** computes ending inventory given sales amounts. The gross profit is subtracted from sales to determine cost of sales. The gross profit method is used when the inventory has been destroyed or stolen. It is also often used in the preparation of interim statements.

       1) EXAMPLE: Assume beginning inventory of 10,000, purchases of 20,000, and sales of 50,000, given a 100% markup on cost. Because the cost of goods sold was 25,000 (50% of sales), ending inventory was 5,000 (30,000 goods available − 25,000 CGS). The easy way to work this type of problem is to prepare the cost of goods sold section of an income statement and solve algebraically for those amounts that are not known.

  8. Stop and review! You have completed the outline for this subunit. Study multiple-choice questions 12 through 22 beginning on page 190.

## 4.3 INVESTMENTS

  1. According to **IAS 27**, *Consolidated Financial Statements and Accounting for Investments in Subsidiaries*, a parent is an enterprise that controls at least one other enterprise (a subsidiary). A parent should present consolidated financial statements, which are financial statements of a group reported as one enterprise.

   a. "**Control** is the power to govern the financial and operating policies of an enterprise so as to obtain benefits from its activities."

   b. A wholly, or virtually wholly, owned subsidiary need not present consolidated statements, provided owners of any minority interest consent.

   c. If consolidated statements are issued, they should include all subsidiaries unless

       1) Control of a subsidiary is intended to be temporary because it was acquired exclusively for disposal in the near future.

       2) Severe long-term restrictions significantly impair transfers of funds to the parent.

   d. **Consolidation procedures** include combining like items, eliminating the investment in each subsidiary and the parent's share of each subsidiary's equity, identifying minority interests in net profit and net assets of consolidated subsidiaries, eliminating intragroup balances and transactions and unrealized profits in full, and eliminating unrealized losses on intragroup transactions to the extent cost can be recovered.

   e. An investment in an enterprise is accounted for as prescribed in IAS 39 (described on the next page) when it no longer qualifies as a subsidiary or an associate (as outlined in IAS 28).

   f. **Minority interests** are separately presented in the consolidated balance sheet and income statement. A minority interest is the portion of net operating results and net assets of a subsidiary not directly or indirectly owned by the parent.

   g. Investments in subsidiaries, whether or not consolidated, are reported in the **parent's separate financial statements** at cost, using the equity method, or as available-for-sale financial assets.

2.    According to **IAS 28**, *Accounting for Investments in Associates*, an associate is an enterprise over which the investor exercises significant influence and that is not a subsidiary or a joint venture. **Significant influence** is "the power to participate in the financial and operating policy decisions of the investee, but is not control over those policies."

    a.    In its consolidated financial statements, an enterprise should account for an investment in an associate using the equity method, unless the investment was acquired exclusively to be disposed of in the near future or the associate is subject to severe long-term restrictions that significantly impair its ability to transfer funds to the investor. Significant influence is presumed, barring a clear demonstration otherwise, when the investor holds directly or indirectly **20% or more of the voting power** of the investee.

        1)    However, if the investor issues consolidated statements but also includes the investment in its separate financial statements, the presentation in the separate statements may be based on the cost method or the equity method, or it may reflect the accounting for an available-for-sale financial asset.

        2)    If the investment in an associate is included in the financial statements of an investor that does not issue consolidated statements, it may be accounted for using the cost method or the equity method or as either an available-for-sale or trading financial asset.

    b.    The **equity method** recognizes both distributed and undistributed amounts arising from an investment in an associate. The investment is recorded initially at cost and is subsequently adjusted for the investor's undistributed share of the associate's profits or losses. The income statement also reflects the investor's share of the associate's operating results. Distributions from the associate reduce the investment balance.

        1)    A difference between the cost of the investment in an associate and the investor's share of the fair value of the associate's identifiable net assets is treated as goodwill or negative goodwill. Adjustments to the investor's share of profits or losses are made for depreciation of the associate's depreciable assets based on fair values and for amortization of the difference between the investment's cost and the investor's share of the fair value of the identifiable net assets.

            a)    Unrealized profits and losses from transactions between the investor and the associate are eliminated to the extent of the investor's interest.

    c.    In contrast, the **cost method** recognizes only distributions from the associate's accumulated net profits as income. Distributions exceeding those profits are reductions in the investment balance. However, the applicability of the cost method has been narrowed by the requirement that equity securities with reliably measurable fair values that do not confer significant influence be carried at fair value (see IAS 39).

3.    **IAS 39**, *Financial Instruments: Recognition and Measurement*, applies to most financial instruments and enterprises but not to accounting for subsidiaries, associates, joint ventures, most aspects of leases, employer accounting for employee benefit plans, insurance contracts, equity instruments issued by the reporting enterprise, certain financial guarantees, and various other matters.

    a.    A **financial instrument** is a contract that results in a financial asset of one enterprise and a financial liability or equity instrument of another enterprise. A **financial asset** is cash, a contract right to receive cash or another financial asset, a contract right to exchange financial instruments under potentially favorable conditions, or another enterprise's equity instrument. A **financial liability** is a contractual obligation to deliver cash or another financial asset or to exchange financial instruments under potentially unfavorable conditions. An **equity instrument** is a contract that is evidence of a residual interest in an enterprise's net assets.

b. A **derivative**, for example, a futures, forward, swap, or option contract, is a financial instrument whose value changes with the change in the **underlying** (a specified interest rate, security price, foreign currency exchange rate, price index, commodity price, etc.), that requires **little or no initial net investment** compared with contracts having similar responses to changing market conditions, and that is characterized by **future settlement**.

   1) An **embedded derivative** is one that is combined with a **host contract** so that some cash flows of the instrument vary in the same way as those of a stand-alone derivative.

      a) The embedded derivative and the host contract are accounted for separately if the economic characteristics and risks of the derivative are not closely related to the host contract, a separate instrument with the same terms would qualify as a derivative, and the hybrid instrument is not measured at fair value with changes therein included in net profit or loss. Examples are convertible debt or a put option on an equity instrument.

      b) If the criteria for separate treatment are met but the components cannot be separately measured, the combined instrument is classified as held for trading.

c. The types of financial assets include the following:

   1) **Financial assets or liabilities held for trading** are intended to result in profits from short-term changes in prices or dealer's margins. Regardless of intent, however, a financial asset is held for trading if it is included in a portfolio with a recent pattern of short-term profit taking. Derivatives are also deemed to be held for trading unless they are designated and effective as hedging instruments.

   2) **Held-to-maturity investments** have fixed or determinable payments and a fixed maturity. Moreover, the enterprise must have a positive intent and ability to hold such investments to maturity. However, this classification excludes loans and receivables originated by the enterprise.

   3) **Loans and receivables originated by the enterprise** result from providing money, goods, or services directly to a debtor, excluding those that are held for trading.

   4) **Available-for-sale financial assets** are those that do not fall within one of the other classifications.

d. A financial asset or liability is **initially recognized** only when the enterprise is a party to the contract. Thus, rights and obligations pertaining to derivatives are recognized as assets and liabilities, but a firm commitment to buy or sell goods or services does not result in recognition until at least one party has performed and is entitled or obligated to receive or disburse an asset.

e. **Derecognition of a financial asset** occurs when the enterprise loses control of the contractual rights the asset represents.

f. **Derecognition of a financial liability** is discussed later in this study unit.

g. **Initial measurement** of financial assets and liabilities is at cost, which equals the fair value given for assets and the fair value received for liabilities. Transaction costs are also included in this measurement.

h.   **Subsequent measurement of financial assets** depends on their type.

1)   Available-for-sale and held-for-trading financial assets are measured at fair value unless they do not have quoted market prices in an active market and their fair values cannot be reliably measured.

2)   Loans and receivables originated by the enterprise and not held for trading, held-to-maturity investments, and financial assets otherwise not qualifying for fair value measurement are measured at amortized cost using the effective interest rate method if they have a fixed maturity. If they do not, they are measured at cost.

   a)   However, loans and receivables originated by the enterprise and not held for trading are measured at amortized cost without consideration of whether the enterprise intends to hold them to maturity.

i.   **Reclassifications**.

1)   If investments no longer qualify as held to maturity, they should be remeasured at fair value.

2)   If the fair value of financial assets becomes reliably measurable, they are remeasured at fair value.

3)   If it becomes appropriate to carry financial assets at amortized cost, the fair value on that date becomes the amortized cost. Any previous gain or loss recognized directly in equity is amortized over the remaining useful life of held-to-maturity investments or, if the financial assets do not have a fixed maturity, the full amount is included in net profit or loss when the assets are disposed of.

4)   A financial asset should not be reclassified out of the trading category. It should be reclassified into the trading category only given a recent actual pattern of short-term profit-taking.

j.   **Subsequent measurement of financial liabilities**, except of those held for trading and derivatives, is at amortized cost.

1)   Financial assets and liabilities that are hedged items are subject to special hedge accounting rules.

k.   **Remeasurement to fair value** of financial assets or liabilities that are not part of a hedge results in recognition of a gain or loss in net profit or loss if the items are held for trading.

1)   A gain or loss on an available-for-sale financial asset may be recognized in net profit or loss when it arises or directly in equity through the statement of changes in equity. In the latter case, the accumulated remeasurement gain or loss is included in net profit or loss when the asset is disposed of or is impaired.

l.   An enterprise assesses whether a financial asset is impaired at each balance sheet date. **Impairment** occurs when the carrying amount exceeds the estimated recoverable amount.

1)   For financial assets carried at amortized cost, such as short-term receivables, the procedure is to reduce the carrying amount to the undiscounted estimated recoverable amount.

2)   For financial assets not carried at fair value because it is not reliably measurable, the impairment loss equals the carrying amount minus the recoverable amount (expected future cash flows discounted at the current market rate).

        3)   If a financial asset remeasured at fair value has suffered a holding loss recognized directly in equity, and objective evidence of an impairment exists, the accumulated net loss is recognized in net profit or loss. The amount recognized equals acquisition cost (minus repayment of principal and amortization) minus current fair value of equity instruments or recoverable amount (expected future cash flows discounted at the current market rate) of debt instruments.

            a)   A reversal in a subsequent period may be included in net profit or loss if it is objectively related to an event occurring after recognition of the original loss in net profit or loss.

4.    Stop and review! You have completed the outline for this subunit. Study multiple-choice questions 23 through 26 beginning on page 195.

## 4.4 PROPERTY, PLANT, AND EQUIPMENT

1.    According to **IAS 16**, *Property, Plant, and Equipment*, items of property, plant, and equipment (PPE) that meet the recognition criteria are initially measured at cost. The cost includes the purchase price (minus trade discounts and rebates, plus purchase taxes) and the directly attributable costs of bringing the assets to working condition for their intended use. Directly attributable costs include site preparation, installation, initial delivery and handling, architects' and engineers' fees, costs of removing the assets and restoring the site, etc.

    a.   Administration, general overhead, and pre-production costs are excluded unless directly attributable, and initial operating losses are expensed.

        1)   The costs of self-constructed assets are calculated based on the same principles. Thus, internal profits and abnormal waste of resources are excluded. Furthermore, **borrowing costs** are expensed under the benchmark treatment provided for by **IAS 23**, *Borrowing Costs*, but capitalization of borrowing costs for qualifying assets is permitted if the criteria specified in the allowed alternative treatment are met. Qualifying assets are those that require a substantial time to prepare for their intended use or sale.

            a)   Borrowing costs minus investment income on funds obtained specifically to acquire a qualifying asset may be capitalized. Moreover, if funds obtained by general borrowing are used for a qualifying asset, the capitalized amount will also include the product of a weighted-average of general borrowing rates for the period and the expenditures for the asset. However, the capitalized amount may not exceed the periodic amount incurred.

            b)   Capitalization begins when expenditures for the asset and borrowing costs are being incurred and activities to prepare the asset for its intended use have begun. Capitalization ends upon substantial completion of the asset.

    b.   **Subsequent expenditures** are added to the carrying amount of an item of PPE if it is probable that, as a result, future economic benefits will exceed the originally assessed standard of performance, for example, because of an extended useful life, improved output quality, or reduced operating costs.

        1)   If a major component of an item of PPE has a different useful life from the item to which it relates, it is treated as a separate asset. Its replacement is accounted for as an acquisition of a separate asset, and the existing carrying amount is written off.

       c.   Expenditures to restore or maintain the originally assessed standard of performance are expensed.

       d.   **Government grants related to assets**, including nonmonetary grants at fair value, are those made on condition that the enterprise acquire long-term assets. They are accounted for as deferred income or as a subtraction from the carrying amount of the assets. An alternative allowed treatment is to record the asset and the grant at a nominal amount.

2.   An item of PPE may be obtained for a dissimilar item of PPE or another asset. The transaction is measured at the fair value of the item received, which equals the fair value of the item surrendered adjusted for any cash transferred.

       a.   However, the exchange of similar items (those with similar uses in the same line of business and with similar fair values) is not a culmination of an earning process; thus, the exchange of such assets does not result in gain or loss, and the new asset is recorded at the carrying amount of the asset surrendered.

           1)   Nevertheless, if a loss is indicated on an exchange of similar items of PPE because the fair value of the asset received evidences an impairment of the asset surrendered, the latter is written down and the reduced amount is recorded for the asset received.

           2)   Inclusion of other assets, such as cash, in the exchange suggests that the exchanged items do not have similar value.

3.   According to the benchmark treatment prescribed by the IASs, an item of PPE is carried at cost minus any accumulated depreciation and impairment losses. Under the allowed alternative treatment, an item of PPE may be carried at a **revalued amount** equal to fair value at the revaluation date minus any subsequent accumulated depreciation and impairment losses.

       a.   Fair value is usually market value determined by an appraisal. Absent a market value, depreciated replacement cost is the value used.

       b.   Revaluation is needed whenever fair value and the asset's carrying amount differ materially. Some assets may be revalued as often as annually.

           1)   Accumulated depreciation is restated proportionately or eliminated.

           2)   If an item of PPE is revalued, all of the items in its class (e.g., land, buildings, office equipment, etc.) also should be revalued.

       c.   A revaluation increase is credited directly to equity (revaluation surplus), but a reversal of a previous decrease is recognized as income.

           1)   A revaluation decrease is treated as an expense after any revaluation surplus is reduced to zero.

           2)   The revaluation surplus may be transferred directly to retained earnings upon its realization, for example, after disposal of the asset or through the difference between revalued depreciation and original-cost depreciation.

4.   **Depreciation** systematically allocates the depreciable amount of an item of PPE over its useful life. It is not a process of valuation. The periodic charge for depreciation is offset by a credit to accumulated depreciation, a contra-asset account.

       a.   Depreciation does not provide resources for asset replacement. Except to the extent that it is tax deductible and reduces cash outlays for taxes, it does not affect cash flows.

       b.   Depreciation is not always expensed. For example, under the full-cost method, depreciation on a factory building and machinery used in production of inventory would be charged to overhead, which in turn would be applied to work-in-progress.

    c.    The amount to be depreciated over the asset's useful life equals the cost, or other financial statement amount, minus the residual value estimated at the acquisition date. But if items of PPE are revalued, a new estimate of the residual value is made.

        1)   The consumption of the economic benefits represented by an asset's recorded value follows a pattern that is unique to each asset. The most common factors to which that pattern may be related are the passage of time (months or years), units of production (e.g., units of output by a machine), and amount of service (hours of operation or miles driven).

    d.    **Methods of allocating the depreciable amount**. The method chosen for depreciating an asset should reflect the pattern in which economic benefits are consumed.

        1)   **Straight-line**. Under this method, depreciation is a constant amount (depreciable amount ÷ estimated useful life) for each period.

        2)   **Accelerated methods** are time-based techniques that result in decreasing depreciation charges over the life of the asset.

            a)   **Diminishing-balance (DB)** determines periodic depreciation by multiplying the carrying amount (NOT a depreciable amount equal to cost minus residual value) at the beginning of each period by some percentage (e.g., 200%, 150%, or 125%) of the straight-line rate.

                i)    The carrying amount decreases by the depreciation recognized, and the result is the use of a constant rate against a diminishing balance.

                ii)   Residual value is ignored in determining the carrying amount, but the asset is not depreciated below residual value.

            b)   **Sum-of-the-years'-digits (SYD)** multiplies a constant depreciable base (cost − residual value) by a diminishing fraction. It is a diminishing-rate, diminishing-charge method.

                i)    The SYD fraction's numerator for a given year equals the number of years of remaining useful life.

                ii)   If n is the total useful life of the asset, the formula to compute the denominator is

$$n \frac{(n + 1)}{2}$$

        3)   The **sum-of-the-units** method calculates depreciation as a function of an asset's use or output rather than the time it has been held.

    e.    Periodic review of the **useful life** results in adjustment of current and future depreciation if expectations differ significantly from prior estimates.

    f.    Periodic review of the **depreciation method** results in a change of method if the expected pattern of economic benefits has changed significantly. This change in method is treated as a change in estimate.

5.   **Retirements and Disposals**. When an item of PPE is disposed of or when it is withdrawn from use and has no future economic benefits, it is no longer reported on the balance sheet.

    a.   The gain or loss from retirement or disposal equals estimated net disposal proceeds minus the carrying amount. It should be recognized as income or expense.

    b.   If an item of PPE is retired and held for disposal, it is reported at its carrying amount on the retirement date. It should also be tested for impairment at least every year-end.

6.   Stop and review! You have completed the outline for this subunit. Study multiple-choice questions 27 through 37 beginning on page 196.

## 4.5 INTANGIBLE ASSETS

1.   **IAS 38**, *Intangible Assets*, defines an intangible asset as "an identifiable nonmonetary asset without physical substance held for use in the production or supply of goods or services, for rental to others, or for administrative purposes." It must also meet the definition of an asset: control over a resource from which future economic benefits will flow. However, IAS 38 does not apply to financial assets; mineral rights and expenditures for exploration or development of oil and gas, other minerals, etc.; insurance contracts; deferred tax assets; acquired goodwill; and certain leases. Examples of intangible assets to which IAS 38 applies include

    a.   Intangibles arising from development (but not research) if certain criteria are met

    b.   Licenses

    c.   Patents

    d.   Computer software not integral to the related hardware (but an operating system is an item of PPE)

    e.   Copyrights

    f.   Franchises

    g.   Trademarks and trade names

    h.   Water rights

    i.   Customer lists obtained from others

    j.   Mortgage servicing rights

2.   An intangible asset is measured initially at **cost**, including the purchase price (including purchase taxes and import duties) and any directly attributable expenditures to prepare the asset for its intended use, such as legal fees.

    a.   If an intangible asset is obtained in a **business combination accounted for as an acquisition**, its cost is its fair value at the date of acquisition.

        1)   The intangible asset need not have been recognized on the books of the acquiree.

        2)   The asset is included in goodwill if its fair value is not reliably measurable.

            a)   Unless an active market exists for the intangible asset, the amount recognized must not increase negative goodwill.

    b.   **Exchanges** of intangible assets are accounted for in the same manner as exchanges of items of PPE.

    c.   An intangible asset acquired through a **government grant**, e.g., airport landing rights or a broadcast license, also may be accounted for in the same manner as a grant of an item of PPE.

3.   **Internally generated goodwill** is not an asset.  However, internally generated intangible assets may be recognized in certain cases.

   a.   **Research** is "original and planned investigation undertaken with the prospect of gaining new scientific or technical knowledge and understanding."  Expenditures on research are expensed when incurred.

   b.   **Development** is "the application of research findings or other knowledge to a plan or design for the production of new or substantially improved materials, devices, products, processes, systems, or services prior to the commencement of commercial production or use."  Development results in recognition of an intangible asset if the enterprise can demonstrate the technical feasibility of completion of the asset, the intent to complete, the ability to use or sell the asset, how it will generate probable future economic benefits, the availability of resources to complete and use or sell the asset, and the ability to measure reliably expenditures attributable to the asset.

   c.   Intangible assets are not recognized for internally generated brands, mastheads, publishing titles, customer lists, and similar items.

4.   Expenditures for an intangible item are expensed unless the foregoing recognition criteria are met or the item is obtained in a business combination accounted for as an acquisition and cannot be recognized as an intangible asset.

   a.   In the latter circumstance, the expenditures (part of the acquisition cost) are included in the amount attributable to goodwill or negative goodwill.

   b.   Items expensed as incurred include expenditures for research and for

      1)   Startup activities (unless included in an item of PPE)
      2)   Training
      3)   Advertising and promotion
      4)   Relocating or reorganizing part or all of an enterprise

5.   Once expenditures for an intangible item have been expensed, they may not subsequently be capitalized.

6.   **Subsequent expenditures** for an intangible asset are expensed when incurred unless it is probable that, as a result, future economic benefits generated by the asset will exceed the originally assessed standard of performance.  The expenditures must also be reliably measurable and attributable to the asset.

7.   According to the benchmark treatment, an intangible asset is carried at cost minus any accumulated amortization and impairment losses.

   a.   The allowed alternative treatment of intangible assets (revaluation) is similar to that for items of PPE.  However, fair value should be determined based on an active market.

8.   **Amortization** of an intangible asset begins when it is available for use.  Its depreciable amount (cost – residual value) is systematically allocated as expense over the best estimate of its **useful life**, which is rebuttably presumed to be no more than 20 years from when it is available for use.

   a.   If an intangible asset represents legal rights effective only for a finite period, the useful life cannot exceed the legal life unless the rights are renewable and renewal is virtually certain.

9.   The **amortization period** for an intangible asset should reflect the pattern of consumption of the economic benefits.  But if a reliable determination cannot be made, the straight-line method is used.

10.  The **residual value** is presumed to be zero barring a third-party commitment to purchase or the existence of an active market for the asset that will probably exist at the end of the useful life.

11. The amortization period and method should be reviewed at least at each balance sheet date. Any changes should be treated as changes in estimate.

12. The treatment of retirements and disposal of intangible assets is similar to that for items of PPE.

13. **Goodwill arising from a business combination accounted for as an acquisition**. Under **IAS 22**, *Business Combinations*, goodwill is recognized as an asset equal to the excess of the cost over the acquirer's interest in the fair value of the identifiable assets and liabilities acquired.

    a.  The carrying amount equals cost minus any accumulated amortization and impairment losses.

    b.  Amortization is expensed on a systematic basis over the useful life, rebuttably presumed to be no more than 20 years. Straight-line amortization is recognized except in the rare situations when another method is more appropriate.

    c.  The amortization period and method should be reviewed at least annually. Any change is a change in accounting estimate. An annual determination of the recoverable amount of goodwill amortized over a period greater than 20 years is also required even if no evidence of its impairment exists.

    d.  **Negative goodwill** is presented as a deduction from assets. It is the excess of the acquirer's interest in the fair value of the identifiable assets and liabilities acquired over the cost.

        1)  To the extent negative goodwill relates to expected future losses and expenses that are reliably measurable but were not identifiable liabilities at the acquisition date, it should be recognized as income when those losses and expenses are recognized. Otherwise, negative goodwill

            a)  Not in excess of the fair value of the identifiable nonmonetary assets acquired is systematically recognized as income over the weighted-average useful life of the identifiable acquired depreciable or amortizable assets.

            b)  In excess of such fair value is recognized immediately as income.

14. Stop and review! You have completed the outline for this subunit. Study multiple-choice questions 38 through 42 beginning on page 200.

## 4.6 AGRICULTURE

1.  **IAS 41**, *Agriculture*, prescribes the accounting treatment of **biological assets** (living plants and animals) and **agricultural produce** (the harvested product of biological assets) at the point of harvest.

2.  **Initial recognition** of biological assets and agricultural produce is appropriate when

    a.  Past events result in the enterprise's having control of the assets,
    b.  Future economic benefits are probable, and
    c.  The asset's fair value or cost is reliably measurable.

3.  **Measurement** of biological assets upon initial recognition (but see 5. on the next page) and agricultural produce from the enterprise's biological assets at the point of harvest is at fair value minus estimated point-of-sale costs (e.g., commissions, transfer taxes, or levies by a commodities exchange but not transport costs).

    a.  Biological assets are also remeasured at subsequent balance sheet dates at fair value minus estimated point-of-sale costs.

4.  **Recognition of gains and losses** on biological assets may result from initial recognition at, or from a change in, fair value minus estimated point-of-sale costs.  These gains and losses should be included in the determination of net profit or loss when they occur.

    a.   A gain or loss resulting from the initial recognition of agricultural produce is included in the determination of net profit or loss when it occurs.

5.  The presumption that the fair value of a biological asset is reliably measurable is rebuttable but only upon initial recognition.  If market prices are unavailable and other measures of fair value are clearly unreliable, measurement is at cost minus accumulated depreciation and impairment losses.  If the fair value becomes reliably measurable, a biological asset should then be measured at fair value minus estimated point-of-sale costs.

6.  A **government grant** may be related to a biological asset measured at fair value minus estimated point-of-sale costs.  If the grant is unconditional, it is recognized as income when it is receivable.  If it is conditional, income is recognized when the conditions are satisfied.

7.  Stop and review!  You have completed the outline for this subunit.  Study multiple-choice questions 43 and 44 on page 202.

## 4.7 FINANCIAL AND OTHER LIABILITIES

1.  **IAS 32**, *Financial Instruments:  Disclosure and Presentation*, defines a **financial liability** as a contractual obligation "to deliver cash or another financial asset to another enterprise or to exchange financial instruments with another enterprise under conditions that are potentially unfavorable."

    a.   Liabilities, for example, deferred revenue and liabilities under operating leases, commodity futures contracts, and most warranties, that are to be settled by transferring nonfinancial assets or rendering services are not financial liabilities.

    b.   Noncontractual liabilities, such as income taxes payable, are not financial liabilities.

    c.   A contingent obligation may satisfy the definition of a financial liability.  For example, a financial guarantee is a contract arising from a past transaction or event and is therefore classified as a financial liability even though the requirement to perform is contingent upon the debtor's future default.

    d.   An enterprise's obligation to issue its own equity instruments, e.g., a share option or warrant, is not a financial liability because cash or another financial asset is not to be delivered.

    e.   **Liability v. Equity**.  Whether a financial instrument, or its components, is a liability or an equity item depends on its substance, not its legal form, at the time of initial recognition.

        1)   For example, if the issuer must redeem preferred shares, or if the holder has a right to redemption, and the amount and date of redemption are fixed or determinable, the shares are liabilities.  Moreover, such a contractual obligation may be established indirectly, as when an optional redemption is rendered highly likely by the circumstances.

        2)   **Compound Instruments**.  If a financial instrument has both equity and liability components, they are presented separately in the issuer's balance sheet.  An example is a bond convertible to common shares of the issuer.  This instrument is equivalent to the separate issuance of debt with an early settlement clause and common share warrants or to the issuance of debt with detachable warrants.

3)   **Interest, dividends, losses, and gains** related to a financial liability are reported as income or expense, but distributions on an equity instrument are debited to equity. Accordingly, dividends on shares classified as liabilities are items of expense, and gains and losses on their redemption or refinancing are also included in the income statement. The effects of redemption or refinancing of an equity instrument, however, are included directly in equity.

f.   Typical financial liabilities include trade accounts payable, notes payable, loans payable, and bonds payable.

g.   An enterprise initially recognizes a financial liability only when it becomes a party to the contract. Initial measurement is at cost (fair value received, adjusted for transaction costs). The fair value is normally determined by reference to the transaction price or other market values. However, if these amounts are not readily determinable, a financial liability is measured at present value using an appropriately imputed interest rate. Subsequent measurement is at amortized cost, so their imputed interest rate is not changed.

2.   A **current liability** is an obligation that is expected to be settled within the normal operating cycle or is due to be settled within 12 months of the balance sheet date. Any other liability is noncurrent.

a.   Some current liabilities are included in the working capital employed in the normal operating cycle, e.g., trade payables and accrued employee operating costs.

b.   Current liabilities not settled within the normal operating cycle include the current part of interest-bearing debt, dividends, income taxes, and bank overdrafts.

c.   **Refinancing.** Some noncurrent, interest-bearing liabilities due to be settled within 12 months should nevertheless continue to be classified as noncurrent if the original term exceeded 12 months, the enterprise intends to refinance on a long-term basis, and its intent is supported by an agreement to refinance or reschedule payments. This agreement must be consummated before the financial statements are authorized for issue.

d.   **Obligations Callable because of Breach.** A debtor may breach a covenant in a long-term borrowing agreement regarding its financial position, for example, the maintenance of certain financial ratios. In this situation, the agreement may stipulate that the debt becomes payable on demand after breach. Accordingly, the liability should be reclassified as current unless

1)   The lender has agreed, prior to the authorization of the financial statements for issue, not to demand payment, and

2)   Additional breaches are not probable within 12 months of the balance sheet date.

3.   The most common financial liabilities are **accounts payable** or trade payables, which are obligations to sellers that are incurred when an enterprise purchases inventory, supplies, or services on credit. These liabilities arise when the goods or services have been received or supplied and have been invoiced or formally agreed with the supplier.

a.   Short-term liabilities, such as accounts payable, are usually not interest bearing (unless the accounts are not settled when due) and are usually not secured by collateral.

    b.   The **gross method** records purchases and accounts payable without regard to purchase discounts available, for example, cash discounts for early payment.

       1)   Purchases and accounts payable may be accounted for using the gross method or the net method.

          a)   In a periodic system, purchase discounts taken are credited to a contra purchases account and closed to cost of goods sold. In a perpetual system, they are credited to inventory.

       2)   The **net method** records purchases and accounts payable at the cash (discounted) price. The advantage of the net method is that it isolates purchase discounts lost, which are treated as financing charges.

    c.   The timing of recognition of accounts payable may depend on the **shipping terms**, that is, whether title and risk of loss pass at the point of shipment or at the ultimate destination.

4.  **Accrued Expenses**. Ordinarily, accrued expenses are liabilities for goods or services received or supplied, but not paid, invoiced, or formally agreed with the supplier, that otherwise meet the recognition criteria in the current period. They are accounted for using basic accrual entries.

    a.   **Reversing entries** may be used to facilitate accounting for accrued expenses in the next period. For example, if wages payable are accrued at year-end (the adjusting entry is to debit wages expense and credit wages payable), the reversing entry at the beginning of the next period is to debit the liability and credit wages expense. If the reversing entry is made, no allocation between the liability and wages expense is needed when wages are paid in the subsequent period (the entry will simply be to debit wages expense and to credit cash).

       1)   If accrual entries are reversed, all expenses paid in the next period can be charged to expense.

       2)   If reversing entries are not made, either of the following methods is used in the next period:

          a)   The liability is debited when the accrued expense is actually paid. For example, the first wages payment of the year will be accounted for by debiting wages expense and wages payable and crediting cash. Thus, this entry will differ from subsequent entries recording the payment of wages.

          b)   Payments are recorded by debiting expense for the full amounts paid. At year-end, the liability is adjusted to the balance owed at that date. For example, if the liability for accrued wages has decreased, the adjusting entry will be to debit wages payable and credit wages expense.

    b.   If an entity fails to accrue expenses at year-end, income is overstated in that period and understated in the next period (when they are paid and presumably expensed).

       1)   Moreover, expenses incurred but unpaid and not recorded result in understated accrued liabilities and possibly understated assets (for example, if the amounts should be inventoried). In addition, working capital (current assets – current liabilities) will be overstated, but cash flows will not be affected.

5.   **Taxes Payable**. Accounting for deferred income taxes is explained in Study Unit 5. Employment-related taxes such as unemployment tax and withholding tax are expenses incurred as employees earn wages, but they are paid only periodically. Accordingly, liabilities should also be accrued for these expenses as well as for wages earned but not paid.

   a.   Property taxes are usually accrued over the tax authority's fiscal period.

   b.   Purchase taxes may be levied on certain goods and services. Ordinarily, the tax is paid by the customer but is collected and remitted by the seller periodically.

6.   **Short-term employee benefits** expected to be paid as a result of service rendered during the period ordinarily should be recognized as an expense and a liability (accrued expense).

   a.   For **short-term compensated absences**, the timing of recognition depends on whether the benefits **accumulate**. If they accumulate, the expected cost is recognized when services are rendered that increase the employees' entitlement to future compensated absences.

   b.   The obligation is recognized whether it is vesting (the employee is entitled to a cash payment for an unused entitlement upon leaving the enterprise) or not vesting, and the amount should not be discounted. It equals the additional amount expected to be paid as a result of the unused accumulated entitlement at the balance sheet date.

7.   **Deferred Revenues**. If the recognition criteria are not met, advance receipts are treated as liabilities (deferred revenues). Recognition is deferred until the obligation is partly or wholly satisfied, that is, when the increase in future economic benefits becomes reliably measurable.

   a.   Cash received in advance may initially be credited to a deferred revenue (liability) account. At the end of the accounting period, revenue is recognized by a debit to deferred revenue and a credit to revenue. However, a reversing entry is not appropriate if advance receipts are initially credited to a deferred revenue (a permanent or real account).

8.   **Derecognition of a financial liability** (or a part) occurs only by **extinguishment**. This condition is satisfied only when the debtor pays the creditor or is legally released from primary responsibility either by the creditor or through the legal process.

   a.   An extinguishment and derecognition of the old debt and recognition of new debt occurs when the borrower and lender exchange debt instruments with substantially different terms, that is, when the respective discounted cash flows differ by at least 10%.

      1)   A substantial modification of terms is also an extinguishment.

   b.   The difference between the carrying amount (including unamortized costs) of a liability (or part thereof) that has been extinguished or transferred and the amount paid is included in net profit or loss.

   c.   The treatment of derecognition of part of a financial liability is the same as that for a financial asset.

9.   Stop and review! You have completed the outline for this subunit. Study multiple-choice questions 45 through 53 beginning on page 202.

## 4.8 PROVISIONS AND CONTINGENCIES

1.  **Provisions** are defined in **IAS 37**, *Provisions, Contingent Liabilities, and Contingent Assets*, as liabilities of uncertain timing or amount that are not covered by another IAS and that do not result from financial instruments carried at fair value, from executory contracts (unless onerous), or from insurance contracts with policyholders. Examples of provisions are liabilities for violations of environmental law, nuclear plant decommissioning costs, warranties, and restructurings.

    a.  Provisions differ from trade payables and accruals because of their greater uncertainty. They differ from contingent liabilities because they are present obligations that meet the recognition criteria, whereas contingencies are possible obligations or do not meet the recognition criteria.

    b.  **Recognition** of provisions is appropriate when the enterprise has a legal or constructive present obligation resulting from a past event (called an obligating event), it is probable that an outflow of economic benefits will be necessary to settle the obligation, and its amount can be reliably estimated.

        1)  A **past event** leads to a **present obligation** if the enterprise has no realistic alternative to settlement.

        2)  For purposes of IAS 37, **probable** means "more likely than not." Moreover, a past event is deemed to result in a present obligation if, given all the available evidence, it is more likely than not that a present obligation exists.

        3)  A **legal obligation** is based on a contract, legislation, or other operation of law.

        4)  A **constructive obligation** results when the enterprise has indicated to other parties, e.g., by an established pattern of practice or by published policies, that it accepts certain responsibilities and has thereby created a valid expectation of fulfilling them.

2.  A **contingent liability** is a possible obligation arising from past events and the existence of which will be confirmed only by uncertain future events not wholly within the enterprise's control. A liability is also contingent if it does not meet the recognition criteria.

    a.  For example, if the enterprise and other parties are jointly and severally liable on an obligation, the amount expected to be paid by the other parties is a contingent liability.

    b.  A contingent liability is not recognized. However, it should be disclosed unless the possibility of resource outflows is **remote**. **Disclosures** include estimated financial effects, any uncertainties related to timing or amount, and the possibility of reimbursement.

3.  A **contingent asset** is a possible asset arising from past events and the existence of which will be confirmed only by uncertain future events not wholly within the enterprise's control. An example is a potential recovery on a legal claim with an uncertain outcome.

    a.  A contingent asset is not recognized but should be disclosed if an inflow of economic benefits is probable. Disclosures include a description of the contingent asset and an estimate of its financial effects.

4.  **Measurement**. A provision is measured in accordance with the **best estimate** of the amount needed to settle the obligation. The best estimate is the pre-tax amount "that an enterprise would rationally pay to settle the obligation at the balance sheet date or to transfer it to a third party at that date."

    a.  If the population of items being measured is large, an **expected value** computation is appropriate. However, even if a single obligation is being estimated, a range of outcomes, not just the single most likely outcome, is considered.

    b.   **Risks and uncertainties** are considered in calculating the best estimate, but they should not result in deliberate overstatement.

    c.   The measurement should be at the **present value** of the outflows needed to settle the obligation if the effects of discounting are material.

    d.   The settlement amount may include the effects of **future events** if sufficient objective evidence of their occurrence is available.

    e.   **Gains on disposal** of assets are not anticipated in measuring the provision.

5.   **An expected reimbursement** of an amount required to settle a provision is recognized only if receipt of the reimbursement is **virtually certain**. In this case, the expected reimbursement is recognized as a separate asset.

    a.   The debit to expense for a provision is net of a recognized reimbursement.

    b.   Reimbursements may result from, for example, insurance, indemnity clauses in contracts, or suppliers' warranties.

6.   A provision is adjusted at the balance sheet date to the current best estimate. If the recognition criteria are no longer met, the provision is reversed.

    a.   If a present value measurement has been made, the periodic increase resulting from the reduction in the discount period is treated as a borrowing cost.

7.   **Future operating losses** are not an appropriate basis for a provision.

8.   An **onerous contract** is one for which the unavoidable costs of performance exceed the expected benefits. The unavoidable costs equal the least net cost of terminating the contract.

    a.   The present obligation of an onerous contract is treated as a provision.

    b.   An example of an onerous contract is a noncancelable lease of a factory building that cannot be sublet after the enterprise has moved its operations to a new site.

9.   A **restructuring** is a program planned and controlled by management that materially changes the scope of a business or the way it is conducted, for example, selling a line of business, relocating activities from one region or country to another, eliminating management layers, or fundamentally reorganizing the enterprise. A provision for restructuring is recognized when the recognition criteria are satisfied.

    a.   If the following conditions are met, a constructive obligation to restructure is created:

        1)   The enterprise has a detailed formal plan.

        2)   A valid expectation has been raised in those affected because the enterprise has begun implementation of the plan or has announced its main features.

    b.   However, no obligation is created relative to the sale of an operation unless a binding sale agreement has been reached.

    c.   The restructuring provision includes only the **direct expenditures** of restructuring, that is, those necessary to the restructuring and not associated with ongoing activities.

        1)   The provision excludes such costs as marketing, retraining employees, relocating employees, and new systems. It also excludes identifiable future operating losses up to the date of the restructuring and any gains on an expected disposal of assets.

10.   Stop and review! You have completed the outline for this subunit. Study multiple-choice questions 54 through 59 beginning on page 206.

## 4.9 BONDS

1. Bonds are debt instruments within the scope of **IAS 39**, *Financial Instruments: Recognition and Measurement*. When bonds are issued on an interest payment date, the entry is to debit cash and credit bonds payable. Any difference is debited to a discount or credited to a premium. If **bonds** are issued at a discount or a premium, the **effective interest method** of amortization should be used (unless the results of another method are not materially different). Under this method, interest expense changes every period, but the interest rate is constant.

   a. Bonds are sold at the sum of the present values of the maturity amount and the interest payments (if interest-bearing). The difference between the nominal amount and the selling price of bonds is either a discount or a premium.

      1) Bonds are sold at a **discount** when they sell for less than the nominal amount, that is, when the contract (stated) interest rate is less than the market (effective) interest rate.

      2) Bonds are sold at a **premium** (in excess of the nominal amount) when the stated rate exceeds the effective rate.

      3) The bond discount or premium should appear as a direct deduction from, or addition to, the nominal amount of the bond payable.

   b. When bonds are issued between interest payment dates, the price includes accrued interest.

   c. Interest expense is equal to the carrying amount of the bond at the beginning of the period times the yield (market) interest rate.

   d. Interest paid remains constant and is equal to the nominal amount of the bond times the stated rate.

   e. The difference between interest expense and interest paid is the discount or premium amortization.

      1) When bonds are carried at a discount, interest expense exceeds interest (cash) paid.

      | | | |
      |---|---|---|
      | Interest expense | $XXX | |
      | Discount on bonds paid | | $XXX |
      | Cash | | XXX |

      2) When bonds are carried at a premium, interest (cash) paid exceeds interest expense.

      | | | |
      |---|---|---|
      | Interest expense | $XXX | |
      | Premium on bonds paid | XXX | |
      | Cash | | $XXX |

   f. For bonds issued at a discount, the carrying amount will increase as the discount is amortized. The result is a higher interest expense each interest payment period. Because the discount amortized is the excess of an increasing interest expense over the constant amount of interest paid, the amortization will increase with each payment.

g.   For bonds issued at a premium, the carrying amount will decrease as the premium is amortized. The result is a lower interest expense each interest payment period. Because the premium amortized is the excess of the constant amount of interest paid over a decreasing amount of interest expense, the premium amortization also will increase with each payment.

h.   The periodic reduction of the discount (premium) will cause the carrying amount of the bonds to be higher (lower) than the carrying amount at the previous period-end. At the maturity date, the discount or premium will be fully amortized to zero, and the carrying amount will be equal to the face value of the bonds.

2.   **Transaction costs**, such as issue costs, are included in the initial measurement of financial liabilities, such as bonds. Financial liabilities are subsequently measured at amortized cost.

a.   Issue costs are incurred to bring a bond to market and include printing and engraving costs, legal fees, accountants' fees, underwriters' commissions, registration fees, and promotional costs.

b.   Although the effective-interest method is theoretically superior, issue costs are customarily amortized using the straight-line method.

3.   **Compound Instruments**. The initial total carrying amount of convertible debt or of debt instruments issued with detachable share purchase warrants should be allocated between the debt instruments and the equity feature, and these debt and equity components should be separately accounted for. The total assigned initially to the instrument as a whole equals the fair value of the consideration received. However, the IASs do not stipulate a method for making the allocation.

a.   One approach is to assign to the less easily measurable component a residual amount after determining the amount of the more readily measurable component. For example, the future payments on the financial liability might be discounted at the market rate for a similar instrument without an equity feature. This amount would then be subtracted from the amount of the compound instrument as a whole to determine the carrying amount of the equity feature.

b.   A second approach is to measure the components separately and then to allocate the total assigned to the instrument as a whole on a basis proportionate to the separate measurements. For example, if the compound instrument is a convertible bond (a financial liability combined with a call option granting the right of conversion to the issuer's common shares), the value of the equity feature might be determined by reference to the fair value of a similar option or to an option-pricing model. The liability might be measured by discounting future cash outflows. These amounts would then be adjusted pro rata so that their sum equals the carrying amount of the compound instrument as a whole.

4.   Stop and review! You have completed the outline for this subunit. Study multiple-choice questions 60 through 71 beginning on page 209.

## 4.10 EQUITY

1.  Equity consists of share capital; items of income, expense, gain, or loss, reported directly in equity; retained earnings; and, possibly, treasury shares.

    Share capital

    | | | | |
    |---|---|---|---|
    | Preferred shares | XXX | | |
    | Share premium | XXX | XXX | |
    | Common shares | XXX | | |
    | Share premium | XXX | XXX | |
    | Total share capital | | | XXX |

    Reserves

    | | | |
    |---|---|---|
    | Revaluation surplus | XXX | |
    | Foreign currency translation adjustment | XXX | |
    | Total reserves | | XXX |

    Retained earnings

    | | | |
    |---|---|---|
    | Retained earnings appropriated for... | XXX | |
    | Unappropriated retained earnings | XXX | |
    | Total unretained earnings | | XXX |

    | | |
    |---|---|
    | Treasury shares (at cost) | (XXX) |
    | Total equity | XXX |

2.  **Share capital** (issued capital) is one of the required line items in the balance sheet. It represents investments by owners in exchange for shares.

    a.  One share capital account shows the par or stated value of all shares outstanding (if shares have no par or stated value, the amount received is given).

        1)  Amounts for each class of share capital, such as common and preferred shares, are usually separately listed.

    b.  Share premium consists of the sources of issued capital in excess of par or stated value. These sources may include

        1)  Amounts in excess of par or stated value received for the enterprise's shares
        2)  Debits for receipts less than par or stated value
        3)  Amounts attributable to treasury share transactions
        4)  Transfers from retained earnings upon the issuance of share dividends

3.  The term **reserve** is used in the Framework to refer to capital maintenance adjustments and to appropriations of retained earnings, but in the illustrative matter in IAS 1 and in this text it also applies to items recognized directly in equity.

    a.  IAS 1 states that reserves must be presented on the face of the balance sheet. Disclosures that must be made in the notes or on the face of the balance sheet are as follows.

        1)  Related party receivables and payables should be separately disclosed.
        2)  The enterprise should disclose shares authorized, issued, fully paid, or not paid; par value (or that there is none); a reconciliation of shares outstanding at the beginning and end of the period; rights of, and restrictions on, shares; shares held by the enterprise itself or its subsidiaries and associates; shares reserved under option and sales contracts; reserves of equity; dividends proposed or declared; and unrecognized cumulative preference dividends.

4.  **Retained earnings** is increased by net profit and decreased by net loss, dividends, and certain transactions in treasury shares.

    a.  According to the benchmark treatment prescribed in **IAS 8**, *Net Profit or Loss for the Period, Fundamental Errors, and Changes in Accounting Policies*, **fundamental errors** and the cumulative effect of changes in accounting policies result in adjustments to the beginning balance of retained earnings.

    b.  An enterprise may **appropriate** retained earnings to, for example, comply with a bond indenture, retain assets for expansion, anticipate losses, or adhere to legal restrictions.

        1)  The appropriation limits dividends but does not set aside assets. Moreover, any such transfer is excluded from the determination of net profit or loss.

5.  **Treasury shares** are the enterprise's own equity instruments reacquired for various purposes, e.g., mergers, options, or share dividends.

    a.  After treasury shares are reacquired by the issuer or a consolidated subsidiary, they are legally available to be reissued even if the intention is to cancel them.

    b.  The acquisition of treasury shares results in a direct change in equity. Furthermore, no gain or loss is recognized in the income statement for any transfer of treasury shares, for example, a sale, other issuance, or cancelation, and the consideration received is also recorded as a direct change in equity.

        1)  Recognition of gain or loss on treasury share transactions is inappropriate because they represent a shifting of interests among shareholders. Thus, the Framework defines income to exclude contributions from equity participants and expense to exclude distributions to equity participants.

    c.  **Disclosure**. Treasury shares are reported as a subtraction from equity on the balance sheet, and the amounts of reductions in equity are disclosed in the notes or on the face of the balance sheet. Whether the enterprise or its subsidiary holds treasury shares obtained from a party able to exercise significant influence or control should also be disclosed.

        1)  The effect of treasury shares is disclosed on the balance sheet or in the notes for all categories of equity. The acquisition cost of treasury shares may be presented in various ways. The following are examples:

            a)  A single line item may be presented as an adjustment to equity for the total cost.

            b)  An amount equal to par value, if any, may be reported as a subtraction from share capital, with adjustments made to other categories of equity (e.g., share premium and retained earnings) for the effects of premiums or discounts.

            c)  An adjustment may be made to each category of equity.

    d.  The enterprise's cost of acquiring a **right** to purchase treasury shares is a direct subtraction from equity. Moreover, such a right is not within the definition of a financial asset because the enterprise will not receive cash or another financial asset through exercise of the right. The definition of a financial asset excludes the enterprise's own equity instruments. Also, the exchange is not potentially favorable given the reduction in equity and outflow of assets.

e. Common means of accounting for treasury shares are the cost and par value methods. Under the **cost method**, the acquisition of treasury shares is recorded as a debit to a treasury shares account and a credit to cash. No other accounts are affected.

1) When the treasury shares are subsequently reissued for cash at a price in excess of their acquisition cost, the difference between the cash received and the carrying amount is credited to share premium from treasury share transactions.

2) If the treasury shares are subsequently reissued for an amount less than their acquisition cost, the difference between the acquisition cost and the reissuance price is debited to share premium from treasury share transactions. After this account is reduced to a zero balance, the remaining debit is to retained earnings.

3) Treasury shares accounted for at cost reduce total equity.

f. The **par value method** treats the acquisition of treasury shares as a constructive retirement and the resale as a new issuance. Upon acquisition, the entry originally made to issue shares is reversed by offsetting the appropriate share capital account, e.g., common shares, with treasury shares at par value and removing the share premium recorded when the shares were originally issued.

1) Any difference between the original issuance price and the reacquisition price is ordinarily adjusted through share premium accounts and retained earnings. Premiums are credited to share premium from treasury share transactions, and discounts are debited to the same account but only to the extent of prior premiums. If the credit balance in the account is insufficient to absorb the discount, retained earnings will be debited for the remainder.

2) Subsequent reissuance removes the treasury shares at par value and reestablishes share premium for any excess of the reissuance price over par value. If the reissuance price is less than par, the debit is to a share premium account or to retained earnings.

3) Treasury shares stated at par is a direct reduction of the appropriate share capital account.

6. Upon **issuance of shares**, cash is debited, the appropriate class of share capital is credited for any par or stated value, and the difference is credited to share premium.

a. Shares may be issued in exchange for services or property as well as for cash. The transaction should be recorded at the more clearly determinable of the fair values of the shares or the property or services received.

b. **Donated assets**. Contributions received appear to fall within the definition of income, which consists of increases in economic benefits that result in increases in equity, other than those from contributions by equity participants. They should be measured at fair value.

1) However, a contribution of treasury shares is, in effect, a transfer of equity instruments among owners, not a gain or loss by the enterprise.

7. **Retirement**. When shares are retired, cash (or treasury shares) is credited. The appropriate class of share capital account is debited for any par or stated value. Share premium is debited to the extent it exists from the original issuance. Any remainder is debited to retained earnings or credited to premium from share retirement.

a. No gain or loss is reported on transactions in an enterprise's own shares. However, the transfer of nonmonetary assets in exchange for shares requires recognition of any holding gain or loss on the nonmonetary assets.

8.  **Cash dividends** cannot be rescinded. Thus, when they are declared, a liability to owners is credited and retained earnings is debited, resulting in a decrease in retained earnings.

    a.  When cash dividends are paid, the dividends payable account is debited and cash is credited. Hence, at the payment date, retained earnings is not affected.

    b.  If dividends on preferred shares are **cumulative**, dividends in arrears and the preferred dividends for the current period must be paid before common shareholders may receive dividends. Dividends in arrears are not a liability until they are declared and are not recognized in the financial statements.

    c.  If preferred shares are **participating**, they may share equally in a cash dividend after a basic return has been paid to holders of both common and preferred shares at the preference rate for the preferred. The remainder is allocated, for example, in proportion to the par values of the outstanding shares.

9.  **Property Dividends**. A nonreciprocal transfer of nonmonetary assets to owners should be recorded at the fair value of the asset transferred on the declaration date. For example, if the property has appreciated, it should first be written up to fair value and a gain recognized.

10. **Liquidating dividends** are repayments of capital. They are distributions in excess of retained earnings. Because the effect of a liquidating dividend is to decrease share capital, share premium is debited first to the extent available before other equity accounts are charged.

11. A **share dividend** provides evidence to the shareholders of their interest in retained earnings without distribution of cash or other property. Share dividends are accounted for as a reclassification of shareholders' equity, not as liabilities.

    a.  The recipient of a share dividend should not recognize income. After receipt of the dividend, the shareholder has the same proportionate interest in the enterprise and the same total carrying amount as before the declaration of the share dividend.

12. **Share splits** are issuances of shares that do not affect any aggregate par value of shares issued and outstanding or total shareholders' equity.

    a.  No entry is made for share splits, and no transfer from retained earnings to share capital occurs, but a memorandum change of any par value or stated value is made.

13. **Rights**. In a rights offering, each shareholder is issued a certificate or **warrant** that is a call option to buy a certain number of shares at a fixed price. If the rights are exercised, the issuer will reflect the proceeds received as an increase in share capital at par value or stated value, if any, with any remainder credited to share premium.

    a.  However, if the rights previously issued without consideration are allowed to lapse, share capital is unaffected.

    b.  Until the issue date, the shares typically trade rights-on. After the issue date, the shares usually trade ex-rights because the rights can be sold separately.

    c.  The recipient of share rights must allocate the carrying amount of the shares owned between those shares and the rights based on their relative fair values. The portion of the price allocated to the rights increases (decreases) the discount (premium) on the investment.

    d.  Transaction costs of redeeming share rights reduce equity.

14. **IAS 19**, *Employee Benefits*, addresses, among many other things, **equity compensation benefits** for employees. However, it does not prescribe recognition and measurement principles applicable to employer accounting for equity compensation benefits. The required disclosures are discussed in Study Unit 3.

15. Stop and review! You have completed the outline for this subunit. Study multiple-choice questions 72 through 80 beginning on page 213.

---

NOTE:   Study Units 3 through 5 cover International Accounting Standards. In keeping with the way in which IASs present information, we have omitted all currency symbols. In some situations, this treatment may seem awkward for candidates accustomed to seeing items presented with monetary units indicated. Be prepared for exam questions that may or may not include monetary units.

---

## QUESTIONS

### 4.1 Receivables

**1.** An enterprise offers its customers credit terms of a 2% discount if paid within 10 days, or the full balance is due within 30 days (2/10, n/30). If some customers take advantage of the cash discount and others do not, which of the following accounts will appear on the income statement if the net method of recording receivables is employed?

| | Sales Discounts | Sales Discounts Forfeited |
|---|---|---|
| A. | Yes | Yes |
| B. | Yes | No |
| C. | No | No |
| D. | No | Yes |

Answer (D) is correct. *(CIA, adapted)*
**REQUIRED:** The account(s) appearing on the income statement if the net method is used.
**DISCUSSION:** The gross method accounts for receivables at their face value. If a discount is taken, a sales discount is recorded and classified as an offset to sales in the income statement to yield net sales. The net method records receivables net of the applicable discount. If the payment is not received during the discount period, an interest revenue account, such as sales discounts forfeited, is credited at the end of the discount period or when the payment is received. Accordingly, the application of the net method requires a sales discount forfeited but not a sales discount account.

**2.** An internal auditor is deriving cash flow data based on an incomplete set of facts. Bad debt expense was 2,000. Additional data for this period follows:

| | |
|---|---|
| Net profit | 100,000 |
| Accounts receivable beginning balance | 5,000 |
| Allowance for bad debts beginning balance | (500) |
| Accounts receivable written off | 1,000 |
| Increase in net accounts receivable (after subtraction of allowance for bad debts) | 30,000 |

How much cash was collected this period?

A. 67,000

B. 68,500

C. 68,000

D. 70,000

Answer (D) is correct. *(CIA, adapted)*
**REQUIRED:** The cash collected on accounts receivable.
**DISCUSSION:** The cash collected equals net profit adjusted for the change in net accounts receivable (gross A/R – allowance for bad debts). An increase in net accounts receivable implies that cash collected was less than net profit. Hence, cash collected was 70,000 (100,000 – 30,000 increase in net A/R). Write-offs (debit the allowance, credit A/R) do not affect the computation of cash collected because the allowance and gross accounts receivable are reduced by the same amount. Moreover, recognition of bad debt expense (debit bad debt expense, credit the allowance) is not included in this calculation because it is already reflected in the net accounts receivable balance.
Answer (A) is incorrect because 67,000 results from subtracting the write-offs and the bad debt expense from the sum of net income and beginning net accounts receivable. Answer (B) is incorrect because 68,500 assumes a zero balance in the beginning allowance account and deducts bad debt expense from the sum of net profit and beginning net accounts receivable. Answer (C) is incorrect because 68,000 deducts bad debt expense from the sum of net profit and beginning net accounts receivable.

**3.** An analysis of an enterprise's 150,000 accounts receivable at year-end resulted in a 5,000 ending balance for its allowance for uncollectible accounts and a bad debt expense of 2,000. During the past year, recoveries on bad debts previously written off were correctly recorded at 500. If the beginning balance in the allowance for uncollectible accounts was 4,700, what was the amount of accounts receivable written off as uncollectible during the year?

A. 1,200

B. 1,800

C. 2,200

D. 2,800

Answer (C) is correct. *(CIA, adapted)*
**REQUIRED:** The amount of accounts receivable written off during the year.
**DISCUSSION:** Under the allowance method, uncollectible accounts are written off by a debit to the allowance account and a credit to accounts receivable. The 500 of recovered bad debts is accounted for by a debit to accounts receivable and a credit to the allowance account. The 2,000 bad debt expense is also credited to the allowance account. The amount of accounts receivable written off as uncollectible is 2,200 [5,000 ending allowance – (4,700 beginning allowance + 500 recoveries + 2,000 bad debt expense)].
Answer (A) is incorrect because 1,200 results from subtracting the recoveries instead of adding them. Answer (B) is incorrect because 1,800 results from subtracting bad debt expense from the allowance account. Answer (D) is incorrect because 2,800 results from subtracting the recoveries and bad debt expense from the allowance account.

Questions 4 through 6 are based on the following information. An enterprise sells goods on an installment basis. The table below includes information about the level of installment sales, the cost of the goods sold on installment, and the cash receipts on installment sales for 2003 through 2005. All cash receipt amounts shown are net of any interest charges.

|                              | 2003   | 2004  | 2005   |
| ---------------------------- | ------ | ----- | ------ |
| Installment sales            | 10,000 | 5,000 | 20,000 |
| Cost of installment sales    | 6,000  | 4,000 | 10,000 |
|                              |        |       |        |
| Cash receipts on 2003 sales  | 2,000  | 4,000 | 4,000  |
| Cash receipts on 2004 sales  |        | 1,000 | 2,000  |
| Cash receipts on 2005 sales  |        |       | 4,000  |

**4.** The rate of gross profit on 2004 installment sales is

A. 20%

B. 40%

C. 50%

D. 80%

Answer (A) is correct. *(CIA, adapted)*
**REQUIRED:** The rate of gross profit on 2004 installment sales.
**DISCUSSION:** The rate of gross profit on 2004 installment sales is 20% [(5,000 of 2004 installment sales – 4,000 cost of 2004 installment sales) ÷ 5,000 of 2004 installment sales].
Answer (B) is incorrect because 40% is the gross profit on 2003 installment sales. Answer (C) is incorrect because 50% is the gross profit on 2005 installment sales. Answer (D) is incorrect because 80% is the ratio of the cost of 2004 installment sales to 2004 installment sales.

**5.** The amount of gross profit to be recognized in 2003 on 2003 installment sales is

A. 800

B. 2,000

C. 3,200

D. 4,000

Answer (A) is correct. *(CIA, adapted)*
**REQUIRED:** The amount of gross profit to be recognized in 2003 on 2003 installment sales.
**DISCUSSION:** In 2003, cash receipts were 2,000 from 2003 installment sales. The gross profit realized is the gross profit on the portion of sales for which payment has been received. This amount equals the 2003 gross profit percentage multiplied by the cash receipts, or 800 {[(10,000 – 6,000) ÷ 10,000] × 2,000}.
Answer (B) is incorrect because 2,000 is the amount of cash receipts during 2003 on 2003 installment sales. Answer (C) is incorrect because 3,200 is the amount of the total gross profit on 2003 installment sales that is deferred to future periods.
Answer (D) is incorrect because 4,000 is the total gross profit on 2003 installment sales.

**6.** The gross profit amount from 2005 sales to be deferred to future years would be

A. 2,000

B. 3,000

C. 8,000

D. 10,000

Answer (C) is correct. *(CIA, adapted)*
**REQUIRED:** The gross profit amount from 2005 sales to be deferred to future years.
**DISCUSSION:** The total gross profit on 2005 sales is 10,000 (20,000 sales – 10,000 cost), and the amount realized is 2,000 {[(20,000 – 10,000) ÷ 20,000] × 4,000 of 2005 cash receipts}. Accordingly, the amount deferred is 8,000 (10,000 – 2,000).
Answer (A) is incorrect because 2,000 is the realized gross profit on 2005 sales. Answer (B) is incorrect because 3,000 equals total receipts for 2004 and 2005 on 2004 sales.
Answer (D) is incorrect because 10,000 is the total gross profit on 2005 sales.

**7.** At the end of September, an enterprise has outstanding accounts receivable of 350 on third-quarter credit sales, composed as follows:

| Month | Credit Sales | Still Outstanding at the End of September |
|---|---|---|
| July | 600 | 100 |
| August | 900 | 170 |
| September | 500 | 80 |

The percentage of receivables in the 31-to-60-day age group at the end of September is

A. 22.86%

B. 28.57%

C. 48.57%

D. 71.43%

Answer (C) is correct. *(CIA, adapted)*
**REQUIRED:** The percentage of receivables in the 31-to-60-day age group.
**DISCUSSION:** Receivables from August sales still outstanding at the end of September are in the 31-to-60-day age group. This group represents 48.57% of total receivables [170 ÷ (100 + 170 + 80)].
Answer (A) is incorrect because 22.86% is the proportion of receivables in the 0-to-30-day age group at the end of September. Answer (B) is incorrect because 28.57% is the proportion of receivables in the 61-to-90-day age group at the end of September. Answer (D) is incorrect because 71.43% is the proportion of outstanding receivables that are from 0 to 60 days old at the end of September.

**8.** An enterprise sells inventory for 80,000 that had an inventory cost of 40,000. The terms of the sale involve payments receivable of 10,000 in the first year, 45,000 in the second year, and 25,000 in the third year. The buyer of the inventory is a new firm with no credit history. If the cost-recovery method of revenue recognition is used, the amount of gross profit to be recognized in the second year is

A. 0

B. 5,000

C. 15,000

D. 45,000

Answer (C) is correct. *(CIA, adapted)*
**REQUIRED:** The gross profit in the second year under the cost-recovery method.
**DISCUSSION:** The profit recognized in the second year equals the cumulative payments received minus the seller's cost, or 15,000 [(10,000 + 45,000) − 40,000].
Answer (A) is incorrect because under the cost-recovery method, profit is recognized in the second year when cash payments by the buyer exceed the seller's cost of merchandise. Answer (B) is incorrect because 5,000 is the profit to be recognized without consideration of the payment received in the first year. Answer (D) is incorrect because 45,000 is the payment received in the second year.

**9.** When a right of return exists, an enterprise may recognize revenue from a sale of goods at the time of sale only if

A. The amount of future returns can be reliably estimated.

B. The seller retains the risks and rewards of ownership.

C. The buyer resells the goods.

D. The seller believes returns will not be material.

Answer (A) is correct. *(CIA, adapted)*
**REQUIRED:** The condition for revenue recognition when a right of return exists.
**DISCUSSION:** One condition for recognition of revenue from the sale of goods is the transfer of the significant risks and rewards of ownership. Retention of significant risk may occur when, for example, the buyer may rescind the purchase for a reason stipulated in the contract, and the buyer is uncertain about the probability of return. However, if the enterprise can reliably estimate future returns and recognizes a liability for returns based on experience and other pertinent information, revenue may be recognized at the time of sale if the other conditions for revenue recognition are also met.
Answer (B) is incorrect because the risks and rewards of ownership must be transferred. Answer (C) is incorrect because this contingency is an example of retention of significant risk. Answer (D) is incorrect because returns may be material if they can be reliably estimated.

**10.** If a transfer of receivables with recourse qualifies to be recognized as a sale, the proceeds from the sale are

A. Accounted for as a collateralized borrowing.

B. Recorded at fair value for the assets obtained and liabilities incurred.

C. Recorded at the historical cost of the assets obtained.

D. Reduced by the fair value of the recourse obligation.

Answer (D) is correct. *(CMA, adapted)*
**REQUIRED:** The accounting for the proceeds of the sale of receivables with recourse.
**DISCUSSION:** When a transfer of receivables with recourse meets the criteria to be accounted for as a sale, the enterprise derecognizes the financial assets it no longer controls. After derecognition, periodic net profit or loss will include the difference between the carrying amount transferred and the proceeds, plus or minus any prior adjustment reflecting the fair value of the asset that had been reported in equity. If a new financial asset is created or a new financial liability is assumed, the calculation is adjusted for the fair value of the asset or liability. Thus, the proceeds of the sale are reduced by the fair value of the recourse obligation (a new financial liability). When the transfer does not meet these criteria, the transfer is accounted for as a collateralized borrowing.

**11.** A transferor enterprise most likely should continue to recognize a transferred financial asset if

A. The transferor may reacquire the asset, and the asset is readily obtainable in the market.

B. The transferee may sell or pledge the full fair value of the asset.

C. The transferor may reacquire the asset, and the reacquisition price is fair value.

D. The transferor is entitled and obligated to repurchase the asset, and the transferee receives a lender's return.

Answer (D) is correct. *(Publisher)*
**REQUIRED:** The circumstances in which a transferred financial asset most likely should not be derecognized.
**DISCUSSION:** An enterprise derecognizes a financial asset if it loses control of the contractual rights the asset represents. Control is lost when the enterprise realizes the rights to the specified contractual benefits, the rights expire, or it surrenders the rights. A transferor has not lost control and does not derecognize the financial asset if it is entitled and obligated to repurchase or redeem the asset, and the terms of this transaction in effect allow the transferee to obtain a lender's return on the assets it receives in exchange for the transferred financial asset.
Answer (A) is incorrect because a financial asset should be derecognized despite the transferor's right to reacquire it if the asset is readily obtainable in the market. Answer (B) is incorrect because control is lost when the transferee has the ability to obtain the benefits of the asset, for example, when the transferee may sell or pledge the full fair value of the asset. Answer (C) is incorrect because a financial asset should be derecognized despite the transferor's right to reacquire it if the price is fair value at the date of reacquisition.

## 4.2 Inventory

**12.** A retail enterprise maintains a markup of 25% based on cost. The enterprise has the following information for the current year:

| | |
|---|---|
| Purchases of merchandise | 690,000 |
| Freight-in on purchases | 25,000 |
| Sales | 900,000 |
| Ending inventory | 80,000 |

Beginning inventory was

A. 40,000

B. 85,000

C. 110,000

D. 265,000

Answer (B) is correct. *(CIA, adapted)*
**REQUIRED:** The beginning inventory.
**DISCUSSION:** Cost of goods sold equals beginning inventory, plus purchases (including freight-in), minus ending inventory. Given that sales reflect 125% of cost, cost of goods sold must equal 720,000 (900,000 sales ÷ 1.25). Consequently, the beginning inventory must have been 85,000 (720,000 CGS + 80,000 EI – 690,000 purchases – 25,000 freight-in).
Answer (A) is incorrect because 40,000 is based on a 25% markup on sales. Answer (C) is incorrect because 110,000 omits the freight-in from the computation of cost of goods available for sale. Answer (D) is incorrect because 265,000 uses the sales figure for cost of goods sold.

**13.** Which inventory pricing method generally approximates current cost for each of the following?

| | Ending Inventory | Cost of Goods Sold |
|---|---|---|
| A. | FIFO | FIFO |
| B. | LIFO | FIFO |
| C. | FIFO | LIFO |
| D. | LIFO | LIFO |

Answer (C) is correct. *(CIA, adapted)*
**REQUIRED:** The inventory pricing method.
**DISCUSSION:** FIFO assigns the most recent purchase prices to ending inventory and the earliest purchase prices to cost of goods sold. LIFO uses the earliest acquisition costs to price the ending inventory. Thus, FIFO approximates current cost for ending inventory, and LIFO approximates current cost of goods sold.

**14.** The cost of materials has risen steadily over the year. Which of the following methods of estimating the ending balance of the materials inventory account will result in the highest net profit, assuming all other variables remain constant?

A. Last-in, first-out (LIFO).

B. First-in, first-out (FIFO).

C. Weighted average.

D. Specific identification.

Answer (B) is correct. *(CIA, adapted)*
**REQUIRED:** The inventory flow assumption yielding the highest net profit given rising prices.
**DISCUSSION:** Net profit will be higher when cost of goods sold is lower, other factors held constant. Cost of goods sold equals beginning inventory, plus purchases, minus ending inventory. Accordingly, cost of goods sold will be lowest when the ending inventory is highest. Ending inventory is highest under FIFO because the older, less expensive items are deemed to have been sold, leaving the more expensive items in the ending inventory.
Answer (A) is incorrect because LIFO yields the lowest net profit. Answer (C) is incorrect because weighted average averages inventory, so it results in a lower net profit than FIFO. Answer (D) is incorrect because, under specific identification, the newest (most expensive) items are not necessarily in the ending inventory. The result is a higher cost of goods sold and lower net profit than under FIFO.

**15.** A physical inventory count showed an enterprise had inventory costing 1,000,000 on hand at December 31, 2003. Excluded from this amount were the following:

- Goods costing 82,000, shipped to a customer free on board (FOB) shipping point on December 28, 2003. They were expected to be received by the customer on January 4, 2004.
- Goods costing 122,000, shipped to a customer free on board (FOB) destination December 30, 2003. They were expected to be received by the customer on January 5, 2004.

Compute the correct ending inventory to be reported on the shipper's balance sheet at December 31, 2003.

A. 1,000,000

B. 1,082,000

C. 1,122,000

D. 1,204,000

Answer (C) is correct. *(CIA, adapted)*
**REQUIRED:** The correct ending inventory balance.
**DISCUSSION:** The goods shipped FOB shipping point should be counted in the buyer's, not the seller's, inventory because title and risk of loss pass at the time and place of shipment. These goods were properly excluded from ending inventory. The goods shipped FOB destination were improperly excluded from the seller's ending inventory. The title and risk of loss did not pass until the time and place where the goods reached their destination and were duly tendered. Thus, the correct ending inventory is 1,122,000 (1,000,000 beginning balance + 122,000 goods shipped FOB destination).
Answer (A) is incorrect because 1,000,000 excludes the goods shipped FOB destination. Answer (B) is incorrect because 1,082,000 excludes the goods shipped FOB destination and fails to exclude the goods shipped FOB shipping point. Answer (D) is incorrect because 1,204,000 includes the goods shipped FOB shipping point.

**16.** When a perpetual inventory system is used and a difference exists between the perpetual inventory amount balance and the physical inventory count, a separate entry is needed to adjust the perpetual inventory amount. Which of the following demonstrates that adjusting entry?

    A. Inventory over and short
          Inventory

    B. Extraordinary loss due to write-down of
          inventory
          Inventory

    C. Extraordinary loss due to write-down of
          inventory
          Allowance for inventory shortages

    D. Cost of goods sold
          Retained earnings appropriated for
            shortages

Answer (A) is correct. *(CIA, adapted)*
    **REQUIRED:** The separate entry to adjust the perpetual inventory amount.
    **DISCUSSION:** The entry to record a write-down is a debit to inventory over and short and a credit to inventory. This amount is reported as an adjustment of cost of goods sold or as an other expense on the income statement.
    Answer (B) is incorrect because a difference between a physical count and a perpetual inventory balance is common. Reasons include normal and expected shrinkage, breakage, shoplifting, and faulty record keeping. Thus, it is not an extraordinary item. Answer (C) is incorrect because a difference between a physical count and a perpetual inventory balance is common. Reasons include normal and expected shrinkage, breakage, shoplifting, and faulty record keeping. Thus, it is not an extraordinary item. Answer (D) is incorrect because, although the debit to cost of goods sold is acceptable, the credit should be to inventory. Also, any appropriation of retained earnings would also have to involve the unappropriated retained earnings account.

**17.** An enterprise had the following selected per-unit data relating to work-in-process:

| | |
|---|---|
| Selling price | 100 |
| Completion costs | 10 |
| Historical cost | 91 |
| Replacement cost | 108 |
| Normal gross profit | 20 |
| Selling cost | 5 |

In comparison with historical cost, what will be the per-unit impact on gross profit of measuring ending inventory?

    A. No effect.

    B. Reduction of 6.

    C. Reduction of 26.

    D. Increase of 5.

Answer (B) is correct. *(CIA, adapted)*
    **REQUIRED:** The per-unit impact on gross profit of valuing ending inventory.
    **DISCUSSION:** Inventories are measured at the lower of cost or net realizable value (NRV). NRV equals selling price minus completion and selling costs. Given that historical cost is 91 and NRV is 85 (price of 100 – 10 completion cost – 5 selling cost), the effect on per-unit gross profit is a reduction of 6. This amount is the writedown expensed.
    Answer (A) is incorrect because no effect implies that NRV is at least as high as cost. Answer (C) is incorrect because a reduction of 26 results from treating normal gross profit as if it were a completion or selling cost. Answer (D) is incorrect because an increase is permissible only to the extent of a prior writedown.

Questions 18 and 19 are based on the following information. Illustrated below is a perpetual inventory card for the current year.

| Date | Units Purchased | Units Sold | Units Balance |
|---|---|---|---|
| January 1 | | | - 0 - |
| January 12 | 1,000 @ 2.00 | | 1,000 |
| March 15 | | 300 | 700 |
| May 5 | 500 @ 2.20 | | 1,200 |
| July 8 | | 500 | 700 |
| November 24 | 1,000 @ 1.65 | | 1,700 |

Additional Information:

The enterprise had no opening inventory.

The items sold on March 15 were purchased on January 12.

The items sold on July 8 were purchased on May 5.

**18.** The ending inventory balance under the first-in, first-out (FIFO) method of inventory valuation is

A. 3,050

B. 3,150

C. 3,230

D. 3,430

Answer (B) is correct. *(CIA, adapted)*
    **REQUIRED:** The ending inventory balance under FIFO.
    **DISCUSSION:** Under the FIFO method, the 1,700 units of ending inventory are valued at the most recent prices. Ending inventory is assumed to include 1,000 units purchased November 24, 500 units purchased May 5, and 200 units purchased January 12. Hence, the ending inventory is 3,150 [(1,000 × 1.65) + (500 × 2.20) + (200 × 2.00)].
    Answer (A) is incorrect because 3,050 is the ending inventory under the specific identification method. Answer (C) is incorrect because 3,230 is the ending inventory under the weighted-average method. Answer (D) is incorrect because 3,430 is the ending inventory under the LIFO method.

**19.** The cost of goods sold under the specific identification method of inventory valuation is

A. 1,320

B. 1,520

C. 1,600

D. 1,700

Answer (D) is correct. *(CIA, adapted)*
    **REQUIRED:** The cost of goods sold under the specific identification method.
    **DISCUSSION:** Of the 800 units sold during the period, the 300 units sold on March 15 were purchased on January 12 at a cost of 2.00 per unit. The remaining 500 units were purchased on May 5 at a cost of 2.20 per unit. The cost of goods sold under the specific identification method is therefore 1,700 [(300 units × 2.00) + (500 units × 2.20)].
    Answer (A) is incorrect because 1,320 is the cost of goods sold under the LIFO method. Answer (B) is incorrect because 1,520 is the cost of goods sold under the weighted-average method. Answer (C) is incorrect because 1,600 is the cost of goods sold under the FIFO method.

Questions 20 and 21 are based on the following information. An enterprise started in 2004 with 200 scented candles on hand at a cost of 3.50 each. These candles sell for 7.00 each. The following schedule represents the purchases and sales of candles during 2004:

| Transaction Number | Quantity Purchased | Unit Cost | Quantity Sold |
|---|---|---|---|
| 1 | --- | --- | 150 |
| 2 | 250 | 3.30 | --- |
| 3 | --- | --- | 100 |
| 4 | 200 | 3.10 | --- |
| 5 | --- | --- | 200 |
| 6 | 350 | 3.00 | --- |
| 7 | --- | --- | 300 |

**20.** If the enterprise uses perpetual LIFO inventory pricing, the cost of goods sold for 2004 is

A. 2,330

B. 2,805

C. 2,375

D. 2,445

Answer (C) is correct. *(CIA, adapted)*
REQUIRED: The cost of goods sold using perpetual LIFO inventory pricing.
DISCUSSION: LIFO assumes that the latest goods purchased are the first sold. In a perpetual system, purchases are directly recorded in the inventory account, and cost of goods sold is determined as each sale is made. Accordingly, the cost of goods sold using perpetual LIFO is 2,375.

| Units Sold | | Unit Cost | | |
|---|---|---|---|---|
| 150 | × | 3.50 | = | 525 |
| 100 | × | 3.30 | = | 330 |
| 200 | × | 3.10 | = | 620 |
| 300 | × | 3.00 | = | 900 |
| | | | | 2,375 |

Answer (A) is incorrect because 2,330 is based on periodic LIFO inventory pricing. Answer (B) is incorrect because 2,805 is the FIFO gross profit. Answer (D) is incorrect because 2,445 is the FIFO cost of goods sold.

**21.** If the enterprise uses periodic FIFO inventory pricing, the gross profit for 2004 would be

A. 2,755

B. 2,805

C. 2,854

D. 2,920

Answer (B) is correct. *(CIA, adapted)*
REQUIRED: The gross profit using periodic FIFO inventory pricing.
DISCUSSION: The FIFO method assumes that the first goods purchased are the first goods sold and that ending inventory consists of the latest purchases. Moreover, whether the inventory system is periodic or perpetual does not affect FIFO valuation. The cost of goods sold is 2,445 {beginning inventory (200 units × 3.50) + purchases [(250 units × 3.30) + (200 units × 3.10) + (350 units × 3.00)] – ending inventory (250 units × 3.00)}. Thus, the gross profit for 2004 using FIFO is 2,805 [sales (750 units × 7.00) – cost of goods sold of 2,445].
Answer (A) is incorrect because 2,755 equals sales minus purchases. Answer (C) is incorrect because 2,854 uses a weighted-average ending inventory and part of the cost of goods sold calculation. Answer (D) is incorrect because 2,920 uses a periodic LIFO inventory value.

**22.** The following data are available from the records of a department store for the year ended December 31, 2003:

|  | At cost | At retail |
|---|---|---|
| Merchandise inventory, as of January 1, 2003 | 9,000 | 13,000 |
| Purchases | 33,000 | 46,000 |
| Markups (net) |  | 1,000 |
| Markdowns (net) |  | 4,000 |
| Sales |  | 48,000 |

Using the retail method to approximate valuation at lower of average cost or net realizable value, the department store's merchandise inventory at December 31, 2003, is

A. 8,400

B. 8,000

C. 6,000

D. 5,600

Answer (D) is correct. *(CIA, adapted)*
**REQUIRED:** The year-end inventory value using the retail method.
**DISCUSSION:** The version of the retail method that approximates a lower-of-average-cost-or-NRV valuation includes markups but not markdowns in the cost-to-retail ratio. Thus, the cost of the inventory at December 31, 2003 is 5,600.

|  | Cost | Retail |
|---|---|---|
| Inventory, January 1, 2003 | 9,000 | 13,000 |
| Purchases | 33,000 | 46,000 |
| Markups, net |  | 1,000 |
|  | 42,000 | 60,000 |
| Sales |  | (48,000) |
| Markdowns, net |  | (4,000) |
| Inventory at retail, December 31, 2003 |  | 8,000 |
| Cost-to-retail ratio (42,000 ÷ 60,000) |  | × .70 |
| Inventory at cost, December 31, 2003 |  | 5,600 |

Answer (A) is incorrect because 8,400 neglects to subtract the net markdowns to compute the merchandise inventory at retail at December 31, 2003. Answer (B) is incorrect because 8,000 is the inventory at retail at December 31, 2003. Answer (C) is incorrect because 6,000 is computed by including the net markdowns in the cost-to-retail ratio.

## 4.3 Investments

**23.** When the equity method is used to account for the investment in an associate, the recording of the receipt of a cash distribution from the investee will result in

A. The recognition of investment income.

B. A reduction in the investment balance.

C. An increase in a liability account.

D. An increase in a special equity account.

Answer (B) is correct. *(CIA, adapted)*
**REQUIRED:** The effect under the equity method of the receipt of a cash distribution.
**DISCUSSION:** When the equity method is used, the investment is initially recorded at cost on the enterprise's books. The carrying amount is subsequently adjusted to recognize the profits or losses of the associate after the date of acquisition. Dividends received from an associate reduce the carrying amount.
Answer (A) is incorrect because, when the equity method is used, investment income (loss) is recognized for the investee's share of the profits or losses of the associate. Dividends received from the investee are recorded as a reduction of the investment account. Answer (C) is incorrect because the investment account is credited. Answer (D) is incorrect because the investment account is credited.

**24.** Derivatives that are not hedging instruments are always classified in which category of financial instruments?

A. Financial assets or liabilities held for trading.

B. Held-to-maturity investments.

C. Loans and receivables originated by the enterprise.

D. Available-for-sale financial assets.

Answer (A) is correct. *(Publisher)*
**REQUIRED:** The category including derivatives that are not hedging instruments.
**DISCUSSION:** Financial assets or liabilities held for trading are intended to result in profits from short-term changes in prices or dealer's margins. Regardless of intent, however, a financial asset is held for trading if it is included in a portfolio with a recent pattern of short-term profit taking. Derivatives are also deemed to be held for trading unless they are designated and effective as hedging instruments.
Answer (B) is incorrect because held-to-maturity investments have fixed or determinable payments and a fixed maturity. Moreover, the enterprise must have a positive intent and ability to hold such investments to maturity. However, this classification excludes loans and receivables originated by the enterprise. Answer (C) is incorrect because loans and receivables originated by the enterprise result from providing money, goods, or services directly to a debtor, excluding those that are held for trading. Answer (D) is incorrect because available-for-sale financial assets are those that do not fall within one of the other classifications.

**25.** Subsequent to their initial recognition, which financial assets with quoted market prices in an active market are measured at fair value?

|  | Held-to-Maturity Investments | Loans and Receivables Originated by the Enterprise and not Held for Trading | Available-for-Sale Financial Assets | Financial Assets Held for Trading |
|---|---|---|---|---|
| A. | Yes | Yes | Yes | No |
| B. | Yes | Yes | No | No |
| C. | No | No | Yes | Yes |
| D. | No | No | No | Yes |

Answer (C) is correct. *(Publisher)*
**REQUIRED:** The financial assets accounted for at fair value subsequent to initial recognition.
**DISCUSSION:** Subsequent measurement of financial assets depends on their type. Available-for-sale and held-for-trading financial assets are measured at fair value unless they do not have quoted market prices in an active market and their fair values cannot be reliably measured. Loans and receivables originated by the enterprise and not held for trading, held-to-maturity investments, and financial assets otherwise not qualifying for fair value measurement are measured at amortized cost using the effective interest rate method if they have a fixed maturity. If they do not, they are measured at cost. However, loans and receivables originated by the enterprise and not held for trading are measured at amortized cost without consideration of whether the enterprise intended to hold them to maturity.

**26.** Assuming an available-for-sale financial asset that is not part of a hedge is remeasured to fair value at the balance sheet, the gain or loss

A. Must be recognized in net profit or loss.

B. Must be recognized directly in equity.

C. May be recognized in net profit or loss or directly in equity.

D. Must be recognized in net profit or loss if the result is a loss and directly in equity if the result is a gain.

Answer (C) is correct. *(Publisher)*
**REQUIRED:** The treatment of a gain or loss remeasured to fair value.
**DISCUSSION:** Available-for-sale and held-for-trading financial assets are measured at fair value unless they do not have quoted market prices in an active market and their fair values cannot be reliably measured. Remeasurement to fair value of financial assets or liabilities that are not part of a hedge results in recognition of a gain or loss in net profit or loss if the items are held for trading. A gain or loss on an available-for-sale financial asset may be recognized in net profit or loss when it arises or directly in equity through the statement of changes in equity. In the latter case, the accumulated remeasurement gain or loss is included in net profit or loss when the asset is disposed of or is impaired. An enterprise should choose either immediate recognition of remeasurement gain or loss in net profit or loss or recognition directly in equity. The chosen accounting policy should then be applied to all available-for-sale financial assets not part of a hedging relationship.

## 4.4 Property, Plant, and Equipment

**27.** An enterprise is depreciating an asset with a 5-year useful life. It cost 100,000 and has no residual value. If the <List A> method is used, depreciation in the second year will be <List B>.

| | List A | List B |
|---|---|---|
| A. | Sum-of-years'-digits | 20,000 |
| B. | Sum-of-years'-digits | 40,000 |
| C. | 200% diminishing-balance | 16,000 |
| D. | 200% diminishing-balance | 24,000 |

Answer (D) is correct. *(CIA, adapted)*
**REQUIRED:** The appropriate matching of depreciation expense in the second year with a depreciation method.
**DISCUSSION:** The 200% diminishing-balance method uses twice the straight-line rate. Accordingly, first-year depreciation expense is 40,000 (100,000 × 20% × 2). In the second year, the depreciation base is reduced by the amount of depreciation already taken in the first year. Thus, depreciation expense in year two is 24,000 [(2 × 20%) × (100,000 − 40,000)].
Answer (A) is incorrect because depreciation in year two will be 20,000 under the straight-line method. Answer (B) is incorrect because, under the SYD method, second-year depreciation will be 26,667 [(4 ÷ 15) × 100,000]. Answer (C) is incorrect because 16,000 is based on the 100% diminishing-balance method.

**28.** Which of the following is not an appropriate basis for measuring the cost of property, plant, and equipment?

A. The purchase price, freight costs, and installation costs of a productive asset should be included in the asset's cost.

B. Proceeds obtained in the process of readying land for its intended purpose, such as from the sale of cleared timber, should be recognized immediately as income.

C. The costs of improvements to equipment incurred after its acquisition should be added to the asset's cost if they increase future service potential.

D. All costs incurred in the construction of a plant building, from excavation to completion, should be considered as part of the asset's cost.

Answer (B) is correct. *(CIA, adapted)*
**REQUIRED:** The basis that is inappropriate for measuring the cost of property, plant, and equipment.
**DISCUSSION:** Accordingly, items of property, plant, and equipment (PPE) that meet the recognition criteria are initially measured at cost. The cost includes the purchase price (minus trade discounts and rebates, plus purchase taxes) and the directly attributable costs of bringing the assets to working condition for their intended use. Directly attributable costs include site preparation, installation, initial delivery and handling, architect and equipment fees, costs of removing the assets and restoring the site, etc. Accordingly, the cost of land includes the cost of obtaining the land and readying it for its intended uses, but it is inappropriate to recognize the proceeds related to site preparation immediately as income. They should be treated as reductions in the price of the land.
Answer (A) is incorrect because the purchase price, freight costs, and installation costs of a productive asset are included in the asset's cost. Answer (C) is incorrect because subsequent expenditures are added to the carrying amount of an item of PPE if it is probable that, as a result, future economic benefits will exceed the originally assessed standard of performance, for example, because of an extended useful life, improved output quality, or reduced operating costs. Answer (D) is incorrect because all costs of construction should be included as a part of the asset's cost.

**29.** A depreciable asset has an estimated 20% residual value. At the end of the asset's estimated useful life, the accumulated depreciation will equal the original cost of the asset under which of the following depreciation methods?

| | Diminishing-Balance | Sum-of-the-Years'-Digits (SYD) |
|---|---|---|
| A. | Yes | Yes |
| B. | Yes | No |
| C. | No | Yes |
| D. | No | No |

Answer (D) is correct. *(CIA, adapted)*
**REQUIRED:** The depreciation method under which accumulated depreciation equals the original cost of the asset at the end of its estimated useful life.
**DISCUSSION:** At the end of the estimated useful life of a depreciable asset, the amount of accumulated depreciation should equal the depreciable cost (original cost – estimated residual value), regardless of the depreciation method used. Periodic diminishing-balance depreciation is calculated without regard to residual value, but the asset is not depreciated below its residual value. The SYD method uses a depreciable base equal to cost minus residual value.

**30.** If an enterprise employs the sum-of-the-years'-digits (SYD) method of depreciation for an asset with an estimated useful life of 4 years, the percentage of the total depreciable cost that will be expensed in the third year is

A. 10%
B. 25%
C. 20%
D. 70%

Answer (C) is correct. *(CIA, adapted)*
**REQUIRED:** The percentage of depreciable cost expensed using the SYD method.
**DISCUSSION:** Under the SYD method, the amount of the depreciable cost that is expensed each year is the remaining useful life at the beginning of that year divided by the sum of the years of useful life. For the third year, the portion expensed is 20% [2 ÷ (1 + 2 + 3 + 4)].
Answer (A) is incorrect because 10% is the amount expensed in the last year. Answer (B) is incorrect because 25% is the percentage expensed each year under the straight-line method. Answer (D) is incorrect because 70% is the total amount expensed in the first 2 years.

**31.** An enterprise donated land to a municipality for a park. The acquisition cost of the land was 75,000, and the market value at the time of the donation was 200,000 as determined by a professional appraisal. If the enterprise has adopted the allowed alternative treatment for measurement of property, plant, and equipment subsequent to initial recognition, the journal entry to record the disposition of the land is

A. Expense                         75,000
    Land                                          75,000

B. Land                            125,000
    Revaluation surplus                           125,000
   Revaluation surplus             125,000
    Income                                        125,000
   Expense                         200,000
    Land                                          200,000

C. Land                            125,000
    Revaluation surplus                           125,000
   Expense                         200,000
    Land                                          200,000

D. Donation expense                200,000
    Land                                          75,000
    Income                                        125,000

Answer (C) is correct. *(CIA, adapted)*
**REQUIRED:** The journal entry to record the donation of appreciated property.
**DISCUSSION:** According to the benchmark treatment prescribed by the IASs, an item of PPE is carried at cost minus any accumulated depreciation and impairment losses. Under the allowed alternative treatment, an item of PPE may be carried at a revalued amount equal to fair value at the revaluation date minus any subsequent accumulated depreciation and impairment losses. Land is not depreciated, so it should be carried at its revalued amount. This amount should be determined by a professional appraisal. The revaluation increased the carrying amount and is therefore credited directly to equity as revaluation surplus. Accordingly, the entry is to debit land and credit revaluation surplus for 125,000. The entire surplus is realized at the date of disposition, at which time it may be transferred to retained earnings (but not through the income statement). Upon disposal, the asset should be removed from the balance sheet, and the resulting loss (revalued carrying amount of 200,000 – 0 net disposal proceeds = 200,000) should be recognized as expense in the income statement.
Answer (A) is incorrect because the revaluation of the land must be recognized. Answer (B) is incorrect because the revaluation surplus is not transferred through the income statement. Answer (D) is incorrect because the revaluation surplus is not transferred through the income statement.

**32.** An enterprise sells a piece of machinery, for cash, prior to the end of its estimated useful life. The sale price is less than the carrying amount of the asset on the date of sale. The entry that the enterprise uses to record the sale is

A. Cash
   Accumulated depreciation -- machinery
   Expense-disposal of machinery
    Machinery

B. Cash
   Accumulated depreciation -- machinery
    Income-disposal of machinery
    Machinery

C. Cash
   Expense-disposal of machinery
    Accumulated depreciation -- machinery
    Machinery

D. Cash
   Machinery
    Accumulated depreciation -- machinery
    Expense-disposal of machinery

Answer (A) is correct. *(CIA, adapted)*
**REQUIRED:** The entry to record sale of machinery at less than book value.
**DISCUSSION:** The cash account is debited for the amount of the sale proceeds. The machinery account and the related accumulated depreciation account are eliminated by a credit and a debit, respectively. Because the sale price was less than the carrying amount of the asset on the date of sale, a loss on disposal should be recognized as an expense of the income statement.
Answer (B) is incorrect because a loss on disposal should be recognized as an expense of the income statement. Answer (C) is incorrect because accumulated depreciation should be debited. Answer (D) is incorrect because an expense and accumulated depreciation should be debited.

**33.** In making a cash flow analysis of property, plant, and equipment (PPE), the internal auditor discovered that depreciation expense for the period was 10,000. PPE with a cost of 50,000 and related accumulated depreciation of 30,000 was sold for a gain of 1,000. If the carrying amount of PPE increased by 80,000 during the period, how much PPE was purchased this period?

A. 91,000

B. 100,000

C. 110,000

D. 119,000

Answer (C) is correct. *(CIA, adapted)*
REQUIRED: The amount of property, plant, and equipment purchased.
DISCUSSION: The carrying amount of the PPE account, net of accumulated depreciation, is increased by the cost of purchases and decreased by the carrying amount of items of PPE sold and depreciation. The net PPE decreased by the carrying amount of items sold, or 20,000 (50,000 cost – 30,000 accumulated depreciation), and by the 10,000 of depreciation. If PPE still increased by 80,000, 110,000 (30,000 total decrease + 80,000 increase) of equipment must have been purchased.
Answer (A) is incorrect because 91,000 ignores the carrying amount of items sold and includes the gain in the computation. Answer (B) is incorrect because 100,000 ignores the depreciation expense for the period. Answer (D) is incorrect because 119,000 double counts depreciation expense and deducts the gain.

**34.** A theme park purchased a new, exciting ride and financed it through the manufacturer. The following facts pertain:

| | |
|---|---|
| Purchase price | 800,000 |
| Delivery cost | 50,000 |
| Installation cost | 70,000 |
| Cost of trial-runs | 40,000 |
| Interest charges for first year | 60,000 |

The straight-line method is to be used. Compute the depreciation on the equipment for the first year assuming an estimated service life of 5 years.

A. 160,000

B. 184,000

C. 192,000

D. 204,000

Answer (C) is correct. *(CIA, adapted)*
REQUIRED: The depreciation expense.
DISCUSSION: Under the straight-line method, the annual depreciation expense for an asset equals the asset's amount (cost – residual value) divided by the asset's estimated useful life. The cost of the asset includes its price and the directly attributable costs of bringing it to working condition for intended use. Thus, the depreciation expense is 192,000 [(800,000 purchase price + 50,000 delivery cost + 70,000 installation cost + 40,000 trial-run cost) ÷ 5-year estimated service life]. Borrowing costs incurred after the asset is prepared for its intended use are expensed even if the allowed alternative treatment of such costs is followed and the asset otherwise satisfies the criteria for capitalization expensed.
Answer (A) is incorrect because 160,000 excludes the delivery, installation, and trial-run costs. Answer (B) is incorrect because 184,000 excludes the trial-run cost. Answer (D) is incorrect because 204,000 includes the borrowing costs.

**35.** On January 1, 2000, an enterprise purchased an abandoned quarry for 1,200,000 to be used as a landfill to service its trash collection contracts with nearby cities for the next 20 years. The enterprise depletes the quarry using the sum-of-the-units method based on a surveyor's measurements of volume of the quarry's pit. This amount was 500,000 cubic yards when purchased and 350,000 cubic yards at year-end 2004. What is the net amount that should be shown on the enterprise's December 31, 2004, balance sheet for the quarry?

A. 1,200,000

B. 900,000

C. 840,000

D. 360,000

Answer (C) is correct. *(CIA, adapted)*
REQUIRED: The carrying amount of the quarry.
DISCUSSION: The sum-of-the-units method allocates cost based on output. The net amount reported as an asset for the quarry using this method is 840,000 [(350,000 cubic yards ÷ 500,000 total cubic yards) × 1,200,000].
Answer (A) is incorrect because 1,200,000 is the purchase price of the quarry. Answer (B) is incorrect because 900,000 results from using straight-line depletion. Answer (D) is incorrect because 360,000 equals {1,200,000 – [(350,000 ÷ 500,000) × 1,200,000]}. The 350,000 cubic yards is the volume remaining in the quarry's pit at year-end 2004, not the volume depleted.

**36.** An enterprise installed an assembly line in 2000. Four years later, 100,000 was invested to automate the line. The automation increased the market value and productive capacity of the assembly line but did not affect its useful life. Proper accounting for the cost of the automation should be to

A. Report it as an expense in 2004.

B. Establish a separate account for the 100,000.

C. Allocate the cost of automation between the asset and accumulated depreciation accounts.

D. Debit the cost to the property, plant, and equipment account.

Answer (D) is correct. *(CIA, adapted)*
**REQUIRED:** The proper accounting for the cost of the automation.
**DISCUSSION:** Subsequent expenditures are added to the carrying amount of an item of PPE if it is probable that, as a result, future economic benefits will exceed the originally assessed standard of performance, for example, because of an extended useful life, improved output quantity or quality, or reduced operating costs.
Answer (A) is incorrect because the cost should be capitalized. Answer (B) is incorrect because the same account should be used. Answer (C) is incorrect because allocation is not an accepted procedure.

**37.** An enterprise purchased new equipment on July 1, 2004, having a list price of 52,500. The enterprise traded old equipment that was being depreciated using the straight-line method and paid 35,000 in cash. The following information pertains to the old equipment:

| | |
|---|---|
| Cost on January 1, 2001 | 38,900 |
| Estimated useful life | 5 years |
| Residual value | 2,900 |
| Fair value on July 1, 2004 | 16,000 |

If the old and new equipment are dissimilar, the enterprise will record the new equipment at

A. 45,100

B. 48,700

C. 51,000

D. 52,500

Answer (C) is correct. *(CIA, adapted)*
**REQUIRED:** The amount recorded for new equipment if it is dissimilar to the old equipment that was traded.
**DISCUSSION:** An exchange of dissimilar items of PPE is considered the culmination of an earning process. Thus, the transaction should be recorded at the fair value of the asset received, which is equivalent to the fair value of the asset surrendered adjusted for any cash transferred. Hence, the enterprise will record the new equipment at the fair value of the old asset plus cash paid, or 51,000 (16,000 + 35,000).
Answer (A) is incorrect because 45,100 equals the book value of the old equipment after being depreciated for 4 years plus the cash paid for the new equipment. Answer (B) is incorrect because 48,700 equals the carrying amount of the old equipment after being depreciated for 3.5 years plus cash paid for the new equipment. Answer (D) is incorrect because 52,500 is the list price of the new equipment.

## 4.5 Intangible Assets

**38.** Which of the following is not considered to be an intangible asset?

A. Goods on consignment.

B. Patents.

C. Copyrights.

D. Trademarks.

Answer (A) is correct. *(CIA, adapted)*
**REQUIRED:** The item not an intangible asset.
**DISCUSSION:** IAS 38, *Intangible Assets*, defines an intangible asset as "an identifiable nonmonetary asset without physical substance held for use in the production or supply of goods or services, for rental to others, or for administrative purposes." Inventory is a tangible asset. Thus, goods on consignment are not intangible assets.
Answer (B) is incorrect because patents are intangible assets. Answer (C) is incorrect because copyrights are intangible assets. Answer (D) is incorrect because trademarks are intangible assets.

**39.** The costs of start-up activities, including fees of attorneys, should be

A. Capitalized, but not amortized, because of the indefinite life of the business.

B. Capitalized and amortized.

C. Capitalized and deferred until liquidation of the business.

D. Expensed when incurred.

Answer (D) is correct. *(CIA, adapted)*
**REQUIRED:** The proper accounting treatment of the costs of start-up activities.
**DISCUSSION:** Expenditures on start-up activities are expensed when incurred unless they are included in the cost of an item of property, plant, and equipment. They include the costs of establishing a new legal entity, such as legal and secretarial costs; pre-opening costs of an enterprise's new business facility; and the pre-operating costs of new operations, products, or processes.

**40.** The amortization of intangible assets over their useful lives is justified by the

    A.  Economic entity assumption.

    B.  Going concern assumption.

    C.  Monetary unit assumption.

    D.  Historical cost assumption.

Answer (B) is correct. *(CIA, adapted)*
**REQUIRED:** The reason for amortizing intangibles.
**DISCUSSION:** Every business is assumed to be a going concern that will continue operating indefinitely. Thus, liquidation values are not important. If an enterprise is not a going concern, its intangible assets are reported at liquidation values, not at historical cost net of amortization.
Answer (A) is incorrect because the economic entity assumption is that every enterprise's affairs are separate from those of its owners. Answer (C) is incorrect because the monetary unit assumption provides that all transactions and events can be measured in terms of money. Answer (D) is incorrect because the historical cost principle deems cost to be the most objective and reliable measure.

**41.** The restriction that manufacturers should not market a new product that is illegally similar to that of another company's product is due to which public policy instrument?

    A.  Copyright.

    B.  Minimum standards for product warranties.

    C.  Anti-merger laws.

    D.  Patent laws.

Answer (D) is correct. *(CIA, adapted)*
**REQUIRED:** The public policy instrument prohibiting sales of products illegally similar to those of other sellers.
**DISCUSSION:** A patent is the exclusive legal right to use or sell an invention, such as a device or process. A patent may be given to any new and useful process, machine, manufacture, or composition of matter, and any infringement of a patent is a basis for a lawsuit. Thus, patent laws require that enterprises not design new products that are illegally similar to those of other enterprises that enjoy patent protection.
Answer (A) is incorrect because a copyright provides legal protection for tangible expressions of ideas, e.g., novels, songs, and software. Answer (B) is incorrect because laws establishing minimum warranty standards do not limit the similarity of product offerings. Answer (C) is incorrect because anti-merger laws can affect the ability of one enterprise to acquire another enterprise producing similar products if the result will be to lessen competition, but they do not affect the design of new products.

**42.** MNO purchased all of XYZ's 100,000 outstanding common shares for 40 per share on August 31. On this date, XYZ's balance sheet showed total assets of 5,000,000 and total liabilities of 2,000,000. The fair value of XYZ's identifiable assets on this date was 550,000 greater than their carrying amount. The amount that should be reported on MNO's consolidated balance sheet on August 31 for goodwill is

    A.  0

    B.  450,000

    C.  550,000

    D.  1,000,000

Answer (B) is correct. *(CIA, adapted)*
**REQUIRED:** The amount of goodwill reported.
**DISCUSSION:** Goodwill is recognized as an asset equal to the excess of the cost over the acquirer's interest in the fair value of the identifiable assets and liabilities acquired. The cost of 4,000,000 (40 × 100,000) is in excess of the 3,550,000 (5,000,000 + 550,000 – 2,000,000) fair value of the identifiable assets and liabilities by 450,000. This excess is goodwill.
Answer (A) is incorrect because cost in excess of fair value of the identifiable assets and liabilities is reported as goodwill. Answer (C) is incorrect because 550,000 is the excess of fair value over the carrying amount of the identifiable assets and liabilities on the seller's books. Answer (D) is incorrect because the purchase price of 4,000,000 exceeds the seller's 3,000,000 carrying amount by 1,000,000.

## 4.6 Agriculture

**43.** According to IAS 41, *Agriculture*, the usual measurement of

A. Agricultural produce is at fair value at the point of harvest.

B. Agricultural produce is at fair value minus point-of-sale costs at the point of harvest and at each subsequent balance sheet date.

C. Biological assets is at fair value minus estimated point-of-sale costs at initial recognition and at each subsequent balance sheet date.

D. Biological assets is at cost minus accumulated depreciation and impairment losses.

Answer (C) is correct. *(Publisher)*
**REQUIRED:** The usual measurement of agricultural produce or biological assets.
**DISCUSSION:** Measurement of biological assets upon initial recognition and agricultural produce from the enterprise's biological assets at the point of harvest ordinarily is at fair value minus estimated point-of-sale costs. Biological assets are also remeasured at subsequent balance sheet dates at fair value minus estimated point-of-sale costs.
Answer (A) is incorrect because agricultural produce is measured at fair value minus estimated point-of-sale costs at the point of harvest. Answer (B) is incorrect because agricultural produce is measured at fair value minus estimated point-of-sale costs at the point of harvest. It is not remeasured for subsequent changes. Answer (D) is incorrect because biological assets are measured at cost minus accumulated depreciation and impairment losses only if the presumption that their fair value is reliably measurable is rebutted. Such rebuttal is permissible only upon initial recognition.

**44.** A gain or loss may be included in the determination of net profit or loss for

I. Initial recognition of a biological asset at fair value minus estimated point-of-sale costs

II. A change in fair value minus estimated point-of-sale costs of a biological asset

III. Initial recognition of agricultural produce at fair value minus estimated point-of-sale costs

IV. A change in fair value minus estimated point-of-sale costs of agricultural produce

A. I and II only.

B. II and IV only.

C. I, II, and III only.

D. I, II, III, and IV.

Answer (C) is correct. *(Publisher)*
**REQUIRED:** The circumstances in which gain or loss may be recognized.
**DISCUSSION:** Recognition of gains and losses on biological assets may result from initial recognition at, or from a change in, fair value minus estimated point-of-sale costs. These gains and losses should be included in net profit or loss as they occur. A gain or loss from the initial recognition of agricultural produce is included in net profit or loss as it occurs. However, agricultural produce is measured only at the point of harvest.
Answer (A) is incorrect because a gain or loss may be reported in net profit or loss for initial recognition of agricultural produce at fair value minus estimated point-of-sale costs. Answer (B) is incorrect because agricultural produce is measured only at the point of harvest. Answer (D) is incorrect because agricultural produce is measured only at the point of harvest.

## 4.7 Financial and Other Liabilities

**45.** An enterprise introduced a new product that carries a 2-year warranty against defects. It estimates that warranty costs will be 2% of sales in the year of sale and 3% of sales in the year following the year of sale. Sales in year 1 and year 2 were 5 million and 7 million, respectively. Actual costs of servicing the warranty in year 1 and year 2 were 110,000 and 260,000, respectively. What provision for warranty costs must the enterprise recognize in year 2?

A. 260,000

B. 290,000

C. 350,000

D. 370,000

Answer (C) is correct. *(CIA, adapted)*
**REQUIRED:** The warranty provision.
**DISCUSSION:** The warranty provision must be matched with revenue in the year of sale. Thus, the provision related to year 2 sales must be recognized in year 2 even if actual expenditures will not occur until year 3. The provision related to year 2 sales equals 350,000 [7,000,000 × (2% for the year of sale + 3% for the year after the year of sale)].
Answer (A) is incorrect because 260,000 is the actual cost of servicing the warranty in year 2. Answer (B) is incorrect because 290,000 equals the sum of 2% of year 2 sales and 3% of year 1 sales. Answer (D) is incorrect because 370,000 equals the actual cost of servicing the warranty in year 1 and year 2.

**46.** On December 31, 2000, XYZ issued 5-year bonds with a face amount of 1 million. The bonds carry a stated interest rate of 10% and were sold at par. Interest is payable annually on December 31. According to the provisions of the bond indenture, XYZ was to make annual deposits into a bond sinking fund (beginning December 31, 2001) to accumulate the funds necessary to retire the bonds at their maturity. On December 31, 2004, all required interest payments and sinking-fund payments due to date had been made on schedule. If the sinking-fund assets are properly classified as noncurrent, how should the balance of bonds payable be classified on the December 31, 2004 balance sheet?

   A. Current liability.

   B. Long-term liability.

   C. Contra to long-term investments.

   D. Deferred credit.

Answer (A) is correct. *(CIA, adapted)*
   **REQUIRED:** The classification of the balance of bonds payable.
   **DISCUSSION:** A current liability is an obligation that is expected to be settled within the normal operating cycle or is due to be settled within 12 months of the balance sheet date. Any other liability is noncurrent. Some current liabilities are included in the working capital employed in the normal operating cycle, e.g., trade payables and accrued employee operating costs. Current liabilities not settled within the normal operating cycle include the current part of interest-bearing debt, dividends, income taxes, and bank overdrafts. Thus, the bonds payable should be classified as current because they are due to be settled within 12 months. Under the IASs, the classification of the sinking-fund assets is irrelevant to the classification of the bond payable.
   Answer (B) is incorrect because the bonds should be classified as a current liability. Answer (C) is incorrect because offsetting assets and liabilities is rarely acceptable. Answer (D) is incorrect because the bonds are a liability and should not be put in an ambiguous category such as deferred credits.

**47.** On August 1, 2000, an enterprise issued 5-year bonds with a face amount of 10 million. The bonds carry a stated interest rate of 10% and interest is payable annually on July 31. Which is the appropriate classification of bonds payable and the related accrued interest payable on the December 31, 2004 balance sheet?

| Classification Table | Bonds Payable | Interest Payable |
|---|---|---|
| Classification A | Current liability | Current liability |
| Classification B | Current liability | Long-term liability |
| Classification C | Long-term liability | Current liability |
| Classification D | Long-term liability | Long-term liability |

   A. Classification A.

   B. Classification B.

   C. Classification C.

   D. Classification D.

Answer (A) is correct. *(CIA, adapted)*
   **REQUIRED:** The appropriate classification of bonds payable and the related accrued interest payable on the balance sheet.
   **DISCUSSION:** A current liability is an obligation that is expected to be settled within the normal operating cycle or is due to be settled within 12 months of the balance sheet date. Any other liability is noncurrent. Some current liabilities are included in the working capital employed in the normal operation cycle, e.g., trade payables and accrued employee operating costs. Current liabilities not settled within the normal operating cycle include the current part of interest-bearing debt, dividends, income taxes, and bank overdrafts. Given that the bonds payable and interest payable are due within 12 months, they should be classified and current.
   Answer (B) is incorrect because the interest payable should be classified as a current liability. It is due within a year after the balance sheet date. Answer (C) is incorrect because the balance of bonds payable should be classified as a current liability. The bonds are due within a year after the balance sheet date. Answer (D) is incorrect because both the balance of bonds payable and interest payable should be classified as current liabilities.

**48.** A manufacturer produces a quality product for which it charges a little more than some competing items but gives its consumers a more liberal warranty policy. The product carries a 5-year warranty that covers both labor and materials charges. Which of the following defines the appropriate method of accounting for the warranty?

    A.  Cash basis.

    B.  Recognition of a provision.

    C.  Sales warranty.

    D.  Tax basis.

Answer (B) is correct. *(CIA, adapted)*
**REQUIRED:** The proper accounting treatment of a warranty.
**DISCUSSION:** A provision is a liability of uncertain timing and amount. A liability is a present obligation arising from past events, the settlement of which is expected to result in an outflow of resources embodying economic benefits. Whether a past event results in a present obligation is usually clear. Thus, it is clear from the circumstances that the enterprise's sale of goods without warranty is an obligating event that resulted in a present obligation for the issuance of warranty costs. Recognition of provisions is appropriate when the enterprise has a legal or constructive present obligation resulting from a past event (called an obligating event), it is probable that an outflow of economic benefits will be necessary to settle the obligation, and its amount can be reliably estimated. Assuming that the amount of warranty costs can be reliably estimated (although they are uncertain in timing and amount compared with a trade payable, for example) and that the outflow is probable (in these circumstances, "more likely than not"), the manufacturer's contractual present obligation should result in recognition of a provision.
    Answer (A) is incorrect because the cash basis calls for recognizing warranty expense as labor and materials are expended to satisfy the warranty. Answer (C) is incorrect because the sales warranty method is appropriate for situations when a warranty is sold separately from the product. Answer (D) is incorrect because the method of accounting for warranties for tax purposes is the cash basis. The cash basis is unacceptable for accounting purposes because it violates the matching principle.

**49.** At its balance sheet date, an enterprise reliably estimates that the expected cost of compensated absences resulting from short-term disability will be 100,000. This unused entitlement arose from employee services rendered during the period and is accumulating. How should it be accounted for?

    A.  Only a disclosure should be made because recognition does not occur until the absences occur.

    B.  An expense should be recorded for 100,000.

    C.  An asset of 100,000 should be recognized.

    D.  A direct reduction to retained earnings of 100,000 should occur.

Answer (B) is correct. *(CIA, adapted)*
**REQUIRED:** The accounting for an entitlement to compensated absences for short-term disability.
**DISCUSSION:** Short-term employee benefits expected to be paid as a result of service rendered during the period ordinarily should be recognized as an expense and a liability (accrued expense). For short-term compensated absences, the timing of recognition depends on whether the benefits accumulate. If the benefits for compensated absences accumulate, the expected cost of short-term compensated absences is recognized when services are rendered that increase the employees' entitlement to future compensated absences. The obligation is recognized whether it is vesting (the employee is entitled to a cash payment for an unused entitlement upon leaving the enterprise) or not vesting. The amount should not be discounted. It equals the additional amount expected to be paid as a result of the unused accumulated entitlement at the balance sheet date. Hence, the enterprise should debit expense and credit liability for 100,000 because the entitlement accumulates and the employees have rendered services during the period that increase their future entitlement.
    Answer (A) is incorrect because recognition occurs at the time of the absences if the benefits are not accumulating. Answer (C) is incorrect because a liability rather than an asset is recognized. Answer (D) is incorrect because the expense is recognized in the income statement.

**50.** A company allows customers to redeem 20 coupons for a toy (cost 3.00). Estimates are that 40% of coupons distributed will result in redemption. Since beginning the promotion this year, 4 million coupons were distributed and 1 million coupons redeemed. The adjusting entry to accrue for unredeemed coupons at year-end is

A. Premium expense      90,000
    Provision
      for premiums                90,000

B. Sales                  90,000
    Provision
      for premiums                90,000

C. Premium expense    1,800,000
    Provision
      for premiums            1,800,000

D. Sales              1,800,000
    Provision
      for premiums            1,800,000

Answer (A) is correct. *(CIA, adapted)*
**REQUIRED:** The adjusting entry to accrue for unredeemed coupons at year-end.
**DISCUSSION:** An expense and a provision should be accrued for the coupons still outstanding that are expected to be redeemed. Of the 4 million coupons distributed, 40%, or 1.6 million, are estimated to be redeemable. Of those, 1 million have already been redeemed, and 600,000 more are expected to be redeemed. The promotion requires 20 coupons to receive one toy, so 30,000 (600,000 ÷ 20) more toys will be required. Each toy costs 3.00, creating a provision of 90,000 (30,000 × 3.00).
Answer (B) is incorrect because the debit should be to an expense. Answer (C) is incorrect because, although an expense should be accrued, the amount is incorrect. Answer (D) is incorrect because the debit should be to an expense, and the amount is incorrect.

**51.** The publisher of a popular magazine offers a special discounted price for a 3-year subscription. At the balance sheet date, the amount that has already been collected but pertains to future periods is best referred to as

A. Accrued subscriptions revenue (an asset account).

B. Deferred subscriptions revenue (a liability account).

C. Earned subscriptions revenue (a revenue account).

D. Precollected subscriptions receivable (a deferred asset account).

Answer (B) is correct. *(CIA, adapted)*
**REQUIRED:** The best description of revenue that has already been collected but pertains to future periods.
**DISCUSSION:** Income, which includes revenue and gains, is recognized in the income statement when an increase in future economic benefits related to an increase in an asset or a decrease in a liability can be reliably measured. Revenue is recognized (reported as revenue) in the period in which the recognition criteria are met; therefore, when it is received in advance, the amount applicable to future periods is deferred. This deferral reflects the uncertainty of the reliable measurement of the future economic benefits. The uncertainty arises because the enterprise still must satisfy an obligation to perform in the future before it is entitled to the future economic benefits. The amount received in advance is considered a liability because it represents a present obligation arising from a past event. Accordingly, deferred or unearned revenue is an amount that has been received but that has not met the recognition criteria for revenue.
Answer (A) is incorrect because an accrued revenue is revenue that has met the recognition criteria but has not been received. Answer (C) is incorrect because the revenue will be recognized in future periods when forthcoming issues of the magazine are published and distributed to the subscribers. Answer (D) is incorrect because there is no such thing as a precollected receivable. Precollected revenue is deferred revenue, which is an amount received that has not met the recognition criteria (classified as a liability). A subscription receivable (an asset) would arise from accrued revenue, which is revenue not yet received.

**52.** A cable television enterprise receives deposits from customers that are refunded when service is terminated. The average customer stays with the enterprise 8 years. How should these deposits be shown on the financial statements?

    A. Operating revenue.

    B. Other revenue.

    C. Share capital.

    D. Liability.

Answer (D) is correct. *(CIA, adapted)*
    **REQUIRED:** The reporting of deposits from customers of a cable television enterprise.
    **DISCUSSION:** Liabilities are present obligations arising from past events, the settlement of which is expected to result in an outflow of resources embodying economic benefits. Customers' deposits must be returned or credited to their accounts. The deposits should therefore be recorded as liabilities.
    Answer (A) is incorrect because deposits meet the definition of liabilities, not revenue. Revenue is income that arises in the ordinary activities of the enterprise. Income is an increase in economic benefits in the form of inflows or enhancements of assets or decreases of liabilities that result in an increase in equity (excluding transactions with owners). Answer (B) is incorrect because deposits meet the definition of liabilities, not revenue. Revenue is income that arises in the ordinary activities of the enterprise. Income is an increase in economic benefits in the form of inflows or enhancements of assets or decreases of liabilities that result in an increase in equity (excluding transactions with owners). Answer (C) is incorrect because deposits are liabilities, not equity items. The equity of an enterprise is the residual interest in the assets of an enterprise that remains after deducting its liabilities.

**53.** In performing an audit, you encounter an adjusting journal entry recorded at year-end that contains a debit to rental revenue and a credit to deferred rental revenue. The purpose of this journal entry is to record

    A. An accrued revenue.

    B. An unexpired expense.

    C. An expired expense.

    D. A liability.

Answer (D) is correct. *(CIA, adapted)*
    **REQUIRED:** The purpose of an adjusting entry debiting rental revenue and crediting deferred revenue rental.
    **DISCUSSION:** A deferred revenue is a revenue item that has been received but has not met the recognition criteria. The journal entry described in the question is an adjusting entry to transfer an amount from the revenue account to a liability (deferred revenue) account. The initial collection of cash in advance from the tenant was apparently recorded by a credit to revenue. An adjusting entry is therefore required at year-end to transfer any remaining amount that does not qualify for revenue recognition.
    Answer (A) is incorrect because an accrued revenue has met the recognition criteria but has not yet been received. The journal entry described indicates that collection has been made. Answer (B) is incorrect because the entry concerns a revenue rather than an expense transaction. Answer (C) is incorrect because the entry concerns a revenue rather than an expense transaction.

## 4.8 Provisions and Contingencies

**54.** Because of a defect discovered in its seat belts in December 2004, an automobile manufacturer believes it is probable that it will be required to recall its products. The final decision on the recall is expected to be made in March 2005. The cost of the recall is reliably estimated to be 2.5 million. How should this information be reported in the December 31, 2004 financial statements?

    A. As a loss of 2.5 million and a provision of 2.5 million.

    B. As an adjustment of the opening balance of retained earnings equal to 2.5 million.

    C. As an appropriation of retained earnings of 2.5 million.

    D. It should not be disclosed because it has not yet happened.

Answer (A) is correct. *(CIA, adapted)*
    **REQUIRED:** The reporting of a probable loss from a product recall.
    **DISCUSSION:** A provision is a liability of uncertain timing or amount. Recognition of provisions is appropriate when the enterprise has a legal or constructive present obligation resulting from a past event (called an obligating event), it is probable that an outflow of economic benefits will be necessary to settle the obligation, and its amount can be reliably estimated. Consequently, the company must recognize a loss and a liability for 2.5 million.
    Answer (B) is incorrect because such an adjustment is appropriate for fundamental errors and changes in accounting policies (under the benchmark treatments). Answer (C) is incorrect because an appropriation of retained earnings is permissible although not required, but the enterprise must still recognize a loss and a provision. Moreover, no part of the appropriation may be transferred to income, and no loss may be charged to an appropriation of retained earnings. Answer (D) is incorrect because, if the loss is probable and can be reliably estimated, it should be recognized by a charge to income.

**55.** An enterprise is subject to warranty claims. A reliable estimate is that between 1 million and 3 million will probably be paid out. No estimate of loss within this range is more likely than any other. The enterprise should

   A. Make no journal entry at this time.

   B. Disclose only a possible loss.

   C. Defer a provision of 1 million to 3 million depending on the applicable national accounting standards.

   D. Recognize a provision of 1 million to 3 million depending on the applicable national accounting standards.

Answer (D) is correct. *(CIA, adapted)*
   **REQUIRED:** The proper accounting for warranty claims.
   **DISCUSSION:** A provision is a liability of uncertain timing or amount. Recognition of provisions is appropriate when the enterprise has a legal or constructive present obligation resulting from a past event (called an obligating event), it is probable that an outflow of economic benefits will be necessary to settle the obligation, and its amount can be reliably estimated. Thus, a provision should be recognized. Moreover, the amount recognized should be the best estimate of the expenditure required to settle the obligation. However, the amount within the reliable estimate of the range of the obligation that will be recognized will vary from country to country.
   Answer (A) is incorrect because the criteria for recognition of a provision have been met, including a reliable estimate of the range of the obligation. Answer (B) is incorrect because the loss is probable. Answer (C) is incorrect because the loss is not deferred; it is accrued.

**56.** Which one of the following will usually be accounted for by recognizing a provision?

   A. Just prior to the balance sheet date, the board decided to close a division. No implementation steps have been taken.

   B. As of the balance sheet date, the board was aware that a new law would require the enterprise to fit smoke filters to its factories within the next year. No such filters have been fitted.

   C. A law requires an airline to overhaul its aircraft once every 3 years.

   D. Premiums offered to customers.

Answer (D) is correct. *(CIA, adapted)*
   **REQUIRED:** The item that is usually recognized as a provision.
   **DISCUSSION:** When premiums are offered to customers, for example, upon redemption of coupons, the enterprise can usually establish that it has a legal present obligation resulting from a past event and that an outflow of economic benefits is probable. Furthermore, if the enterprise has prior experience with such offers or information about the experience of similar enterprises, a reliable estimate of the obligation should be feasible. If no obligating event has occurred, the enterprise could avoid the future expenditure by its future actions.

**57.** Which of the following is not a factor, with respect to pending litigation, that must be considered in determining whether a provision should be recognized?

   A. The time period in which the underlying cause of action occurred.

   B. The probability of an unfavorable outcome.

   C. The ability to make a reliable estimate of the amount of loss.

   D. The number of parties involved in the litigation.

Answer (D) is correct. *(CIA, adapted)*
   **REQUIRED:** The item not a factor in determining whether a provision should be recognized.
   **DISCUSSION:** The number of parties involved in the litigation is irrelevant. For example, the same accounting treatment is applied whether a claim is brought by an individual or in a class action suit.
   Answer (A) is incorrect because the time period in which the obligating event occurred is relevant. If it arose after the date of the financial statements, a provision may not be recognized in those statements. Answer (B) is incorrect because a provision is not recognized unless it is probable that an outflow of resources embodying economic benefits will be required to settle a present obligation arising from a past event. Answer (C) is incorrect because a provision is not recognized unless it is probable that an outflow of resources embodying economic benefits will be required to settle a present obligation arising from a past event. Moreover, the amount of the obligation should be capable of reliable estimation.

**58.** An enterprise has been sued for 100 million for producing and selling an unsafe product. Attorneys for the enterprise cannot reliably predict the outcome of the litigation. In its financial statements, the enterprise should

A.  Make the following journal entry, and disclose the existence of the lawsuit in a footnote.

  Estimated loss
    from litigation          100,000,000

      Estimated provision
        for litigation loss              100,000,000

B.  Disclose the existence of the lawsuit in a note without making a journal entry.

C.  Neither make a journal entry nor disclose the lawsuits in a note because bad publicity will hurt the enterprise.

D.  Make the following journal entry, and disclose the existence of the lawsuit in a note.

  Cost of goods
    sold                    100,000,000

      Estimated provision
        for litigation loss              100,000,000

Answer (B) is correct.  *(CIA, adapted)*
   **REQUIRED:** The financial statement treatment of a loss from pending litigation.
   **DISCUSSION:** In the very rare case in which a reliable estimate of an obligation that otherwise qualifies for treatment as a provision cannot be determined, no liability is recognized. Instead, the existing liability is disclosed as a contingent liability (unless the possibility of any outflow in settlement is remote).
   Answer (A) is incorrect because a journal entry is made when the outflow in settlement is probable and can be reliably estimated. Answer (C) is incorrect because a disclosure must be made of a contingent liability. Answer (D) is incorrect because a journal entry is made when the outflow in settlement is probable and can be reliably estimated.

**59.** An enterprise is currently being sued by a customer. A reliable estimate can be made of the costs that would result from a ruling unfavorable to the enterprise, and the amount involved is material. The enterprise's managers, lawyers, and auditors agree that the likelihood of an unfavorable ruling is remote. This contingent liability

A.  Should be disclosed in a note.

B.  Should be disclosed as a parenthetical comment in the balance sheet.

C.  Need not be disclosed.

D.  Should be disclosed by an appropriation of retained earnings.

Answer (C) is correct.  *(Publisher)*
   **REQUIRED:** The proper treatment of a contingent liability that is reliably estimable but remote in probability.
   **DISCUSSION:** A contingent liability includes a present obligation for which an outflow of resources embodying economic benefits is not probable. A contingent liability is not recognized but is disclosed unless the possibility of the outflow is remote.

## 4.9 Bonds

**60.** In November of the current year, the vice-president of a local bank reviews the bank's mortgage portfolio prior to the December 31 year-end. The bank's largest client has mortgages on buildings in three cities. The client has incurred net losses for the past 3 years and is now experiencing serious cash flow problems. For the past 6 months, no payments have been made on any of the three mortgages. The vice-president reluctantly concludes that it is probable that the full amount of principal and interest will not be collected. What is the impact of this conclusion on the local bank's current year financial statements?

A. No accounting or disclosure of a possible loss in value is necessary.

B. Contingency note disclosure of a possible impairment is required.

C. The carrying amount of the mortgages should be reduced, with a charge directly to retained earnings.

D. The carrying amount of the mortgages should be reduced, with a charge to the income statement.

Answer (D) is correct. *(CIA, adapted)*
**REQUIRED:** The effect of determining that the full amount of principal and interest probably will not be collected.
**DISCUSSION:** A financial asset, such as a lender's mortgage receivable, is impaired if its carrying amount at the balance sheet date exceeds its estimated recoverable amount. If it is probable that all amounts due on such a held-to-maturity investment (a financial asset carried at amortized cost) cannot be collected, the loss should be included in net profit or loss. The loss equals the difference between the carrying amount and the present value of the expected future cash flows discounted at the original effective interest rate. The carrying amount of the asset should be reduced to its estimated recoverable amount directly or by crediting an allowance account.

**61.** If bonds are initially sold at a discount and the effective-interest method of amortization is used,

A. Interest expense in the earlier periods will be less than interest expense in the later periods.

B. Interest expense in the earlier periods will be greater than interest expense in the later periods.

C. Interest expense will equal the cash interest payment each period.

D. Interest expense will be less than the cash interest payment each period.

Answer (A) is correct. *(CIA, adapted)*
**REQUIRED:** The effect on interest expense if bonds are initially sold at a discount and the effective-interest method of amortization is used.
**DISCUSSION:** Interest expense equals the carrying amount of the liability at the beginning of the period times the effective interest rate. The carrying amount of the liability equals the face amount of the bond minus the discount. As the discount is amortized over the life of the bond, the carrying amount increases. Consequently, the interest expense increases over the term of the bond.
Answer (B) is incorrect because interest expense will increase over the term of the bonds. Answer (C) is incorrect because interest expense exceeds the cash interest payment when bonds are issued at a discount. The reason is that the effective rate is higher than the nominal rate. The excess of interest expense over the cash payment is the amount of discount amortized each period. Answer (D) is incorrect because interest expense exceeds the cash interest payment when bonds are issued at a discount. The reason is that the effective rate is higher than the nominal rate. The excess of interest expense over the cash payment is the amount of discount amortized each period.

**62.** An enterprise issues 10-year bonds with a face value of 1 million, dated January 1, 2004 and bearing interest at an annual rate of 12% payable semiannually on January 1 and July 1. The full interest amount will be paid each due date. The market rate of interest on bonds of similar risk and maturity, with the same schedule of interest payments, is also 12%. If the bonds are issued on February 1, 2004, the amount the issuing enterprise receives from the buyers of the bonds on that date is

A. 990,000

B. 1,000,000

C. 1,010,000

D. 1,020,000

Answer (C) is correct. *(CIA, adapted)*
**REQUIRED:** The amount received when bonds are issued subsequent to the date printed on the face of the bonds.
**DISCUSSION:** The amount the issuing enterprise receives on 2/1/04 is the face amount of the issue plus 1 month of accrued interest, or 1,010,000 {1,000,000 + [(1,000,000 × 12%) ÷ 12]}.
Answer (A) is incorrect because 990,000 is the result if 1 month of accrued interest is deducted from, rather than added to, the amount received. Answer (B) is incorrect because the purchasers must pay for the accrued interest from the last interest date to the issue date. They will receive 6 months' interest on July 1 despite holding the bonds for 5 months. Answer (D) is incorrect because 1,020,000 results from adding 2 months of accrued interest to the face amount.

**63.** If bonds payable with a carrying amount equal to par value are refunded by use of a call provision, the call premium of the refunded issue should be

A. Amortized over the remaining original life of the extinguished issue.

B. Amortized over the life of the new issue.

C. Recognized currently in net profit or loss as an extraordinary item.

D. Recognized currently in net profit or loss.

Answer (D) is correct. *(CIA, adapted)*
**REQUIRED:** The accounting treatment of the call premium of refunded bonds.
**DISCUSSION:** An enterprise should remove a financial liability from its balance sheet only when it is extinguished, for example, when the creditor is paid. The difference between the carrying amount and the amount paid should be included in net profit or loss for the period.
Answer (A) is incorrect because the excess of the reacquisition price over the net carrying amount of the old bonds is recognized in full in net profit or loss for the period. Answer (B) is incorrect because the excess of the reacquisition price over the net carrying amount of the old bonds is recognized in full in net profit or loss for the period. Answer (C) is incorrect because an extraordinary item is income or an expense arising from events or transactions that are clearly distinct from the ordinary activities of the enterprise and are not expected to recur frequently or regularly.

**64.** At December 31, 2003, an enterprise had the following obligations that were expected to be refinanced:

| | |
|---|---|
| 17% note payable | 140,000 |
| 15% note payable | 200,000 |

The 17% note payable was issued on October 1, 2002 and matures on July 1, 2004. The 15% note payable was issued on May 1, 2002 and matures on May 1, 2004. On February 1, 2004, the entire 140,000 balance of the 17% note payable was refinanced by issuance of a long-term debt instrument. On February 7, 2004, the enterprise entered into a noncancelable agreement with a lender to refinance the 15% note payable on a long-term basis. The financial statements were authorized to be issued on March 1, 2004. The total amount of obligations that may be properly excluded from current liabilities on the enterprise's December 31, 2003 balance sheet is

A. 0

B. 140,000

C. 200,000

D. 340,000

Answer (D) is correct. *(CIA, adapted)*
**REQUIRED:** The total amount of obligations that may be properly excluded from current liabilities.
**DISCUSSION:** Some noncurrent, interest-bearing liabilities due to be settled within 12 months should nevertheless continue to be classified as noncurrent if the original term exceeded 12 months, the enterprise intends to refinance on a long-term basis, and its intent is supported by an agreement to refinance or reschedule payments. This agreement must be consummated before the financial statements are authorized for issue. Thus, 340,000 (140,000 + 200,000) may be excluded from current liabilities.
Answer (A) is incorrect because 340,000 may be excluded from current liabilities. Answer (B) is incorrect because the 15% note is also excluded from current liabilities. Answer (C) is incorrect because the 17% note is also excluded from current liabilities.

**65.** An enterprise most likely may derecognize a financial liability if it

    A.  Transfers amounts to a trust to be used to repay the obligation.

    B.  Exchanges debt instruments with the lender with substantially similar terms.

    C.  Exchanges debt instruments with the lender with substantially different terms.

    D.  Transfers amounts in a transaction that meets the requirements of an in-substance defeasance.

Answer (C) is correct. *(Publisher)*
**REQUIRED:** The circumstances in which an enterprise may derecognize a financial liability.
**DISCUSSION:** Derecognition of a financial liability (or a part thereof) occurs only by means of extinguishment. This condition is satisfied only when the debtor pays the creditor or is legally released from primary responsibility either by the creditor or through the legal process. An extinguishment and derecognition of the old debt and recognition of new debt occurs when the borrower and lender exchange debt instruments with substantially different terms, that is, when the respective discounted cash flows differ by at least 10%.
Answer (A) is incorrect because payment to a third party such as a trust (also known as an in-substance defeasance) does not by itself extinguish the obligation absent a legal release. Answer (B) is incorrect because the terms should be substantially different. Answer (D) is incorrect because payment to a third party such as a trust (also known as an in-substance defeasance) does not by itself extinguish the obligation absent a legal release.

**66.** An enterprise has a 100,000 liability on the books. In 12 months, 110,000 will be due, including 10% interest. The enterprise negotiates settlement of the debt today by exchanging customer receivables with a carrying amount of 90,000. What is the journal entry today?

    A.

| | | |
|---|---|---|
| Liability | 110,000 | |
|   Receivables | | 99,000 |
|   Gain | | 11,000 |

    B.

| | | |
|---|---|---|
| Liability | 100,000 | |
|   Receivables | | 99,000 |
|   Gain | | 1,000 |

    C.

| | | |
|---|---|---|
| Liability | 110,000 | |
|   Receivables | | 90,000 |
|   Gain | | 20,000 |

    D.

| | | |
|---|---|---|
| Liability | 100,000 | |
|   Receivables | | 90,000 |
|   Gain | | 10,000 |

Answer (D) is correct. *(CIA, adapted)*
**REQUIRED:** The journal entry to record settlement of a liability by exchanging customer receivables.
**DISCUSSION:** An enterprise may derecognize a financial liability when it is extinguished. This condition is met when the debtor discharges the debt by paying the creditor, such as with cash, other financial assets (e.g., receivables), goods, or services. Consequently, the liability should be debited for its 100,000 balance. Receivables with a 90,000 balance are given up, so that account should be credited. The difference is a gain.
Answer (A) is incorrect because the liability and receivables should not be increased by the 10% interest rate. Answer (B) is incorrect because the receivables should not be increased by the 10% interest rate. Answer (C) is incorrect because the liability should not be increased by the 10% interest rate.

**67.** How will net profit or loss be affected by the amortization of a premium on bonds payable?

    A.  Interest expense is decreased, so net profit or loss is increased.

    B.  Interest expense is increased, so net profit or loss is decreased.

    C.  Interest income is increased, so net profit or loss is increased.

    D.  Interest income is decreased, so net profit or loss is decreased.

Answer (A) is correct. *(CIA, adapted)*
**REQUIRED:** The effect on net profit or loss of the amortization of a premium on bonds payable.
**DISCUSSION:** The entry is to debit interest expense, debit bond premium, and credit cash paid. Thus, the amortization of a premium on bonds payable reduces the interest expense, thereby increasing net profit or loss.
Answer (B) is incorrect because the amortization of a premium on bonds payable reduces interest expense. Answer (C) is incorrect because interest income is not affected by the amortization of a premium on bonds payable. Answer (D) is incorrect because interest income is not affected by the amortization of a premium on bonds payable.

**68.** What is the preferred method of handling unamortized discount, unamortized issue costs, and the costs of implementing a conversion of debt into common shares?

A. Expense them in the period bonds are converted.

B. Amortize them over the remaining life of the issue retired.

C. Amortize them over a period not to exceed 40 years.

D. Charge them to share premium in excess of the par value of the shares issued.

Answer (D) is correct. *(Publisher)*
**REQUIRED:** The preferred handling of unamortized discount, unamortized issue costs, and the costs of converting debt into common shares.
**DISCUSSION:** The conversion of debt into common shares is ordinarily based upon the carrying amount of the debt at the time of issuance. Because the carrying amount is based on all related accounts, the debit balances of unamortized bond discount, unamortized issue costs, and conversion costs should be considered reductions in the net carrying amount at the time of conversion. Consequently, these items should be reflected as reductions in the share premium in excess of par account.
Answer (A) is incorrect because this amount is not expensed. In effect, it reduces the amount at which the shares are issued. Answer (B) is incorrect because this amount is not expensed. In effect, it reduces the amount at which the shares are issued. Answer (C) is incorrect because this amount is not expensed. In effect, it reduces the amount at which the shares are issued.

**69.** On May 1, 2004, an enterprise issued, at 103 plus accrued interest, 500 of its 12%, 1,000 bonds. The bonds are dated January 1, 2004 and mature on January 1, 2009. Interest is payable semiannually on January 1 and July 1. The journal entry to record the issuance of the bonds and the receipt of the cash proceeds is

A. 
| Cash | 515,000 | |
| Interest payable | 20,000 | |
| Bonds payable | | 500,000 |
| Premium on bonds payable | | 35,000 |

B. 
| Cash | 525,000 | |
| Bonds payable | | 500,000 |
| Premium on bonds payable | | 15,000 |
| Interest payable | | 10,000 |

C. 
| Cash | 535,000 | |
| Bonds payable | | 500,000 |
| Premium on bonds payable | | 15,000 |
| Interest payable | | 20,000 |

D. 
| Cash | 535,000 | |
| Bonds payable | | 500,000 |
| Premium on bonds payable | | 35,000 |

Answer (C) is correct. *(CIA, adapted)*
**REQUIRED:** The journal entry to record the issuance of a bond at a premium plus accrued interest.
**DISCUSSION:** The face amount of the 500 bonds is equal to 500,000 (500 × 1,000). The cash proceeds excluding interest from the issuance of the bonds are 515,000 (103% × 500,000). The 15,000 premium is the difference between the cash issuance proceeds and the face amount of the bonds. Because the bonds were issued between interest payment dates, the issuer is also entitled to receive accrued interest for the 4 months between the prior interest date and the issuance date. The accrued interest is 20,000 [500 bonds × 1,000 face value × 12% stated rate × (4 ÷ 12)]. The issuing company will therefore receive 535,000 in cash (515,000 + 20,000). The resulting journal entry includes a 535,000 debit to cash, a 500,000 credit to bonds payable, a 15,000 credit to premium, and a 20,000 credit to either interest payable or interest expense.
Answer (A) is incorrect because the bond premium is 15,000 (500,000 × .03), and interest payable should be credited. Answer (B) is incorrect because interest payable should be 20,000 [500,000 × .12 × (4 ÷ 12)]. Answer (D) is incorrect because the premium on bonds payable should not include interest payable.

**70.** An enterprise received a 2-year, 190,000 note on January 1, 2002 in exchange for property it sold. According to the terms of the note, interest of 5% is payable annually on January 1, 2003 and January 1, 2004, when the face amount is also due. There was no established exchange price for the property. The prevailing rate of interest for a note of this type was 12% at the beginning of 2002 and 14% at the beginning of 2003. What interest rates should be used to calculate the amount of interest income from this transaction for the years ended December 31, 2002 and 2003, respectively?

A. 0% and 5%.

B. 5% and 5%.

C. 12% and 12%.

D. 12% and 14%.

Answer (C) is correct. *(CIA, adapted)*
**REQUIRED:** The interest rates used to calculate interest income for successive years if the prevailing rate changes.
**DISCUSSION:** When the nominal interest rate on a note is not equal to the prevailing market rate for this type of note, the face amount of the note is not equal to its fair value or present value. In this case, the present value of the note should be determined by discounting the 190,000 maturity value and the 9,500 annual interest payments using an appropriately imputed rate of interest. Given that 12% was the prevailing rate of interest for a note of that type at the issuance date, 12% should be used to determine both the fair value and the interest income during the life of the note, regardless of fluctuations in prevailing interest rates.

**71.** Debtor owes Bank on a 10-year, 15% note in the amount of 100,000, plus 30,000 accrued interest. Because of financial difficulty, Debtor has been unable to make annual interest payments for the past 2 years, and the note is due today. Accordingly, Bank legally agreed to restructure Debtor's debt as follows:

- The 30,000 of accrued interest was forgiven.
- Debtor was given 3 more years to pay off the debt at 8% interest. Payments are to be made annually at year-end. The present value of the payments using the prevailing rate for similar instruments of an issuer with a similar credit rating is 84,018.

At the date of the restructuring, Debtor properly records

    A. A loss of 30,000.

    B. A gain of 30,000.

    C. A gain of 45,982.

    D. No gain or loss because no extinguishment occurred.

Answer (C) is correct. *(Publisher)*
**REQUIRED:** The entry for the restructuring of a debt if accrued interest is forgiven, the interest rate is lowered, and the payment period is extended.
**DISCUSSION:** Derecognition of a financial liability (or a part thereof) occurs only by means of extinguishment. This condition is satisfied only when the debtor pays the creditor or is legally released from primary responsibility either by the creditor or through the legal process. An extinguishment and derecognition of the old debt and recognition of new debt occurs when the borrower and lender exchange debt instruments with substantially different terms, that is, when the respective discounted cash flows differ by at least 10%. A substantial modification of terms is also accounted for as an extinguishment. The difference between the carrying amount (including unamortized costs) of a liability (or part thereof) that has been extinguished or transferred and the amount paid is included in net profit or loss. This transaction qualifies as an extinguishment based on a substantial modification of terms because the discounted cash flow from the old debt (130,000 due immediately) and the new debt (given as 84,018) differ by at least 10%. Hence, the amount included by Debtor in net profit or loss at the date of the restructuring is a 45,982 gain (130,000 – 84,018), that is, the difference between the carrying amount extinguished and the amount paid (the present value of the new debt instrument determined by discounting the cash outflows at the prevailing rate for similar instruments of an issuer with a similar credit rating). The entry is to debit the extinguished liability for accrued interest and principal (130,000), debit discount on note payable (15,982), credit note payable (100,000), and credit gain (45,982).
Answer (A) is incorrect because 30,000 is the difference between the sum of the existing liabilities and the face amount of the note with modified terms. Moreover, a gain should be recognized. Answer (B) is incorrect because 30,000 is the difference between the sum of the existing liabilities and the face amount of the note with modified terms. Moreover, a gain should be recognized. Answer (D) is incorrect because the terms were substantially different. Thus, an extinguishment occurred.

## 4.10 Equity

**72.** During the year, an enterprise's balance sheet accounts increased by the following amounts:

| | |
|---|---|
| Assets | 180,000 |
| Liabilities | 50,000 |
| Common shares | 90,000 |
| Share premium | 15,000 |

Net profit for the year was 42,000. The only other change in retained earnings was for the declaration of cash dividends. The amount of dividends declared was

    A. 2,000

    B. 17,000

    C. 33,000

    D. 67,000

Answer (B) is correct. *(CIA, adapted)*
**REQUIRED:** The amount of dividends declared.
**DISCUSSION:** Assets equals liabilities plus equity. Given an increase of 180,000 in assets, the sum of liabilities and equity must also have increased by 180,000. Because liabilities, share capital, and share premium increased by 155,000 (50,000 + 90,000 + 15,000), retained earnings must have increased by 25,000 (180,000 – 155,000). Given net profit of 42,000, dividends declared must have been 17,000 (42,000 – 25,000).
Answer (A) is incorrect because 2,000 ignores the 15,000 increase in share premium. Answer (C) is incorrect because 33,000 equals the increase in assets minus the sum of the increases in share capital accounts and net profit. Answer (D) is incorrect because 67,000 equals net profit plus the increase in net assets other than from owner contributions.

**73.** At December 31, year 1, an enterprise had the following equity accounts:

| | |
|---|---:|
| Common shares, 10 par, 100,000 shares authorized, 40,000 shares issued and outstanding | 400,000 |
| Share premium from issuance of common shares | 640,000 |
| Retained earnings | 1,000,000 |
| | |
| Total equity | 2,040,000 |

Each of the 40,000 common shares outstanding was issued at a price of 26. On January 2, year 2, 2,000 shares were reacquired for 30 per share. The cost method is used in accounting for these treasury shares. Which of the following correctly describes the effect of the acquisition of the treasury shares?

A. Common shares is reduced by 20,000.

B. Share premium from issuance of common shares is reduced by 32,000.

C. The retained earnings account balance is reduced by 8,000.

D. Total equity is reduced by 60,000.

Answer (D) is correct. *(CIA, adapted)*
**REQUIRED:** The effect of the acquisition of the treasury shares under the cost method.
**DISCUSSION:** Using the cost method, the journal entry to record the acquisition of the treasury shares includes a debit to treasury shares for 60,000. The balance of the treasury shares account is classified as a contra equity item. Thus, the acquisition of the treasury shares reduces total equity by 60,000 (30 × 2,000 shares = 60,000).
Answer (A) is incorrect because the common shares account balance is not affected when treasury shares are acquired. Answer (B) is incorrect because share premium is not affected when treasury shares are acquired and accounted for by the cost method. Answer (C) is incorrect because retained earnings is not affected by treasury share acquisitions when the cost method is used.

**74.** At December 31, year 1, an enterprise has the following account balances:

| | |
|---|---:|
| Common shares (10 par, 50,000 shares issued) | 500,000 |
| 8% preferred shares (50 par, 10,000 shares issued) | 500,000 |
| Share premium on common shares | 640,000 |
| Share premium on preferred shares | 20,000 |
| Retained earnings | 600,000 |

The preferred shares are cumulative and nonparticipating, and has a call price of 55 per share. The journal entry to record the redemption of all preferred shares on January 2, year 2 pursuant to the call provision is

A.
| | | |
|---|---:|---:|
| Preferred shares | 500,000 | |
| Share premium: preferred | 20,000 | |
| Discount on preferred shares | 30,000 | |
|     Cash | | 550,000 |

B.
| | | |
|---|---:|---:|
| Preferred shares | 500,000 | |
| Share premium: preferred | 20,000 | |
| Loss on redemption of preferred shares | 30,000 | |
|     Cash | | 550,000 |

C.
| | | |
|---|---:|---:|
| Preferred shares | 500,000 | |
| Loss on redemption of preferred shares | 50,000 | |
| Retained earnings | 300,000 | |
|     Cash | | 550,000 |
|     Share premium: preferred | | 300,000 |

D.
| | | |
|---|---:|---:|
| Preferred shares | 500,000 | |
| Share premium: preferred | 20,000 | |
| Retained earnings | 30,000 | |
|     Cash | | 550,000 |

Answer (D) is correct. *(CIA, adapted)*
**REQUIRED:** The journal entry to record the redemption of preferred shares pursuant to the call provision.
**DISCUSSION:** The exercise of the call provision resulted in the redemption of the 10,000 preferred shares issued and outstanding at the call price of 550,000 (10,000 shares × 55 call price per share). To eliminate the carrying amount of the preferred shares and recognize the cash paid in this transaction, the required journal entry is to debit preferred shares for 500,000, debit share premium: preferred for 20,000, and credit cash for 550,000. The difference of 30,000 (550,000 cash – 520,000 carrying amount of the preferred shares) is charged to retained earnings. No loss is reported because an Interpretation of IAS 32 does not permit the recognition of a gain or loss on transactions involving an enterprise's own shares.
Answer (A) is incorrect because the 30,000 excess of cash paid over the carrying amount of the redeemed shares should be debited to retained earnings. Answer (B) is incorrect because the 30,000 excess of cash paid over the carrying amount of the redeemed shares should be debited to retained earnings. Answer (C) is incorrect because the premium on the preferred shares must be debited for only 20,000. Moreover, retained earnings must also be debited for the difference of 30,000.

**75.** Enterprise X effects self-insurance against loss from fire by appropriating an amount of retained earnings each year equal to the amount that would otherwise be paid out as fire insurance premiums. The procedure used by Enterprise X is

A. Prohibited for external reporting purposes.

B. Acceptable provided that fire losses are not charged against the appropriation.

C. Acceptable provided that fire losses are charged against the appropriation.

D. Acceptable if the amount is shown outside the equity section of the balance sheet.

Answer (B) is correct. *(Publisher)*
   **REQUIRED:** The true statement about an appropriation of retained earnings to disclose self-insurance against fire loss.
   **DISCUSSION:** Accrual of an expense prior to the occurrence of the event for which an enterprise is self-insured should not be permitted. This rule holds because the fair value of the property diminishes only if the event actually occurs. But an appropriation of retained earnings is acceptable to disclose the self-insurance policy if, when a fire loss occurs, the entry appropriating retained earnings is reversed, and the loss is charged against income of the period of loss and not against retained earnings.
   Answer (A) is incorrect because an appropriation of retained earnings for self-insurance is permissible. Answer (C) is incorrect because fire losses may never be charged against the appropriation of retained earnings. Answer (D) is incorrect because the procedure is acceptable only if the appropriation is shown within the equity section of the balance sheet.

**76.** Unlike a share split, a share dividend requires a formal journal entry in the financial accounting records because share

A. Dividends increase the relative carrying amount of an individual's share holding.

B. Splits increase the relative carrying amount of an individual's share holdings.

C. Dividends are payable on the date they are declared.

D. Dividends represent a transfer from retained earnings to share capital.

Answer (D) is correct. *(CIA, adapted)*
   **REQUIRED:** The reason a share dividend requires a formal journal entry and a share split does not.
   **DISCUSSION:** The purpose of a share dividend is to provide evidence to the shareholders of their interest in accumulated earnings without distribution of cash or other property. Share dividends are typically accounted for by a transfer from retained earnings at fair value.
   Answer (A) is incorrect because share dividends have no effect on total equity or on the carrying amount of an individual shareholder's investment. Answer (B) is incorrect because share splits have no effect on total equity or on the carrying amount of an individual shareholder's investment. Answer (C) is incorrect because dividends, whether of shares, cash, or property, are usually payable on a date different from the declaration date.

**77.** Enterprise UK has 6,000 shares of 5% cumulative, 100 par value preferred shares outstanding and 200,000 common shares outstanding. The board of directors last declared dividends for the year ended May 31, 2002, and there were no dividends in arrears. For the year ended May 31, 2004, UK had net profit of 1,750,000. The board of directors is declaring a dividend for common shareholders equivalent to 20% of net profit. The total amount of dividends to be paid by UK at May 31, 2004 is

A. 350,000

B. 380,000

C. 206,000

D. 410,000

Answer (D) is correct. *(CMA, adapted)*
   **REQUIRED:** The total amount of dividends to be paid given cumulative preferred shares.
   **DISCUSSION:** If an enterprise has cumulative preferred shares, all preferred dividends for the current and any unpaid prior years must be paid before any dividends can be paid on common shares. The total preferred dividends that must be paid equal 60,000 (2 years × 5% × 100 par × 6,000 shares), and the common dividend is 350,000 (1,750,000 × 20%), for a total of 410,000.
   Answer (A) is incorrect because 350,000 is the common shares dividend. Answer (B) is incorrect because 380,000 omits the 30,000 of cumulative dividends for 2002. Answer (C) is incorrect because 206,000 is based on a flat rate of 1 per share.

**78.** Early in its fiscal year, Starr purchased 1,000 shares of Pack common shares for 54,000. In the same transaction, Starr acquired 2,000 detachable share purchase warrants. Two of the warrants are required to purchase one additional Pack common share. The market price without the warrants was 49 per share. The market price of the warrants was 3.50 per warrant. Starr sold 50% of the warrants several weeks later. If the proceeds received by Starr equaled 4,000, it recognized a realized gain of

A.  3,000

B.  625

C.  500

D.  0

Answer (B) is correct. *(Publisher)*
**REQUIRED:** The gain on sale of detachable warrants.
**DISCUSSION:** The recipient of share purchase warrants should allocate the carrying amount of the shares owned between those shares and the rights based on their relative fair values. Thus, the amounts to be allocated to the common shares and warrants are 47,250 ({[(49 × 1,000) ÷ [(49 × 1,000) + (3.50 × 2,000)]} × 54,000) and 6,750 (54,000 − 47,250), respectively. The realized gain is therefore 625 [4,000 − (6,750 × 50%)].
Answer (A) is incorrect because 3,000 is the excess of the fair value of 2,000 rights over the sale price of 1,000 rights. Answer (C) is incorrect because 500 equals the excess of the sale price of 1,000 rights over their fair value. Answer (D) is incorrect because Starr should recognize a realized gain for the excess of the price over the carrying amount.

---

Questions 79 and 80 are based on the following information. An enterprise has issued 1,000 common shares with a par value of 10, and its credit balance in retained earnings is 5,000. Two proposals are under consideration. The first is a share split giving each shareholder two new shares for each share formerly held. The second is to declare and distribute a 10% share dividend.

---

**79.** The share split proposal will <List A> earnings per share by <List B> than will the share dividend proposal.

|   | List A | List B |
|---|--------|--------|
| A. | Increase | More |
| B. | Increase | Less |
| C. | Decrease | More |
| D. | Decrease | Less |

Answer (C) is correct. *(CIA, adapted)*
**REQUIRED:** The effect of a share split and a share dividend on earnings per share.
**DISCUSSION:** The share split will double the number of shares outstanding to 2,000. The 10% share dividend will increase the number of outstanding shares to 1,100. The higher number of shares in the split will result in a lower earnings per share than will result from the share dividend.

**80.** Under the share <List A>, the par value per outstanding share will <List B>.

|   | List A | List B |
|---|--------|--------|
| A. | Dividend | Increase |
| B. | Split | Increase |
| C. | Dividend | Decrease |
| D. | Split | Decrease |

Answer (D) is correct. *(CIA, adapted)*
**REQUIRED:** The effect of a share split and a share dividend on par value.
**DISCUSSION:** A share split results in a lower par value per share because the total number of shares increases but the total par value of outstanding share does not change.
Answer (A) is incorrect because par value per share does not change following a share dividend. Answer (B) is incorrect because par value per share decreases following a share split. Answer (C) is incorrect because par value per share does not change following a share dividend.

---

Use Gleim's *CIA Test Prep* for interactive testing with over 2,000 additional multiple-choice questions!

# STUDY UNIT FIVE
# FINANCIAL ACCOUNTING -- SPECIAL TOPICS

(23 pages of outline)

Study Unit 5 is the last of three study units pertaining to financial accounting. It addresses topics listed or suggested in the CSO that were not covered in the preceding study units. The first subunit applies to changes in accounting estimates, fundamental errors, and changes in accounting policies. The next two subunits concern pensions and leases, which are important sources of liabilities that may or may not be fully reflected in the balance sheet. The fourth subunit outlines the fundamentals of statement analysis, a topic that also relates to the study unit on finance. The next subunit concerns accounting for deferred income tax amounts. The final three subunits contain outlines of advanced accounting topics.

**NOTE:** In keeping with the way in which IASs present information, we have omitted most currency symbols. In some situations, this treatment may seem awkward for candidates accustomed to seeing items presented with monetary units indicated. Be prepared for exam questions that may or may not include monetary units.

## 5.1 ACCOUNTING CHANGES

1. A **change in accounting estimate** is a normal, recurring revision resulting from changes in circumstances, additional experience, new information, or subsequent events. It is neither a fundamental error nor an extraordinary item. The effect of a change in estimate is included in the determination of net profit or loss in the period of change (if the change affects that period only) or in the period of change and in future periods (if the change affects both the current and future periods). A change in accounting estimate should be reflected in the financial statements prospectively.

   a. Examples of estimates are uncollectible receivables, inventory obsolescence, service lives and residual values of depreciable assets, warranty costs, periods benefited by a deferred cost, and recoverable mineral reserves.

   b. If distinguishing between a change in estimate and a change in accounting policy is difficult, the change is accounted for as a change in estimate and properly disclosed.

   c. A change in an accounting estimate does not result in a change in its income statement classification.

2.    **Fundamental errors** are those "discovered in the current period that are of such significance that the financial statements of one or more prior periods can no longer be considered to have been reliable at the date of their issue" (IAS 8).

   a.    Typical errors are mistakes in mathematical calculations, in the application of accounting policies, or in factual interpretation. Other examples are fraud or simple oversight. Such errors are usually recognized in current-period net profit or loss.

      1)    However, in rare circumstances, errors may be of such magnitude that they rendered prior-period statements unreliable, for example, because of recognition of material work-in-progress and receivables related to fraudulent contracts.

      2)    A change in estimate is distinct from a fundamental error. An estimate is an amount expected to require revision, such as the gain or loss recognized after the outcome of a contingency that previously could not be reliably estimated.

   b.    According to the **benchmark treatment**, the correction of a fundamental error is recognized as an adjustment of the opening balance of retained earnings to the extent it affects prior periods.

      1)    Comparative information should be restated if practicable. Furthermore, national law may require the amendment of statements filed with regulators or approved by shareholders.

      2)    Thus, under the benchmark treatment, the amount of the correction of a fundamental error that pertains to a given prior period is included in net profit or loss for that period, provided that restated financial statements for the period are presented comparatively. The amount of the correction related to periods prior to those for which restated information is presented comparatively is an adjustment of the opening balance of retained earnings for the earliest period presented.

   c.    According to the **allowed alternative treatment**, the full amount of the correction required for a fundamental error is included in the current period's net profit or loss.

      1)    Comparative information for prior periods is not restated. However, if practicable, additional **pro forma information** should be prepared and disclosed in accordance with the benchmark treatment.

      2)    The allowed alternative treatment may be necessary in countries where the comparative information must agree with the previously issued financial statements.

3.    **Changes in Accounting Policies.** Accounting policies are "specific principles, bases, conventions, rules, and practices adopted by an enterprise in preparing and presenting financial statements" (IAS 8). To facilitate comparison of an enterprise's financial information over time, the same accounting policies ordinarily are followed from period to period.

   a.    A change in accounting policy is indicated only if the result will be a more appropriate, that is, a more reliable and relevant, presentation of events or transactions or if required by statute or by a standard-setting body.

      1)    A change in policy has not been made when a policy is chosen to account for events or transactions differing in substance from prior events or transactions or for events or transactions that have not previously occurred or that were not material.

       2) The adoption of a policy to carry property, plant, and equipment or intangible assets at revalued amounts is treated in accordance with the revaluation provisions of specifically applicable IASs rather than as a change in accounting policy.

       3) A change in accounting policy pursuant to a new IAS should be accounted for in accordance with its transition provisions.

  b. **Other Changes in Accounting Policies.** According to the benchmark treatment, a change in accounting policy is applied retrospectively unless any adjustment relating to prior periods is not reasonably determinable. The resulting adjustment is to the opening balance of retained earnings for the earliest period presented. If practicable, comparative information is restated.

       1) Retrospective application means that the policy is applied as if it had always been in force.

       2) If the adjustment to the opening balance of retained earnings is not reasonably determinable, application of the new policy is prospective.

  c. **Other Changes in Accounting Policies.** According to the **allowed alternative treatment**, retrospective treatment is required unless any adjustment relating to prior periods is not reasonably determinable.

       1) If retrospective treatment is not appropriate, the resulting adjustment is recognized in net profit or loss for the period. The amount recognized is the cumulative effect of the change.

       2) Comparative information for prior periods is not restated, but pro forma comparative information prepared in accordance with the benchmark treatment is presented if practicable.

       3) If the cumulative amount to be included in current net profit or loss is not reasonably determinable, the new policy should be applied prospectively.

4. **Error Analysis.** The analysis of accounting errors addresses such issues as whether an error affects prior-period financial statements, the timing of error detection, whether comparative financial statements are presented, and whether the error is counterbalancing.

  a. An error affecting prior-period statements may or may not affect net profit or loss. For example, misclassifying an item as a gain rather than a revenue does not affect income and is readily correctable. No adjustment is required.

  b. An error that affects prior-period net profit or loss is counterbalancing if it self-corrects over two periods. For example, understating ending inventory for one period (and the beginning inventory of the next period) understates the net profit or loss and retained earnings of the first period but overstates the net profit or loss and retained earnings of the next period by the same amount (assuming no tax changes). However, despite the self-correction, the financial statements remain misstated. They should be restated if presented comparatively in a later period.

       1) An example of a noncounterbalancing error is a misstatement of depreciation. Such an error does not self-correct over two periods. Thus, an adjustment will be necessary.

       2) In principle, a counterbalancing error requires no correcting entry if detection occurs two or more periods afterward (assuming no tax changes). Earlier detection necessitates a correcting entry.

5. Stop and review! You have completed the outline for this subunit. Study multiple-choice questions 1 through 10 beginning on page 239.

## 5.2 EMPLOYER ACCOUNTING FOR POSTEMPLOYMENT BENEFITS

1.   The applicable pronouncement is **IAS 19**, *Employee Benefits*. Examples of postemployment benefits are pensions and other retirement benefits, life insurance, and medical care. An arrangement to provide these benefits to employees is a postemployment benefit plan. Such a plan may be a defined contribution plan or a defined benefit plan.

   a.   Under a **defined contribution plan**, the enterprise's maximum legal or constructive obligation equals its agreed contributions to a fund (a separate entity). The benefits to be received by employees are determined by the contributions made (including any made by the employees) and by the investment returns thereon. Accordingly, actuarial risk and investment risk are borne by the employees.

   b.   Under a **defined benefit plan**, the enterprise is responsible for providing the agreed benefits and therefore bears **actuarial risk and investment risk**.

   c.   If a **multiemployer plan** is a defined benefit plan, the enterprise should use defined benefit plan accounting for its proportionate share of the defined benefit obligation, plan assets, and cost. If the information available does not suffice for this purpose, the employer should account for the plan as a defined contribution plan.

      1)   A **state plan** created legislatively and operated by a government or other body is accounted for as a multiemployer plan.

      2)   The employer may pay **insurance** premiums to fund the plan. In this case, the employer should account for the plan as a defined contribution plan. However, it should account for the plan as a defined benefit plan if it will have a legal or constructive obligation to pay benefits directly when they are due or to make additional contributions if the insurer does not pay all future benefits.

2.   **Defined Contribution Plan Accounting.** The employer recognizes an expense and a liability for the contribution payable in exchange for an employee's services performed during the period. The amount is determined after subtracting any contribution already made. However, if the contribution made exceeds the amount due, the excess is treated as a prepaid expense.

3.   **Defined Benefit Plan Accounting.** The employer must estimate the benefits attributable to the current and prior periods as a result of employee services rendered. Thus, it must make **actuarial assumptions** about such variables as employee turnover, mortality, the discount rate, future increases in compensation, the expected rate of return on plan assets, and increases in medical costs. Furthermore, the benefits must be discounted and determinations must be made of the fair value of plan assets, of total actuarial gains and losses and the amount to be recognized, of past service cost when a plan has been initiated or amended, and of any gain or loss after a curtailment or settlement.

   a.   The amount of the **defined benefit liability** recognized equals the present value of the defined benefit obligation at the balance sheet date, plus (minus) unrecognized actuarial gains (losses), minus unrecognized past service cost, minus the fair value of plan assets at the balance sheet date.

      1)   If this amount is negative, it is an **asset**. However, the maximum amount recognizable for such an asset is the sum of unrecognized actuarial losses, unrecognized past service cost, and the present value of future refunds from the plan or reductions in future contributions.

2)  The **defined benefit obligation** (DBO) consists of future amounts required to settle the obligation arising from services provided by employees in the current and prior periods. The **projected unit credit method** should be used to determine the present value of the DBO, current service cost, and past service cost.

a)  Each service period results in a unit of benefit, with each unit separately measured to determine the total obligation. Furthermore, the plan's benefit formula is used to attribute benefits to service periods. Nevertheless, if service in later years will result in materially greater benefits than in earlier years, benefits should be attributed on a straight-line basis until the date when additional service will no longer create an entitlement to material incremental benefits.

b)  The measurement of a postemployment benefit obligation includes estimates of future salary increases, the benefits defined in the plan, the benefits arising from any constructive obligation beyond the terms of the plan, and estimates of future changes in state benefits that affect the level of plan benefits.

c)  The possibility that nonvested projected benefits will not vest is a factor in the measurement of the DBO, but it does not affect the existence of the obligation.

b.  Income (subject to the maximum recognizable for a defined benefit asset) or expense is recognized for the sum of the following:

1)  **Current service cost** is the increase in the present value of the DBO arising from services rendered by employees in the current period.

2)  **Interest cost** is the increase in the present value of the DBO because settlement is one period closer.

3)  The **expected return on plan assets** is determined with regard to market expectations for returns on the fair value of plan assets held after allowing for actual contributions paid into, and actual benefits paid out of, the fund.

4)  **Actuarial gains and losses** recognized under the "corridor" approach. Actuarial gains and losses include the effects of changes in actuarial assumptions and adjustments for actual experience different from that previously assumed. Hence, the difference between the actual and expected return on plan assets is an actuarial gain or loss.

a)  Part of the actuarial gains and losses should be recognized as income or expense if the net cumulative unrecognized amount at the close of the prior period exceeds the "corridor" amount: the greater of 10% of the present value of the DBO at that date or 10% of the fair value of plan assets at that date.

i)  Thus, the difference between the actual and expected returns on plan assets for the current period is not included in the "corridor" amount and is not recognized as part of the minimum expense or income.

b)  The minimum to be recognized equals the amount outside of the "corridor" divided by the average expected remaining working life of plan participants. However, the enterprise may apply any systematic method that results in faster recognition.

5) **Past service cost** recognized. Past service cost is the increase in the present value of the DBO related to prior employee service that arises in the current period from the introduction of, or an amendment to, postemployment benefits.

   a) Past service cost is expensed on a straight-line basis over the average period until vesting. To the extent it is vested upon introduction of, or amendment to, a plan, past service cost is immediately recognized.

6) **Curtailment or settlement** effects. A curtailment arises from a reduction in covered employees or amendment of the plan to reduce benefits for future service. A settlement is a transaction that eliminates the DBO for part or all of plan benefits.

   a) When a curtailment or settlement occurs, the gain or loss recognized encompasses the change in the present value of the DBO, the change in the fair value of plan assets, and previously unrecognized related actuarial gains and losses and past service cost.

c. **Transitional liability**. Upon initial adoption of IAS 19, the transitional liability equals the present value of the DBO, minus the fair value of plan assets, minus any past service cost to be recognized in future periods.

   1) If this liability is greater than the liability that would have been recognized under the previous accounting policy, the enterprise must make an irrevocable choice regarding recognition of the excess as part of the defined benefit liability. The decision is between immediate recognition in full as a change in accounting policy or straight-line amortization of expense over a maximum of 5 years. If the latter choice is made, the enterprise

      a) Limits any asset to be recognized when the defined benefit liability is negative to the maximum amount.

      b) Limits recognition of actuarial gains (but not negative past service cost) under the "corridor" approach. The actuarial gain that otherwise would be recognized under that approach is limited to the excess of the net cumulative unrecognized actuarial gains over the unrecognized transitional liability.

      c) Includes the related part of the unrecognized transitional liability in the calculation of a settlement or curtailment gain or loss.

   2) If the transitional liability is less than the liability under the previous accounting policy, the decrease is immediately recognized as a change in accounting policy.

4. Stop and review! You have completed the outline for this subunit. Study multiple-choice questions 11 through 19 beginning on page 243.

## 5.3 LEASES

1. A **lease** is an agreement by which a lessor (owner) conveys the right to a lessee to use an asset for an agreed period in exchange for a payment or series of payments. The accounting for leases is based on the substance of the transaction. A lease may be, in effect, the financing of a purchase or a rental agreement.

2.  **Lessee Accounting for Finance Leases**.  A lease may be classified as either a finance lease or an operating lease by a lessee.  A **finance lease** transfers substantially all of the risks and rewards of ownership of the asset to the lessee.

    a.  A finance lease should be accounted for by the lessee as the acquisition of an asset and the incurrence of a liability.  In subsequent periods, the lessee should depreciate the asset and recognize finance (interest) expense on the liability.  Depreciation should be consistent with the accounting policy for owned assets.  Absent a reasonable certainty that the lessee will own the asset at the end of the lease term, it should be fully depreciated over the shorter of the useful life or the lease term.

3.  A lease is classified at its **inception**.  It is normally classified as a finance lease if, for example,

    a.  The lease provides for the **transfer of ownership** of the leased asset by the end of the lease term.

        1)  Leases of land and buildings are subject to the same rules as leases of other assets.  However, given that land ordinarily has an indefinite economic life, if ownership does not pass to the lessee at the end of the lease term, the lease is not a finance lease because substantially all of the risks and rewards of ownership will not be transferred.

    b.  The lease contains a **bargain purchase option**; i.e., the lessee has the option to purchase at a price expected to be sufficiently below the fair value of the exercise date that, at the lease's inception, exercise is reasonably certain.

    c.  The **lease term** is for the major part of the economic life of the leased asset.

    d.  The **present value of the minimum lease payments** is at least substantially all of the fair value of the leased asset at the inception of the lease.

    e.  The leased asset is such that it can be used only by the lessee without major modification.

4.  Other factors also may indicate classification as a finance lease:

    a.  Lessor losses from cancelation of the lease are borne by the lessee.
    b.  The lessee bears the risk of fluctuations in the fair value of the residual value.
    c.  The lessee may renew the lease at a rent substantially below the market rent.

5.  The lessee records a finance lease as an asset and a liability at the inception of the lease at the **fair value of the leased property** (not to exceed the present value of the minimum lease payments).

    a.  The **discount factor** used to calculate present value is the interest rate implicit in the lease (if practicable to determine).  The implicit rate is the discount rate that equates the fair value of the leased asset at the lease's inception with the sum of the present values of the minimum lease payments and the unguaranteed residual value.  The alternative is to use the lessee's incremental borrowing rate.

6.  The lessee's **minimum lease payments** include required payments (excluding contingent rent and costs for services and taxes to be paid by and reimbursed to the lessor) during the lease term and the amount of a bargain purchase option.

    a.  If no bargain purchase option exists, the minimum lease payments equal the sum of the minimum payments payable over the lease term and any amounts guaranteed by the lessee or by a party related to the lessee.

    b.  From the **lessor's perspective**, the minimum lease payments (absent a bargain purchase option) include the residual value guaranteed by the lessee, a party related to the lessee, or a financially capable third party unrelated to the lessor or lessee.

7.   A **periodic lease payment** has two components: the finance charge and the reduction of the outstanding liability. This charge should be allocated so that a constant periodic rate of interest is maintained on the diminishing liability balance. Under the effective-interest method, the appropriate interest rate is applied to the carrying amount of the lease liability at the beginning of the interest period to calculate finance expense.

   a.   The portion of the minimum lease payment greater than the finance expense reduces the balance sheet liability for the finance lease.

8.   **Lessor Accounting for Finance Leases**. Lessors also classify most leases as either an operating or a finance lease.

   a.   Under a finance lease, the lessor recognizes a net receivable equal to the **net investment** in the lease: **gross investment** (minimum lease payments from the lessor's perspective plus unguaranteed residual value) minus unearned finance income.

      1)   **Unearned finance income** equals the difference between the gross investment and its present value. Finance income is recognized so as to provide a constant periodic rate of return on the carrying amount of the net investment. Thus, lease payments (minus costs for services) are applied to reduce the principal and the unearned finance income.

      2)   The **initial direct costs** of entering into a finance lease, e.g., commissions and legal fees, may be recognized immediately or allocated over the lease term. One possibility is to recognize the expense as incurred while also recognizing as income in the same period an equal amount of the unearned finance income.

   b.   When a **manufacturer or dealer** lessor accounts for a finance lease, selling profit or loss should be recognized in income as if an outright sale had occurred. If a rate lower than the commercial rate is charged, the selling profit (sales revenue minus cost of sale) is limited to the amount that would have resulted from use of the commercial rate.

      1)   The initial direct costs are expensed at the lease's inception.

      2)   Sales revenue is the fair value of the asset or, if lower, the present value of the minimum lease payments based on a commercial interest rate.

      3)   The cost of sale equals the cost or carrying amount of the leased property minus the present value of the unguaranteed residual value.

   c.   The following are the basic lessor entries:

| Lessor not a Manufacturer/Dealer | | | Manufacturer/Dealer | | |
|---|---|---|---|---|---|
| Lease payments | | | Cost of sale | XXX | |
|   receivable | XXX | |   Asset | | XXX |
|     Asset | | XXX | | | |
| | | | Lease payments receivable | XXX | |
|     Unearned finance | | |     Sales revenue | | XXX |
|       income | | XXX |     Unearned finance income | | XXX |

9.   **Operating leases** do not meet the criteria for classification as finance leases. They do not transfer substantially all the risks and rewards of ownership.

   a.   Under an operating lease, the lessee records no liability except for rental expense accrued at the end of an accounting period. Thus, an operating lease is a form of off-balance-sheet financing. The lessor continues to recognize and depreciate an asset, and a manufacturer or dealer lessor recognizes no selling profit.

b. Rent is reported as expense or income by the lessee or lessor on a straight-line basis unless another systematic basis is representative of, respectively, the time pattern of the user's benefit or the time pattern in which the use benefit from the asset is reduced.

c. If initial direct costs are incurred for the purpose of obtaining revenues from an operating lease, the lessor may expense them immediately or amortize them over the lease term in proportion to rent income.

10. A **sale-leaseback** involves the sale by the owner and a lease of the asset back to the seller. In a sale-leaseback transaction, if the lease qualifies as a finance lease, any excess of the proceeds over the carrying amount is deferred and amortized by the seller-lessee over the lease term.

    a. If the sale-leaseback results in an operating lease, and the transaction is clearly at fair value, profit or loss is recognized immediately.

        1) If the sale price is below fair value, profit or loss is recognized immediately unless a loss is to be offset by future lease payments at less than market price. In that case, the loss is amortized proportionately to the lease payments over the asset's period of use.

        2) If the sale price exceeds fair value, the excess over fair value is amortized over the asset's period of use.

    b. If the sale-leaseback gives rise to an operating lease, and the fair value is below the carrying amount, a loss equal to the difference is recognized immediately.

11. Stop and review! You have completed the outline for this subunit. Study multiple-choice questions 20 through 29 beginning on page 246.

## 5.4 STATEMENT ANALYSIS

1. The essence of financial statement analysis is the calculation of financial ratios. These ratios establish relationships among financial statement accounts at a moment in time or for a given accounting period. Once calculated, the enterprise's ratios can be compared with its historical data and with its projections for the future. Moreover, ratios can also be evaluated by comparison with those for other enterprises or with industry averages. However, users of such information must be aware of the limitations of ratio analysis, for example, those arising from differences in the nature of the enterprises being compared, changes in accounting policies, and the effects of changing price levels. Ratios must also be evaluated in terms of broad economic and strategic factors and from the unique perspectives of particular users.

2. **Liquidity (solvency) ratios** measure the short-term viability of the business, i.e., its ability to continue in the short term by paying its obligations.

    a. **Current ratio**     $\dfrac{Current\ assets}{Current\ liabilities}$

        1) If the current ratio is less than 1.0, a transaction that results in equal increases (decreases) in the numerator and denominator increases (decreases) the ratio. However, if the current ratio is more than 1.0, equal increases (decreases) in the numerator and denominator decrease (increase) the ratio.

    b. **Acid test or quick ratio**     $\dfrac{Current\ assets\ -\ Inventory}{Current\ liabilities}$

        1) A more conservative computation limits the numerator to certain financial assets, such as those held for trading, net receivables, and cash equivalents.

    c.    **Defensive-interval ratio**     $\dfrac{Defensive\ assets}{Average\ daily\ operating\ costs}$

         1)    Defensive assets include cash, financial assets held for trading, and net short-term receivables.

    d.    **Working capital**     *Current assets – Current liabilities*

         1)    Working capital identifies the relatively liquid portion of the capital of the enterprise available for meeting obligations within the operating cycle.

3.    **Asset management ratios** measure the enterprise's ability to generate income.

    a.    **Inventory turnover**     $\dfrac{Cost\ of\ sales}{Average\ inventory}$

         1)    A high turnover implies that the enterprise does not hold excessive stocks of inventories that are unproductive (obsolete or not marketable) and lessen its profitability.

    b.    **Number of days of inventory** (inventory conversion period)    $\dfrac{365,\ 360,\ or\ 300}{Inventory\ turnover}$

         1)    The days in a year may be 365, 360 (a banker's year), or 300 (business days).

    c.    **Accounts receivable turnover**     $\dfrac{Net\ credit\ sales}{Average\ accounts\ receivable}$

    d.    **Number of days of receivables** (receivables collection period)

$$\dfrac{365,\ 360,\ or\ 300}{Accounts\ receivable\ turnover}$$

    e.    **Operating cycle**     *Days of inventory + Days of receivables*

         1)    An alternative, more accurate concept is the **cash conversion cycle**. It equals the inventory conversion period, plus the receivables collection period, minus the payables deferral period (average time between resource purchases and payment of cash for them).

    f.    **Total assets turnover**     $\dfrac{Net\ sales}{Average\ total\ assets}$

    g.    **Fixed assets turnover**     $\dfrac{Net\ sales}{Net\ fixed\ assets}$

4.    **Leverage ratios** measure the use of debt to finance assets and operations. Trading on the equity (leverage) is the financial strategy in which fixed-charge securities, such as debt or preferred shares, are used to finance assets with the hope that the return on the assets will be greater than the fixed charges.

    a.    **Debt-to-equity ratio**     $\dfrac{Total\ liabilities}{Total\ equity}$

    b.    **Debt ratio**     $\dfrac{Total\ liabilities}{Total\ assets}$

   c.   **Times-interest-earned ratio**

$$\frac{Net\ profit\ +\ Interest\ expense\ +\ Income\ tax\ expense}{Interest\ expense}$$

      1)   If net profit declines sufficiently, no income tax expense will be recognized.

   d.   **Fixed-charge coverage**

$$\frac{Net\ profit\ +\ Interest\ expense\ +\ Income\ tax\ expense\ +\ Lease\ obligations}{Interest\ expense\ +\ Lease\ obligations}$$

   e.   **Leverage factor (equity multiplier)**   $\dfrac{Average\ total\ assets}{Average\ common\ equity}$

5.   **Profitability ratios** measure net profit on a relative basis.

   a.   **Profit margin on sales**   $\dfrac{Net\ profit\ after\ interest\ and\ taxes}{Net\ sales}$

   b.   **Return on total assets**   $\dfrac{Net\ profit\ after\ interest\ and\ taxes}{Average\ total\ assets\ (carrying\ amount)}$

   c.   The **basic Du Pont equation** relates the return on average total assets, the total assets turnover, and the profit margin on sales.

$$\frac{Net\ profit\ after\ interest\ and\ taxes}{Average\ total\ assets} = \frac{Net\ sales}{Average\ total\ assets} \times \frac{Net\ profit\ after\ interest\ and\ taxes}{Net\ sales}$$

   d.   If the basic Du Pont equation is combined with the leverage factor, the result is the **return on common equity** (after adjustment for any preferred dividends).

$$\frac{Net\ profit\ after\ interest\ and\ taxes\ -\ Preferred\ dividends}{Average\ common\ equity}$$

      1)   The leverage factor and return on equity may also be calculated for total equity.

6.   **Growth ratios** measure the changes in the enterprise's economic status over a period of years. Enterprises compare their growth in sales, operating profit, net profit, EPS, and dividends per share with the results of competitors and the economy as a whole.

   a.   **Basic earnings per share (BEPS)**

$$\frac{Net\ profit\ attributable\ to\ ordinary\ shareholders}{Weighted-average\ outstanding\ ordinary\ shares}$$

      1)   In some cases, **diluted earnings per share (DEPS)** is also required.

          a)   The denominator is increased by the weighted-average number of ordinary shares that might be issued upon conversion of dilutive potential ordinary shares. Conversion is deemed to have occurred at the beginning of the period or the date of issue of the potential shares, if later.

b) The numerator is adjusted for the after-tax effects of hypothetically converting dilutive potential ordinary shares to ordinary shares. Thus, interest and dividends related to the potential shares are added back, and an adjustment is made for any other changes in income or expense that would result from conversion.

c) The exercise of dilutive options and other dilutive potential ordinary shares should be assumed. The assumed proceeds are deemed to be from the issue of shares at fair value. The difference between the shares issued and the number issued at fair value is regarded as an issue for no consideration. Thus, if the fair value (average price for the period) is greater than the option price, the number of ordinary shares deemed to be issued for no consideration is added to the EPS denominator. They have no effect on the numerator.

d) If the shares outstanding change as a result of a capitalization or bonus issue (sometimes called a stock dividend or share dividend) or a share split or reverse share split, the calculations of BEPS and DEPS for all periods presented are adjusted retrospectively.

e) Potential ordinary shares are dilutive only when their conversion decreases net profit per share from continuing ordinary operations.

b. **Cash flow per share**

$$\frac{Net\ cash\ provided\ by\ operations\ Preference\ dividends}{Weighted-average\ outstanding\ common\ shares}$$

c. **Dividend payout ratio for common shares**

$$\frac{Cash\ dividends\ to\ common\ shareholders}{Net\ profit-Preference\ dividends}$$

d. **Dividend yield**   $\dfrac{Cash\ dividends\ per\ common\ share}{Market\ price\ per\ common\ share}$

7. **Valuation ratios** reflect the basic principle that management's goal is to maximize shareholder value.

a. **Book value per common share**

$$\frac{Net\ assets\ available\ to\ common\ shareholders}{Shares\ outstanding}$$

1) Assets available to common shareholders are assets, minus liabilities, minus assets required to redeem preferred shareholders' shares.

b. **Price-earnings ratio**   $\dfrac{Market\ price\ per\ common\ share}{EPS}$

1) P-E ratios tend to be higher for growth companies.

8. **Limitations of Ratio Analysis**

a. Development of ratios for comparison with industry averages is more useful for enterprises that operate within a particular industry than for conglomerates.

b. Inflation misstates the balance sheet and income statement because of the effects on fixed assets, depreciation, inventory, long-term debt, and profitability.

    c.    Seasonal factors affect results. For example, inventory and receivables may vary widely, and year-end balances may not reflect the periodic averages.

    d.    An enterprise's management has an incentive to **window dress** financial statements.

    e.    Comparability of financial statement amounts and the ratios derived from them is impaired if different enterprises choose different accounting policies.

    f.    The ratios that are strong indicators of an enterprise's financial position may vary from one industry, enterprise, or division to another.

    g.    Ratios are constructed from accounting data subject to estimation.

    h.    Trends may be misinterpreted absent sufficient years of analysis.

    i.    Ratio analysis may be distorted by failing to use an average or weighted average.

    j.    Misleading conclusions may result if improper comparisons are selected.

    k.    Whether a certain level of a ratio is favorable depends on the underlying circumstances.

    l.    Different ratios may yield opposite conclusions about an enterprise's financial health. Thus, the net effects of a set of ratios should be analyzed.

    m.    Industry averages may include data from capital-intensive and labor-intensive enterprises and from enterprises with divergent policies about leverage.

    n.    Some data may be presented either before or after taxes.

    o.    Comparability among enterprises may be impaired if they have different fiscal years.

    p.    The geographical locations of enterprises may affect comparability because of differences in labor markets, price levels, regulation, taxation, etc.

    q.    Size differentials among enterprises affect comparability because of differences in access to and cost of capital, economies of scale, and width of markets.

9.    **Comparative analysis** includes horizontal (trend) analysis that compares analytical data over time and vertical analysis that makes comparisons among one year's data.

    a.    Comparing an enterprise's performance with respect to its industry may identify its strengths and weaknesses. Horizontal analysis of the industry may identify industrywide trends and practices.

    b.    **Common-size financial statements** compare enterprises of different sizes by expressing items as percentages of corresponding base-year figures. The base amount is assigned the value of 100%.

          1)    The **horizontal** form evaluates trends. The amounts for subsequent years are stated in percentages of a base-year amount.

          2)    **Vertical** common-size analysis presents figures for one year expressed as percentages of a base amount on the balance sheet (e.g., total assets) and on the income statement (e.g., sales).

10.    Stop and review! You have completed the outline for this subunit. Study multiple-choice questions 30 through 45 beginning on page 250.

# 5.5 INCOME TAXES

1.    **Objective**. The carrying amount of an asset or liability is expected to be recovered (consumed) or settled, respectively. Under **IAS 12**, *Income Taxes*, a deferred tax liability or asset ordinarily is recognized when future tax payments probably will differ as a result of such recovery or settlement from what they would have been if the recovery or settlement had no tax consequences.

    a.    The tax consequences of transactions and other events are accounted for in the same way as the transactions and other events. For example, if the transactions and other events are included in the income statement or directly in equity, the related tax effects are also included in the income statement or directly in equity.

2.  **Income taxes** are all domestic and foreign taxes on taxable profits. **Tax expense or tax income** for the period consists of current and deferred components.

    a.  **Current tax** is the income tax payable or recoverable with regard to taxable profit or tax loss.

        1)  **Taxable profit or tax loss** is calculated based on rules prescribed by the tax authorities.

    b.  A liability is recognized for the unpaid amount of current tax for current and prior periods. An asset is recognized to the extent the amount paid exceeds the amount due. An asset also is recognized for the benefit of a tax loss carryback that recovers current tax of a prior period.

    c.  A **deferred tax liability** is an amount of income taxes payable in the future with regard to a taxable temporary difference, and a **deferred tax asset** is an amount of income taxes recoverable in the future with regard to a deductible temporary difference or the carryforward of unused tax losses or credits.

        1)  The difference between the carrying amount of an asset or liability and its tax base is a **temporary difference (TD)**. A taxable (deductible) TD results in taxable (deductible) amounts in the future when the carrying amount of the asset or liability is recovered or settled.

        2)  The **tax base** is the amount attributed for tax purposes to an asset or liability. The tax base of an asset is the amount deductible against future taxable economic benefits when the asset's carrying amount is recovered. The tax base of a liability is the portion of the carrying amount that will not be deductible against future taxable economic benefits for tax purposes. The tax base of revenue received in advance (a liability) is the portion of the carrying amount taxable in the future.

3.  A deferred tax liability (DTL) is recognized for most taxable TDs. However, no DTL is recognized when it arises from **goodwill** if the amortization of the goodwill is not deductible for tax purposes. The reason is that the recognition of a DTL would increase goodwill. In a business combination that is an acquisition, goodwill equals the excess of the acquisition cost over the acquirer's interest in the fair value of the identifiable net assets of the acquiree.

    a.  A DTL also is not recognized if it results from the initial recognition of an asset or liability that is not part of a business combination and, at the date of the transaction, affects neither accounting profit (net profit or loss before subtracting tax expense) nor taxable profit or tax loss.

        1)  With exceptions for goodwill and negative goodwill, deferred tax items may arise in a business combination that is an acquisition.

        2)  Most deferred tax items arise when accounting profit and taxable profit or tax loss are both affected but in different periods.

        3)  In other cases, no DTL is recognized because the carrying amount of the asset would have to be adjusted, with a consequent loss of transparency.

4.  A deferred tax asset (DTA) is recognized for most deductible TDs and for the carryforward of unused tax losses and credits, but only to the extent it is probable that taxable profit will be available to permit the use of those amounts. However, no DTA is recognized when it arises from **negative goodwill** treated as deferred income. The reason is that the recognition of a DTA would increase negative goodwill. In a business combination that is an acquisition, negative goodwill equals the excess of the acquirer's interest in the fair value of the identifiable net assets of the acquiree over the acquisition cost.

    a.  A DTA also is not recognized in the circumstances described for DTLs.
    b.  An unrecognized DTA is reassessed at the balance sheet date.

5. **Measurement**. A **current tax liability or asset** for the current and prior periods is the amount to be paid to, or recovered from, the taxation authorities, based on tax laws and rates enacted or substantively enacted as of the balance sheet date.

    a. A **DTA or DTL** is measured at the rates expected to apply when it is realized or settled, based on tax laws and rates enacted or substantively enacted as of the balance sheet date. If different rates apply to different taxable profit levels, a DTA or DTL is measured based on the average rates expected to apply in the periods when the TDs are expected to reverse.

    b. The tax rate or tax base may vary with the manner of recovery or settlement. For example, one tax rate may apply if an asset is sold immediately and another may apply if it is to be recovered through continued use.

    c. Deferred tax items are not discounted.

    d. A DTA is reviewed at the balance sheet date to determine whether it is probable that sufficient taxable profit will be available to permit the benefit of the DTA to be used. Any resulting reduction in the DTA may subsequently be reversed to the extent the availability criterion is satisfied.

6. **Recognition**. Current tax and deferred tax are included in net profit or loss as income or expense. However, a tax that arises from a transaction or event recognized directly in equity is itself debited or credited directly to equity.

    a. The carrying amount of a deferred tax item may change even though the amount of the related TD has not changed, for example, because of a change in a tax law or rate, a reassessment of recoverability of a deferred tax asset, or a change in the expected manner of recovery.

7. **Presentation**. Tax assets and liabilities are presented separately in the balance sheet from other assets and liabilities, and deferred tax items are reported separately from current tax items. An enterprise that distinguishes between current and noncurrent items should not classify deferred tax items as current.

    a. Current tax items should be offset given a legally enforceable right to do so and an intent to settle on a net basis or to realize the asset and settle the liability at the same time.

    b. Deferred tax items should be offset given a legally enforceable right to do so, provided the amounts relate to taxes imposed by the same tax authority on either the same taxable entity or on different entities that intend either to settle current amounts on a net basis or to realize assets and settle liabilities simultaneously in each future period in which significant amounts are involved.

    c. Tax expense or tax income for profit or loss from ordinary activities is reported on the income statement.

8. Stop and review! You have completed the outline for this subunit. Study multiple-choice questions 46 through 54 beginning on page 255.

## 5.6 EXCHANGE RATES

1. **IAS 21**, *The Effects of Changes in Foreign Exchange Rates*, applies to foreign currency transactions and to translation of the statements of foreign operations included in the enterprise's statements.

    a. A **foreign currency** is any currency that is not the reporting currency.

    b. A **foreign operation** is a subsidiary, associate, joint venture, or branch whose activities are not in the reporting enterprise's country.

    c. A foreign operation is classified as a **foreign entity** if its activities are not integral to the reporting enterprise.

2.    The **initial recognition** of a **foreign currency transaction** is at the spot exchange rate at the transaction date (or at an approximation, such as an average, if rates do not vary materially).

   a.    At the balance sheet date, **monetary items** are reported at the **closing rate** (spot rate on the balance sheet date).

      1)    **Nonmonetary items measured at historical cost** are reported at the rate on the transaction date.

      2)    **Nonmonetary items measured at fair value** are reported at the rates when the fair values were measured.

   b.    An **exchange difference** arises when a given amount of a foreign currency is reported in the reporting currency at different exchange rates.

      1)    Exchange differences are ordinarily recognized as **income or expense** when they arise, that is, upon

         a)    Settlement of a monetary item or
         b)    Reporting of a monetary item at a closing rate different from the initial rate.

            i)    Thus, the exchange difference recorded in a period is based on the change in rates for that period.

      2)    An exchange difference with respect to a monetary item that is part of a **net investment in a foreign entity** (a share of its net assets) is recorded in **equity** until disposal of the investment.

         a)    Upon disposal of the net investment, the cumulative amounts are recorded as income or expense.

         b)    Such a monetary item is typically a long-term receivable or payable not likely to be settled in the foreseeable future.

         c)    The same treatment is given to an exchange difference on a foreign currency liability that is a **hedge** of a net investment in a foreign entity.

      3)    **Allowed alternative treatment.** An exchange difference is included in the **carrying amount of an asset** when

         a)    It results from severe devaluation of a currency.

         b)    Hedging is impracticable, for example, because exchange controls limit the availability of foreign currency.

         c)    The devaluation affects a liability that cannot be settled and that arose directly from a recent asset acquisition.

         d)    The ceiling on the adjusted carrying amount is the lower of replacement cost or the amount recoverable from the sale or use of the asset.

3.    **Translation**

   a.    If the **foreign operation is integral to the reporting enterprise**, its transactions are treated as if they had been executed by the reporting enterprise. Thus, the accounting rules for initial recognition of, and exchange differences arising from, foreign currency transactions apply.

   b.    If the foreign operation is a **foreign entity**, the reporting enterprise

      1)    Translates **all assets and liabilities** of the foreign entity at the closing rate.

      2)    Translates **all items of income and expense** of the foreign entity at the rates in effect when the transactions occurred.

         a)    An approximate rate, such as an average, is often used in practice.

b) If the foreign entity's reporting currency is that of a **hyperinflationary economy**, the closing rate is used.

    i) The foreign entity's financial statements must first be **restated** before being translated into the reporting currency. Under **IAS 29**, *Financial Reporting in Hyperinflationary Economics*, these statements should be stated in terms of the measuring unit current at the balance sheet date. This approach is necessary whether the statements are presented on the historical-cost or current-cost basis.

    3) Reports **exchange differences** in equity until the net investment in the foreign entity is disposed of.

4. Stop and review! You have completed the outline for this subunit. Study multiple-choice questions 55 and 56 beginning on page 258.

## 5.7 JOINT VENTURES

1. **IAS 31**, *Financial Reporting of Interests in Joint Ventures*, applies to reporting of joint venture assets, liabilities, income, and expenses by venturers and investors.

    a. A **joint venture** "is a contractual arrangement whereby two or more parties undertake an economic activity that is subject to joint control."

        1) A **venturer** is a party to the venture who has joint control.
        2) An **investor** is a party to the venture who lacks joint control.
        3) **Control** is power over the policies of an economic activity that permits the controlling party to obtain benefits.

2. **Jointly Controlled Operations**

    a. In this type of joint venture, the venturers operate separately without establishing an organization or financial structure distinct from themselves. An example is the production of an aircraft, with each venturer responsible for different aspects of the process.

    b. Accordingly, each venturer reports in its separate and consolidated financial statements

        1) The assets it controls.
        2) The liabilities and expenses it incurs.
        3) Its share of the joint venture's income.

3. **Jointly Controlled Assets**

    a. This kind of joint venture also does not involve establishing an organization or financial structure distinct from the venturers. However, the venturers may jointly control (and own) assets. An example is joint operation of an oil pipeline.

    b. In this case, each venturer reports in its separate and consolidated financial statements

        1) Its share of the jointly controlled assets classified by the nature of the assets.
        2) The liabilities it has incurred, including liabilities incurred jointly as part of the venture.
        3) Income from its share of the output of the venture and its share of the expenses of the venture.
        4) Expenses with respect to its interest in the venture, such as charges related to the financing of a share in the assets and costs of selling the venture's output.

4. **Jointly Controlled Entities**

    a.    The venturers establish a separate entity in which each has an interest and that operates in the same manner as other entities. For example, two venturers may transfer assets and liabilities in a given line of business to a jointly controlled entity.

    b.    **Benchmark treatment.** A venturer should adopt one of two formats for **proportional consolidation**. Thus, a venturer reports in its consolidated financial statements its share of the jointly controlled entity's assets, liabilities, income, and expenses.

        1)    These amounts may be combined with the other similar line items in the venturer's consolidated statements.

        2)    These amounts may be reported as separate line items.

        3)    Proportional consolidation is discontinued when the venturer's joint control ends.

    c.    **Allowed alternative treatment.** A venturer may apply the **equity method** of accounting for its interest in a jointly controlled entity.

        1)    Use of the equity method must end when the venturer no longer has significant influence.

    d.    When a jointly controlled entity becomes a **subsidiary** of the venturer, **consolidation** is required.

    e.    The pronouncement on **financial instruments** (IAS 39) applies to an interest in a jointly controlled entity.

        1)    Acquired and held solely for near-term disposal.

        2)    Operating under "severe long-term restrictions that significantly impair its ability to transfer funds to the venturer."

5. In a **transaction between a venturer and a joint venture**, accounting for gain or loss on a transfer of assets to the joint venture reflects the substance of the transaction. If ownership risks and rewards have been transferred, the gain or loss recognized excludes the amount attributable to the interest of the transferor.

    a.    The **full loss** is recognized when the transfer evidences reduction in the net realizable value of current assets or an impairment loss.

    b.    In a **purchase of assets** from a joint venture, the venturer does not record its share of the venture's profit or loss until the assets are sold to an independent party.

        1)    A loss is recognized immediately when it reflects a reduction in the net realizable value of current assets or an impairment loss.

6. An **investor** in a joint venture without joint control should report its interest in accordance with the pronouncement on financial instruments (**IAS 39**).

    a.    If the investor has **significant influence**, the pronouncement on investments in affiliates applies (IAS 28).

    b.    An investor that issues consolidated statements may also report the investment at **cost** in its separate statements.

7. An **operator** or manager of a joint venture that is paid fees records revenue. The joint venture records an expense.

8. Stop and review! You have completed the outline for this subunit. Study multiple-choice question 57 on page 259.

## 5.8 BUSINESS COMBINATIONS

1. According to **IAS 22**, *Business Combinations*,

   a. A **business combination** creates one economic entity from previously separate enterprises. The combination results when one enterprise

      1) Unites with another or
      2) Obtains control over the other's net assets and operations.

   b. In an **acquisition**, the **acquirer** gains control over the net assets and operations of the **acquired**. Control is obtained by transferring assets, issuing equity, or incurring liabilities. The **acquisition date** is when the acquirer effectively gains control.

   c. In a **uniting of interests**, the shareholders of the enterprises involved combine control over the whole of their net assets and operations. The result is mutual sharing of risks and rewards, with no enterprise serving as the acquirer.

   d. **Control** "is the power to govern the financial and operating policies of an enterprise so as to obtain benefits from its activities."

      1) An acquisition of more than 50% of voting rights is rebuttably presumed to confer control.

   e. A **parent** has at least one **subsidiary**, an enterprise controlled by the parent.

   f. A **minority interest** arises when part of the net results of operations and of the net assets of a subsidiary is not directly or indirectly owned by the parent.

2. An **acquisition** is accounted for by the **purchase method**.

   a. Beginning with the **acquisition date**, the acquirer includes the acquiree's

      1) Results of operations in the income statement and
      2) Liabilities in the balance sheet.

         a) Goodwill or negative goodwill resulting from the acquisition is also recognized.

   b. The purchase method involves accounting for the acquisition by recognizing the following elements of **cost**:

      1) Cash or cash equivalents paid
      2) Fair value of other consideration at the exchange date
      3) Direct costs other than the purchase price, e.g., professional fees and securities issuance costs.

   c. The acquiree's **identifiable assets and liabilities**, whether or not recognized by the acquiree, are recognized only if

      1) Their cost or fair value is reliably measurable.
      2) In the case of assets, the acquirer will receive future economic benefits.
      3) In the case of liabilities, the acquirer will have to surrender resources representing future economic benefits.

         a) Liabilities resulting from the acquirer's intentions or actions ordinarily are not recognized. Expected losses or costs resulting from the acquisition also are not recognized.

d.  **Exception**. At the acquisition date, the acquirer may recognize a **restructuring provision** (that was not a liability of the acquiree) for **plans** integral to the acquisition and related to the **acquiree's business**. The present obligation embodied in the provision must result directly from the acquisition.

1)  By the acquisition date, the acquirer must have defined the **main features of a plan** to reduce or end the acquiree's activities. The plan must relate to, and the provision must cover only the costs of,

    a)  Employee termination payments,
    b)  Facilities closure,
    c)  Elimination of product lines, or
    d)  Contract termination when the acquirer has communicated the intent to terminate to the other party by the acquisition date.

2)  The acquirer must have **announced** the main features of the plan by the acquisition date. Parties affected must, as a result, have a **valid expectation** of plan implementation.

3)  The acquirer must have developed a **detailed formal plan** by the earlier of

    a)  3 months after the acquisition date or
    b)  Approval of the annual financial statements.

4)  The acquirer's detailed formal plan must, at a minimum, state

    a)  The parts of the business and locations affected
    b)  The locations, functions, and number of employees receiving termination benefits
    c)  Expected expenditures
    d)  The timing of implementation

e.  **Allocation of acquisition cost.**

1)  **Benchmark treatment**. The identifiable assets and liabilities acquired are stated at the sum of

    a)  **Fair value** as of the date of exchange to the extent of the acquirer's interest, and
    b)  The percentage of the **carrying amount** of the acquiree's net identifiable assets that is attributable to the **minority interest**.

2)  **Allowed alternative treatment**. All of the identifiable assets and liabilities are stated at fair value.

    a)  The minority interest is allocated its percentage of the fair value of the net identifiable assets.

f.  **Goodwill** is an asset measured initially as the excess of acquisition cost over the acquirer's interest in the fair value of the net identifiable assets at the exchange date.

1)  Goodwill is **amortized** systematically over its useful life (rebuttably presumed to be a period of no more than 20 years).

    a)  The **straight-line method** is used unless another method more appropriately reflects the pattern of consumption of the economic benefits.
    b)  Periodic amortization is **expensed**.
    c)  The amortization period and method are reviewed at least at year-end. Changes are treated as changes in estimates.

2) The acquirer should apply the principles stated in **IAS 36**, *Impairment of Assets*, to goodwill.

    a) Under IAS 36, the **recoverable amount** of an asset is the higher of the net selling price or the **value in use** (present value of estimated cash flows from the use and disposal of the asset). In general, impairment loss expensed equals the excess of the recoverable amount over the carrying amount.

    b) **Impairment loss of a cash-generating unit.** Because goodwill does not produce cash flows by itself, the recoverable amount is calculated for the cash-generating unit to which the goodwill relates. Any impairment loss is allocated first to reduce any goodwill allocated to the unit (but not below zero) and then to the other assets on a pro rata basis.

        i) **Bottom-up test.** The enterprise determines whether goodwill can be **reasonably and consistently allocated** to the unit. If so, it compares the unit's carrying amount (including goodwill) with the unit's recoverable amount.

        ii) **Top-down test.** If no goodwill allocation to the unit under review is possible under the bottom-up test, the enterprise identifies the smallest cash-generating unit (containing the unit reviewed) to which goodwill can be reasonably and consistently allocated. The enterprise then compares the larger unit's carrying amount (including goodwill) with that unit's recoverable amount.

        iii) If goodwill cannot be allocated reasonably and consistently using the bottom-up test, **both tests** are applied. Thus, any impairment loss for the cash-generating unit reviewed (the smaller unit) will be recognized even though no goodwill is allocated.

    c) At least at each year-end, the enterprise must estimate the recoverable amount of goodwill with an **amortization period greater than 20 years from initial recognition**. Accordingly, this test is made even in the absence of any indication of impairment.

g. **Negative goodwill** is presented as a deduction from assets. It is the excess of the acquirer's interest in the fair value of the net identifiable assets acquired over the cost.

    1) Negative goodwill may relate to **expected future losses and expenses** that are identified in the acquirer's plan and are reliably measurable but were not identifiable liabilities at the acquisition date. To that extent, it should be recognized as income when those losses and expenses are recognized. Otherwise, negative goodwill

        a) Not in excess of the fair value of the **identifiable nonmonetary assets** acquired is systematically recognized as income over the weighted-average useful like of the identifiable acquired depreciable or amortizable assets.

        b) In excess of such fair value is recognized immediately as income.

h. **Purchase consideration contingent** on future events may be an adjustment to the cost of the purchase at the acquisition date.

1) For example, the future event might be attainment of an earnings target or a securities price. The cost is adjusted if

   a) The adjustment is probable, and
   b) The amount is reliably measurable.

2) If estimate must be revised, the acquisition cost (and any goodwill or negative goodwill) is adjusted.

i. A **subsequent change in the acquisition cost** is indicated when a relevant contingency is resolved.

1) The acquisition cost (and any goodwill or negative goodwill) is adjusted when

   a) Payment of the amount of the purchase consideration is probable, and
   b) The amount can be reliably estimated.

2) An acquirer may have agreed that, if the market price of securities issued as part of the consideration falls below a specified level, additional securities will be issued to make up the difference.

   a) Hence, the acquisition cost remains the same, and no adjustment to goodwill or negative goodwill is required.
   b) The issuance of additional securities reduces the premium or increases the discount on the original issuance.

j. **Subsequent recognition of identifiable assets and liabilities** is appropriate when they satisfy the recognition criteria after the acquisition date.

1) **Subsequent changes in the carrying amounts of identifiable assets and liabilities** are made when additional relevant evidence about their fair values is obtained.

2) **Goodwill or negative goodwill** may be adjusted in either of these circumstances (but not above its recoverable amount).

   a) This adjustment ordinarily may be made only during the first annual accounting period after the acquisition date.

      i) After this period ends, any such adjustment is recognized as income or expense.

3) A **restructuring provision** for plans related to the acquirer's business may have been recognized at the acquisition date.

   a) **Reversal** is appropriate only if

      i) The outflow of economic benefits is not probable or
      ii) The detailed plans is not carried out within the time limit or in the way described.

   b) The reversal requires an adjustment to **goodwill or negative goodwill** (and minority interests), not a recognition of income or expense.

      i) Adjusted goodwill is amortized prospectively.
      ii) Adjusted negative goodwill is accounted for using the principles that apply when the negative goodwill does not relate to identifiable expected losses and expenses.

3. A **uniting of interests** is accounted for by the **pooling-of-interests method**.

   a. The **financial statements** of the combining enterprises issued for the period of the combination should be reported as if the pooling had occurred at the beginning of the earliest period presented.

      1) The statements of an enterprise do not reflect a pooling occurring after the date of the most recent balance sheet presented.

   b. The combined entity applies one set of **accounting principles**. Accordingly, the carrying amounts of the combined assets, liabilities, and equity are adjusted only as necessary to conform the accounting policies and apply them to the periods presented.

      1) A pooling does not create goodwill or negative goodwill.
      2) The effects of interenterprise transactions are eliminated.
      3) The sum of **share capital** issued and any additional consideration may differ from the amount recorded for share capital acquired.

         a) This difference is adjusted through the equity accounts.

   c. The **expenditures to effect a pooling** are expensed when incurred. They include registration fees, consultants' fees, cost of combining operations, etc.

4. Stop and review! You have completed the outline for this subunit. Study multiple-choice questions 58 through 60 beginning on page 259.

## QUESTIONS

### 5.1 Accounting Changes

**1.** Changes in accounting estimates are viewed as

A. Extraordinary items.

B. Errors in reported amounts in prior periods.

C. Catch-up adjustments related to amounts reported in prior periods.

D. Normal recurring revisions.

Answer (D) is correct. *(CIA, adapted)*
   **REQUIRED:** The nature of changes in accounting estimates.
   **DISCUSSION:** A change in accounting estimate is a normal, recurring revision resulting from changes in circumstances, additional experience, new information, or subsequent events. It is neither a fundamental error nor an extraordinary item. The effect of a change in estimate is included in the determination of net profit or loss in the period of change, if the change affects that period only, or in the period of change and in future periods, if the change affects both the current and future periods. In other words, a change in accounting estimate should be reflected in the financial statements prospectively.
   Answer (A) is incorrect because extraordinary items are clearly distinct from ordinary activities and not expected to recur frequently or regularly. Changes in accounting estimates are normal and recurring. Answer (B) is incorrect because changes in accounting estimates are not errors. They are responses to new information, subsequent events, additional experience, or changes in circumstances. Answer (C) is incorrect because catch-up adjustments to prior reported amounts are retroactive. Changes in accounting estimates are accounted for prospectively.

**2.** The following financial statement notes are extracts from the audited financial statements of public enterprises. Which note describes a change in accounting estimate?

A. The enterprise changed its amortization of capital assets based on a reassessment of the useful lives of the assets. Accordingly, the enterprise changed its rate of amortization from 5% and 6% to 8% and 10%, for machinery and equipment.

B. Prior to 2001, plant and equipment (other than customer service replacement parts) were depreciated using the diminishing-balance method. Plant and equipment are now depreciated on a straight-line basis.

C. During the year, the enterprise changed its method of accounting for noninterest-bearing, nonrecourse loans due from employees, pursuant to a change in an International Accounting Standard.

D. Effective January 1, 2001, the enterprise changed to the LIFO method of inventory valuation. Prior to 2001, the FIFO method was used.

Answer (A) is correct. *(CIA, adapted)*
**REQUIRED:** The note describing a change in accounting estimate.
**DISCUSSION:** Accounting estimates, e.g., service lives, residual values, warranty costs, uncollectible accounts, and inventory obsolescence, are a necessary part of preparing financial statements. However, they inevitably change as new events occur and as additional experience and information are obtained. When altered conditions require a change in estimate, it is accounted for prospectively. Thus, a change in the estimate of the service lives of depreciable assets is a change in accounting estimate.
Answer (B) is incorrect because a change from diminishing-balance depreciation to straight-line depreciation is a change in accounting policy. Answer (C) is incorrect because changing an accounting method due to a change in an IAS is a change in accounting policy. Answer (D) is incorrect because a change from FIFO to LIFO inventory valuation is a change in accounting policy.

**3.** On January 1, 2000, an enterprise purchased a machine for 10,000. The estimated useful life was 10 years, with no residual value. The enterprise depreciates its property, plant, and equipment using the straight-line method. On January 1, 2004, it was estimated that the machine had a remaining useful life of 3 years. Compute the enterprise's 2004 depreciation expense for the machine.

A. 1,000

B. 2,000

C. 3,000

D. 6,000

Answer (B) is correct. *(CIA, adapted)*
**REQUIRED:** The depreciation expense.
**DISCUSSION:** The machine's net carrying amount at January 1, 2004 is 6,000 (10,000 cost – 4,000 accumulated depreciation for 4 years). A change in accounting estimate is applied prospectively. Thus, depreciation expense is 2,000 per year for the next 3 years.
Answer (A) is incorrect because 1,000 assumes no change in estimate. Answer (C) is incorrect because 3,000 assumes a 2-year remaining useful life. Answer (D) is incorrect because 6,000 is the carrying amount at January 1, 2004.

**4.** When financial statements are being prepared, which of the following items requires that accountants estimate the effects of future conditions and events?

A. The purchase price for an acquired building.

B. The price of a marketable security.

C. The amount of recoverable mineral reserves.

D. The physical quantity of inventory.

Answer (C) is correct. *(CIA, adapted)*
**REQUIRED:** The item requiring that accountants estimate the effects of future conditions and events.
**DISCUSSION:** Changes in estimates used in accounting are necessary consequences of periodic presentations of financial statements. Preparing financial statements requires estimating the effects of future events. Examples of items for which estimates are necessary are uncollectible receivables, inventory obsolescence, service lives and residual values of depreciable assets, warranty costs, periods benefited by a deferred cost, and recoverable mineral reserves.
Answer (A) is incorrect because the purchase price for an acquired building can be ascertained with certainty. No estimate is required. Answer (B) is incorrect because the price of a marketable security can be calculated with certainty. No estimate is required. Answer (D) is incorrect because the physical quantity of inventory as of the balance sheet date can be measured. Although some estimation of the correct amount may be required, the estimates will not depend on future conditions and events but on current conditions and measurement methods.

**5.** In the prior accounting period, an enterprise incorrectly expensed a newly purchased piece of equipment rather than establishing an asset balance and beginning to depreciate it over the estimated useful life of the item. To correct this fundamental error in the single-period financial statements of the current period, the enterprise records which entry if it uses the benchmark treatment?

  A.  Debit equipment
     Credit retained earnings
     Credit accumulated depreciation – equipment

  B.  Debit retained earnings
     Debit accumulated depreciation – equipment
     Credit equipment

  C.  Debit equipment
     Debit retained earnings
     Credit accumulated depreciation – equipment

  D.  Debit equipment
     Debit accumulated depreciation – equipment
     Credit equipment

Answer (A) is correct. *(CIA, adapted)*
  **REQUIRED:** The entry to correct a fundamental error.
  **DISCUSSION:** The benchmark treatment of fundamental errors requires retrospective treatment. To correct the fundamental error, the enterprise must debit equipment for its cost and credit accumulated depreciation for the depreciation expense appropriate for the first year of the estimated useful life. Retained earnings must be credited because the error understated net profit or overstated net loss in the prior period.
  Answer (B) is incorrect because this entry is the reverse of the correct entry. Answer (C) is incorrect because retained earnings should be credited. Answer (D) is incorrect because accumulated depreciation and retained earnings should be credited.

**6.** A retrospective change in an accounting policy in the current period should be accounted for in comparative reports by

  A.  An adjustment directly to retained earnings and restatement of prior years' statements.

  B.  A line item on the current income statement for the cumulative effect of the change.

  C.  Presentation of pro forma comparative information.

  D.  Note disclosure only in the current period.

Answer (A) is correct. *(CIA, adapted)*
  **REQUIRED:** The treatment of a retrospective change in an accounting policy in comparative reports.
  **DISCUSSION:** According to the benchmark treatment, a change in accounting policy is applied retrospectively unless any adjustment relating to prior periods is not reasonably determinable. The resulting adjustment is to the opening balance of retained earnings for the earliest period presented. If practicable, comparative information is restated.
  Answer (B) is incorrect because reporting the cumulative effect is the allowed alternative treatment for a change in an accounting policy. Answer (C) is incorrect because this answer describes one of the requirements under the allowed alternative treatment for a change in an accounting policy. Answer (D) is incorrect because a change in an accounting policy qualifying for retrospective application requires an adjustment to retained earnings.

**7.** An accounting change requiring retrospective treatment is a change in

  A.  The residual value of equipment.

  B.  Depreciation methods from straight-line to diminishing-balance.

  C.  An accounting policy inseparable from a change in an accounting estimate.

  D.  A provision for warranty costs.

Answer (B) is correct. *(CMA, adapted)*
  **REQUIRED:** The accounting change requiring retrospective treatment.
  **DISCUSSION:** A change in depreciation methods is reported as a change in accounting policy. According to the benchmark treatment, a change in accounting policy is applied retrospectively unless any adjustment relating to prior periods is not reasonably determinable. The resulting adjustment is to the opening balance of retained earnings for the earliest period presented. If practicable, comparative information is restated.
  Answer (A) is incorrect because the residual value of equipment is a change in estimate that is accounted for on a prospective basis (in the future). Answer (C) is incorrect because, if distinguishing between a change in estimate and a change in accounting policy is difficult, the change is accounted for as a change in estimate and properly disclosed. Answer (D) is incorrect because a provision for warranty costs is a change in estimate that is accounted for on a prospective basis (in the future).

**8.** If ending inventory is underestimated due to an error in the physical count of items on hand, the cost of goods sold for the period will be <List A> and net earnings will be <List B>.

|     | List A | List B |
| --- | --- | --- |
| A. | Underestimated | Underestimated |
| B. | Underestimated | Overestimated |
| C. | Overestimated | Underestimated |
| D. | Overestimated | Overestimated |

Answer (C) is correct. *(CIA, adapted)*
**REQUIRED:** The effect of underestimating ending inventory.
**DISCUSSION:** Cost of goods sold equals beginning inventory, plus purchases, minus ending inventory. If ending inventory is underestimated, cost of goods sold will be overestimated for the period. If cost of goods sold is overestimated, the net earnings for the period will be underestimated.
Answer (A) is incorrect because cost of goods sold will be overestimated. Answer (B) is incorrect because cost of goods sold will be overestimated and net earnings will be underestimated. Answer (D) is incorrect because net earnings will be underestimated.

**9.** The failure to record an accrued expense at year-end will result in which of the following overstatement errors in the financial statements prepared at that date?

|     | Net Profit | Working Capital | Cash |
| --- | --- | --- | --- |
| A. | No | No | Yes |
| B. | No | Yes | No |
| C. | Yes | No | No |
| D. | Yes | Yes | Yes |

Answer (D) is correct. *(CIA, adapted)*
**REQUIRED:** The overstatement errors resulting from the failure to record an accrued expense at year-end.
**DISCUSSION:** An accrued expense is an expense that has been incurred but not paid. The appropriate adjusting entry to record an accrued expense will increase an expense account and increase a liability account. The failure to record an accrued expense will result in an understatement of expenses leading to an overstatement of net profit. The failure to record the increase in a liability account will result in an understatement of current liabilities leading to an overstatement of working capital. There will be no effect on cash.
Answer (A) is incorrect because the failure to record an accrued expense will result in an overstatement of net profit and an overstatement of working capital, and will have no effect on cash. Answer (B) is incorrect because the failure to record an accrued expense will result in an overstatement of net profit. Answer (C) is incorrect because the failure to record an accrued expense will result in an overstatement of working capital.

**10.** Which of the following errors is not self-correcting over two accounting periods?

A. Failure to record accrued wages.

B. Failure to record depreciation.

C. Overstatement of inventory.

D. Failure to record prepaid expenses.

Answer (B) is correct. *(CIA, adapted)*
**REQUIRED:** The error not self-correcting over two accounting periods.
**DISCUSSION:** A failure to record depreciation must be corrected because the effects of the error do not automatically reverse in future periods. Expenses are understated in the year of the error, but no corresponding overstatement of expenses occurs in later years.
Answer (A) is incorrect because understatement of accrued wages is a self-correcting error. Future wage expense will be overstated, future cost of goods sold will be overstated, and future expenses will be understated, respectively. Answer (C) is incorrect because overstatement of inventory and the consequent understatement of cost of goods sold is a self-correcting error. Future wage expense will be overstated, future cost of goods sold will be overstated, and future expenses will be understated, respectively. Answer (D) is incorrect because understatement of prepaid expenses (overstatement of expenses) is a self-correcting error. Future wage expense will be overstated, future cost of goods sold will be overstated, and future expenses will be understated, respectively.

## 5.2 Employer Accounting for Postemployment Benefits

**11.** Which of the following statements is true for a defined contribution postemployment benefit plan?

   A. The employer is required to contribute a certain amount each period based on the plan's formula.

   B. The employer bears the risk of the plan's investment performance.

   C. Postemployment benefits received by employees are defined by the plan's formula.

   D. The employer and employees are required to contribute equal amounts to the fund.

Answer (A) is correct. *(CIA, adapted)*
**REQUIRED:** The true statement about a defined contribution plan.
**DISCUSSION:** A defined contribution plan provides benefits in exchange for services, provides an account for each participant, and specifies how contributions are to be determined. Postemployment benefits depend only on contributions, returns on investment, and allocated forfeitures of other participants' benefits. Thus, employees have the benefit of gain and the risk of loss.
Answer (B) is incorrect because the employees bear the risk of the plan's investment performance. Answer (C) is incorrect because, under a defined benefit plan, the postemployment benefits received by employees are defined by the plan's formula. Answer (D) is incorrect because equal contributions are not required for a defined contribution plan.

**12.** The defined postemployment benefit obligation of an enterprise includes benefit obligations to <List A> employees at <List B> salary levels.

| | List A | List B |
|---|---|---|
| A. | Vested | Current |
| B. | Vested | Future |
| C. | Vested and nonvested | Current |
| D. | Vested and nonvested | Future |

Answer (D) is correct. *(CIA, adapted)*
**REQUIRED:** The nature of the defined postemployment benefit.
**DISCUSSION:** The measurement of a postemployment benefit obligation estimates of future salary increases, the benefits defined in the plan, the benefits arising from any constructive obligation beyond the terms of the plan, and estimates of future changes in state benefits that affect the level of plan benefits. The possibility that nonvested projected benefits will not vest is a factor in the measurement of the DBO, but it does not affect the existence of the obligation.

**13.** An employee's right to obtain postemployment benefits regardless of whether (s)he remains employed is known as his/her

   A. Past service cost.

   B. Defined benefit plan.

   C. Vested benefits.

   D. Additional minimum liability.

Answer (C) is correct. *(CIA, adapted)*
**REQUIRED:** The term defined as the right to obtain postemployment benefits regardless of future employment.
**DISCUSSION:** Vested benefits are those earned postemployment benefits owed to an employee that are not contingent upon the employee's continued service. Whether benefits have vested affects the measurement of the employer's defined benefit obligation but not its existence. Moreover, vesting affects the accounting for past service cost. Past service cost is amortized as an expense over the average period until the benefits are vested.
Answer (A) is incorrect because past service cost relates to benefits for employee service provided prior to the adoption or amendment of a defined benefit plan. Answer (B) is incorrect because a defined benefit plan provides a defined benefit based on one or more factors, such as level of compensation, years of service, or age. Answer (D) is incorrect because, under IAS 19, the employer does not recognize an additional minimum liability.

**14.** An employer sponsors a defined postemployment benefit plan. If the given amount of the present value of the defined benefit obligation exceeds the given amount of the fair value of plan assets, the defined benefit liability to be recognized in the balance sheet is greatest when the employer has

A. Net unrecognized actuarial gains and no past service cost.

B. Net unrecognized actuarial losses and no past service cost.

C. Net unrecognized actuarial losses and unrecognized past service cost.

D. No unrecognized actuarial gains or losses and unrecognized past service cost.

Answer (A) is correct.  *(Publisher)*
**REQUIRED:** The computation reflecting the greatest defined benefit liability.
**DISCUSSION:** The amount of the defined benefit liability recognized equals the present value of the defined benefit obligation at the balance sheet date, plus (minus) unrecognized actuarial gains (losses), minus unrecognized past service cost, minus the fair value of plan assets at the balance sheet date. If this amount is negative, it represents an asset. However, the maximum that may be recognized for such an asset is the sum of unrecognized actuarial losses, unrecognized past service cost, and the present value of future refunds from the plan or reductions in future contributions. Thus, if the excess of the DBO over the fair value of plan assets is constant, net unrecognized actuarial gains will increase the liability. Net unrecognized actuarial losses and unrecognized past service cost decrease the liability.
Answer (B) is incorrect because net unrecognized actuarial losses decrease the liability. Answer (C) is incorrect because net unrecognized actuarial losses and unrecognized past service cost decrease the liability. Answer (D) is incorrect because net unrecognized actuarial gains increase the liability.

**15.** The following information relates to the activity of the defined postemployment benefit plan of Twain Publishers, Ltd.:

| | |
|---|---|
| Current service cost | 120,000 |
| Expected return on plan assets | 30,000 |
| Interest cost on defined benefit obligation | 40,000 |
| Amortization of net actuarial loss | 10,000 |
| Past service cost | 5,000 |

Twain's expense recognized in the income statement is

A. 120,000

B. 135,000

C. 140,000

D. 145,000

Answer (D) is correct.  *(Publisher)*
**REQUIRED:** The recognized expense related to a defined postemployment benefit plan.
**DISCUSSION:** Components of the expense are current service cost, interest cost, the expected return on plan assets, past service cost (recognition in full of vested amounts and amortization of nonvested amounts). Current service cost, interest cost, the amortization of actuarial loss, and the past service cost increase the expense. The expected return on plan assets decreases the expense.

| | |
|---|---|
| Current service cost | 120,000 |
| Return on plan assets | (30,000) |
| Interest cost | 40,000 |
| Amortization of actuarial loss | 10,000 |
| Past service cost | 5,000 |
| Expense | 145,000 |

Answer (A) is incorrect because 120,000 includes only the current service cost component. Answer (B) is incorrect because 135,000 excludes the amortization of the actuarial loss. Answer (C) is incorrect because 140,000 excludes the past service cost.

**16.** At the start of its current fiscal year, Emper Corporation amended its defined postemployment benefit plan, resulting in an increase in the present value of the DBO. The benefits become vested after 6 years of service. Past service cost arising from the plan amendment includes 400,000 of benefits that are already vested and 200,000 of nonvested benefits. If the average period until vesting is 4 years, the minimum past service cost to be recognized in the first year is

A. 50,000

B. 200,000

C. 450,000

D. 600,000

Answer (C) is correct.  *(Publisher)*
**REQUIRED:** The minimum amount of past service cost to be recognized.
**DISCUSSION:** Past service cost is the increase in the present value of the DBO related to prior employee service that arises in the current period from the introduction of, or an amendment to, postemployment benefits. Accordingly, 400,000 should be recognized immediately to reflect the vested benefits and amortization of the nonvested benefits equals 50,000 (200,000 ÷ 4), a total of 450,000.
Answer (A) is incorrect because 50,000 is the periodic amortization of nonvested benefits. Answer (B) is incorrect because 200,000 is the amount of the nonvested benefits. Answer (D) is incorrect because 600,000 includes nonvested benefits not yet required to be amortized.

**17.** At end of the year, Employer's defined benefit obligation (DBO) was determined to be 1,500,000, which was 200,000 higher than had been expected. The defined benefit plan's assets had a fair value of 1,250,000. No other actuarial gains and losses have occurred. If the average remaining working life is 20 years, the minimum required amortization of the unrecognized net actuarial gains and losses in the next year will be

A. 20,000

B. 3,750

C. 2,500

D. 0

Answer (C) is correct. *(Publisher)*
**REQUIRED:** The minimum required amortization of unrecognized net actuarial gains and losses.
**DISCUSSION:** At a minimum, amortization of the cumulative unrecognized net actuarial gains and losses must be included as income or expense if, as of the close of the prior period, that unrecognized gain or loss exceeds 10% of the greater of the present fair value of the DBO or the fair value of plan assets. At year-end, the present value of the DBO was 200,000 greater than estimated (a 200,000 liability loss). Given that no other gain or loss has occurred, the unrecognized actuarial net loss to be amortized beginning next year is 200,000. The corridor amount is 150,000 (10% of the greater of 1,500,000 present value of the DBO or 1,250,000 fair value of plan assets). The amount outside the corridor is 50,000 (200,000 – 150,000), and the amount to be amortized is therefore 2,500 (50,000 ÷ 20 years of average remaining working life).
Answer (A) is incorrect because 20,000 is the result of using the full 200,000 liability loss without regard to the corridor amount and assumes an amortization period of 10 years instead of 20. Answer (B) is incorrect because 3,750 is the result of using 125,000 (10% × 1,250,000 plan assets) as the corridor amount instead of 150,000. Answer (D) is incorrect because 50,000 of the liability loss must be amortized over the average remaining working life beginning the year following the loss.

**18.** For an enterprise with a defined postemployment benefit plan, the fair value of plan assets at the beginning of the year was 500,000. No unrecognized net cumulative actuarial gain or loss existed. On the last day of the fiscal year, the fair value of plan assets was 620,000. Benefits paid equaled 100,000, and the enterprise made 120,000 in contributions. The discount rate was 10%, and the expected long-term rate of return on plan assets was 12%. The actual return on plan assets was

A. 50,000

B. 60,000

C. 75,000

D. 100,000

Answer (D) is correct. *(Publisher)*
**REQUIRED:** The actual return on plan assets.
**DISCUSSION:** The actual return on plan assets is equal to the difference between the fair value of plan assets at the beginning and the end of the year adjusted for contributions and benefits paid. The actual return thus is 100,000.

| | |
|---|---:|
| FV, end of year | 620,000 |
| Benefits paid | 100,000 |
| Contributions | (120,000) |
| FV, beginning of year | (500,000) |
| Actual return | 100,000 |

Answer (A) is incorrect because 50,000 equals 10% of the beginning fair value. Answer (B) is incorrect because 60,000 equals 12% of the beginning fair value. Answer (C) is incorrect because 75,000 is a nonsense number.

**19.** An enterprise that sponsors a defined benefit postemployment benefit plan has discontinued a segment of its business. As a result, the employees of that segment will not be able to earn additional benefits. On the date of the discontinuance, the present value of the DBO was 10,000,000, the fair value of the plan assets was 8,500,000, and the net unrecognized actuarial gain was 500,000, and the unrecognized past service cost was 100,000. The effect of the discontinuance was to reduce the present value of the DBO by 10%. The portions of the unrecognized actuarial gain and past service cost related to the portion of the DBO that was eliminated also equaled 10%. Accordingly, the enterprise should recognize what net defined benefit liability immediately after the discontinuance?

A. 410,000

B. 860,000

C. 900,000

D. 950,000

Answer (B) is correct. *(Publisher)*
**REQUIRED:** The defined benefit liability immediately after the discontinuance.
**DISCUSSION:** A curtailment arises from a reduction in covered employees or amendment of the plan to reduce benefits for future service. A settlement is a transaction that eliminates the DBO for part or all of plan benefits. When a curtailment or settlement occurs, the gain or loss recognized encompasses the change in the present value of the DBO, the change in the fair value of plan assets, and previously unrecognized related actuarial gains and losses and past service cost. Thus, the present value of the DBO after the curtailment was 9,000,000 [10,000,000 – (10% × 10,000,000)]. The fair value of plan assets was given as 8,500,000. The unrecognized actuarial gain was reduced to 450,000. The unrecognized past service cost was reduced to 90,000. Accordingly, the defined benefit liability immediately after the discontinuance was 860,000 (9,000,000 – 8,500,000 + 450,000 – 90,000).
Answer (A) is incorrect because 410,000 omits the remaining unrecognized actuarial gain. Answer (C) is incorrect because 900,000 is 10% of the present value of the remaining DBO. Answer (D) is incorrect because 950,000 omits past service cost from the calculation.

## 5.3 Leases

**20.** If a lease agreement transfers substantially all of the risks and rewards of ownership of the asset to the lessee, the asset value is recognized on the lessee's records as a(n) <List A> asset, and the lease is referred to as a <List B> lease.

| | List A | List B |
|---|---|---|
| A. | Tangible | Finance |
| B. | Intangible | Finance |
| C. | Tangible | Operating |
| D. | Intangible | Operating |

Answer (A) is correct.  *(CIA, adapted)*
**REQUIRED:** The type of lease that transfers substantially all of the risks and rewards of ownership.
**DISCUSSION:** When a lease agreement transfers the risks and rewards of ownership of the asset to the lessee, the lease is treated as a finance lease because the transaction is in essence an installment purchase. Accordingly, the lessee records a depreciable asset and a liability. Moreover, IAS 38, *Intangible Assets*, specifically does not apply to leases that are within the scope of IAS 17, *Leases*. A finance lease is therefore regarded as a tangible asset.
Answer (B) is incorrect because the recorded asset is a tangible asset. Answer (C) is incorrect because, if it transfers substantially all of the risks and rewards of ownership, the lease is a finance lease. Answer (D) is incorrect because, if it transfers substantially all of the risks and rewards of ownership, the lease is a finance lease.

**21.** Finance and operating leases differ in that the lessor

A. Obtains use of the asset only under a finance lease.

B. Is using the lease as a source of financing only under an operating lease.

C. Makes rent payments that are actually installment payments constituting a payment of both principal and interest only under a finance lease.

D. Finances the transaction through the leased asset only under a finance lease.

Answer (D) is correct.  *(CIA, adapted)*
**REQUIRED:** The difference between finance and operating leases.
**DISCUSSION:** A lease is a rental or sub-purchase arrangement between a lessor (the owner or seller of the property) and a lessee (the renter or purchaser). The issue in all leases is whether the risks and rewards of ownership have been transferred from the lessor to the lessee; if so, the lease should be accounted for as a sale-purchase, i.e., a finance lease. If the risks and rewards of ownership have not transferred, the lease is a rental arrangement and is called an operating lease. In effect, the lessor provides financing for an installment purchase, and the lessee's payments include both principal and interest components.
Answer (A) is incorrect because the lessee obtains use of the asset. Answer (B) is incorrect because the lessee uses the lease as a source of financing under a finance lease, not an operating lease. Answer (C) is incorrect because the lessee makes payments to the lessor.

**22.** Which of the following statements is false of a finance lease?

A. The lessor capitalizes the net investment in the lease.

B. The lessor records the leased item as an asset.

C. The lessee records depreciation or finance cost allowance on the leased asset.

D. The lease arrangement represents a form of financing.

Answer (B) is correct.  *(CIA, adapted)*
**REQUIRED:** The false statement about a finance lease.
**DISCUSSION:** When a transaction meets the criteria of a finance lease, the lessor removes the leased item from the books and records lease payments receivable regardless of whether the lessor is a manufacturer or dealer. The lessee records and depreciates the leased item under a finance lease.
Answer (A) is incorrect because, under a finance lease, the lessor recognizes a net receivable equal to the net investment in the lease: gross investment (minimum lease payments from the lessor's perspective plus unguaranteed residual value) minus unearned finance income. Answer (C) is incorrect because the lessee records depreciation on the leased asset under a finance lease. This process is separate from the accounting for the lease obligation. Answer (D) is incorrect because, in essence, the leased asset is being purchased when a lease meets the criteria for capitalization. Hence, the lease agreement represents a form of financing.

**23.** At the inception of a finance lease, how should the lessee account for guaranteed residual value?

A. As part of minimum lease payments at present value.

B. As part of minimum lease payments at future value.

C. As part of minimum lease payments at future value of an annuity due.

D. As not a part of the lease contract.

Answer (A) is correct. *(CIA, adapted)*

**REQUIRED:** The accounting treatment of the guaranteed residual value at the inception of a finance lease.

**DISCUSSION:** The lessee records a finance lease as an asset and a liability at the inception of the lease at the fair value of the leased property (not to exceed the present value of the minimum lease payments). The lessee's minimum lease payments include required payments (excluding contingent rent and costs for services and taxes to be paid by and reimbursed to the lessor) during the lease term and the amount of a bargain purchase option. If no bargain purchase option exists, the minimum lease payments equal the sum of the minimum payments payable over the lease term and any amounts guaranteed by the lessee or by a party related to the lessee.

Answer (B) is incorrect because the guaranteed residual must be discounted to present value. Answer (C) is incorrect because the guaranteed residual must be discounted to present value. Answer (D) is incorrect because guaranteed residuals are part of the lease contract.

**24.** Which of the following leases ordinarily should be classified as a finance lease by the lessee?

| | Lease A | Lease B | Lease C | Lease D |
|---|---|---|---|---|
| Contains a bargain purchase option? | Yes | No | No | No |
| Lease term is for the major part of the economic life of the leased asset | No | No | Yes | No |
| Present value of the minimum lease payments is substantially all of the fair value of the leased asset | No | No | No | Yes |
| Leased asset usable only by lessor without major modification | No | Yes | Yes | No |

A. Lease A only.

B. Lease B only.

C. Leases A, C, and D.

D. Leases C and D only.

Answer (C) is correct. *(CIA, adapted)*

**REQUIRED:** The lease(s) meeting a capitalization criterion.

**DISCUSSION:** A lease should be classified as a finance lease by a lessee if it transfers substantially all of the risks and rewards of ownership. A lease is classified at its inception. It normally is classified as a finance lease if, for example, the lease provides for the transfer of ownership of the leased asset by the end of the lease term; the lease contains a bargain purchase option, i.e., the lessee has the option to purchase at a price expected to be sufficiently below the fair value of the exercise date that, at the lease's inception, exercise is reasonably certain; the lease term is for the major part of the economic life of the leased asset; the present value of the minimum lease payments is at least substantially all of the fair value of the leased asset at the inception of the lease; or the leased asset is such that it can be used only by the lessee without major modification. Lease A is a finance lease because the terms of the lease include a bargain purchase option. Lease C passes the economic life test, and lease D passes the recovery of investment test.

Answer (A) is incorrect because Leases C and D are also finance leases. Answer (B) is incorrect because B is the only operating lease in the set. If it were usable by the lessee (not the lessor) without major modification, it would normally be classified as a finance lease. Answer (D) is incorrect because Lease A contains a bargain purchase option, so it qualifies as a finance lease.

**25.** ABC Enterprises, a manufacturer lessor, leased a machine to XYZ on January 1. The lease meets the criteria for a finance lease. Title to the asset will automatically pass to the lessee at the end of the lease term. Other details are as follows:

| | |
|---|---|
| Lease term | 10 years |
| Useful life of the asset | 10 years |
| Cost of the leased asset to the lessor | 55,000 |
| Annual payment payable at the beginning of each year, beginning January 1 | 10,000 |
| Implicit interest rate | 10% |
| Present value of an annuity due of 1 discounted for 10 years at 10% | 6.7590 |
| Present value of 1 due in 10 years discounted at 10% | .3855 |

Assuming the fair value of the asset is at least equal to the present value of the minimum lease payments, the journal entry to record the inception of this lease on the lessor's books at January 1 is

A.
| | | |
|---|---|---|
| Leased machine | 67,590 | |
| Lease liability | | 57,590 |
| Cash | | 10,000 |

B.
| | | |
|---|---|---|
| Lease payments receivable | 90,000 | |
| Cash | 10,000 | |
| Cost of sales | 55,000 | |
| Inventory | | 55,000 |
| Unearned finance income--leases | | 45,000 |
| Sales | | 55,000 |

C.
| | | |
|---|---|---|
| Lease payments receivable | 90,000 | |
| Cash | 10,000 | |
| Finance income | | 32,410 |
| Gross profit on lease | | 12,590 |
| Inventory | | 55,000 |

D.
| | | |
|---|---|---|
| Lease payments receivable | 90,000 | |
| Cash | 10,000 | |
| Cost of sales | 55,000 | |
| Sales | | 67,590 |
| Inventory | | 55,000 |
| Unearned finance income--leases | | 32,410 |

Answer (D) is correct. *(CIA, adapted)*
**REQUIRED:** The manufacturer-lessor's journal entry at the inception of a finance lease.
**DISCUSSION:** For this finance lease, the manufacturer-lessor should record

1. As gross investment, the minimum lease payments because there is no residual value

2. As net investment, the difference between the gross investment in the lease (a debit to a receivable) and unearned finance income (a credit to a liability)

3. As unearned finance income, the difference between the gross investment and its present value

4. As sales revenue, the fair value of the asset or, if lower, the present value of the minimum lease payments computed at the interest rate implicit in the lease

5. As cost of goods sold, the cost of the leased asset

Because the first payment is made at the inception of the lease, the payment structure is that of an annuity due. Sales revenue is therefore equal to the 10,000 periodic payment times the present value of an annuity due of 1 discounted for 10 years at 10% (10,000 × 6.7590 = 67,590).

Given that cash is paid at the beginning of the year, the initial 10,000 cash debit immediately decreases the gross investment in the lease (lease payments receivable) from 100,000 to 90,000. The cost of the leased asset (55,000) must also be charged to cost of sales and credited to inventory. Finally, at the inception of the lease, unearned finance income equals the difference between the gross investment and the sales price (100,000 – 67,590 = 32,410).

Answer (A) is incorrect because it is the lessee's journal entry. Answer (B) is incorrect because the sale should be recorded at the present value of the minimum lease payments, and the unearned finance income should be recorded as the difference between the gross lease payments receivable and the present value of this gross investment. Answer (C) is incorrect because the lease should reflect both cost of goods sold and sales, not the netted gross profit on the lease.

---

**26.** On August 1, Jones leased property to Smith for a 5-year period. The annual 20,000 lease payment is payable at the end of each year. The expected residual value at the end of the lease term is 10,000. Jones's implicit interest rate is 12%. The cost of the property to Jones was 50,000, which is the fair value at the lease date. The present value of an ordinary annuity of 1 for five periods is 3.605. The present value of 1 at the end of five periods is .567. At the inception of the lease, the recorded gross investment is

A. 110,000

B. 100,000

C. 72,100

D. 90,000

Answer (A) is correct. *(J.O. Hall)*
**REQUIRED:** The amount to be recorded.
**DISCUSSION:** For a finance lease, the lessor should record the gross investment in the lease at the undiscounted sum of the minimum lease payments (the total of the lessee's required payments, excluding contingent rent and costs for services and taxes to be paid by and reimbursed to the lessor, and any guaranteed residual value) and any unguaranteed residual value. The gross investment is the same regardless of whether any residual value is guaranteed. The five periodic payments of 20,000 equal 100,000. The expected residual value including guaranteed and unguaranteed portions equals 10,000. The gross investment should be 110,000 (100,000 + 10,000).

Answer (B) is incorrect because it fails to include the residual value in the gross investment. Answer (C) is incorrect because the annual lease payments should be recorded at their undiscounted value. Answer (D) is incorrect because the residual value is added to, not subtracted from, the undiscounted lease payments.

**27.** KW Ltd. leased equipment under a 4-year, noncancelable lease properly classified as a finance lease. The lease does not transfer ownership or contain a bargain purchase option. The equipment had an estimated economic life of 5 years and an estimated residual value of 20,000. Terms of the lease included a guaranteed residual value of 50,000. KW initially recorded the leased equipment at 240,000, and its depreciation policy for owned assets is to use the straight-line method. Thus, the amount of depreciation that should be charged each year is

A. 55,000

B. 47,500

C. 44,000

D. 38,000

Answer (B) is correct. *(H.F. Bush)*
    **REQUIRED:** The amount of depreciation to be recorded on a finance lease.
    **DISCUSSION:** Depreciation should be consistent with the accounting policy for owned assets. Absent a reasonable certainty that the lessee will own the asset at the end of the lease term, it should be fully depreciated over the shorter of the useful life or the lease term. The lease does not transfer ownership or contain a bargain purchase option. Accordingly, the period of amortization should be the lease term. In accordance with the straight-line method used by KW for owned assets, the depreciable base for this finance lease is equal to the 240,000 initially recorded minus the 50,000 guaranteed residual value allocated equally over the 4-year lease term. Consequently, annual depreciation expense is 47,500 [(240,000 − 50,000) ÷ 4 years].
    Answer (A) is incorrect because the guaranteed residual value, not the estimated residual value, must be subtracted from the amount initially recorded. Answer (C) is incorrect because the guaranteed residual value, not the estimated residual value, must be subtracted from the initially recorded amount, and the term of the lease, not the estimated economic life, is used as the denominator in the depreciation calculation. Answer (D) is incorrect because the term of the lease, not the estimated economic life, must be used as the denominator in the depreciation calculation.

---

Questions 28 and 29 are based on the following information.

On January 1, Plantation Partners is planning to enter as the lessee into the two lease agreements described in the opposite column. Each lease is noncancelable, and Plantation does not receive title to either leased property during or at the end of the lease term. All payments required under these agreements are due on January 1 each year.

| Lessor | Lease A | Lease B |
|---|---|---|
| Type of property | Oven | Computer |
| Yearly rental | 15,000 | 4,000 |
| Lease term | 10 years | 3 years |
| Economic life | 15 years | 5 years |
| Purchase option | None | 3,000 |
| Renewal option | None | None |
| Fair value at inception of lease | 125,000 | 10,200 |
| Unguaranteed residual value | None | 2,000 |
| Lessee's incremental borrowing rate | 10% | 10% |
| Executory costs paid by | Lessee | Lessor |
| Annual executory costs | 800 | 500 |
| Present value factor at 10% (of an annuity due) | 6.76 | 2.74 |

**28.** Plantation should treat Lease A as a(n)

A. Finance lease with an initial asset value of 101,400.

B. Operating lease, charging 14,200 in rental expense and 800 in executory costs to annual operations.

C. Operating lease, charging the present value of the yearly rental expense to annual operations.

D. Operating lease, charging 15,000 in rental expense and 800 in executory costs to annual operations.

Answer (D) is correct. *(CMA, adapted)*
    **REQUIRED:** The true statement about Lease A.
    **DISCUSSION:** Lease A is an operating lease with a 15,000 annual rental expense with annual executory costs (e.g., maintenance, insurance, and taxes) of 800 to be paid by the lessee. An operating lease does not transfer the risks and rewards of ownership to the lessee. Lease A is nothing more than a rental arrangement. Circumstances in which the risks and rewards of ownership are normally deemed to be transferred include the following: the lease transfers title to the lessee, the lease has a bargain purchase option, the lease term is for the major part of the useful life of the leased asset, the present value of the minimum lease payments is at least substantially all of the asset's fair value, or the asset is usable only by the lessee without major modification.
    Answer (A) is incorrect because Lease A does not qualify as a finance lease. Answer (B) is incorrect because rental expense is 15,000. Answer (C) is incorrect because the actual cash outlay for rent, 15,000, is charged to expense.

**29.** Refer to the information preceding question 28. Plantation should treat Lease B as a(n)

A. Finance lease with an initial asset value of 10,960.

B. Finance lease with an initial asset value of 10,200.

C. Operating lease, charging 3,500 in rental expense and 500 in executory costs to annual operations.

D. Finance lease with an initial asset value of 9,590.

Answer (D) is correct.   *(CMA, adapted)*
**REQUIRED:** The true statement about Lease B.
**DISCUSSION:** A finance lease is one in which the risks and rewards of ownership are transferred to the lessee. For accounting purposes, the lessee treats a finance lease as similar to the purchase of an asset capitalized at the fair value of the leased asset or, if lower, the present value of the minimum lease payments. The lessee's minimum lease payments include the required payments, excluding contingent rent and executory costs (e.g., taxes and insurance), plus any amounts guaranteed by the lessee or a related party. If a bargain purchase option exists, however, minimum lease payments equal the required payments plus the amount of the option. If the present value of the minimum lease payments (calculated without guaranteed amounts or a bargain purchase option) is substantially all of the asset's fair value, the lease normally is accounted for as a finance lease. Given that the executory costs associated with the lease are to be paid by the lessor, a portion of the lease rental price is for those costs, not for the asset. Consequently, the annual minimum lease payment equals the annual payment minus the executory costs, or 3,500 (4,000 yearly rental – 500). The present value of the minimum lease payments is therefore 9,590 (2.74 × 3,500), which is substantially all of the fair value of the asset. Thus, the lease should be capitalized. The appropriate amount of the initial asset value is the present value of the minimum lease payments calculated above.
Answer (A) is incorrect because the initial asset value cannot exceed the fair value of the leased asset. Moreover, 10,960 includes the present value of the executory costs. Answer (B) is incorrect because 10,200 is the fair value of the leased asset. Answer (C) is incorrect because the lease meets the criteria of a finance lease.

## 5.4 Statement Analysis

**30.** An enterprise has a high fixed-assets turnover ratio. What conclusion can a financial analyst draw from this?

A. The enterprise may be overcapitalized.

B. The enterprise may have a problem with employees converting inventory to personal use.

C. The enterprise may be undercapitalized.

D. The enterprise has favorable profitability.

Answer (C) is correct.   *(CIA, adapted)*
**REQUIRED:** The implication of a high fixed-assets turnover ratio.
**DISCUSSION:** The fixed-assets turnover ratio equals net sales divided by net fixed assets. A high ratio indicates either that the enterprise is undercapitalized, that is, it cannot afford to buy enough fixed assets, or that it uses fixed assets efficiently.
Answer (A) is incorrect because the ratio may indicate undercapitalization. Answer (B) is incorrect because fluctuations in inventory do not affect fixed-assets turnover. Answer (D) is incorrect because the fixed-assets turnover ratio is not a profitability indicator. It measures the efficiency of asset management.

**31.** The times-interest-earned ratio is primarily an indication of

A. Solvency.

B. Liquidity.

C. Asset management.

D. Profitability.

Answer (A) is correct.   *(CIA, adapted)*
**REQUIRED:** The purpose of the times-interest-earned ratio.
**DISCUSSION:** The times-interest-earned ratio equals net profit before taxes and interest divided by interest. It measures the extent to which operating profit can decline before the enterprise is unable to meet its annual interest cost. Thus, it is a measure of debt-paying capacity (solvency).
Answer (B) is incorrect because liquidity ratios, e.g., the current ratio, indicate the relationship of current assets to current liabilities. Answer (C) is incorrect because asset management ratios indicate how effectively the enterprise is using its assets. Answer (D) is incorrect because profitability ratios measure operating results.

**32.** An enterprise's receivables collection period is equal to

- A. The inventory conversion period.
- B. The cash conversion cycle.
- C. The day's sales outstanding.
- D. The inventory divided by average daily sales.

Answer (C) is correct. *(CIA, adapted)*
**REQUIRED:** The receivables collection period.
**DISCUSSION:** The day's sales outstanding (days of receivables) may be stated as the accounts receivable balance divided by average credit sales per day or as days in the year divided by the receivables turnover. It is the average time required to convert the enterprise's receivables into cash. Thus, it is also called the receivables collection period.

Answer (A) is incorrect because the inventory conversion period (days of inventory) is the average time required to convert materials into finished goods and then to sell them. This process typically occurs before the receivables collection period, and the amount of time in one period does not necessarily bear any relationship to the other. Answer (B) is incorrect because the cash conversion cycle equals the inventory conversion period, plus the receivables collection period, minus the payables deferral period (average time between resource purchases and payment of cash for them). It estimates the time between when the enterprise makes payments and when it receives cash inflows. Answer (D) is incorrect because the inventory divided by the sales per day is the inventory conversion period (days of inventory).

**33.** Which of the following is true about the impact of price inflation on financial ratio analysis?

- A. Inflation has no impact on financial ratio analysis.
- B. Inflation affects financial ratio analysis for one enterprise over time but not comparative analysis of enterprises of different ages.
- C. Inflation affects financial ratio analysis for one enterprise over time, as well as comparative analysis of enterprises of different ages.
- D. Inflation affects comparative analysis of enterprises of different ages but not financial ratio analysis for one enterprise over time.

Answer (C) is correct. *(CIA, adapted)*
**REQUIRED:** The true statement about the impact of price inflation on financial ratio analysis.
**DISCUSSION:** Inflation is the diminution over time of the purchasing power of money. Because balance sheet amounts are expressed in terms of money, historical cost amounts for different periods are measured in units representing different levels of purchasing power. Net profit is also distorted because of inflation's impact on depreciation expense and inventory costs. Inflation therefore impairs the comparability of financial statement items, whether for the same enterprise over time or for enterprises of differing ages.

Answer (A) is incorrect because inflation badly distorts balance sheets, depreciation charges, inventory costs, and profits. Answer (B) is incorrect because inflation affects any financial ratio analysis involving comparisons of prior-period with current-period monetary amounts. Answer (D) is incorrect because inflation affects any financial ratio analysis involving comparisons of prior-period with current-period monetary amounts.

**34.** An investor has been given several financial ratios for an enterprise but none of the financial reports. Which combination of ratios can be used to derive return on equity?

- A. Market-to-book-value ratio and total-debt-to-total-assets ratio.
- B. Price-to-earnings ratio, earnings per share, and net profit margin.
- C. Price-to-earnings ratio and return-on-assets ratio.
- D. Net profit margin, total assets turnover, and equity multiplier.

Answer (D) is correct. *(CIA, adapted)*
**REQUIRED:** The combination of ratios used to derive return on equity.
**DISCUSSION:** The net profit margin equals the net profit available to common shareholders divided by sales, the total assets turnover equals sales divided by total assets, and the product of these two ratios is the return on assets. This result is the basic Du Pont equation. In the extended Du Pont equation, the return on assets is multiplied by the leverage factor, also called the equity multiplier (total assets ÷ common equity at carrying amount). The extended Du Pont equation gives the return on common equity. This result is obtained because the total assets and sales factors cancel in the multiplication of the three ratios.

Answer (A) is incorrect because the market-to-carrying-amount ratio and the total-debt-to-total-assets ratio do not provide any information about net profit available to shareholders. Answer (B) is incorrect because the price-to-earnings ratio, EPS, and the net profit margin do not provide information about the carrying amount of common equity. Answer (C) is incorrect because the price-to-earnings ratio and the return-on-assets ratio do not provide information about the carrying amount of common equity.

**35.** The following ratios relate to an enterprise's financial situation compared with that of its industry:

|  | The Company | Industry Average |
|---|---|---|
| Return on Assets (ROA) | 7.9% | 9.2% |
| Return on Equity (ROE) | 15.2% | 12.9% |

What conclusion could a financial analyst validly draw from these ratios?

A. The enterprise's product has a high market share, leading to higher profitability.

B. The enterprise uses more debt than does the average enterprise in the industry.

C. The enterprise's profits are increasing over time.

D. The enterprise's shares have a higher market value to carrying amount than does the rest of the industry.

Answer (B) is correct. *(CIA, adapted)*
**REQUIRED:** The conclusion from comparing ROA and ROE with industry averages.
**DISCUSSION:** The use of financial leverage has a multiplier effect on the return on assets. The extended Du Pont formula illustrates this point by showing that the return on equity equals the return on assets times the leverage factor, also called the equity multiplier (total assets ÷ common equity). Thus, greater use of debt increases the equity multiplier and the return on equity. In this example, the equity multiplier is 1.92 (15.2% ROE ÷ 7.9% ROA), and the industry average is 1.40 (12.9% ROE ÷ 9.2% ROA). The higher equity multiplier indicates that the enterprise uses more debt than the industry average.
Answer (A) is incorrect because the question gave no information about market share. Answer (C) is incorrect because this comparison is with an industry average, not over time. Answer (D) is incorrect because share valuation is a response to many factors. The higher-than-average return on equity does not mean that the enterprise has a more favorable market-to-carrying-amount ratio.

**36.** All else being equal, an enterprise with a higher dividend-payout ratio will have a <List A> debt-to-assets ratio and a <List B> current ratio.

|  | List A | List B |
|---|---|---|
| A. | Higher | Higher |
| B. | Higher | Lower |
| C. | Lower | Higher |
| D. | Lower | Lower |

Answer (B) is correct. *(CIA, adapted)*
**REQUIRED:** The implications of a higher dividend-payout ratio.
**DISCUSSION:** An enterprise with a higher dividend-payout ratio is distributing more of its earnings as dividends to common shareholders. It will have less cash and less total assets than a comparable enterprise with a lower payout ratio. The debt-to-assets ratio will be higher because total assets are lower, and the current ratio will be lower because cash is lower.
Answer (A) is incorrect because the current ratio will be lower. Answer (C) is incorrect because the debt-to-assets ratio will be higher and the current ratio will be lower. Answer (D) is incorrect because the debt-to-assets ratio will be higher.

**37.** The following account balances represent the December 31 balance sheet of an enterprise.

| | |
|---|---|
| Accounts payable | 67,000 |
| Accounts receivable (net) | 115,000 |
| Accumulated depreciation -- building | 298,500 |
| Accumulated depreciation -- equipment | 50,500 |
| Cash | 27,500 |
| Common shares (10 par value) | 100,000 |
| Deferred income taxes payable | 37,500 |
| Equipment | 136,000 |
| Income taxes payable | 70,000 |
| Inventory | 257,000 |
| Land and building | 752,000 |
| Long-term notes payable | 123,000 |
| Financial assets held for trading | 64,000 |
| Notes payable within 1 year | 54,000 |
| Other current liabilities | 22,500 |
| Share premium | 150,000 |
| Prepaid expenses | 27,000 |
| Retained earnings | 403,500 |

The quick ratio for this year is

A. 1.42

B. 1.08

C. 0.97

D. 0.82

Answer (C) is correct. *(CIA, adapted)*
**REQUIRED:** The quick ratio.
**DISCUSSION:** The acid test (quick) ratio equals quick assets (cash, financial assets held for trading, and accounts receivable) divided by current liabilities. Quick assets total 206,500 (27,500 cash + 64,000 financial assets held for trading + 115,000 net accounts receivable). Given current liabilities of 213,500 (67,000 accounts payable + 54,000 current notes payable + 70,000 income taxes payable + 22,500 other current liabilities), the quick ratio is 0.967 (206,500 ÷ 213,500).
Answer (A) is incorrect because 1.42 excludes the income taxes payable from the current liabilities. Answer (B) is incorrect because 1.08 includes prepaid expenses in the quick assets and excludes income taxes payable in the current liabilities. Answer (D) is incorrect because 0.82 includes deferred income taxes payable in the current liabilities.

Questions 38 through 40 are based on the following information.

An enterprise's financial statements for the current year are as follows:

**Statement of Income and Retained Earnings**

| | |
|---|---:|
| Sales | 3,000 |
| Cost of goods sold | 1,600 |
| Gross profit | 1,400 |
| Operating expenses | 970 |
| Operating profit | 430 |
| Interest expense | 30 |
| Profit before tax | 400 |
| Income tax | 200 |
| Net profit | 200 |
| Plus Jan. 1 retained earnings | 150 |
| Minus dividends | 100 |
| Dec. 31 retained earnings | 250 |

**Balance Sheet**

| | |
|---|---:|
| Cash | 100 |
| Accounts receivable | 200 |
| Inventory | 50 |
| Net fixed assets | 600 |
| Total | 950 |
| Accounts payable | 140 |
| Long-term debt | 300 |
| Share capital | 260 |
| Retained earnings | 250 |
| Total | 950 |

**38.** The enterprise has a dividend-payout ratio of

A. 19.6%

B. 28.6%

C. 40.0%

D. 50.0%

Answer (D) is correct. *(CIA, adapted)*
REQUIRED: The dividend-payout ratio.
DISCUSSION: The dividend-payout ratio is the ratio of dividends paid to net profit for the period. Hence, it equals 50.0% (100 dividends ÷ 200 net profit).
Answer (A) is incorrect because 19.6% is the ratio of dividends paid to the December 31 carrying amount of common equity. Answer (B) is incorrect because 28.6% is the ratio of dividends paid to the sum of beginning retained earnings and net profit. Answer (C) is incorrect because 40.0% is the ratio of dividends paid to the December 31 retained earnings.

**39.** The enterprise has return on assets of

A. 21.1%

B. 39.2%

C. 42.1%

D. 45.3%

Answer (A) is correct. *(CIA, adapted)*
REQUIRED: The return on assets.
DISCUSSION: The return on assets is the ratio of net profit to total assets. It equals 21.1% (200 net profit ÷ 950 total assets).
Answer (B) is incorrect because 39.2% is the ratio of net profit to common equity. Answer (C) is incorrect because 42.1% is the ratio of profit before tax to total assets. Answer (D) is incorrect because 45.3% is the ratio of profit before interest and tax to total assets.

**40.** The enterprise has a profit margin of

A. 6.67%

B. 13.33%

C. 14.33%

D. 46.67%

Answer (A) is correct. *(CIA, adapted)*
REQUIRED: The profit margin.
DISCUSSION: The profit margin is the ratio of net profit to sales. It equals 6.67% (200 net profit ÷ 3,000 sales).
Answer (B) is incorrect because 13.33% is the ratio of profit before tax to sales. Answer (C) is incorrect because 14.33% is the ratio of profit before interest and taxes to sales. Answer (D) is incorrect because 46.67% is the ratio of gross profit to sales.

**41.** An enterprise has 100,000 outstanding common shares with a market value of 20 per share. Dividends of 2 per share were paid in the current year, and the enterprise has a dividend-payout ratio of 40%. The price-to-earnings ratio of the enterprise is

A. 2.5

B. 4

C. 10

D. 50

Answer (B) is correct. *(CIA, adapted)*
REQUIRED: The P-E ratio.
DISCUSSION: The P-E ratio equals the share price divided by EPS. If the dividends per share equaled 2 and the dividend-payout ratio was 40%, EPS must have been 5 (2 ÷ .4). Accordingly, the P-E ratio is 4 (20 share price ÷ 5 EPS).
Answer (A) is incorrect because 2.5 equals EPS divided-by dividends per share. Answer (C) is incorrect because 10 equals share price divided by dividends per share. Answer (D) is incorrect because 50 equals price per share divided by the dividend-payout percentage.

**42.** The following are the January 1 and June 30 balance sheets of an enterprise:

| Assets (in millions) | Jan. 1 | June 30 |
|---|---|---|
| Cash | 3 | 4 |
| Accounts receivable | 5 | 4 |
| Inventories | 8 | 10 |
| Fixed assets | 10 | 11 |
| Total assets | 26 | 29 |
| | | |
| Accounts payable | 2 | 3 |
| Notes payable | 4 | 3 |
| Accrued wages | 1 | 2 |
| Long-term debt | 9 | 11 |
| Equity | 10 | 10 |
| Total liabilities and equity | 26 | 29 |

From January 1 to June 30, the net working capital

- A. Decreased by 1 million.
- B. Stayed the same.
- C. Increased by 1 million.
- D. Increased by 2 million.

Answer (C) is correct. *(CIA, adapted)*
**REQUIRED:** The behavior of the net working capital.
**DISCUSSION:** Net working capital equals current assets (cash, accounts receivable, inventories for this enterprise) minus current liabilities (accounts payable, notes payable, accrued wages). From January 1 to June 30, the net working capital increased by 1,000,000 {[(4 + 4 + 10) − (3 + 3 + 2)] − [(3 + 5 + 8) − (2 + 4 + 1)]}.
Answer (A) is incorrect because a decrease of 1,000,000 results from omitting inventories. Answer (B) is incorrect because the difference between all assets and all liabilities stayed the same. Answer (D) is incorrect because an increase of 2,000,000 results from omitting accrued wages.

---

Questions 43 and 44 are based on the following information.

An enterprise has a current ratio of 1.4, a quick, or acid test, ratio of 1.2, and the following partial summary balance sheet:

| | | | |
|---|---|---|---|
| Cash | 10 | Current liabilities | ____ |
| | | Long-term | |
| Accounts receivable | ____ | liabilities | 40 |
| Inventory | ____ | Equity | 30 |
| Fixed assets | ____ | Total liabilities | |
| Total assets | 100 | and equity | ____ |

---

**43.** The enterprise has an accounts receivable balance of

- A. 12
- B. 26
- C. 36
- D. 66

Answer (B) is correct. *(CIA, adapted)*
**REQUIRED:** The accounts receivable balance.
**DISCUSSION:** Total assets equal total liabilities and equity. Hence, if total assets equal 100, total liabilities and equity must equal 100, and current liabilities must equal 30 (100 − 40 − 30). Because the quick ratio equals the quick assets (cash + accounts receivable) divided by current liabilities, the quick assets must equal 36 (30 × 1.2 quick ratio), and the accounts receivable balance is 26 (36 − 10 cash).
Answer (A) is incorrect because 12 equals current assets minus current liabilities. Answer (C) is incorrect because 36 equals the quick assets. Answer (D) is incorrect because 66 equals the sum of the quick assets and current liabilities.

**44.** The enterprise has a fixed assets balance of

A. 0

B. 16

C. 58

D. 64

Answer (C) is correct. *(CIA, adapted)*
 **REQUIRED:** The fixed assets balance.
 **DISCUSSION:** Total assets (given as 100) equals the sum of cash (given as 10), accounts receivable (26), inventory, and fixed assets. Inventory can be determined because it is included in current, but not quick, assets, and the current and quick ratios are known. Current assets equal 42 (1.4 current ratio × 30 current liabilities), and the quick assets equal 36 (1.2 quick ratio × 30 current liabilities). Thus, inventory, which is the only difference in this question between current and quick assets, equals 6 (42 – 36). Fixed assets must then equal 58 (100 total assets – 10 cash – 26 accounts receivable – 6 inventory).
 Answer (A) is incorrect because the sum of cash, accounts receivable, and inventory is less than 100. Answer (B) is incorrect because 16 is the result of neglecting to subtract the equity balance when calculating the current liability balance. Answer (D) is incorrect because 64 assumes that inventory is 0.

**45.** A growing enterprise is assessing current working capital requirements. An average of 58 days is required to convert raw materials into finished goods and to sell them. Then an average of 32 days is required to collect on receivables. If the average time the enterprise takes to pay for its raw materials is 15 days after they are received, the total cash conversion cycle is

A. 11 days.

B. 41 days.

C. 75 days.

D. 90 days.

Answer (C) is correct. *(CIA, adapted)*
 **REQUIRED:** The total cash conversion cycle.
 **DISCUSSION:** The cash conversion cycle is the length of time between paying for purchases and receiving cash from the sale of finished goods. It equals the inventory conversion period, plus the receivables collection period, minus the payables deferral period, or 75 days (58 days + 32 days – 15 days).
 Answer (A) is incorrect because 11 days results from subtracting the receivables collection period. Answer (B) is incorrect because 41 days results from subtracting the receivables collection period and adding the payables deferral period. Answer (D) is incorrect because 90 days omits the payables deferral period.

## 5.5 Income Taxes

**46.** Which one of the following statements best describes the asset-liability method of accounting for deferred income taxes?

A. The amount of deferred tax is based on tax rates in effect when temporary differences originate.

B. The amount of deferred tax is based on the tax rates expected to be in effect during the periods in which the deferred tax liability is settled or the deferred tax asset is realized.

C. The tax effects of temporary differences are not reported separately but are reported as adjustments to the amounts of specific assets and liabilities and the related revenues and expenses.

D. The appropriate tax rate to be reported on the income statement is the tax actually levied in that year, meaning no deferred taxes would be reported.

Answer (B) is correct. *(CIA, adapted)*
 **REQUIRED:** The description of the asset-liability method of accounting for deferred income taxes.
 **DISCUSSION:** A DTA or DTL is measured at the rates expected to apply when it is realized or settled, based on tax laws and rates enacted or substantively enacted as of the balance sheet date. If different rates apply to different taxable profit levels, a DTA or DTL is measured based on the average rates expected to apply in the periods when the TDs are expected to reverse. The tax rate or tax base may vary with the manner of recovery or settlement. For example, one tax rate may apply if an asset is sold immediately and another may apply if it is to be recovered through continued use.
 Answer (A) is incorrect because this statement describes the deferred method of accounting for deferred income taxes. Answer (C) is incorrect because this statement describes the net-of-tax method, which recognizes that future taxability and deductibility are important factors in the valuation of individual assets and liabilities. Answer (D) is incorrect because this statement describes the nonallocation or flow-through approach, which does not support the calculation and reporting of deferred income tax.

**47.** Which one of the following temporary differences will result in a deferred tax asset?

A. Use of the straight-line depreciation method for determining accounting profit and an accelerated method for determining taxable profit (tax loss).

B. Installment sale profits accounted for on the accrual basis for determining accounting profit and on a cash basis for determining taxable profit (tax loss).

C. Advance rental receipts accounted for on the accrual basis for financial statement purposes and on a cash basis for tax purposes.

D. Prepaid expenses accounted for on the accrual basis for determining accounting profit and on a cash basis for determining taxable profit (tax loss).

Answer (C) is correct.  *(CMA, adapted)*
**REQUIRED:** The temporary difference that will result in a deferred tax asset.
**DISCUSSION:** A deferred tax asset records the deferred tax consequences attributable to deductible temporary differences and carryforwards. Advance rental receipts accounted for on the accrual basis for determining accounting profit and on a cash basis for determining taxable profit (tax loss) would give rise to a deferred tax asset. The financial statements would show no income and no related tax expense because the rental payments apply to future periods. The tax return, however, would show the rent as income when the cash was received, and a tax would be due in the year of receipt. Because the tax is paid prior to recording accounting profits, it represents an asset that will be recognized as an expense when income is finally recorded.
Answer (A) is incorrect because using an accelerated depreciation method for determining taxable profit (tax loss) results in a deferred tax liability. Answer (B) is incorrect because recognizing installment income on the financial statements but not the tax return results in a taxable temporary difference. Answer (D) is incorrect because recognizing prepaid expenses earlier on the tax return than on the financial statements (a situation akin to the accelerated depreciation of fixed assets) gives rise to a deferred tax liability.

**48.** At December 31, SCM Ltd., a calendar-year enterprise, reported the following accounts for which the carrying amount differed from the tax base:

|  | Carrying Amount | Tax Base |
|---|---|---|
| Depreciable assets (net) | 150,000 | 80,000 |
| Deferred rental income | 40,000 | 0 |

What taxable and deductible amounts are related to these temporary differences?

|  | Taxable Amounts | Deductible Amounts |
|---|---|---|
| A. | 40,000 | 70,000 |
| B. | 70,000 | 40,000 |
| C. | 0 | 110,000 |
| D. | 110,000 | 0 |

Answer (B) is correct.  *(Publisher)*
**REQUIRED:** The taxable and deductible amounts arising from the temporary differences.
**DISCUSSION:** The difference between the carrying amount of an asset or liability and its tax base is a temporary difference (TD). A taxable (deductible) TD results in taxable (deductible) amounts in the future when the carrying amount of the asset or liability is recovered or settled. The tax base is the amount attributed for tax purposes to an asset or liability. The tax base of an asset is the amount deductible against future taxable economic benefits when the asset's carrying amount is recovered. The tax base of a liability is the portion of the carrying amount that will not be deductible against future taxable economic benefits for tax purposes. The tax base of revenue received in advance (a liability) is the portion of the carrying amount taxable in the future. Thus, the 70,000 temporary difference (150,000 carrying amount – 80,000 tax base) related to the depreciable assets is classified as a taxable amount. When income, such as rental income, is taxable before being recognized in accounting profit, future sacrifices to provide the rental service or refund amounts paid will result in future tax deductible amounts when the liability is settled. Thus, the 40,000 temporary difference (40,000 carrying amount – 0 tax base) related to the deferred rental revenue is classified as a deductible amount.

**49.** Which of the following results in a tax base of zero?

A. Trade receivables have a carrying amount of 1,000, and the related revenue has been included in full in the determination of taxable profit.

B. A loan receivable has a carrying amount of 1,000, and repayment has no tax effects.

C. Unearned interest revenue has a carrying amount of 1,000, and the related interest revenue was included in full in the determination of taxable profit.

D. Accrued expenses have a carrying amount of 1,000, and the related expense has been included in full in the determination of taxable profit.

Answer (C) is correct.  *(Publisher)*
**REQUIRED:** The balance sheet item with a tax base of zero.
**DISCUSSION:** The difference between the carrying amount of an asset or liability and its tax base is a temporary difference (TD). A taxable (deductible) TD results in taxable (deductible) amounts in the future when the carrying amount of the asset or liability is recovered or settled. The tax base is the amount attributed for tax purposes to an asset or liability. The tax base of an asset is the amount deductible against future taxable economic benefits when the asset's carrying amount is recovered. The tax base of a liability is the portion of the carrying amount that will not be deductible against future taxable economic benefits for tax purposes. The tax base of revenue received in advance (a liability) is the portion of the carrying amount taxable in the future. For unearned interest revenue for which the related interest revenue was taxed on a cash basis, the tax base equals zero (1,000 carrying amount – 1,000 not taxable in the future).

Questions 50 and 51 are based on the following information. An enterprise has purchased an asset with a 10-year useful life. It will use an accelerated depreciation method for determining taxable profit or tax loss. For determining accounting profit, it will use straight-line depreciation.

**50.** During the 10-year life of the asset, the enterprise will report as deferred tax an amount that

A. Increases steadily for the 10 years.

B. Is constant.

C. Increases and then decreases.

D. Decreases and then increases.

Answer (C) is correct. *(CIA, adapted)*
REQUIRED: The deferred tax amount reported.
DISCUSSION: The cumulative deferred tax increases, peaks, and then decreases to zero over the life of the asset. In the early years, the asset is depreciated more quickly for tax purposes than for financial reporting purposes. This temporary difference reverses in later years. Hence, in the early years, actual taxes payable will be less than tax expense reported in the financial statements, and a deferred tax liability will be recognized. By the end of the asset's useful life, cumulative actual taxes paid will equal cumulative reported tax expense, so the deferred tax balance will be zero.

**51.** When determining cash flows accruing to the enterprise, using financial statements prepared for tax purposes will result in

A. No effect on cash flow amounts.

B. An overstatement of cash flows throughout the economic life of the asset.

C. An understatement of cash flows throughout the economic life of the asset.

D. An overstatement of cash flows in the early years and then an understatement of cash flows in the later years of the economic life of the asset.

Answer (A) is correct. *(CIA, adapted)*
REQUIRED: The effect on cash flows of using financial statements prepared for tax purposes.
DISCUSSION: Cash flows are not affected by the basis of accounting used to prepare the financial statements. Accordingly, whether the financial statements are prepared based on the tax basis, the cash basis, or accounting principles generally accepted in a given country, cash flows should be the same. For example, the cash inflow or outflow resulting from using an accelerated depreciation method to determine actual tax expense or benefit (the amount paid to or refunded by the taxing authority) is completely unaffected by the depreciation method used in the financial statements. However, if cash flows are derived indirectly by adjusting net profit or loss reported in the financial statements, different adjustments are necessary to arrive at the same cash flow amounts if different bases of accounting are used in the preparation of the financial statements.

**52.** Based on its current operating levels, Glucose Plc estimates that its annual level of taxable profit in the foreseeable future will be 200,000 annually. Enacted tax rates for the tax jurisdiction in which Glucose operates are 15% for the first 50,000 of taxable profit, 25% for the next 50,000 of taxable profit, and 35% for taxable profit in excess of 100,000. Which tax rate should Glucose use to measure a deferred tax liability or asset?

A. 15%

B. 25%

C. 27.5%

D. 35%

Answer (C) is correct. *(Publisher)*
REQUIRED: The tax rate applicable to the measurement of a deferred tax liability or asset.
DISCUSSION: In measuring a deferred tax liability or asset, the objective is to use the enacted or substantively enacted tax rate(s) expected to apply to taxable profit in the periods in which the deferred tax liability or asset is expected to be settled or realized. If different rates apply to different taxable profit levels, a DTA or DTL is measured based on the average rates expected to apply in the periods when the TDs are expected to reverse. Accordingly, the applicable tax rate is 27.5%.

| Taxable Profit | | Tax Rate | | |
|---|---|---|---|---|
| 50,000 | × | 15% | = | 7,500 |
| 50,000 | × | 25% | = | 12,500 |
| 100,000 | × | 35% | = | 35,000 |
| 200,000 | | | | 55,000 |

$$55,000 \div 200,000 = 27.5\%$$

Answer (A) is incorrect because 15% is the tax rate for the first 50,000 of taxable profit. Answer (B) is incorrect because 25% is the tax rate for taxable profit over 50,000 but less than 100,000. Answer (D) is incorrect because 35% is the tax rate for taxable profit over 100,000.

**53.** When an enterprise reports deferred tax assets and liabilities, deferred tax expense or income should be disclosed equal to the

   A.   Decrease in the deferred tax assets.

   B.   Sum of the net changes in deferred tax assets and deferred tax liabilities.

   C.   Increase in the deferred tax liabilities.

   D.   Amount of the total tax liability.

Answer (B) is correct.   *(Publisher)*
**REQUIRED:** The deferred tax expense or income disclosed.
**DISCUSSION:** The deferred tax expense or income disclosed is the sum of the net changes in the deferred tax assets and deferred tax liabilities. This amount is the deferred tax expense or income relating to the origination or reversal of temporary differences. For example, the reduction in a deferred tax asset or an increase in a deferred tax liability increases deferred tax expense.
Answer (A) is incorrect because the deferred tax expense or income is equal to the sum of the net changes in the deferred tax assets and deferred tax liabilities. Answer (C) is incorrect because the deferred tax expense or income is equal to the sum of the net changes in the deferred tax assets and deferred tax liabilities. Answer (D) is incorrect because the total tax liability includes both the current and deferred tax expense or income for the year.

**54.** On December 31, year 1, Health Enterprises reported a 150,000 warranty expense in its income statement. The expense was based on actual warranty costs of 30,000 in year 1 and expected warranty costs of 35,000 in year 2, 40,000 in year 3, and 45,000 in year 4. For tax purposes, warranty costs are not deductible until paid. At December 31, year 1, deferred taxes should be based on a

   A.   120,000 deductible temporary difference.

   B.   150,000 deductible temporary difference.

   C.   120,000 taxable temporary difference.

   D.   150,000 taxable temporary difference.

Answer (A) is correct.   *(Publisher)*
**REQUIRED:** The taxable (deductible) temporary difference resulting from a warranty.
**DISCUSSION:** At year-end year 1, Health Enterprises should report a 120,000 warranty liability in its balance sheet. The warranty liability is equal to the 150,000 warranty expense minus the 30,000 warranty cost actually incurred in year 1. Because warranty costs are not deductible until paid, the tax base of the warranty liability is 0. The result is a 120,000 temporary difference (120,000 carrying amount – 0 tax base). When the liability is settled through the actual incurrence of warranty costs, the amounts will be deductible. Thus, the temporary difference should be classified as a deductible temporary difference.
Answer (B) is incorrect because 150,000 equals the warranty expense, not the payable. Answer (C) is incorrect because warranty costs will result in a deductible amount. Answer (D) is incorrect because the warranty costs will result in a deductible amount, and the 30,000 actual warranty costs is currently deductible.

## 5.6 Exchange Rates

**55.** On September 22, 20X2, Yumi Corp. purchased merchandise from an unaffiliated foreign company for 10,000 units of the foreign company's local currency. On that date, the spot rate was $.55. Yumi paid the bill in full on March 20, 20X3, when the spot rate was $.65. The spot rate was $.70 on December 31, 20X2. What amount should Yumi report as a foreign currency transaction loss in its income statement for the year ended December 31, 20X2?

   A.   $0

   B.   $500

   C.   $1,000

   D.   $1,500

Answer (D) is correct.   *(CPA, adapted)*
**REQUIRED:** The amount of foreign currency transaction loss to be reported in the income statement.
**DISCUSSION:** SFAS 52 requires that a receivable or payable denominated in a foreign currency be adjusted to its current exchange rate at each balance sheet date. The resulting gain or loss should ordinarily be included in determining net income. It is the difference between the spot rate on the date the transaction originates and the spot rate at year-end. Thus, the 20X2 transaction loss for Yumi Corp. is $1,500 [($0.55 – $0.70) × 10,000 units].
Answer (A) is incorrect because a loss resulted when the spot rate increased. Answer (B) is incorrect because $500 results from using the spot rates at 12/31/X2 and 3/20/X3. Answer (C) is incorrect because $1,000 results from using the spot rates at 9/22/X2 and 3/20/X3.

**56.** XYZ Company purchased $10,000 of British pounds and $25,000 of land in euros on June 1 of the current year. At the end of XYZ Company's fiscal year on December 31, the spot rate for the British pounds was $12,000. The land had a value of $27,500 in euros. XYZ Company records its nonmonetary items at historical cost. Which of the following is the correct presentation of this transaction on XYZ Company's balance sheet?

|    | British Pounds | Land     |
|----|----------------|----------|
| A. | $10,000        | $25,000  |
| B. | $10,000        | $27,500  |
| C. | $12,000        | $25,000  |
| D. | $12,000        | $27,500  |

Answer (C) is correct. *(Publisher)*
**REQUIRED:** The correct recognition of foreign currency transactions on the balance sheet.
**DISCUSSION:** At the balance sheet date, monetary items are reported at the closing rate which is often the spot rate on the balance sheet date. Nonmonetary items measured at historical cost are reported at the rate on the transaction date. Therefore, the British pounds are reported at $12,000 and the land is reported at $25,000.
Answer (A) is incorrect because the British pounds are reported at the spot rate on the date of the balance sheet. Answer (B) is incorrect because the British pounds are reported at the spot rate on the balance sheet date and the land is valued at the date of purchase. Answer (D) is incorrect because the land is reported based upon the historical cost on the purchase date.

## 5.7 Joint Ventures

**57.** Which of the following is true with regard to joint ventures?

A. The establishment of a separate financial structure is necessary when joint venturers own joint assets.

B. Two venturers are not allowed to transfer assets and liabilities in a given line of business to a jointly controlled entity.

C. When a jointly controlled entity becomes a subsidiary of the venturer, consolidation is required.

D. An investor is a party to the venture who has joint control.

Answer (C) is correct. *(Publisher)*
**REQUIRED:** The true statement with regard to joint ventures.
**DISCUSSION:** A joint venture "is a contractual arrangement whereby two or more parties undertake an economic activity that is subject to joint control." When a jointly controlled entity becomes a subsidiary of the venturer, consolidation is required.
Answer (A) is incorrect because jointly controlled assets do not require the establishment of an organization or financial structure separate from the venturers. Answer (B) is incorrect because the venturers may establish a separate entity in which each has an interest and that operates in the same manner as other entities if they choose to have a jointly controlled entity. Answer (D) is incorrect because an investor is a party to the venture who lacks joint control.

## 5.8 Business Combinations

**58.** To effect a business combination initiated on July 1, 2004, Proper Co. acquired all the outstanding common shares of Scapula Co. for cash equal to the carrying amount of Scapula's net assets. The carrying amounts of Scapula's assets and liabilities approximated their fair values, except that the carrying amount of its building was more than fair value. In preparing Proper's December 31, 2004 consolidated income statement, what is the effect of recording the assets acquired and liabilities assumed at fair value and should goodwill amortization be recognized?

|    | Depreciation Expense | Goodwill Amortization |
|----|----------------------|-----------------------|
| A. | Lower                | Yes                   |
| B. | Higher               | Yes                   |
| C. | Lower                | No                    |
| D. | Higher               | No                    |

Answer (C) is correct. *(CPA, adapted)*
**REQUIRED:** The adjustments made in preparing the consolidated income statement.
**DISCUSSION:** A business combination initiated after June 30, 2001 is accounted for as a purchase regardless of the form of consideration given. Under purchase accounting, assets acquired and liabilities assumed should be recorded at their fair values. The differences between fair values and carrying amounts will affect net income when related expenses are incurred. The effect of recording the building at fair value in the consolidated balance sheet instead of its higher carrying amount on Scapula's books will be to decrease future depreciation. If the building is to be used, fair value is its current replacement cost for similar capacity unless expected use indicates a lower value to the acquirer. If the building is to be sold, it should be reported at fair value minus cost to sell. The excess of the cost over fair value of the net assets acquired will be recognized as goodwill, but, under SFAS 142, this amount will be tested for impairment but not amortized.
Answer (A) is incorrect because depreciation will decrease, and goodwill will be recognized but not amortized. Answer (B) is incorrect because depreciation will decrease, and goodwill will be recognized but not amortized. Answer (D) is incorrect because depreciation will decrease, and goodwill will be recognized but not amortized.

**59.** Pellew Corp. paid $600,000 for the outstanding common stock of Samos Co. in a business combination initiated and completed in December 2004. At that time, Samos had the following condensed balance sheet:

|  | Carrying Amounts |
| --- | --- |
| Current assets | $ 80,000 |
| Plant and equipment, net | 760,000 |
| Liabilities | 400,000 |
| Equity | 440,000 |

The fair value of the plant and equipment was $120,000 more than its carrying amount. The fair values and carrying amounts were equal for all other assets and liabilities. What amount of goodwill, related to Samos's acquisition, should Pellew report in its consolidated balance sheet?

A. $40,000

B. $80,000

C. $120,000

D. $160,000

Answer (A) is correct.   *(CPA, adapted)*
**REQUIRED:** The amount of goodwill reported in the consolidated balance sheet.
**DISCUSSION:** A business combination initiated after June 30, 2001 is accounted for as a purchase regardless of the form of the consideration given. Under purchase accounting, assets acquired and liabilities assumed should be recorded at their fair values. Any excess of cost over the fair value of the net assets acquired is recorded as goodwill. After adjusting the net plant and equipment, and given that other items are stated at fair value, the fair value of the net assets acquired is $560,000 [$80,000 current assets + ($760,000 + $120,000) plant and equipment – $400,000 liabilities]. Hence, goodwill is $40,000 ($600,000 cost – $560,000).
Answer (B) is incorrect because $80,000 is the amount of current assets. Answer (C) is incorrect because $120,000 is the amount plant and equipment is undervalued. Answer (D) is incorrect because $160,000 is the difference between the $600,000 cost and the $440,000 carrying amount of the net assets.

**60.** In a business combination, the sum of the amounts assigned by the acquiring entity to assets acquired and liabilities assumed exceeds the cost of the acquired entity. The excess should be reported as a

A. Deferred credit.

B. Reduction of the amounts assigned to current assets and a deferred credit for any unallocated portion.

C. Reduction of the amounts assigned to certain acquired assets and an extraordinary gain for any unallocated portion.

D. Pro rata reduction of the amounts assigned to all acquired assets and an extraordinary gain for any unallocated portion.

Answer (C) is correct.   *(CPA, adapted)*
**REQUIRED:** The accounting for the excess of the fair value of acquired net assets over cost.
**DISCUSSION:** In a business combination, any excess of the fair value assigned to the net assets acquired over the cost of the purchase must be allocated proportionately to reduce the amounts otherwise assignable to all of the acquired assets except (a) financial assets (excluding equity-method investments), (b) assets to be disposed of by sale, (c) deferred tax assets, (d) prepaid assets relating to post-retirement benefit plans, and (e) other current assets. Any remainder after the amounts otherwise assignable to those assets have been reduced to zero is reported as an extraordinary gain (SFAS 141).
Answer (A) is incorrect because a deferred credit is never recognized for the excess of the fair value of acquired net assets over cost. Answer (B) is incorrect because the allocated portion is reported as an extraordinary gain, not as a deferred credit. Answer (D) is incorrect because the amounts assigned to certain acquired assets (most financial assets, assets to be disposed of by sale, etc.) are not reduced.

# STUDY UNIT SIX
# FINANCE

(32 pages of outline)

The emphasis of this study unit is on the financing of an enterprise. Sources of funds may be internal or external, short-term or long-term, and debt or equity. Selecting the appropriate types and amounts of available financing sources is necessary to minimize the firm's cost of capital and maximize shareholder value.

In the **formative stage** of the **business development life cycle**, the emerging firm most likely relies on the personal resources of its owners, assistance from governmental agencies, and trade credit for its financing needs. If the firm is successful and enters the stage of **rapid growth**, internal financing becomes feasible, and trade credit continues to be used. Moreover, the firm's performance may enable it to secure bank credit to meet seasonal needs and intermediate-term loans. Such a firm may also attract equity financing from venture capitalists. If the firm is extremely successful, it may be able to issue securities that are publicly traded. Thus, the firm may enter the formal capital and money markets. These markets provide financing at lower cost than venture capitalists. At this stage, however, the firm must consider the limitations of the **product life cycle**. Absent the development of new products, growth will not continue, and the firm will enter the **product maturity and decline stage**. The financing pattern at this stage usually includes internal financing, diversification, share repurchases, and mergers.

## 6.1 LONG-TERM FINANCING

1. A firm may have long-term funding requirements that it cannot, or does not want to, meet using retained earnings. It must therefore issue equity or debt securities. Certain hybrid forms are also used for long-term financing, e.g., convertible securities.

2. The principal considerations when reviewing financing choices are cost, risk, and the lender's (the investor's) view of the financing device.

3. **Common Shares**. The common shareholders are the owners of the corporation, and their rights as owners, although reasonably uniform, depend on the laws where the firm is incorporated. Equity ownership involves risk because holders of common shares are not guaranteed a return and are last in priority in a liquidation. Equity provides the cushion for creditors if any losses occur on liquidation.

   a. Advantages of common shares to the issuer

      1) Dividends are not fixed. They are paid from profits when available.
      2) There is no fixed maturity date for repayment of the capital.
      3) The sale of common shares increases the creditworthiness of the firm by providing more equity.

4) Common shares are frequently more attractive to investors than debt because it grows in value with the success of the firm.

   a) The higher the common share value, the more advantageous equity financing is over debt financing.

b. Disadvantages of common shares to the issuer

   1) Control (voting rights) is usually diluted as more common shares are sold.
   2) New common shares dilute earnings available to existing shareholders because of the greater number of shares outstanding.
   3) Underwriting costs are typically higher for common share issues.
   4) Too much equity may raise the average cost of capital of the firm above its optimal level.
   5) Common share cash dividends may not be deductible as an expense and are after-tax cash deductions to the firm.

c. Common shareholders ordinarily have **preemptive rights**.

   1) Preemptive rights give common shareholders the right to purchase any additional issuances in proportion to their current ownership.
   2) If applicable law or the corporate charter does not provide preemptive rights, the firm may nevertheless sell to the common shareholders in a **rights** offering. Each shareholder is issued a certificate or warrant that is an option to buy a certain number of shares at a fixed price within a given time.

      a) Until the rights are actually issued, the shares trade **rights-on**; that is, the shares and the rights are not separable. After the rights are received, the shares trade **ex-rights** because the rights can be sold separately. The price of a share right sold rights-on is

$$\frac{P - S}{N + 1}$$

   If: P = value of a share rights-on
       S = subscription price of a share
       N = number of rights needed to buy a share

4. **Preferred shares** are a hybrid of debt and equity. They have a fixed charge and increase leverage, but payment of dividends is not a legal obligation.

   a. Advantages of preferred shares to the issuer

      1) They are a form of equity and therefore build the creditworthiness of the firm.
      2) Control is still held by common shareholders.
      3) Superior earnings of the firm are usually still reserved for the common shareholders.

   b. Disadvantages of preferred shares to the issuer

      1) Preferred share cash dividends paid are not tax deductible in most countries. The result is a substantially greater cost relative to bonds.
      2) In periods of economic difficulty, accumulated (past) dividends may create major managerial and financial problems for the firm.

c. Typical provisions of preferred share issues

1) **Par value**. Par value is the liquidation value, and a percentage of par equals the preferred dividend.

2) **Priority** in assets and earnings. If the firm goes bankrupt, the preferred shareholders have priority over common shareholders.

3) **Accumulation of dividends**. If preferred dividends in arrears are cumulative, they must be paid before any common dividends can be paid.

4) **Convertibility**. Preferred share issues may be convertible into common shares at the option of the shareholder.

5) **Participation**. Preferred shares may participate with common in excess earnings of the company. For example, 8% participating preferred shares might pay a dividend each year greater than 8% when the corporation is extremely profitable. But nonparticipating preferred shares will receive no more than is stated on the face of the share.

6) **Redeemability**. Some preferred shares may be redeemed at a given time or at the option of the holder or otherwise at a time not controlled by the issuer. This feature makes preferred shares more nearly akin to debt, particularly in the case of **transient preferred stock**, which must be redeemed within a short time (e.g., 5 to 10 years).

7) **Voting rights**. These may be conferred if preferred dividends are in arrears for a stated period.

8) **Callability**. The issuer may have the right to repurchase the shares. For example, the shares may be noncallable for a stated period after which they may be called if the issuer pays a call premium.

9) **Maturity**. Preferred shares may have a sinking fund that allows for the purchase of a given annual percentage of the outstanding shares.

d. Holding preferred shares rather than bonds may provide corporations a tax advantage. A portion of dividends received from preferred shares may be tax deductible, whereas all bond interest received ordinarily is taxable.

5. **Bonds** are long-term debt instruments. They are similar to term loans except that they are usually offered to the public and sold to many investors.

a. Advantages of bonds to the issuer

1) Basic control of the firm is not shared with the debtholder.

2) Cost of debt is limited. Bondholders usually do not participate in the superior earnings of the firm.

3) Ordinarily, the expected yield of bonds is lower than the cost of shares.

4) Interest paid on debt is usually tax deductible.

5) Debt may add substantial flexibility in the financial structure of the corporation through the use of call provisions.

b. Disadvantages of bonds to the issuer

1) Debt has a fixed charge. If the earnings of the firm fluctuate, the risk of insolvency is increased by the fixed interest obligation.

2) Debt adds risk to a firm. Shareholders will consequently demand higher capitalization rates on equity earnings, which may result in a decline in the market price of shares.

3) Debt usually has a maturity date.

4) Debt is a long-term commitment, a factor that can affect risk profiles. Debt originally appearing to be profitable may become a burden and drive the firm into bankruptcy.

5) Certain managerial prerogatives are usually surrendered in the contractual relationship defined in the bond indenture.

a) For example, specific ratios may have to remain above a certain level during the term of the loan.

6) The amount of debt financing available to the individual firm is limited. Generally accepted standards of the investment community will usually dictate a certain debt-equity ratio for a firm. Beyond this limit, the cost of debt may rise rapidly, or debt financing may not be available.

c. The **bond indenture** is the contractual arrangement between the issuer and the bondholders. It contains restrictive covenants intended to prevent the issuer from taking actions contrary to the interests of the bondholders. A trustee, often a bank, is appointed to ensure compliance.

1) **Call provisions** give the corporation the right to redeem bonds. If interest rates decline, the company can call high-interest bonds and replace them with low-interest bonds.

2) Bonds are **putable** or redeemable if the holder has the right to exchange them for cash. This option is usually activated only if the issuer takes a stated action, for example, greatly increasing its debt or being acquired by another entity.

3) **Sinking fund** requirements provide for the firm to retire a certain portion of its bonds each year or to set aside money for repayment in the future. Such terms increase the probability of repayment for bondholders but require the use of capital by the firm.

4) The issuer may be required to maintain its financial ratios, e.g., times-interest-earned, at specified levels.

5) Dividends may be limited if earnings do not meet specified requirements.

6) The amount of new bonds issued may be restricted to a percentage of bondable property (fixed assets).

d. Types of bonds

1) A **mortgage bond** is a pledge of certain assets for a loan. It is usually secured by real property as a condition of the loan.

2) A **debenture** is a long-term bond not secured by specific property. Only companies with the best credit ratings can issue debentures because holders will be general creditors. They will have a status inferior to that of secured parties and creditors with priorities in bankruptcy.

3) **Subordinated debentures** normally have a higher yield than secured bonds because they are subordinated (inferior) to the claims of other general creditors, secured parties, and persons with priorities in bankruptcy. The bond indenture specifies the claims (senior debt) to which these bonds are subordinate. They are usually issued only when the company has some debt instrument outstanding that prohibits the issuance of additional regular bonds.

4) An **income bond** pays interest only if the issuing company has earnings. Such bonds are riskier than other bonds.

5) **Serial bonds** have staggered maturities. These bonds permit investors to choose the maturity dates that meet their needs.

6) **Registered bonds** are issued in the name of the owner. Interest payments are sent directly to the owner. When the owner sells registered bonds, the bond certificates must be surrendered and new certificates issued.

    a) They differ from **coupon (bearer) bonds**, which can be freely transferred and have a detachable coupon for each interest payment.

7) **Participating bonds** participate in excess earnings of the debtor as defined in the indenture.

8) **Indexed bonds** (purchasing power bonds) pay interest that is indexed to a measure of general purchasing power, such as the Consumer Price Index.

9) **Zero-coupon bonds** pay no interest but sell at a deep discount from face value.

    a) The need to reinvest the periodic payments from normal bonds makes their final return uncertain because future reinvestment rates are uncertain. But investors know the exact return on a zero-coupon bond. Investors might therefore be willing to pay a premium for them, which in turn might lead firms to issue them.

    b) The lack of interest payments means the firm faces no additional insolvency risk from the issue until it matures.

10) **Junk bonds** are very high-risk, high-yield securities issued to finance leveraged buyouts and mergers. They are also issued by troubled companies. They exploit the large tax deductions for interest paid by entities with high debt ratios.

11) **International bonds** exist in two forms: foreign bonds and Eurobonds. **Foreign bonds** are denominated in the currency of the nation in which they are sold. **Eurobonds** are denominated in a currency other than that of the nation where they are sold.

    a) For example, foreign bonds issued in the United States and denominated in dollars must be registered with the SEC, but such extensive disclosure is not required in most European nations. Thus, a U.S. company may elect to issue Eurobonds denominated in dollars in a foreign nation because of the convenience of not having to comply with registration requirements.

6. Share rights and convertibility are among the common financing arrangements used to increase investor interest in corporate securities. The objective is a lower interest rate on bonds or a higher selling price for shares.

    a. **Share rights** evidenced by **warrants** are options that are distributed with debt or preferred shares. They permit a holder to share in a company's prosperity through a future purchase of shares at a special low price. They should be distinguished from put and call options.

        1) A **put option** is a right traded in the shares market to sell shares at a given price within a specified period.

        2) A **call option** is a right to purchase shares at a given price within a specified period.

        3) Neither a put nor a call is issued by the company whose shares are the subject of the option.

    b. **Convertibility.** Bonds or preferred shares may be exchangeable (by the investor) into common shares under certain conditions.

    c. Both the issuance of rights and a conversion feature offer a corporation a means of delayed equity financing when market prices are unfavorable. When the market price rises above the conversion price, holders will presumably exercise the rights or convert the securities.

7.   **Intermediate-term financing** refers to debt issues having approximate maturities of greater than 1 but less than 10 years. The principal types of intermediate-term financing are term loans and lease financing. Major lenders under term agreements are commercial banks, life insurance companies, and, to some extent, pension funds.

   a.   **Term loans**. One possible feature of term loans is tying the interest payable on the loan to a variable rate. This **floating rate**, usually stated as some percentage over the prime, may result in extremely high borrowing costs.

      1)   This risk must be traded off against

         a)   The need of the firm to obtain the loan
         b)   The flexibility inherent in term borrowing
         c)   The ability of the firm to borrow in the capital market
         d)   Other available types of debt financing
         e)   The amount of privacy desired

      2)   Term loans are private contracts between private firms, whereas long-term debt securities usually involve governmental regulation, often including disclosure.

      3)   Variable or floating rate loans are advantageous to lenders because they permit better matching of interest costs and revenues. The market values of these loans also tend to be more stable than those for fixed rate loans.

         a)   The disadvantages include a heightened risk of default, losses of expected revenues if interest rates decline or if market rates rise above the ceiling specified in the agreement, and the difficulty of working with a more complex product.

      4)   Borrowers may benefit from the lower initial costs of these loans but must accept increased interest rate risk, the difficulty of forecasting cash flows, a possible loss of creditworthiness if interest rates are expected to rise, and the burden of more complex financing arrangements.

      5)   If the interest rate is variable but the monthly loan payment is fixed, an increase in the rate means that the interest component of the payment and the total interest for the loan term will be greater.

         a)   The term of the loan will also be extended, and the principal balance will increase because amortization is diminished. Indeed, negative amortization may occur if the interest rate increase is great enough.

   b.   **Lease financing** offers a variety of tax and other benefits. If leases are not accounted for as installment purchases, they provide off-balance-sheet financing. Thus, under an operating lease, the lessee need not record an asset or a liability, and rent expense rather than interest is recognized.

8.   **Maturity matching** (equalizing the life of an asset acquired with the debt instrument used to finance it) is an important factor in choosing the source of funds. Financing long-term assets with long-term debt allows the company to generate sufficient cash flows from the assets to satisfy obligations as they mature.

9. **Venture Capital**. Venture capital firms invest in new enterprises that might not be able to obtain funds in the usual capital markets due to the riskiness of new products. Placements of securities with venture capital firms are usually private placements and not subject to government regulation.

    a.   Venture capitalists accept low liquidity for their investments and high risk.

    b.   The payoff may be substantial if the company does succeed.

    c.   Venture capital is usually sought during the rapid growth stage of the firm's development.

10. Stop and review! You have completed the outline for this subunit. Study multiple-choice questions 1 through 12 beginning on page 292.

## 6.2 SHORT-TERM FINANCING

1.   Short-term credit is debt scheduled to be repaid within 1 year. Three main sources of this credit are trade credit, commercial banks, and commercial paper, but many other sources are available.

    a.   The terms of **trade credit** are set by suppliers.

        1)   EXAMPLE: If 2/10, net/30 were the method of payment, the buyer has 10 days to take a 2% discount. If it is not taken, the full price must be paid within 30 days. Advantages of this arrangement are that trade credit may be the only source of financing available and that the first 10 days of credit are free. The disadvantage is that the 20 additional days of credit are costly.

        2)   Payments should be made within discount periods if the cost of not taking discounts exceeds the firm's cost of capital.

            a)   The cost of not taking discounts is approximately

$$\frac{360}{(Total\ pay\ period\ -\ Discount\ period)} \times \frac{Discount\ \%}{(100\%\ -\ Discount\ \%)}$$

            b)   In this example, the cost of not taking the discount is

$$\frac{360}{(30\ -\ 10)} \times \frac{2}{(100\ -\ 2)} = 36.7\%$$

            c)   A more accurate calculation of the cost of not taking discounts considers the effects of compounding. In this example, annualizing this cost means that 18 payments are deemed to occur during the year. The annual effective rate is

$$Rate = [1.0 + (2 \div 98)]^{18} - 1.0 = 43.8\%$$

b.  **Commercial banks** have traditionally offered savings (time deposit) and checking (demand deposit) accounts and served as lenders for a variety of purposes. Thus, they have been instrumental in governmental efforts to manage the money supply. However, other financial institutions have emerged that perform such functions. Furthermore, commercial banks have expanded their operations to include stock brokerage, insurance, and other services.

1)  Commercial bank lending is very significant to firms needing sources of short-term and intermediate-term financing. It is second only to trade credit as a source of financing.

a)  The majority of lending by commercial banks is on a short-term basis. Many short-term loans are written for a term of 90 days.

b)  The loan is obtained by signing a **promissory note**. Repayment is made in a lump sum at the maturity date, or installments are paid.

c)  A **line of credit** may be extended to a borrowing firm. An amount is credited to the borrower's checking account for business use. At the maturity date, the checking account is charged the amount constituting repayment, usually principal and interest.

i)  A revolving credit agreement (committed line of credit) imposes a legal obligation on the bank, but the borrower pays a commitment fee.

d)  Commercial banks typically require **compensating balances** in checking accounts equal to some percentage of the loan. The result is an increase in the effective interest rate.

e)  The interest rate at which the bank will lend to a firm will depend on the firm's financial strength. The interest rate may be anywhere from the **prime interest rate** to 2 or 3 points above it. The prime interest rate is the rate charged by commercial banks to their best (the largest and financially strongest) business customers. It is traditionally the lowest rate charged by banks. However, in recent years, banks have been making loans at still lower rates in response to competition from the commercial paper market.

f)  The cost of a bank loan may be determined in several ways. **Simple interest** is based on the borrowed amount and is paid at the end of the loan term. **Discounted interest** is based on the borrowed amount but is paid in advance. The add-on interest rate for an installment loan equals the interest divided by the average balance. Furthermore, **compounding** (periodically adding interest to the carrying amount) increases the effective rate, and the more frequent the compounding, the higher the rate.

i)  Simple interest rate for a 1-year loan:
$$\frac{Interest}{Borrowed\ amount}$$

ii)  Discounted interest rate for a 1-year loan:
$$\frac{Interest}{Borrowed\ amount\ -\ Interest}$$

iii)  Add-on installment interest rate for a 1-year loan:
$$\frac{Interest}{Average\ borrowed\ amount}$$

iv) The present value and future value formulas with which accountants should be very familiar illustrate compounding. However, they are not repeated here.

2) When choosing a commercial lender, a borrower should consider the following:

a) The bank's policy toward risk

b) The additional services and counseling the bank provides to customers

c) The support a bank will provide in times of financial distress. Will the bank pressure a firm to repay its loans on time or negotiate extensions?

d) The degree of loan specialization provided by a bank. For example, a bank may specialize in loans to companies in a given line of business.

e) The size of the bank and its lending capacity. Thus, given that a bank cannot lend more than 15% of its capital to one customer, a large company ordinarily will choose a large bank.

f) The financial strength of the bank

c. **Commercial paper** consists of short-term, unsecured, notes payable issued in large denominations ($100,000 or more) by large companies with high credit ratings to other companies and institutional investors, such as pension funds, banks, and insurance companies. The maturity date of commercial paper is normally less than 270 days. Commercial paper is traded in **money markets** and thus is highly liquid. Commercial paper is a lower cost source of funds than bank loans. It is usually issued at below the prime rate.

1) Advantages are that it affords broad and efficient distribution, provides large sums (at a given cost), and avoids costly financing arrangements.

2) Disadvantages are that it trades in an impersonal market and that the amount available is limited to the excess liquidity of big corporations.

d. Many other types of short-term financing are in use.

1) **Bankers' acceptances** are drafts drawn on deposits at a bank. The acceptance by the bank is a guarantee of payment at maturity.

2) **Repurchase agreements** involve sales by a dealer in government securities who agrees to repurchase at a given time for a specific price. Maturities may be very short-term. This arrangement is in essence a secured loan.

3) **Pledging or assigning receivables** involves securing loans with receivables. A bank will often lend up to 80% of outstanding receivables. Receivables may also be **factored** (sold).

4) **Money-market mutual funds** invest in portfolios of short-term securities.

5) **Warehouse financing** uses inventory as security for the loan. A third party, for example, a public warehouse, holds the collateral and serves as the creditor's agent. The creditor receives the warehouse receipts evidencing rights in the collateral. Security for inventory financing may also be in other forms.

a) A **blanket (floating) lien** against all inventory of the debtor nevertheless permits sale of the inventory. Thus, the value of the collateral may be reduced.

b) A **trust receipt** is an instrument in which the debtor acknowledges that the inventory is held in trust for the creditor. Proceeds of sale of the specified goods are remitted promptly to the creditor. Dealer financing of an automobile purchase uses this method.

c) A **field warehousing arrangement** provides for on-site control and supervision of specified goods by a third party.

6) **Agency securities** are issued by government agencies. An example in the U.S. is the Federal National Mortgage Association (Fannie Mae), which issues mortgage-backed securities. Agency securities may be long- or short-term.

7) National governments may issue long and short-term debt. Examples in the U.S. are **treasury bills**, which are short-term U.S. government obligations issued by the Treasury at a discount from their face value and **treasury notes and bonds**, which are long-term investments.

8) Local governmental entities issue short-term securities that are exempt from taxation.

9) **Chattel mortgages** are loans secured by movable personal property (e.g., equipment or livestock).

2. Stop and review! You have completed the outline for this subunit. Study multiple-choice questions 13 through 20 beginning on page 296.

## 6.3 OPTIMAL CAPITALIZATION

1. The **financial structure** of a firm encompasses the right-hand side of the balance sheet, which describes how the firm's assets are financed. Capital structure is the permanent financing of the firm and is represented primarily by

   a. Long-term debt

      1) Most firms renew (roll over) their long-term obligations. Thus, long-term debt is often effectively permanent.

   b. Preferred stock

   c. Common equity

      1) Common stock
      2) Additional paid-in capital
      3) Retained earnings

2. The following factors influence financial structure:

   a. Growth rate and stability of future sales
   b. Competitive structures in the industry
   c. Asset makeup of the individual firm
   d. Attitude toward risk of owners and management
   e. Control position of owners and management
   f. Lenders' attitudes toward the industry and a particular firm
   g. Tax considerations

3. **Leverage** is the relative amount of the fixed cost of capital, principally debt, in a firm's capital structure. Leverage, by definition, creates financial risk, which relates directly to the question of the cost of capital. The more leverage, the higher the financial risk, and the higher the cost of debt capital.

   a. **Earnings per share** will ordinarily be higher if debt is used to raise capital instead of equity, provided that the firm is not over-leveraged. The reason is that the cost of debt is lower than the cost of equity because interest is tax deductible. However, the prospect of higher EPS is accompanied by greater risk to the firm resulting from required interest costs, creditors' liens on the firm's assets, and the possibility of a proportionately lower EPS if sales volume fails to meet projections.

   b. **The degree of financial leverage (DFL)** is the percentage change in earnings available to common shareholders that is associated with a given percentage change in net operating income. The second formula on the next page can be derived from the first (the derivation is not given).

c.

$$DFL = \frac{\% \; \Delta \; in \; net \; income}{\% \; \Delta \; in \; net \; operating \; income} = \frac{EBIT}{EBIT - I}$$

1) Net income means earnings available to common shareholders.
2) Operating income equals earnings before interest and taxes (EBIT).
3) I equals interest expense. If the company has preferred stock, the second formula is further modified as follows (if P = preferred dividends and T is the tax rate):

$$\frac{EBIT}{EBIT - I - [P \div (1 - T)]}$$

4) The greater the DFL, the riskier the firm.

d. If the return on assets exceeds the cost of debt, additional leverage is favorable.

e. Operating leverage concerns the extent to which fixed costs are used in the production process. A company with a high percentage of fixed costs is more risky than a firm in the same industry that relies more on variable costs to produce.

1) **The degree of operating leverage (DOL)** is the percentage change in net operating income associated with a given percentage change in sales. The formula following the one below can be derived from the first (the derivation is not given).

2)

$$DOL = \frac{\% \; \Delta \; in \; net \; operating \; income}{\% \; \Delta \; in \; sales} = \frac{Contribution \; Margin}{Contribution \; Margin - Fixed \; Costs}$$

a) EXAMPLE: If operating income increases 20% with a 10% increase in sales, DOL is 2.0.

f. **The degree of total leverage (DTL)** combines the DFL and the DOL. It equals the degree of financial leverage times the degree of operating leverage. Thus, it also equals the percentage change in net income that is associated with a given percentage change in sales.

1)

$$DTL = DFL \times DOL = \frac{\% \; \Delta \; in \; net \; income}{\% \; \Delta \; in \; sales}$$

a) EXAMPLE: If net income increases 15% with a 5% increase in sales, DTL is 3.0.

2) Firms with a high degree of operating leverage do not usually employ a high degree of financial leverage and vice versa. One of the most important considerations in the use of financial leverage is operating leverage.

a) EXAMPLE: A firm has a highly automated production process. Because of automation, the degree of operating leverage is 2. If the firm wants a degree of total leverage not exceeding 3, it must restrict its use of debt so that the degree of financial leverage is not more than 1.5. If the firm had committed to a production process that was less automated and had a lower DOL, more debt could be employed, and the firm could have a higher degree of financial leverage.

4.    **Cost of Capital**. Managers must know the cost of capital in making investment (long-term funding) decisions because investments with a return higher than the cost of capital will increase the value of the firm (shareholders' wealth). The theory underlying the cost of capital applies to new, long-term funding because long-term funds finance long-term investments. Short-term funds are used to meet working capital and other temporary needs. Cost of capital is of less concern for short-term funding.

   a.    The cost of capital is a weighted average of the various debt and equity components. The **weighted-average cost of capital** weights the percentage cost of each component by the percentage of that component in the financial structure.

      1)    The **cost of debt** equals the interest rate times one minus the marginal tax rate because interest is a tax deduction. Hence, an increase in the tax rate decreases the cost of debt.

      2)    The **cost of retained earnings** is an opportunity cost. It is the rate that investors can earn elsewhere on investments of comparable risk. The cost of internally generated funds is an imputed cost.

      3)    The **cost of new external common equity** is higher than the cost of retained earnings because of stock flotation costs.

         a)    Providers of equity capital are exposed to more risk than lenders are because the firm is not obligated to pay them a return. Also, in case of liquidation, creditors are paid before equity investors. Thus, equity financing is more expensive than debt because equity investors require a higher return to compensate for the greater risk assumed.

      4)    The **cost of preferred stock** equals the preferred dividend divided by the net issuance price. No tax adjustment is necessary because preferred dividends paid are not deductible.

   b.    Standard financial theory states that an **optimal capital structure** exists.

      1)    The optimal capital structure minimizes the weighted average cost of capital and thereby maximizes the value of the firm's stock.

         a)    The optimal capital structure does not maximize EPS. Greater leverage maximizes EPS but also increases risk. Thus, the highest stock price is not reached by maximizing EPS.

      2)    The optimal capital structure usually involves some debt, but not 100% debt.

      3)    The relevant relationships are depicted below.

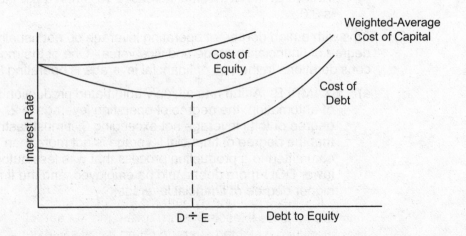

D ÷ E represents the lowest weighted-average cost of capital and is therefore the firm's optimal capital structure.

4) Ordinarily, firms cannot identify this optimal point precisely. Thus, they should attempt to find an optimal range for the capital structure.

c. The required **rate of return on equity capital (R)** can be estimated as follows.

1) The **Capital Asset Pricing Model (CAPM)** adds the risk-free rate (determined by government securities) to the product of the beta coefficient (a measure of the firm's risk) and the difference between the market return and the risk-free rate. Below is the basic equilibrium equation for the CAPM.

$$R = R_F + \beta(R_M - R_F)$$

a) The **market risk premium** $(R_M - R_F)$ is the amount above the risk-free rate required to induce average investors to enter the market.

b) The **beta coefficient ($\beta$)** of an individual stock is the correlation between the volatility (price variation) of the stock market and the volatility of the price of the individual stock.

i) EXAMPLE: If an individual stock rises 10% and the stock market rises 10%, the beta coefficient is 1.0. If the stock rises 15% and the stock market only rises 10%, beta is 1.5.

c) EXAMPLE: Assuming a beta of 1.20, a market rate of return of approximately 17%, and an expected risk-free rate of 12%, the required rate of return on equity capital is .12 + 1.20 (.17 − .12), or 18%.

d) The graph of this equation (with interest rates plotted on the vertical axis and betas on the horizontal axis) is the **Security Market Line**. The slope of the SML equals the market risk premium, and the y-intercept is the risk-free rate.

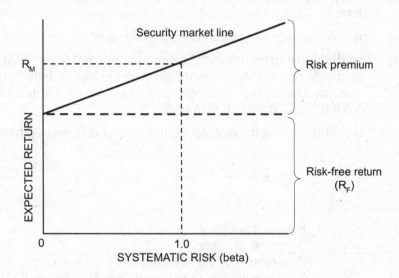

e) **Risk premium** is the difference in expected rates of return on a risky asset and a less risky asset.

2) **Arbitrage pricing theory (APT)** is based on the assumption that an asset's return is based on multiple systematic risk factors. In contrast, the CAPM is a model that uses just one systematic risk factor to explain the asset's return. That factor is the expected return on the market portfolio, i.e., the market-valued weighted average return for all securities available in the market.

a) The difference between actual and expected returns on an asset is attributable to systematic and unsystematic risks. **Unsystematic risk** (also called company-specific risk or diversifiable risk) is specific to a particular asset and can be eliminated by sufficient diversification. However, **systematic risk** (also called market risk or nondiversifiable risk) affects many assets and is undiversifiable. Thus, investors must be paid a risk premium to compensate them for systematic (market) risk.

b) Accordingly, APT provides for a separate beta and a separate risk premium for each systematic risk factor identified in the model. Examples of the many potential systematic risk factors are the gross domestic product (GDP), inflation, and real interest rates. The APT for a three-factor model may be formulated as follows:

$$R = R_F + \beta_1 k_1 + \beta_2 k_2 + \beta_3 k_3$$

If:  $R$ = expected rate of return
 $R_F$ = risk-free rate
 $\beta_{1,2,3}$ = individual factor beta coefficients
 $k_{1,2,3}$ = individual factor risk premiums

c) EXAMPLE: Assume $R_F$ = 9% and

| | | | | |
|---|---|---|---|---|
| $k_1$ | = | 2% | $\beta_1$ = .6 |
| $k_2$ | = | 5% | $\beta_2$ = .4 |
| $k_3$ | = | 8% | $\beta_3$ = .2 |

Applying the above values, the expected rate of return is .09 + (.6)(.02) + (.4)(.05) + (.2)(.08), or 13.8%.

3) R may also be estimated by adding a percentage to the firm's long-term cost of debt.

a) A 3% to 5% premium is frequently used.

4) The **dividend growth model** estimates the cost of retained earnings using the dividends per share, the expected growth rate, and the market price. To justify retention of earnings, management must expect a return at least equal to the dividend yield plus a growth rate.

a) The formula for calculating the cost of retained earnings is

$$R = \frac{D_1}{P_0} + G$$

If:  $P_0$ = current price
 $D_1$ = next dividend
 $R$ = required rate of return
 $G$ = growth rate in dividends per share (but the model assumes that the dividend payout ratio, retention rate, and therefore the EPS growth rate are constant).

i) EXAMPLE: If a company's dividend is expected to be $4 while the market price is $50 and the dividend is expected to grow at a constant rate of 6%, the required rate of return would be $4 ÷ $50 + .06, or 14%.

b) To determine the cost of new common stock (external equity), the model is altered to incorporate the flotation cost. As the flotation cost rises, R increases accordingly.

$$R = \frac{D_1}{P_0(1 - Flotation\ cost)} + G$$

c) The dividend growth model is also used for stock price evaluation. The formula can be restated in terms of $P_0$ as follows:

$$P_0 = \frac{D_1}{R - G}$$

d) The stock price is affected by the dividend payout ratio because some investors may want capital gains, but others may prefer current income. Thus, investors will choose stocks that give the proper mix of capital gains and dividends.

e) A concept relevant to securities valuation is the **efficient markets hypothesis (EMH)**. It states that current share prices immediately and fully reflect all relevant information. Hence, the market is continuously using new information to correct pricing errors, and securities prices are always in equilibrium. The reason is that securities are intensely analyzed by many highly trained individuals. These analysts work for institutions with the resources to take very rapid action when new information is available.

i) The EMH states that abnormal returns cannot be obtained consistently with either fundamental or technical analysis. **Fundamental analysis** evaluates a security's future price based upon sales, internal developments, industry trends, the general economy, and expected changes in each factor. **Technical analysis** evaluates a security's future price based on the sales price and number of shares traded in recent transactions.

ii) Under the EMH, the expected return of each security is equal to the return required by the marginal investor given the risk of the security. Moreover, the price equals its fair value as perceived by investors.

iii) Under the **strong form** of the EMH, all public and private information is instantaneously reflected in securities' prices. Thus, insider trading is assumed not to result in abnormal returns. The **semistrong form** states that all publicly available data are reflected in security prices, but private or insider data are not immediately reflected. Accordingly, insider trading can result in abnormal returns. The **weak form** states that current prices reflect all recent past price data, so technical analysis will not provide a basis for abnormal returns.

iv) Empirical data have refuted only the strong form of the EMH.

v) The price of a security reflects the present value of its future cash flows. If that price is accurate, the net present value of the investment is $0. Thus, if all prices are accurate, every security has an NPV of $0, and all securities are therefore perfect substitutes.

d.  The **marginal cost of capital**. The cost of capital to the firm for the next dollar of new capital increases because lower-cost capital sources are used first.

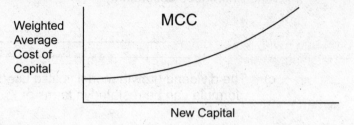

e.  The **marginal efficiency of investment**. The return on additional dollars of capital investment decreases because the most profitable investments are made initially.

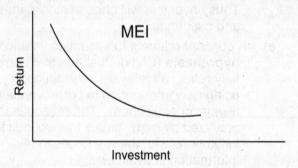

f.  Combining the MCC and MEI schedules (graphs) produces the equilibrium investment level for the firm (Q*) at a particular interest rate (i) and the capital budget.

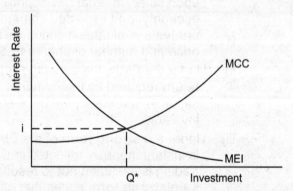

5.  The foregoing outline describes the traditional approach to analysis of capital structure. A contrary view is asserted in the **Modigliani-Miller Hypothesis**, a proposition largely responsible for winning Nobel prizes for its authors. It states that, in an efficient capital market with no tax distortions, the relative proportion of debt and equity in a corporate capitalization does not affect the total market value of the firm, which is dependent on its profitability and risk. Thus, no unique capital structure maximizes firm value.

a.  In a world with no taxes, leverage raises the required rate of return on equity by increasing the risk of equity. In other words, the weighted average cost of capital is constant because the cost of equity will increase as the cost of debt decreases. The implication is that issuing debt is not advantageous merely because its cost is low. Nevertheless, corporate financial officers and financial engineers continue to search for market inefficiencies and tax-related opportunities that can lower a corporation's cost of capital in the real world.

b. Dividends play no role in the Modigliani-Miller analysis because the cost of capital is the same regardless of the source.

c. The hypothesis also assumes that there are no transaction costs for selling equity or debt securities.

6. Stop and review! You have completed the outline for this subunit. Study multiple-choice questions 21 through 32 beginning on page 299.

## 6.4 CASH MANAGEMENT

1. The **cash budget** details projected receipts and disbursements, preferably with a view to planning the synchronization of inflows and outflows.

    a. It is based on the projected sales and credit terms, collection percentages, and estimated purchases and payment terms.

    b. Cash outflows are budgeted based on the level of sales.

    c. Cash budgeting is an ongoing, cumulative activity.

        1) Budgets must be for a specified period of time, and the units of time must be short enough to assure that all cash payments can be made.

2. **Holding cash** is done for the following reasons:

    a. As a **medium of exchange**. Cash is still needed for some business transactions.

    b. As a **precautionary measure**. Cash or a money-market fund can be held for emergencies. Normally, investment in high-grade, short-term securities is a better alternative to holding cash.

        1) Years ago, in face of cash shortages, money was literally held, as a precaution against bank closings.

        2) Today, if the banks fail, paper money will be worthless; thus, there is no precautionary reason to hoard paper currency.

    c. For **speculation**. Cash may be held to take advantage of bargain-purchase opportunities. However, for this purpose too, short-term, highly liquid securities are preferable.

    d. As a **compensating balance** in exchange for a bank's services or loans

3. **Cash collections** should be expedited.

    a. Invoices should be mailed promptly.

    b. Credit terms must be competitive but geared to encourage prompt payment.

    c. A **lockbox system** may be used to expedite the receipt of funds. A company maintains mailboxes, often in numerous locations around the country, to which customers send payments. A bank checks these mailboxes several times a day, and funds received are immediately deposited to the company's account without first being processed by the company's accounting system, thereby hastening availability of the funds. In addition, having several lockboxes throughout the country reduces the time a payment is in the postal system.

        1) **Concentration banking** may be useful in this context. Regional concentration banks may serve as centers for the transfer of lockbox receipts. A disbursement account at the regional center will then expedite the use of the receipts for payments in that region. Such use might be delayed if all receipts were transmitted to a national central bank.

    d. Transfer of monies by wire expedites cash management. A **wire transfer** is any electronic funds transfer by means of a two-way system. An example in the U.S. is the Federal Reserve Wire Transfer System (Fedwire).

e. **Electronic Data Interchange (EDI)** is the communication of electronic documents directly from one computer to another. **Electronic funds transfer (EFT)** and customer debit cards are applications of EDI that expedite cash inflows. With the recent widespread growth of **electronic commerce** (the buying and selling of products and services over the Internet) by individuals, the use of electronic funds transfer has mushroomed. Companies such as PayPal enable individuals to transfer funds to each other at little or no cost.

f. **Automated clearing houses (ACHs)** are electronic networks that facilitate the reading of data among banks. In the U.S., the 32 regional ACH associations guarantee 1-day clearing of checks. Except for the New York ACH, they are operated by the Federal Reserve.

4. **Slowing cash disbursements** increases available cash.

a. Payment beyond normal credit terms, however, creates vendor ill will and may incur interest charges.

b. Payments should be made within discount periods if the cost of not taking a discount exceeds the firm's cost of capital.

c. Payment by **draft** (a three-party instrument in which the drawer orders the drawee to pay money to the payee) is a means of slowing cash outflows.

1) A check is the most common draft. **Check float** arises from the delay between an expenditure or receipt by check and the clearing of the check.

a) The effect is an interest-free loan to the payor.

b) Accordingly, companies attempt to maximize **disbursements float** (the period from when checks are written to when they are deducted from the bank balance) and minimize **collections float**, which consists of the sum of the time checks are in the mail, internal processing time, and the time required for clearing through the banking system.

2) **Payable through drafts (PTDs)** are also drafts, but they differ from checks because they are not payable on demand, and the drawee is the payor, not a bank. After presentment to a bank, a PTD must be presented to the issuer. If the latter chooses to accept the instrument, it will deposit the necessary funds. Consequently, use of PTDs allows a firm to postpone the deposit of funds and therefore to maintain lower cash balances.

a) The drawbacks of PTDs are that suppliers prefer checks. Furthermore, banks impose greater charges for processing PTDs.

d. When **compensating balances** are negotiated with banks, use of average rather than absolute compensating balances frees most of the compensating balance as a contingency fund.

1) The flexible compensating balance can be used as a cushion for the days when cash demands are greatest and deposits fail to materialize.

2) The effective interest rate on loans requiring compensating balances equals total interest cost divided by total principal.

a) $\dfrac{\text{Total interest cost}}{\text{Total principal}}$

b) Total principal is reduced by the account's ordinary balance, and total interest cost is reduced by the amount of interest that the company would earn on its ordinary balance.

e. **Zero-balancing checking accounts** are disbursement accounts (for example, payroll) offered by some banks. The account balance is maintained at zero until a check comes in. The resulting overdraft is covered by a transfer from a master (parent) account earning interest.

   1) The disadvantages are that the bank may charge a fee for this service and the amount needed in the master account still needs to be estimated.

5. The amount of cash to keep on hand should be determined by cost-benefit analysis.

   a. The reduction in average cash times the interest rate (cost of capital or investment yield rate) is the benefit.

   b. Costs of having insufficient cash include incremental personnel cost, lost discounts, and lost vendor goodwill.

   c. The **economic order quantity (EOQ)** model is applicable to cash management.

      1) It can be stated in terms of the following assumptions:

         a) A known demand for cash

         b) A given carrying (interest) cost

         c) The flat amount (cost) of converting other assets to cash, such as the broker's fee for sale of marketable securities (assumed to be constant regardless of the transaction size)

      2) One such EOQ-type model is the **Baumol Cash Management Model**. The Baumol model attempts to minimize the total of the costs of securities transactions and the opportunity costs of holding cash (the return forgone by not investing in marketable securities or the cost of borrowing cash). If *OC* is the optimal cash level, *b* is the cost per transaction (a fixed amount per transaction), *i* is the interest rate on marketable securities or the cost of borrowing cash, and *T* is the total cash demand for the period, the formula is

$$OC = \sqrt{\frac{2bT}{i}}$$

3) The Baumol model, like the EOQ model, is deterministic and relies on simplifying assumptions. For example, the demand for cash must be known. If such information is not known, the **Miller-Orr Cash Management Model** can be used. The Miller-Orr model assumes uncertain cash flows that are random in amount and direction and are normally distributed as the number of periods increases. It provides for cost efficient cash balances by determining an upper limit and lower limit for cash balances. The target cash balance is between these two limits. As long as cash is between the two limits, no transaction to replenish or invest the cash balance occurs.

    a) The diagram below illustrates the Miller-Orr Model. The objective of the model is to minimize the expected cost of holding cash by choosing appropriate values for two variables: the upper limit (H) and the return point (Z). The lower limit (L) is given. When the cash balance reaches H, sufficient cash is invested to reduce the balance to Z. When the balance falls to L, sufficient assets are sold to increase the balance.

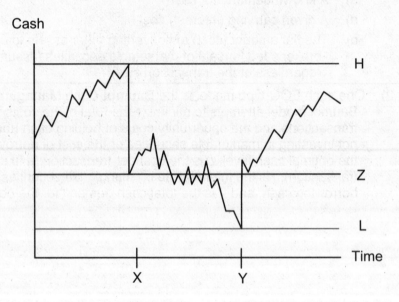

6. A firm's excess cash should be placed in an investment with a high return and little risk, such as those listed below.

    a. **Treasury bills** are short-term government debt securities guaranteed explicitly by the U.S. government and exempt from state and local taxation. They are sold on a discount basis.

        1) Obligations of federal agencies are not guaranteed by the U.S. government but only by the agency itself.

    b. **Certificates of deposit** are a form of savings deposit that cannot be withdrawn before maturity without a high penalty. However, negotiable CDs are subject to government securities regulation.

    c. **Money-market accounts** are similar to checking accounts but pay higher interest.

    d. **High-grade commercial paper** consists of unsecured, short-term notes issued by large companies that are very good credit risks. However, commercial paper may yield a higher return than CDs because it is riskier.

    e. A firm with excessive cash might tend to be an attractive takeover target.

7. Interest rate expectation theory states that long-term interest rates are usually a geometric average of expected future short-term interest rates.

8. Stop and review! You have completed the outline for this subunit. Study multiple-choice questions 33 through 39 beginning on page 303.

## 6.5 MARKETABLE SECURITIES MANAGEMENT

1. Short-term marketable securities (e.g., U.S. T-bills and CDs) are sometimes held as substitutes for cash but are more likely to be acquired as temporary investments.

   a. Most firms avoid large cash balances and prefer borrowing to meet short-term needs.

   b. As temporary investments, marketable securities may be purchased with maturities timed to meet seasonal fluctuations, to pay off a bond issue, to make tax payments, or otherwise to satisfy anticipated needs.

2. Marketable securities should be chosen with a view to the risk of default (**financial risk**).

   a. U.S. government securities are the least risky.

3. **Interest-rate risk** should be minimized given the reasons for holding marketable securities.

   a. Short-term securities are less likely to fluctuate in value because of changes in the general level of interest rates.

4. Changes in the general price level (inflation) determine the purchasing power of payments on investments (principal and interest) and thus the types of securities chosen and the rates charged.

5. The degree of marketability of a security determines its **liquidity**, that is, the ability to resell at the quoted market price.

6. The firm's tax position will influence its choice of securities; for example, a firm with net loss carryforwards may prefer a higher-yielding taxable security to a tax-exempt municipal bond.

7. Short-term marketable securities are usually chosen for reasons that make high-yield, high-risk investments unattractive. Hence, a higher return may be forgone in exchange for greater safety. Given the various options available, a company should have an **investment policy statement** to provide continuing guidance to management regarding the risk-return trade-off.

   a. Thus, speculative tactics, such as selling short (borrowing and selling securities in the expectation that their price will decline by the time they must be replaced) and margin trading (borrowing from a broker to buy securities) are avoided.

8. Stop and review! You have completed the outline for this subunit. Study multiple-choice question 40 on page 305.

## 6.6 RECEIVABLES MANAGEMENT

1. The **objective** of managing accounts receivable is to have both the optimal amount of receivables outstanding and the optimal amount of bad debts.

   a. This balance requires a trade-off between the benefits of credit sales, such as more sales, and the costs of accounts receivable, e.g., collection, interest, and bad debt costs. The appropriate policy does not seek merely to maximize sales or to minimize default risk.

   b. Thus, a firm should extend credit until the marginal benefit (profit) is zero (considering opportunity costs of alternative investments).

2. Credit terms, collection policies, etc., are frequently determined by competitors. A firm must match such inducements to make sales. Firms often use a statistical technique called **credit scoring** to determine whether to extend credit to a specific customer. Credit scoring assigns numerical values to the elements of credit worthiness, e.g., income, length of time employed in the same job, occupation, and home ownership.

3. The objective of receivables management is to maximize the accounts receivable turnover ratio, that is, to shorten the average time receivables are held.

   a. The **accounts receivable turnover ratio** equals net credit sales divided by average accounts receivable.

   b. A common analytical tool is an **aging schedule** developed from a company's accounts receivable ledger. It stratifies the accounts depending on how long they have been outstanding.

   c. The **number of days of receivables** equals the number of days in the year (365, 360, or 300) divided by the receivables turnover ratio. This ratio can be compared with the seller's credit terms to determine whether most customers are paying on time.

      1) It is the average number of days to collect a receivable (collection period).
      2) It may also be computed as average accounts receivable divided by average daily sales (net credit sales ÷ days in a year).

   d. **Average gross receivables** is calculated by multiplying average daily sales by the average collection period.

4. The following are different types of credit instruments used in receivables management:

   a. An **invoice** is a bill issued by a company that has provided goods or services to a customer. It includes the prices, terms, and types of goods. In asset-based lending (such as factoring), an invoice means an account receivable.

   b. A **promissory note** is a two-party negotiable instrument that contains an unconditional promise to pay a fixed sum of money at a definite time.

   c. A **conditional sales contract** is a financing method often used by sellers of equipment. The buyer receives possession and use of the goods. The seller initially receives a promissory note but retains title until the installment debt is paid. Retention of title facilitates repossession.

5. Other tools of credit such as bank charge cards should be evaluated as an alternative to charge accounts.

   a. Banks charge a fee equal to 3% to 5% of charge sales.
   b. Charge tickets can be deposited at a bank in the same way as customer checks.
   c. Money is instantly available to the seller.

6. Stop and review! You have completed the outline for this subunit. Study multiple-choice questions 41 through 45 beginning on page 306.

## 6.7 VALUATION AND PRICING BUSINESS COMBINATIONS

1. The most fundamental approach to valuing a business combination is **capital budgeting analysis**. If the net present value is positive, that is, if the present value of the estimated incremental cash flows from the combination exceeds the present value of the amounts to be paid for the acquired firm, the investment is financially sound for the acquirer. The shareholders of the acquired firm should perform a similar analysis and compare the result with the net present value of remaining an independent entity. Accordingly, the analysis must emphasize

   a. Accurate estimates of expected cash flows
   b. The effect on the cost of capital and the optimal capital structure of the acquirer

    c.    How the combination will be financed

    d.    The price to be paid

        1)    If the combination is synergistic or otherwise results in the creation of new value, a **premium** can be paid to the shareholders of the acquired firm while still permitting the shareholders of the acquiring firm to benefit. However, most of the gain in value usually is paid to the acquired firm's shareholders as an inducement to sell.

2.    Crucial aspects of valuation analysis are the estimates of the **incremental cash flows** from the combination and the **required rate of return** (cost of capital) for those incremental cash flows. This rate is the discount rate to be used in calculating the net present value.

    a.    Projecting incremental cash flows from the combination becomes relatively more difficult when the firms' operations are to be merged or if the acquired firm's operations are to be changed.

        1)    The cash flow analysis should also consider the **transaction costs** involved.

    b.    In comparison with the usual capital budgeting analysis, a combination often requires consideration of more **complex debt arrangements**. The debt acquired will have different rates from that held by the acquiring firm, debt may be issued to finance the combination, and new debt may be issued to finance expansion of the acquired firm. Accordingly, the projected cash flow analysis should incorporate **interest**. Because the net cash flows will be calculated after subtraction of interest, the valuation will reflect the equity residual, i.e., the value to the shareholders of the acquiring firm.

    c.    The **forecast** of the incremental cash flows available to the acquiring firm's shareholders should be based on analyses of the sensitivity of the net present value to changes in the crucial variables. It should also consider the range of the probable values of these variables based on their probability distributions. Consequently, a **computer simulation** may be a useful technique for evaluating the combination, assuming probabilities can be estimated for the components of the projected cash flows.

    d.    If the net incremental cash flows to the acquiring firm's shareholders are to be calculated, the **discount rate** used should be the **cost of equity capital**. Moreover, this rate should reflect the risk associated with the use of funds rather than their source. The rate therefore should not be the cost of capital of the acquiring firm but rather the cost of equity of the combined firm after the combination. This calculation requires a new estimate of **beta** to be used in the **Capital Asset Pricing Model**.

    e.    Estimating the value of the combination using discounted cash flows should not ignore the **market prices** of comparable investments. If the market is efficient, market prices should equal the values of those investments. This analysis should include the P-E ratio, price-to-book-value ratio, and price-to-sales ratio.

    f.    The **nature of the bid** for the acquired firm (cash, stock, debt, or a combination) has important effects on

        1)    The combined firm's capital structure

        2)    The tax position of the acquiring company and the shareholders of the acquired company

        3)    Whether the acquired firm's shareholders will benefit from postcombination gains by the combined firm

        4)    The extent of governmental regulatory involvement

3.    Stop and review! You have completed the outline for this subunit. Study multiple-choice questions 46 and 47 on page 307.

## 6.8 DERIVATIVE FINANCIAL INSTRUMENTS

1. Options and futures are derivative securities. They are not claims on business assets, such as those represented by equity securities. Instead, they are created by the parties who trade in them.

    a. An **American option** is a contractual arrangement that gives the owner the right to buy or sell an asset at a fixed price at any moment in time before or on a specified date. A **European option** is exercisable only at the expiration date.

    b. **Exercise** of an option is the act of buying or selling the asset underlying the option contract. An **open interest** is the total number of option or futures contracts that have not expired, been exercised, or been fulfilled by delivery.

    c. An option is a right of the owner, not an obligation.

    d. The **exercise or strike (striking) price** is the price at which the owner can purchase the asset underlying the option contract. The **option price**, also called **option premium**, is the amount paid to acquire an option.

        1) The **bid-ask spread** is the difference between what a buyer is willing to bid and what a seller is asking.

    e. An option usually has an expiration date after which it can no longer be exercised.

    f. The longer the time before its expiration, the more valuable the option. The reason is the increased time available for the asset's price to rise or fall.

    g. A **covered option** is one that is written against stock held in the option writer's portfolio.

    h. A **naked (uncovered) option** is one that does not have the backing of stock.

    i. A **call option** is the most common type of option. It gives the owner the right to purchase the underlying asset at a fixed price. Thus, it represents a **long position** because the owner gains from a price increase. The profit is the difference between the price paid and the value at the closing date, minus the brokerage fee.

        1) Call options usually involve common stock as the underlying asset; however, any type of asset may underlie an option.

        2) If the value of the asset underlying a call option is less than the exercise price of the option, the option is **out-of-the-money**, or not worth exercising. If the value of the asset underlying the option is greater than the exercise price, it is **in-the-money** and can earn the owner a profit.

        3) A call option's expiration value equals the excess of the current price of the asset over the exercise price. If the exercise price exceeds the current price, the option is worthless.

    j. A **put option** gives the owner the right to sell the underlying asset for a fixed price. It represents a **short position** because the owner benefits from a price decrease.

        1) If the value of the asset underlying a put option is greater than its exercise price, the put is out of the money.

        2) If the value of the asset underlying the put option is less than the exercise price of the put option, the put is in the money. **Intrinsic value** is the difference between the exercise price and the market price of the underlying security.

        3) A put option's expiration value equals either zero or the excess of the exercise price over the current market price.

k.  A **stock option** is an option to buy a specific stock at some future time.  An **index option** is an option whose underlying security is an index.  If exercised, settlement is made by cash payment because physical delivery is not possible.  **Long-Term Equity Anticipation Securities (LEAPS)** are examples of long-term stock options or index options, with expiration dates up to three years away.  **Foreign currency options** give the holder the right to buy a specific foreign currency at a designated exchange rate.

l.  **Put-call parity**.  For European options, given market equilibrium for all relevant prices (no arbitrage possibilities), equal exercise prices for the put and the call, and the same expiration date, the put-call parity theorem states that a fixed relationship applies to the market values of the put and call options on a security.  For example, a strategy of selling one call option, buying one share of the stock, and buying one put option should result in a risk-free return.  The gain (loss) from the stock and the put should equal the gain (loss) on the call.  If $V_S$ is the value of the stock, $V_P$ is the value of the put, $V_C$ is the value of the call, and $PV_E$ is the present value of the exercise price (the time interval is the time to expiration), the formula for put-call parity may be stated as follows:

$$V_S + V_P - V_C = PV_E$$

m.  The value of a call option is based on its exercise price, its expiration date, the price of the underlying asset, the variability of that asset, and the risk-free interest rate.  The well-known **Black-Scholes Option-Pricing Model** uses these factors.

1)  If **C** is the current value of a call option with time **t** in years until expiration, **S** is the current stock price, **N ($d_i$)** is the cumulative probability that a deviation less than $d_i$ will occur in a standardized normal distribution [N ($d_i$) is an area to the left of $d_i$ under the curve for the standard normal distribution], **E** is the call's exercise price, **e** is a constant (approximately 2.7183), **r** is the annualized continuous risk-free rate of return, **ln (S/E)** is the natural logarithm of S/E, and $\sigma^2$ is the variance of the continuous rate of return on the stock, the Black-Scholes formula is

$$C = SN(d_1) - Ee^{-rt}N(d_2) \qquad d_1 = \frac{\ln(S/E) + [r + (\sigma^2 \div 2)]t}{\sigma\sqrt{t}} \qquad d_2 = d_1 - \sigma\sqrt{t}$$

a)  In effect, the first term of the equation for C is the expected present value of the final stock price, and the second term is essentially the present value of the exercise price.

2.  A futures contract is a specific kind of **forward contract**, which is simply an executory contract.  The parties to a forward contract agree to the terms of a purchase and sale, but performance, i.e., payment by the buyer and delivery by the seller, is deferred.  A **futures contract** is a definite agreement that allows a trader to purchase or sell an asset at a fixed price during a specific future month.  Futures contracts for agricultural commodities, metals, oil, and financial assets are traded on numerous exchanges.

a.  One characteristic of a futures contract is that it may be highly leveraged.  The initial **margin** paid may be a very small percentage of the price.  Thus, the risk of either gain or loss to a speculator may be great.

b.  A futures contract differs from a forward contract in part because it is **traded on an exchange**.  The result is a liquid market in futures that permits buyers and sellers to net out their positions.  For example, a party who has sold a contract can net out his/her position by buying a futures contract.

c.   Because futures contracts are for **delivery during a given month**, not a specific day, they are more flexible arrangements than forward contracts.  The seller notifies the exchange clearinghouse when delivery is to be made, and the clearinghouse randomly matches the seller with a buyer who has purchased a contract for the same month.

d.   Another distinguishing feature of futures contracts is that their prices are **marked to market** at the close of every day.  Thus, the market price is posted at the close of business each day.  A mark-to-market provision minimizes a futures contract's chance of default because profits and losses on the contracts must be received or paid each day through a clearinghouse.  This requirement of **daily settlement** is necessary because futures contracts are sold on margin (i.e., they are highly leveraged).

1)   **Cover** is the cancelation of a short position in any futures contract by the purchase of an equal quantity of the same futures contract.  It is a means of closing out a futures position.

2)   Another means of closing a futures position is **delivery**.  It is the tender and receipt of the actual commodities or, in the case of agricultural commodities, warehouse receipts covering such commodities, in settlement of a futures contract.  Some contracts settle in cash (cash delivery), in which case open positions are marked to market on the last day of the contract based on the cash market close.

e.   A futures contract is entered into as either a speculation or a hedge.  A financial manager can protect a company against adverse changes in prices and interest rates by hedging in the futures market.  **Hedging** is the process of using offsetting commitments to minimize or avoid the impact of adverse price movements.

1)   **Long hedges** are futures contracts that are purchased to protect against price increases.

2)   **Short hedges** are futures contracts that are sold to protect against price declines.

3)   EXAMPLE:  In the commodities market, a company might have a contract with a farmer to buy soybeans at a future date.  The price is agreed upon as the current price.  The company would lose money if the soybean prices declined before the beans were delivered.  To avoid any loss (or gain), the company could sell soybeans in the future at today's price.  If the price of soybeans does decline before the delivery date, the company will lose money on the beans bought from the farmer, but it will gain money on the beans sold through the futures contract by buying cheap beans in the future to cover the delivery.

a)   Because commodities can be bought and sold on margin, considerable leverage is involved.  This high degree of leverage is most beneficial to the speculator who is looking for large returns and is willing to bear the risk to get them.  For hedgers, however, the small margin requirement is useful only because the risk can be hedged without tying up a large amount of cash.

4)   The **delta** or **hedge ratio** is the change in price of a call option for every one-point movement in the price of the underlying security.  It is equal to $N(d_1)$ in the Black-Scholes Option-Pricing Model.  **Gamma** is a measurement of how fast delta changes, given a unit change in the underlying futures price.

f.   **Interest rate futures contracts** involve risk-free bonds such as U.S. Treasury bonds, T-bills, Ginnie-Maes, and money-market certificates.

1)   The quantity traded is either $100,000 or $1,000,000, depending on which market is used.

2) EXAMPLE: If a corporation wants to borrow money in 6 months for a major project, but the lender refuses to commit itself to an interest rate, the interest rate futures market can be used to hedge the risk that interest rates might increase in the interim. The company agrees to sell Treasury bonds in 6 months. If interest rates do increase over the period, the value of the Treasury bonds will decline. The company can buy Treasury bonds in 6 months and use them to cover the delivery that it had promised in the futures contract. Because the price of Treasury bonds has declined over the period, the company will make a profit on their delivery. The interest rates that the company will have to pay on the upcoming loan will be higher, however. It has cost the company money to wait 6 months for the loan. The profit from the futures contract should approximately offset the loss resulting from the higher interest loan. If interest rates had declined, the company would have had the benefit of a lower interest loan but would have lost money on the Treasury bonds. The goal of any such hedging operation is to break even on the change in interest rates.

   a) By hedging, the financial manager need not worry about fluctuations in interest rates but can concentrate instead on the day-to-day operations of the company.

g. **Duration hedging** involves hedging interest-rate risk. **Duration**, also known as **Macaulay duration**, is the weighted average of the times to interest and principal payments. If duration increases, the volatility of the price of the debt instrument increases. Duration is not the time to maturity except for a zero-coupon bond.

   1) Duration is lower if the nominal rate on the instrument is higher because more of the return is received earlier. The formula for duration is as follows if $C_T$ is the interest or principal payment, T is the time to the payment, n is the time to maturity, r is the yield to maturity, and V is the value of the instrument:

$$\sum_{T=1}^{n} \left( \frac{C_T \times T}{(1 + r)^T} \right) \div V$$

   2) The goal of duration hedging is not to equate the duration of assets and the duration of liabilities but for the following relationship to apply:

$$\left( Value\ of\ assets \right) \times \left( Duration\ of\ assets \right) = \left( Value\ of\ liabilities \right) \times \left( Duration\ of\ liabilities \right)$$

   a) The firm is immunized against interest-rate risk when the total price change for assets equals the total price change for liabilities.

   3) **Modified duration** is a measure of the price sensitivity of a bond to interest rate movements. It is equal to the Macaulay duration divided by [1+ (bond yield ÷ k)], if k is the number of compounding periods per year. Modified duration is therefore inversely proportional to the approximate percentage change in price for a given change in yield.

h.   **Swaps** are contracts to hedge risk by exchanging cash flows. The simplest form, sometimes called a **plain vanilla swap**, is an exchange of interest rates without any change in the initial debt arrangement.

1)   In an **interest-rate swap**, one firm exchanges its fixed interest payments for a series of payments based on a floating rate. Such contracts are highly customized. If a firm has debt with fixed charges, but its revenues fluctuate with interest rates, it may prefer to swap for cash outflows based on a floating rate. The advantage is that revenues and the amounts of debt service will then move in the same direction, and interest-rate risk will be reduced. The specified dollar amount on which the exchanged interest payments are based is called the **notional principle** amount.

a)   The steps to **valuation of swaps** include

i)    Identifying the cash flows over time.

ii)   Constructing the swap curve, obtained from the government yield curve and the swap spread curve.

iii)  Constructing a zero-coupon curve from the swap curve.

iv)   Determining the present value of the cash flows using the zero-coupon rates.

b)   The **swap spread** is obtained from market makers. It is the market-determined additional yield that compensates counter-parties who receive fixed payments in a swap for the credit risk involved in the swap. The swap spread will differ with the creditworthiness of the counter-party.

c)   Most swaps are **priced** to be at-the-money at inception, meaning that the value of the floating rate cash flows is the same as the value of the fixed rate cash flows at the inception of the deal. Naturally, as interest rates change, the relative value may shift. Receiving the fixed rate flow will become more valuable than receiving the floating rate flow if interest rates drop or if credit spreads tighten.

d)   Investment banks and commercial banks are the **market makers** for most swaps. The market makers generally warehouse the risk in portfolios, managing the residual interest rate risk of the cash flows.

2)   A **currency swap** is an exchange of an obligation to pay out cash flows denominated in one currency for an obligation to pay in another. For example, a U.S. firm with revenues in euros has to pay suppliers and workers in dollars, not euros. To minimize exchange-rate risk, it might agree to exchange euros for dollars held by a firm that needs euros. The exchange rate will be an average of the rates expected over the life of the agreement.

3)   A **swaption** is an option on a swap, usually on an interest-rate swap, that provides the holder with the right to enter into a swap at a specified future date at specified terms (freestanding option on a swap) or to extend or terminate the life of an existing swap (embedded option on a swap).

i.   **Arbitrage** is the simultaneous purchase and sale of identical or equivalent financial instruments or commodity futures to benefit from a discrepancy in their price relationship. This sometimes involves selling in one market while simultaneously buying in another market.

j.   **Program trading**, also known as index arbitrage or computer-assisted trading, exploits the price discrepancies between indexes of stocks and futures contracts by using sophisticated computer models to hedge positions. Program trading arose with the advent of telecommunication technology that permits transactions in different markets to be monitored simultaneously.

    k.    An **interest rate cap** is an option that limits the risk of interest rate increases. If interest rates rise above a certain level, the cap holder receives the excess of the actual interest rate over a designated interest rate (the strike or cap rate) based on the notional principal amount. The cap holder's loss is limited to the premium paid to the cap writer. The cap writer has unlimited risk from potential increases in interest rates above the specified rate.

    l.    An **interest rate floor** is an option that limits the risk of interest rate decreases. If rates fall below a specified level, the floor holder receives cash payments equal to the excess of a designated rate (the strike or floor rate) over the actual rate based on the notional principal amount. The buyer pays the writer a premium to receive this right, and the floor writer faces significant risk from potential decreases in rates below the specified rate.

    m.    A **collar** is an option that combines the strategies of a cap and a floor. The buyer acquires a cap and writes a floor. The writer writes a cap and buys a floor. Collars fix the rate a variable-rate lender will receive or a borrower will pay between the cap and floor rate levels. Collars help reduce the cost of buying outright a cap or floor. Because a borrower or lender is usually only interested in protecting against movements in interest rates in one direction, the premium received for writing a cap or floor serves to reduce the cost of the cap or floor purchased.

3.    Stop and review! You have completed the outline for this subunit. Study multiple-choice questions 48 through 59 beginning on page 308.

## 6.9 PORTFOLIO THEORY

1.    The **expected rate of return** on an investment is determined using an expected value calculation. If $k_i$ is the return from the ith possible outcome and if $p_i$ is its probability, the expected return ($\hat{k}$) may be expressed as

$$\hat{k} = \sum_{i=1}^{n} k_i \, p_i$$

    a.    The greater the **standard deviation** of the expected return, the wider the range of possible returns, and the riskier the investment. The standard deviation ($\sigma$) is the square root of the variance. If $k_i$ is the return from the ith outcome, $p_i$ is its probability, and $\hat{k}$ is the expected (mean) return, the variance ($\sigma^2$) is

$$\sigma^2 = \sum_{i=1}^{n} (k_i - \hat{k})^2 p_i$$

    b.    The **coefficient of variation** is useful when the rates of return and standard deviations of two investments differ. It measures the risk per unit of return because it divides the standard deviation ($\sigma$) by the expected return ($\hat{k}$).

2.    Whether the expected return entices an investor depends on its risk, the risks and returns of alternative investments, and the investor's attitude toward risk.

    a.    Most serious investors are risk averse. They have a diminishing marginal utility for wealth (the utility of additional wealth decreases). The utility of a gain is therefore less than the disutility of a loss of the same amount.

    b.    Due to this risk aversion, risky securities must have higher expected returns.

3.    When a **portfolio** of investments is held, risk and return should be evaluated for the entire portfolio, not for individual assets. Thus, the expected return on a portfolio is the weighted average of the returns on the individual assets.

a.    However, the risk of the portfolio is usually not an average of the standard deviations of the particular assets. Thanks to the **diversification effect**, combining assets results in a portfolio risk that is less than the average of the standard deviations because the returns are imperfectly correlated.

1)    Given perfect positive correlation (r = 1.0), risk for a two-stock portfolio with equal investments in each would be the same as that for the individual assets.

2)    Given perfect negative correlation, risk would in theory be eliminated.

3)    In practice, assets are usually positively but imperfectly correlated. The normal range for the correlation of two randomly selected stocks is .50 to .70. The result is a reduction in, but not elimination of, risk.

b.    The measurement of the standard deviation of a portfolio's returns is based on the same formula as that for a single security. Another important measurement used in portfolio analysis is the **covariance**. It measures the volatility of returns together with their correlation with the returns of other securities. For two stocks X and Y, if $\hat{k}$ is the expected return, $k_i$ is a given outcome, and $p_i$ is its probability, the covariance of X and Y is

$$COV(XY) = \sum_{i=1}^{n} (k_{xi} - \hat{k}_x)(k_{yi} - \hat{k}_y)p_i$$

1)    The **correlation coefficient (r)** standardizes the covariance by dividing by the product of the standard deviations of the two assets.

$$r_{xy} = \frac{COV_{XY}}{\sigma_X \ \sigma_Y}$$

4.    Portfolio management involves determining how much to invest and which securities to choose so as to maximize expected return and minimize risk. An **efficient portfolio** is a feasible portfolio that offers the highest expected return for a given risk or the least risk for a given expected return. The **optimal portfolio** is a portfolio that is selected from the efficient set of portfolios because it is tangent to the investor's highest indifference curve.

a.    An indifference curve represents combinations of portfolios having equal utility. Given that risk and returns are plotted on the horizontal and vertical axes, respectively, and that the investor is risk averse, the curve has an increasingly positive slope. As risk increases, the additional required return per unit of additional risk also increases.

1)    The steeper the slope, the more risk averse an investor is.

2)    The higher the curve, the greater is the investor's level of utility.

3) A, B, C, D, and E are indifference curves. A represents the highest level of utility and E the lowest. On a given curve, each point represents the same total utility to a risk-averse investor. For example, points 1, 2, and 3 are different combinations of risk and return that yield the same utility.

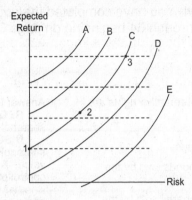

5. The investment in securities should be based on expected net cash flows and cash flow uncertainty evaluations. Arranging a portfolio so that the maturity of funds will coincide with the need for funds will maximize the average return on the portfolio and provide increased flexibility. Maturity matching ensures that securities will not have to be sold unexpectedly.

   a. If its cash flows are relatively uncertain, a security's marketability and market risk are important factors. Transaction costs are also a consideration. Thus, higher-yield long-term securities provide less certainty.

   b. When cash flows are relatively certain, the maturity date is a paramount concern.

6. **Company-specific (investee-specific) risk** or **unsystematic risk** is associated with a specific company's (investee's) operations: new products, patents, acquisitions, competitors, activities, etc.

   a. This risk can be largely eliminated by proper diversification of investments.

   b. The relevant risk of an individual security held in a portfolio is its contribution to the overall risk of the portfolio.

   c. When much of a security's risk can be eliminated by diversification, its relevant risk is low.

   d. In principle, diversifiable risk should continue to decrease as the number of different securities held increases. In practice, the benefits of diversification become extremely small when more than 30 to 40 different securities are held.

7. The risk of an individual security that is unaffected by diversification is **market** or **systematic risk** and is measured by the **beta coefficient**.

   a. According to the Capital Asset Pricing Model, beta measures the volatility of the returns of a security relative to the returns on the market portfolio (a portfolio of all securities). An average-risk stock has a beta of 1.0 because its returns are perfectly positively correlated with those on the market portfolio. For example, if the market return increases by 20%, the return on the security increases by 20%.

   b. The word **beta** is derived from the regression equation for regressing the return of an individual security (the dependent variable) to the overall market return. The beta coefficient is the slope of the regression line.

      1) The beta for a security may also be calculated by dividing the covariance of the return on the market and the return on the security by the variance of the return on the market.

c.   Beta is the best measure of the risk of an individual security held in a **diversified portfolio** because it determines how the security affects the risk of the portfolio. The **beta of a portfolio** is the weighted average of the betas of the individual securities. For example, adding high-beta securities to a portfolio tends to increase its risk.

8.   Stop and review! You have completed the outline for this subunit. Study multiple-choice questions 60 through 64 beginning on page 312.

## QUESTIONS

### 6.1 Long-Term Financing

**1.** Common shareholders with preemptive rights are entitled to

A.   Vote first at annual meetings.

B.   Purchase any additional bonds sold by the firm.

C.   Purchase any additional shares sold by the firm.

D.   Gain control of the firm in a proxy fight.

Answer (C) is correct.  *(CIA, adapted)*
   **REQUIRED:** The privilege enjoyed by common shareholders with preemptive rights.
   **DISCUSSION:** Preemptive rights protect common shareholders' proportional ownership interests from dilution in value. A secondary purpose is to maintain the shareholders' control of the company. Accordingly, the preemptive right, whether granted by statute or by the corporate charter, grants common shareholders the power to acquire on a pro rata basis any additional common shares sold by the firm. Preemptive rights also apply to debt convertible into common shares.
   Answer (A) is incorrect because there is no prescribed order of shareholder voting. Answer (B) is incorrect because preemptive rights concern only equity ownership. Thus, they do not apply to nonconvertible debt. Answer (D) is incorrect because a proxy fight is an attempt to gain control of a company by persuading shareholders to grant their voting rights to others.

**2.** Participating preferred shareholders are entitled to

A.   Monitor any sinking funds for the purchase and retirement of debt.

B.   Vote at all annual meetings.

C.   Convert their shares into common shares.

D.   Share in the firm's earnings beyond the stated dividend level.

Answer (D) is correct.  *(CIA, adapted)*
   **REQUIRED:** The right of participating preferred shareholders.
   **DISCUSSION:** Participating preferred shareholders are entitled to share in the earnings of the firm. They participate in earnings distributions under set terms and conditions. Hence, after the stated preferred dividend is paid, and common shareholders receive an equal dividend, any remaining dividends are allocated to all shareholders in proportion to the par values of their shares.
   Answer (A) is incorrect because the participation privilege is unrelated to monitoring privileges. Answer (B) is incorrect because preferred shareholders do not have voting rights except in circumstances in which the firm has not paid the preferred share dividends for a specified period. Answer (C) is incorrect because a conversion feature, not a participation feature, allows conversion to common stock.

**3.** A company has recently purchased some shares of a competitor as part of a long-term plan to acquire the competitor. However, it is somewhat concerned that the market price of the shares could decrease over the short run. The company could hedge against the possible decline in the market price by

A.   Purchasing a call option on the shares.

B.   Purchasing a put option on the shares.

C.   Selling a put option on the shares.

D.   Obtaining a warrant option on the shares.

Answer (B) is correct.  *(CIA, adapted)*
   **REQUIRED:** The means of hedging against the possible decline in the share's market price.
   **DISCUSSION:** A put option is the right to sell shares at a given price within a certain period. If the market price falls, the put option may allow the sale of shares at a price above market, and the profit of the option holder will be the difference between the price stated in the put option and the market price, minus the cost of the option, commissions, and taxes.
   Answer (A) is incorrect because a call option is the right to purchase shares at a given price within a specified period. It hedges against a price increase. Answer (C) is incorrect because selling a put option could force the company to purchase additional shares if the option is exercised. Answer (D) is incorrect because a warrant gives the holder a right to purchase shares from the issuer at a given price (it is usually distributed along with debt).

**4.** A call option on a common share is more valuable when there is a lower

    A. Market value of the underlying share.

    B. Exercise price on the option.

    C. Time to maturity on the option.

    D. Variability of market price on the underlying share.

Answer (B) is correct. *(CIA, adapted)*
    **REQUIRED:** The circumstance under which a call option is more valuable.
    **DISCUSSION:** The lower the exercise price, the more valuable the call option. The exercise price is the price at which the call holder has the right to purchase the underlying share.
    Answer (A) is incorrect because a call option is the right to purchase a common share at a set price for a set time period. If the underlying share has a lower market value, the call option is less, not more, valuable. Answer (C) is incorrect because a call option is less, not more, valuable given less time to maturity. When the option has less time to maturity, the chance that the share price will rise is smaller. Answer (D) is incorrect because a call option is less, not more, valuable if the price of the underlying share is less variable. Less variability means a lower probability of a price increase.

**5.** Preferred shares are securities with characteristics of both common shares and bonds. Preferred shares have <List A> like common shares and <List B> like bonds.

| | List A | List B |
|---|---|---|
| A. | A maturity date | A fixed periodic payment |
| B. | No maturity date | No fixed periodic payment |
| C. | A maturity date | No fixed periodic payment |
| D. | No maturity date | A fixed periodic payment |

Answer (D) is correct. *(CIA, adapted)*
    **REQUIRED:** The characteristics of preferred shares.
    **DISCUSSION:** Like common shares (but unlike bonds), preferred shares have no maturity date, although certain preferred shares (transient preferred shares) must be redeemed within a short time (e.g., 5 to 10 years). Like bonds (but unlike common shares), preferred shares have a fixed periodic payment. The fixed payment is in the form of a stated dividend in the case of the preferred shares and interest payments in the case of bonds. However, preferred dividends, unlike interest, do not become an obligation unless declared.
    Answer (A) is incorrect because preferred shares do not have a maturity date. Answer (B) is incorrect because preferred shares have fixed periodic dividend payments. Answer (C) is incorrect because preferred shares do not have a maturity date but do have fixed periodic dividend payments.

**6.** Which of the following is usually not a feature of cumulative preferred shares?

    A. Has priority over common shares with regard to earnings.

    B. Has priority over common shares with regard to assets.

    C. Has voting rights.

    D. Has the right to receive dividends in arrears before common share dividends can be paid.

Answer (C) is correct. *(CIA, adapted)*
    **REQUIRED:** The item not usually a feature of cumulative preferred shares.
    **DISCUSSION:** Preferred shares do not usually have voting rights. Preferred shareholders are usually given the right to vote for directors only if the company has not paid the preferred dividend for a specified period of time, such as 10 quarters. Such a provision is an incentive for management to pay preferred dividends.
    Answer (A) is incorrect because preferred shares have priority over common shares with regard to earnings, so dividends must be paid on preferred shares before they can be paid on common shares. Answer (B) is incorrect because preferred shares have priority over common shares with regard to assets. In the event of liquidation, for example, because of bankruptcy, the claims of preferred shareholders must be satisfied in full before the common shareholders receive anything. Answer (D) is incorrect because cumulative preferred shares have the right to receive any dividends not paid in prior periods before common share dividends are paid.

**7.** If a company has outstanding bonds with a sinking fund provision and if interest rates have <List A> since the bonds were issued, the company would realize a savings in meeting its sinking fund obligations by <List B>.

|  | List A | List B |
|---|---|---|
| A. | Increased | Buying back bonds in the open market |
| B. | Remained constant | Calling in a portion of the bonds at face value |
| C. | Increased | Calling in a portion of the bonds at face value |
| D. | Decreased | Buying back bonds in the open market |

Answer (A) is correct. *(CIA, adapted)*

**REQUIRED:** The appropriate match of the movement of interest rates, if any, and redemptions or bond market purchases.

**DISCUSSION:** If interest rates have increased, the prices of outstanding bonds must decrease so that their yields will reach the market rate. Hence, the bonds will be selling at a discount (below face value) in the open market. Retiring a portion of the outstanding bonds by buying them in the open market at the discounted price will be cheaper than calling a portion of the bonds at face value.

Answer (B) is incorrect because, if interest rates have remained constant, the bonds will still be selling at face value in the open market. The cost of buying bonds on the open market will be the same as the cost of calling a portion of the bonds at face value. Answer (C) is incorrect because, if interest rates have increased, buying bonds in the open market will be the cheaper strategy. Answer (D) is incorrect because, if interest rates have decreased, the bonds will be selling at a premium in the open market. Retiring a portion of the bonds by purchasing them on the open market will be more costly than calling a portion of the bonds at face value.

**8.** Convertible bonds and bonds issued with warrants differ in that

A. Convertible bonds have lower coupon rates than straight bonds, while bonds issued with warrants have higher coupon rates than straight bonds.

B. Convertible bonds have higher coupon rates than straight bonds, while bonds issued with warrants have lower coupon rates than straight bonds.

C. Convertible bonds remain outstanding after the bondholder exercises the right to become a common shareholder, while bonds that are issued with warrants do not.

D. Bonds that are issued with warrants remain outstanding after the bondholder exercises the right to become a common shareholder, while convertible bonds do not.

Answer (D) is correct. *(CIA, adapted)*

**REQUIRED:** The difference between convertible bonds and bonds issued with warrants.

**DISCUSSION:** Warrants are usually detachable. They are options to purchase equity securities and should be separately accounted for. A capital gain results if the share price rises above the option price. The bonds remain outstanding if the warrants are exercised. Convertible bonds must be surrendered when the conversion privilege is exercised. The equity feature of convertible bonds is not separately accounted for.

Answer (A) is incorrect because bonds issued with warrants and convertible bonds have lower coupon rates than conventional bonds. Answer (B) is incorrect because bonds issued with warrants and convertible bonds have lower coupon rates than conventional bonds. Answer (C) is incorrect because convertible bonds do not remain outstanding.

**9.** Zero-coupon bonds

A. Sell for a small fraction of their face value because their yield is much lower than the market rate.

B. Increase in value each year as they approach maturity, providing the owner with the total payoff at maturity.

C. Are redeemable in measures of a commodity such as barrels of oil, tons of coal, or ounces of rare metal (e.g., silver).

D. Are high-interest-rate, high-risk, unsecured bonds that have been used extensively to finance leveraged buyouts.

Answer (B) is correct. *(CIA, adapted)*

**REQUIRED:** The feature of zero-coupon bonds.

**DISCUSSION:** Zero-coupon bonds sell at a deep discount and increase in value each year until maturity. These bonds do not pay interest.

Answer (A) is incorrect because deep discount bonds pay interest significantly below the market rate, whereas zero-coupon bonds do not pay interest. Answer (C) is incorrect because commodity-backed bonds are redeemable in measures of a commodity. Answer (D) is incorrect because junk bonds are high-interest-rate, high-risk, unsecured bonds.

**10.** Bondholders are assured of protection against inflation if they hold

   A. Income bonds.

   B. Convertible bonds.

   C. Mortgage bonds.

   D. Indexed bonds.

Answer (D) is correct. *(CIA, adapted)*
**REQUIRED:** The bonds that provide protection against inflation.
**DISCUSSION:** The interest payments on indexed or purchasing power bonds are based on an inflation index, such as the consumer price index. Thus, interest paid to bondholders rises automatically when the inflation rate rises.
Answer (A) is incorrect because income bonds pay interest to the holder only if the interest is earned. The interest paid is not inflation adjusted. Answer (B) is incorrect because convertible bonds can be redeemed for the common shares of the issuer at the option of the holder. Interest payments are not inflation adjusted. Answer (C) is incorrect because mortgage bonds are secured by fixed assets of the issuer. Thus, they provide greater security to bondholders, but the interest payments are not inflation adjusted.

**11.** From the viewpoint of the investor, which of the following securities provides the least risk?

   A. Mortgage bond.

   B. Subordinated debenture.

   C. Income bond.

   D. Debentures.

Answer (A) is correct. *(CIA, adapted)*
**REQUIRED:** The least risky security from the viewpoint of the investor.
**DISCUSSION:** A mortgage bond is secured with specific fixed assets, usually real property. Thus, under the rights enumerated in the bond indenture, creditors will be able to receive payments from liquidation of the property in case of default. In a bankruptcy proceeding, these amounts are paid before any transfers are made to other creditors, including those preferences. Hence, mortgage bonds are less risky than the others listed.
Answer (B) is incorrect because a debenture is long-term debt that is not secured (collateralized) by specific property. Subordinated debentures have a claim on the debtor's assets that may be satisfied only after senior debt has been paid in full. Debentures of either kind are therefore more risky than mortgage bonds. Answer (C) is incorrect because an income bond pays interest only if the debtor earns it. Such bonds are also more risky than secured debt. Answer (D) is incorrect because unsecured debt is riskier than a mortgage bond.

**12.** Which of the following classes of securities are listed in order from lowest risk/opportunity for return to highest risk/opportunity for return?

   A. U.S. Treasury bonds; corporate first mortgage bonds; corporate income bonds; preferred shares.

   B. Corporate income bonds; corporate mortgage bonds; convertible preferred shares; subordinated debentures.

   C. Common shares; corporate first mortgage bonds; corporate second mortgage bonds; corporate income bonds.

   D. Preferred shares; common shares; corporate mortgage bonds; corporate debentures.

Answer (A) is correct. *(CIA, adapted)*

**REQUIRED:** The correct listing of classes of securities from lowest to highest risk/opportunity for return.

**DISCUSSION:** The general principle is that risk and return are directly correlated. For example, U.S. Treasury securities are backed by the full faith and credit of the U.S. government and are therefore the least risky form of investment listed. However, their return is correspondingly lower. Corporate first mortgage bonds are less risky than income bonds or shares because they are secured by specific property. In the event of default, the bondholders can have the property sold to satisfy their claims. Holders of first mortgages have rights paramount to those of any other parties, such as holders of second mortgages. Income bonds pay interest only in the event the corporation earns income. Thus, holders of income bonds have less risk than shareholders because meeting the condition makes payment of interest mandatory. Preferred shareholders receive dividends only if they are declared, and the directors usually have complete discretion in this matter. Also, shareholders have claims junior to those of debtholders if the enterprise is liquidated.

Answer (B) is incorrect because the proper listing is mortgage bonds, subordinated debentures, income bonds, and preferred shares. Debentures are unsecured debt instruments. Their holders have enforceable claims against the issuer even if no income is earned or dividends declared. Answer (C) is incorrect because the proper listing is first mortgage bonds, second mortgage bonds, income bonds, and common shares. The second mortgage bonds are secured, albeit junior, claims. Answer (D) is incorrect because the proper listing is mortgage bonds, debentures, preferred shares, and common shares. Holders of common shares cannot receive dividends unless the holders of preferred shares receive the stipulated periodic percentage return, in addition to any arrearages if the preferred shares are cumulative.

## 6.2 Short-Term Financing

**13.** The correct equation for calculating the approximate percentage cost, on an annual basis, of not taking trade discounts is

   A. $$\dfrac{\text{Discount \%}}{100 - \text{Discount \%}} \times \dfrac{360}{[\text{Days credit is outstanding} - \text{Discount period}]}$$

   B. $$\dfrac{\text{Discount \%}}{100} \times \dfrac{360}{[\text{Days credit is outstanding} - \text{Discount period}]}$$

   C. $$\dfrac{100 - \text{Discount \%}}{\text{Discount \%}} \times \dfrac{360}{[\text{Days credit is outstanding} - \text{Discount period}]}$$

   D. $$\dfrac{\text{Discount \%}}{100 - \text{Discount \%}} \times \dfrac{[\text{Days credit is outstanding} - \text{Discount period}]}{360}$$

Answer (A) is correct. *(CIA, adapted)*

**REQUIRED:** The equation for calculating the percentage cost of not taking trade discounts.

**DISCUSSION:** The first term of the formula represents the periodic cost of the trade discount, calculated as the cost per unit of trade credit (discount %) divided by the funds made available by not taking the discount (100 – discount %). The second term represents the number of times per year this cost is incurred. The multiple of these terms is the approximate annual percentage cost of not taking the trade discount. A precise formula would incorporate the effects of compounding when calculating the annual cost.

Answer (B) is incorrect because the denominator of the first term should represent the funds made available by not taking the discount (100 – discount %). Answer (C) is incorrect because the first term is the reciprocal of the correct term. Answer (D) is incorrect because the second term is the reciprocal of the correct term.

**14.** A company obtaining short-term financing with trade credit will pay a higher percentage financing cost, everything else being equal, when

- A. The discount percentage is lower.
- B. The items purchased have a higher price.
- C. The items purchased have a lower price.
- D. The supplier offers a longer discount period.

Answer (D) is correct. *(CIA, adapted)*
**REQUIRED:** The factor resulting in a higher cost of trade credit.
**DISCUSSION:** If the discount period is longer, the days of extra credit obtained by forgoing the discount are fewer. Assuming other factors are constant, the result is that the cost of trade credit, that is, the cost of not taking the discount, is greater.
Answer (A) is incorrect because the lower the discount percentage, the lower the opportunity cost of forgoing the discount and using the trade credit financing. Answer (B) is incorrect because percentage financing cost is unaffected by the purchase price of the items. Answer (C) is incorrect because percentage financing cost is unaffected by the purchase price of the items.

**15.** A company has accounts payable of $5 million with terms of 2% discount within 15 days, net 30 days (2/15 net 30). It can borrow funds from a bank at an annual rate of 12%, or it can wait until the 30th day when it will receive revenues to cover the payment. If it borrows funds on the last day of the discount period in order to obtain the discount, its total cost will be

- A. $51,000 less.
- B. $75,500 less.
- C. $100,000 less.
- D. $24,500 more.

Answer (B) is correct. *(CIA, adapted)*
**REQUIRED:** The effect on total cost of taking a cash discount.
**DISCUSSION:** The interest cost of borrowing $4,900,000 (98% × $5,000,000) to take advantage of the discount is $24,500 [$4,900,000 × 12% × (15 ÷ 360)], and the total cost will be $4,924,500. The total cost if the discount is not taken will be $5,000,000, a difference of $75,500.
Answer (A) is incorrect because $51,000 less is based on a 30-day borrowing period. Answer (C) is incorrect because $100,000 less does not consider the interest paid. Answer (D) is incorrect because $24,500 more reflects interest paid but ignores the discounted price.

**16.** A short-term bank loan will have a higher effective financing cost if it has which combination of characteristics?

- A. A 10% compensating balance and regular interest.
- B. A 10% compensating balance and discount interest.
- C. A 20% compensating balance and regular interest.
- D. A 20% compensating balance and discount interest.

Answer (D) is correct. *(CIA, adapted)*
**REQUIRED:** The characteristics resulting in a higher effective financing cost.
**DISCUSSION:** The most costly combination of characteristics is a higher compensating balance and discount interest. The higher the compensating balance, the higher the portion of the loan funds that must be left on deposit with the lender. Hence, the interest paid is charged on a smaller amount of funds available to be used by the borrower, and the effective cost is higher. Also, discount interest is deducted from the loan funds in advance, resulting in a further increase in the effective financing cost.

**17.** The credit instrument known as a banker's acceptance

- A. Calls for immediate payment upon delivery of the shipping documents to the bank's customer and acceptance of goods by the bank.
- B. Involves an invoice being signed by the banker upon receipt of goods, after which both the banker and the seller record the transaction on their respective books.
- C. Is a time draft payable on a specified date and guaranteed by the bank.
- D. Is a method of sales financing in which the bank retains title to the goods until the buyer has completed payment.

Answer (C) is correct. *(CIA, adapted)*
**REQUIRED:** The nature of a banker's acceptance.
**DISCUSSION:** A time draft (trade acceptance) is a form of commercial draft because it is drawn by a seller on the buyer; that is, it calls for the buyer to pay a specified amount. The draft and the shipping documents related to the goods are then sent to the buyer's bank, which transmits the draft to the buyer. The buyer accepts the draft by signing it. A time draft, however, is similar to a promissory note because it is payable at a specific time in the future rather than upon acceptance by the buyer, which is characteristic of a sight draft. If a seller is reluctant to ship goods because of concern about the buyer's ability to pay a time draft, the seller's bank may, for a fee, guarantee payment. This banker's acceptance is an assumption of the obligation to pay at the due date.
Answer (A) is incorrect because a sight draft calls for immediate payment upon delivery of the shipping documents to, and the acceptance of the draft by, the buyer. Answer (B) is incorrect because an open account is a credit arrangement involving only the signing of an invoice by the buyer. Answer (D) is incorrect because the description is of a conditional sales contract except that the seller, not the bank, retains title to the goods until the buyer has completed payment.

**18.** An example of secured short-term financing is

    A. Commercial paper.

    B. A warehouse receipt.

    C. A revolving credit agreement.

    D. Trade credit.

Answer (B) is correct. *(CIA, adapted)*
    **REQUIRED:** The example of secured short-term financing.
    **DISCUSSION:** A document of title is usually issued by a bailee covering goods in the bailee's possession or care (UCC 1-201). It represents ownership of the goods and is ordinarily needed to obtain the goods from the bailee. The two major types of documents of title are bills of lading (issued by carriers) and warehouse receipts. A warehouse receipt is issued by a person engaged in the business of storing goods for hire. Security for short-term inventory financing can be arranged if the debtor places its inventory under the control of the lender or its agent (e.g., a public warehouse), and the lender holds the warehouse receipts.
    Answer (A) is incorrect because commercial paper is a type of unsecured, short-term promissory note issued by large firms to other firms, insurance companies, mutual funds, etc. Answer (C) is incorrect because a revolving credit agreement is a formal line of credit, usually with a bank, that large firms often use. Answer (D) is incorrect because accounts payable, or trade credit, is the most common source of unsecured short-term financing.

**19.** Factoring is the

    A. Selling of accounts receivable by one company to another.

    B. Selling of inventory by one company to another.

    C. Conversion of accounts receivable to bad debt on financial statements for accounts that are long overdue.

    D. Adjustment of inventories on financial statements for supplies that have become obsolete.

Answer (A) is correct. *(CIA, adapted)*
    **REQUIRED:** The definition of factoring.
    **DISCUSSION:** A factor purchases a company's accounts receivable and assumes the risk of collection. The seller receives money immediately to reinvest in new inventories. The financing cost is usually high: about 2 points or more above prime, plus a fee for collection. Factoring has been traditional in the textile industry for years, and recently companies in many industries have found it an efficient means of operation. A company that uses a factor can eliminate its credit department, accounts receivable staff, and bad debts. These reductions in costs can more than offset the fee charged by the factor, which can often operate more efficiently than its clients because of the specialized nature of its service.

**20.** The following forms of short-term borrowing are available to a firm:

- Floating lien
- Factoring
- Revolving credit
- Chattel mortgages
- Bankers' acceptances
- Lines of credit
- Commercial paper

The forms of short-term borrowing that are unsecured credit are

    A. Floating lien, revolving credit, chattel mortgage, and commercial paper.

    B. Factoring, chattel mortgage, bankers' acceptances, and line of credit.

    C. Floating lien, chattel mortgage, bankers' acceptances, and line of credit.

    D. Revolving credit, bankers' acceptances, line of credit, and commercial paper.

Answer (D) is correct. *(CMA, adapted)*
    **REQUIRED:** The forms of short-term borrowing that are unsecured credit.
    **DISCUSSION:** An unsecured loan is a loan made by a bank based on credit information about the borrower and the ability of the borrower to repay the obligation. The loan is not secured by collateral, but is made on the signature of the borrower. Unsecured credit is not backed by collateral. Revolving credit, bankers' acceptances, lines of credit, and commercial paper are all unsecured means of borrowing. A chattel mortgage is a loan secured by personal property (movable property such as equipment or livestock). A floating lien is also secured by property, such as inventory, the composition of which may be constantly changing. Factoring is a form of financing in which receivables serve as security.

## 6.3 Optimal Capitalization

**21.** A company has made the decision to finance next year's capital projects through debt rather than additional equity. The benchmark cost of capital for these projects should be

A. The before-tax cost of new-debt financing.

B. The after-tax cost of new-debt financing.

C. The cost of equity financing.

D. The weighted-average cost of capital.

**Answer (D) is correct.** *(CIA, adapted)*
**REQUIRED:** The benchmark cost of capital.
**DISCUSSION:** A weighted average of the costs of all financing sources should be used, with the weights determined by the usual financing proportions. The terms of any financing raised at the time of initiating a particular project do not represent the cost of capital for the firm. When a firm achieves its optimal capital structure, the weighted-average cost of capital is minimized. The cost of capital is a composite, or weighted average, of all financing sources in their usual proportions. The cost of capital should also be calculated on an after-tax basis.

**22.** When a company increases its degree of financial leverage (DFL),

A. The equity beta of the company falls.

B. The systematic risk of the company falls.

C. The systematic risk of the company rises.

D. The standard deviation of returns on the equity of the company rises.

**Answer (D) is correct.** *(CIA, adapted)*
**REQUIRED:** The effect of increasing the DFL.
**DISCUSSION:** The DFL equals the percentage change in EPS (earnings available to common shareholders) divided by the percentage change in net operating profit. When the DFL rises, fixed interest charges and the riskiness of the firm rise. As a result, the variability of returns will increase. In other words, the standard deviation of returns of the company rises.
Answer (A) is incorrect because an increase in the DFL increases the riskiness of the firm's shares. Thus, beta rises. Beta is a measure of the volatility of a firm's share price relative to the average share. Answer (B) is incorrect because systematic risk, also known as market risk, is unrelated to the DFL. Systematic risk is not specific to a company. It is the risk associated with a company's shares that cannot be diversified because it arises from factors that affect all shares. Answer (C) is incorrect because systematic risk, also known as market risk, is unrelated to the DFL. Systematic risk is not specific to a company. It is the risk associated with a company's shares that cannot be diversified because it arises from factors that affect all shares.

**23.** In its first year of operations, a firm had $50,000 of fixed operating costs. It sold 10,000 units at a $10 unit price and incurred variable costs of $4 per unit. If all prices and costs will be the same in the second year and sales are projected to rise to 25,000 units, what will the degree of operating leverage (the extent to which fixed costs are used in the firm's operations) be in the second year?

A. 1.25

B. 1.50

C. 2.0

D. 6.0

**Answer (B) is correct.** *(CIA, adapted)*
**REQUIRED:** The degree of operating leverage (DOL) in the second year.
**DISCUSSION:** The DOL may be calculated as the contribution margin (sales – variable cost) divided by the excess of the contribution margin over fixed costs. The contribution margin is $150,000 [25,000 units × ($10 unit price – $4 unit variable cost)]. Hence, the DOL in the second year is 1.50 [$150,000 CM ÷ ($150,000 – $50,000 FC)].
Answer (A) is incorrect because 1.25 ignores variable costs. Answer (C) is incorrect because 2.0 uses the first-year sales level and ignores variable costs. Answer (D) is incorrect because 6.0 uses the first-year sales level.

**24.** If a company has a higher dividend-payout ratio, then, if all else is equal, it will have

A. A higher marginal cost of capital.

B. A lower marginal cost of capital.

C. A higher investment opportunity schedule.

D. A lower investment opportunity schedule.

**Answer (A) is correct.** *(CIA, adapted)*
**REQUIRED:** The effect of a higher dividend-payout ratio.
**DISCUSSION:** The higher the dividend-payout ratio, the sooner retained earnings are exhausted and the company must seek external financing. Assuming the same investments are undertaken, the result is a higher marginal cost of capital because lower-cost capital sources will be used up earlier.
Answer (B) is incorrect because the marginal cost of capital is higher. Answer (C) is incorrect because the existence of investment opportunities is unrelated to the dividend payout. Answer (D) is incorrect because the existence of investment opportunities is unrelated to the dividend payout.

**25.** If two companies, company X and company Y, are alike in all respects except that company X employs more debt financing and less equity financing than company Y does, which of the following statements is true?

A. Company X has more net earnings variability than company Y.

B. Company X has more operating earnings variability than company Y.

C. Company X has less operating earnings variability than company Y.

D. Company X has less financial leverage than company Y.

Answer (A) is correct.  *(CIA, adapted)*
**REQUIRED:** The true statement regarding a company's debt and equity financing.
**DISCUSSION:** Given that company X is more highly leveraged, it has greater fixed financing charges than company Y. Interest payments are fixed financing charges, but common share dividends are not. As a result, company X will be more risky and therefore will have a more volatile net income stream than company Y, if other factors are constant.
Answer (B) is incorrect because the level of fixed financing charges does not affect operating income variability. Answer (C) is incorrect because the level of fixed financing charges does not affect operating income variability. Answer (D) is incorrect because company X has greater, not less, financial leverage than company Y. Greater use of debt financing means that a company has greater financial leverage.

**26.** The market value of a firm's outstanding common shares will be higher, everything else equal, if

A. Investors have a lower required return on equity.

B. Investors expect lower dividend growth.

C. Investors have longer expected holding periods.

D. Investors have shorter expected holding periods.

Answer (A) is correct.  *(CIA, adapted)*
**REQUIRED:** The item resulting in a higher market value for common shares.
**DISCUSSION:** The dividend growth model is used to calculate the cost of equity. The simplified formula is

$$R = \frac{D}{P} + G$$

R is the required rate of return, D is the next dividend, P is the share's price, and G is the growth rate in earnings per share. The equation is also used to determine the share price.

$$P = \frac{D}{R - G}$$

Thus, when investors have a lower required return on equity, the denominator is smaller, which translates into a higher market value.
Answer (B) is incorrect because, if investors expect lower dividend growth, the market value of common shares will decrease. Answer (C) is incorrect because the expected holding periods of investors are not related to the market value of the common shares. Answer (D) is incorrect because the expected holding periods of investors are not related to the market value of the common shares.

**27.** Assume that nominal interest rates just increased substantially but that the expected future dividends for a company over the long run were not affected. As a result of the increase in nominal interest rates, the company's share price should

A. Increase.

B. Decrease.

C. Stay constant.

D. Change, but in no obvious direction.

Answer (B) is correct.  *(CIA, adapted)*
**REQUIRED:** The effect on a company's share price of an increase in nominal interest rates.
**DISCUSSION:** The dividend growth model is used to calculate the price of a share.

$$P_0 = \frac{D_1}{R_s - G}$$

If:  $P_0$ = current price
     $D_1$ = next dividend
     $R_s$ = required rate of return
     $G$ = EPS growth rate

Assuming that $D_1$ and G remain constant, an increase in $R_s$ resulting from an increase in the nominal interest rate will cause $P_0$ to decrease. A higher interest rate raises the required return of investors, which results in a lower share price.

**28.** A company has 10,000 outstanding shares with a market value of $25 each. It just paid a $1 per share dividend. Dividends are expected to grow at a constant rate of 10%. If flotation costs are 5% of the selling price, the cost of new equity financing is calculated by the following formula:

A.
$$\frac{Dividend\ at\ time\ zero}{Market\ price} + Dividend\ growth\ rate$$

$$= \left(\$1.10 \div \$25\right) + .10$$

$$= .04 + .10 = 14.00\%$$

B.
$$\frac{Dividend\ at\ time\ zero}{Net\ proceeds} + Dividend\ growth\ rate$$

$$= \left(\$1 \div \$23.75\right) + .10$$

$$= .0421 + .10 = 14.21\%$$

C.
$$\frac{Expected\ dividend\ at\ end\ of\ period}{Market\ price} + Dividend\ growth\ rate$$

$$= \left(\$1.10 \div \$25\right) + .10$$

$$= .044 + .10 = 14.40\%$$

D.
$$\frac{Expected\ dividend\ at\ end\ of\ period}{Net\ proceeds\ issuing\ one\ share} + Dividend\ growth\ rate$$

$$= \left[\$1(1.1) \div \$23.75\right] + .10$$

$$= .0463 + .10 = 14.63\%$$

Answer (D) is correct. *(CIA, adapted)*
**REQUIRED:** The cost of new equity financing.
**DISCUSSION:** The cost of new equity is calculated by adding the expected dividend yield, based on the net proceeds of the new issue, to the expected dividend growth rate. The expected dividend at the end of the period equals the dividend at time zero times one plus the expected dividend growth rate. Net proceeds received by the firm when issuing one common share equals the market price of a share times one minus the flotation cost percentage. Flotation costs include items such as underwriting fees, printing, and advertising. The calculation of the cost of new equity is as follows:

$$\frac{Expected\ dividend\ at\ end\ of\ period}{Net\ proceeds\ issuing\ one\ share} + Dividend\ growth\ rate$$

$$= \frac{\$1(1 + .10)}{\$25(1 - .05)} + 10\%$$

$$= 14.63\%$$

Answer (A) is incorrect because the end-of-period expected dividend and the net proceeds of the issue should be included in calculating the dividend yield. Answer (B) is incorrect because the end-of-period expected dividend should be included in calculating the dividend yield. Answer (C) is incorrect because the net proceeds, not market price, should be included in calculating the dividend yield.

**29.** The marginal cost of debt for a firm is defined as the interest rate on <List A> debt minus the <List B>.

| | List A | List B |
|---|---|---|
| A. | New | Firm's marginal tax rate |
| B. | Outstanding | Firm's marginal tax rate |
| C. | New | Interest rate times the firm's marginal tax rate |
| D. | Outstanding | Interest rate times the firm's marginal tax rate |

Answer (C) is correct. *(CIA, adapted)*
**REQUIRED:** The definition of the marginal cost of debt.
**DISCUSSION:** The marginal cost of debt must equal the cost of new debt minus the tax savings. Hence, marginal cost equals the cost of new debt times one minus the marginal tax rate, or $K_d(1 - T)$. This expression equals $K_d - K_dT$. The marginal cost of debt financing is the interest rate on new debt minus the firm's marginal tax rate multiplied by the interest rate. Moreover, the marginal or incremental cost of debt to the firm is based on the cost of newly issued debt, not on the cost of outstanding debt.

Questions 30 through 32 are based on the following information.

A company has the following three investment projects available:

| Project | Cost | Internal Rate of Return |
|---------|------|-------------------------|
| A | $ 50 million | 14% |
| B | $ 75 million | 12% |
| C | $125 million | 8% |

The company has a 40% debt and 60% equity capital structure. Each dollar of investment funds will be raised in these proportions (40 cents of debt and 60 cents of equity).
    The marginal cost of financing increases with the amount of new funds raised, as follows:

| Interval | Amount Raised | Weighted-Average Cost of Capital |
|----------|---------------|----------------------------------|
| 1 | First $ 75 million | 6% |
| 2 | Next $100 million | 10% |
| 3 | Over $175 million | 12% |

These investment opportunities and financing costs are shown in the graph below:

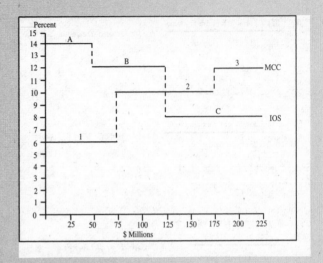

MCC = Marginal cost of capital
IOS = Investment opportunity schedule

**30.** The investment opportunity schedule (IOS) shows, in rank order, how much money the company would invest at different rates of return. Such schedules can be drawn only for a set of projects that

A. Have the same investment cost.

B. Are mutually exclusive.

C. Have the same net present value.

D. Are independent.

Answer (D) is correct. *(CIA, adapted)*
    **REQUIRED:** The characteristics of projects on an IOS.
    **DISCUSSION:** An IOS schedule is drawn for a set of independent projects. The decision to be made is whether to accept or reject each project without regard to other investment opportunities. Thus, the cash flows of one independent project are not influenced by those of another. Independence should be distinguished from mutual exclusivity. Projects are mutually exclusive if acceptance of one requires rejection of the other.
    Answer (A) is incorrect because IOS schedules do not require that all projects have the same investment cost. The steps of the schedule can be of varying lengths. Answer (B) is incorrect because IOS schedules cannot be drawn for mutually exclusive projects. Answer (C) is incorrect because IOS schedules do not require that all projects have the same NPV. The NPV of each project depends on the investment cost and on the present value of the expected cash flows. Both costs and cash flows can vary for projects on an IOS.

**31.** The company should invest in Project(s) <List A> and has an optimal capital budget of <List B> million dollars.

|   | List A | List B |
|---|--------|--------|
| A. | B only | 75 |
| B. | A and B only | 125 |
| C. | A and C only | 175 |
| D. | C only | 125 |

Answer (B) is correct. *(CIA, adapted)*
    **REQUIRED:** The project(s) in which the company should invest and its optimal capital budget.
    **DISCUSSION:** The intersection of the IOS and MCC schedules determines the cost of capital and the optimal capital budget. The company should begin with the project having the highest return and continue accepting projects as long as the IRR exceeds the MCC. The highest ranked project is A, with a $50 million cost and a 14% IRR. The MCC is only 6% over this range of financing. The next highest ranked project is B, with a $75 million cost and a 12% IRR. When $125 million has been invested, the marginal cost of the next dollar of capital is 10%, so Project B is also acceptable, bringing the optimal capital budget to $125 million. Project C is not acceptable because it has an 8% return. The MCC is 10% for the first $50 million invested in this project and 12% for the remaining $75 million.
    Answer (A) is incorrect because both A and B should be undertaken. Answer (C) is incorrect because A is acceptable, but C is not. Answer (D) is incorrect because C is not acceptable. It offers an IRR less than the marginal cost of financing the project.

**32.** Without prejudice to your answer to any other question, assume that the optimal capital budget for the company is $150 million. The marginal cost of capital and the appropriate discount rate to use in evaluating investment proposals for this company would be

A. 6%

B. 8%

C. 10%

D. 12%

Answer (C) is correct. *(CIA, adapted)*
**REQUIRED:** The marginal cost of capital and the appropriate discount rate.
**DISCUSSION:** The appropriate discount rate (the cost of capital used in capital budgeting) theoretically is determined at the intersection of the IOS and MCC schedules. This intersection is at an MCC of 10% and an optimal capital budget of $125 million. However, if the optimal capital budget is assumed to be $150 million, the company is still in the second interval of the MCC schedule. The marginal cost of financing in this part of the schedule is 10%.
Answer (A) is incorrect because 6% applies only to the first $75 million of new financing. Given that the optimal capital budget exceeds $75 million, 6% cannot be the discount rate. Answer (B) is incorrect because 8% is the IRR of Project C. Answer (D) is incorrect because at an investment level of $150 million, the MCC is 10%.

## 6.4 Cash Management

**33.** The most direct way to prepare a cash budget for a manufacturing firm is to include

A. Projected sales, credit terms, and net income.

B. Projected net income, depreciation, and goodwill amortization.

C. Projected purchases, percentages of purchases paid, and net income.

D. Projected sales and purchases, percentages of collections, and terms of payments.

Answer (D) is correct. *(CMA, adapted)*
**REQUIRED:** The most direct way of preparing a cash budget for a manufacturing firm.
**DISCUSSION:** The most direct way of preparing a cash budget requires incorporation of sales projections and credit terms, collection percentages, estimated purchases and payment terms, and other cash receipts and disbursements. In other words, preparation of the cash budget requires consideration of both inflows and outflows.
Answer (A) is incorrect because net income includes noncash elements, e.g., goodwill amortization and depreciation. Answer (B) is incorrect because net income includes noncash elements, e.g., goodwill amortization and depreciation. Answer (C) is incorrect because collection percentages must be considered, and net income includes noncash elements.

**34.** Cleveland Masks and Costumes Inc. (CMC) has a majority of its customers located in the states of California and Nevada. Keystone National Bank, a major west coast bank, has agreed to provide a lockbox system to CMC at a fixed fee of $50,000 per year and a variable fee of $0.50 for each payment processed by the bank. On average, CMC receives 50 payments per day, each averaging $20,000. With the lockbox system, the company's collection float will decrease by 2 days. The annual interest rate on money market securities is 6%. If CMC makes use of the lockbox system, what would be the net benefit to the company? Use 365 days per year.

A. $59,125

B. $60,875

C. $50,000

D. $120,000

Answer (B) is correct. *(CMA, adapted)*
**REQUIRED:** The net benefit to the company if a lockbox system is adopted.
**DISCUSSION:** If payments are collected 2 days earlier, the company can earn $120,000 ($20,000 × 50 payments per day × 2 days × .06) at a cost of $59,125 [$50,000 + (50 payments × 365 days × $.50)], a gain of $60,875.
Answer (A) is incorrect because $59,125 is the annual lockbox cost. Answer (C) is incorrect because $50,000 is the annual fixed fee. Answer (D) is incorrect because $120,000 is the annual savings without regard to costs.

**35.** DLF is a retail mail order firm that currently uses a central collection system that requires all checks to be sent to its Boston headquarters. An average of 6 days is required for mailed checks to be received, 3 days for DLF to process them, and 2 days for the checks to clear through its bank. A proposed lockbox system would reduce the mailing and processing time to 2 days and the check clearing time to 1 day. DLF has an average daily collection of $150,000. If DLF adopts the lockbox system, its average cash balance will increase by

A. $1,200,000

B. $750,000

C. $600,000

D. $450,000

Answer (A) is correct. *(Publisher)*
**REQUIRED:** The average increase in cash after the adoption of a lockbox system.
**DISCUSSION:** Checks are currently tied up for 11 days (6 for mailing, 3 for processing, and 2 for clearing). If that period were reduced to 3 days, DLF's cash balance would increase by $1,200,000 (8 days × $150,000 per day).
Answer (B) is incorrect because the decrease is 8 days, not 5. Answer (C) is incorrect because $600,000 represents only a 4-day savings. Answer (D) is incorrect because the lockbox system will result in an additional 8 days of savings, not 3.

**36.** Assume that each day a company writes and receives checks totaling $10,000. If it takes 5 days for the checks to clear and be deducted from the company's account, and only 4 days for the deposits to clear, what is the float?

A. $10,000

B. $0

C. $(10,000)

D. $50,000

Answer (A) is correct. *(CMA, adapted)*
**REQUIRED:** The net float when checks clear more slowly than deposits.
**DISCUSSION:** The float period is the time between when a check is written and when it clears the payor's checking account. Check float results in an interest-free loan to the payor because of the delay between payment by check and its deduction from the bank account. If checks written require one more day to clear than checks received, the net float equals one day's receipts. The company will have free use of the money for one day. In this case, the amount is $10,000.
Answer (B) is incorrect because the company enjoys one day's net float because its checks clear more slowly than its deposits. Answer (C) is incorrect because the net float is positive. The company can write checks (up to $10,000) even when it has no money because the checks do not clear until a day after deposits clear. Answer (D) is incorrect because the net float represents the difference between when deposits clear and when disbursements clear.

**37.** A company obtained a short-term bank loan of $250,000 at an annual interest rate of 6%. As a condition of the loan, the company is required to maintain a compensating balance of $50,000 in its checking account. The company's checking account earns interest at an annual rate of 2%. Ordinarily, the company maintains a balance of $25,000 in its checking account for transaction purposes. What is the effective interest rate of the loan?

A. 6.44%

B. 7.00%

C. 5.80%

D. 6.66%

Answer (A) is correct. *(CMA, adapted)*
**REQUIRED:** The effective interest rate on a loan that requires a compensating balance of $25,000 above the company's normal working balance.
**DISCUSSION:** The $50,000 compensating balance requirement is partially satisfied by the company's practice of maintaining a $25,000 balance for transaction purposes. Thus, only $25,000 of the loan will not be available for current use, leaving $225,000 of the loan usable. At 6% interest, the $250,000 loan would require an interest payment of $15,000 per year. This is partially offset by the 2% interest earned on the $25,000 incremental balance, or $500. Subtracting the $500 interest earned from the $15,000 of expense results in net interest expense of $14,500 for the use of $225,000 in funds. Dividing $14,500 by $225,000 produces an effective interest rate of 6.44%.
Answer (B) is incorrect because 7.00% fails to consider that the $25,000 currently being maintained counts toward the compensating balance requirement. Answer (C) is incorrect because 5.8% fails to consider the compensating balance requirement. Answer (D) is incorrect because 6.66% fails to consider the interest earned on the incremental balance being carried.

**38.** Which one of the following is not a characteristic of a negotiable certificate of deposit? Negotiable certificates of deposit

    A. Have a secondary market for investors.

    B. Are regulated by the Federal Reserve System.

    C. Are usually sold in denominations of a minimum of $100,000.

    D. Have yields considerably greater than bankers' acceptances and commercial paper.

Answer (D) is correct. *(CMA, adapted)*
    **REQUIRED:** The item not a characteristic of a negotiable certificate of deposit.
    **DISCUSSION:** A certificate of deposit (CD) is a form of savings deposit that cannot be withdrawn before maturity without incurring a high penalty. A negotiable CD can be traded. CDs usually have a fairly high rate of return compared with other savings instruments because they are for fixed, usually long-term periods. However, their yield is less than that of commercial paper and bankers' acceptances because they are less risky.
    Answer (A) is incorrect because negotiable CDs do have a secondary market (i.e., they are negotiable). Answer (B) is incorrect because negotiable CDs are regulated. Answer (C) is incorrect because negotiable CDs are typically issued in a denomination of $100,000.

**39.** A firm has daily cash receipts of $300,000. A bank has offered to provide a lockbox service that will reduce the collection time by 3 days. The bank requires a monthly fee of $2,000 for providing this service. If money market rates are expected to average 6% during the year, the additional annual income (loss) of using the lockbox service is

    A. $(24,000)

    B. $12,000

    C. $30,000

    D. $54,000

Answer (C) is correct. *(Publisher)*
    **REQUIRED:** The amount a company will gain or lose by hiring a bank lockbox service to process cash collections.
    **DISCUSSION:** Because collections will be accelerated by 3 days at a rate of $300,000 per day, the company will have an additional $900,000 to invest. At a rate of 6%, the interest earned will be $4,000 per year. However, the bank will charge $24,000 (12 months × $2,000 per month) for its services. Thus, the firm wil increase its income by $30,000 ($54,000 – $24,000).
    Answer (A) is incorrect because $(24,000) ignores the additional interest revenue from investing the increased funds. Answer (B) is incorrect because $12,000 is based on 2 days of accelerated inflows rather than 3. Answer (D) is incorrect because $54,000 ignores the $24,000 bank service charge.

## 6.5 Marketable Securities Management

**40.** When managing cash and short-term investments, a corporate treasurer is primarily concerned with

    A. Maximizing rate of return.

    B. Minimizing taxes.

    C. Investing in Treasury bonds since they have no default risk.

    D. Liquidity and safety.

Answer (D) is correct. *(CMA, adapted)*
    **REQUIRED:** The primary concern when managing cash and short-term investments.
    **DISCUSSION:** Cash and short-term investments are crucial to a firm's continuing success. Sufficient liquidity must be available to meet payments as they come due. At the same time, liquid assets are subject to significant control risk. Therefore, liquidity and safety are the primary concerns of the treasurer when dealing with highly liquid assets. Cash and short-term investments are held because of their ability to facilitate routine operations of the company. These assets are not held for purposes of achieving investment returns.
    Answer (A) is incorrect because most companies are not in business to earn high returns on liquid assets (i.e., they are held to facilitate operations). Answer (B) is incorrect because the holding of cash and cash-like assets is not a major factor in controlling taxes. Answer (C) is incorrect because investments in Treasury bonds do not have sufficient liquidity to serve as short-term assets.

## 6.6 Receivables Management

**41.** Garo Company, a retail store, is considering foregoing sales discounts in order to delay using its cash. Supplier credit terms are 2/10, net 30. Assuming a 360-day year, what is the annual cost of credit if the cash discount is not taken and Garo pays net 30?

A. 24.0%

B. 24.5%

C. 36.0%

D. 36.7%

Answer (D) is correct.   *(CMA, adapted)*
**REQUIRED:** The annual cost of credit if cash discounts are not taken when terms are 2/10, net 30.
**DISCUSSION:** On a $1,000 invoice, the company could save $20 by paying within the discount period. Thus, an immediate payment of $980 would save the company $20, and the interest rate charged for holding $980 an additional 20 days (30 − 10) is 2.04% ($20/$980). Because the number of 20-day periods in a year is 18 (360/20), the annual rate is 36.7% (18 × 2.04%).
Answer (A) is incorrect because the length of the extra credit period is 20 days, not 30 days. Answer (B) is incorrect because the length of the extra credit period is 20 days, not 30 days. Answer (C) is incorrect because 36.0% calculates the interest rate based on the full invoice price.

**42.** The sales manager at Ryan Company feels confident that, if the credit policy at Ryan's were changed, sales would increase and, consequently, the company would utilize excess capacity. The two credit proposals being considered are as follows:

|  | Proposal A | Proposal B |
| --- | --- | --- |
| Increase in sales | $500,000 | $600,000 |
| Contribution margin | 20% | 20% |
| Bad debt percentage | 5% | 5% |
| Increase in operating profits | $75,000 | $90,000 |
| Desired return on sales | 15% | 15% |

Currently, payment terms are net 30. The proposed payment terms for Proposal A and Proposal B are net 45 and net 90, respectively. An analysis to compare these two proposals for the change in credit policy would include all of the following factors except the

A. Cost of funds for Ryan.

B. Current bad debt experience.

C. Impact on the current customer base of extending terms to only certain customers.

D. Bank loan covenants on days' sales outstanding.

Answer (B) is correct.   *(CMA, adapted)*
**REQUIRED:** The factor not considered in an analysis of proposed credit policies.
**DISCUSSION:** All factors should be considered that differ between the two policies. Factors that do not differ, such as the current bad debt experience, are not relevant. Ryan must estimate the expected bad debt losses under each new policy.
Answer (A) is incorrect because the cost of funds is an obvious element in the analysis of any investment. Answer (C) is incorrect because the impact on the current customer base of extending terms to only certain customers is relevant. The current customers may demand the same terms. Answer (D) is incorrect because existing loan agreements may require Ryan to maintain certain ratios at stated levels. Thus, Ryan's ability to increase receivables and possible bad debt losses may be limited.

**43.** The average collection period for a firm measures the number of days

A. After a typical credit sale is made until the firm receives the payment.

B. For a typical check to "clear" through the banking system.

C. Beyond the end of the credit period before a typical customer payment is received.

D. Before a typical account becomes delinquent.

Answer (A) is correct.   *(CMA, adapted)*
**REQUIRED:** The meaning of a firm's average collection period.
**DISCUSSION:** The average collection period measures the number of days between the date of sale and the date of collection. It should be related to a firm's credit terms. For example, a firm that allows terms of 2/15, net 30, should have an average collection period of somewhere between 15 and 30 days.
Answer (B) is incorrect because it describes the concept of float. Answer (C) is incorrect because the average collection period includes the total time before a payment is received, including the periods both before and after the end of the normal credit period. Answer (D) is incorrect because it describes the normal credit period.

**44.** Best Computers believes that its collection costs could be reduced through modification of collection procedures. This action is expected to result in a lengthening of the average collection period from 28 days to 34 days; however, there will be no change in uncollectible accounts. The company's budgeted credit sales for the coming year are $27,000,000, and short-term interest rates are expected to average 8%. To make the changes in collection procedures cost beneficial, the minimum savings in collection costs (using a 360-day year) for the coming year would have to be

A. $30,000.

B. $360,000.

C. $180,000.

D. $36,000.

Answer (D) is correct. *(CMA, adapted)*
**REQUIRED:** The minimum savings in collection costs that would be necessary to make the lengthened credit period beneficial.
**DISCUSSION:** Given sales of $27,000,000, the average amount of daily sales must be $75,000 ($27,000,000 ÷ 360 days). The increased accounts receivable balance is therefore $450,000 (6 days × $75,000). With an additional $450,000 of capital invested in receivables, the company's interest cost will increase by $36,000 per year (8% × $450,000). Thus, the company must save at least $36,000 per year to justify the change in procedures.

**45.** A firm averages $4,000 in sales per day and is paid, on an average, within 30 days of the sale. After they receive their invoice, 55% of the customers pay by check, while the remaining 45% pay by credit card. Approximately how much would the company show in accounts receivable on its balance sheet on any given date?

A. $4,000

B. $120,000

C. $48,000

D. $54,000

Answer (B) is correct. *(CMA, adapted)*
**REQUIRED:** The average balance in accounts receivable given the average payment period and sales per day.
**DISCUSSION:** If sales are $4,000 per day, and customers pay in 30 days, 30 days of sales are outstanding, or $120,000. Whether customers pay by credit card or cash, collection requires 30 days.
Answer (A) is incorrect because $4,000 is only one day's sales. Answer (C) is incorrect because invoices are outstanding for 30 days, not 12 days. Answer (D) is incorrect because $54,000 is based on the 45% of collections via credit card.

## 6.7 Valuation and Pricing Business Combinations

**46.** A common mistake in valuing the firm to be acquired in a business combination is

A. Using market values in the valuation.

B. Including incremental cash flows in the valuation.

C. Using the acquiring firm's discount rate when valuing the incremental cash flows.

D. Including all related transaction costs associated with an acquisition.

Answer (C) is correct. *(Publisher)*
**REQUIRED:** The common mistake in valuing the acquired firm.
**DISCUSSION:** If the net incremental cash flows to the acquiring firm's shareholders are to be valued, the discount rate used should be the cost of equity capital. Moreover, this rate should reflect the risk associated with the use of funds rather than their source. The rate therefore should not be the cost of capital of the acquiring firm but rather the cost of equity of the combined firm after the combination. This calculation requires a new estimate of beta to be used in the Capital Asset Pricing Model.

**47.** For the past several years, M.F.S. Company has invested in the common stock of Annabelle Company. M.F.S. currently owns approximately 13% of the total of Annabelle's outstanding voting common stock. Recently, managements of the two companies have discussed a possible combination of the two entities. If they do decide to combine, the resulting combination should be accounted for as a

A. Pooling of interests.

B. Purchase.

C. Part purchase, part pooling.

D. Joint venture.

Answer (B) is correct. *(Publisher)*
**REQUIRED:** The accounting for a business combination, given 13% ownership of one combining entity by the other.
**DISCUSSION:** SFAS 141, *Business Combinations*, requires that all business combinations be accounted for using the purchase method.
Answer (A) is incorrect because the pooling-of-interests method is no longer an acceptable method of accounting for business combinations. Answer (C) is incorrect because accounting for a business combination as part purchase and part pooling is not allowed. Answer (D) is incorrect because a business combination cannot be accounted for as a joint venture.

## 6.8 Derivative Financial Instruments

**48.** A company has recently purchased some stock of a competitor as part of a long-term plan to acquire the competitor. However, it is somewhat concerned that the market price of this stock could decrease over the short run. The company could hedge against the possible decline in the stock's market price by

A. Purchasing a call option on that stock.

B. Purchasing a put option on that stock.

C. Selling a put option on that stock.

D. Obtaining a warrant option on that stock.

**Answer (B) is correct.** *(CIA, adapted)*
**REQUIRED:** The means of hedging against the possible decline in the stock's market price.
**DISCUSSION:** A put option is the right to sell stock at a given price within a certain period. If the market price falls, the put option may allow the sale of stock at a price above market, and the profit of the option holder will be the difference between the price stated in the put option and the market price, minus the cost of the option, commissions, and taxes. The company that issues the stock has nothing to do with put (and call) options.
Answer (A) is incorrect because a call option is the right to purchase shares at a given price within a specified period. Answer (C) is incorrect because selling a put option could force the company to purchase additional stock if the option is exercised. Answer (D) is incorrect because a warrant gives the holder a right to purchase stock from the issuer at a given price (it is usually distributed along with debt).

**49.** If a call option is "out-of-the-money,"

A. The option has expired.

B. The value of the underlying asset is less than the exercise price.

C. The option no longer exists.

D. The option has become a put option.

**Answer (B) is correct.** *(Publisher)*
**REQUIRED:** The meaning behind a call option being "out-of-money."
**DISCUSSION:** When the value of the asset underlying a call option is less than the exercise price of the option, the option is "out-of-money."
Answer (A) is incorrect because an out-of-the-money option may not have expired. Answer (C) is incorrect because the option does exist; it is just not worth exercising. Answer (D) is incorrect because call options do not change into put options.

**50.** The type of option that does not have the backing of stock is called a(n)

A. Covered option.

B. Unsecured option.

C. Naked option.

D. Put option.

**Answer (C) is correct.** *(Publisher)*
**REQUIRED:** The type of option that does not have the backing of stock.
**DISCUSSION:** A naked or uncovered option is a call option that does not have the backing of stock. Thus, the option writer will have to purchase the underlying stock if the call option is exercised.
Answer (A) is incorrect because a covered option is one that is written against stock held in the option writer's portfolio. Answer (B) is incorrect because an unsecured option is a nonsense term. Answer (D) is incorrect because a put option is an option that gives the owner the right to sell the underlying asset for a fixed price.

**51.** A contractual arrangement that gives the owner the right to buy or sell an asset at a fixed price at any moment in time before or on a specified date is a(n)

A. European option.

B. Foreign option.

C. Future option.

D. American option.

**Answer (D) is correct.** *(Publisher)*
**REQUIRED:** The type of option that can be exercised at any time before or on a specified date.
**DISCUSSION:** An American option is a contractual arrangement that gives the owner the right to buy or sell an asset at a fixed price at any moment in time before or on a specified date.
Answer (A) is incorrect because a European option is exercisable only at the expiration date. Answer (B) is incorrect because a foreign option is a nonsense term. Answer (C) is incorrect because although an option can be exercised in the future, it is not called a future option.

**52.** The use of derivatives to either hedge or speculate results in

A. Increased risk regardless of motive.

B. Decreased risk regardless of motive.

C. Offset risk when hedging and increased risk when speculating.

D. Offset risk when speculating and increased risk when hedging.

Answer (C) is correct. *(Publisher)*
**REQUIRED:** The effects of hedging and speculating on risk.
**DISCUSSION:** Derivatives, including options and futures, are contracts between the parties who contract. Unlike stocks and bonds, they are not claims on business assets. A futures contract is entered into as either a speculation or a hedge. Speculation involves the assumption of risk in the hope of gaining from price movements. Hedging is the process of using offsetting commitments to minimize or avoid the impact of adverse price movements.
Answer (A) is incorrect because hedging decreases risk by using offsetting commitments that avoid the impact of adverse price movements. Answer (B) is incorrect because speculation involves the assumption of risk in the hope of gaining from price movements. Answer (D) is incorrect because speculating increases risk while hedging offsets risk.

**53.** An automobile company that uses the futures market to set the price of steel to protect a profit against price increases is an example of

A. A short hedge.

B. A long hedge.

C. Selling futures to protect the company from loss.

D. Selling futures to protect against price declines.

Answer (B) is correct. *(Publisher)*
**REQUIRED:** The example of the use of the futures market to protect a profit.
**DISCUSSION:** A change in prices can be minimized or avoided by hedging. Hedging is the process of using offsetting commitments to minimize or avoid the impact of adverse price movements. The automobile company desires to stabilize the price of steel so that its cost to the company will not rise and cut into profits. Accordingly, the automobile company uses the futures market to create a long hedge, which is a futures contract that is purchased to protect against price increases.
Answer (A) is incorrect because a short hedge is a futures contract that is sold to protect against price declines. The automobile company wishes to protect itself against price increases. Answer (C) is incorrect because the automobile company needs to purchase futures in order to protect itself from loss, not sell futures. Selling futures protects against price declines. Answer (D) is incorrect because it is the definition of a short hedge, which is used for avoiding price declines. The automobile company wants to protect itself against price increases.

**54.** If a corporation holds a forward contract for the delivery of U.S. Treasury bonds in 6 months and, during those 6 months, interest rates decline, at the end of the 6 months the value of the forward contract will have

A. Decreased.

B. Increased.

C. Remained constant.

D. Any of the answers may be correct, depending on the extent of the decline in interest rates.

Answer (B) is correct. *(Publisher)*
**REQUIRED:** The impact of an interest rate decline on the value of a forward contract.
**DISCUSSION:** Interest rate futures contracts involve risk-free bonds, such as U.S. Treasury bonds. When interest rates decrease over the period of a forward contract, the value of the bonds and the forward contract increase.
Answer (A) is incorrect because the value of the forward contract will increase when interest rates decrease. Answer (C) is incorrect because the value of the forward contract will not remain constant if interest rates decline. Answer (D) is incorrect because any decline in interest rates increases the value of the bonds.

**55.** A company wishes to price a call option written on a nondividend-paying stock. The current stock price is $50, the exercise price is $48, the risk-free interest rate is 5.0%, the option expires in 1 year, and the cumulative probabilities used to calculate the present values of the final stock price and the exercise price are .65 and .58, respectively. According to the Black-Scholes Option Pricing Model, the current value of the call option is

A.  $6.02

B.  $4.66

C.  $4.02

D.  $2.00

Answer (A) is correct. *(Publisher)*
**REQUIRED:** The current value of the call option according to the Black-Scholes Option Pricing Model.
**DISCUSSION:** The basic formula is

$$C = SN(d_1) - Ee^{(-rt)}N(d_2)$$

If C is the current value of a call option with time t in years until expiration, S is the current stock price, N ($d_i$) is the cumulative probability that a i deviation less than $d_i$ will occur in a standardized normal distribution [N ($d_i$) is an area to the left of d under the curve for the standard normal distribution], E is the call's exercise price, e is a constant (approximately 2.7183), and r is the annualized continuous risk-free rate of return, the value of the call is

$$
\begin{aligned}
C &= (\$50 \times .65) - (\$48 \times 2.7183^{(-.05 \times 1)} \times .58) \\
&= \$32.50 - (\$48 \times .9512 \times .58) \\
&= \$32.50 - \$26.48 \\
&= \$6.02
\end{aligned}
$$

Answer (B) is incorrect because $4.66 results from omitting the term $e^{(-rt)}$ power from the equation. Answer (C) is incorrect because $4.02 equals the estimated call price minus the difference between the current stock price and the exercise price. Answer (D) is incorrect because $2.00 is the difference between the current stock price and the exercise price.

**56.** A company has purchased a $1,000, 7%, 5-year bond at par that pays interest annually. The discount factors for the present value of $1 at 7% for five periods are as follows:

| Period | Factor |
| --- | --- |
| 1 | .935 |
| 2 | .873 |
| 3 | .816 |
| 4 | .763 |
| 5 | .713 |

For purposes of duration hedging, the duration of the bond is

A.  5.39 years.

B.  5.00 years.

C.  4.39 years.

D.  3.81 years.

Answer (C) is correct. *(Publisher)*
**REQUIRED:** The duration of the bond.
**DISCUSSION:** Duration hedging involves hedging interest-rate risk by matching the duration and value of assets with the duration and value of liabilities. Duration is the weighted average of the times to interest and principal payments. If duration increases, the volatility of the price of the debt instrument increases. Duration is lower if the nominal rate on the instrument is higher because more of the return is received earlier. The formula for duration is as follows if $C_T$ is the interest or principal payment, T is the time to the payment, n is the time to maturity, r is the yield to maturity, and V is the value of the instrument:

$$\sum_{t=1}^{n} \left[ \frac{C_T \times T}{(1 + r)^T} \right] \div V$$

Because the expression $1 \div (1 + r)^T$ is the present value of $1, the weighted present values of the payments can be calculated as follows: $65.45 (7% × $1,000 × 1 period × .935), $122.22 (7% × $1,000 × 2 periods × .873), $171.36 (7% × $1,000 × 3 periods × .816), $213.64 (7% × $1,000 × 4 periods × .763), and $3,814.55 (107% × $1,000 × 5 periods × .713). The total is $4,387.22. The value of the bond is $1,000 {[[$70 × (.935 + .873 + .816 + .763 + .713)] + ($1,000 × .713)}. Thus, the duration is approximately 4.39 years ($4,387.22 ÷ $1,000).
Answer (A) is incorrect because 5.39 years results from adding $1,000 to the numerator of the calculation. Answer (B) is incorrect because 5.00 years is the term of the bond. Answer (D) is incorrect because 3.81 years equals the weighted present value of the final payment divided by $1,000.

**57.** Herbert Corporation was a party to the following transactions during November and December 2002. Which of these transactions is most likely to be defined as a derivative?

  A. Purchased 1,000 shares of common stock of a public corporation based on the assumption that the stock will increase in value.

  B. Purchased a term life insurance policy on the company's chief executive officer to protect the company from the effects of an untimely demise of this officer.

  C. Agreed to cosign the note of its 100%-owned subsidiary to protect the lender from the possibility that the subsidiary might default on the loan.

  D. Based on its forecasted need to purchase 300,000 bushels of wheat in 3 months, entered into a 3-month forward contract to purchase 300,000 bushels of wheat to protect itself from changes in wheat prices during the period.

Answer (D) is correct. *(Publisher)*
**REQUIRED:** The transaction resulting in an investment in a derivative instrument.
**DISCUSSION:** SFAS 133 defines a derivative as a financial instrument or other contract that (1) has (a) one or more underlyings and (b) one or more notional amounts or payment provisions, or both; (2) requires either no initial net investment or an immaterial net investment; and (3) requires or permits net settlement. An underlying may be a specified interest rate, security price, commodity price, foreign exchange rate, index of prices or rates, or other variable. A notional amount is a number of currency units, shares, bushels, pounds, or other units specified. Settlement of a derivative is based on the interaction of the notional amount and the underlying. The purchase of the forward contract as a hedge of a forecasted need to purchase wheat meets the criteria prescribed by SFAS 133.
Answer (A) is incorrect because it involves a net investment equal to the fair value of the stock. Answer (B) is incorrect because insuring the CEO's life is a transaction based on identifiable events, not underlyings. Answer (C) is incorrect because cosigning a subsidiary's note is a transaction based on identifiable events, not underlyings.

**58.** On December 1, 2004, Lombardi Company, a calendar-year-end firm, entered into a derivative contract designed to hedge the risk of cash flows associated with the forecast future sale of 300,000 bushels of wheat. The anticipated sales date is February 1, 2005. The notional amount of the derivative contract is 300,000 bushels, the underlying is the price of the same variety and grade of wheat that Lombardi expects to sell, and the settlement date of the derivative is February 1, 2005. The fair value of the derivative contract on December 31, 2004 increased by $30,000, an amount equal to the decrease in the fair value of the wheat. The fair value of the derivative contract had increased by an additional $25,000 on February 1, 2005, also an amount equal to the decrease in the fair value of the wheat. On February 1, 2005, the wheat was sold and the derivative contract was settled. The gains attributable to the increase in the fair value of the derivative that should be recognized in 2004 and 2005 earnings, respectively, are

|    | 2004 | 2005 |
|----|------|------|
| A. | $30,000 | $25,000 |
| B. | $0 | $55,000 |
| C. | $55,000 | $0 |
| D. | $0 | $0 |

Answer (B) is correct. *(Publisher)*
**REQUIRED:** The gains resulting from the increase in the fair value of a hedging derivative to be included in earnings for the periods during which it was outstanding.
**DISCUSSION:** A cash flow hedge is a hedge of an exposure to variability in the cash flows of a recognized asset or liability or a forecasted transaction. The accounting treatment of gains and losses arising from changes in fair value of a derivative designated as a cash flow hedge varies for the effective and ineffective portions. The effective portion initially is reported as other comprehensive income. It is reclassified into earnings when the forecasted transaction affects earnings. The ineffective portion is immediately included in earnings. This hedge has no ineffective portion. Given that the sale occurred in 2005, the $30,000 gain in 2004 is recognized as other comprehensive income in 2004. It is reclassified and included in earnings in 2005. Thus, 2005 earnings include the $30,000 reclassified from other comprehensive income and the $25,000 gain attributable to the increase in fair value in 2005. Given that the hedge was fully effective, the $55,000 gain should be recognized in the period in which the forecasted transaction affects earnings.

**59.** At the beginning of period 1, Forecast Corporation enters into a qualifying cash flow hedge of a transaction it expects to occur at the beginning of period 4. Forecast assesses hedge effectiveness by comparing the change in present value (PV) of the expected cash flows associated with the forecasted transaction with all of the hedging derivative's gain or loss (change in fair value). The change in those cash flows that occurs for any reason has been designated as the hedged risk. The following information about the periodic changes hedging relationship is available:

| Period | Change in Fair Value of the Derivative | Change in PV of Expected Cash Flows from the Forecasted Transactions |
|--------|----------------------------------------|---------------------------------------------------------------------|
| 1 | $50,000 | $(48,000) |
| 2 | 47,000 | (51,000) |
| 3 | (81,000) | 80,000 |

Given that the hedge is effective to the extent it offsets the change in the present value of the expected cash flows on the forecasted transaction, Forecast should

A. Recognize a loss of $2,000 in earnings for period 1.

B. Report a balance in other comprehensive income (OCI) of $16,000 at the end of period 3.

C. Recognize a gain of $47,000 in earnings for period 2.

D. Record other comprehensive income of $97,000 for period 2.

Answer (B) is correct. *(Publisher)*
**REQUIRED:** The appropriate accounting for a cash flow hedge of a forecasted transaction.
**DISCUSSION:** The effective portion of a cash flow hedge of a forecasted transaction is included in OCI until periods in which the forecasted transaction affects earnings. At the end of period 3, the net change in the hedging derivative's fair value is $16,000 ($50,000 + $47,000 – $81,000), and the change in the PV of the expected cash flows on the forecasted transaction is $-19,000 ($80,000 – $48,000 – $51,000). Thus, the hedge is effective at the end of period 3 to the extent it offsets $16,000 of the net $19,000 decrease in the cash flows of the forecasted transaction that are expected to occur in period 4.
Answer (A) is incorrect because Forecast should recognize earnings for period 1 of $2,000. The increase in fair value of the derivative exceeds the decrease in PV of the cash flows by $2,000. The derivative is adjusted to fair value by a $50,000 debit, OCI is credited for $48,000, and earnings is credited for $2,000. Answer (C) is incorrect because the entry for period 2 is to debit the derivative for $47,000, debit earnings for $2,000, and credit OCI for $49,000 ($50,000 + $47,000 – $48,000 credit in period 1). Answer (D) is incorrect because, at the end of period 2, OCI should have a credit balance of $97,000 (the extent of the hedge's effectiveness).

## 6.9 Portfolio Theory

Questions 60 through 62 are based on the following information.

Techspace has been a successful stock over the past few years despite its riskiness. The state of the economy has a tremendous effect on the expected returns for Techspace:

| Probability | State of the Economy | Techspace Returns |
|-------------|----------------------|-------------------|
| .05 | Depression | –45% |
| .15 | Recession | –10% |
| .20 | Minimal Slowdown | 5% |
| .40 | Stable | 10% |
| .15 | Expansion | 30% |
| .05 | Significant Expansion | 35% |

**60.** What is the expected rate of return on Techspace shares?

A. 7.5%

B. 15%

C. 35%

D. 25%

Answer (A) is correct. *(Publisher)*
**REQUIRED:** The expected rate of return on shares given probabilities for different situations and corresponding returns.
**DISCUSSION:** The expected rate of return on an investment is determined using an expected value calculation. It is an average of the outcomes weighted according to their probabilities. For Techspace, the average is accomplished by multiplying each probability by the corresponding return for each state of the economy and then calculating the sum of the products. Numerically, the calculation is performed as follows: .05(-.45) + .15(-.10) + .2(.05) + .4(.10) + .15(.30) + .05(.35) = .075 = 7.5%.
Answer (B) is incorrect because 15% adds positive products instead of negative products for the first two states. Answer (C) is incorrect because 35% is the sum of the returns (assuming all are positive) minus 1. Answer (D) is incorrect because 25% is the sum of the returns.

**61.** The variance of Techspace returns is

A. .1735

B. .0301

C. .075

D. .2738

Answer (B) is correct. *(Publisher)*
**REQUIRED:** The variance of returns given probabilities for different situations and corresponding returns.
**DISCUSSION:** The variance ($\sigma^2$) is calculated using the equation

$$\sigma^2 = \sum_{i=1}^{n}\left(k_i - \hat{k}\right)^2 p_i$$

If: $k_i$ is the return for the ith outcome, $\hat{k}$ is the expected return, and $p_i$ is the probability of the ith outcome.

$$\hat{k} = \sum_{i=1}^{n} k_i p_i \qquad \text{or} \quad .05(-.45) + .15(-.10) + .2(.05)$$

$+ .4(.10) + .15(.30) + .05(.35) = .075$

$\sigma^2 = .05(-.45 - .075)^2 + .15(-.1 - .075)^2$
$+ .2(.05 - .075)^2 + .4(.1 - .075)^2 + .15(.30 - .075)^2$
$+ .05(.35 - .075)^2 = .0301$

Answer (A) is incorrect because .1735 is the standard deviation of Techspace returns. Answer (C) is incorrect because .075 is the expected return. Answer (D) is incorrect because .2738 is the square root of the expected return.

**62.** The standard deviation of Techspace returns is

A. 7.5%

B. 17.35%

C. 3.01%

D. None of the answers are correct.

Answer (B) is correct. *(Publisher)*
**REQUIRED:** The standard deviation.
**DISCUSSION:** The standard deviation ($\sigma$) gives an exact value for the tightness of the distribution and the riskiness of the investment. It is calculated by taking the square root of the variance. Given that the variance is .0301, the standard deviation is .1735, or 17.35%.
Answer (A) is incorrect because 7.5% is the expected return. Answer (C) is incorrect because 3.01% is the variance. Answer (D) is incorrect because the standard deviation is 17.35%.

**63.** If the covariance of share A with share B is -.0076, then what is the covariance of share B with share A?

A. +.0076

B. -.0076

C. Greater than .0076.

D. Less than -.0076.

Answer (B) is correct. *(Publisher)*
**REQUIRED:** The covariance of two investments.
**DISCUSSION:** The covariance measures the volatility of returns together with their correlation with the returns of other securities. It is calculated with the following equation:

$$COV(XY) = \sum_{i=1}^{n}\left(k_{xi} - \hat{k}_x\right)\left(k_{yi} - \hat{k}_y\right)p_i$$

The covariance of two shares is the same regardless of which share is compared with the other.

**64.** A feasible portfolio that offers the highest expected return for a given risk or the least risk for a given expected return is a(n)

A. Optimal portfolio.

B. Desirable portfolio.

C. Efficient portfolio.

D. Effective portfolio.

Answer (C) is correct. *(Publisher)*
**REQUIRED:** The term for a portfolio that offers the highest expected return for a given risk.
**DISCUSSION:** A feasible portfolio that offers the highest expected return for a given risk or the least risk for a given expected return is called an efficient portfolio.
Answer (A) is incorrect because an optimal portfolio is a portfolio selected from the efficient set of portfolios because it is tangent to the investor's highest indifference curve. Answer (B) is incorrect because a desirable portfolio is a nonsense term. Answer (D) is incorrect because an effective portfolio is a nonsense term.

# STUDY UNIT SEVEN
# MANAGERIAL ACCOUNTING

(34 pages of outline)

Study Unit 7 covers basic concepts of managerial accounting. One basic concept is cost behavior, that is, whether costs are fixed, variable, or some combination. Cost behavior must be understood to plan for firm profitability. This study unit also addresses cost allocation methods. These methods are used to assign indirect costs to cost objects. Other subunits apply to costing systems, budgeting, certain analytical methods, transfer pricing, and responsibility systems.

## 7.1 COST-VOLUME-PROFIT (CVP) ANALYSIS

1. CVP (breakeven) analysis predicts the relationships among revenues, variable costs, and fixed costs at various production levels. It determines the probable effects of changes in sales volume, sales price, product mix, etc.

2. The **variables** include

   a. Revenue as a function of price per unit and quantity produced
   b. Fixed costs
   c. Variable cost per unit or as a percentage of sales
   d. Profit per unit or as a percentage of sales

3. The inherent simplifying **assumptions** used in CVP analysis are the following:

   a. Costs and revenues are predictable and are linear over the relevant range.
   b. **Total variable costs** change proportionally with volume, but **unit variable costs** are constant over the relevant range.
   c. Changes in inventory are insignificant in amount.
   d. **Total fixed costs** remain constant over the relevant range of volume, but **unit fixed costs** vary indirectly with volume.
   e. Selling prices remain fixed.
   f. Production equals sales.
   g. The product mix is constant, or the firm makes only one product.
   h. A relevant range exists in which the various relationships are true for a given time span.
   i. All costs are either fixed or variable relative to a given cost object.
   j. Productive efficiency is constant.

    k.    Costs vary only with changes in physical sales volume.

    l.    The breakeven point is directly related to costs and indirectly related to the budgeted margin of safety and the contribution margin.

## 4.  Definitions

    a.    The **relevant range** is the set of limits within which the cost and revenue relationships remain linear and fixed costs are fixed.

    b.    The **breakeven point** is the sales level at which total revenues equal total costs.

    c.    The **margin of safety** is the excess of budgeted sales dollars over breakeven sales dollars (or budgeted units over breakeven units).

    d.    The **sales mix** is the composition of total sales in terms of various products, i.e., the percentages of each product included in total sales.  It is maintained for all volume changes.

    e.    The **unit contribution margin (UCM)** is the unit selling price minus the unit variable cost.  It is the contribution from the sale of one unit to cover fixed costs (and possibly a targeted profit).

        1)    It is expressed as either a percentage of the selling price (**contribution margin ratio**) or a dollar amount.

        2)    The UCM is the slope of the total cost line plotted so that volume is on the x axis and dollar value is on the y axis.

## 5.  Breakeven Formula

    a.  $P = S - FC - VC$
        $S = XY$

        If:    $P$ = profit (zero at breakeven)
                $S$ = sales
                $FC$ = fixed costs
                $VC$ = variable costs
                $X$ = quantity of units sold
                $Y$ = unit sales price

## 6.  Applications

    a.    The basic problem equates sales with the sum of fixed and variable costs.

        1)    EXAMPLE:  Given a selling price of $2.00 per unit and variable costs of 40%, what is the breakeven point if fixed costs are $6,000?

$$\begin{aligned} S &= FC + VC \\ \$2.00X &= \$6,000 + \$.80X \\ \$1.20X &= \$6,000 \\ X &= 5,000 \text{ } units\text{ }at\text{ }breakeven\text{ }point \end{aligned}$$

        2)    The same result can be obtained by dividing fixed costs by the UCM.

        3)    The breakeven point in dollars can be calculated by dividing fixed costs by the contribution margin ratio.

    b.    An amount of profit, either in dollars or as a percentage of sales, may be required.

        1)    EXAMPLE:  If units are sold at $6.00 and variable costs are $2.00, how many units must be sold to realize a profit of 15% ($6.00 × .15 = $.90 per unit) before taxes, given fixed costs of $37,500?

$$\begin{aligned} S &= FC + VC + P \\ \$6.00X &= \$37,500 + \$2.00X + \$.90X \\ \$3.10X &= \$37,500 \\ X &= 12,097 \text{ } units\text{ }at\text{ }breakeven\text{ }to\text{ }earn\text{ }a\text{ }15\%\text{ }profit \end{aligned}$$

2) The desired profit of $.90 per unit is treated as a variable cost. If the desired profit were stated in total dollars rather than as a percentage, it would be treated as a fixed cost.

3) Selling 12,097 units results in $72,582 of sales. Variable costs are $24,194 and profit is $10,888 ($72,582 × 15%). The proof is that fixed costs of $37,500, plus variable costs of $24,194, plus profit of $10,888 equals $72,582 of sales.

c. Multiple products may be involved in calculating a breakeven point.

1) EXAMPLE: If A and B account for 60% and 40% of total sales, respectively, and the variable cost ratios are 60% and 85%, respectively, what is the breakeven point, given fixed costs of $150,000?

$$S = FC + VC$$
$$S = \$150,000 + .6(.6S) + .85(.4S)$$
$$S = \$150,000 + .36S + .34S$$
$$.30S = \$150,000$$
$$S = \$500,000$$

a) In effect, the result is obtained by calculating a weighted-average contribution margin ratio (30%) and dividing it into the fixed costs to arrive at the breakeven point in sales dollars.

b) Another approach is to divide fixed costs by the UCM for a composite unit (when unit prices are known) to determine the number of composite units. The number of individual units can then be calculated based on the stated mix.

d. Sometimes breakeven analysis is applied to analysis of the profitability of special orders. This application is essentially contribution margin analysis.

1) EXAMPLE: What is the effect of accepting a special order for 10,000 units at $8.00, given the following unit operating data?

|  | Per Unit |
| --- | --- |
| Sales | $12.50 |
| Manufacturing costs -- variable | (6.25) |
| -- fixed | (1.75) |
| Gross profit | $ 4.50 |
| Selling expenses -- variable | (1.80) |
| -- fixed | (1.45) |
| Operating profit | $ 1.25 |

a) The assumptions are that idle capacity is sufficient to manufacture 10,000 extra units, that sale at $8.00 per unit will not affect the price or quantity of other units sold, and that no additional selling expenses are incurred.

b) Because the variable cost of manufacturing is $6.25, the UCM is $1.75 ($8 special-order price − $6.25), and the increase in operating profit is $17,500 ($1.75 × 10,000 units).

7. Stop and review! You have completed the outline for this subunit. Study multiple-choice questions 1 through 5 beginning on page 349.

## 7.2 VARIABLE AND ABSORPTION COSTING

1. These methods result in different inventory values and net profits. They also result in income statements in which the classification and order of costs are different. Under **absorption (full) costing**, all factory overhead costs are assigned to products.

2.    However, **variable (direct) costing** has won increasing support. This method assigns variable but not fixed factory overhead to products.

    a.    The term **direct costing** may be misleading because it suggests traceability, which is not what cost accountants mean when they speak of direct costing. Many accountants believe that **variable costing** is a more suitable term, and some even call the method **contribution margin reporting**.

3.    Variable and absorption costing are just two of a continuum of possible inventory costing methods. At one extreme is **supervariable costing**, which treats direct materials as the only variable cost. At the other extreme is **superabsorption costing**, which treats costs from all links in the value chain as inventoriable.

4.    Under variable costing, all direct labor, direct materials, variable factory overhead costs, and selling and administrative costs are handled in precisely the same manner as under absorption costing. Only fixed factory overhead costs are treated differently. They are expensed when incurred.

    a.    EXAMPLE: A firm, during its first month in business, produced 100 units of product X and sold 80 units while incurring the following costs:

| | |
|---|---:|
| Direct materials | $100 |
| Direct labor | 200 |
| Variable factory overhead | 150 |
| Fixed factory overhead | 300 |

        1)    Given total costs of $750, the absorption cost per unit is $7.50 ($750 ÷ 100 units). Thus, total ending inventory is $150 (20 × $7.50). Using variable costing, the cost per unit is $4.50 ($450 ÷ 100 units), and the total value of the remaining 20 units is $90.

        2)    If the unit sales price is $10, and the company incurred $20 of variable selling expenses and $60 of fixed selling expenses, the following income statements result from using the two methods:

| Variable Cost | | | Absorption Cost | | |
|---|---:|---:|---|---:|---:|
| Sales | | $800 | Sales | | $800 |
|   Beginning inventory | $ 0 | |   Beginning inventory | $ 0 | |
|   Variable cost of | | |   Cost of goods | | |
|     manufacturing | 450 | |     manufactured | 750 | |
| | $450 | |   Cost of goods available | | |
|   Ending inventory | (90) | |     for sale | $750 | |
|   Variable cost of goods cost | | (360) |   Ending inventory | (150) | |
| Manufacturing contribution | | | Cost of goods sold | | (600) |
|   margin | | $440 | Gross margin | | $200 |
| Variable selling expenses | | (20) | Selling expenses | | (80) |
| Contribution margin | | $420 |   Operating profit | | $120 |
| Fixed factory overhead | | (300) | | | |
| Fixed selling expenses | | (60) | | | |
|   Operating profit | | $ 60 | | | |

        3)    The $60 difference in operating profit ($120 – $60) is the difference between the two ending inventory values ($150 – $90). In essence, the absorption method treats 20% of the fixed factory overhead costs (20% × $300 = $60) as an asset (inventory) because 20% of the month's production (100 – 80 sold = 20) is still on hand. The variable-costing method assumes that the fixed factory overhead costs are not product costs because they would have been incurred even if no production had occurred.

4) The **contribution margin** is an important element in the variable costing income statement. It equals sales minus total variable costs. It indicates how much sales contribute toward covering fixed costs and providing a profit.

5. Variable costing permits the adoption of the **contribution approach** to performance measurement. This approach is emphasized because it focuses on controllability. Fixed costs are much less controllable than variable costs, so the contribution margin (revenues – all variable costs) may therefore be a fairer basis for evaluation than gross margin (also called gross profit), which equals revenues minus cost of sales.

   a. Allocation of **central administration costs** (allocated common costs) is a fundamental issue in responsibility accounting. It has often been made based on budgeted revenue or contribution margin. If allocation is based on actual sales or contribution margin, a responsibility center that surpasses expectations will be penalized (charged with increased overhead).

      1) Research has shown that central administrative costs are **allocated** to organizational subunits for the following reasons:

         a) The allocation reminds managers that such costs exist and that the managers would incur these costs if their operations were independent.

         b) The allocation also reminds managers that profit center earnings must cover some amount of support costs.

         c) Organizational subunits should be motivated to use central administrative services appropriately.

         d) Managers who must bear the costs of central administrative services that they do not control may be encouraged to exert pressure on those who do.

      2) If central administrative or other fixed costs are **not allocated**, responsibility centers might reach their revenue or contribution margin goals without covering all fixed costs, a necessity to operate in the long run.

      3) Allocation of overhead, however, is **motivationally negative**; central administrative or other fixed costs may appear noncontrollable and be unproductive. Furthermore,

         a) Managers' morale may suffer when allocations depress operating results.

         b) Dysfunctional conflict may arise among managers when costs controlled by one are allocated to others.

         c) Resentment may result if cost allocation is perceived to be arbitrary or unfair. For example, an allocation on an ability-to-bear basis, such as operating profit, penalizes successful managers and rewards underachievers and may therefore have a demotivating effect.

      4) A much preferred alternative is to budget a certain amount of the contribution margin earned by each responsibility center to the central administration based on **negotiation**. The hoped-for result is for each subunit to see itself as contributing to the success of the overall entity rather than carrying the weight (cost) of central administration.

         a) The central administration can then make the decision whether to expand, divest, or close responsibility centers.

6. Stop and review! You have completed the outline for this subunit. Study multiple-choice questions 6 through 10 beginning on page 351.

## 7.3 OVERHEAD ALLOCATION

1.  Factory overhead consists of indirect manufacturing costs that cannot be assigned to specific units of production but are incurred as a necessary part of the production process. Allocation bases (activity levels) in traditional cost accounting include direct labor hours, direct labor cost, machine hours, materials cost, and units of production. An allocation base should have a high correlation with the incurrence of overhead.

2.  The distinction between variable and fixed factory overhead rates should be understood. Variable factory overhead per unit of the allocation base is assumed to be constant within the relevant range of activity. Thus, estimation of the variable factory overhead rate emphasizes the per-unit amount. However, fixed factory overhead is assumed to be constant in total over the relevant range. Accordingly, the fixed factory overhead rate is calculated by dividing the total budgeted cost by the appropriate denominator (capacity) level.

    a.  The use of an annual predetermined fixed factory overhead application rate is often preferred. It smooths cost fluctuations that would otherwise occur as a result of fluctuations in production from month to month. Thus, higher overhead costs are not assigned to units produced in low production periods and vice versa. The denominator of the fixed factory overhead rate may be defined in terms of various capacity concepts.

        1)  **Theoretical or ideal capacity** is the level at which output is maximized assuming perfectly efficient operations at all times. This level is impossible to maintain and results in underapplied overhead.

        2)  **Practical capacity** is theoretical capacity minus idle time resulting from holidays, downtime, changeover time, etc., but not from inadequate sales demand.

        3)  **Normal capacity** is the level of activity that will approximate demand over a period of years. It includes seasonal, cyclical, and trend variations. Deviations in one year will be offset in other years.

        4)  **Expected actual activity** is a short-run activity level. It minimizes under- or overapplied overhead but does not provide a consistent basis for assigning overhead cost. Per-unit overhead will fluctuate because of short-term changes in the expected production level.

3.  **Overapplied** overhead (a credit balance in factory overhead) results when product costs are overstated because the activity level was higher than expected or actual overhead costs were lower than expected.

    a.  **Underapplied** overhead (a debit balance in factory overhead) results when product costs are understated because the activity level was lower than expected or actual overhead costs were higher than expected.

    b.  Unit variable factory overhead costs and total fixed factory overhead costs are expected to be constant within the relevant range. Accordingly, when actual activity is significantly greater or less than planned, the difference between the actual and predetermined fixed factory overhead rates is likely to be substantial. However, a change in activity, by itself, does not affect the variable rate.

    c.  The treatment of over- or underapplied overhead depends on the materiality of the amount. If the amount is immaterial, it may be debited or credited to cost of goods sold.

        1)  If the amount is material, it should theoretically be allocated to work-in-process, finished goods, and cost of goods sold on the basis of the currently applied overhead in each of the accounts. This procedure will restate inventory costs and cost of goods sold to the amounts actually incurred. An alternative is to prorate the variance based on the total balances in the accounts.

4. Two factory overhead accounts may be used: factory overhead control and factory overhead applied.

   a. As actual overhead costs are incurred, they are debited to the control account. As overhead is applied (transferred to work-in-process) based on a predetermined rate, the factory overhead applied account is credited.

   b. Assuming proration of under- or overapplied overhead, the entry to close the overhead accounts is

   | | | |
   |---|---|---|
   | Cost of goods sold (Dr or Cr) | $XXX | |
   | Work-in-process (Dr or Cr) | XXX | |
   | Finished goods (Dr or Cr) | XXX | |
   | Factory overhead applied | XXX | |
   | Factory overhead control | | $XXX |

5. The improvements in information technology and decreases in its cost have made a **restated allocation rate** method more appealing. This approach is implemented at the end of the period to calculate the actual overhead rates and then restate every entry involving overhead. The effect is that job-cost records, the inventory accounts, and cost of goods sold are accurately stated with respect to actual overhead. This means of disposing of variances is costly but has the advantage of improving the analysis of product profitability.

6. The foregoing discussion assumes that **normal costing** methods are applied. Under normal costing, amounts are recorded for direct costs at actual rates and prices times actual inputs. For indirect costs, budgeted rates are used.

   a. Under **actual costing**, however, actual rates are used to record indirect costs.

   b. Under **budgeted costing**, budgeted rates and prices are used for direct costs, and budgeted rates are used for indirect costs.

   c. In practice, organizations may combine these methods in various ways.

7. The foregoing discussion also emphasizes cost control systems for manufacturing entities. However, the basic concepts are also applicable to service and retailing organizations, although without the complications resulting from the need to account for inventories. For example, job-order costing principles apply to an audit by an accounting firm, whereas the costs of routine mail delivery may be controlled using process costing techniques.

8. Stop and review! You have completed the outline for this subunit. Study multiple-choice questions 11 through 13 beginning on page 354.

## 7.4 PROCESS COSTING AND JOB-ORDER COSTING

1. **Process cost accounting** is used to assign costs to products or services. It is applicable to relatively homogeneous items that are mass produced on a continuous basis (e.g., refined oil).

   a. The objective is to determine the portion of cost that is to be expensed because the products or services were sold and the portion that is to be deferred.

   b. Process costing is an averaging process that calculates the average cost of all units. Thus, the costs are accumulated by cost centers, not jobs. Moreover, in a manufacturing setting, work-in-process (WIP) inventory is stated in terms of equivalent units of production (EUP) so that average costs may be calculated.

c.   A manufacturing entity's direct materials, direct labor, and factory overhead are debited to WIP when they are committed to the process.

1)   The sum of these costs and the beginning WIP (BWIP) is the total production cost to be accounted for in any one period. This total is allocated to finished goods and to ending WIP (EWIP), which may be credited for abnormal spoilage.

2)   Direct materials are usually accounted for in a separate account.

| | | |
|---|---|---|
| Direct materials inventory | $XXX | |
| Accounts payable or cash | | $XXX |

3)   When direct materials are transferred to WIP, the inventory account is credited.

4)   Direct labor is usually debited directly to WIP when the payroll is recorded. Any wages not attributable directly to production, e.g., those for janitorial services, are considered indirect labor and debited to overhead. Shift differentials and overtime premium are likewise deemed to be overhead. However, shift differentials and overtime premium are charged to a specific job when a customer requirement, rather than a management decision, causes the differential in the overtime.

| | | |
|---|---|---|
| WIP | $XXX | |
| Factory overhead | XXX | |
| Wages payable | | $XXX |
| Payroll taxes payable | | XXX |

5)   Indirect costs were traditionally debited to a single factory overhead control account. However, under activity-based costing (ABC), many such accounts are used.

a)   They include supplies, plant depreciation, etc.

| | | |
|---|---|---|
| Factory overhead | $XXX | |
| Insurance expense | | $XXX |
| Supplies expense | | XXX |
| Depreciation expense (or accum. dep.) | | XXX |

b)   To charge all factory overhead incurred over a period, such as a year, to WIP, factory overhead is credited and WIP is debited on some systematic basis.

| | | |
|---|---|---|
| WIP | $XXX | |
| Factory overhead | | $XXX |

6)   **Transferred-in costs** are similar to direct materials added at a point in the process because both attach to (become part of) the product at that point, usually the beginning of the process. However, transferred-in costs are dissimilar because they attach to the units of production that move from one process to another. Thus, they are the basic units being produced. By contrast, direct materials are added to the basic units during processing.

7)   As goods are completed, their cost is credited to WIP and debited to finished goods. When the finished goods are sold, their cost is debited to cost of sales. The deferred manufacturing costs are held in the ending WIP, finished goods inventory, and direct materials inventory accounts.

| | | |
|---|---|---|
| Finished goods inventory | $XXX | |
| WIP | | $XXX |
| Cost of goods sold | $XXX | |
| Finished goods inventory | | $XXX |

8) In the following T account illustration, each arrow represents a journal entry to record a transfer. It indicates a credit to the original account and a debit to the next account in the sequence.

FLOW OF COSTS THROUGH ACCOUNTS

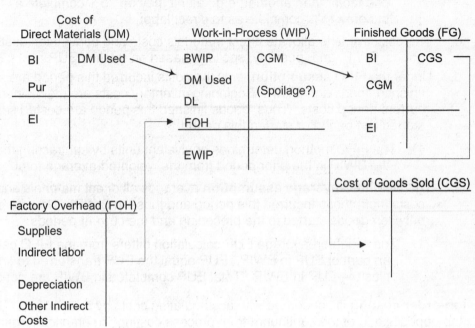

a) Cost of goods manufactured (CGM) equals the costs of goods completed in the current period and transferred to finished goods (BWIP + DM + DL + FOH − EWIP).

b) For simplicity, a single overhead account is shown. However, many accountants prefer to accumulate actual costs (debits) in the overhead control account and the amounts charged to WIP in a separate overhead applied account. This account will have a credit balance. Overhead applied is based on a predetermined rate.

c) The debits to WIP are the total costs incurred. They equal the sum of the CGM, EWIP, and abnormal spoilage.

d) Abnormal spoilage is not inherent in the particular process. It is charged to a loss in the period in which detection occurs. However, normal spoilage is a product cost included in CGM and EWIP.

2. **Equivalent units of production (EUP)** measure the amount of work performed in each production phase in terms of fully processed units during a given period. An equivalent unit is a set of inputs required to manufacture one physical unit. Calculating EUP for each factor of production facilitates measurement of output and cost allocation when WIP exists.

a. Incomplete units are restated as the equivalent amount of completed units. The calculation is made separately for direct materials (transferred-in costs are treated as direct materials for this purpose) and conversion cost (direct labor and factory overhead).

    b.    One equivalent unit is the amount of conversion cost (direct labor and factory overhead) or direct materials cost required to produce one finished unit.

        1)    EXAMPLE: If 10,000 units in EWIP are 25% complete, they equal 2,500 (10,000 × 25%) equivalent units.

        2)    Some units may be more advanced in the production process with respect to one factor than another; e.g., a unit may be 75% complete as to direct materials but only 15% complete as to direct labor.

    c.    The objective is to allocate direct materials costs and conversion costs to finished goods, EWIP, and, possibly, spoilage based on relative EUP.

    d.    Under the **FIFO assumption**, only the costs incurred this period are allocated between finished goods and EWIP. Beginning inventory costs are maintained separately from current-period costs. Thus, goods finished this period are costed separately as either started last period or started this period.

        1)    The FIFO method determines equivalent units by subtracting the work done on the BWIP in the prior period from the weighted-average total.

    e.    The **weighted-average assumption** averages all direct materials and all conversion costs (both those incurred this period and those in BWIP). No differentiation is made between goods started in the preceding and the current periods.

        1)    The weighted-average EUP calculation differs from the FIFO calculation by the amount of EUP in BWIP. EUP equal the EUP transferred to finished goods plus the EUP in EWIP. Total EUP completed in BWIP are not deducted.

3.    **Job-order costing** is concerned with accumulating costs by specific job. This method is at the opposite end of the continuum from process costing. In practice, organizations tend to combine elements of both approaches. However, a job-order costing orientation is appropriate when an entity's products or services have individual characteristics or when identifiable groupings are possible, e.g., when the entity produces batches of certain styles or types of furniture.

    a.    Units (jobs) should be dissimilar enough to warrant the special record keeping required by job-order costing. Costs are recorded by classification (direct materials, direct labor, and factory overhead) on a job-cost sheet specifically prepared for each job.

    b.    The difference between process and job-order costing is often overemphasized. Job-order costing simply requires subsidiary ledgers to record the additional details needed to account for specific jobs. However, the totals of subsidiary ledger amounts should equal the balances of the related general ledger control accounts. The latter are the basic accounts used in process costing. For example, the total of all amounts recorded on job-cost sheets for manufacturing jobs in process equals the balance in the WIP control account.

    c.    Source documents for costs incurred include stores' requisitions for direct materials and work (or time) tickets for direct labor.

    d.    Overhead is usually assigned to each job through a predetermined overhead rate, e.g., $3 of overhead for every direct labor hour.

    e.    Journal entries record direct materials, direct labor, and factory overhead used for a specific job. They are similar to the entries used in process costing.

    f.    Evaluating the efficiency of the production process under a job-order system can be accomplished through the use of a standard cost system or by budgeting costs for each job individually, based on expected materials and labor usage.

g.   A summary of the accounting process for a manufacturer's job-order system follows:

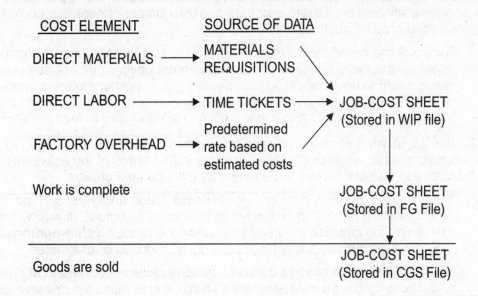

4.   Stop and review!  You have completed the outline for this subunit.  Study multiple-choice questions 14 through 18 beginning on page 355.

## 7.5 ACTIVITY-BASED COSTING (ABC)

1.   **Key Terms**

a.   **Cost objects** are the intermediate and final dispositions of cost pools.  Intermediate cost objects receive temporary accumulations of costs as the cost pools move from their originating points to the final cost objects.  A final cost object, such as a job, product, or process, should be logically linked with the cost pool based on a cause-and-effect relationship.

b.   A **cost pool** is an account in which a variety of similar costs are accumulated prior to allocation to cost objects.  It is a grouping of costs associated with an activity.  The overhead account is a cost pool into which various types of overhead are accumulated prior to their allocation.

2.   **Activity-based costing (ABC)** may be used by manufacturing, service, or retailing entities and in job-order or process costing systems.  It has been popularized because of the rapid advance of technology, which has led to a significant increase in the incurrence of indirect costs and a consequent need for more accurate cost assignment.  However, developments in computer and related technology (such as bar coding) also allow management to obtain better and more timely information at relatively low cost.

a.   ABC is one means of improving a cost system to avoid what has been called **peanut-butter costing**.  Inaccurately averaging or spreading costs like peanut butter over products or service units that use different amounts of resources results in **product-cost cross-subsidization**.

1)   This term describes the condition in which the miscosting of one product causes the miscosting of other products.  In the traditional systems previously discussed, direct labor and direct materials are traced to products or service units, a single pool of costs (overhead) is accumulated for a given organizational unit, and these costs are then assigned using an allocative rather than a tracing procedure.  The effect is an averaging of costs that may result in significant inaccuracy when products or service units do not use similar amounts of resources.

3.   To improve its costing system, an organization can attempt to identify as many direct costs as economically feasible. It can also increase the number of separate pools for costs not directly attributable to cost objects.

   a.   Each of these pools should be homogeneous; that is, each should consist of costs that have substantially similar relationships with the driver or other base used for assignment to cost objects. Thus, choosing the appropriate base, preferably one with a driver or cause-and-effect relationship (a high correlation) between the demands of the cost object and the costs in the pool, is another way to improve a costing system.

4.   ABC attempts to improve costing by assigning costs to activities rather than to an organizational unit. Accordingly, ABC requires identification of the activities that consume resources and that are subject to demands by ultimate cost objects.

   a.   Design of an ABC system starts with **process value analysis**, a comprehensive understanding of how an organization generates its output. It involves a determination of which activities that use resources are **value-adding** or **nonvalue-adding** and how the latter may be reduced or eliminated.

      1)   This linkage of product costing and continuous improvement of processes is **activity-based management (ABM)**. It encompasses driver analysis, activity analysis, and performance measurement.

5.   Once an ABC system has been designed, costs may be assigned to the identified activities, costs of related activities that can be reassigned using the same driver or other base are combined in **homogeneous cost pools**, and an overhead rate is calculated for each pool.

   a.   The next step, as in traditional methods, is to assign costs to ultimate cost objects. In other words, cost assignment is a two-stage process: First, costs are accumulated for an activity based on the resources it can be directly observed to use and on the resources it can be assumed to use based on its consumption of **resource drivers** (factors that cause changes in the costs of an activity); second, costs are reassigned to ultimate cost objects on the basis of **activity drivers** (factors measuring the demands made on activities).

      1)   In ABC, these objects may include not only products and services but also customers, distribution channels, or other objects for which activity and resource costs may be accumulated.

6.   An essential element of ABC is **driver analysis** that emphasizes the search for the cause-and-effect relationship between an activity and its consumption of resources and for an activity and the demands made on it by a cost object. For this purpose, activities and their drivers have been classified in accounting literature as follows:

   a.   **Unit-level** (volume-related) activities occur when a unit is produced, e.g., direct labor and direct materials activities.

   b.   **Batch-level** activities occur when a batch of units is produced, e.g., ordering, setup, or materials handling.

   c.   **Product- or service-level** (product- or service-sustaining) activities provide support of different kinds to different types of output, e.g., engineering changes, inventory management, or testing.

   d.   **Facility-level** (facility-sustaining) activities concern overall operations, e.g., management of the physical plant, personnel administration, or security arrangements.

7.   Using this model, activities are grouped by level, and drivers are determined for the activities. Within each grouping of activities, the cost pools for activities that can use the same driver are combined into homogeneous cost pools. In contrast, traditional systems assign costs largely on the basis of unit-level drivers.

a.　At the unit level, examples of drivers are direct labor hours or dollars, machine hours, and units of output.

b.　At the batch level, drivers may include number or duration of setups, orders processed, number of receipts, weight of materials handled, or number of inspections.

c.　At the product level, drivers may include design time, testing time, number of engineering change orders, or number of categories of parts.

d.　At the facility level, drivers may include any of those used at the first three levels.

8.　A difficulty in applying ABC is that, whereas the first three levels of activities pertain to specific products or services, facility-level activities do not. Thus, facility-level costs are not accurately assignable to products. The theoretically sound solution may be to treat these costs as **period costs**. Nevertheless, organizations that apply ABC ordinarily assign them to products to obtain a full absorption cost suitable for external financial reporting in accordance with GAAP.

9.　Organizations most likely to benefit from using ABC are those with products or services that vary significantly in volume, diversity of activities, and complexity of operations; relatively high overhead costs; or operations that have undergone major technological or design changes.

a.　However, service organizations may have some difficulty in implementing ABC because they tend to have relatively high levels of facility-level costs that are difficult to assign to specific service units. They also engage in many nonuniform human activities for which information is not readily accumulated. Furthermore, output measurement is more problematic in service than in manufacturing entities. Nevertheless, ABC has been adopted by various insurers, banks, railroads, and health care providers.

10.　Stop and review! You have completed the outline for this subunit. Study multiple-choice questions 19 through 22 beginning on page 357.

## 7.6 SERVICE COST ALLOCATION

1.　Service (support) department costs are considered part of overhead (indirect costs). Thus, they cannot feasibly be traced to cost objects and therefore must be allocated to the operating departments that use the services.

a.　When service departments also render services to each other, their costs may be allocated to each other before allocation to operating departments.

2.　Four criteria are used to allocate costs.

a.　**Cause and effect** should be used if possible because of its objectivity and acceptance by operating management.

b.　**Benefits received** is the most frequently used criterion when cause and effect cannot be determined. However, it requires an assumption about the benefits of costs, for example, that advertising promoting the company but not specific products increased sales by the various divisions.

c.　**Fairness** is sometimes mentioned in government contracts but appears to be more of a goal than an objective allocation base.

d.　**Ability to bear** (based on profits) is usually unacceptable because of its dysfunctional effect on managerial motivation.

3.  The **direct method** is the simplest and most common method of service cost allocation.  It allocates costs directly to the producing departments without recognition of services provided among the service departments.

    a.  No attempt is made to allocate the costs of service departments to other service departments under the direct method.

    b.  Allocations of service department costs are made only to production departments based on their relative use of services.

4.  The **step** or **step-down method** includes an allocation of service department costs to other service departments in addition to the producing departments.

    a.  The allocation may begin with the costs of the service department that

        1)  Provides the highest percentage of its total services to other service departments,

        2)  Provides services to the greatest number of other service departments, or

        3)  Has the greatest dollar cost of services provided to other service departments.

    b.  The costs of the remaining service departments are then allocated in the same manner, but no cost is assigned to service departments whose costs have already been allocated.

    c.  The process continues until all service department costs are allocated.

5.  The **reciprocal method** is the most theoretically sound.  It allows reflection of all reciprocal services among service departments.  It is also known as the simultaneous-solution method, cross-allocation method, matrix-allocation method, or double-distribution method.

    a.  The step method considers only services rendered among service departments in one direction, but the reciprocal method considers services in both directions.

        1)  If all reciprocal services are recognized, linear algebra may be used to reach a solution.  The typical problem on a professional examination can be solved using two or three simultaneous equations.

6.  Stop and review!  You have completed the outline for this subunit.  Study multiple-choice questions 23 through 25 beginning on page 360.

## 7.7 JOINT PRODUCTS AND BY-PRODUCTS

1.  **Definitions**

    a.  When two or more separate products are produced by a common manufacturing process from a common input, the outputs from the process are **joint products**.  The joint costs of two or more joint products with significant values are usually allocated to the joint products at the point at which they became separate products.

    b.  **By-products** are one or more products of relatively small total value that are produced simultaneously from a common manufacturing process with products of greater value and quantity (joint products).

    c.  **Joint costs** (sometimes called common costs) are incurred prior to the split-off point to produce two or more goods manufactured simultaneously by a single process or series of processes.  Joint costs, which include direct materials, direct labor, and overhead, are not separately identifiable and must be allocated to the individual joint products.

    d.   At the **split-off point**, the joint products acquire separate identities. Costs incurred after split-off are separable costs.

    e.   **Separable costs** can be identified with a particular joint product and allocated to a specific unit of output. They are the costs incurred for a specific product after the split-off point.

2.   Several methods are used to allocate joint costs. Each assigns a proportionate amount of the total cost to each product on a quantitative basis.

    a.   The **physical-unit method** is based on some physical measure such as volume, weight, or a linear measure.

    b.   The **sales-value method** is based on the relative sales values of the separate products at split-off.

    c.   The **estimated net realizable value (NRV)** method is based on final sales value minus separable costs.

    d.   The **constant gross margin percentage NRV** method is based on allocating joint costs so that the percentage is the same for every product.

        1)   This method determines the overall percentage, deducts the appropriate gross margin from the final sales value of each product to calculate total costs for that product, and then subtracts the separable costs to arrive at the joint cost amount.

3.   Joint costs are normally allocated to joint products but not by-products. The most cost-effective method for the initial recognition of by-products is to account for their value at the time of sale as a reduction in the cost of goods sold or as a revenue. Thus, cost of sales does not exist for by-products.

    a.   The alternative is to recognize their value at the time of production, a method that results in the recording of by-product inventory. Under this method, the value of the by-product may also be treated as a reduction in cost of goods sold or as a separate revenue item. The value to be reported for by-products may be sales revenue, sales revenue minus a normal profit, or estimated net realizable value.

    b.   Regardless of the timing of their recognition in the accounts, by-products usually do not receive an allocation of joint costs because the cost of this accounting treatment ordinarily exceeds the benefit. However, allocating joint costs to by-products is acceptable. In that case, they are treated as joint products despite their small relative values.

    c.   Although scrap is similar to a by-product, joint costs are almost never allocated to scrap.

4.   The relative sales value method is the most frequently used way to allocate joint costs to joint products. It allocates joint costs based upon each product's proportion of total sales revenue.

    a.   For joint products salable at the split-off point, the relative sales value is the selling price at split-off.

    b.   If further processing is needed, the relative sales value may be approximated by subtracting the additional anticipated processing and marketing costs from the final sales value to arrive at the estimated net realizable value.

    c.   Thus, the allocation of joint costs to Product X is determined as follows:

$$\frac{\textit{Sales value or NRV of X}}{\textit{Total sales value or NRV of joint products}} \times \textit{Joint costs}$$

5.  In determining whether to sell a product at the split-off point or process the item further at additional cost, the joint cost of the product is irrelevant because it is a sunk (already expended) cost.

    a.  The cost of additional processing (incremental costs) should be weighed against the benefits received (incremental revenues). The sell-or-process decision should be based on that relationship.

6.  Stop and review! You have completed the outline for this subunit. Study multiple-choice questions 26 through 29 beginning on page 361.

## 7.8 STANDARD COSTING AND VARIANCE ANALYSIS

1.  Standard costs are budgeted unit costs established to motivate optimal productivity and efficiency. A standard cost system is designed to alert management when the actual costs of production differ significantly from target or standard costs.

    a.  A standard cost is a monetary measure with which actual costs are compared.

    b.  A standard cost is not an average of past costs but a scientifically determined estimate of what costs should be.

    c.  A standard cost system can be used in both job-order and process costing systems to isolate variances.

    d.  Because of the effect of fixed costs, standard costing is most effective in a flexible budgeting system.

    e.  When actual costs and standard costs differ, the difference is a variance.

        1)  A favorable (unfavorable) variance arises when actual costs are less (greater) than standard costs.

        2)  Management will usually set standards so that they are currently attainable.

            a)  If standards are set too high (or tight), they may be ignored by workers, or morale may suffer.

        3)  Standard costs must be kept current. If prices have changed considerably for a particular raw material, there will always be a variance if the standard cost is not changed. Much of the usefulness of standard costs is lost if a large variance is always expected.

    f.  Standard costs are usually established for materials, labor, and factory overhead.

2.  **Direct materials variances** are usually divided into price and efficiency components. Part of a total materials variance may be attributed to using more raw materials than the standard and part to a cost that was higher than standard.

    a.  The **direct materials quantity (usage) variance** (an efficiency variance) is the actual quantity minus standard quantity, times standard price: $(AQ - SQ)SP$.

    b.  The **direct materials price variance** is the actual price minus the standard price, times the actual quantity: $(AP - SP)AQ$.

        1)  The price variance may be isolated either at the time of purchase or at the time of transfer to WIP. The advantage of the former method is that the variance is identified earlier.

            a)  Normal spoilage is considered in the calculation of standard direct materials cost per unit.

c. The direct materials quantity (usage) variance is sometimes supplemented by the direct materials mix variance and the direct materials yield variance.

1) These variances are calculated only when the production process involves combining several materials in varying proportions (when substitutions are allowable in combining materials).

2) The **direct materials mix variance** equals total actual quantity times the difference between the weighted-average unit standard cost of the budgeted mix of ingredients and the weighted-average unit standard cost of the actual mix.

3) The **direct materials yield variance** is the weighted-average unit standard cost of the budgeted mix multiplied by the difference between the actual quantity of materials used and the standard quantity.

4) Certain relationships may exist among the various materials variances. For instance, an unfavorable price variance may be offset by a favorable mix or yield variance because materials of better quality and higher price are used. Also, a favorable mix variance may result in an unfavorable yield variance, or vice versa.

3. **Direct labor variances** are similar to direct materials variances. For example, the direct labor rate and efficiency variances are calculated in much the same way as the direct materials price and quantity variances, respectively.

4. **Factory overhead variances** include variable and fixed components.

a. The total **variable factory overhead variance** is the difference between actual variable factory overhead and the amount applied based on the budgeted application rate and the standard input allowed for the actual output.

1) In **four-way analysis of variance**, it includes the

a) **Spending variance** -- the difference between actual variable factory overhead and the product of the budgeted application rate and the actual amount of the allocation base (activity level or amount of input)

b) **Efficiency variance** -- the budgeted application rate times the difference between the actual input and the standard input allowed for the actual output

i) Variable factory overhead applied equals the flexible-budget amount for the actual output level. The reason is that unit variable costs are assumed to be constant within the relevant range. The third column in the diagram below gives the flexible budget amount (also the amount applied).

ii) If variable factory overhead is applied on the basis of output, not inputs, no efficiency variance arises.

iii) Diagram of variable factory overhead variances

| Actual Variable<br>Factory Overhead | Actual Input<br>×<br>Budgeted Application Rate | Standard Input Allowed<br>for Actual Output<br>×<br>Budgeted Application Rate |
|---|---|---|
| | Spending<br>Variance | Efficiency<br>Variance |

b. The **total fixed factory overhead variance** is the difference between actual fixed factory overhead and the amount applied based on the budgeted application rate and the standard input allowed for the actual output.

1) In four-way analysis of variance, it includes the

a) **Budget variance** (spending variance) -- the difference between actual fixed factory overhead and the amount budgeted

b) **Volume variance** (idle capacity variance, production volume variance, or output-level variance) -- the difference between budgeted fixed factory overhead and the product of the budgeted application rate and the standard input allowed for the actual output

i) Fixed factory overhead applied does not necessarily equal the flexible-budget amount for the actual output. The reason is that the latter amount is assumed to be constant over the relevant range of output. Thus, the second column in the diagram below represents the flexible-budget amount, and the third column represents the amount applied.

ii) No efficiency variance is calculated because budgeted fixed factory overhead is a constant at all relevant output levels.

2) Diagram of fixed factory overhead variances

| Actual Fixed Factory Overhead | Budgeted Fixed Factory Overhead | Standard Input Allowed for Actual Output × Budgeted Application Rate |
|---|---|---|
| | Budget Variance | Volume Variance |

c. The total overhead variance also may be divided into two or three variances (but one variance is always the fixed overhead volume variance).

1) **Three-way analysis** divides the total overhead variance into volume, efficiency, and spending variances.

a) The spending variance combines the fixed overhead budget and variable overhead spending variances.

b) The variable overhead efficiency and fixed overhead volume variances are the same as in four-way analysis.

2) **Two-way analysis** divides the total overhead variance into two variances: volume and controllable (the latter is sometimes called the budget, total overhead spending, or flexible-budget variance).

a) The variable overhead spending and efficiency variances and the fixed overhead budget variance are combined.

5. **Sales variances** are used to evaluate the selling departments. If a firm's sales differ from the amount budgeted, the difference could be attributable to either the **sales price variance** or the **sales volume variance** (sum of the sales mix and quantity variances). The analysis of these variances concentrates on contribution margins because fixed costs are assumed to be constant.

a. EXAMPLE (single product): A firm has budgeted sales of 10,000 units at $17 per unit. Variable costs are expected to be $10 per unit, and fixed costs are budgeted at $50,000. Thus, the company anticipates a contribution margin of $70,000 and a net income of $20,000. However, the actual results are

| | |
|---|---:|
| Sales (11,000 units) | $ 176,000 |
| Variable costs | (110,000) |
| Contribution margin | $ 66,000 |
| Fixed costs | (50,000) |
| Net income | $ 16,000 |

1) Sales were greater than predicted, but the contribution margin is less than expected. The $4,000 discrepancy can be analyzed in terms of the sales price variance and the sales volume variance.

2) For a single-product firm, the **sales price variance** is the reduction in the contribution margin because of the change in selling price. In the example, the actual selling price of $16 per unit is $1 less than expected. Thus, the sales price variance is $1 times 11,000 units actually sold, or $11,000 unfavorable.

3) For the single-product firm, the **sales volume variance** is the change in contribution margin caused by the difference between the actual and budgeted volume. In this case, it is $7,000 favorable ($7 budgeted UCM × 1,000-unit increase in volume).

4) The sales mix variance is zero because the firm sells one product only. Hence, the sales volume variance equals the **sales quantity variance**.

5) The sales price variance ($11,000 unfavorable) combined with the sales volume variance ($7,000 favorable) equals the total change in the contribution margin ($4,000 unfavorable).

6) The same analysis may be done for cost of goods sold. The average production cost per unit is used instead of the average unit selling price, but the quantities for production volume are the same as those used for sales quantity. Accordingly, the overall variation in gross profit is the sum of the variation in revenue plus the variation in CGS.

b. If a company produces two or more products, the sales variances reflect not only the effects of the change in total unit sales but also any difference in the mix sold.

1) In the multiproduct case, the **sales price variance** may be calculated as in 5.a.2) for each product. The results are then added.

2) One way to calculate the multiproduct **sales volume variance** is to determine the variance for each product as in 5.a.3) above and to add the results.

3) The **sales quantity variance** (the sales volume variance for a single-product company) is the difference between the budgeted contribution margin based on actual unit sales and the budgeted contribution margin based on expected sales, assuming that the budgeted sales mix is constant. One way to calculate this variance is to multiply the budgeted UCM for each product times the difference between the budgeted unit sales of the product and its budgeted percentage of actual total unit sales and then to add the results.

4) The **sales mix variance** is the difference between the budgeted contribution margin for the actual mix and actual total quantity of products sold and the budgeted contribution margin for the expected mix and actual total quantity of products sold. One way to calculate this variance is to multiply the budgeted UCM for each product times the difference between actual unit sales of the product and its budgeted percentage of actual total unit sales and then to add the results.

c. The components of the sales quantity variance are the market size and the market share variances.

1) The **market size variance** equals the budgeted market share percentage, times the difference between the actual market size in units and the budgeted market size in units, times the budgeted weighted-average UCM.

2) The **market share variance** equals the difference between the actual market share percentage and the budgeted market share percentage, times the actual market size in units, times the budgeted weighted-average UCM.

6. **Journal Entries.** Variances usually do not appear on the financial statements. They are used for managerial control and are recorded in the ledger accounts.

a. When standard costs are recorded in inventory accounts, variances are also recorded. Thus, direct labor is recorded as a liability at actual cost, but it is charged to WIP control at its standard cost for the standard quantity used. The direct labor rate and efficiency variances are recognized at that time.

1) Direct materials, however, should be debited to materials control at standard prices at the time of purchase. The purpose is to isolate the direct materials price variance as soon as possible. When direct materials are used, they are debited to WIP at the standard cost for the standard quantity, and the materials quantity variance is then recognized.

b. Actual overhead costs are debited to overhead control and credited to accounts payable, wages payable, etc. Applied overhead is credited to an overhead applied account and debited to WIP control.

1) The simplest method of recording the overhead variances is to wait until year-end. The variances can then be recognized separately when the overhead control and overhead applied accounts are closed (by a credit and a debit, respectively). The balancing debits or credits are to the variance accounts.

c. The following are the entries to record variances. Favorable variances are credits and unfavorable variances are debits:

1)
| | | |
|---|---|---|
| Materials control (AQ × SP) | $XXX | |
| Direct materials price variance (Dr or Cr) | XXX | |
| Accounts payable (AQ × AP) | | $XXX |

2)
| | | |
|---|---|---|
| WIP control (SQ × SP) | XXX | |
| Direct materials quantity variance (Dr or Cr) | XXX | |
| Direct labor rate variance (Dr or Cr) | XXX | |
| Direct labor efficiency variance (Dr or Cr) | XXX | |
| Materials control (AQ × SP) | | XXX |
| Wages payable (AQ × AP) | | XXX |

3)
| | | |
|---|---|---|
| Overhead control (actual) | XXX | |
| Wages payable (actual) | | XXX |
| Accounts payable (actual) | | XXX |

4)
| | | |
|---|---|---|
| WIP control (standard) | XXX | |
| Overhead applied (standard) | | XXX |

5)
| | | |
|---|---|---|
| Overhead applied (standard) | XXX | |
| Variable overhead spending variance (Dr or Cr) | XXX | |
| Variable overhead efficiency variance (Dr or Cr) | XXX | |
| Fixed overhead budget variance (Dr or Cr) | XXX | |
| Fixed overhead volume variance (Dr or Cr) | XXX | |
| Overhead control (actual) | | XXX |

6) The result of the foregoing entries is that WIP contains standard costs only.

d. **Disposition of variances**. Immaterial variances are customarily closed to cost of goods sold or income summary.

1) Variances that are material may be prorated. A simple approach to proration is to allocate the total net variance to work-in-process, finished goods, and cost of goods sold based on the balances in those accounts. However, more complex methods of allocation are possible.

e. Several alternative approaches to the timing of recognition of variances are possible. For example, direct materials and labor might be transferred to WIP at their actual quantities. In that case, the direct materials quantity and direct labor efficiency variances might be recognized when goods are transferred from WIP to finished goods.

1) Furthermore, the direct materials price variance might be isolated at the time of transfer to WIP. These methods, however, delay the recognition of variances. Early recognition is desirable for control purposes.

7. Stop and review! You have completed the outline for this subunit. Study multiple-choice questions 30 through 35 beginning on page 363.

## 7.9 TYPES OF BUDGETS

1.  A **budget (profit plan)** is a realistic plan for the future expressed in quantitative terms. Top management can use a budget to plan for the future and communicate objectives and goals to all levels of the organization, to motivate employees, to control organizational activities, and to evaluate performance. The annual budget should be based upon an organization's goals and objectives. Thus, the annual budget is usually based on a combination of financial, quantitative, and qualitative measures.

2.  The **operating budget sequence** is the part of the master budget process that begins with the sales budget and culminates in the pro forma income statement. Its emphasis is on obtaining and using resources. It includes budgets for sales, production, and cost of goods sold.

    a.  **Other budgets** prepared during the operating budget sequence are those for R&D, design, marketing, distribution, customer service, and administrative costs. These budgets, the sales budget, and the cost of goods sold budget are needed to prepare a pro forma operating income statement.

3.  The **sales budget** is usually the first budget prepared. Accordingly, accurate sales forecasts are crucial. Once a firm can estimate sales, the next step is to decide how much to produce or purchase.

    a.  Sales are usually budgeted by product or department.

    b.  Sales volume affects production and purchasing levels, operating expenses, and cash flow.

4.  The **production budget** (for a manufacturer) is based on the sales forecast, **in units**, plus or minus the desired inventory change.

    a.  It is prepared for each department and is used to plan when items will be produced.

    b.  When the production budget has been completed, it is used in conjunction with the **ending inventory budget** to prepare three additional budgets.

        1)  Direct materials usage, together with beginning inventory and targeted ending inventory data, determines the **direct materials budget**.

        2)  The **direct labor budget** depends on wage rates, amounts and types of production, employees to be hired, etc.

        3)  The **factory overhead budget** is a function of how factory overhead varies with particular cost drivers.

5.  The **cost of goods sold budget** reflects direct materials usage, direct labor, factory overhead, and the change in finished goods inventory.

6.  The **financial budget sequence** is the part of the master budget process that incorporates the cash budget, capital budget, and pro forma financial statements. Its emphasis is on obtaining the funds needed to purchase operating assets.

7.  The **capital budget** is not part of the operating budget because it is not part of normal operations. The capital budget may be prepared more than a year in advance to allow sufficient time to

    a.  Plan financing of major expenditures for long-term assets such as equipment, buildings, and land

    b.  Receive custom orders of specialized equipment, buildings, etc.

8. The **cash budget** is vital because an organization must have adequate cash at all times. Even with plenty of other assets, an organization with a temporary shortage of cash can be driven into bankruptcy. Proper planning can keep an entity from financial embarrassment. Thus, cash budgets are prepared not only for annual and quarterly periods but also for monthly and weekly periods.

   a. A cash budget projects cash flows for planning and control purposes. Hence, it helps prevent not only cash emergencies but also excessive idle cash.

   b. It cannot be prepared until the other budgets have been completed.

   c. Almost all organizations, regardless of size, prepare a cash budget.

   d. It is particularly important for organizations operating in seasonal industries.

   e. Cash budgeting facilitates planning for loans and other financing.

9. The following is a summary of the operating budget sequence for a manufacturing firm that includes all elements of the value chain:

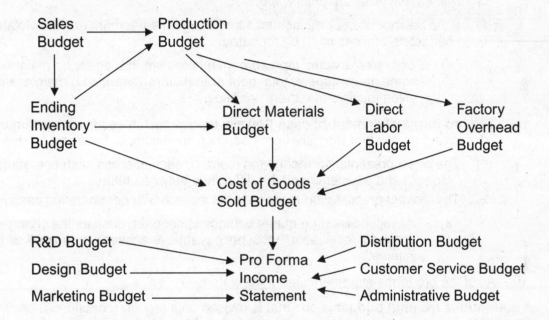

10. The following summarizes the financial budget sequence:

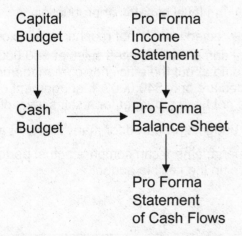

11. Once the individual budgets are complete, budgeted financial statements can be prepared. They are often called **pro forma** statements because they are prepared before actual activities commence.

   a. The **pro forma income statement** is the culmination of the operating budget sequence. It is the pro forma operating income statement adjusted for interest and taxes.

      1) It is used to decide whether the budgeted activities will result in an acceptable level of income.

      2) If it shows an unacceptable level of income, the whole budgeting process must begin again.

   b. The **pro forma balance sheet** is prepared using the cash and capital budgets and the pro forma income statement. Thus, it and the pro forma statement of cash flows culminate the financial budget sequence. The pro forma balance sheet is the beginning of the period balance sheet updated for projected changes in cash, receivables, payables, inventory, etc.

      1) If the balance sheet indicates that a contractual agreement may be violated, the budgeting process must be repeated.

         a) For example, some loan agreements require that equity be maintained at some percentage of total debt or that current assets be maintained at a given multiple of current liabilities.

   c. The **pro forma statement of cash flows** classifies cash receipts and disbursements depending on whether they are from operating, investing, or financing activities.

      1) The direct presentation reports the major classes of gross cash operating receipts and payments and the difference between them.

      2) The indirect presentation reconciles net income with net operating cash flow.

         a) The reconciliation requires balance sheet data, such as the changes in accounts receivable, accounts payable, and inventory, as well as net income.

   d. All of the pro forma statements are interrelated.

12. A **continuous (rolling) budget** is one that is revised on a regular (continuous) basis. Typically, a company extends such a budget for another month or quarter in accordance with new data as the current month or quarter ends. For example, if the budget is for 12 months, a budget for the next 12 months will be available continuously as each month ends.

13. A **fixed budget** is based on only one level of sales or production.

   a. It is not very useful if the expected level is not reached or is exceeded.

   b. EXAMPLE: Assume that a company budgeted sales at $80,000 and supplies expense at $6,000. What can be said about the efficiency of management if supplies expense is actually $480 when sales are only $40,000? Management cannot evaluate the variance because it does not have a budget for a sales level of $40,000.

14. A **flexible budget** is a series of budgets prepared for many levels of activity.

   a. At the end of the period, management can compare actual performance with the appropriate budgeted level in the flexible budget.

    b.    A flexible budget is designed to allow adjustment of the budget to the actual level of activity before comparing the budgeted activity with actual results.

        1)    EXAMPLE: Assume that a $175,000 estimate of manufacturing costs was based on expected production of 25,000 units at $7 per unit. Actual production was 25,500 units. Production cost should have been $178,500 ($7 × 25,500). Given budgeted and actual selling and administration costs of $85,000 and $83,000 respectively, the **flexible budget variance** is $2,500 F.

| | Budget | Flexible Budget | Actual | Variance |
|---|---|---|---|---|
| Variable expenses | $175,000 | $178,500 | $178,000 | $ 500 F |
| Selling and administration | 85,000 | 85,000 | 83,000 | 2,000 F |
| | $260,000 | $263,500 | $261,000 | $2,500 F |

15.  **Zero-base budgeting (ZBB)** is a budget and planning process in which each manager must justify a department's entire budget every year (or period).

    a.    ZBB differs from traditional **incremental budgeting** in which the current budget is simply adjusted to allow for changes planned for the coming year.

    b.    Under ZBB, a manager must build the budget every year from a base of zero. All expenditures must be justified regardless of the variance from previous years.

16.  A **life-cycle budget** estimates a product's revenues and expenses over its entire life cycle beginning with research and development and ending with withdrawal of customer support.

    a.    Life-cycle budgeting is intended to account for the costs at all stages of the **value chain** (R&D, design, production, marketing, distribution, and customer service). This information is important for pricing decisions because revenues must cover costs incurred in each stage of the value chain, not just production.

    b.    Life-cycle budgeting also highlights the potential for **locking in** (designing in) future costs.

17.  **Activity-based budgeting** applies activity-based costing principles to budgeting. It focuses on the numerous activities necessary to produce and market goods and services. This approach contrasts with the traditional emphasis on functions or spending categories.

    a.    Thus, activity-based budgeting provides greater detail, especially regarding indirect costs, because it permits the isolation of numerous cost drivers. A cost pool is established for each activity, and a cost driver is identified for each pool.

    b.    The budgeted cost for each pool is determined by multiplying the demand for the activity by the estimated cost of a unit of the activity.

18.  The Japanese term **kaizen** means continuous improvement, and **kaizen budgeting** assumes the continuous improvement of products and processes. It requires estimates of the effects of improvements and the costs of their implementation. Accordingly, kaizen budgeting is based not on the existing system but on changes yet to be made, and budget targets cannot be reached unless those improvements occur.

19.  **Governmental budgeting** differs from private-sector budgeting. A governmental budget is not only a financial plan and a basis for evaluating performance, but is also an expression of public policy and a form of control having the force of law.

20.  Stop and review! You have completed the outline for this subunit. Study multiple-choice questions 36 through 42 beginning on page 365.

## 7.10 CAPITAL BUDGETING

1. Capital budgeting is the process of planning expenditures for assets, the returns on which are expected to continue beyond 1 year. Accurate forecasting is needed to anticipate changes in product demand so that full economic benefits flow to the firm when the capital asset is available for use and to allow for possible changes in capital markets, inflation, interest rates, and the money supply.

2. **Types of Costs Considered in Capital Budgeting Analysis**

   a. An **avoidable cost** may be eliminated by ceasing an activity or by improving efficiency.

   b. A **common cost** is shared by all options and is not clearly allocable.

   c. The **cost of capital** is the weighted average of the interest cost of debt (net of tax) and the implicit cost of equity capital to be invested in long-term assets. It is the minimum return on a new investment that maintains shareholder value.

   d. A **deferrable cost** may be shifted to the future with little effect on current operations.

   e. A **fixed cost** does not vary with the level of activity within the relevant range.

   f. An **imputed cost** may not entail a specified dollar outlay formally recognized by the accounting system, but it is nevertheless relevant to establishing the economic reality analyzed in the decision-making process.

   g. An **incremental cost** is the difference in cost resulting from selecting one option instead of another.

   h. An **opportunity cost** is the benefit forgone, for example, the contribution to income, by not selecting the best alternative use of scarce resources.

   i. **Relevant costs** vary with the action. Other costs are constant and therefore do not affect the decision.

   j. A **sunk cost** cannot be avoided because an expenditure or an irrevocable decision to incur the cost has been made.

   k. **Taxes.** As with every other decision, the tax consequences of a new investment (and possible disinvestment of a replaced asset) must be considered.

3. Capital budgeting requires choosing among investment proposals. Thus, a ranking procedure for such decisions is needed.

   a. Determine the asset cost or net investment.

      1) The net investment is the net outlay, or gross cash requirement, minus cash recovered from the trade or sale of existing assets, with any necessary adjustments for applicable tax consequences. Cash outflows in subsequent periods must also be considered.

      2) The investment required also includes funds to provide for increases in working capital, for example, the additional receivables and inventories resulting from the acquisition of a new manufacturing plant. This investment in working capital is treated as an initial cost of the investment (a cash outflow) that will be recovered at the end of the project.

   b. Calculate estimated cash flows, period by period, using the acquired assets.

      1) Reliable estimates of cost savings or revenues are necessary.

      2) Net cash flow is the economic benefit or cost, period by period, resulting from the investment.

      3) **Economic life** is the time period over which the benefits of the investment proposal are expected to be obtained, as distinguished from the physical or technical life of the asset involved.

4) **Depreciable life** is the period used for accounting and tax purposes over which cost is to be systematically and rationally allocated. It is based upon permissible or standard guidelines and may have no particular relevance to economic life.

c. Relate the cash-flow benefits to their cost by using a method to evaluate the advantage of purchasing the asset.

d. Rank the investments.

4. The rating methods can sometimes yield different solutions to an investment problem. Managers should therefore use all the methods and then apply their judgment in making the final decision. All of these techniques consider only the economic factors in a decision, but sometimes noneconomic factors can take precedence.

5. **Techniques for Ranking Investment Proposals**

a. **Payback** is the number of periods required to complete the return of the original investment, i.e., the time it takes for a new asset to pay for itself. This measure is computed by dividing the initial net investment by the periodic constant expected cash flow to be generated.

1)
$$\frac{Initial\ net\ investment}{Periodic\ constant\ expected\ cash\ flow}$$

2) If periodic cash flows are not constant, the calculation must be in cumulative form.

3) It ignores cash flows after the payback period and the time value of money.

4) The longer the payback period, the more risky the investment.

5) The payback reciprocal (1 ÷ payback) is sometimes used as an estimate of the internal rate of return.

6) The **bailout payback** incorporates the salvage value of the asset into the calculation. It measures the length of the payback period when the periodic cash inflows are combined with the salvage value.

7) **Breakeven time** is the period required for the discounted cumulative cash inflows on a project to equal the discounted cumulative cash outflows (usually the initial cost). Thus, it is the time necessary for the present value of the discounted cash flows to equal zero. This period begins at the outset of a project, not when the initial cash outflow occurs.

a) An alternative that results in a longer breakeven time is to consider the time required for the present value of the cumulative cash inflows to equal the present value of all the expected future cash outflows.

b. **Net present value (NPV)** is broadly defined as the difference between the present value of the estimated net cash inflows and the present value of the net cash outflows.

1) The NPV method is used when the desired rate of return (also known as the discount rate or hurdle rate) is specified. The weighted-average cost of capital is frequently specified.

2)
$$NPV = \sum_{t=0}^{n} \frac{PCF_t}{(1 + k)^t}$$

If: n = number of periods of future cash flows
PCF$_t$ = periodic cash flow for period t
k = discount rate
t = time period

3) The reinvestment rate often becomes critical when choosing between the NPV and IRR methods. NPV assumes the cash flows from the investment can be reinvested at the particular project's cost of capital.

4) Present value tables are used to reduce the future cash flows to current dollars.

5) If the NPV is positive, the project should be accepted. If the NPV is negative, the project should be rejected.

6) NPV is the best method for **capital rationing** situations. Capital rationing exists when a firm sets a limit on the amount of funds to be invested during a given period. Under capital rationing, a firm will not undertake all projects that are viewed as profitable. Only those projects that will return the greatest NPV for the limited capital available can be undertaken.

c. **Internal rate of return (IRR)** is an interest rate (r) computed such that the net present value (NPV) of the investment is zero. Hence, the present value of the expected cash outflows equals the present value of the expected cash inflows.

1)
$$\sum_{t=0}^{n} \frac{PCF_t}{(1 + IRR)^t} = 0$$

If:  $n$ = number of periods of future cash flows
   $PCF_t$ = periodic cash flow for period t
   $IRR$ = internal rate of return
   $t$ = time period

2) The IRR can be found by trial and error using arbitrarily selected interest rates.

a) As long as r is greater than k, NPV must be greater than zero.

b) The IRR and NPV methods rank projects differently if

i) The cost of one project is greater than the cost of another.

ii) The timing of cash flows differs among projects.

3) The IRR method assumes that the cash flows will be reinvested at the internal rate of return (r). If the project's funds are not reinvested at the IRR, the ranking calculations obtained may be in error.

a) The NPV method is better in many decision situations because the reinvestment is assumed to be the cost of capital (k).

4) Under some circumstances, IRR is not totally reliable because it can give multiple answers for the same set of facts. This anomaly occurs when more than one change in the direction of net periodic cash flows occurs. For example, one direction change occurs when an initial net cash outflow is followed by a series of net inflows. However, if a negative net cash flow occurs in a later period, another direction change and a second solution result. The number of solutions to the IRR formula equals the number of changes in the direction of the net cash flows.

a) The reason multiple solutions may arise is that the IRR equation has n roots (solutions). All of these roots except one are imaginary numbers when one change in the direction of cash flows occurs. If more than one direction change occurs, the number of real roots increases on a one-to-one basis.

d. **Profitability or excess present value index** is the ratio of the present value of future net cash inflows to the discounted initial net investment.

1)
$$\frac{PV \ of \ future \ net \ cash \ inflows}{Discounted \ initial \ net \ investment}$$

2) This variation of the net present value method facilitates comparison of different-sized investments.

    e.   **Accounting rate of return** (also called unadjusted rate of return or book value rate of return) is the increase in accounting net profit divided by the required investment.

        1)   Sometimes the denominator is the average investment rather than the initial investment.

        2)   The accounting rate of return ignores the effects of the time value of money.

6.   Stop and review! You have completed the outline for this subunit. Study multiple-choice questions 43 through 45 beginning on page 368.

## 7.11 RELEVANT COSTS

1.   The typical problem for which relevant costs are considered involves incremental (differential or marginal) analysis. The quantitative analysis emphasizes the ways in which costs and benefits vary with the option chosen. Thus, the focus is on incremental, not total, costs because the former, not the latter, are relevant.

    a.   EXAMPLE: A firm's product has the following unit costs:

| | |
|---|---|
| Raw materials | $2.00 |
| Direct labor | 3.00 |
| Variable overhead | .50 |
| Fixed overhead | 2.50 |
| Total cost | $8.00 |

        1)   The product normally sells for $10 per unit. An application of incremental cost analysis is necessary if a foreign buyer, who has never before been a customer, offers to pay $5.75 per unit for a **special order** of the firm's product. The immediate reaction might be to refuse the offer because the selling price is less than the average cost of production by a considerable amount. However, incremental cost analysis results in a different decision.

        2)   Only the relevant costs should be considered. In this example, the only relevant costs are for raw materials, direct labor, and variable overhead. No additional fixed overhead costs will be incurred. Because the $5.75 selling price (incremental revenue) exceeds the $5.50 of relevant costs ($2 materials + $3 labor + $.50 variable OH), accepting the special order will be profitable.

2.   In addition to special-order situations, incremental costing can be used in decisions to make or buy (insourcing or outsourcing), add or drop product lines, sell or process further, acquire or divest a segment, or select a market channel.

3.   Caution must always be used in applying incremental cost analysis because of the many nonquantitative factors that must be considered, including

    a.   Whether price concessions violate federal law
    b.   The effect of government contract pricing regulations
    c.   The effect of special customer sales on the firm's regular market
    d.   Whether regular customers will demand equal terms
    e.   Whether sales of other product lines will suffer if a product line is dropped

4. The concept behind a **make-or-buy** decision is to use available resources as efficiently as possible before outsourcing. Often, an array of products can be produced efficiently if production capacity is available. If not enough capacity is available to produce them all, the products that are produced least efficiently should be outsourced (or capacity should be expanded).

   a. If the total relevant costs of production are less than the cost to buy the item, it should be insourced. The key variable is relevant costs, not total costs.

      1) Past (sunk) costs are irrelevant.

      2) Opportunity costs are important because they represent the forgone opportunities of the firm. For example, if the firm chooses not to produce the most profitable item, the opportunity cost is the profit on that item.

      3) When excess capacity is available, allocated fixed factory overhead is an irrelevant cost. This cost will be incurred whether the product is made or bought. However, at full capacity, the allocation of fixed factory overhead must be considered.

5. **Disinvestment** decisions are the opposite of capital budgeting decisions, i.e., to terminate rather than start an operation.

   a. Four steps should be taken in making a disinvestment decision:

      1) Identify fixed expenses that would be curtailed by the disinvestment decision, e.g., depreciation and insurance on equipment used.

      2) Determine the revenue needed to justify continuing operations (variable cost of production).

      3) Establish the disinvestment flows, such as salvage value, return of working capital, tax consequences, employee severance payments, and restoration costs.

      4) Determine if the book value of the assets is equal to the economic value of the capital. If not, reevaluate the decision using current fair value rather than the book value.

   b. When a firm disinvests, excess capacity exists unless another project uses this capacity immediately. The cost of idle capacity should be treated as a relevant cost.

   c. In general, if the marginal cost of a project is greater than the marginal revenue, the firm should disinvest.

6. Stop and review! You have completed the outline for this subunit. Study multiple-choice questions 46 through 53 beginning on page 369.

## 7.12 TRANSFER PRICING

1. Transfer prices are the amounts charged by one segment of an organization for goods and services it provides to another segment of the same organization.

   a. Transfer prices are used by profit and investment centers.

      1) In a decentralized system, each responsibility center theoretically may be a completely separate entity. Thus, Division A should charge the same price to Division B as would be charged to an outside buyer.

      2) The reason for decentralization is to motivate managers to achieve the best results. The best interests of Division A may not be served by giving a special discount to Division B if the goods can be sold at the regular price to outside buyers. However, it may be to the overall company's advantage to have A sell at a special price to B.

b. A transfer price should permit a segment to operate independently and meet its goals while serving the best interests of the firm. Hence, transfer pricing should motivate managers; it should encourage goal congruence and managerial effort.

1) Goal congruence is agreement regarding the goals of the organization or the segment by both supervisors and subordinates. Performance is assumed to be optimized when the parties understand that personal and segmental goals should be consistent with those of the organization.

2) Managerial effort is the extent to which a manager attempts to accomplish a goal. It may include psychological as well as physical commitment to a goal.

3) Motivation is the desire of managers to attain a specific goal (goal congruence) and the commitment to accomplish the goal (managerial effort). Managerial motivation is therefore a combination of managerial effort and goal congruence.

c. Transfer prices can be determined in a number of ways. They may be based on

1) A market price, assuming that a market exists

2) Differential outlay cost plus opportunity cost to the seller

a) For example, if a good costing $4 can be sold for $10, the outlay cost is $4 and the seller's opportunity cost is $6 (given no idle capacity).

3) Full absorption cost, including materials, labor, and a full allocation of manufacturing overhead

4) Cost plus a lump sum or a markup percentage

a) Cost may be either the standard or the actual cost. The former has the advantage of isolating variances. Actual costs give the selling division little incentive to control costs.

b) A cost-based price ignores market prices and may not promote long-term efficiencies.

5) Negotiation

a) A negotiated price may result when organizational subunits are free to determine the prices at which they buy and sell internally. Hence, a transfer price may simply reflect the best bargain that the parties can strike between themselves. It need not be based directly on particular market or cost information. A negotiated price may be especially appropriate when market prices are subject to rapid fluctuation.

d. The choice of a transfer pricing policy (which type of transfer price to use) is normally decided by top management at the corporate level. The decision will typically include consideration of the following:

1) **Goal congruence factors.** Will the transfer price promote the goals of the company as a whole?

2) **Segmental performance factors.** The segment making the transfer should be allowed to recover its incremental cost plus its opportunity cost of the transfer. The opportunity cost is the benefit forgone by not selling to an outsider.

a) For this purpose, the transfer should be at market price.

b) The selling manager should not lose income by selling within the company.

c) Properly allocating revenues and expenses through appropriate transfer pricing also facilitates evaluation of the performance of the various segments.

     3)  **Negotiation factors**. If the purchasing segment could purchase the product or service outside the company, it should be permitted to negotiate the transfer price.

        a)  The purchasing manager should not have to incur greater costs by purchasing within the company.

     4)  **Capacity factors**. Does the seller have excess capacity?

        a)  If Division A has excess capacity, it should be used for producing products for Division B.

        b)  If Division A is operating at full capacity and selling its products at the full market price, profitable work should not be abandoned to produce for Division B.

     5)  **Cost structure factors**. What portions of production costs are variable and fixed?

        a)  If Division A has excess capacity and an opportunity arises to sell to Division B at a price in excess of the variable cost, the work should be performed for Division B because a contribution to cover the fixed costs will result.

     6)  **Tax factors**. A wide range of tax issues on the interstate and international levels may arise, e.g., income taxes, sales taxes, value-added taxes, inventory and payroll taxes, and other governmental charges.

        a)  In the international context, exchange rate fluctuations and limits on transfers of profits outside the host country are additional concerns.

e.  **Dual pricing** is another internal price-setting alternative. For example, the seller could record the transfer to another segment at the usual market price that would be paid by an outsider. The buyer, however, would record a purchase at the variable cost of production.

     1)  Each segment's performance would be improved by the use of a dual-pricing scheme.

     2)  The company would benefit because variable costs would be used for decision-making purposes. In a sense, variable costs would be the relevant price for decision-making purposes, but the regular market price would be used for evaluation of production divisions.

     3)  Under a dual-pricing system, the profit for the company will be less than the sum of the profits of the individual segments.

     4)  In effect, the seller is given a corporate subsidy under the dual-pricing system.

     5)  The dual-pricing system is rarely used because the incentive to control costs is reduced. The seller is assured of a high price, and the buyer is assured of an artificially low price. Thus, neither manager must exert much effort to show a profit on segmental performance reports.

2.  Stop and review! You have completed the outline for this subunit. Study multiple-choice questions 54 through 56 beginning on page 373.

## 7.13 RESPONSIBILITY SYSTEMS

1.  A responsibility system should encourage the efficient achievement of organizational goals. Thus, managerial control should promote **goal congruence** and **managerial effort**. All managers should be motivated to expend the necessary effort to reach common goals. The goals should be specific, objective, and verifiable. Conversely, the system should discourage effort directed toward incongruent goals. Suboptimization occurs when one segment of a firm takes action that is in its own best interests but is detrimental to the firm as a whole.

    a.  A key issue for organizations is how to promote goal congruence while securing the benefits of appropriate decentralization. Providing subunit managers with significant autonomy may result in greater awareness of the needs of important constituencies (e.g., customers, suppliers, and employees), faster decisions, more rapid management development, and greater management initiative.

    b.  One means of attaining goal congruence is to harmonize the measures used to evaluate managers with the measures used in top management's decision models. For example, the transfer price charged by a selling division to a buying division of a company should be set so that individual managers acting in their own best interests will further the objectives of the company. This result will be reached when maximizing the performance measure for a manager also provides the greatest benefit for the organization.

2.  The alignment of managerial with organizational goals requires assigning responsibility for activities, delegating the authority to perform necessary tasks, establishing accountability, and measuring and evaluating performance. The result is a structure within which individual efforts can be coordinated to attain ultimate organizational goals.

    a.  **Authority** is the power to direct and exact performance from others. It includes the right to prescribe the means and methods by which work will be done. However, the authority to direct is only as good as one individual's willingness to accept direction from another. Moreover, with authority comes responsibility and accountability.

    b.  **Responsibility** is the obligation to perform.

        1)  In the classical view, this obligation formally comes down from a superior position and is inherent in any job (it has its origins in the rights of private property as defined by the appropriate laws).

        2)  In the behavioral view, responsibility must and should be delegated; a successive dividing and passing down of obligation occurs.

            a)  The appropriate amount of authority or power must be delegated with the responsibility.

            b)  However, a higher position can never rid itself of ultimate responsibility.

    c.  **Accountability** is the liability for failure to meet the obligation. In practice, accountability is

        1)  The duty to report performance to one's superior

            a)  The principle of single accountability or unity of command means that each subordinate should report to only one superior.

            b)  The principle of unity of command permits more than one person to act as a subordinate's superior only under conditions in which there is complete coordination of plans so that no conflicting or contradicting instructions are given.

        2)  The physical means for reporting or being able to substantiate performance, i.e., record keeping

3.    **Controllability** is another concept important to the understanding of a responsibility system.  It is the extent to which a manager can influence activities.

    a.    Managerial performance theoretically should be evaluated only on the basis of those factors controllable by the manager.  Thus, managers may control revenues, costs, or investment in resources.  For example, a controllable cost is one that is directly regulated by a specific manager at a given level of production within a given time span.  However, controllability and responsibility are rarely coextensive.  One reason is that more than one manager may influence an activity.

    b.    If responsibility exceeds the extent to which a manager can influence an activity, the result may be reduced morale, a decline in managerial effort, and poor performance.  Such a manager encounters greater risk because his/her success depends on uncontrollable factors.  Thus, a manager in these circumstances should be compensated for the incremental risk assumed.

    c.    However, if a manager is accountable solely for activities over which (s)he has extensive influence, the manager may develop too narrow a focus.

        1)    For example, the manager of a cost center may make decisions based only on cost efficiency and ignore the overall effectiveness goals of the organization.  By extending the manager's responsibility to profits as well as costs, the organization may encourage desirable behavior congruent with overall goals, such as improved coordination with marketing personnel, even though the manager still does not control revenues.

        2)    Furthermore, a manager who does not control an activity may nevertheless be the individual who is best informed about it.  Thus, a purchasing agent may be in the best position to explain price variances even though (s)he cannot control them.

4.    A well-designed responsibility accounting system establishes responsibility centers within the organization.  A responsibility center is an organizational subunit, such as a department, plant, division, or segment, whose manager has authority over, and is responsible and accountable for, a defined group of activities.  Responsibility centers may be classified as follows:

    a.    A **cost center** is responsible for costs only.  A maintenance department is an example.

    b.    A **revenue center** is responsible for revenues but not costs other than those attributable to marketing.  A specialty clothing department of a department store is an example.

    c.    A **profit center** is responsible for revenues and expenses.  An appliance department in a retail store is an example.

    d.    An **investment center** is responsible for revenues, expenses, and invested capital.  A branch office is an example.

    e.    A **service center** exists primarily and sometimes solely to provide specialized support to other organizational subunits.  It is usually operated as a cost center.  A maintenance department is also an example of a service center.

5.    Stop and review!  You have completed the outline for this subunit.  Study multiple-choice questions 57 through 59 beginning on page 374.

## QUESTIONS

### 7.1 Cost-Volume-Profit (CVP) Analysis

**1.** Presented below is a cost-volume-profit chart for a firm. Various reference points are marked on the chart with letters.

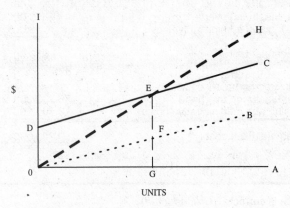

UNITS

The letters CEH on the chart represent the

A. Total sales.

B. Total expenses.

C. Area of the chart where total sales exceed total expenses.

D. Area of the chart where total expenses exceed total sales.

Answer (C) is correct. *(CIA, adapted)*
  **REQUIRED:** The meaning of the letters CEH on the chart.
  **DISCUSSION:** A cost-volume-profit chart contains elements (lines, points, axes) that identify variable cost, fixed cost, the breakeven point, total revenue, profit, and volume in units. When the total sales revenue line rises above the total expense line, a company will have positive net income.
  Answer (A) is incorrect because line HEO represents total sales. Answer (B) is incorrect because line CED represents total expenses. Answer (D) is incorrect because the loss area, i.e., the area of the chart where total expenses exceed sales, is represented by the area OED.

**2.** A company manufactures a single product. Estimated cost data regarding this product and other information for the product and the company are as follows:

| | |
|---|---|
| Sales price per unit | $40 |
| Total variable production cost per unit | $22 |
| Sales commission (on sales) | 5% |
| Fixed costs and expenses: | |
|   Manufacturing overhead | $5,598,720 |
|   General and administrative | $3,732,480 |
| Effective income tax rate | 40% |

The number of units the company must sell in the coming year in order to reach its breakeven point is

A. 388,800 units.

B. 518,400 units.

C. 583,200 units.

D. 972,000 units.

Answer (C) is correct. *(CIA, adapted)*
  **REQUIRED:** The number of units to reach the break-even point.
  **DISCUSSION:** The breakeven point is determined by dividing total fixed costs by the unit contribution margin. The total fixed costs are $9,331,200 ($5,598,720 manufacturing overhead + $3,732,480 general and administrative). The contribution margin is $16.00 ($40 sales price – $22 variable production cost – $2.00 commission). Thus, the breakeven point is 583,200 units ($9,331,200 ÷ $16).
  Answer (A) is incorrect because 388,800 units results from not subtracting the variable costs per unit from sales price. Answer (B) is incorrect because 518,400 units does not reflect the sales commissions in the total variable costs. Answer (D) is incorrect because 972,000 units includes taxes in the total variable costs, which understates the unit contribution margin.

Questions 3 and 4 are based on the following information.

A company that sells its single product for $40 per unit uses cost-volume-profit analysis in its planning. The company's after-tax net income for the past year was $1,188,000 after applying an effective tax rate of 40%. The projected costs for manufacturing and selling its single product in the coming year are listed.

Variable costs per unit:

| | |
|---|---:|
| Direct material | $ 5.00 |
| Direct labor | 4.00 |
| Manufacturing overhead | 6.00 |
| Selling and administrative costs | 3.00 |
| Total cost per unit | $18.00 |

Annual fixed operating costs:

| | |
|---|---:|
| Manufacturing overhead | $6,200,000 |
| Selling and administrative costs | 3,700,000 |
| Total annual fixed cost | $9,900,000 |

---

**3.** The dollar sales volume required in the coming year to earn the same after-tax net profit as the past year is

A.  $20,160,000

B.  $21,600,000

C.  $23,400,000

D.  $26,400,000

Answer (B) is correct.  *(CIA, adapted)*
   **REQUIRED:** The dollar sales volume required in the coming year to earn the same after-tax net profit as the past year.
   **DISCUSSION:** The desired after-tax net profit is $1,188,000 (the past year's amount). Given a 40% tax rate, the pretax equivalent is $1,980,000 [$1,188,000 ÷ (1.0 − .40)]. Pretax net profit equals dollar sales (unit sales × $40), minus total fixed costs, minus total variable costs (unit sales × unit variable cost). Hence, the contribution margin (sales − variable costs) is equated with the sum of fixed costs and the targeted pretax net profit. Unit sales (S) equal 540,000, and sales dollars equal $21,600,000 ($40 × 540,000 units).

$$\$40S - \$9,900,000 - \$18S = \$1,980,000$$
$$\$22S = \$11,880,000$$
$$S = 540,000\ units$$

   Answer (A) is incorrect because $20,160,000 does not adjust after-tax net profit to pretax net profit. Answer (C) is incorrect because $23,400,000 results from adjusting after-tax net profit by dividing by the tax rate rather than one minus the tax rate. Answer (D) is incorrect because $26,400,000 results from equating the sum of the desired pretax net profit and total fixed costs with total variable costs instead of the contribution margin.

---

**4.** The company has learned that a new direct material is available that will increase the quality of its product. The new material will increase the direct material costs by $3 per unit. The company will increase the selling price of the product to $50 per unit and increase its marketing costs by $1,575,000 to advertise the higher-quality product. The number of units the company has to sell in order to earn a 10% before-tax return on sales would be

A.  337,500 units.

B.  346,875 units.

C.  425,000 units.

D.  478,125 units.

Answer (D) is correct.  *(CIA, adapted)*
   **REQUIRED:** The number of units the company has to sell to earn a 10% before-tax return on sales.
   **DISCUSSION:** Pretax net profit (10% of dollar sales) equals dollar sales (unit sales × $50), minus total fixed costs (increased by $1,575,000 of marketing costs), minus total variable costs (increased by $3 per unit). Unit sales (S) therefore equal 478,125 units.

$$.10(\$50S) = \$50S - (\$9,900,000 + \$1,575,000) - (\$18 + \$3)S$$
$$\$24S = \$11,475,000$$
$$S = 478,125\ units$$

   Answer (A) is incorrect because 337,500 units results from using the wrong sign for the pretax net profit. Answer (B) is incorrect because 346,875 units results from subtracting, not adding, the incremental marketing costs to determine total fixed costs. Answer (C) is incorrect because 425,000 units fails to adjust for the increase in direct materials costs.

**5.** A retail company determines its selling price by marking up variable costs 60%. In addition, the company uses frequent selling price markdowns to stimulate sales. If the markdowns average 10%, what is the company's contribution margin ratio?

A. 27.5%

B. 30.6%

C. 37.5%

D. 41.7%

Answer (B) is correct. *(CIA, adapted)*
    **REQUIRED:** The contribution margin ratio.
    **DISCUSSION:** The contribution margin equals revenues minus variable costs. The CMR equals the UCM divided by the selling price. For example, if variable costs average $10 per unit, the average selling price is $16 (1.60 × $10). However, the 10% markdown implies that the actual average selling price is $14.40 (.90 × $16). The CMR is therefore 30.6% [($14.40 − $10.00) ÷ $14.40].
    Answer (A) is incorrect because 27.5% omits markdowns from the denominator. Answer (C) is incorrect because 37.5% ignores markdowns. Answer (D) is incorrect because 41.7% omits markdowns from the numerator.

## 7.2 Variable and Absorption Costing

Questions 6 and 7 are based on the following information. A company manufactures and sells a single product. Planned and actual production in its first year of operation was 100,000 units. Planned and actual costs for that year were as follows:

|  | Manufacturing | Nonmanufacturing |
|---|---|---|
| Variable | $600,000 | $500,000 |
| Fixed | 400,000 | 300,000 |

The company sold 85,000 units of product at a selling price of $30 per unit.

**6.** Using absorption costing, the company's operating profit was

A. $750,000

B. $900,000

C. $975,000

D. $1,020,000

Answer (B) is correct. *(CIA, adapted)*
    **REQUIRED:** The absorption costing operating profit.
    **DISCUSSION:** Under absorption costing, product costs include fixed and variable manufacturing costs. The unit product cost under absorption costing is $10 [($600,000 + $400,000) ÷ 100,000 units produced]. All nonmanufacturing costs are expensed in the period incurred. Thus, operating profit is $900,000.

| | |
|---|---|
| Revenue (85,000 units × $30) | $2,550,000 |
| Cost of goods sold (85,000 units × $10) | (850,000) |
| Nonmanufacturing costs | |
| ($500,000 + $300,000) | (800,000) |
| | |
| Operating profit | $ 900,000 |

    Answer (A) is incorrect because $750,000 equals absorption costing net profit minus ending inventory ($15,000 units × $10). Answer (C) is incorrect because $975,000 treats the variable nonmanufacturing costs as manufacturing costs. Answer (D) is incorrect because $1,020,000 assumes that all costs are manufacturing costs.

**7.** Refer to the information preceding question 6. Using variable costing, the company's operating profit was

   A.  $750,000

   B.  $840,000

   C.  $915,000

   D.  $975,000

Answer (B) is correct.  *(CIA, adapted)*
   **REQUIRED:** The variable costing operating profit.
   **DISCUSSION:** Under variable costing, the product cost includes only variable manufacturing costs. All fixed costs are expensed in the period incurred. Unit product cost under variable costing is $6 ($600,000 ÷ 100,000 units produced).

| | |
|---|---:|
| Revenue (85,000 units × $30) | $2,550,000 |
| Variable cost of goods sold | |
|   (85,000 units × $6) | (510,000) |
| Variable nonmanufacturing costs | (500,000) |
| Contribution margin | $1,540,000 |
| Fixed costs | (700,000) |
| Operating profit | $ 840,000 |

   Answer (A) is incorrect because $750,000 equals variable costing net profit minus ending inventory (15,000 units × $6). Answer (C) is incorrect because $915,000 treats all variable costs as manufacturing costs. Answer (D) is incorrect because $975,000 treats all variable costs and fixed manufacturing costs as product costs.

**8.** During its first year of operations, a company produced 275,000 units and sold 250,000 units. The following costs were incurred during the year:

Variable costs per unit:
| | |
|---|---:|
|   Direct materials | $15.00 |
|   Direct labor | 10.00 |
|   Manufacturing overhead | 12.50 |
|   Selling and administrative | 2.50 |

Total fixed costs:
| | |
|---|---:|
|   Manufacturing overhead | $2,200,000 |
|   Selling and administrative | 1,375,000 |

The difference between operating profit calculated on the absorption-costing basis and on the variable-costing basis is that absorption-costing operating profit is

   A.  $200,000 greater.

   B.  $220,000 greater.

   C.  $325,000 greater.

   D.  $62,500 less.

Answer (A) is correct.  *(CIA, adapted)*
   **REQUIRED:** The difference between absorption-costing and variable-costing operating profit.
   **DISCUSSION:** Absorption-costing operating profit will exceed variable-costing operating income because production exceeds sales, resulting in a deferral of fixed manufacturing overhead in the inventory calculated using the absorption method. The difference of $200,000 is equal to the fixed manufacturing overhead per unit ($2,200,000 ÷ 275,000 = $8.00) times the difference between production and sales (275,000 − 250,000 = 25,000, which is the inventory change in units).
   Answer (B) is incorrect because units produced, not units sold, should be used as the denominator to calculate the fixed manufacturing cost per unit. Answer (C) is incorrect because fixed selling and administrative costs are not properly inventoriable under absorption costing. Answer (D) is incorrect because variable selling and administrative costs are period costs under both variable- and absorption-cost systems in the determination of operating profit.

Questions 9 and 10 are based on the following information.

A and B are autonomous divisions of a corporation. They have no beginning or ending inventories, and the number of units produced is equal to the number of units sold. Following is financial information relating to the two divisions.

|  | A | B |
|---|---|---|
| Sales | $150,000 | $400,000 |
| Other revenue | 10,000 | 15,000 |
| Direct materials | 30,000 | 65,000 |
| Direct labor | 20,000 | 40,000 |
| Variable factory overhead | 5,000 | 15,000 |
| Fixed factory overhead | 25,000 | 55,000 |
| Variable S&A expense | 15,000 | 30,000 |
| Fixed S&A expense | 35,000 | 60,000 |
| Central corporate expenses (allocated) | 12,000 | 20,000 |

**9.** What is the total contribution to corporate profits generated by Division A before allocation of central corporate expenses?

A. $18,000

B. $20,000

C. $30,000

D. $90,000

Answer (C) is correct. *(CIA, adapted)*
**REQUIRED:** The total contribution to profits by A.
**DISCUSSION:** Division A's total contribution to corporate profits includes everything except the central corporate expense allocation. Thus, the total contribution is $30,000 ($150,000 sales + $10,000 other revenue – $30,000 direct materials – $20,000 direct labor – $5,000 variable overhead – $25,000 fixed overhead – $15,000 variable S&A expense – $35,000 fixed S&A expense).
Answer (A) is incorrect because $18,000 is the result of deducting the central corporate expenses. Answer (B) is incorrect because $20,000 is the result of excluding other revenue. Answer (D) is incorrect because $90,000 is the result of failing to deduct the fixed costs.

**10.** What is the contribution margin of Division B?

A. $150,000

B. $205,000

C. $235,000

D. $265,000

Answer (D) is correct. *(CIA, adapted)*
**REQUIRED:** The contribution margin of B.
**DISCUSSION:** The contribution margin equals revenue minus variable costs. Thus, Division B's contribution margin is $265,000 ($400,000 sales + $15,000 other revenue – $65,000 direct materials – $40,000 direct labor – $15,000 variable overhead – $30,000 variable S&A expense).
Answer (A) is incorrect because $150,000 is the result of subtracting fixed costs. Answer (B) is incorrect because $205,000 is the result of subtracting fixed S&A costs. Answer (C) is incorrect because $235,000 is the result of subtracting fixed S&A costs but not variable S&A costs.

## 7.3 Overhead Allocation

**11.** A company allocates overhead to jobs in process using direct labor costs, raw material costs, and machine hours. The overhead application rates for the current year are

> 100% of direct labor
> 20% of raw materials
> $117 per machine hour

A particular production run incurred the following costs:

> Direct labor, $8,000
> Raw materials, $2,000
> A total of 140 machine hours were required for the production run

What is the total cost that would be charged to the production run?

- A. $18,000
- B. $18,400
- C. $24,780
- D. None of the answers are correct.

**Answer (C) is correct.** *(CIA, adapted)*
**REQUIRED:** The total cost for a production run given overhead application rates.
**DISCUSSION:** The total cost is $34,780. It consists of direct labor ($8,000), raw materials ($2,000), and factory overhead ($24,780). The overhead applied is calculated as follows:

| | | |
|---|---|---|
| 100% × $8,000 of direct labor | = | $ 8,000 |
| 20% × $2,000 of raw materials | = | 400 |
| $117 × 140 machine hours | = | 16,380 |
| | | $24,780 |

Answer (A) is incorrect because $18,000 includes only $8,000 for overhead (based on 100% of direct labor). Answer (B) is incorrect because $18,400 includes only $8,400 for overhead (based on 100% of direct labor and 20% of raw materials). Answer (D) is incorrect because total cost is $34,780.

**12.** A company manufactures plastic products for the home and restaurant market. The company also does contract work for other customers and uses a job-order costing system. The flexible budget covering next year's expected range of activity is

| Direct labor hours | 50,000 | 80,000 | 110,000 |
|---|---|---|---|
| Machine hours | 40,000 | 64,000 | 88,000 |
| Variable O/H costs | $100,000 | $160,000 | $220,000 |
| Fixed O/H costs | 150,000 | 150,000 | 150,000 |
| Total O/H costs | $250,000 | $310,000 | $370,000 |

A predetermined overhead rate based on direct labor hours is used to apply total overhead. Management has estimated that 100,000 direct labor hours will be used next year. The predetermined overhead rate per direct labor hour to be used to apply total overhead to the individual jobs next year is

- A. $3.36
- B. $3.50
- C. $3.70
- D. $3.88

**Answer (B) is correct.** *(CIA, adapted)*
**REQUIRED:** The predetermined overhead rate per direct labor hour.
**DISCUSSION:** The predetermined overhead rate is calculated by dividing the total fixed overhead by the activity level to arrive at a unit fixed overhead cost that is added to the unit variable overhead cost. The unit variable overhead rate is the same at each activity level. Thus, the predetermined overhead rate is $3.50 [($150,000 FOH ÷ 100,000 hrs.) + ($220,000 VOH ÷ 110,000 hrs.)].
Answer (A) is incorrect because $3.36 per direct labor hour is based on use of an activity level of 110,000 direct labor hours to determine the fixed overhead rate. Answer (C) is incorrect because $3.70 is the result of assuming that $220,000 of variable overhead will be incurred for 100,000 (not 110,000) direct labor hours. Answer (D) is incorrect because $3.88 (rounded) results from using an activity level of 80,000 direct labor hours to determine the fixed overhead rate.

**13.** At the beginning of the year, Smith Inc. budgeted the following:

| | |
|---|---:|
| Units | 10,000 |
| | |
| Sales | $100,000 |
| Minus: | |
|    Total variable expenses | 60,000 |
|    Total fixed expenses | 20,000 |
| | |
| Net income | $ 20,000 |
| | |
| Factory overhead: | |
|    Variable | $ 30,000 |
|    Fixed | 10,000 |

There were no beginning inventories. At the end of the year, no work was in process, total factory overhead incurred was $39,500, and underapplied factory overhead was $1,500. Factory overhead was applied on the basis of budgeted unit production. How many units were produced this year?

A. 10,250

B. 10,000

C. 9,875

D. 9,500

Answer (D) is correct. *(Publisher)*
**REQUIRED:** The number of units produced given various overhead data.
**DISCUSSION:** Given actual overhead of $39,500 and underapplied overhead of $1,500, overhead applied was $38,000 ($39,500 – $1,500). Overhead is applied at the rate of $4 per unit ($40,000 budgeted overhead ÷ 10,000 budgeted units). Accordingly, 9,500 units were produced ($38,000 applied overhead ÷ $4 per unit application rate).
Answer (A) is incorrect because 10,250 would have been produced if overhead had been overapplied by $1,500 [($39,500 + $1,500) ÷ $4]. Answer (B) is incorrect because 10,000 is the result of dividing budgeted, not applied, overhead by the application rate. Answer (C) is incorrect because 9,875 units would have been produced if $39,500 had been the amount of applied overhead.

## 7.4 Process Costing and Job-Order Costing

Questions 14 through 18 are based on the following information.

Kimbeth Manufacturing uses a process cost system to manufacture Dust Density Sensors for the mining industry. The following information pertains to operations for the month of May:

| | Units |
|---|---:|
| Beginning work-in-process inventory, May 1 | 16,000 |
| Started in production during May | 100,000 |
| Completed production during May | 92,000 |
| Ending work-in-process inventory, May 31 | 24,000 |

The beginning inventory was 60% complete for materials and 20% complete for conversion costs. The ending inventory was 90% complete for materials and 40% complete for conversion costs.

Costs pertaining to the month of May are as follows:

- Beginning inventory costs are materials, $54,560; direct labor, $20,320; and factory overhead, $15,240.
- Costs incurred during May are materials used, $468,000; direct labor, $182,880; and factory overhead, $391,160.

**14.** Using the first-in, first-out (FIFO) method, the equivalent units of production (EUP) for materials are

A. 97,600 units.

B. 104,000 units.

C. 107,200 units.

D. 108,000 units.

Answer (B) is correct. *(CMA, adapted)*
**REQUIRED:** The equivalent units of production for materials under FIFO.
**DISCUSSION:** Under FIFO, EUP are based solely on work performed during the current period. The EUP equals the sum of the work done on the beginning work-in-process inventory, units started and completed in the current period, and the ending work-in-process inventory. Given that beginning work-in-process was 60% complete as to materials, the current period is charged for 6,400 EUP (40% × 16,000 units). Because 92,000 units were completed during the period, 76,000 (92,000 – 16,000 in BWIP) must have been started and completed during the period. They represent 76,000 EUP. Finally, the EUP for ending work-in-process equal 21,600 (90% × 24,000 units). Thus, total EUP for May are 104,000 (6,400 + 76,000 + 21,600).
Answer (A) is incorrect because 97,600 units omits the 6,400 EUP added to beginning work-in-process. Answer (C) is incorrect because 107,200 units assumes beginning work-in-process was 40% complete. Answer (D) is incorrect because 108,000 units equals the sum of the physical units in beginning work-in-process and the physical units completed.

**15.** Refer to the information preceding question 14. Using the FIFO method, the equivalent units of production for conversion costs are

A. 85,600 units.

B. 88,800 units.

C. 95,200 units.

D. 98,400 units.

Answer (D) is correct.    *(CMA, adapted)*
 **REQUIRED:** The equivalent units of production for conversion costs under FIFO.
 **DISCUSSION:** The beginning inventory was 20% complete as to conversion costs. Hence, 12,800 EUP (80% × 16,000 units) were required for completion. EUP for units started and completed equaled 76,000 [100% × (92,000 completed units – 16,000 units in BWIP)]. The work done on ending work-in-process totaled 9,600 EUP (40% × 24,000 units). Thus, total EUP for May are 98,400 (12,800 + 76,000 + 9,600).
 Answer (A) is incorrect because 85,600 units omits the work done on beginning work-in-process. Answer (B) is incorrect because 88,800 units omits the work done on ending work-in-process. Answer (C) is incorrect because 95,200 units assumes the beginning work-in-process was 40% complete as to conversion costs.

**16.** Refer to the information preceding question 14. Using the FIFO method, the equivalent unit cost of materials for May is

A. $4.12

B. $4.50

C. $4.60

D. $4.80

Answer (B) is correct.    *(CMA, adapted)*
 **REQUIRED:** The equivalent unit cost of materials under FIFO.
 **DISCUSSION:** Under the FIFO method, EUP for materials equal 104,000 [(16,000 units in BWIP × 40%) + (76,000 units started and completed × 100%) + (24,000 units in EWIP × 90%)]. Consequently, the equivalent unit cost of materials is $4.50 ($468,000 total materials cost in May ÷ 104,000 EUP).
 Answer (A) is incorrect because $4.12 is based on EUP calculated under the weighted-average method. Answer (C) is incorrect because $4.60 is the weighted-average cost per equivalent unit. Answer (D) is incorrect because $4.80 omits the 6,400 EUP added to beginning work-in-process.

**17.** Refer to the information preceding question 14. Using the FIFO method, the equivalent unit conversion cost for May is

A. $5.65

B. $5.83

C. $6.00

D. $6.20

Answer (B) is correct.    *(CMA, adapted)*
 **REQUIRED:** The conversion cost per equivalent unit under FIFO.
 **DISCUSSION:** Under the FIFO method, EUP for conversion costs equal 98,400 [(16,000 units in BWIP × 80%) + (76,000 units started and completed × 100%) + (24,000 units in EWIP × 40%)]. Conversion costs incurred during the current period equal $574,040 ($182,880 DL + $391,160 FOH). Hence, the equivalent unit cost for conversion costs is $5.83 ($574,040 ÷ 98,400).
 Answer (A) is incorrect because $5.65 is based on EUP calculated under the weighted-average method. Answer (C) is incorrect because $6.00 is the cost per equivalent unit calculated under the weighted-average method. Answer (D) is incorrect because $6.20 results from combining conversion costs for May with those in beginning work-in-process and dividing by 98,400 EUP.

**18.** Refer to the information preceding question 14. Using the FIFO method, the total cost of units in the ending work-in-process inventory at May 31 is

A. $153,168

B. $154,800

C. $155,328

D. $156,960

Answer (A) is correct.    *(CMA, adapted)*
 **REQUIRED:** The total cost of units in ending work-in-process under FIFO.
 **DISCUSSION:** The FIFO costs per equivalent unit for materials and conversion costs are $4.50 and $5.83, respectively. EUP for materials in ending work-in-process equal 21,600 (90% × 24,000). Thus, total FIFO materials cost is $97,200 (21,600 EUP × $4.50). EUP for conversion costs in ending work-in-process equal 9,600 (40% × 24,000). Total conversion costs are therefore $55,968 (9,600 EUP × $5.83). Consequently, total work-in-process costs are $153,168 ($97,200 + $55,968).
 Answer (B) is incorrect because $154,800 is based on a FIFO calculation for materials and a weighted-average calculation for conversion costs. Answer (C) is incorrect because $155,328 is based on a weighted-average calculation for materials and a FIFO calculation for conversion costs. Answer (D) is incorrect because $156,960 is the weighted-average cost of ending work-in-process.

## 7.5 Activity-Based Costing (ABC)

Questions 19 and 20 are based on the following information. Believing that its traditional cost system may be providing misleading information, an organization is considering an activity-based costing (ABC) approach. It now employs a full cost system and has been applying its manufacturing overhead on the basis of machine hours.

The organization plans on using 50,000 direct labor hours and 30,000 machine hours in the coming year. The following data show the manufacturing overhead that is budgeted.

| Activity | Cost Driver | Budgeted Activity | Budgeted Cost |
|---|---|---|---|
| Material handling | No. of parts handled | 6,000,000 | $ 720,000 |
| Setup costs | No. of setups | 750 | 315,000 |
| Machining costs | Machine hours | 30,000 | 540,000 |
| Quality control | No. of batches | 500 | 225,000 |
| | Total manufacturing overhead cost: | | $1,800,000 |

Cost, sales, and production data for one of the organization's products for the coming year are as follows:

Prime costs:

| | |
|---|---|
| Direct material cost per unit | $4.40 |
| Direct labor cost per unit .05 DLH @ $15.00/DLH | .75 |
| Total prime cost | $5.15 |

Sales and production data:

| | |
|---|---|
| Expected sales | 20,000 units |
| Batch size | 5,000 units |
| Setups | 2 per batch |
| Total parts per finished unit | 5 parts |
| Machine hours required | 80 MH per batch |

**19.** If the organization uses the traditional full cost system, the cost per unit for this product for the coming year will be

A. $5.39

B. $5.44

C. $6.11

D. $6.95

Answer (C) is correct. *(CIA, adapted)*
**REQUIRED:** The unit cost under traditional full costing.
**DISCUSSION:** Given that manufacturing overhead is applied on the basis of machine hours, the overhead rate is $60 per hour ($1,800,000 ÷ 30,000) or $.96 per unit [($60 × 80 machine hours per batch) ÷ 5,000 units per batch]. Accordingly, the unit full cost is $6.11 ($5.15 unit price cost + $.96).
Answer (A) is incorrect because $5.39 assumes that 80 machine hours are required for the total production of 20,000 units. Answer (B) is incorrect because $5.44 is based on the machining overhead rate ($18). Answer (D) is incorrect because $6.95 is based on the direct labor hour manufacturing overhead rate.

**20.** If the organization employs an activity-based costing system, the cost per unit for the product described for the coming year will be

A. $6.00

B. $6.08

C. $6.21

D. $6.30

Answer (D) is correct. *(CIA, adapted)*
**REQUIRED:** The unit cost under the ABC system.
**DISCUSSION:** Materials handling cost per part is $.12 ($720,000 ÷ 6,000,000), cost per setup is $420 ($315,000 ÷ 750), machining cost per hour is $18 ($540,000 ÷ 30,000), and quality cost per batch is $450 ($225,000 ÷ 500). Hence, total manufacturing overhead applied is $22,920 [(5 parts per unit) × 20,000 units × $.12) + (4 batches × 2 setups per batch × $420) + (4 batches × 80 machine hours per batch × $18) + (4 batches × $450)]. The total unit cost is $6.296 [$5.15 prime cost + ($22,920 ÷ 20,000 units) overhead].
Answer (A) is incorrect because $6.00 assumes one setup per batch and 80 total machine hours. Answer (B) is incorrect because $6.08 assumes that only 80 machine hours were used. Answer (C) is incorrect because $6.21 assumes one setup per batch.

Questions 21 and 22 are based on the following information. This information was presented as part of Question 3 on Part 3 of the June 1992 CMA examination, which covered activity-based costing.

Alaire Corporation manufactures several different types of printed circuit boards; however, two of the boards account for the majority of the company's sales. The first of these boards, a television (TV) circuit board, has been a standard in the industry for several years. The market for this type of board is competitive and therefore price-sensitive. Alaire plans to sell 65,000 of the TV boards next year at a price of $150 per unit. The second high-volume product, a personal computer (PC) circuit board, is a recent addition to Alaire's product line. Because the PC board incorporates the latest technology, it can be sold at a premium price; plans include the sale of 40,000 PC boards at $300 per unit.

Alaire's management group is meeting to discuss strategies, and the current topic of conversation is how to spend the sales and promotion dollars for next year. The sales manager believes that the market share for the TV board could be expanded by concentrating Alaire's promotional efforts in this area. In response to this suggestion, the production manager said, "Why don't you go after a bigger market for the PC board? The cost sheets that I get show that the contribution from the PC board is more than double the contribution from the TV board. I know we get a premium price for the PC board; selling it should help overall profitability."

Alaire uses a standard cost system, and the following data apply to the TV and PC boards:

|  | TV Board | PC Board |
|---|---|---|
| Direct materials | $80 | $140 |
| Direct labor | 1.5 hours | 4 hours |
| Machine time | .5 hours | 1.5 hours |

Variable factory overhead is applied on the basis of direct labor hours. For next year, variable factory overhead is budgeted at $1,120,000, and direct labor hours are estimated at 280,000. The hourly rates for machine time and direct labor are $10 and $14, respectively. Alaire applies a materials handling charge at 10% of materials cost; this materials handling charge is not included in variable factory overhead. Total annual expenditures for materials are budgeted at $10,600,000.

Ed Welch, Alaire's controller, believes that, before the management group proceeds with the discussion about allocating sales and promotional dollars to individual products, they should consider the activities involved in their production. As Welch explained to the group, "Activity-based costing integrates the cost of all activities, known as cost drivers, into individual product costs rather than including these costs in overhead pools." Welch has prepared the schedule shown below to help the management group understand this concept.

"Using this information," Welch explained, "we can calculate an activity-based cost for each TV board and each PC board and then compare it with the standard cost we have been using. The only cost that remains the same for both cost methods is the cost of direct materials. The cost drivers will replace the direct labor, machine time, and overhead costs in the standard cost."

| Budgeted Cost | | Cost Driver | Annual Activity for Cost Driver |
|---|---|---|---|
| Materials overhead: | | | |
| Procurement | $  400,000 | Number of parts | 4,000,000 parts |
| Production scheduling | 220,000 | Number of boards | 110,000 boards |
| Packaging and shipping | 440,000 | Number of boards | 110,000 boards |
| | $1,060,000 | | |
| | | Number of setups | 278,750 setups |
| | | Pounds of waste | 16,000 pounds |
| Variable overhead: | | Number of inspections | 160,000 inspections |
| Machine setup | $  446,000 | Number of boards | 110,000 boards |
| Hazardous waste disposal | 48,000 | | |
| Quality control | 560,000 | | |
| General supplies | 66,000 | Number of parts | 3,000,000 parts |
| | | Number of parts | 1,000,000 parts |
| | $1,120,000 | Number of boards | 110,000 boards |
| Manufacturing: | | | |
| Machine insertion | $1,200,000 | | |
| Manual insertion | 4,000,000 | | |
| Wave soldering | 132,000 | | |
| | $5,332,000 | | |

| Required per unit | TV Board | PC Board |
|---|---|---|
| Parts | 25 | 55 |
| Machine insertions | 24 | 35 |
| Manual insertions | 1 | 20 |
| Machine setups | 2 | 3 |
| Hazardous waste | .02 lb. | .35 lb. |
| Inspections | 1 | 2 |

**21.** On the basis of standard costs, the total contribution budgeted for the TV board is

A. $1,950,000

B. $2,275,000

C. $2,340,000

D. $2,470,000

Answer (A) is correct.  *(Publisher)*
**REQUIRED:** The total contribution budgeted for the TV board on a standard cost basis.
**DISCUSSION:** As calculated below, the budgeted standard unit cost of a TV board is $120. This amount includes $6 of variable overhead [1.5 DLH × ($1,120,000 total VOH ÷ 280,000 DLH)]. Given a unit price of $150, the unit contribution margin is therefore $30. Total budgeted contribution is $1,950,000 ($30 UCM × 65,000 budgeted units).

| | |
|---|---:|
| Direct materials | $ 80 |
| DM handling (10% × $80) | 8 |
| Direct labor (1.5 hr. × $14) | 21 |
| Machine time (.5 hr. × $10) | 5 |
| Variable overhead (1.5 hr. × $4) | 6 |
| Budgeted unit cost | $120 |

Answer (B) is incorrect because $2,275,000 excludes the cost of machine time ($5 × 65,000 units = $325,000). Answer (C) is incorrect because $2,340,000 excludes the variable overhead ($6 × 65,000 units = $390,000). Answer (D) is incorrect because $2,470,000 excludes the direct materials handling cost ($8 × 65,000 units = $520,000).

**22.** On the basis of activity-based costs (ABC), the total contribution budgeted for the TV board is

A. $1,594,000

B. $1,950,000

C. $2,037,100

D. $2,557,100

Answer (D) is correct.  *(Publisher)*
**REQUIRED:** The total contribution budgeted for the TV board on an ABC basis.
**DISCUSSION:** As calculated below, the budgeted activity-based unit cost of a TV board is $110.66. Given a unit price of $150, the unit contribution margin is $39.34. Total budgeted contribution is $2,557,100 ($39.34 UCM × 65,000 budgeted units).

| | |
|---|---:|
| Direct materials | $ 80.00 |
| Procurement [($400,000 ÷ 4,000,000 parts) × 25 parts] | 2.50 |
| Scheduling ($220,000 ÷ 110,000 boards) | 2.00 |
| Packaging and shipping ($440,000 ÷ 110,000 boards) | 4.00 |
| Setups [($446,000 ÷ 278,750 setups) × 2 setups] | 3.20 |
| Waste disposal [($48,000 ÷ 16,000 lb.) × .02] | .06 |
| Quality control ($560,000 ÷ 160,000 inspections) | 3.50 |
| General supplies ($66,000 ÷ 110,000 boards) | .60 |
| Machine insertion [(1,200,000 ÷ 3,000,000 parts) × 24 parts] | 9.60 |
| Manual insertion ($4,000,000 ÷ 1,000,000 parts) | 4.00 |
| Soldering ($132,000 ÷ 110,000 boards) | 1.20 |
| Budgeted ABC unit cost | $110.66 |

Answer (A) is incorrect because $1,594,000 is the CM for the PC board based on an ABC calculation. Answer (B) is incorrect because $1,950,000 is the CM for the TV board based on a standard-cost calculation. Answer (C) is incorrect because $2,037,100 erroneously includes $8 per board for materials handling ($8 × 65,000 units = $520,000).

## 7.6 Service Cost Allocation

Questions 23 and 24 are based on the following information. Fabricating and Finishing are the two production departments of a manufacturing company. Building Operations and Information Services are service departments that provide support to the two production departments as well as to each other. The company employs departmental overhead rates in the two production departments to allocate the service department costs to the production departments. Square footage is used to allocate building operations, and computer time is used to allocate information services. The costs of the service departments and relevant operating data for the departments are as follows:

|  | Building Operations | Information Services | Fabricating | Finishing |
|---|---|---|---|---|
| Labor and benefit costs | $200,000 | $ 300,000 | | |
| Other traceable costs | 350,000 | 900,000 | | |
| Total | $550,000 | $1,200,000 | | |
| Square feet occupied | 5,000 | 10,000 | 16,000 | 24,000 |
| Computer time (in hours) | 200 | | 1,200 | 600 |

**23.** If the company employs the direct method to allocate the costs of the service departments, then the amount of Building Operations costs allocated to Fabricating would be

A. $140,000

B. $160,000

C. $176,000

D. $220,000

Answer (D) is correct. *(CIA, adapted)*
**REQUIRED:** The amount of Building Operations costs allocated to Fabricating under the direct method.
**DISCUSSION:** The direct method does not allocate service costs to other service departments. Hence, the allocation base is the square footage in the two production departments. Fabricating's share is 40% (16,000 ÷ 40,000) of the total cost incurred by Building Operations, or $220,000 (40% × $550,000).
Answer (A) is incorrect because $140,000 is 40% of other traceable costs. Answer (B) is incorrect because $160,000 assumes an allocation base of 55,000 square feet. Answer (C) is incorrect because $176,000 assumes an allocation base of 50,000 square feet.

**24.** If the company employs the step method to allocate the costs of the service departments and if Information Services costs are allocated first, then the total amount of service department costs (information services and building operations) allocated to Finishing would be

A. $657,000

B. $681,600

C. $730,000

D. $762,000

Answer (D) is correct. *(CIA, adapted)*
**REQUIRED:** The total service department costs.
**DISCUSSION:** The step method of service department cost allocation is a sequential (but not a reciprocal) process. These costs are allocated to other service departments as well as to users. The process usually starts with the service department that renders the greatest percentage of its services to other service departments, the department that provides services to the greatest number of other departments, or the department with the greatest costs of services provided to other service departments. If the $1,200,000 of Information Services costs is allocated first, the allocation base is 2,000 computer hours (200 + 1,200 + 600). Thus, $120,000 [(200 ÷ 2,000) × $1,200,000] will be allocated to Building Operations and $360,000 [(600 ÷ 2,000) × $1,200,000] to Finishing. The total of the Building Operations costs to be allocated to production equals $670,000 ($550,000 + $120,000). The allocation base will be 40,000 square feet because no costs are allocated back to Information Services. Accordingly, the total of service costs allocated to Finishing equals $762,000 {$360,000 + [$670,000 × (24,000 ÷ 40,000)]}.
Answer (A) is incorrect because $657,000 results from allocating Building Operations costs first. Answer (B) is incorrect because $681,600 results from allocating Building Operations costs to Information Services. Answer (C) is incorrect because $730,000 allocates the costs of both service departments according to the direct method rather than the step method.

**25.** The step-down method of service department cost allocation often begins with allocation of the costs of the service department that

A. Provides the greatest percentage of its services to the production departments.

B. Provides the greatest percentage of its services to other service departments.

C. Provides the greatest total output of services.

D. Has the highest total costs among the service departments.

Answer (B) is correct. *(CIA, adapted)*
**REQUIRED:** The basis for determining the order of step-down allocation.
**DISCUSSION:** The step-down method may start with the department that renders the highest percentage of its total services to other service departments. It then progresses in descending order to the service department rendering the least percentage of its services to the other service departments. An alternative is to begin with the department that renders the highest dollar value of services to other service departments. A third possibility is to begin with the department that renders service to the greatest number of other service departments.
Answer (A) is incorrect because the step-down method may start with the department that renders the highest percentage of its total services to other service (not production) departments. Answer (C) is incorrect because beginning with the service department with the greatest output is not customary. Answer (D) is incorrect because beginning with the service department with the highest costs is not customary.

## 7.7 Joint Products and By-Products

Questions 26 through 29 are based on the following information.

Atlas Foods produces three supplemental food products simultaneously through a refining process costing $93,000.

The joint products, Alfa and Betters, have a final selling price of $4 per pound and $10 per pound, respectively, after additional processing costs of $2 per pound of each product are incurred after the split-off point. Morefeed, a by-product, is sold at the split-off point for $3 per pound.

| | |
|---|---|
| Alfa | 10,000 pounds of Alfa, a popular but relatively rare grain supplement having a caloric value of 4,400 calories per pound. |
| Betters | 5,000 pounds of Betters, a flavoring material high in carbohydrates with a caloric value of 11,200 calories per pound. |
| Morefeed | 1,000 pounds of Morefeed, used as a cattle feed supplement with a caloric value of 1,000 calories per pound. |

**26.** Assuming Atlas Foods inventories Morefeed, the by-product, the joint cost to be allocated to Alfa, using the net realizable value method is

A. $3,000

B. $30,000

C. $31,000

D. $60,000

Answer (B) is correct. *(CMA, adapted)*
**REQUIRED:** The joint cost allocated to Alfa based on net realizable values if the by-product is inventoried.
**DISCUSSION:** The NRV at split-off for each of the joint products must be determined. Given that Alfa has a $4 selling price and an additional $2 of processing costs, the value at split-off is $2 per pound. The total value at split-off for 10,000 pounds is $20,000. Betters has a $10 selling price and an additional $2 of processing costs. Thus, the value at split-off is $8 per pound. The total value of 5,000 pounds of Betters is therefore $40,000. The 1,000 pounds of Morefeed has a split-off value of $3 per pound, or $3,000. Assuming that Morefeed (a by-product) is inventoried (recognized in the accounts when produced) and treated as a reduction of joint costs, the allocable joint cost is $90,000 ($93,000 – $3,000). (NOTE: Other methods of accounting for by-products are possible.) The total net realizable value of the main products is $60,000 ($20,000 Alfa + $40,000 Betters). The allocation to Alfa is $30,000 [($20,000 ÷ $60,000) × $90,000].
Answer (A) is incorrect because $3,000 is the value of the by-product. Answer (C) is incorrect because $31,000 fails to adjust the joint processing cost for the value of the by-product. Answer (D) is incorrect because $60,000 is the amount allocated to Betters.

**27.** Refer to the information preceding question 26. Assuming Atlas Foods inventories Morefeed, the by-product, the joint cost to be allocated to Alfa, using the physical quantity method is

- A. $3,000
- B. $30,000
- C. $31,000
- D. $60,000

Answer (D) is correct.  *(CMA, adapted)*
**REQUIRED:** The joint cost allocated to Alfa based on the physical quantity method if the by-product is inventoried.
**DISCUSSION:** Joint cost is $93,000, and Morefeed has a split-off value of $3,000. Assuming the latter amount is treated as a reduction in joint cost, the allocable joint cost is $90,000. The total physical quantity (volume) of the two joint products is 15,000 pounds (10,000 Alfa + 5,000 Betters). Hence, $60,000 [(10,000 ÷ 15,000) × $90,000] of the net joint costs should be allocated to Alfa.
Answer (A) is incorrect because $3,000 is the value of the by-product. Answer (B) is incorrect because $30,000 is based on the net realizable value method. Answer (C) is incorrect because $31,000 is based on the net realizable value method and fails to adjust the joint processing cost for the value of the by-product.

**28.** Refer to the information preceding question 26. Assuming Atlas Foods inventories Morefeed, the by-product, the joint cost to be allocated to Betters using the weighted quantity method based on caloric value per pound is

- A. $39,208
- B. $39,600
- C. $50,400
- D. $52,080

Answer (C) is correct.  *(CMA, adapted)*
**REQUIRED:** The joint cost allocated to Betters based on the weighted quantity method.
**DISCUSSION:** The net allocable joint cost is $90,000. The caloric value of Alfa is 44,000,000 (4,400 × 10,000 pounds), the caloric value of Betters is 56,000,000 (11,200 × 5,000 pounds), and the total is 100,000,000. Of this total volume, Alfa makes up 44% and Betters 56%. Thus, $50,400 (56% × $90,000) should be allocated to Betters.
Answer (A) is incorrect because $39,208 is the amount allocated to Alfa if the 1,000,000 calories attributable to Morefeed is included in the computation. Answer (B) is incorrect because $39,600 is the allocation to Alfa. Answer (D) is incorrect because $52,080 is the allocation to Betters if the joint cost is not adjusted for the value of the by-product.

**29.** Refer to the information preceding question 26. Assuming Atlas Foods inventories Morefeed, the by-product, the joint cost to be allocated to Alfa using the gross market value method is

- A. $36,000
- B. $40,000
- C. $41,333
- D. $50,000

Answer (B) is correct.  *(CMA, adapted)*
**REQUIRED:** The joint cost allocated to Alfa using the gross market value method if the by-product is inventoried.
**DISCUSSION:** Alfa has a gross sales value of $40,000 ($4 × 10,000 pounds), Betters has a gross sales value of $50,000 ($10 × 5,000 pounds), and Morefeed has a split-off value of $3,000. If the value of Morefeed is inventoried and treated as a reduction in joint cost, the allocable joint cost is $90,000 ($93,000 − $3,000). The total gross sales value of the two main products is $90,000 ($40,000 + $50,000). Of this total value, $40,000 should be allocated to Alfa [($40,000 ÷ $90,000) × $90,000].
Answer (A) is incorrect because $36,000 is based on 40%, not 4/9. Answer (C) is incorrect because $41,333 fails to adjust the joint cost by the value of the by-product. Answer (D) is incorrect because $50,000 is the joint cost allocated to Betters.

## 7.8 Standard Costing and Variance Analysis

Questions 30 and 31 are based on the following information.

A company produces a gasoline additive. The standard costs and input for a 500-liter batch of the additive are presented below.

| Chemical | Standard Input Quantity in Liters | Standard Cost per Liter | Total Cost |
|---|---|---|---|
| Echol | 200 | $.200 | $ 40.00 |
| Protex | 100 | .425 | 42.50 |
| Benz | 250 | .150 | 37.50 |
| CT-40 | 50 | .300 | 15.00 |
| | 600 | | $135.00 |

The quantities purchased and used during the current period are shown below. A total of 140 batches were made during the current period.

| Chemical | Quantity Pur-chased (Liters) | Total Purchase Price | Quantity Used (Liters) |
|---|---|---|---|
| Echol | 25,000 | $ 5,365 | 26,600 |
| Protex | 13,000 | 6,240 | 12,880 |
| Benz | 40,000 | 5,840 | 37,800 |
| CT-40 | 7,500 | 2,220 | 7,140 |
| Total | 85,500 | $19,665 | 84,420 |

**30.** What is the materials mix variance for this operation?

    A. $294 favorable.

    B. $388.50 favorable.

    C. $94.50 unfavorable.

    D. $219.50 favorable.

Answer (B) is correct. *(Publisher)*
**REQUIRED:** The materials mix variance.
**DISCUSSION:** The materials mix variance equals the actual total quantity used times the difference between the budgeted weighted- average standard unit cost for the budgeted mix and the budgeted weighted-average standard unit cost for the actual mix. This variance is favorable if the standard weighted-average cost for the actual mix is less than the standard weighted-average cost for the budgeted mix. The standard mix weighted-average standard unit cost is $.225 per liter ($135 standard total cost ÷ 600 liters).
    The standard cost of the actual quantity used was $18,606 (see below). Thus, the actual mix weighted-average standard unit cost was $.220398 ($18,606 ÷ 84,420 liters used), and the mix variance was $388.50 favorable [($.220398 – $.225) × 84,420 liters].

$$
\begin{array}{rl}
.200 \times 26,600 = & \$ 5,320.00 \\
.425 \times 12,880 = & 5,474.00 \\
.150 \times 37,800 = & 5,670.00 \\
.300 \times 7,140 = & 2,142.00 \\
\hline
& \$18,606.00 \\
\end{array}
$$

    Answer (A) is incorrect because $294 favorable is the materials quantity variance. Answer (C) is incorrect because $94.50 unfavorable is the materials yield variance. Answer (D) is incorrect because $219.50 favorable is based on the actual mix of purchases.

**31.** What is the materials yield variance for this operation?

    A. $294.50 favorable.

    B. $388.50 favorable.

    C. $94.50 unfavorable.

    D. $219.50 favorable.

Answer (C) is correct. *(Publisher)*
**REQUIRED:** The materials yield variance.
**DISCUSSION:** The materials yield variance equals the difference between the actual input and the standard input allowed for the actual output, times the budgeted weighted-average standard cost per input unit at the standard mix. The standard input for the actual output was 84,000 liters (140 batches × 600 liters per batch). The standard mix budgeted weighted-average standard unit cost is $.225 per liter ($135 total cost ÷ 600 liters). Thus, the yield variance is $94.50 unfavorable [(84,420 liters used – 84,000 liters allowed) × $.225].
    Answer (A) is incorrect because $294.50 favorable is the materials quantity variance. Answer (B) is incorrect because $388.50 favorable is the materials mix variance. Answer (D) is incorrect because $219.50 favorable is based on the actual mix of purchases.

**32.** The following is a standard cost variance analysis report on direct labor cost for a division of a manufacturing company:

| Job | Actual Hours at Actual Wages | Actual Hours at Standard Wages | Standard Hours at Standard Wages |
|---|---|---|---|
| 213 | $3,243 | $3,700 | $3,100 |
| 215 | $15,345 | $15,675 | $15,000 |
| 217 | $6,754 | $7,000 | $6,600 |
| 219 | $19,788 | $18,755 | $19,250 |
| 221 | $3,370 | $3,470 | $2,650 |
| Totals | $48,500 | $48,600 | $46,600 |

What is the total flexible budget direct labor variance for the division?

A. $100 favorable.

B. $1,900 unfavorable.

C. $1,900 favorable.

D. $2,000 unfavorable.

Answer (B) is correct.  *(CIA, adapted)*
REQUIRED:  The total flexible budget direct labor variance.
DISCUSSION:  The total flexible budget direct labor variance equals the difference between total actual direct labor cost and standard direct labor cost allowed for the actual output.  It combines the direct labor rate and efficiency variances.  For this company, the variance is $1,900 unfavorable ($48,500 actual wages at actual hours – $46,600 standard wages at standard hours).
Answer (A) is incorrect because the direct labor rate variance is $100 favorable ($48,500 – $48,600).  Answer (C) is incorrect because the total labor variance is unfavorable.  Answer (D) is incorrect because the direct labor efficiency variance is $2,000 unfavorable.

---

Questions 33 through 35 are based on the following information.

Water Control Inc. manufactures water pumps and uses a standard cost system.  The standard factory overhead costs per water pump are based on direct labor hours and are as follows:

| | |
|---|---|
| Variable overhead (4 hours at $8/hour) | $32 |
| Fixed overhead (4 hours at $5*/hour) | 20 |
| Total overhead cost per unit | $52 |

*Based on a capacity of 100,000 direct labor hours per month.

The following additional information is available for the month of November:

- 22,000 pumps were produced although 25,000 had been scheduled for production.
- 94,000 direct labor hours were worked at a total cost of $940,000.
- The standard direct labor rate is $9 per hour.
- The standard direct labor time per unit is 4 hours.
- Variable overhead costs were $740,000.
- Fixed overhead costs were $540,000.

---

**33.** The fixed overhead spending variance for November was

A. $40,000 unfavorable.

B. $70,000 unfavorable.

C. $460,000 unfavorable.

D. $240,000 unfavorable.

Answer (A) is correct.  *(CMA, adapted)*
REQUIRED:  The fixed overhead spending variance.
DISCUSSION:  The fixed overhead spending (budget) variance is the difference between actual and budgeted fixed factory overhead.  Actual fixed overhead was $540,000.  Budgeted fixed overhead was $5 per hour based on a capacity of 100,000 direct labor hours per month, or $500,000.  Because these costs are fixed, the budgeted fixed overhead is the same at any level of production.  Hence, the variance is $40,000 unfavorable ($540,000 – $500,000).
Answer (B) is incorrect because $70,000 unfavorable is the difference between actual fixed overhead and the product of the standard rate and the actual direct labor hours.  Answer (C) is incorrect because $460,000 unfavorable is the volume variance.  Answer (D) is incorrect because $240,000 unfavorable is the difference between actual variable overhead and budgeted fixed overhead.

**34.** The variable overhead spending variance for November was

    A. $60,000 favorable.

    B. $12,000 favorable.

    C. $48,000 unfavorable.

    D. $40,000 unfavorable.

Answer (B) is correct. *(CMA, adapted)*
    **REQUIRED:** The variable overhead spending variance.
    **DISCUSSION:** The variable overhead spending variance is the difference between actual variable overhead and the variable overhead based on the standard rate and the actual activity level. Thus, the variable overhead spending variance was $12,000 favorable [$740,000 actual cost – ($8 standard rate × 94,000 actual hours)]. Because actual is less than standard, the variance was favorable.
    Answer (A) is incorrect because $60,000 favorable is based on 100,000 hours, not the actual hours of 94,000. Answer (C) is incorrect because $48,000 unfavorable is the variable overhead efficiency variance. Answer (D) is incorrect because $40,000 unfavorable is the fixed overhead spending variance.

**35.** The variable overhead efficiency variance for November was

    A. $48,000 unfavorable.

    B. $60,000 favorable.

    C. $96,000 unfavorable.

    D. $200,000 unfavorable.

Answer (A) is correct. *(CMA, adapted)*
    **REQUIRED:** The variable overhead efficiency variance.
    **DISCUSSION:** The variable overhead efficiency variance equals the standard price ($8 an hour) times the difference between the actual hours and the standard hours allowed for the actual output. Thus, the variance is $48,000 {$8 × [94,000 actual hours – (4 standard hours per unit × 22,000 units produced)]}. The variance is unfavorable because actual hours exceeded standard hours.
    Answer (B) is incorrect because $60,000 favorable is the variable overhead spending variance calculated based on capacity, not actual hours. Answer (C) is incorrect because $96,000 unfavorable is based on the difference between standard hours allowed for the actual output and capacity hours. Answer (D) is incorrect because $200,000 unfavorable is the excess of actual direct labor costs over actual variable overhead costs.

## 7.9 Types of Budgets

**36.** Individual budget schedules are prepared to develop an annual comprehensive or master budget. The budget schedule that would provide the necessary input data for the direct labor budget would be the

    A. Sales forecast.

    B. Raw materials purchases budget.

    C. Schedule of cash receipts and disbursements.

    D. Production budget.

Answer (D) is correct. *(CMA, adapted)*
    **REQUIRED:** The budget schedule that would provide the input data for the direct labor budget.
    **DISCUSSION:** A master budget typically begins with the preparation of a sales budget. The next step is to prepare a production budget. Once the production budget has been completed, the next step is to prepare the direct labor, raw material, and overhead budgets. Thus, the production budget provides the input necessary for the completion of the direct labor budget.
    Answer (A) is incorrect because the sales forecast is insufficient for completion of the direct labor budget. Answer (B) is incorrect because the raw material purchases budget is not needed to prepare a direct labor budget. Answer (C) is incorrect because the schedule of cash receipts and disbursements cannot be prepared until after the direct labor budget has been completed.

Questions 37 and 38 are based on the following information.

The Raymar Company is preparing its cash budget for the months of April and May. The firm has established a $200,000 line of credit with its bank at a 12% annual rate of interest on which borrowings for cash deficits must be made in $10,000 increments. There is no outstanding balance on the line of credit loan on April 1. Principal repayments are to be made in any month in which there is a surplus of cash. Interest is to be paid monthly. If there are no outstanding balances on the loans, Raymar will invest any cash in excess of its desired end-of-month cash balance in U.S. Treasury bills. Raymar intends to maintain a minimum balance of $100,000 at the end of each month by either borrowing for deficits below the minimum balance or investing any excess cash. Expected monthly collection and disbursement patterns are shown in the columns to the right.

- *Collections.* 50% of the current month's sales budget and 50% of the previous month's sales budget.
- *Accounts Payable Disbursements.* 75% of the current month's accounts payable budget and 25% of the previous month's accounts payable budget.
- All other disbursements occur in the month in which they are budgeted

### Budget Information

|  | March | April | May |
|---|---|---|---|
| Sales | $40,000 | $50,000 | $100,000 |
| Accounts payable | 30,000 | 40,000 | 40,000 |
| Payroll | 60,000 | 70,000 | 50,000 |
| Other disbursements | 25,000 | 30,000 | 10,000 |

**37.** In April, Raymar's budget will result in

A. $45,000 in excess cash.

B. A need to borrow $50,000 on its line of credit for the cash deficit.

C. A need to borrow $100,000 on its line of credit for the cash deficit.

D. A need to borrow $90,000 on its line of credit for the cash deficit.

Answer (C) is correct. *(CMA, adapted)*
**REQUIRED:** The effect on cash by the end of April.
**DISCUSSION:** Assuming Raymar maintained a $100,000 cash balance at the end of March, the amount to be borrowed or invested in April is the difference between cash receipts and disbursements. April's cash collections are $45,000 [(50% × $50,000 April sales) + (50% × $40,000 March sales)]. Disbursements for accounts payable are $37,500 [(75% × $40,000 April payables) + (25% × $30,000 March payables)]. In addition to the accounts payable disbursements, payroll and other disbursements will require an additional $100,000. Hence, total disbursements are estimated to be $137,500. The net negative cash flow (amount to be borrowed to reach the required minimum cash balance of $100,000) is $92,500 ($137,500 – $45,000). Because the line of credit must be drawn upon in $10,000 increments, the loan must be for $100,000.
Answer (A) is incorrect because $45,000 equals cash receipts. Answer (B) is incorrect because the cash deficit will be $92,500 without borrowing. Answer (D) is incorrect because a loan of only $90,000 would still leave a negative cash balance of $2,500.

**38.** In May, Raymar will be required to

A. Repay $20,000 principal and pay $1,000 interest.

B. Repay $90,000 principal and pay $100 interest.

C. Pay $900 interest.

D. Borrow an additional $20,000 and pay $1,000 interest.

Answer (D) is correct. *(CMA, adapted)*
**REQUIRED:** The transaction required in May.
**DISCUSSION:** The company will have to borrow $100,000 in April, which means that interest will have to be paid in May at the rate of 1% per month (12% annual rate). Consequently, interest expense is $1,000 (1% × $100,000). May receipts are $75,000 [(50% × $100,000 May sales) + (50% × $50,000 April sales)]. Disbursements in May are $40,000 [(75% × $40,000 May payables) + (25% × $40,000 April payables)]. In addition to the May accounts payable disbursements, payroll and other disbursements are $60,000, bringing total disbursements to $101,000 ($60,000 + $40,000 + $1,000). Thus, disbursements exceed receipts by $26,000 ($101,000 – $75,000). However, cash has a beginning surplus balance of $7,500 ($100,000 April loan – $92,500 negative cash flow for April). As a result, the company needs to borrow an additional $18,500 to eliminate its cash deficit. Given the requirement that loans be in $10,000 increments, the May loan must be for $20,000.
Answer (A) is incorrect because no funds are available to repay the loan. May receipts are less than May disbursements. Answer (B) is incorrect because the 1% interest is calculated on a $100,000 loan, not a $90,000 loan. Answer (C) is incorrect because the 1% interest is calculated on a $100,000 loan, not a $90,000 loan.

**39.** When sales volume is seasonal in nature, certain items in the budget must be coordinated. The three most significant items to coordinate in budgeting seasonal sales volume are

A. Production volume, finished goods inventory, and sales volume.

B. Direct labor hours, work-in-process inventory, and sales volume.

C. Raw material inventory, direct labor hours, and manufacturing overhead costs.

D. Raw material inventory, work-in-process inventory, and production volume.

Answer (A) is correct. *(CMA, adapted)*
**REQUIRED:** The three most significant items to coordinate in budgeting seasonal sales volume.
**DISCUSSION:** The most difficult items to coordinate in any budget, particularly for a seasonal business, are production volume, finished goods inventory, and sales. Budgets usually begin with sales volume and proceed to production volume, but the reverse is sometimes used when production is more of an issue than generation of sales. Inventory levels are also important because sales cannot occur without inventory, and the maintenance of high inventory levels is costly.
Answer (B) is incorrect because direct labor hours and work-in-process are only two components of a production budget. Answer (C) is incorrect because sales is usually the most important aspect of any budget. Answer (D) is incorrect because sales is usually the most important aspect of any budget.

**40.** Butteco has the following cost components for 100,000 units of product for 1998:

| | |
|---|---|
| Raw materials | $200,000 |
| Direct labor | 100,000 |
| Manufacturing overhead | 200,000 |
| Selling/administrative expense | 150,000 |

All costs are variable except for $100,000 of manufacturing overhead and $100,000 of selling and administrative expenses. The total costs to produce and sell 110,000 units during 1998 are

A. $650,000

B. $715,000

C. $695,000

D. $540,000

Answer (C) is correct. *(CMA, adapted)*
**REQUIRED:** The flexible budget costs for producing and selling a given quantity.
**DISCUSSION:** Raw materials unit costs are strictly variable at $2 ($200,000 ÷ 100,000 units). Similarly, direct labor has a variable unit cost of $1 ($100,000 ÷ 100,000 units). The $200,000 of manufacturing overhead for 100,000 units is 50%. The variable unit cost is $1. Selling costs are $100,000 fixed and $50,000 variable for production of 100,000 units, and the variable unit selling expense is $.50 ($50,000 ÷ 100,000 units). The total unit variable cost is therefore $4.50 ($2 + $1 + $1 + $.50). Fixed costs are $200,000. At a production level of 110,000 units, variable costs are $495,000 ($4.50 × 110,000 units). Hence, total costs are $695,000 ($495,000 + $200,000).
Answer (A) is incorrect because $650,000 is the cost at a production level of 100,000 units. Answer (B) is incorrect because $715,000 assumes a variable unit cost of $6.50 with no fixed costs. Answer (D) is incorrect because total costs are $695,000 based on a unit variable cost of $4.50 each.

**41.** Barnes Corporation expected to sell 150,000 board games during the month of November, and the company's master budget contained the following data related to the sale and production of these games:

| | |
|---|---|
| Revenue | $2,400,000 |
| Cost of goods sold | |
| Direct materials | 675,000 |
| Direct labor | 300,000 |
| Variable overhead | 450,000 |
| Contribution | $ 975,000 |
| Fixed overhead | 250,000 |
| Fixed selling/administration | 500,000 |
| Operating income | $ 225,000 |

Actual sales during November were 180,000 games. Using a flexible budget, the company expects the operating income for the month of November to be

A. $225,000

B. $270,000

C. $420,000

D. $510,000

Answer (C) is correct. *(CMA, adapted)*
**REQUIRED:** The expected operating income based on a flexible budget at a given production level.
**DISCUSSION:** Revenue of $2,400,000 reflects a unit selling price of $16 ($2,400,000 ÷ 150,000 games). The contribution margin is $975,000, or $6.50 per game ($975,000 ÷ 150,000 games). Thus, unit variable cost is $9.50 ($16 − $6.50). Increasing sales will result in an increased contribution margin of $195,000 (30,000 × $6.50). Assuming no additional fixed costs, net income will increase to $420,000 ($225,000 originally reported + $195,000).
Answer (A) is incorrect because $225,000 is the net income before the increase in sales. Answer (B) is incorrect because net income was originally $1.50 per game. The $270,000 figure simply extrapolates that amount to sales of 180,000 games. Answer (D) is incorrect because $510,000 assumes that variable overhead is fixed. Variable overhead is a $3 component ($450,000 ÷ 150,000 units) of unit variable cost.

**42.** The major feature of zero-base budgeting (ZBB) is that it

A. Takes the previous year's budgets and adjusts them for inflation.

B. Questions each activity and determines whether it should be maintained as it is, reduced, or eliminated.

C. Assumes all activities are legitimate and worthy of receiving budget increases to cover any increased costs.

D. Focuses on planned capital outlays for property, plant, and equipment.

Answer (B) is correct.  *(CIA, adapted)*
**REQUIRED:** The major feature of ZBB.
**DISCUSSION:** ZBB is a planning process in which each manager must justify his/her department's full budget for each period.  The purpose is to encourage periodic reexamination of all costs in the hope that some can be reduced or eliminated.
Answer (A) is incorrect because traditional or incremental budgeting takes the previous year's budgets and adjusts them for inflation.  Answer (C) is incorrect because traditional or incremental budgeting assumes all activities are legitimate and worthy of receiving budget increases to cover any increased costs.  Answer (D) is incorrect because it is a definition of a capital budget.

## 7.10 Capital Budgeting

Questions 43 and 44 are based on the following information.  A firm with an 18% cost of capital is considering the following projects (on January 1, 2001):

| | January 1, 2001 Cash Outflow (000's Omitted) | December 31, 2005 Cash Inflow (000's Omitted) | Project Internal Rate of Return |
|---|---|---|---|
| Project A | $3,500 | $7,400 | 16% |
| Project B | 4,000 | 9,950 | ? |

Present Value of $1 Due at the End of "N" Periods

| N | 12% | 14% | 15% | 16% | 18% | 20% | 22% |
|---|---|---|---|---|---|---|---|
| 4 | .6355 | .5921 | .5718 | .5523 | .5158 | .4823 | .4230 |
| 5 | .5674 | .5194 | .4972 | .4761 | .4371 | .4019 | .3411 |
| 6 | .5066 | .4556 | .4323 | .4104 | .3704 | .3349 | .2751 |

**43.** Using the net-present-value (NPV) method, project A's net present value is

A. $316,920

B. $23,140

C. $(265,460)

D. $(316,920)

Answer (C) is correct.  *(CIA, adapted)*
**REQUIRED:** The net present value of project A.
**DISCUSSION:** The cash inflow occurs 5 years after the cash outflow, and the NPV method uses the firm's cost of capital of 18%.  The present value of $1 due at the end of 5 years discounted at 18% is .4371.  Thus, the NPV of project A is $(265,460) [(.4371 × $7,400,000 cash inflow) – $3,500,000 cash outflow].
Answer (A) is incorrect because $316,920 discounts the cash inflow over a 4-year period.  Answer (B) is incorrect because $23,140 assumes a 16% discount rate.  Answer (D) is incorrect because $(316,920) discounts the cash inflow over a 4-year period and also subtracts the present value of the cash inflow from the cash outflow.

**44.** Project B's internal rate of return is closest to

A. 15%

B. 16%

C. 18%

D. 20%

Answer (D) is correct.  *(CIA, adapted)*
**REQUIRED:** The percentage closest to project B's internal rate of return.
**DISCUSSION:** The internal rate of return is the discount rate at which the NPV is zero.  Consequently, the cash outflow equals the present value of the inflow at the internal rate of return.  The present value of $1 factor for project B's internal rate of return is therefore .4020 ($4,000,000 cash outflow ÷ $9,950,000 cash inflow).  This factor is closest to the present value of $1 for 5 periods at 20%.
Answer (A) is incorrect because 15% results in a positive NPV for project B.  Answer (B) is incorrect because 16% is the approximate internal rate of return for project A.  Answer (C) is incorrect because 18% is the company's cost of capital.

**45.** Everything else being equal, the internal rate of return (IRR) of an investment project will be lower if

A. The investment cost is lower.

B. Cash inflows are received later in the life of the project.

C. Cash inflows are larger.

D. The project has a shorter payback period.

Answer (B) is correct. *(CIA, adapted)*
**REQUIRED:** The true statement about the IRR.
**DISCUSSION:** The IRR is the discount rate at which the net present value is zero. Because the present value of a dollar is higher the sooner it is received, projects with later cash flows will have lower net present values for any given discount rate than will projects with earlier cash flows, if other factors are constant. Hence, projects with later cash flows will have a lower IRR.
Answer (A) is incorrect because the present value of the cash inflows is inversely related to the discount rate; that is, if the discount rate is higher, the present value of the cash inflows is lower. If the investment cost is lower, a higher discount rate (the IRR) will be required to set the net present value equal to zero. Answer (C) is incorrect because the larger the cash inflows, the higher the IRR will be. Higher cash inflows have a higher present value at any given discount rate. A higher discount rate will be required to set the net present value equal to zero. Answer (D) is incorrect because projects with shorter payback periods have higher cash inflows early in the life of the project. Projects with earlier cash inflows have higher IRRs.

## 7.11 Relevant Costs

**46.** A manufacturing company's primary goals include product quality and customer satisfaction. The company sells a product, for which the market demand is strong, for $50 per unit. Due to the capacity constraints in the Production Department, only 300,000 units can be produced per year. The current defective rate is 12% (i.e., of the 300,000 units produced, only 264,000 units are sold and 36,000 units are scrapped). There is no revenue recovery when defective units are scrapped. The full manufacturing cost of a unit is $29.50, including

| | |
|---|---|
| Direct materials | $17.50 |
| Direct labor | 4.00 |
| Fixed manufacturing overhead | 8.00 |

The company's designers have estimated that the defective rate can be reduced to 2% by using a different direct material. However, this will increase the direct materials cost by $2.50 per unit to $20 per unit. The net benefit of using the new material to manufacture the product will be

A. $(120,000)

B. $120,000

C. $750,000

D. $1,425,000

Answer (C) is correct. *(CIA, adapted)*
**REQUIRED:** The net benefit of using the new material.
**DISCUSSION:** If a different direct material is used, incremental revenue will be $1,500,000 {[(12% defect rate – 2%) × 300,000 units] × $50}. Incremental cost will be $750,000 ($2.50 × 300,000 units). Thus, the net benefit will be $750,000 ($1,500,000 – $750,000).
Answer (A) is incorrect because $(120,000) considers only the production costs of the good units sold. Moreover, it includes fixed overhead, a cost that is not affected by the choice of materials. Answer (B) is incorrect because $120,000 considers only the variable costs of the good units produced. Answer (D) is incorrect because $1,425,000 includes only the incremental direct materials cost of the increase in the number of good units produced.

Questions 47 through 49 are based on the following information. The segmented income statement for a retail company with three product lines is presented below:

| | Total Company | Product Line 1 | Product Line 2 | Product Line 3 |
|---|---|---|---|---|
| Volume (in units) | | 20,000 | 28,000 | 50,000 |
| Sales revenue | $2,000,000 | $800,000 | $700,000 | $500,000 |
| Costs & expenses: | | | | |
| Administrative | $ 180,000 | $ 60,000 | $ 60,000 | $ 60,000 |
| Advertising | 240,000 | 96,000 | 84,000 | 60,000 |
| Commissions | 40,000 | 16,000 | 14,000 | 10,000 |
| Cost of sales | 980,000 | 360,000 | 420,000 | 200,000 |
| Rent | 280,000 | 84,000 | 140,000 | 56,000 |
| Salaries | 110,000 | 54,000 | 32,000 | 24,000 |
| Total costs & expenses | $1,830,000 | $670,000 | $750,000 | $410,000 |
| Operating income (loss) | $ 170,000 | $130,000 | $ (50,000) | $ 90,000 |

The company buys the goods in the three product lines directly from manufacturers' representatives. Each product line is directed by a manager whose salary is included in the administrative expenses. Administrative expenses are allocated to the three product lines equally because the administration is spread evenly among the three product lines. Salaries represent payments to the workers in each product line and therefore are traceable costs of each product line. Advertising promotes the entire company rather than the individual product lines. As a result, the advertising is allocated to the three product lines in proportion to the sales revenue. Commissions are paid to the salespersons in each product line based on 2% of gross sales. Rent represents the cost of the retail store and warehouse under a lease agreement with 5 years remaining. The product lines share the retail and warehouse space, and the rent is allocated to the three product lines based on the square footage occupied by each of the product lines.

**47.** The company has an opportunity to promote one of its product lines by making a one-time $7,000 expenditure. The company can choose only one of the three product lines to promote. The incremental sales revenue that would be realized from this $7,000 promotion expenditure in each of the product lines is estimated as follows:

| | Increase in Sales Revenue |
|---|---|
| Product Line 1 | $15,000 |
| Product Line 2 | 20,000 |
| Product Line 3 | 14,000 |

In order to maximize profits, the promotion expenditure should be spent on <List A>, resulting in an increase in operating income of <List B>.

| | List A | List B |
|---|---|---|
| A. | Product Line 2 | $13,000 |
| B. | Product Line 2 | $ 5,000 |
| C. | Product Line 3 | $ 1,400 |
| D. | Product Line 3 | $ 1,120 |

Answer (D) is correct.   *(CIA, adapted)*

**REQUIRED:** The product line to be promoted by a one-time advertising expenditure and the resulting income increase.

**DISCUSSION:** Fixed costs should be ignored. Thus, the increase in sales revenue should be multiplied by the contribution margin ratio for each product line. The incremental promotion cost ($7,000) is subtracted from this amount to determine the marginal benefit of promoting each product line. Hence, Product Line 3 has an increased profit of $1,120.

Calculation of Contribution Margin

| | Total Company | Product Line 1 | Product Line 2 | Product Line 3 |
|---|---|---|---|---|
| Sales revenue | $2,000,000 | $800,000 | $700,000 | $500,000 |
| Variable costs | | | | |
| Commissions | $ 40,000 | $ 16,000 | $ 14,000 | $ 10,000 |
| Cost of sales | 980,000 | 360,000 | 420,000 | 200,000 |
| Total | $1,020,000 | $376,000 | $434,000 | $210,000 |
| CM | $ 980,000 | $424,000 | $266,000 | $290,000 |
| CMR | 49% | 53% | 38% | 58% |
| Revenue | | $ 15,000 | $ 20,000 | $ 14,000 |
| CMR | | .53 | .38 | .58 |
| CM | | $ 7,950 | $ 7,600 | $ 8,120 |
| Promotion cost | | 7,000 | 7,000 | 7,000 |
| Increased profits | | $ 950 | $ 600 | $ 1,120 |

Answer (A) is incorrect because Product Line 2 has an increased profit of $600. Answer (B) is incorrect because Product Line 2 has an increased profit of $600. Answer (C) is incorrect because $1,400 omits the commissions from the calculation.

**48.** One company executive has expressed concern about the operating loss that has occurred in Product Line 2 and has suggested that Product Line 2 be discontinued. If Product Line 2 is dropped, the manager of the line would be retained and assigned other duties with the company, but the other employees would not be retained. Management has indicated that the nature of the company's advertising might change with the elimination of Product Line 2, but the total dollar amount would not change. If Product Line 2 were to be dropped, the operating income of the company would

A. Increase by $50,000.

B. Decrease by $94,000.

C. Decrease by $234,000.

D. Increase by $416,000.

Answer (C) is correct. *(CIA, adapted)*
REQUIRED: The operating income effect of dropping a product line.
DISCUSSION: The operating income will decrease. Product Line 2 income will be lost, but only the traceable costs of commissions, cost of sales, and salaries will be avoided. Accordingly, the decrease will be $234,000 [-$700,000 + ($14,000 + 420,000 + 32,000)]. The other shared costs will have to be absorbed by the two remaining product lines.
Answer (A) is incorrect because an increase of $50,000 assumes the revenue will be lost and all of its costs will be avoided. Answer (B) is incorrect because a decrease of $94,000 results from treating rent as an avoidable cost. Answer (D) is incorrect because an increase of $416,000 subtracts the costs that will not be avoided if Product Line 2 is dropped from the lost sales revenue.

**49.** A customer, operating in an isolated foreign market, has approached the head salesperson for Product Line 1 and offered to purchase 4,000 units of a special-order product over the next 12 months. This product would be sold in the same manner as Product Line 1's other products except that the customer is hoping for a price break. Product Line 1's cost to purchase this product (cost of sales) would be $14.70. Product Line 1 has excess capacity, meaning that the rate or amount of the remaining operating costs would not change as a consequence of the purchase and sale of this special-order product. The minimum selling price for this special-order product would be

A. $15.00

B. $17.30

C. $27.50

D. $30.20

Answer (A) is correct. *(CIA, adapted)*
REQUIRED: The minimum selling price for a special-order product.
DISCUSSION: Product Line 1 needs to cover its variable out-of-pocket costs as a minimum on this special-order product; therefore, any selling price greater than the variable cost will contribute towards profits. Thus, the minimum selling price of the special-order product is the variable cost divided by 1 minus the commission rate, or $15 [$14.70 ÷ (1.0 − .02)].
Answer (B) is incorrect because $17.30 includes the average cost of salaries (at the new volume level of 24,000 units) as a cost that needs to be covered when determining the minimum selling price. Answer (C) is incorrect because $27.50 is calculated based on a full cost approach. Answer (D) is incorrect because $30.20 adds all costs and expenses (except cost of sales) and divides them by the original volume level of 20,000 units to determine the average operating costs. The new cost of sales is added to the average operating costs to determine the minimum selling price.

**50.** The ABC Company manufactures components for use in producing one of its finished products. When 12,000 units are produced, the full cost per unit is $35, separated as follows:

| | |
|---|---|
| Direct materials | $ 5 |
| Direct labor | 15 |
| Variable overhead | 10 |
| Fixed overhead | 5 |

The XYZ Company has offered to sell 12,000 components to ABC for $37 each. If ABC accepts the offer, some of the facilities currently being used to manufacture the components can be rented as warehouse space for $40,000. However, $3 of the fixed overhead currently applied to each component would have to be covered by ABC's other products. What is the differential cost to the ABC Company of purchasing the components from the XYZ Company?

A. $8,000

B. $20,000

C. $24,000

D. $44,000

Answer (B) is correct. *(CIA, adapted)*
REQUIRED: The differential cost of purchasing the components.
DISCUSSION: Differential (incremental) cost is the difference in total cost between two decisions. The relevant costs do not include unavoidable costs, such as the $3 of fixed overhead. It would cost ABC an additional $20,000 to purchase, rather than manufacture, the components.

| | |
|---|---|
| Cost to purchase ($37 × 12,000) | $444,000 |
| Minus rental income | (40,000) |
| | $404,000 |
| Cost to manufacture ($32 × 12,000) | $384,000 |
| Cost differential | $ 20,000 |

Answer (A) is incorrect because $8,000 assumes that $3 of fixed overhead is avoidable. Answer (C) is incorrect because $24,000 compares the full cost of manufacturing with cost to purchase. Answer (D) is incorrect because $44,000 ignores the opportunity cost.

Questions 51 and 52 are based on the following information.

A business needs a computer application that can be either developed internally or purchased. Suitable software from a vendor costs $29,000. Minor modifications and testing can be conducted by the systems staff as part of their regular workload.

If the software is developed internally, a systems analyst would be assigned full time, and a contractor would assume the analyst's responsibilities. The hourly rate for the regular analyst is $25. The hourly rate for the contractor is $22. The contractor would occupy an empty office. The office has 100 square feet, and occupancy cost is $45 per square foot.

Other related data are as follows. Computer time is charged using predetermined rates. The organization has sufficient excess computer capacity for either software development or modification/testing of the purchased software.

|  | Internal Development | Purchased Software |
|---|---|---|
| Systems analyst time in hours |  |  |
| Development | 1,000 | N/A |
| Modifications and testing | N/A | 40 |
| Computer charges | $800 | $250 |
| Additional hardware purchases | $3,200 | N/A |
| Incidental supplies | $500 | $200 |

**51.** When applying the cost-benefit approach to a decision, the primary criterion is how well management goals will be achieved in relation to costs. Costs include all expected

A. Variable costs for the courses of action but not expected fixed costs because only the expected variable costs are relevant.

B. Incremental out-of-pocket costs as well as all expected continuing costs that are common to all the alternative courses of action.

C. Future costs that differ among the alternative courses of action plus all qualitative factors that cannot be measured in numerical terms.

D. Historical and future costs relative to the courses of action including all qualitative factors that cannot be measured in numerical terms.

Answer (C) is correct. *(CIA, adapted)*
REQUIRED: The costs included in the cost-benefit approach.
DISCUSSION: The analysis of a make-or-buy decision is based on relevant costs. If costs do not vary with the option chosen, they are irrelevant. Moreover, the decision may be based on nonquantitative factors, for example, the desire to maintain a relationship with a vendor or to assume control over development of a product.
Answer (A) is incorrect because variable and fixed costs may be relevant or irrelevant. Answer (B) is incorrect because expected incremental out-of-pocket expenses should be considered, but common costs should not. Answer (D) is incorrect because historical costs are not relevant to cost-benefit analysis because they are sunk costs.

**52.** Based solely on the cost figures presented, the cost of developing the computer application will be

A. $3,500 less than acquiring the purchased software package.

B. $500 less than acquiring the purchased software package.

C. $1,550 more than acquiring the purchased software package.

D. $3,550 more than acquiring the purchased software package.

Answer (A) is correct. *(CIA, adapted)*
REQUIRED: The comparison of the costs of developing and purchasing software.
DISCUSSION: Development cost equals the cost of the outside contractor plus the costs for hardware and supplies. Computer charges are transfer prices and do not require additional expenditures, given idle capacity. The relevant cost of supplies is $300 ($500 – $200 cost if the software is purchased). The contractor's use of an otherwise idle office is not relevant. Thus, the relevant cost of development is $25,500 [($22 hourly cost of the contractor × 1,000 hours) + $3,200 hardware purchases + $300 incremental cost of supplies]. This amount is $3,500 less than the $29,000 cost of purchase. A systems analyst's work on the new software is not relevant. It is part of the regular workload.
Answer (B) is incorrect because the contractor is not paid $25 per hour. Answer (C) is incorrect because $550 in computer charges and $4,500 in occupancy charges should not be included. Answer (D) is incorrect because the contractor is not paid $25 per hour, and 40 hours of modification and testing, $550 of the computer charges, and the occupancy costs are irrelevant.

**53.** A company manufactures a product that is sold for $37.95. It uses an absorption-cost system. Plant capacity is 750,000 units annually, but normal volume is 500,000 units. Costs at normal volume are given below.

| | Unit Cost | Total Cost |
|---|---|---|
| Direct materials | $ 9.80 | $4,900,000 |
| Direct labor | 4.50 | 2,250,000 |
| Manufacturing overhead | 12.00 | 6,000,000 |
| Selling and administrative: Variable | 2.50 | 1,250,000 |
| Fixed | 4.20 | 2,100,000 |
| Total cost | $33.00 | $16,500,000 |

Fixed manufacturing overhead is budgeted at $4.5 million. A customer has offered to purchase 100,000 units at $25.00 each to be packaged in large cartons, not the normal individual containers. It will pick up the units in its own trucks. Thus, variable selling and administrative expenses will decrease by 60%. The company should compare the total revenue to be derived from this order with the total relevant costs of

A. $1,830,000

B. $1,880,000

C. $2,930,000

D. $3,150,000

Answer (A) is correct. *(CIA, adapted)*
REQUIRED: The total relevant costs of the special order.
DISCUSSION: The necessary assumptions are that all fixed costs and the unit variable costs of direct materials, direct labor, and variable manufacturing overhead are not affected by the special order. Hence, the fixed costs are not relevant. The unit costs of direct materials and direct labor are given as $9.80 and $4.50, respectively. The unit variable manufacturing overhead cost is $3.00 [($6,000,000 total manufacturing overhead – $4,500,000 total fixed manufacturing overhead) ÷ 500,000 units normal volume]. The unit variable selling and administrative cost is $1.00 [$2.50 × (1.0 – .6)]. Consequently, the total relevant cost of the special order is $1,830,000 [100,000 units × ($9.80 + $4.50 + $3.00 + $1.00)].
Answer (B) is incorrect because variable manufacturing per unit is determined by using normal volume, not plant capacity, as the denominator level. Answer (C) is incorrect because the total relevant cost of the special order is $1,830,000 [100,000 units × ($9.80 + $4.50 + $3.00 + $1.00)]. Answer (D) is incorrect because fixed selling and administrative expenses of $4.20 per unit should not be included. Furthermore, variable manufacturing of $3 per unit, not total manufacturing overhead of $12 per unit, should be used in the calculation of relevant costs.

## 7.12 Transfer Pricing

**54.** A large manufacturing company has several autonomous divisions that sell their products in perfectly competitive external markets as well as internally to the other divisions of the company. Top management expects each of its divisional managers to take actions that will maximize the organization's goals as well as their own goals. Top management also promotes a sustained level of management effort of all of its divisional managers. Under these circumstances, for products exchanged between divisions, the transfer price that will generally lead to optimal decisions for the manufacturing company would be a transfer price equal to the

A. Full cost of the product.

B. Full cost of the product plus a markup.

C. Variable cost of the product plus a markup.

D. Market price of the product.

Answer (D) is correct. *(CIA, adapted)*
REQUIRED: The optimal transfer price.
DISCUSSION: A market price transfer price promotes goal congruence and a sustained level of management effort. It is also consistent with divisional autonomy. A market transfer price is most appropriate when the market is competitive, interdivisional dependency is low, and buying in the market involves no marginal costs or benefits.
Answer (A) is incorrect because a transfer at full cost means that the selling division will not make a profit. In addition, the selling division may be forgoing profits that could be obtained by selling to outside customers. Thus, full-cost transfer prices can lead to suboptimal decisions. Answer (B) is incorrect because a transfer at full cost plus markup results in no incentive for the selling division to control its costs. Hence, a sustained level of management effort may not be maintained. Answer (C) is incorrect because a transfer at variable cost plus markup has the same weaknesses as full cost plus markup.

**55.** The Eastern division sells goods internally to the Western division of the same company. The quoted external price in industry publications from a supplier near Eastern is $200 per ton plus transportation. It costs $20 per ton to transport the goods to Western. Eastern's actual market cost per ton to buy the direct materials to make the transferred product is $100. Actual per ton direct labor is $50. Other actual costs of storage and handling are $40. The company president selects a $220 transfer price. This is an example of

A. Market-based transfer pricing.

B. Cost-based transfer pricing.

C. Negotiated transfer pricing.

D. Cost-plus-20% transfer pricing.

Answer (A) is correct. *(CIA, adapted)*
**REQUIRED:** The type of transfer price.
**DISCUSSION:** A transfer price is the price charged by one segment of an organization for a product or service supplied to another segment of the same organization. The three basic criteria that the transfer pricing system in a decentralized company should satisfy are to (1) provide information allowing central management to evaluate divisions with respect to total company profit and each division's contribution to profit, (2) stimulate each manager's efficiency without losing each division's autonomy, and (3) motivate each divisional manager to achieve his/her own profit goal in a manner contributing to the company's success. Because the $220 transfer price selected is based on the quoted external price (market), it is an example of market-based transfer pricing.
Answer (B) is incorrect because the cost-based price would be $210 ($100 + $50 + $40 + $20). Answer (C) is incorrect because no negotiations took place. Answer (D) is incorrect because cost plus 20% would be $252 ($210 × 1.20).

**56.** Division A of a company is currently operating at 50% capacity. It produces a single product and sells all its production to outside customers for $13 per unit. Variable costs are $7 per unit, and fixed costs are $6 per unit at the current production level. Division B, which currently purchases this product from an outside supplier for $12 per unit, would like to purchase the product from Division A. Division A will operate at 80% capacity to meet outside customers' and Division B's demand. What is the minimum price that Division A should charge Division B for this product?

A. $7.00 per unit.

B. $10.40 per unit.

C. $12.00 per unit.

D. $13.00 per unit.

Answer (A) is correct. *(CIA, adapted)*
**REQUIRED:** The minimum price that should be charged by one division of a company to another.
**DISCUSSION:** From the seller's perspective, the price should reflect at least its incremental cash outflow (outlay cost) plus the contribution from an outside sale (opportunity cost). Because A has idle capacity, the opportunity cost is $0. Thus, the minimum price Division A should charge Division B is $7.00.
Answer (B) is incorrect because $7.00 is the minimum that should be charged. Answer (C) is incorrect because Division A should not include any fixed costs in its transfer price because Division A has idle capacity. Answer (D) is incorrect because, since Division A has idle capacity, the minimum transfer price should recover Division A's variable (outlay) costs.

## 7.13 Responsibility Systems

**57.** A segment of an organization is referred to as a service center if it has

A. Responsibility for developing markets and selling the output of the organization.

B. Responsibility for combining the raw materials, direct labor, and other factors of production into a final output.

C. Authority to make decisions affecting the major determinants of profit including the power to choose its markets and sources of supply.

D. Authority to provide specialized support to other units within the organization.

Answer (D) is correct. *(CMA, adapted)*
**REQUIRED:** The definition of a service center.
**DISCUSSION:** A service center exists primarily and sometimes solely to provide specialized support to other units within the organization. Service centers are usually operated as cost centers.
Answer (A) is incorrect because a service center has no responsibility for developing markets or selling. Answer (B) is incorrect because a production center is engaged in manufacturing. Answer (C) is incorrect because a profit center can choose its markets and sources of supply.

**58.** Which of the following techniques would be best for evaluating the management performance of a department that is operated as a cost center?

    A. Return on assets ratio.

    B. Return on investment ratio.

    C. Payback method.

    D. Variance analysis.

Answer (D) is correct. *(CIA, adapted)*
**REQUIRED:** The best method for evaluating a cost center.
**DISCUSSION:** A cost center is a responsibility center that is responsible for costs only. Of the alternatives given, variance analysis is the only one that can be used in a cost center. Variance analysis involves comparing actual costs with predicted or standard costs.
Answer (A) is incorrect because return on assets cannot be computed for a cost center. The manager is not responsible for revenue (return) or the assets available. Answer (B) is incorrect because return on investments cannot be computed for a cost center. The manager is not responsible for revenue (return) or the assets available. Answer (C) is incorrect because the payback method is a means of evaluating alternative investment proposals.

**59.** Decentralized firms can delegate authority and yet retain control and monitor managers' performance by structuring the organization into responsibility centers. Which one of the following organizational segments is most like an independent business?

    A. Revenue center.

    B. Profit center.

    C. Cost center.

    D. Investment center.

Answer (D) is correct. *(CMA, adapted)*
**REQUIRED:** The organizational segment most like an independent business.
**DISCUSSION:** An investment center is the organizational type most like an independent business because it is responsible for its own revenues, costs incurred, and capital invested. The other types of centers do not incorporate all three elements.
Answer (A) is incorrect because a revenue center is responsible only for revenue generation, not for costs or capital investment. Answer (B) is incorrect because a profit center is responsible for revenues and costs but not for invested capital. Answer (C) is incorrect because a cost center is evaluated only on the basis of costs incurred. It is not responsible for revenues or invested capital.

---

Use Gleim's *CIA Test Prep* for interactive testing with over 2,000 additional multiple-choice questions!

# STUDY UNIT EIGHT
# REGULATORY, LEGAL, AND ECONOMIC ISSUES

(17 pages of outline)

This study unit discusses the impact of government regulation and the economic environment on business. The first subunit covers major organizations and treaties that affect international trade and the trade restrictions that they attempt to reduce. The next subunit discusses various tax structures and their effects on business. The third subunit describes key economic indicators such as the gross domestic product and other national income concepts, various forecasting measures, inflation indexes, the balance of payments, and the definitions of the money supply. The fourth subunit outlines the legal rules of evidence. The next subunit addresses the nature and essential elements of contract-based agreements. The final subunit applies to internal audit engagements for monitoring and evaluating the performance of certain contracts.

## 8.1 INTERNATIONAL TRADE INSTITUTIONS AND AGREEMENTS

1. **International Monetary System**

    a. Subsequent to World War II, international monetary crises have periodically been in the news. Economic conditions have changed rapidly. Following is a brief description of events that have helped shape today's monetary situation.

    1) Prior to 1944, the world was on a **gold standard** under which the basic unit of currency was equal to and exchangeable for a specified amount of gold. The monetary system that prevailed in the post-World War II period was devised in 1944. It was a system of fixed exchange rates based on a modified gold standard. International reserves in this system included foreign currencies and the right to borrow in specified situations. The **International Monetary Fund (IMF)** was created and is still active today.

        a) Resources of the IMF consist of a pool of currency from which participating countries can draw during short-term balance of payments difficulties.

        b) The **World Bank** was created at the same time as the IMF. Its purpose is to provide credit for development purposes to underdeveloped countries.

    2) In the post-war years, the U.S. dollar became the world's key currency used for transactions and reserves.

    3) By the mid-1950s, fixed exchange rates and changing economic conditions turned the dollar shortage into a dollar glut. Holders tried to convert dollars to other currencies, causing the dollar to decline in value.

    4) In the early 1970s, convertibility of gold into dollars was abolished by the U.S., breaking down the entire fixed-rate international system. Most countries agreed to allow the currencies to float to determine the new rates, but these countries would frequently intervene in support of their currencies.

5) In 1976, the leading noncommunist nations developed a system called the **Jamaica Agreement**. This agreement moved the world to a system of managed floating exchange rates. Each country had greater autonomy in managing its exchange rate.

b. **Eurodollars** are U.S. dollars held at banks outside of the U.S., either foreign banks or branches of U.S. banks. The growth in the use of Eurodollars has been spectacular because they facilitate the exchange of goods between other nations (often the exchanges use dollars even if the U.S. is not involved in the transaction).

1) Because it is outside the direct control of the U.S. monetary authorities, the Eurodollar market has lower costs. For example, U.S. reserve requirements and Federal Deposit Insurance Corporation (FDIC) premium payments do not apply in this market. A lower cost market can offer depositors higher interest rates.

2) **Eurobonds** are sold in one country but denominated in the currency of another country. Their advantage is that they are usually less stringently regulated than most other bonds. Thus, transaction costs are lower. They are not always denominated in Eurodollars.

c. The **euro** is the new common currency adopted by most members of the European Union. Its phase-in period began in 1999. In 2002, national notes and coins were withdrawn from use and replaced with euro notes and coins.

2. **Multinational Corporations**

a. The **home country** benefits from multinational operations because of improved earnings and exports of products to foreign subsidiaries. A multinational corporation may also be better able to obtain scarce resources than a domestic corporation. The existence of multinationals tends to benefit everyone to the extent they foster more international trade, freer trading policies, a better international monetary system, and improved international understanding.

1) The home country, however, may suffer adverse balance of payments effects as a result of investment in foreign nations. Jobs may be lost to foreign subsidiaries, unions weakened, and tax revenues diminished. The multinational may also have a competitive advantage over domestic rivals. Furthermore, multinationals incur greater risk of expropriation and reduced flexibility of operation in a foreign political system.

b. The **host country** for a multinational operation reaps the advantages of the investment of capital, technology, and management abilities. Output and efficiency often improve along with exports and the balance of payments. The presence of a multinational may stimulate competition, increase tax revenues, and produce a higher standard of living.

1) But payment of royalties, dividends, and profits can result in a net capital outflow. Multinationals sometimes establish economically unreasonable transfer prices among subsidiaries so that profits will be earned where taxes are lowest or restrictions on the export of profits are least stringent. Moreover, multinationals may engage in anticompetitive activities, such as formation of cartels.

3. **International trade agreements** provide regulatory authority for businesses in international trade. Until recently, the broadest and most important of these agreements was the **General Agreement on Tariffs and Trade (GATT)**. Under GATT, the signatory countries agreed to equal treatment of all member nations, multilateral negotiations to reduce tariffs, and the abolition of import quotas.

   a. However, GATT was replaced by the **World Trade Organization (WTO)**. The WTO, which was established on January 1, 1995, is the product of the Uruguay Round of international trade negotiations. It is a permanent body with a secretariat based in Geneva, Switzerland.

      1) The **WTO Agreement** is a permanent set of commitments by more than 120 nations designed to prohibit trade discrimination among member nations and between imported and domestic products. Most of the rules of GATT are still applicable with respect to trade in goods.

         a) The WTO Agreement applies to trade in **services and intellectual property** as well as goods. In addition to market access, the WTO's mandate also extends to antidumping rules, subsidies and countervailing measures, import licensing, rules of origin, technical barriers to trade, sanitary measures, emergency protection from imports ("safeguards"), and preshipment inspection.

         b) A multilateral **dispute settlement** apparatus has been established. If bilateral consultations and mediation efforts fail, a panel is established to examine the case and make recommendations. If a violation is found, trade retaliation by the complainant against an offending country may be approved if that country does not comply with the recommendations.

4. The **North American Free Trade Agreement (NAFTA)** was enacted in late 1993. The agreement essentially provides for free trade among the U.S., Canada, and Mexico. The pact creates the world's largest free trade zone, stretching from the Yukon to the Yucatan. Three nations and 360 million people are linked into one economic unit.

   a. The consensus is that Mexico will benefit the most by the agreement because many U.S. firms are likely to transfer assembly operations to Mexican subsidiaries with lower labor costs.

      1) NAFTA is intended to correct the disparities between the open markets of the U.S. and the relatively closed markets of Mexico. U.S. companies should be able to sell more goods to Mexico because Mexicans will have greater disposable income because new industries will relocate there.

      2) The biggest objection to NAFTA in the U.S. is that it causes the loss of jobs to Mexico due to the lower labor costs and the more lax environmental standards. Supporters of NAFTA claim that the pact will create more jobs in the U.S. than it eliminates, because of the increase in exports. However, trade between the U.S. and Mexico has increased, with the U.S. now exporting considerably more to Mexico.

      3) The U.S. financial services industry, such as mutual funds, banks, and brokers, should benefit by NAFTA because the agreement allows U.S. financial firms, for the first time, to have easy access to Mexican investors. Also, with the opening of Mexico's financial markets, more opportunities for U.S. investors should emerge.

      4) American industries such as shoe makers, apparel manufacturers, and farmers, may be hurt by increased competition from cheaper Mexican products.

      5) High-tech firms in the U.S. may benefit because there will be few Mexican products to compete against and exports will expand. Moreover, NAFTA establishes uniform legal standards for the protection of intellectual property.

   b.  **Transition rules.** NAFTA ended tariffs on about half of the more than 9,000 products covered by the agreement. Tariffs on another 15% of the goods were to end in 1998, and the rest of the products are to be duty-free by 2008.

   1)  One of the biggest controversies during negotiations was determining the products to be protected with the longest tariff phaseouts. The U.S. won long phaseouts for such items as sneakers, household glassware, asparagus, broccoli, peanuts, and orange juice concentrate.

   2)  Negotiation of import and export restrictions was an important aspect of setting the transition rules for NAFTA. For example, the "infant-industry argument" contends that protective tariffs are needed to allow new domestic industries to become established.

   3)  An extension of the infant-industry argument is the "strategic trade policy argument," which contends that a government should use trade barriers strategically to reduce the risk of product development borne by domestic firms, particularly for products involving advanced technology.

   c.  The theory behind **free trade zones** is that they benefit consumers by lowering prices and that manufacturers and workers gain from expanded markets for the items each country produces most efficiently.

5.  **Trade Restrictions**

   a.  Even though individuals (as a whole) are best off under free trade, governments often establish protectionist policies designed to block or restrict the importation of certain products, to encourage exports, or even to restrict exports.

   1)  **Tariffs** are taxes designed to restrict imports and lower consumption.

   a)  **Antidumping rules** prevent foreign producers from selling excess goods on the domestic market at less than cost to eliminate competitors.

   2)  **Import quotas** set fixed limits on different products. In the short run, they help a country's balance of payments by increasing domestic employment, but the prices of the products produced will also increase.

   a)  An **embargo** is a total ban on some kinds of imports.

   3)  **Domestic content rules** require that at least a portion of any imported product be constructed from parts manufactured in the importing nation. This rule is sometimes used by capital-intensive nations. Parts can be produced using idle capacity and then sent to a labor-intensive country for final assembly.

   4)  **Exchange controls** limit the amount of foreign currency transactions. They also set exchange rates with other currencies. These controls limit the ability of a firm selling in a country to repatriate its export earnings.

   5)  **Export subsidies** are payments by the government to producers in certain industries in an attempt to increase exports. A government may also impose **countervailing duties** on imports if those goods were produced in a foreign country with the aid of a subsidy.

   6)  **Special tax benefits to exporters** are an indirect form of export subsidy. For example, Foreign Sales Corporations (FSCs) are entities located in U.S. possessions or in countries with tax information exchange agreements with the U.S. About 15% of their qualified export income is exempt.

   7)  Certain exports may require **licenses**. For example, sales of technology with military applications are limited by western nations that are members of the Coordinating Committee for Multilateral Export Controls. The related U.S. legislation is the Export Administration Act of 1979.

   8)  In the U.S., the **Export Trading Company Act** of 1982 permits competitors to form export trading companies without regard to antitrust legislation.

b.   The **economic effect of trade barriers** is to shift workers from relatively efficient export industries into less efficient protected industries.  Real wage rates will decline as a result, as will total world output.  Domestic producers are not subject to the restrictions and will therefore have an advantage over their foreign competitors.  However, absent such competition, the domestic price of the item will be higher.  Domestic producers will sell more at a higher price, and domestic consumers will consume less following the price increase.

c.   A major reason for trade restrictions is that the costs of competition are direct and concentrated (people lose jobs and firms go out of business), but benefits of unrestricted trade are less noticeable and occur in the future (lower prices, higher wages, more jobs in export industries).

    1)   Special-interest groups are strong and well organized, and they lobby effectively for legislation that is harmful to free trade.

    2)   **Economic integration** is the joining of the markets from two or more nations into a free-trade zone.  Examples of economic blocs of trading nations are the European Union and the North American Free Trade Agreement (NAFTA).  The trading bloc ordinarily provides trading incentives to member nations and discriminates against nonmember nations.

6.   **International Tax Considerations**

a.   Multinational corporations frequently derive income from several countries.  The government of each country in which a corporation does business may enact statutes imposing one or more types of tax on the corporation.

b.   **Treaties**.  To avoid double taxation, two or more countries may adopt treaties to coordinate or synchronize the effects of their taxing statutes.

    1)   Treaties are also used to integrate other governmental goals, e.g., providing incentive for desired investment.

    2)   For example, if a U.S. statute and a treaty to which the U.S. is a party conflict, the one enacted or adopted last controls.

    3)   A treaty might modify the rules in a country's statutes that designate the country that income is sourced to or the country a firm is a resident of.

c.   **Multinational corporations**

    1)   Most countries tax only the income sourced to that country.

    2)   The U.S. taxes worldwide income (from whatever source derived) of a domestic corporation.  Double taxation is avoided by allowing a credit for income tax paid to foreign countries or by treaty provisions.

    3)   In the case of foreign corporations, the U.S. taxes only income sourced to the U.S.  Ordinarily, such income is effectively connected with engaging in a trade or business of the U.S.  Certain U.S. source income, e.g., gain on the sale of most stock, is not taxed by the U.S.

    4)   **Transfer pricing** is an important aspect of the tax calculation for multinational corporations that transfer inventories between branches in different countries.  For example, U.S. tax laws limit the amount of profit that can be transferred from a U.S. parent to a foreign subsidiary or branch.  Although there are exceptions, the basic transfer pricing rules limit the amount of taxable income that can be claimed by the foreign subsidiary to no more than 50% of the total taxable income.  Thus, transfer prices charged to foreign subsidiaries may differ substantially from those charged to domestic subsidiaries.

5)    There are also **nontax aspects** of transfer pricing.  For example, limitations on taking profits out of a foreign country, or currency restrictions, can be avoided by charging the foreign subsidiary a higher transfer price than that charged to domestic subsidiaries.  The reason is that because firms in developing countries are allowed to pay their accounts payable to foreign vendors, but they are not allowed to distribute profits to foreign owners.

6)    The existence of tariffs in the foreign country may necessitate a lower transfer price to reduce a tariff based on the inventory value.

7.    Stop and review!  You have completed the outline for this subunit.  Study multiple-choice questions 1 through 7 beginning on page 393.

## 8.2 METHODS OF TAXATION

1.    Government, at all levels, finances its expenditures by taxation.  Thus, taxes generate government revenues.  National governments also use taxation as a means of implementing fiscal policy regarding inflation, full employment, economic growth, etc.

2.    One rationale for taxation is that individuals should pay tax based on the benefits received from the services (e.g., paying for the use of a public park or swimming pool).  Another view is that consumers should pay taxes based on their ability to pay (e.g., taxes on income and wealth).

3.    **Tax-Rate Structures**

a.    **Progressive**.  With a higher income, individuals pay a higher percentage of their income in taxes.

1)    **Indexing** is a means of avoiding the unfairness that results when inflation increases nominal but not real taxable income, thereby subjecting it to higher tax rates.  Adjusting tax bracket, deduction, and exemption amounts by reference to some index of inflation avoids this problem.

b.    **Proportional**.  At all levels of income, the percentage paid in taxes is constant (e.g., a flat tax on income).

c.    **Regressive**.  As income increases, the percentage paid in taxes decreases (e.g., sales, payroll, property, or excise taxes).  For example, an excise tax is regressive because its burden falls disproportionately on lower-income persons.  As personal income increases, the percentage of income paid declines because an excise tax is a flat amount per quantity of the good or service purchased.

4.    The **marginal tax rate** is the rate applied to the last dollar of taxable income.

a.    The **average tax rate** is the total tax liability divided by the amount of taxable income.

b.    The **effective tax rate** is the total tax liability divided by total economic income (includes amounts that do not have tax consequences).

5.    **Direct taxes** are imposed upon the taxpayer and paid directly to the government, e.g., the personal income tax.

a.    **Indirect taxes** are levied against others and therefore only indirectly on the individual taxpayer, e.g., corporate income taxes.

6.    The **incidence of taxation** refers to who actually bears a particular tax.  Accordingly, the person who actually bears an indirect tax may not be the one who pays the tax to the government.

a.    The incidence of taxation becomes important when a government wants to change the tax structure.  Because taxation is a form of fiscal policy, the government needs to know who will actually bear the incidence of taxation, not just who will statutorily pay the tax.

b. Taxes such as the corporate income tax and corporate property and excise taxes are often shifted to the consumer in the form of higher prices.

   1) However, sellers ordinarily must bear part of the burden. Passing on the entire tax might reduce unit sales unacceptably by raising the price too high. Thus, the effect of the tax is to reduce supply (because suppliers' costs increase) and quantity demanded by buyers (because the price increases). The combined loss of sellers and buyers is called the **deadweight loss** or excess burden of taxation.

c. Taxes such as windfall profits taxes are not shifted to the consumer via higher prices. This type of one-time-only tax levied on part of the output produced does not increase the equilibrium price of the taxed good.

d. Supply-side economists use the **Laffer Curve** to attempt to explain how people react to varying rates of income taxation. For example, if the income tax rate is 0%, zero revenue will be raised. Similarly, if the tax rate is 100%, income tax revenue will probably be zero because an earner who faces a tax rate of 100% will not work.

   1) The optimal income tax rate will bring in the most revenue possible. A rate that is either too high or too low will generate less than optimal tax revenues.

   2) Supply-side economists do not state that lowering income tax rates will bring in more revenue. Instead, they claim that, if the rates are too high, lowering rates will bring in more revenue because output and national income will increase. This result, in theory, should follow because of increased incentives to work, invest, and save.

   3) However, economic policy should not be confused with political considerations. There are obvious political reasons for having higher or lower tax rates on certain income levels. Thus, the theory underlying the Laffer Curve does not address questions of redistributionist politics.

   4) A criticism of the Laffer Curve is that it does not prescribe the optimal tax rate. The only way to know if the current tax rates are too high or too low is to change them and see if revenues increase. Critics also have observed that the incentives provided by tax cuts may have relatively small supply-side effects and that those effects may be felt only in the very long run. Still another potential problem is that cutting taxes in an expanding economy may overstimulate demand, thereby increasing inflation.

7. Many major industrial nations have already adopted a **value-added tax (VAT)**.

   a. The tax is levied on the value added to goods by each business unit in the production and distribution chain. The amount of value added is the difference between sales and purchases. Each firm in the chain collects the tax on its sales, takes a credit for taxes paid on purchases, and remits the difference to the government.

   b. The consumer ultimately bears the incidence of the tax through higher prices.

   c. A VAT encourages consumer savings because taxes are paid only on consumption, not on savings. Because the VAT is based on consumption, people in the lower income groups spend a greater proportion of their income on this type of tax. Thus, the VAT is regressive.

   d. Only those businesses that make a profit have to pay income taxes. The VAT, however, requires all businesses to pay taxes, regardless of income.

   e. The VAT tax is not a useful tool for fiscal policy purposes.

8. Stop and review! You have completed the outline for this subunit. Study multiple-choice questions 8 through 15 beginning on page 395.

## 8.3 ECONOMIC INDICATORS

1. **National income accounting** measures the output and performance of the economy. The **gross domestic product** (GDP) is the principal measure. It is the total market value of all final goods and services produced within the boundaries of a country, whether by domestic or foreign-owned sources, during a specified period of time (usually a year). GDP is calculated without regard to the ownership of productive resources. Thus, the value of the output of a factory abroad is excluded regardless of its ownership, but the output of a foreign-owned factory is included in the host country's GDP.

   a. **Income approach**. GDP equals the sum of the items below, minus income earned abroad.

      1) Employee compensation, interest, and rents
      2) Proprietors' income
      3) Depreciation (consumption of fixed capital)
      4) Indirect business taxes (e.g., sales taxes) and corporate income taxes
      5) Dividends
      6) Undistributed corporate profits

   b. **Expenditure approach.** GDP is also the sum of

      1) Personal consumption expenditures
      2) Gross private domestic investment
      3) Government purchases
      4) Net exports

   c. To avoid double counting, the value added to each good or service at each stage of production over the period must be summed. Alternatively, the total market value of all final goods and services may be added.

   d. GDP is not an ideal measure of economic well-being.

      1) GDP is a monetary measure; therefore, comparing GDP over a period of time requires adjustment for changes in the price level. The **GDP deflator** is a price index used to convert nominal GDP to real GDP.
      2) Increases in GDP often involve environmental damage such as noise, congestion, or pollution.
      3) GDP is not adjusted for changes in the population (which changes per capita income).
      4) Changes in the value of leisure time are not considered.
      5) Some nonmarket transactions are excluded, e.g., the value of homemakers' work.
      6) Military expenditures are included at cost, not incremental total value.

   e. Other national income concepts

      1) **Net domestic product** (NDP) = GDP – depreciation
      2) **National income** (NI) = NDP + net income earned abroad – indirect business taxes (e.g., sales taxes)

         a) NI is the income earned by a nation's resources, whether located at home or abroad.

      3) **Personal income** (PI) = NI – corporate income taxes and undistributed profits – required contributions to governmental social security programs + transfer payments (public and private)
      4) **Disposable income** = PI – personal income taxes

   f. **Real per capita output** is GDP divided by population, adjusted for inflation. It is used as a measure of the standard of living.

2. **Other Economic Indicators**. Economists use a variety of economic measures to forecast turns in the business cycle. They are variables that have had a high correlation with aggregate economic activity. The best known are the composite indexes calculated by **The Conference Board**, a private research group with a worldwide membership.

   a. The Conference Board's **leading indicators** include

      1) Average workweek for production workers
      2) Prices of 500 common stocks
      3) Average weekly initial unemployment insurance claims
      4) New orders for consumer goods and materials (1996 U.S. dollars)
      5) New orders for nondefense capital goods
      6) Building permits for homes
      7) Vendor performance (slower deliveries diffusion index)
      8) Money supply ($M_2$ in 1996 U.S. dollars)
      9) Index of consumer expectations (1966 base year)
      10) Interest rate spread (10-year U.S. Treasury bonds-federal funds rate)

   b. The Conference Board's **lagging indicators** include

      1) Average duration of unemployment in weeks
      2) Change in index of labor cost per unit of output
      3) Average prime rate charged by banks
      4) Ratio of manufacturing and trade inventories to sales (1996 U.S. dollars)
      5) Commercial and industrial loans outstanding (1996 U.S. dollars)
      6) Ratio of consumer installment credit outstanding to personal income
      7) Change in CPI for services

   c. The Conference Board's **coincident indicators** include

      1) Employees on nonagricultural payrolls
      2) Personal income minus transfer payments (1996 U.S. dollars)
      3) Industrial production (based on value added and physical output)
      4) Manufacturing and trade sales (1996 U.S. dollars)

3. **Measuring Inflation**

   a. **The consumer price index (CPI)** measures inflation by a monthly pricing of items on a typical household shopping list.

      1) The current index uses a base year as a reference point. The price in the current year of a market basket of goods and services is determined relative to the same basket for the base year.

      2)
$$\frac{\textit{Price of market basket in a given year}}{\textit{Price of the same market basket in the base year}} \times 100$$

   b. **The wholesale price index (WPI)** measures increases in prices at the wholesale level. It is often accepted as a proxy for future inflation.

   c. The **GDP deflator** is a price index that includes every item produced in the economy at the price at which it entered the GDP account. **Nominal GDP** is stated at the actual prices at time of measurement. **Real GDP**, after application of the deflator, is stated in base-year dollars.

4.   The **balance of payments** includes all international payments made by one nation to another, including those for imports, exports, investments, unilateral transfers, and capital movements. The principal accounts are the current account and the capital account.

   a.   The **current account** records

      1)   Exports (credits) and imports (debits) of goods

         a)   The **balance of trade** is the difference between total exports and total imports of goods.

         b)   A **trade deficit** occurs when a country imports more goods than it exports.

      2)   Exports (credits) and imports (debits) of services

         a)   The **balance on goods and services** is the difference between total exports and total imports of goods and services.

      3)   Interest and dividends received on investments abroad (credits) and interest and dividends paid on foreign investments at home (debits)

      4)   Net unilateral transfers, e.g., foreign aid, pension payments, and remittance to relatives (credits or debits depending on whether the flow is into or out of the country, respectively)

      5)   The balance on the current account

   b.   The **capital account** records capital flows resulting from the purchase and sale of fixed or financial assets.

      1)   Inflows of foreign capital (credits) are effectively exports of stocks and bonds and therefore result in inflows of foreign currencies.

      2)   Outflows of capital (debits) use up supplies of foreign currencies.

      3)   A capital account surplus therefore indicates that inflows exceeded outflows.

   c.   The **balance of payments deficit or surplus** is the net of the current and capital account balances.

   d.   A third account is the **official reserves account**, which keeps track of transactions involving the central bank and its official reserve assets, such as gold and foreign currencies.

      1)   Also included among a central bank's reserves are **special drawing rights**, or SDRs, which are accounting entries established by the International Monetary Fund.

   e.   The references to debits and credits treat the balance of payments account as if it were a revenue or expense account. In other words, a debit is similar to an expense in that it is unfavorable for the country's balance of payments position.

      1)   EXAMPLE: A debit (such as an import) is undesirable because it contributes to an unfavorable balance of payments. The U.S. has an unfavorable balance of payments when payments by the U.S. to foreign countries exceed the payments made from foreign countries to the U.S. It is also unfavorable because foreign currency reserves held by the U.S. must be given up to correct the imbalance.

         a)   A credit in the balance of payments account is desirable (exports, for instance) because foreigners will be paying more to the U.S. than the U.S. is paying out. Thus, the foreign currency reserves available to the U.S. increase.

f.   **Domestic effects**.  In addition to decreasing the reserves of foreign currencies held by a country, an unfavorable balance of payments can also affect the domestic economy.

1)   EXAMPLE:  An excess of imports can cause an unfavorable balance of payments.  At the same time, consumers may not be buying domestic products, which may result in domestic layoffs and production cutbacks.  These in turn will mean less investment opportunity domestically, and investors will begin sending their investment dollars overseas.  The flow of capital overseas compounds the balance of payments problem because investing in a foreign country is essentially the same as importing a product (i.e., the investor is importing foreign stocks and bonds).

2)   Steps to correct an unfavorable balance of payments

a)   Establish import quotas.

i)   One country's unfavorable balance of payments may be caused by another nation's import quotas.  For example, if the U.S. has a continuing unfavorable balance of payments with Japan, it might be possible to encourage Japan to remove the trade barriers set up to keep U.S. electronics products out.  The removal of Japan's trade restrictions would help the U.S. balance of payments (but might result in an unfavorable balance of payments for Japan).

b)   Provide export incentives.

i)   EXAMPLE:  The U.S. tax law provisions for Domestic International Sales Corporations (DISCs) and Foreign Sales Corporations (FSCs) permit exporters to postpone or avoid income taxes on export-related income as long as that income is reinvested in export-related assets.

c)   Develop substitutes for products currently being imported.

i)   EXAMPLE:  The U.S. has tried to develop substitutes or local sources for imported oil.

3)   An **automatic correction** results when a debtor nation's monetary unit declines relative to that of a creditor nation.

g.   A balance of payments deficit (imbalance) must be equalized by shipments of goods or reductions in reserves.

1)   Gifts and grants are also used.

h.   In the 1980s, the U.S. became the nation with the largest foreign debt.  The reasons include the following:

1)   Federal budget deficits financed by foreigners
2)   Growth in the economy that attracted foreign investors
3)   High real interest rates
4)   A strengthened dollar in the early 1980s that encouraged imports
5)   The shift from a manufacturing to a service economy
6)   A decrease in exports of agricultural goods

i.   The following are the actual or potential effects of the U.S.'s debt:

1)   An increase in the percentage of the GDP used for debt service
2)   Reduced reserves leading to a devalued dollar, inflation, and increased exports
3)   A decline in net imports and improvement in the trade balance
4)   Increased savings as a result of economic uncertainty

5) Increased pressure for trade protectionism
6) Potentially high interest rates to curtail inflation and tighten the money supply, with the consequent incentive for foreign investment

5. **Definitions of money** are important because tools for expanding or contracting the money supply are methods of managing a nation's economy.

a. $M_1$ includes

1) Coins and currency
2) Checking deposits (including travelers' checks)

b. The U.S. Federal Reserve's targets for monetary growth emphasize $M_2$, which includes

1) Coins and currency
2) Checking deposits
3) Nonchecking savings
4) Small (less than $100,000) time deposits
5) Money market accounts and money market mutual funds

c. $M_1$ and $M_2$ are the most common measures of money and are reported weekly in the *Wall Street Journal*.

d. $M_3$ includes $M_2$ plus large ($100,000 or more) time deposits.

6. Stop and review! You have completed the outline for this subunit. Study multiple-choice questions 16 through 28 beginning on page 397.

## 8.4 LEGAL RULES OF EVIDENCE

1. The legal rules of evidence are found in statutes, case law, and constitutions. Their essential purpose is to govern the admissibility of evidence in legal proceedings, but they are drafted with a view to protecting the parties as well as ascertaining the truth.

a. **Exclusionary rules** prevent the admission of evidence whose value as proof is offset by its possible prejudicial effect. An internal auditor, however, need not be limited by the legal and constitutional safeguards imposed in court.

1) The internal auditor may examine and evaluate any information until, in his/her professional judgment, sufficient, reliable, relevant, and useful information has been collected.

2) In this text, the word **evidence** is used strictly in the legal context. The word **information** is used to signify the support for the internal auditor's observations, conclusions, and recommendations.

2. Nevertheless, legal and internal auditing concepts share much common ground. Information in the internal auditing context and evidence in the legal context are intended to provide a basis for belief, to prove or disprove something.

3. The legal rules of evidence may be most obviously relevant to internal auditors when they participate in fraud investigations or provide litigation-support services, but such knowledge may also be beneficial in ordinary engagement work.

4. The following are types of evidence:

a. **Best evidence** or **primary evidence** constitutes the most satisfactory and reliable method of proving the matter asserted.

1) The most frequent application of the best evidence rule is to documentary evidence.

2) To prove the content of a writing, the original contract, deed, business record, or other document must be produced if it is available.

    a) The purpose of preventing the admission of testimonial evidence to prove the content of a writing is to avoid misinterpretation.

        i) However, oral evidence may be admissible to explain the terms of a writing when it is subject to more than one reasonable interpretation.

b. **Secondary evidence** is less reliable than primary evidence because it may consist of copies of original documents or oral evidence regarding their content.

    1) Nevertheless, copies may be admissible when the originals

        a) Have been lost or destroyed without wrongful intent by the party proffering the copies

        b) Cannot be obtained through legal or other reasonable means by the party proffering the copies

        c) Are within the control of a public entity

    2) Copies are preferable to written summaries of, or oral testimony about, original writings. However, these types of evidence may be admitted when the originals

        a) Are very voluminous

        b) Cannot be considered by the court within a reasonable time

        c) Are available to be produced for inspection at the court's discretion

    3) Secondary evidence may also be admitted when production of the originals, such as the accounting records of a business, and their possession by the court for a long time might cause undue hardship on a party.

c. **Direct evidence** is proof without presumption or inference.

    1) Examples are original documents and testimony about what a witness him/herself did, saw, or heard.

d. **Circumstantial evidence** is indirect evidence because it proves intermediate facts from which a primary fact that is material to the matter in dispute may be deduce

    1) For example, an alteration of online accounting data protected by password access constitutes circumstantial evidence that an authorized person was responsible. However, this inference may be unsound if an unauthorized person has been able to obtain the necessary password.

e. **Conclusive evidence** is so powerful that it permits only one reasonable conclusion and needs no additional corroboration.

f. **Corroborative evidence** supports other evidence.

    1) For example, the testimony of a second eyewitness to an event may strengthen and confirm the account of the first witness.

g. **Opinion evidence** is usually excluded because of its potentially prejudicial effect.

    1) Witnesses ordinarily are allowed to testify only as to factual matters within their direct experience.

    2) An exception is made for expert opinion. Such testimony is allowed when it

        a) Concerns matters beyond the knowledge of lay people

        b) Is offered by someone whose special expertise and objectivity will assist the court and the jury in the truth ascertainment process

h. **Hearsay evidence** is a statement other than one made by the declarant while testifying at the trial or hearing, offered in evidence to prove the truth of the matter asserted.

   1) For example, if Employee A states that Employee B said that she saw Employee C steal from petty cash, Employee A's statement, if offered to prove that Employee C stole from petty cash, is hearsay.

   2) Hearsay is normally inadmissible because it cannot be tested by cross-examination. Thus, in the example above, Employee A merely heard what B said and therefore cannot be asked questions testing the truth of the matter asserted in the declaration made out of court (or out of the internal auditor's hearing).

   3) Various exceptions to the hearsay rule exist based on circumstances promoting the reliability of the assertions.

      a) For example, documents effectively are hearsay, but documents created in the ordinary course of business are admissible if properly authenticated.

5. Stop and review! You have completed the outline for this subunit. Study multiple-choice questions 29 through 33 beginning on page 401.

## 8.5 CONTRACTS

1. No part of commercial law is more pervasive than **contract law**. Billions of contract-based agreements to transfer property and services are negotiated daily by individuals, businesses, and governments.

   a. Promise keeping is essential for planning in a modern complex society. Without a legal system committed to enforcement of private contractual agreements, everyday transactions in a free-enterprise economy would be impossible. Contemporary contract law allows parties to enter into private agreements with others with assurance that these agreements are enforceable against a party that fails to perform.

2. A **contract** is a promise or an agreement that the law recognizes as establishing a duty of performance. It is enforceable by applying a remedy for its breach.

3. The most basic element of a contract is a voluntary agreement by the parties. **Agreement** requires the mutual assent of the contracting parties reached through an offer by the offeror and acceptance by the offeree.

   a. An **offer** is a statement or other communication that, if not terminated, confers upon the offeree the power of acceptance. An offer need not be in any particular form to be valid but it must

      1) Be communicated to an offeree
      2) Indicate an intent to enter into a contract, and
      3) Be sufficiently definite and certain.

   b. **Communication** of an offer may be done in various ways and may occur over time. However, at some moment in the formation of a contract, each party expresses an intent to enter into a legally binding and enforceable agreement.

      1) Whether an offer has been made is determined by an objective standard that uses the following test: Would a reasonable person assume that the power of acceptance had been conferred upon him/her? An offer must be made with serious intent, not in anger, great excitement, or jest.

        2)   Language constituting an offer should be distinguished from that merely soliciting or inviting offers. Communications between parties may simply be preliminary negotiations concerning a possible contract. A party may initiate negotiations by suggesting the general nature of a possible contract.

    c.   An offer also must be **definite and certain**. If an offer is indefinite or vague or lacking an essential provision, no agreement arises from an attempt to accept it because the courts cannot tell what the parties are bound to do.

        1)   However, minor details left for future determination do not make an agreement too vague to be an offer.

    d.   An offer does not remain effective forever. The **offer will terminate** under any of the following circumstances:

        1)   Revocation by the offeror,
        2)   Rejection or counteroffer by the offeree,
        3)   Death or incompetency of either the offeror or offeree,
        4)   Destruction of the specific subject matter to which the offer relates,
        5)   Subsequent illegality of the offer, or
        6)   Lapse of a specified or reasonable time.

    e.   **Acceptance** of an offer is essential to the formation of a contract. An agreement consists of an offer and an acceptance.

        1)   To be effective, an acceptance must relate to the terms of the offer. The acceptance must be positive, unequivocal, and unconditional. It may not change, subtract from, add to, or qualify in any way the terms of the offer.

4.   **Consideration** is the primary basis for the enforcement of agreements in contract law. It is the "price" paid to make a promise enforceable. Ordinarily, if a promise is not supported by consideration, it is not enforceable.

    a.   One requirement of consideration is **mutuality of obligation**. Both parties must give consideration. Consequently, something of legal value must be given in a bargained-for exchange when the parties intend an exchange.

    b.   The second required element of consideration is **legal sufficiency** (something of legal value). Consideration is legally sufficient to render a promise enforceable if the promisor receives a legal benefit or the promisee incurs a legal detriment.

        1)   To incur a legal detriment, the promisee must do (or promise to do) something that (s)he is not legally obligated to do or not do (or promise not to do) something (s)he is legally entitled to do. A cause-and-effect relationship must exist between the promise made by one party and the detriment incurred by the other.

5.   Parties to a contract must possess legal capacity. **Capacity** is the mental ability to make a rational decision, which includes the ability to perceive and appreciate all relevant facts. Three classes of parties are legally limited in their capacity to contract: minors (also known as infants), mentally incompetent persons, and intoxicated parties.

    a.   For public policy reasons, parties in these three groups are protected from the enforcement of most contracts against them.

6.   **Legality** is an essential requirement for an agreement to be valid and enforceable. Formation or performance of an agreement may violate a criminal law, constitute a civil wrong upon which a suit may be filed, or be determined by a court to be contrary to public policy. Is these instances, the agreement is illegal and unenforceable.

   a.   An agreement that is **contrary to public policy** has a negative impact on society at large that outweighs the interests of the parties. This principle reflects a balancing by the courts of freedom of contract and the public interest. Examples of agreements that may violate public policy are

      1)   Agreements to unduly restrain competition;
      2)   Clauses that excuse one of the parties from any liability;
      3)   Contracts calling for immoral acts; and
      4)   Agreements found to be unfair, oppressive, or unconscionable.

7.   An **oral contract** is as enforceable as a written contract. However, a statute may require that some contracts be **in writing** to be enforceable. For example, statutes may require the following to be in writing:

   a.   Contracts involving an interest in land

   b.   Contracts that by their terms cannot possibly be performed within 1 year (e.g., some employment contracts)

   c.   Collateral promises by which a person promises to answer for the debt or duty of another (e.g., a guarantee)

   d.   Contracts for the sale of goods for more than a stated amount

8.   Stop and review! You have completed the outline for this subunit. Study multiple-choice questions 34 through 39 beginning on page 402.

## 8.6 CONTRACT ENGAGEMENTS

1.   Internal auditors often perform engagements to monitor and evaluate significant **construction contracts** and **operating contracts** that involve the provision of services. The usual types of arrangements for such contracts are lump-sum (fixed-price), cost-plus, and unit-price.

2.   **Lump-sum contracts**. The internal auditor may have little to evaluate when the work is performed in accordance with the contract. However, reviewing such an agreement may call for consideration of

   a.   Progress payments.

   b.   Incentives (e.g., for early completion).

   c.   An escalator clause (e.g., one causing the entire price to be due in the event of some breach of the contract).

   d.   Adjustments for labor costs (e.g., premiums paid to obtain necessary labor).

   e.   Change orders.

3.   **Cost-plus contracts** are ways to cope with uncertainties about costs by setting a price equal to cost plus a fixed amount or cost plus a fixed percentage of cost. A problem is that the contractor may have little incentive for economy and efficiency, a reason for careful review by the internal auditors. These contracts may have provisions for

   a.   Setting cost ceilings, with any savings shared by the parties.

   b.   Incentives for early completion.

4. **Unit-price contracts** are often used when a convenient measure of work is available, such as acres of land cleared, cubic yards of earth moved, or square footage patrolled by a security service.

   a. The key issue is accurate measurement of the work performed.

5. To protect the organization, internal auditors should be involved throughout the contracting process, not merely during the performance phase. They should review the terms of the contract and

   a. Procedures for bidding (e.g., competitive bidding).
   b. Procedures for cost estimation and control.
   c. Budgets and financial forecasts.
   d. The contractor's information and control systems.
   e. The contractor's financial position.
   f. Funding and tax matters.
   g. Progress of the project and costs incurred.

6. Stop and review! You have completed the outline for this subunit. Study multiple-choice questions 40 through 41 beginning on page 404.

## QUESTIONS

### 8.1 International Trade Institutions and Agreements

**1.** In the modern world economy, balance-of-payments deficits and surpluses can be eliminated

A. Through the market mechanism of flexible exchange rates.

B. If all nations adopt tight monetary policies.

C. Only if trade between nations is curtailed.

D. When the opportunity costs of production are made the same in all countries.

Answer (A) is correct. *(CMA, adapted)*
**REQUIRED:** The means by which balance-of-payments deficits and surpluses can be eliminated.
**DISCUSSION:** If exchange rates are allowed to fluctuate, the value of a particular currency will be determined in accordance with the supply of and demand for that currency. For example, if U.S. exports to Japan are greater than imports, the dollar will be in great demand; thus, the dollar will be driven up in price relative to the Japanese yen. This increase in price will discourage the Japanese from buying U.S. goods. The decrease in Japanese purchases will then result, in principle, in less demand for the dollar and a movement back toward equilibrium in the export/import ratio.
Answer (B) is incorrect because tight money policies would not affect the balance of payments but would reduce economic activity generally. Answer (C) is incorrect because deficits can be overcome by less drastic and counterproductive methods than eliminating trade. Answer (D) is incorrect because demand for particular products is as important as relative costs in creating trade deficits.

**2.** What is the role of gold in the present international monetary system?

A. Gold is quoted in United States dollars only.

B. All of the major currencies of the world, except the United States dollar, have a fixed value in terms of gold.

C. Gold is like any other asset whose value depends upon supply and demand.

D. Gold is the reserve asset of the International Monetary Fund.

Answer (C) is correct. *(CMA, adapted)*
**REQUIRED:** The role of gold in the present international monetary system.
**DISCUSSION:** Gold has no special role in the modern international monetary system. The present system is based upon managed floating currency exchange rates. Consequently, gold is treated as a commodity, the price of which depends upon supply and demand.
Answer (A) is incorrect because, although most exchanges quote the price of gold in U.S. dollars, the dollar's value is not linked to that of gold. Answer (B) is incorrect because floating exchange rates have existed since about 1973. Tying currency values to a gold standard, in effect, fixes exchange rates. Answer (D) is incorrect because the only reserves of the IMF are international currencies.

**3.** Interest rates received by depositors on Eurodollar deposits tend to be higher than domestic U.S. rates on equivalent instruments because

   A. Borrowers pay higher rates than domestic U.S. rates on equivalent instruments.

   B. The deposits involve different currencies.

   C. Eurodollar deposits are for smaller amounts.

   D. The Eurodollar market is outside the direct control of the U.S. monetary authorities and has lower costs.

Answer (D) is correct.  *(CIA, adapted)*
**REQUIRED:** The reason that interest rates on Eurodollar deposits exceed U.S. rates.
**DISCUSSION:** Eurodollars are U.S. dollars deposited in banks outside the U.S. Because it is outside the direct control of the U.S. monetary authorities, the Eurodollar market has lower costs. For example, U.S. reserve requirements and FDIC premium payments do not apply in this market. A lower cost market can offer depositors higher interest rates.
Answer (A) is incorrect because Eurodollar borrowers tend to pay lower, not higher, rates. Borrowers and depositors can both receive more favorable rates because, with its lower costs, the Eurodollar market can offer smaller spreads between borrowing and lending rates. Answer (B) is incorrect because U.S. dollars are on deposit in both cases. Answer (C) is incorrect because Eurodollar deposits tend to be for larger, not smaller, amounts. Furthermore, smaller deposits tend to earn lower, not higher, rates than larger deposits.

**4.** Of the following, a characteristic of Eurobonds is that they are

   A. Always denominated in Eurodollars.

   B. Always sold in some country other than the one in whose currency the bond is denominated.

   C. Sold outside the country of the borrower but are denominated in the currency of the country in which the issue is sold.

   D. Generally issued as registered bonds.

Answer (B) is correct.  *(CIA, adapted)*
**REQUIRED:** The characteristic of Eurobonds.
**DISCUSSION:** Eurobonds are, by definition, always sold in some country other than the one in whose currency the bond issue is denominated. Their advantage is that they are customarily less stringently regulated than most other bonds. Hence, transaction costs are lower.
Answer (A) is incorrect because Eurobonds are not always denominated in Eurodollars, which are U.S. dollars deposited outside the U.S. Answer (C) is incorrect because foreign bonds are denominated in the currency of the country in which they are sold. Answer (D) is incorrect because Eurobonds are usually issued not as registered bonds but as bearer bonds, so names and nationalities of the investors are not recorded.

**5.** The World Trade Organization

   A. Introduced fixed exchange rates among the United States, Canada, and members of the European Union.

   B. Created the International Monetary Fund.

   C. Encourages reductions in trade barriers between countries.

   D. Introduced exchange rates that adjust in response to changes in trade deficits and surpluses.

Answer (C) is correct.  *(CMA, adapted)*
**REQUIRED:** The true statement about the World Trade Organization.
**DISCUSSION:** International trade agreements provide regulatory authority for businesses in international trade. The WTO, which was established on January 1, 1995, is the product of the Uruguay Round of international trade negotiations. It is a permanent body with a secretariat based in Geneva, Switzerland. The WTO Agreement is a permanent set of commitments by more than 120 nations designed to prohibit trade discrimination among member nations and between imported and domestic products.
Answer (A) is incorrect because the WTO is a worldwide agreement concerning trade barriers, not exchange rates. Today, moreover, exchange rates are not pegged (fixed) but are allowed to float. Answer (B) is incorrect because the IMF was founded in 1944 to stabilize exchange rates. Answer (D) is incorrect because the WTO is a worldwide agreement concerning trade barriers, not exchange rates.

**6.** What law prohibits U.S. companies from making bribes to foreign officials for the purpose of obtaining or retaining business?

   A. Federal Ethical Standards Act.

   B. Robinson-Patman Act.

   C. Foreign Corrupt Practices Act.

   D. North American Free Trade Agreement.

Answer (C) is correct.  *(Publisher)*
**REQUIRED:** The law that prohibits bribes to foreign officials.
**DISCUSSION:** The Foreign Corrupt Practices Act of 1977 prohibits bribes to foreign officials for purposes of obtaining or retaining business. The Act also requires companies to maintain effective systems of internal control.
Answer (A) is incorrect because the Federal Ethical Standards Act does not deal with international payments. Answer (B) is incorrect because the Robinson-Patman Act of 1936 prohibits price discrimination. Answer (D) is incorrect because the North American Free Trade Agreement (NAFTA), passed in 1993, provides for free trade among the nations of Canada, Mexico, and the U.S.

**7.** Which of the following is not an aspect of the Foreign Corrupt Practices Act of 1977?

- A. It subjects management to fines and imprisonment.

- B. It prohibits bribes to foreign officials.

- C. It requires the establishment of independent audit committees.

- D. It requires an internal control system to be developed and maintained.

Answer (C) is correct. *(Publisher)*
**REQUIRED:** The false statement with respect to the Foreign Corrupt Practices Act.
**DISCUSSION:** The Foreign Corrupt Practices Act of 1977 prohibits bribes to foreign officials and requires firms to have adequate systems of internal control. Violation of the act subjects individual managers to fines and/or imprisonment. The Act does not specifically require the establishment of audit committees, but many firms have established audit committees as one means of dealing with the internal control provisions of the Act.

## 8.2 Methods of Taxation

**8.** An individual had taxable income of $23,000 per year and paid $8,000 in income tax. The individual's taxable income then increased to $30,000 per year resulting in a $10,000 income tax liability. The personal tax system being applied to this individual is

- A. Progressive.

- B. Regressive.

- C. Marginal.

- D. Proportional.

Answer (B) is correct. *(CIA, adapted)*
**REQUIRED:** The nature of the personal tax system.
**DISCUSSION:** The average tax rate of the individual has decreased from 34.8% ($8,000 ÷ $23,000) to 33.3% ($10,000 ÷ $30,000). Under a regressive tax system, the average tax rate falls as income rises, although the amount of tax paid may rise.
Answer (A) is incorrect because, under a progressive tax system, both the amount of tax and the percentage of income paid in tax (the average tax rate) rise as income increases. In the case described, the individual pays a higher amount of tax but a lower percentage of income in tax. Answer (C) is incorrect because marginal is not a type of tax system but a type of tax rate. The marginal tax rate is the tax rate paid on incremental income. Answer (D) is incorrect because, under a proportional income tax system, the average tax rate is the same for all levels of income. The average tax rate of this individual falls as income rises.

**9.** In most countries <List A> taxes tend to be <List B> with respect to income.

|   | List A | List B |
|---|--------|--------|
| A. | General sales | Proportional |
| B. | Property | Regressive |
| C. | Personal income | Proportional |
| D. | Personal income | Regressive |

Answer (B) is correct. *(CIA, adapted)*
**REQUIRED:** The correct match of a tax and its proportion of a taxpayer's income.
**DISCUSSION:** Property taxes tend to be regressive. Taxpayers with lower incomes must pay a higher portion of their incomes for necessities, such as housing.
Answer (A) is incorrect because general sales taxes tend to be regressive. The lower the taxpayer's income, the higher the proportion that is usually paid in sales taxes, which are collected at a flat rate per dollar. Low-income taxpayers are unable to save as high a portion of their income as high-income taxpayers. Thus, the latter are less exposed to general sales taxes because they avoid the tax on the amount saved. Answer (C) is incorrect because personal income taxes tend to be progressive. Higher tax rates are charged on higher incomes. Answer (D) is incorrect because personal income taxes tend to be progressive. Higher tax rates are charged on higher incomes.

**10.** In a <List A> personal tax system, an individual's marginal tax rate is normally <List B> the average tax rate.

|   | List A | List B |
|---|--------|--------|
| A. | Progressive | Greater than |
| B. | Progressive | Equal to |
| C. | Regressive | Equal to |
| D. | Regressive | Greater than |

Answer (A) is correct. *(CIA, adapted)*
**REQUIRED:** The true statement about marginal and average rates in a personal tax system.
**DISCUSSION:** The marginal tax rate is the tax applicable to the last unit of income, whereas the average tax rate is the total tax paid divided by taxable income. In a progressive tax system, higher incomes attract higher tax rates, so the marginal tax rate paid on the last unit of income exceeds the average tax rate.
Answer (B) is incorrect because, in a progressive tax system, the tax rate varies with the level of income, so the marginal and average tax rates differ. Answer (C) is incorrect because, in a regressive tax system, the tax rate varies with the level of income, so the marginal and average tax rates differ. Answer (D) is incorrect because, in a regressive tax system, the marginal tax rate is less than, not greater than, the average tax rate.

**11.** In order to index a progressive tax system to inflation, the government must

    A. Adjust only tax deductions and exemptions.

    B. Adjust only tax brackets.

    C. Adjust deductions, exemptions, and tax brackets.

    D. Ensure that nominal tax receipts grow more slowly than inflation.

Answer (C) is correct. *(CIA, adapted)*
**REQUIRED:** The adjustment(s) needed to index a progressive tax system.
**DISCUSSION:** If tax brackets are not adjusted for inflation, increases in nominal but not real income may push taxpayers into tax brackets with higher (progressive) rates. Additionally, deductions and exemptions must be indexed so that the real incidence of taxation is not increased by inflation. Increases in nominal but not real income will result in higher real taxable income if deductions and exemptions have not been adjusted for inflation.
Answer (A) is incorrect because, if only deductions and exemptions are indexed, real taxes will still increase with inflation as taxpayers experience bracket creep. Answer (B) is incorrect because, if only tax brackets are adjusted, deductions and exemptions will have less real value. Real taxes will rise. Answer (D) is incorrect because indexing does not result in nominal tax receipts growing more slowly than the rate of inflation. Rather, indexing maintains the same real rate of taxation by ensuring that nominal tax receipts keep pace with inflation.

**12.** A value-added tax is collected on the basis of

    A. The difference between the value of a firm's sales and the value of its purchases from other domestic firms.

    B. The difference between the selling price of a real estate property and the amount the firm originally paid for the property.

    C. The value of a firm's sales to related companies.

    D. The profit earned on a firm's sales.

Answer (A) is correct. *(CIA, adapted)*
**REQUIRED:** The basis for collecting a value-added tax.
**DISCUSSION:** A value-added tax (VAT) is collected on the basis of the value created by the firm. This tax is measured by the difference between the value of the firm's sales and the value of its purchases. A VAT is in effect a retail sales tax. Because a consumer can avoid the tax by not purchasing, a VAT encourages saving and discourages consumption.
Answer (B) is incorrect because the difference between the selling price of a real estate property and the amount the firm originally paid for the property is a capital gain. Answer (C) is incorrect because the value of a firm's sales to related companies is the internal transfer price. Answer (D) is incorrect because the profit earned on a firm's sales is subject to the income tax.

**13.** A company purchases $150,000 of inputs from other firms and incurs $500,000 of labor costs in manufacturing its products. It also incurs $100,000 of interest expense. The company sells all of its output for $2.5 million. Rather than paying income tax, the company must pay a 25% value-added tax. How much tax will be due for this year's activities?

    A. $437,500

    B. $462,500

    C. $587,500

    D. $625,000

Answer (C) is correct. *(CIA, adapted)*
**REQUIRED:** The value-added tax due.
**DISCUSSION:** The value added is the difference between the value of the output and the value of the purchased inputs. Value-added tax payable equals the value-added tax rate times value added, or $587,500 [.25 × ($2,500,000 − $150,000)].
Answer (A) is incorrect because $437,500 is 25% of the earnings before tax. Answer (B) is incorrect because $462,500 deducts labor costs as well as purchased inputs. Answer (D) is incorrect because $625,000 is the value-added tax rate multiplied by the output of the firm.

**14.** Which of the following designations refers to taxes that will not necessarily take a larger absolute amount of income as income rises?

    A. Progressive.

    B. Proportional.

    C. Regressive.

    D. Regenerative.

Answer (C) is correct. *(CIA, adapted)*
**REQUIRED:** The taxes that will not necessarily take a larger absolute amount of income as income rises.
**DISCUSSION:** Regressive taxes are those for which the average tax rate falls as income rises. They take a smaller percentage of income as income rises, so they will not necessarily take a larger absolute amount of income as income rises.
Answer (A) is incorrect because progressive taxes, for which the average tax rate rises as income rises, take both a larger percentage of income and a larger absolute amount of income as income rises. Answer (B) is incorrect because proportional taxes, for which the average tax rate is constant for all income levels, always take a larger absolute amount of income as income rises. Answer (D) is incorrect because regenerative is not a term used to designate types of taxes.

**15.** A taxpayer who earns $50,000 during the year and pays a 15% tax rate on the first $30,000 of income and a 30% tax rate on all earnings over $30,000 has a(n)

   A. Marginal tax rate of 15%.

   B. Marginal tax rate of 21%.

   C. Average tax rate of 21%.

   D. Average tax rate of 22.5%.

Answer (C) is correct. *(CIA, adapted)*
   **REQUIRED:** The nature and amount of the tax rate.
   **DISCUSSION:** The average tax rate is calculated using the weighted-average method. The weight assigned to each rate is determined by the proportion of taxable income subject to it. The average tax rate is 21% [.15 × ($30,000 ÷ $50,000) + .30 × ($20,000 ÷ $50,000)].
   Answer (A) is incorrect because the marginal tax rate is 30%. The marginal tax rate equals the highest rate paid. Answer (B) is incorrect because the marginal tax rate is 30%. The marginal tax rate equals the highest rate paid. Answer (D) is incorrect because 22.5% is a simple numerical average.

## 8.3 Economic Indicators

**16.** The narrow definition of money supply, $M_1$, consists only of

   A. Current and demand deposits.

   B. Currency, demand deposits, other checkable deposits, and travelers' checks.

   C. Currency, demand deposits, and small time deposits.

   D. Currency, demand deposits, small time deposits, and Money Market Mutual Fund balances.

Answer (B) is correct. *(CMA, adapted)*
   **REQUIRED:** The narrow definition of money supply.
   **DISCUSSION:** The narrow definition of money supply includes coins, currency, and checking account deposits (including travelers' checks).
   Answer (A) is incorrect because it omits travelers' checks. Answer (C) is incorrect because it includes small time deposits. Answer (D) is incorrect because the broader definition adds small time deposits (e.g., little CDs owned by individuals) and money market funds.

**17.** Some economic indicators lead the economy into a recovery or recession, and some lag it. An example of a lag variable would be

   A. Chronic unemployment.

   B. Orders for consumer and producer goods.

   C. Housing starts.

   D. Consumer expectations.

Answer (A) is correct. *(CIA, adapted)*
   **REQUIRED:** The example of a lag variable.
   **DISCUSSION:** Economists use a variety of economic indicators to forecast turns in the business cycle. Economic indicators are variables that in the past have had a high correlation with aggregate economic activity. The best known are the composite indexes calculated by The Conference Board, a private research group with more than 2,700 corporate and other members worldwide. Indicators may lead, lag, or coincide with economic activity. The Conference Board's lagging indicators include average duration of unemployment in weeks, the change in the index of labor cost per unit of output, the average prime rate charged by banks, the ratio of manufacturing and trade inventories to sales, the commercial and industrial loans outstanding, the ratio of consumer installment credit outstanding to personal income, and the change in the CPI for services.
   Answer (B) is incorrect because orders for consumer and producer goods are leading indicators. Answer (C) is incorrect because housing starts are leading indicators. Answer (D) is incorrect because consumer expectations are leading indicators.

**18.** The two main variables that contribute to increases in real gross domestic product (GDP) derived from labor inputs are labor productivity and

   A. The potential labor force.

   B. The inflation rate.

   C. Quality of output.

   D. Total worker hours.

Answer (D) is correct. *(CIA, adapted)*
   **REQUIRED:** The other main variable contributing to increased real GDP derived from labor inputs.
   **DISCUSSION:** Real GDP increases when resource inputs and their productivity increase. Thus, to the extent that real GDP depends on labor inputs, real GDP equals total worker hours (labor input) times labor productivity (real output per worker per hour).
   Answer (A) is incorrect because the potential labor force is not a factor in the calculation. Rather, real GDP is determined by actual inputs and their productivity. Answer (B) is incorrect because real GDP is adjusted for inflation. Answer (C) is incorrect because national income accounting does not address the quality of output.

**19.** If the government of a country uses its foreign currency reserves to <List A> its own currency in the foreign currency market, the effect is to <List B> domestic aggregate demand.

|    | List A | List B |
|----|--------|--------|
| A. | Purchase | Not affect |
| B. | Purchase | Decrease |
| C. | Sell | Not affect |
| D. | Sell | Decrease |

Answer (B) is correct. *(CIA, adapted)*
**REQUIRED:** The effect on domestic aggregate demand of a government's purchase or sale of its own currency.
**DISCUSSION:** Aggregate demand is the amount of real domestic output that domestic consumers, foreign buyers, governments, and businesses will want to purchase at each price level. One factor that changes aggregate demand is net export spending. Exchange rates are among the determinants of net export spending. When a government intervenes in the foreign currency market to purchase its own currency, it causes an appreciation of that currency. One result is that the trade balance will be affected. Exports will fall as domestic goods become more costly from the perspective of foreign consumers. Imports will rise as foreign goods become less costly for domestic consumers. Consequently, net exports will decline and domestic aggregate demand will also decline.
Answer (A) is incorrect because, if a government increases the demand for its own currency, the currency will appreciate. This action will alter the trade balance and the level of aggregate demand. Answer (C) is incorrect because a sale of the currency by the domestic government will cause the currency to depreciate. This action will alter the trade balance and the level of aggregate demand. Answer (D) is incorrect because, if the government intervenes and causes a depreciation of the domestic currency, exports will rise and imports will fall. Net exports will therefore rise if the currency appreciates, so aggregate demand will increase.

**20.** The sale of final goods is <List A> the gross domestic product, and the sale of intermediate goods is <List B> the gross domestic product.

|    | List A | List B |
|----|--------|--------|
| A. | Included in | Included in |
| B. | Included in | Excluded from |
| C. | Excluded from | Included in |
| D. | Excluded from | Excluded from |

Answer (B) is correct. *(CIA, adapted)*
**REQUIRED:** The treatment of sales of final and intermediate goods in the determination of GDP.
**DISCUSSION:** The sale of final goods is included in, and the sale of intermediate goods is excluded from, GDP. The purpose of this treatment is to avoid double counting. The value of final goods already includes any intermediate transactions involved in their production.

**21.** Under the income approach, gross domestic product (GDP) is measured as

A. *Depreciation charges and indirect business taxes + Wages + Rents + Interest + Profits adjusted for net income earned abroad.*

B. *Wages + Rents + Interest + Profits.*

C. *Depreciation charges and indirect business taxes + Wages + Rents − Interest + Profits.*

D. *Wages + Rents + Interest − Profits adjusted for net income earned abroad.*

Answer (A) is correct. *(CIA, adapted)*
**REQUIRED:** The income approach to measurement of GDP.
**DISCUSSION:** GDP is the total value of goods and services produced within the boundaries of a country. It may be measured using an expenditures approach or an income approach. Under the income approach, GDP equals all income derived from the production of the year's output, with an adjustment for net income earned abroad (a positive or negative amount in theory). Two types of nonincome charges or allocations must be added to incomes (wages, rents, interest, and profits). Depreciation reflects the consumption of fixed capital during the period. It is the part of the year's receipts that must be allocated to replace the machinery, plant, etc., used up in the production of GDP. Indirect business taxes, such as sales, excise, and property taxes, are treated by businesses as a cost of production and form part of the total price of goods and services. Thus, they are not paid as wages, rents, interest, and profits. Accordingly, GDP may be measured as the sum of consumption of fixed capital, indirect business taxes, wages, rents, interest, and profits (proprietors' income, corporate taxes, dividends, and undistributed corporate profits), with an adjustment for net income earned abroad.
Answer (B) is incorrect because nonincome charges and the adjustment for net income earned abroad must also be included in the calculation. Answer (C) is incorrect because interest income is added, not subtracted. Also, the adjustment for net income earned abroad must be considered. Answer (D) is incorrect because profits are added, not subtracted. Also, nonincome charges must be included in the calculation.

**22.** Net domestic product is composed of the total market value of

    A.  All final goods and services produced in the economy in 1 year.

    B.  All goods and services produced in the economy in 1 year.

    C.  All final goods and services produced in the economy in 1 year minus the capital consumption allowance.

    D.  All goods and services produced in the economy in 1 year minus the capital consumption allowance.

Answer (C) is correct. *(CIA, adapted)*
    **REQUIRED:** The composition of net domestic product.
    **DISCUSSION:** Net domestic product is the market value of all final goods and services produced within the boundaries of a country within 1 year minus the capital consumption allowance.
    Answer (A) is incorrect because net domestic product is calculated net of the capital consumption allowance. Answer (B) is incorrect because net domestic product includes only final goods. The inclusion of intermediate goods would involve double counting. Also, net domestic product is calculated net of the capital consumption allowance. Answer (D) is incorrect because net domestic product does not include intermediate goods.

**23.**

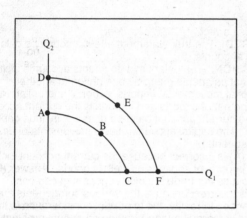

Curves ABC and DEF on the above graph represent production possibility curves for a nation. If point E on curve DEF represents the current combination of goods #1 and #2 consumed by that nation, the nation can reach point B on curve ABC by

    A.  Discovering more or better resources.

    B.  Discovering improved production techniques.

    C.  Incurring a trade deficit.

    D.  Incurring a trade surplus.

Answer (D) is correct. *(CIA, adapted)*
    **REQUIRED:** The method by which a nation can change its production possibilities curve.
    **DISCUSSION:** If a nation's exports are greater than its imports, the combination of goods consumed will be less than the combination produced. Hence, the production possibilities curve will shift inward, for example, to point B on curve ABC.
    Answer (A) is incorrect because the discovery of more or better resources causes an outward shift of the production possibilities curve. Answer (B) is incorrect because the discovery of improved production techniques causes an outward shift of the production possibilities curve. Answer (C) is incorrect because incurring a trade deficit results in consumption of a combination of goods outside the current production possibilities curve.

**24.** A nation's unemployment rate increased from 4% to 6%. The economic cost of this increase in unemployment can be described as the amount by which

    A.  Actual gross domestic product falls short of potential gross domestic product.

    B.  Aggregate expenditures fall short of the full-employment level of net domestic product.

    C.  Aggregate spending exceeds the full-employment level of net domestic product.

    D.  Merchandise imports exceed exports.

Answer (A) is correct. *(CIA, adapted)*
    **REQUIRED:** The economic cost of an increase in unemployment.
    **DISCUSSION:** In macroeconomic terms, the cost of unemployment is lost production. This lost output is measured in terms of the GDP gap, that is, the difference between actual and potential GDP. According to Okun's Law, a 2.5% GDP gap results from every 1% excess of the actual unemployment rate over the natural rate.

**25.** In relation to the balance of trade, all international transactions involving the purchase or sale of physical products between domestic and foreign countries are reflected in

    A. The balance of the capital account.

    B. Official reserves held by the central banks.

    C. The official financing account.

    D. The trade balance in the current account.

Answer (D) is correct.  *(CMA, adapted)*
    **REQUIRED:** The correct account.
    **DISCUSSION:** The balance of payments represents all international payments made by one nation to another, including those for imports, exports, investments, unilateral transfers such as pensions and gifts, and capital movements. The principal accounts are the current account and the capital account. The current account includes a net trade balance in goods, net investment receipts or payments, net receipts or payments for services, and the balance of unilateral transfers.
    Answer (A) is incorrect because the capital account includes capital movements only; the direction of capital movements is influenced by the prevailing interest rates in each nation. Answer (B) is incorrect because official reserves are assets held by central banks and are not necessarily related to current transactions. Answer (C) is incorrect because this is a nonsense answer.

**26.** When analyzing a country's balance of payments accounts, the

    A. "Current account" refers only to merchandise exports and imports.

    B. "Current account" and "trade balance" are the same.

    C. "Capital account" refers to the transactions related to the international movement of financial capital.

    D. Country will be in financial jeopardy unless each component in the balance of payments accounts balances at the end of the year.

Answer (C) is correct.  *(CMA, adapted)*
    **REQUIRED:** The true statement about a country's balance of payments accounts.
    **DISCUSSION:** The balance of payments accounts include all international payments made by one nation to another, including capital movements, imports, exports, and unilateral transfers. The net of exports and imports is the current account balance. The current account balance does not include capital transactions. The capital account reflects movements of financial capital (investments).
    Answer (A) is incorrect because the current account includes exports and imports of services as well as goods. Answer (B) is incorrect because the trade balance concerns goods only. Answer (D) is incorrect because the various components are never in balance. In reality, the important consideration is the total, and that is more of a long-run than an annual problem.

**27.** Which one of the following items represents a credit in the U.S. balance of payment accounts?

    A. U.S. imports of crude oil.

    B. Expenditures of American tourists abroad.

    C. Earnings belonging to foreign businesses that have U.S. plants.

    D. Loans to Americans by foreigners.

Answer (D) is correct.  *(CMA, adapted)*
    **REQUIRED:** The item that represents a credit in the U.S. balance of payments accounts.
    **DISCUSSION:** Basically, exports of goods and services are credited to the U.S. balance of payments accounts and imports are debited. Similarly, capital movements may be debited or credited. For example, transfers of capital from foreigners to Americans, such as loans, are credits in the accounts. In effect, these loans constitute exports of debt instruments and increase the supply of foreign exchange available for the U.S.
    Answer (A) is incorrect because imports are debited. Answer (B) is incorrect because expenditures of American tourists abroad are treated as imports and are therefore debited. Answer (C) is incorrect because earnings of foreigners represent outflows of foreign exchange and are debited.

**28.** The dominant reason countries devalue their currencies is to

    A. Improve the balance of payments.

    B. Discourage exports without having to impose controls.

    C. Curb inflation by increasing imports.

    D. Slow what is regarded as too rapid an accumulation of international reserves.

Answer (A) is correct.  *(CMA, adapted)*
    **REQUIRED:** The dominant reason countries devalue their currencies.
    **DISCUSSION:** Currency devaluations result in a change in the balance of payments. A devaluation means that other currencies will buy more of the devaluing nation's currency, and the prices of goods denominated in the devalued currency are therefore cheaper. A devaluation usually results in an increase in exports, a decrease in imports (caused by higher relative input prices), and an improved balance of trade.
    Answer (B) is incorrect because a devaluation will encourage exports. Answer (C) is incorrect because a devaluation will discourage imports and may encourage domestic inflation. Foreign goods will be more expensive. Answer (D) is incorrect because devaluation most likely occurs when a country is losing its reserves.

## 8.4 Legal Rules of Evidence

**29.** Hearsay

A. Could not consist of evidence of statements made in a court.

B. Is evidence of statements made verbally or nonverbally.

C. Is admissible but not discoverable.

D. Is discoverable but not admissible.

**Answer (B) is correct.** *(Publisher)*
**REQUIRED:** The true statement concerning hearsay.
**DISCUSSION:** Hearsay is a statement other than one made by the declarant while testifying at the trial or hearing, offered in evidence to prove the truth of the matter asserted. The statement alluded to may be a verbal or a nonverbal statement. It might include body language or written statements.

Answer (A) is incorrect because hearsay might involve a statement made in a courtroom at an unrelated trial or hearing. Answer (C) is incorrect because anything which is admissible is also discoverable under the rules of discovery. Answer (D) is incorrect because hearsay is discoverable only if it relates to the subject matter of the pending litigation and is not privileged. Hearsay may be admissible if one of the numerous exceptions to the hearsay rule is applicable.

**30.** Which of the following statements describes an internal control questionnaire? It

A. Provides detailed evidence regarding the substance of the control system.

B. Takes less of the engagement client's time to complete than other control evaluation devices.

C. Requires that the internal auditor be in attendance to properly administer it.

D. Provides indirect evidence that might need corroboration.

**Answer (D) is correct.** *(CIA, adapted)*
**REQUIRED:** The statement that describes an internal control questionnaire.
**DISCUSSION:** An internal control questionnaire consists of a series of questions about the controls designed to prevent or detect errors or irregularities. Answers to the questions help the internal auditor to identify specific internal control policies and procedures relevant to specific assertions and to design tests of controls to evaluate the effectiveness of their design and operation. The questionnaire provides a framework to assure that specific concerns are not overlooked, but it is not a sufficient means of understanding the entire system. Thus, the evidence obtained is indirect and requires corroboration by means of observation, interviews, flowcharting, examination of documents, etc.

Answer (A) is incorrect because questionnaires usually provide for yes/no responses and therefore provide less detailed evidence than some other procedures. Answer (B) is incorrect because questionnaires tend to be lengthy, and their completion is time-consuming. Answer (C) is incorrect because an auditor need not be present.

**31.** During interviews with the inventory management personnel, an internal auditor learned that salespersons often order inventory for stock without receiving the approval of the vice president of sales. Also, detail testing showed that there are no written approvals on purchase orders for replacement parts. The detail testing is a good example of

A. Indirect evidence.

B. Circumstantial evidence.

C. Corroborative evidence.

D. Subjective evidence.

**Answer (C) is correct.** *(CIA, adapted)*
**REQUIRED:** The evidence of which detail testing is a good example.
**DISCUSSION:** Corroborative evidence is evidence from a different source that supplements and confirms other evidence. For example, oral testimony that a certain procedure was not performed may be corroborated by the absence of documentation.

Answer (A) is incorrect because detail testing provides direct evidence that the approvals were not received. Indirect evidence establishes immediately collateral facts from which the main fact may be inferred. Answer (B) is incorrect because circumstantial evidence tends to prove a fact by proving other events or circumstances that afford a basis for a reasonable inference of the occurrence of the fact. Thus, it is also indirect evidence. Answer (D) is incorrect because subjective evidence is opinion-oriented and is not dependable for reaching engagement conclusions. No subjective evidence is present in this situation.

**32.** A contract dispute has arisen between an organization and a major supplier. To resolve the dispute, the most competent evidence is

A. Oral testimony of contracting parties.

B. The original contract.

C. Actions by parties to the contract.

D. A letter from the supplier's attorney.

Answer (B) is correct. *(CIA, adapted)*
**REQUIRED:** The most competent evidence to resolve a contract dispute between a company and a major supplier.
**DISCUSSION:** The best (primary) evidence is the most persuasive evidence. Reliability and the best evidence rule are closely related. The best evidence rule is ordinarily applied only to documentary evidence, especially to proof of the content of a writing. If the original writing is available, the best evidence rule prohibits a party from proving the content of a writing through oral testimony. Therefore, the original writing is the most competent evidence.
Answer (A) is incorrect because, if the original writing is available, oral testimony cannot contradict the content of the writing. Answer (C) is incorrect because the contract itself is the best evidence. Answer (D) is incorrect because the contract itself is the best evidence.

**33.** Much of the internal auditor's work involves accumulation of engagement information. A duplicate of a contract rather than the original is an example of what kind of evidence?

A. Secondary.

B. Circumstantial.

C. Hearsay.

D. Opinion.

Answer (A) is correct. *(CIA, adapted)*
**REQUIRED:** The type of evidence exemplified by the duplicate of a contract.
**DISCUSSION:** Secondary evidence according to the legal view is acceptable if primary evidence (the strongest evidence, e.g., original documents) has been destroyed or is not reasonably procurable. Secondary evidence must be a proper representation of primary evidence, e.g., copies of a contract.
Answer (B) is incorrect because circumstantial evidence inferentially establishes one fact by proving another collateral fact. Answer (C) is incorrect because hearsay is an out-of-court statement offered in evidence to prove the truth of the matter asserted. Answer (D) is incorrect because except for testimony by experts, witnesses may normally testify as to facts only.

## 8.5 Contracts

**34.** Which of the following is not a required element of a contract?

A. Legality.

B. Consideration.

C. Legal capacity.

D. A writing.

Answer (D) is correct. *(Publisher)*
**REQUIRED:** The element not required in a contract.
**DISCUSSION:** The four essential elements of a contract are an agreement (offer and acceptance), consideration, legal capacity of the parties to contract, and a legal objective or purpose. A writing is not required to enter into a contract. However, some contracts are not enforceable unless a writing evidences the contract.
Answer (A) is incorrect because legality is a required element of a contract. Answer (B) is incorrect because consideration is a required element of a contract. Answer (C) is incorrect because legal capacity is a required element of a contract.

**35.** The necessary elements of a contract include

A. Some form of writing, equal consideration, and legal capacity.

B. Formal execution, definite terms, and a valid offer and acceptance.

C. Offer and acceptance, consideration, legal capacity, and mutual assent.

D. Bilateral promises, legal capacity, and legality of purpose.

Answer (C) is correct. *(Publisher)*
**REQUIRED:** The element of a contract that is not necessary.
**DISCUSSION:** Contracts require each of the following:

1. Offer and acceptance
2. Mutual assent (meeting of the minds)
3. Consideration (bargained-for exchange)
4. Legality (legal purpose)
5. Capacity of parties (legal ability)

Answer (A) is incorrect because an oral contract is usually enforceable. Consideration must be legally sufficient and must be bargained for but need not have equal market value. Answer (B) is incorrect because most contracts are informal (simple), and if a term is missing, it can be implied by the court, with the exception of a quantity term. Answer (D) is incorrect because promises can be unilateral or divisible.

**36.** Consideration consists of

    A. Something with monetary value.

    B. Each party's receiving an actual benefit only.

    C. Two promises.

    D. Legal sufficiency and bargained-for exchange.

Answer (D) is correct. *(Publisher)*
**REQUIRED:** The elements of consideration.
**DISCUSSION:** Consideration must be legally sufficient and intended as a bargained-for exchange. A promisee has provided legally sufficient consideration if (s)he incurs a legal detriment or if the promisor receives a legal benefit. An essential aspect of consideration is that it be bargained for, and given in exchange for, the consideration provided by the other party. That is, consideration is mutual.
Answer (A) is incorrect because a promise satisfies the element of legal sufficiency. Monetary value is relatively unimportant. Answer (B) is incorrect because consideration is an exchange of legal benefit that may not have actual benefit. Answer (C) is incorrect because contracts can be unilateral, which involves only one promise.

**37.** Lamar became homeless at a very young age and was taken in by Aunt and Uncle. Many years later, Lamar became a detective in the city police department. When Aunt disappeared and was not heard from for a month, the case was assigned to Lamar. Uncle also came to Lamar and asked him to promise to find Aunt in return for the years of support. Lamar agreed to Uncle's request. Which of the following is true?

    A. Lamar's contractual duty to find Aunt is based on past consideration.

    B. Lamar has no contractual duty to find Aunt.

    C. If Uncle had also promised Lamar $1,000 for finding Aunt, he would be liable when Lamar found her.

    D. Lamar will be liable for breach of contract if he does not find Aunt.

Answer (B) is correct. *(Publisher)*
**REQUIRED:** The true statement regarding Lamar's contractual duty.
**DISCUSSION:** Lamar has a preexisting legal duty to find Aunt. Consideration does not exist if an existing duty was imposed by law or a person is already under a contractual agreement to render a specified performance. Lamar will suffer no new legal detriment by finding Aunt; thus, no contractual obligation exists.
Answer (A) is incorrect because past consideration does not satisfy the consideration requirement for the formation of a contract. Answer (C) is incorrect because Lamar has a preexisting legal duty to find Aunt. Answer (D) is incorrect because Lamar has not made a valid contract with Uncle.

**38.** Which of the following creates a valid contract between the parties?

    A. A reward was posted for the capture of Tom Jones. Maypole Burden, the county sheriff, captured Jones and claimed the reward.

    B. Slim Polestone promised to give Mabel Abbot a wedding present.

    C. Anxious Father promised to pay Albert Niceguy $4,000 to take his daughter to the annual Mulestone Dance. Albert agreed.

    D. Festival Fanny was drowning in her hot tub. Her boyfriend pulled her out. After the rescue, Festival's husband promised to pay her boyfriend $4 for rescuing his wife.

Answer (C) is correct. *(E. Rahm)*
**REQUIRED:** The item that creates a valid contract between the parties.
**DISCUSSION:** A valid contract exists because Anxious Father offered to pay Albert $4,000 for taking his daughter to the dance. This is a unilateral contract supported by the consideration of $4,000. Albert will be entitled to the $4,000 after he takes the daughter to the dance.
Answer (A) is incorrect because the sheriff had a preexisting legal duty to capture the criminal. Answer (B) is incorrect because a promise to make a gift is not enforceable. It lacks the bargain element. Answer (D) is incorrect because past consideration is not consideration.

**39.** Which of the following is a true statement about the legality requirement for a contract?

A. Only agreements to commit a crime or a tort or to violate a statute fail to meet the legality requirement.

B. All contracts in restraint of trade are considered illegal.

C. The illegality that invalidates the contract must be in the consideration for the promise.

D. The general rule is that neither party may be permitted to enforce an illegal agreement.

Answer (D) is correct.  *(Publisher)*
   **REQUIRED:** The true statement regarding the legality requirement for a contract.
   **DISCUSSION:** Legal purpose is requisite to enforceability of a contract.  An agreement that cannot be performed without violating a statute is void, as are agreements that violate public policy.  The state, not a private citizen, prosecutes violations of criminal statutes.  The interest protected is that of society.
   Answer (A) is incorrect because agreements that violate public policy lack legality.  Answer (B) is incorrect because the rule of reason is applied in antitrust cases to allow certain contracts to restrain competition.  Answer (C) is incorrect because lack of legality in formation or performance renders a contract void.

## 8.6 Contract Engagements

**40.** Which of the following types of contracts require an internal auditor to thoroughly review the economy and efficiency of performance of the contract?

A. Lump-sum contracts.

B. Cost-plus contracts.

C. Unit-price contracts.

D. Fixed-price contracts.

Answer (B) is correct.  *(Publisher)*
   **REQUIRED:** The contract requiring careful review of economy and efficiency by the internal auditor.
   **DISCUSSION:** Cost-plus are used in situations where the costs of a project are uncertain.  The price paid to the contractor is usually the cost to perform the contract and a fixed amount or fixed percentage cost.  A problem that may be encountered is that the contractor may not have an incentive to perform the contract efficiently or cost-effectively.  Therefore the internal auditor should review these contracts with more care.
   Answer (A) is incorrect because the internal auditor usually has little to evaluate because the work is performed in accordance with the terms of the contract.  Answer (C) is incorrect because a unit-contract is used when there is a convenient measure of how much work is completed.
   Answer (D) is incorrect because a fixed-price contract is another name for a lump-sum contract.

**41.** Which of the following types of contracts would be most appropriate to measure the work completed on a contract to clear 100 acres of farmland?

A. Fixed-price contract.

B. Lump-sum contract.

C. Cost-plus contract.

D. Unit-price contract.

Answer (D) is correct.  *(Publisher)*
   **REQUIRED:** The most appropriate contract to use when a measure of work is available.
   **DISCUSSION:** Unit-price contracts are often used when a convenient measure of work is available on a contract.  The 100 acres of farmland cleared can be easily measured per acre as the contract is performed.
   Answer (A) is incorrect because a fixed-price contract does not make it easier to measure work completed when a convenient measure of work is available.  Answer (B) is incorrect because a lump-sum contract is another name for a fixed-price contract and neither contract provide for an easy measure of work available on the 100 acres of farmland.  Answer (C) is incorrect because a cost-plus contract is often used when costs are unknown.  However, clearing 100 acres of farmland is not an unknown cost and a cost-plus contract will not help measure the progress on the performance of the contract.

---

Use Gleim's ***CIA Test Prep*** for interactive testing with over 2,000 additional multiple-choice questions!

# STUDY UNIT NINE
# INFORMATION TECHNOLOGY I

(41 pages of outline)

This study unit addresses the nature and modes of computer processing, the elements of the IT function, and basic control concepts. It continues with a treatment of computer hardware and operating systems. The concluding subunits concern various aspects of system security, including planning for business continuity in the event of an interruption of computer processing.

## 9.1 INTRODUCTION TO IT

1. **Characteristics**. The use of computers in business information systems has fundamental effects on the nature of business transacted, the procedures followed, the risks incurred, and the methods of mitigating those risks. These effects flow from the characteristics that distinguish computer-based processing from manual processing.

   a. **Transaction trails**. A complete trail useful for audit and other purposes might exist for only a short time or only in computer-readable form. The nature of the trail is often dependent on the transaction processing mode, for example, whether transactions are batched prior to processing or whether they are processed immediately as they happen.

   b. **Uniform processing of transactions**. Computer processing uniformly subjects like transactions to the same processing instructions and thus virtually eliminates clerical error, but programming errors (or other similar systematic errors in either the hardware or software) will result in all like transactions being processed incorrectly when they are processed under the same conditions.

   c. **Segregation of functions**. Many controls once performed by separate individuals may be concentrated in computer systems. Hence, an individual who has access to the computer may perform incompatible functions. As a result, other controls may be necessary to achieve the control objectives ordinarily accomplished by segregation of functions.

   d. **Potential for errors and fraud**. The potential for individuals, including those performing control procedures, to gain unauthorized access to data, to alter data without visible evidence, or to gain access (direct or indirect) to assets may be greater in computer systems. Decreased human involvement in handling transactions can reduce the potential for observing errors and fraud. Errors or fraud in the design or changing of application programs can remain undetected for a long time.

   e. **Potential for increased management supervision**. Computer systems offer management many analytical tools for review and supervision of operations. These additional controls may enhance internal control. For example, traditional comparisons of actual and budgeted operating ratios and reconciliations of accounts are often available for review on a more timely basis. Furthermore, some programmed applications provide statistics regarding computer operations that may be used to monitor actual processing.

f.  **Initiation or subsequent execution of transactions by computer**. Certain transactions may be automatically initiated or certain procedures required to execute a transaction may be automatically performed by a computer system. The authorization of these transactions or procedures may not be documented in the same way as those in a manual system, and management's authorization may be implicit in its acceptance of the design of the system.

g.  **Dependence of other controls on controls over computer processing**. Computer processing may produce reports and other output that are used in performing manual control procedures. The effectiveness of these controls can be dependent on the effectiveness of controls over the completeness and accuracy of computer processing. For example, the effectiveness of a manual review of a computer-produced exception listing is dependent on the controls over the production of the listing.

2.  **Classification of Controls**. The broad categories are defined beginning below.

    a.  **General controls** apply to all computer activities. They often include controls over the development, modification, and maintenance of computer programs and controls over the use of and changes to data maintained on computer files. General controls encompass

        1)  The plan of organization and operation of the computer activity

            a)  **Organizational controls** address the proper segregation of duties and responsibilities within the computer processing environment.

            b)  **Operating controls** ensure efficient and effective operation within the computer department.

                i)   These controls also assure proper procedures in case of data loss because of error or disaster.

                ii)  Typical operating controls include the proper labeling of all files both internally (machine-readable file header and trailer labels) and externally (halt and error procedures, duplicate files, and reconstruction procedures for files).

        2)  The procedures for documenting, reviewing, testing, and approving systems or programs and changes in them

            a)  **Program development and documentation controls** are concerned with the proper planning, development, writing, and testing of computer application programs.

                i)   These activities require proper documentation, including flowcharts, listings, and run manuals for programs already written.

                ii)  Controls over proper authorization of any changes in existing programs are also necessary.

        3)  Controls built into the equipment by the manufacturer **(hardware controls)**

            a)  Hardware controls assure the proper internal handling of data as they are moved and stored. They include parity checks, echo checks, read-after-write checks, and any other procedure built into the equipment to assure data integrity.

        4)  Controls over access to equipment and data files

            a)  **Access controls** provide assurance that only authorized individuals use the system and that usage is for authorized purposes. Such controls include physical safeguards of equipment, proper library security, and passwords.

5) Other data and procedural controls affecting overall computer operations

b. **Application controls** relate to specific tasks performed by the system. They should provide reasonable assurance that the recording, processing, and reporting of data are properly performed. Application controls relate to individual computerized accounting applications, for example, programmed edit controls for verifying customers' account numbers and credit limits.

   1) **Input controls** provide reasonable assurance that data received for processing have been properly authorized, converted into machine-sensible form, and identified. They also provide reasonable assurance that data (including data transmitted over communication lines) have not been lost, suppressed, added, duplicated, or otherwise improperly changed. Moreover, input controls relate to rejection, correction, and resubmission of data that were initially incorrect.

   2) **Processing controls** provide reasonable assurance that processing has been performed as intended for the particular application. All transactions should be processed as authorized, no authorized transactions should be omitted, and no unauthorized transactions should be added.

   3) **Output controls** provide assurance that the processing result (such as account listings or displays, reports, files, invoices, or disbursement checks) is accurate and that only authorized personnel receive the output.

3. **Functional Areas of IT Operations**. Controls should ensure the efficiency and effectiveness of IT operations. They include proper segregation of the duties within the IT environment. Thus, the responsibilities of systems analysts, programmers, operators, file librarians, the control group, and others should be assigned to different individuals, and proper supervision should be provided.

   a. **Segregation of Duties**. This general control is vital because a segregation of functions (authorization, recording, and access to assets) may not be feasible in an IT environment. For example, a computer may print checks, record disbursements, and generate information for reconciling the account balance, which are activities customarily segregated in a manual system. If the same person provides the input and receives the output for this process, a significant control weakness exists. Accordingly, certain tasks should not be combined.

      1) **Database/network/web administrators**. They are responsible for management, supervision, and oversight of computing facilities.

         a) The **database administrator (DBA)** is the individual who has overall responsibility for developing and maintaining the database and for establishing controls to protect its integrity. Thus, only the DBA should be able to update data dictionaries. In small systems, the DBA may perform some functions of a DBMS. In larger applications, the DBA uses a DBMS as a primary tool.

      2) **Data administrators**. They coordinate activities within the data administration department.

      3) **Systems analysts** are specifically qualified to analyze and design computer information systems. They survey the existing system, analyze the organization's information requirements, and design new systems to meet those needs. These design specifications will guide the preparation of specific programs by computer programmers. Systems analysts should not perform programming tasks or have access to computer equipment, production programs, data files, and input-output controls.

      4) **Programmers** design, write, test, and document the specific programs developed by the analysts. Programmers as well as analysts may be able to modify programs, data files, and controls and should therefore have no access to computer equipment and files or to copies of programs used in production.

5) **Computer (console) operators** are responsible for the actual processing of data in accordance with the program run manual and messages received from the system (preferably in hard copy form for review by the control group). They load data, mount storage devices, and operate the equipment.

   a) Console operators should not be assigned programming duties or responsibility for systems design and should have no opportunity to make changes in programs and systems as they operate the equipment. Ideally, computer operators should not have programming knowledge or access to documentation not strictly necessary for their work.

   b) **Help desks** are usually a responsibility of computer operations because of the operational nature of their functions. A help desk logs reported problems, resolves minor problems, and forwards more difficult problems to the appropriate information systems resources, such as a technical support unit or vendor assistance.

6) **Data conversion operators** perform the tasks of data preparation and transmission, for example, conversion of source data to magnetic disk or tape and entry of transactions from remote terminals.

7) **Librarians** should maintain control over and accountability for documentation, programs, and data files. Librarians should have no access to equipment or the skills to perpetrate fraud.

8) The **data control group** must be independent of systems development, programming, and operations. It receives user input, logs it, transfers it to the computer center, monitors processing, reviews error messages, compares control totals, distributes output, and determines whether error corrections have been made by users.

9) **End users** need access to applications data and functions only.

4. **Data center operations** may occur in a centralized data processing facility that is responsible for the storage, management, and dissemination of data and information. A data center may be either an internal department or a separate organization that specializes in providing data services to others. A data center may operate in several possible modes.

   a. **Batch Mode**. Batch processing is the accumulation and grouping of transactions for processing on a delayed basis. The batch approach is suitable for applications that can be processed at intervals and involve large volumes of similar items, e.g., payroll, sales, inventory, and billing.

      1) **Service bureaus** perform batch processing for subscribers. This off-site mode of processing requires a user to prepare input and then transport it to the bureau, with attendant loss of time and increase in security problems. Employing a service bureau is one means of **outsourcing**. Hiring a **facilities management organization** is another. A facilities management organization operates and manages an internal data processing activity. It may manage hardware, software, system development, system maintenance, and staffing. The facilities manager may own all of the hardware and software and employ all the personnel.

   b. **Online Mode**. An online processing system is in direct communication with the computer, giving it the capability to handle transactions as they are entered. An online system permits both immediate posting (updating) and inquiry of master files as transactions occur.

      1) **Real-time processing** involves processing an input record and receiving the output soon enough to affect a current decision-making process. In a real-time system, the user interacts with the system to control an ongoing activity.

2) The term "online," often used with "real time," indicates that the decision maker is in direct communication with the computer. **Online, real-time systems** usually permit access to the main computer from multiple remote terminals.

c. A **timesharing** system allows many users to have access through remote terminals to a CPU owned by a vendor of computing services. The CPU services them alternately. Timesharing differs from multiprogramming because the CPU devotes a fixed time to each user's program.

d. **Totally Centralized Systems**. All data processing and systems development are done at one data processing center.

    1) All processing is done by one large computer.

    2) Remote users are serviced via data communications channels between themselves and the center.

    3) Terminals at the remote sites are usually dumb terminals (providing communications only, with no stand-alone processing capabilities).

    4) Requests for development of new systems are submitted for the consideration of the centralized systems development group.

    5) The centralized staff is large.

    6) Advantages of total centralization arise primarily from the economies of scale permitted and the strengthening of control.

e. **Totally Decentralized Systems**. Data processing functions are independently developed at each remote site. Each site has its own smaller computer and its own staff.

    1) In a completely decentralized system, each computer stands alone, independent of any centralized or other computer.

    2) The primary advantages of a decentralized system are that

        a) The individual units' personnel identify more closely with the system.

        b) Development projects are more easily accepted and meet local needs better.

f. **Downsizing** consists of moving organization-wide applications to mid-range or networked computers. The purpose is to reduce costs by using less expensive systems that are more versatile than larger, more expensive systems.

    1) Factors to consider when downsizing include the following:

        a) Downsized applications are less reliable than their mainframe predecessors because they usually are newer and thus have not been tested extensively.

        b) Downsized technology is less reliable and lacks the monitoring and control features that permit recovery from minor processing interruptions.

        c) Security is better on larger mainframe systems.

        d) Downsized applications increase complexity because data becomes fragmented across multiple systems.

        e) Applications with very large databases still require very large computers (i.e., mainframes) in order to make data accessible.

        f) Mainframes allow for easier and cheaper data entry.

g. **Distributed Data Processing**

    1) In a distributed data processing system, the organization's processing needs are examined in their totality.

2) Information is analyzed to determine which parts of the application are better performed locally and which parts are better performed at some other, possibly centralized, site.

    a) For example, an organization may prefer to use workstations rather than a mainframe for ad hoc queries to avoid the expense and the possible degradation of response time on the host computer.

    b) An advantage of distributed processing is **fail-soft protection**, that is, the ability to continue processing at all sites except a nonfunctioning one.

3) The key distinction between decentralized and distributed systems is the interconnection among the nodes (sites) in the network.

4) EXAMPLE: In processing a sales order, order entry may be handled by an intelligent terminal. Upon the completion of the sales order, the terminal will transmit it to a computer in a local warehouse. This computer will determine whether the item is available by interrogating an inventory file at the organization's manufacturing plant. If the item is available, the paperwork is produced locally at the warehouse, and the clerk at the terminal is notified. If it is not available, the plant's computer determines the probable delay before the item is available. This information is transmitted via the local warehouse computer to the terminal. If this delay is acceptable to the customer, the production paperwork is performed at the plant. Thus, the actual processing of the order entry is shared by the intelligent terminal, the warehouse computer, and the manufacturing plant computer.

5) The increased **interdependence among processing sites** allows greater flexibility in systems design and the possibility of an optimal distribution of processing tasks. The process of deciding on the best distribution of processing capabilities (hardware), safeguards (controls), information (files and databases), and personnel is complex.

6) **Cooperative processing** is a system in which computers in a distributed processing network can share the use of application programs belonging to another end user. The system assigns different machines the functions they perform best in executing a transaction-based application program. In other words, separate sections of an application may reside on different computers. In contrast, traditional distributed processing performed a task on one computer, with other computers used for communications.

    a) For example, a personal computer may be more cost effective for entering and validating data for the application. It is better suited for frequent screen updating and graphical user interfaces. A mainframe might handle file input and output.

7) Updating data in a distributed system may require special protocols. Thus, a **two-phase commit disk-writing protocol** is used. If data is to be updated in two places, databases in both locations are cleared for updating before either one performs (commits) the update. In the first phase, both locations agree to the update. In the second phase, both perform the update.

8) The development of distributed systems may be hindered because of the existence of legacy systems, which are applications developed with older technology that are an integral part of the entity's computer processing and are difficult to modify or replace. Conversely, less software has been developed for the newer distributed processing technology.

9) **Response times** in distributed networks will depend on the volume of data traffic; i.e., the greater the data traffic, such as transactions, security checking and other network functions, and backups, the longer the response time.

10) **Backing up** software and data files also is a significant issue in distributed and cooperative systems. Because the systems are controlled by users, not a central information processing department, user management must be responsible for adequate backup.

5. Stop and review! You have completed the outline for this subunit. Study multiple-choice questions 1 through 10 beginning on page 445.

## 9.2 OPERATING SYSTEMS AND COMPUTER DEVICES

1. Systems software in machine or assembly language is necessary to facilitate the processing of application programs by the computer. Systems software, which is ordinarily purchased from vendors, performs the fundamental tasks needed to manage computer resources (the CPU, communications devices, and peripherals).

   a. An **operating system** is essential software that acts as an interface between application software and the hardware. It manages access to the computer's resources by concurrent applications and, in a network system, concurrent users.

      1) DOS, Windows, and Unix are examples of operating systems.

2. The **operating system** mediates between the application programs and the computer hardware.

   a. To communicate with the user, the operating system of a PC may include a **graphical user interface (GUI)**. It employs graphical icons to represent activities, programs, and files. The computer mouse is used to select icons. A GUI simplifies computer usage compared with older systems that require the typing of text-based commands on a keyboard.

      1) **Windows** is a GUI shell initially developed by Microsoft to run in conjunction with the DOS operating system.

      2) Windowing is the characteristic that allows a computer to display more than one program on the screen at the same time. Each program has its own section of the screen, but only one program can interact with the user at a given time.

   b. An operating system also manages job scheduling and accounts for computer usage, controls input and output, assigns storage locations in main memory, and protects data in the event of a system malfunction.

   c. Furthermore, an operating system may permit a single configuration of hardware to function in several different modes.

      1) **Batch processing** entails periodic processing of accumulated groups of transactions. It is typical of older systems or of those in which extremely large numbers of transactions must be processed. Contrast **online processing**, which involves immediate and direct entry of transactions.

      2) **Multiprogramming**. The operating system processes a program until an input or output operation is required. Because input or output can be handled by peripheral hardware, the CPU can begin executing another program's instructions while input or output is in progress and thereby increase its throughput. Several programs are being processed concurrently, but only one is actually being executed in the CPU. **Throughput** is the quantity of work processed in a given period. It is used as a measuring tool to evaluate processors.

      3) **Multitasking** is multiprogramming on a single-user operating system. For example, a PC user might be able to display a spreadsheet program and a word processing program on the screen at the same time.

4) **Multiprocessing**. The operating system in conjunction with multiple CPUs executes instructions from more than one program simultaneously.

5) **Virtual storage**. The operating system automatically separates user programs into small fixed-length pages or variable-length segments, allowing the user to have access to a memory virtually equivalent to the total of primary and secondary memories.

6) **Paging**. A page is part of a program. Paging is a memory-swapping technique. The major portion of a program or set of data may be kept in secondary memory while the remainder is held in primary memory. This swapping means that the "virtual" capacity of primary memory is greatly expanded.

3. **Hardware** is the configuration of electronic, magnetic, and mechanical devices that perform input, processing, output, storage, control, communications, and data preparation functions in a computer system.

   a. Fourth-generation hardware uses **very large-scale integrated circuits (VLSIC)** based on silicon chips that contain millions of transistors per chip. This kind of integrated circuit is a **semiconductor**. Thus, memory, logic, and control features can be combined on a chip, or **microprocessor**. This technology has resulted in huge increases in memory size and processing speeds, a rapid decline in computing costs, and the widespread use of microprocessors in everyday products.

   1) Chip speed depends on **word length**, **cycle speed** (measured in megahertz or millions of cycles per second), and **data bus width** (also measured in bits).

   2) **Reduced instruction set computing (RISC)** is another means of increasing chip speed. It reduces the number of instructions hardwired into a chip.

4. All computers have at least one **central processing unit (CPU)** that works in conjunction with peripheral devices.

   a. The CPU is the main element of a computer system. The major function of the CPU is to fetch stored instructions and data, decode the instructions, and carry out the instructions in the **arithmetic-logic unit (ALU)**. The principal components of the CPU are the ALU (one or more) and the control unit.

   1) The **control unit** directs and coordinates the entire computer system.

   2) **Primary storage** is closely connected to the CPU in the central processor. It consists of electronic components that store letters, numbers, and special characters used in processing. The purposes of primary storage are to hold the operating system, part or all of a program being executed, and data used by the program.

      a) Internal primary storage includes **register memory**, used for ultra high-speed and very brief storage of small amounts of data and instructions immediately before use; **cache memory**, used for high-speed storage of frequently used data and programs; and **random-access memory (RAM)**, used to store large quantities of data. Data may be read from or written on RAM. A power interruption causes erasure of RAM.

      b) **Read-only memory (ROM)** is permanent storage used to hold the basic low-level programs and data. ROM can be read from but not written to; ROM chips are obtained from the manufacturer with programs already stored in them. A power interruption does not erase data written on ROM or on magnetic secondary storage devices. However, a power interruption may corrupt the data.

         i) **Programmable ROM** (PROM) can be programmed once.

         ii) **Erasable programmable ROM** (EPROM) can be erased using a special process and then reprogrammed.

b.   Computer systems are typically classified by **computing power** dictated by CPU speed, memory capacity, and hardware architecture (and thus cost).

   1)   **Personal computers (microcomputers)** range in price and performance from low-end personal computers to powerful desktop models. **Workstations** are also desktop machines, but they are often classified separately from personal computers because of their enhanced mathematical and graphical abilities. In addition, workstations have the capacity to execute more complicated tasks simultaneously than a personal computer. Thus, they tend to be used by scientists and engineers, for example, for simulations and computer-aided design, and in the financial services industry.

      a)   Because of the large number of personal computers in use and aggressive pricing strategies, personal computers have become very affordable. Moreover, personal computers have crossed into the minicomputer arena by providing comparable power and multi-user capabilities previously unavailable.

      b)   By adding a modem and communications software, the personal computer can also serve as an interface with other computers. Accordingly, many of the same control and security concerns that apply to larger computers also apply to a personal computer environment.

      c)   **Notebook, laptop, and palmtop computers** are the smallest forms of personal computers.

   2)   **Mainframes** are large, general-purpose computers characterized by large memory sizes and very rapid processing speeds. They often provide data communications, support many terminal users, are capable of handling large databases, and can execute many millions of instructions per second (MIPS).

   3)   **Supercomputers** are ultra powerful machines designed for scientific, military, and business applications involving very large numbers of variables. They can process up to hundreds of billions of instructions per second by using **parallel processing** technology.

   4)   A **server** may be any of the foregoing types of computers. It is specially configured to support a network by permitting users to share files, databases, software, and peripherals.

   5)   A **network computer** is a personal computer that does not store programs and data but rather downloads them via the Internet or a company's own network.

5.   **Peripheral devices** include items of equipment, other than the CPU, that provide for input, storage, output, outside communication, or additional facilities. They function much more slowly than the CPU, and a system is said to be input-output bound when the speed of peripheral devices determines the speed of task completion.

a.   **Data entry devices**

   1)   A **data entry terminal** with a **keyboard** is online equipment that is a common input device. The terminal includes a monitor that allows display of user input and computer output.

   2)   A **magnetic ink character reader (MICR)** is used in the banking industry to read the magnetic ink on checks.

3)   An **optical character reader (OCR)** does not need special ink and can read bar codes and alphanumeric characters.

    a)   A **turnaround document** is computer output prepared in such a way that it can eventually be used as a source document for an input transaction. For example, an optical character recognition document might be used as a sales invoice to be mailed to a customer and returned with the payment. Thus, no new document would have to be prepared to record the payment.

4)   An alternative to keyboard and text-based input is the use of a **computer mouse**. Its point and click function controls a cursor on the video display screen. The user pushes a button on the mouse to choose the command indicated by the cursor.

5)   **Touch screen** technology provides another limited alternative to keyboard input. Commands or data can be entered by touching the sensitized surface of a monitor.

6)   **Digital scanners** convert documents and pictures into digital form.

7)   **Voice recognition** input devices are still another alternative to keyboard input. These systems compare the speaker's voice patterns with prerecorded patterns. Advanced systems now have large vocabularies and shorter training periods. They allow for dictation and are therefore not limited to simple commands.

8)   New forms of mobile data acquisition methods are available.

    a)   **Palmtop computers** are miniature notebook computers with keyboard input.

    b)   **Pen-based input** is possible with devices that have a flat screen on which the user can print directly with a special stylus.

    c)   Other special devices may be used to gather inventory data, read meters, inspect goods, etc. Moreover, manufacturers may use infrared, ultraviolet, and other devices to automate the acquisition of production data.

9)   **Sensors** collect information directly for transmittal to a computer.

10)  **Point-of-sale terminals** and **automated teller machines** are other input devices.

b.  **Output devices**

1)   A **monitor** or **video display terminal** (a cathode ray tube or CRT) can be used to display output and is the most common output device.

2)   **Printers** are also common devices used solely for output. Printers may print one character, one line, or one page at a time at varying speeds and with varying quality. Some newer printers have limited processing ability.

3)   A **plotter** is an output device that draws graphs on paper.

4)   A **voice output device** converts digital data into speech using prerecorded sounds.

 c. **Secondary storage devices**

  1) **Floppy disk drives** serve as low-capacity backup devices for PCs. The most common floppy disk is 3 1/2" with a capacity up to 2.8 MB.

  2) **Hard disk drives** provide a permanent location for data and system files. A vast array of internal and external drives exist, providing gigabytes of flexible storage options. Popular external drives are available with removable cartridges. This trend has created a practically endless amount of storage space. One possibility is a **redundant array of inexpensive disks (RAID)** (also called a redundant array of inexpensive drives or redundant array of independent disks). It is a grouping of numerous hard disk drives, a control chip, and software that allows for data delivery along multiple paths. RAID is used in fault-tolerant systems because, if one drive fails, the other disks can compensate for the loss. It can also improve access time since data can be read simultaneously from multiple disks.

  3) **Magnetic tape drives** are based on older (and cheaper) technology but are still used for system backup and data transfer. Tape density is from 1,600 to 6,250 bytes per inch. However, tape cartridges with much higher densities are now replacing reels in large computers. Small cartridges are used in PCs.

   a) **DAT (digital audiotape)** is primarily used as a backup in imaging systems and as a master for CD-ROM.

  4) **CD-ROM (compact disk/read-only memory) drives**. CD-ROMs are laser-optical disks that are almost identical to CD-audio disks. They provide capacities of over 660 MB.

   a) **WORM (write once/read many)** optical disks allow the user to write once without the possibility of erasure. However, erasable optical disks are also available.

   b) **Digital video (versatile) disks (DVDs)** have greater storage capacity than CD-ROMs. They can store up to 5 gigabytes of video, audio, graphics, and text data.

  5) A multitude of storage devices exists. Capacity, reliability, convenience, and speed are limited only by the amount a user is willing to spend.

 d. **Other peripheral equipment**

  1) **Controllers** are hardware units designed to operate (control) specific input or output units, e.g., terminals and printers. These devices eliminate the need for the CPU to operate such devices. The term "buffers and channels" is also sometimes used to describe devices that link the CPU with input/output devices and storage units.

  2) A **console** consists of a VDT, a keyboard, and a printer. It is used for communication between the operator or maintenance engineer and the computer.

   a) It permits the computer to exchange instructions with the operator, logs jobs, and provides a printout of activity that can be reviewed by auditors and the control group.

  3) A **node** is a hardware device in a network that can act as a message buffer (hold part of the message until the rest is received), switch messages, and serve as an error control. A node can be a computer, controller, or multiplexor.

6. Stop and review! You have completed the outline for this subunit. Study multiple-choice questions 11 through 21 beginning on page 448.

## 9.3 DEVELOPMENT OF SYSTEMS AND APPLICATIONS

1.    **Systems Development**

    a.    The **life-cycle approach** is the traditional methodology applied to the development of large, highly structured application systems.

        1)    A major advantage of the life-cycle approach is enhanced management and control of the development process.  The systems development cycle may be divided into three steps:  (1) definition, (2) development, and (3) installation and operation.

            a)    **Definition**.  The following phases are involved:

                i)    A **proposal** for a new or modified application should be prepared indicating the need for the application, the support for it within the organization, and scheduling considerations (timing of the project, employee availability, etc.).

                ii)    **Feasibility studies** should be conducted to determine whether the system is technically, economically, and operationally feasible.

                iii)    **Information requirements** must be ascertained, including the inquiries to be made by users, reports generated, database needs, and operating characteristics

                iv)    The **general (conceptual) design** contains the users' description of the application, required inputs and outputs, the functions to be carried out, an overview of the processing flow (relationship of the most important programs, files, inputs, and outputs), an overview of controls, and outlines of documentation.

            b)    **Development**

                i)    **Physical system design**

- This phase involves work by specialists to develop specifications for

  - Work flow and programs (but not coding)
  - Controls and points where they should be implemented
  - Hardware
  - Security measures, including backup
  - Data communications
  - Quality assurance testing for the balance of the development process

- One approach to design of the physical system is **top-down design**, which is the practice of defining a system by its general purpose and then progressively refining the level of detail in the form of a hierarchy.

  - The top-down method begins with analysis of broad organizational goals, objectives, and policies as the bases for the design process.  This step requires an understanding of the entity's environment and significant activities.

  - The next step is to determine the decisions to be made by managers and the information required to make those decisions.  The necessary reports, databases, inputs, processing methods, and equipment specifications can then be defined.

■ A weakness of the top-down approach is that it tends to concentrate on managers' information needs at the expense of the design of efficient transaction processing at the operational level.

● **Structured design** of the physical system is a modular approach. Each module (subsystem) is functionally defined, and the degree of interdependence among the modules is minimized. This process simplifies development and enhances adaptability of the components of the system but requires careful definition of modules and the linkages (interfaces) between them.

● **HIPO** (Hierarchy-Input-Process-Output) is a documentation technique developed by IBM that relies on stylized charts depicting increasingly more detailed levels of the system.

ii) **Physical database design** depends on the existing system.

● New files or a new database may have to be designed.

● Modifying an existing database may be feasible.

● If the existing database provides for the new application, modification may not be necessary.

iii) **Procedure development** includes writing technical manuals, forms, and other materials for all persons who will use, maintain, or otherwise work with the system.

● A **printer layout chart** is a gridded spacing chart that is an aid to designing documents and reports generated as hardcopy paper output by a printer.

iv) **Flowcharting** is an essential aid in the development process. A flowchart is a pictorial representation of the definition, analysis, or solution of a problem in which symbols are used to depict operations, data flow, equipment, etc. Flowcharts may be created for a system, program, or document.

v) Other means of documenting the decision logic reflected in systems are matrices (presentations of pairs of conditions and resulting actions), decision tables, decision trees, and pseudocode.

vi) **Data flow diagrams** are employed in **structured systems analysis**. They use just four basic symbols. Data flow diagrams show how data flow to, from, and within the system and the processes that manipulate the data. A data flow diagram can be used to depict lower-level details as well as higher-level processes. A system can be divided into subsystems, and each subsystem can be further subdivided at levels of increasing detail. Thus, any process can be expanded as many times as necessary to show the required level of detail.

● **Action diagrams** are process logic notations that combine graphics and text to support the definition of technical rules.

● **Program structure charts** are graphical depictions of the hierarchy of modules or instructions in a program.

● **Conceptual data modules** are independent definitions of the data requirements that are explained in terms of entities and relationships.

vii) **Program development** entails coding programs in accordance with the specifications in the physical design phase and then testing the results.

- **Structured programming** divides the system's set of programs into discrete modules by functional specifications. The objective is to create modules that are independent logical units, each of which has one entry and one exit point. Data sharing among modules should also be minimized. This method reduces the complexity created when instructions jump back and forth among different sections of the program.

- Structured analysis relies on diagrams, not narrative. See the discussion of data flow diagrams on the previous page.

- Each module can be coded by a separate team to

  - Facilitate security because no one group knows the complete set of programs

  - Expedite the development process because several programming teams can work simultaneously

  - Facilitate maintenance because a change or patch need only be module-specific, a less complicated procedure than fitting a patch to a complex, multifunction program

- **Computer-aided software engineering (CASE)** applies the computer to software design and development. It provides the capacity to maintain on the computer all of the system documentation, e.g., data flow diagrams, data dictionaries, and pseudocode (structured English); to develop executable input and output screens; and to generate program code in at least skeletal form. Thus, CASE facilitates the creation, organization, and maintenance of documentation and permits some automation of the coding process.

- **Object-oriented programming** combines data and the related procedures into an object. Thus, an object's data can be operated on only within the object. If the procedures (called methods) for manipulating the data in an object are changed, no other parts of the program are affected. The idea of limiting code that operates on an object to its own source code unit is called encapsulation.

  - The basic concepts of object-oriented programming are class and inheritance. Programs are written by describing the creation and interaction of objects. One class of objects can inherit the characteristics of a more general class. Thus, a basic advantage of object-oriented programming is that the code is reusable.

  - However, the methods unique to a subclass may override an inherited method. When override occurs, the object responds to the same message but executes its method, not the inherited method. Accordingly, the advantage of having objects that inherit properties is that program code can be written once for the class instead of having to be rewritten for each instance of similar objects in the class.

- **Visual programming** creates programs by choosing objects from a library and arranging them in a desired sequence rather than by writing code. It is an offshoot of object-oriented programming. The process of creating software in this way is sometimes referred to as rapid application development.

c) **Installation and operation**

i) Training and educating system users is important not only for proper use of the system but also to offset the resistance of users whose jobs may have been substantially changed.

ii) Acceptance testing by users of inputs, outputs, programs, and procedures is necessary to determine that the new system meets their needs.

iii) Systems conversion is the final testing and switchover. If a direct cutover (immediate full implementation of and switch to the new system) is not indicated, other options include the following:

- **Parallel operation** is the operation of the old and new systems simultaneously until satisfaction is obtained that the new system is operating as expected.
- **Pilot operation** (modular or phase-in conversion) is the conversion to the new or modified system by module or segment, e.g., one division, department, function, or branch of the company at a time. One disadvantage is the extension of the conversion time.

iv) Systems follow-up or post-audit evaluation is a subsequent review of the efficiency and effectiveness of the system after it has operated for a substantial time (e.g., 1 year).

b. **Prototyping** (an experimental assurance or iterative process) is costly and time-consuming and thus is not currently the most common approach. It entails developing and putting into operation successively more refined versions of the system until sufficient information is obtained to produce a satisfactory design. It is advantageous for smaller applications, especially those involving decision support when end users cannot anticipate how the final system will function.

c. Systems development should be overseen by an **information systems steering committee** consisting of senior managers representing the functional areas of the organization, such as information systems, accounting, and marketing.

1) It provides overall guidance for information systems activities to assure that goals are consistent with those of the organization. Thus, the steering committee establishes priorities for implementing applications and either performs or approves high-level planning.

2.   **Application controls**

a.   Crucial to the development of programs for particular applications is the inclusion of application controls (input, processing, and output controls). **Input controls** provide reasonable assurance that data received for processing have been properly authorized, converted into machine-sensible form, and identified, and that data (including data transmitted over communication lines) have not been lost, suppressed, added, duplicated, or otherwise improperly changed. Input controls also relate to rejection, correction, and resubmission of data that were initially incorrect.

1)   **Edit checks** are programmed into the software. They include

a)   **Error listing**. Editing (validation) of data should produce a cumulative automated error listing that includes not only errors found in the current processing run but also uncorrected errors from earlier runs. Each error should be identified and described, and the date and time of detection should be given. Sometimes, the erroneous transactions may need to be recorded in a suspense file. This process is the basis for developing appropriate reports.

b)   **Field checks** are tests of the characters in a field to verify that they are of an appropriate type for that field. For example, the field for a Social Security number should not contain alphabetic characters.

c)   **Financial totals** summarize dollar amounts in an information field in a group of records.

d)   A **hash total** is a control total without a defined meaning, such as the total of employee numbers or invoice numbers, that is used to verify the completeness of data. Thus, the hash total for the employee listing by the personnel department could be compared with the total generated during the payroll run.

e)   **Limit and range checks** are based on known limits for given information. For example, hours worked per week will not equal 200.

f)   **Preformatting**. To avoid data entry errors in online systems, a screen prompting approach may be used that is the equivalent of the preprinted forms routinely employed as source documents. The dialogue approach, for example, presents a series of questions to the operator. The preformatted screen approach involves the display of a set of boxes for entry of specified data items. The format may even be in the form of a copy of a transaction document.

g)   **Reasonableness (relationship) tests** check the logical correctness of relationships among the values of data items on an input and the corresponding master file record. For example, it may be known that employee John Smith works only in departments A, C, or D; thus, a reasonableness test could be performed to determine that the payroll record contains one of the likely department numbers. In some texts, the term reasonableness test is defined to encompass limit checks.

h)   **Record count** is a control total of the number of records processed during the operation of a program.

i)   **Self-checking digits** may be used to detect incorrect identification numbers. The digit is generated by applying an algorithm to the ID number. During the input process, the check digit is recomputed by applying the same algorithm to the code actually entered.

j)   **Sequence checks** determine that records are in proper order. For example, a payroll input file is likely to be sorted into Social Security number order. A sequence check can then be performed to verify record order.

        k)    **Sign checks** assure that data in a field have the appropriate arithmetic sign. For example, hours worked in a payroll record should always be a positive number.

        l)    **Validity checks** are tests of identification numbers or transaction codes for validity by comparison with items already known to be correct or authorized. For example, Social Security numbers on payroll input records can be compared with Social Security numbers authorized by the personnel department.

2)    **Key verification** entails rekeying input and comparing the results.

3)    A **redundancy check** requires sending additional data items to serve as a check on the other transmitted data; for example, part of a customer name could be matched against the name associated with the transmitted customer number.

4)    An **echo check** is an input control over transmission along communications lines. Data are sent back to the user's terminal for comparison with the transmitted data.

5)    **Completeness checks** of transmission of data determine whether all necessary information has been sent. The software notifies the sender if something is omitted.

        a)    A complementary transmission control numbers and dates each message sent from a given terminal. This procedure allows verification of the completeness of the sequence and establishment of control totals for each terminal.

b.    **Processing controls** provide reasonable assurance that processing has been performed as intended for the particular application, i.e., that all transactions are processed as authorized, that no authorized transactions are omitted, and that no unauthorized transactions are added.

1)    Some input controls are also processing controls, e.g., limit, reasonableness, and sign tests.

2)    Other tests of the logic of processing are posting, cross-footing, and zero-balance checks.

        a)    Comparing the contents of a record before and after updating is a **posting** check.

        b)    **Cross-footing** compares an amount to the sum of its components.

        c)    A **zero-balance check** adds the positive and negative amounts posted. The result should be zero.

3)    **Run-to-run control totals** (e.g., record counts or certain critical amounts) should be generated and checked at designated points during processing.

        a)    **Proof account activity listing**. In an online system, the change in a file for the day can be compared with source information.

4)    **Internal header and trailer labels** ensure that incorrect files are not processed.

        a)    A matching test should make certain an updating transaction is matched with the appropriate master file.

5)    Programs used in processing should be tested, for example, by reprocessing actual data with a known result or by employing test data.

6)    **End-of-file procedures** should be available to avoid errors such as prematurely closing the transaction file when the end of the current master file is reached. The transaction file may contain new records to be added to the master file.

7)    **Concurrency controls** manage situations in which two or more programs attempt to use a file or database at the same time.

8) An **audit trail** should be created through the use of input-output control logs, error listings, transaction logs, and transaction listings.

9) **Key integrity checks** prevent the updating process from creating inaccuracies in keys. Keys are attributes of records that permit them to be sorted. A **primary key** is the data item(s) that is the principal identifier, e.g., the vendor number. A **secondary key** is an alternative used for either sorting or special processing, e.g., the payment date on the vendor's invoice.

c. **Output controls** provide assurance that the processing result (such as account listings or displays, reports, magnetic files, invoices, or disbursement checks) is accurate and that only authorized personnel receive the output.

1) The **data control group** supervises output control.

a) The daily **proof account activity listings** (changes in master files) should be sent to users for review.

b) **Error listings** should be received directly from the system by the control group, which should make any necessary inquiries and send the errors to users for correction and resubmission.

c) The **console log** should be reviewed for unusual interruptions, interventions, or other activity.

d) Output should be distributed in accordance with distribution registers that list authorized users.

e) **End-of-job markers** on the last page of printed output permits verification that the entire report has been received.

f) **Spooler controls** prevent access to spooled output, i.e., to the results of processing that are temporarily stored in an intermediate file rather than immediately printed.

2) An important detective control is **user review** of output. Users should be able to determine when output is incomplete or not reasonable, particularly when the user prepared the input. Thus, users as well as computer personnel have a quality assurance function.

3. **Documentation** supports and explains data processing applications, including systems development. It is helpful to operators and other users, control personnel, new employees, and auditors as well as to programmers and analysts who are maintaining the old or developing a new system. The auditor considers documentation to be an important internal control activity. Documentation should be secured in a library, and access should be carefully controlled. It should be subject to uniform standards regarding flowcharting techniques, coding methods, and modification procedures (including proper authorization).

a. **System documentation** includes narrative descriptions, flowcharts, the system definition used for development, input and output forms, file and record layouts, controls, program change authorizations, and backup procedures.

b. **Program documentation** contains descriptions, program flowcharts and decision tables, program listings or source code, test data, input and output forms, detailed file and record layouts (describing the data structure, e.g., field lengths and types), change requests, operator instructions, and controls.

c. **Operating documentation** (computer run manual) provides information about setup, necessary files and devices, input procedures, console messages and responsive operator actions, run times, recovery procedures, disposal of output, and control.

d. **Procedural documentation** includes the system's master plan and operations to be performed, documentation standards, procedures for labeling and handling files, and standards for systems analysis, programming, operations, security, and data definition.

e. **User documentation** describes the system and procedures for data entry, error checking and correction, and formats and uses of reports.

4. **Systems and program acquisition and development controls**

a. **Standards** for systems design and programming should be established. These standards represent user needs and system requirements determined during the systems analysis.

1) Higher level logical units of the system can be described using **pseudocode**, a structured, informal version of English. Pseudocode can depict the overall design of the software without getting into the details of the particular programming language to be used.

b. Studies of the economic, operational, and technical **feasibility** of new applications will necessarily entail evaluations of existing as well as proposed systems.

c. Changes in the computer system should be subject to strict controls (**change controls**).

d. Proposed programs should be tested with incorrect or incomplete data as well as typical data to determine if controls have been properly implemented in the program.

1) **Test data** should test all branches of the program, including the program's edit capabilities. The edit function includes sequence checks, valid field tests, reasonableness checks, and other tests of the input data.

2) Expected results should be calculated and compared with actual performance. These results should include both accurate output and error messages.

e. To avoid **legal liability**, controls should also be implemented to prevent use of unlicensed software not in the public domain. A **software licensing agreement** permits a user to employ either a specified or an unlimited number of copies of a software product at given locations, at particular machines, or throughout the company. The agreement may restrict reproduction or resale, and it may provide for subsequent customer support and product improvements.

5. **Change control.**

a. Changes in the computer system should be subject to strict controls. For example, a written request for an application program change should be made by a user department and authorized by a designated manager or committee.

1) The program should then be redesigned using a **working copy**, not the version currently in use. Also, the systems documentation must be revised.

2) Changes in the program will be tested by the user, the internal auditor, and a systems employee who was not involved in designing the change.

3) **Approval** of the documented change and the results of testing should be given by a systems manager. The change and test results may then be accepted by the user.

4) Unauthorized program changes can be detected by **code comparison**. The version in use should be periodically compared with a copy controlled by the auditors. Software can be used to perform this procedure.

a) Versions of critical application programs should be stored in **object code**. Most users lack the technical skill to modify object code.

6.   **End-User Computing (EUC).**

   a.   End-user computing involves user-created or -acquired systems that are maintained and operated outside of traditional information systems controls.

      1)   **Environmental control risks** that are more likely in an EUC environment include copyright violations that occur when unauthorized copies of software are made or software is installed on multiple computers.

      2)   **Access** to application programs and related data by unauthorized persons is another concern because of lack of physical access controls, application-level controls, and other controls found in mainframe or networked environments.

      3)   Moreover, an EUC environment may be characterized by inadequate **backup, recovery, and contingency planning** that may result in an inability to re-create the system or its data.

      4)   **Program development, documentation, and maintenance** may also suffer from the lack of centralized control found in larger systems.

         a)   The risk of allowing end users to develop their own **applications** is decentralization of control. End-user-developed applications may not be subject to an independent outside review by systems analysts and are not created in the context of a formal development methodology. These applications may lack appropriate standards, controls, and quality assurance procedures.

         b)   Moreover, when end users create their own applications and files, **private information systems** may proliferate in which data are largely uncontrolled. Systems may contain the same information, but end-user applications may update and define the data in different ways. Thus, determining the location of data and ensuring data consistency become more difficult.

         c)   The auditors should determine that the EUC applications contain **controls** that allow users to rely on the information produced. Identification of applications is more difficult than in a traditional centralized computing environment because few people know about and use them. The auditor's first concern is to discover their existence and their intended functions. One approach is to take an organization-wide inventory of major EUC applications. An alternative is to review major EUC applications in concert with the function or department that is the major user.

            i)   The next step is **risk assessment**. The EUC applications that represent high-risk exposures are chosen for audit, for example, because they support critical decisions or are used to control cash or physical assets.

            ii)  The third step is to review the controls included in the applications chosen in the second phase.

      5)   In a personal computer setting, the user is often the programmer and operator. Thus, the protections afforded by segregation of duties are eliminated.

      6)   The **audit trail** is diminished because of the lack of history files, incomplete printed output, etc.

      7)   In general, available security features for stand-alone machines are limited compared with those in a network configuration.

b. **Application software** includes the programs that perform the tasks required by end users, e.g., standard accounting operations.

    1) Applications may be developed internally or purchased from vendors.

        a) Vendor-produced software is in either **source code** (not machine language) or **object code** (machine language), but vendors prefer to sell the latter.

        b) Application software production is a vital aspect of system development, and control over its maintenance (changes to meet new user needs) after implementation is likewise crucial.

    2) A **spreadsheet** is one type of application software that is especially helpful to accountants, auditors, and business people. It displays an on-screen financial model in which the data are presented in a grid of columns and rows. An example is a financial statement spreadsheet.

        a) An electronic spreadsheet permits the creation of a template containing the model of the mathematical relationships among the variables as defined by the user. It specifies the inputs, the computational algorithms, and the format of the output. The effects of changes in assumptions can be seen instantly because a change in one value results in an immediate recomputation of related values.

        b) Thus, in designing a spreadsheet model, the first step is to define the problem. This step is followed by an identification of relevant inputs and outputs, and the development of assumptions and decision criteria. Finally, formulas must be documented.

        c) Excel and Lotus 1-2-3 are common spreadsheet programs.

    3) Software is **copyrightable**, but a substantial amount is in the public domain. Networks of computer users may share such software.

        a) **Shareware** is software made available for a fee (usually with an initial free trial period) by the owners to users through a distributor (or web sites or electronic bulletin board services).

        b) **Software piracy** is a problem for vendors. The best way to detect an illegal copy of application software is to compare the serial number on the screen with the vendor's serial number.

        c) Use of unlicensed software increases the risk of introducing computer viruses into the organization. Such software is less likely to have been carefully tested.

        d) Diskless workstations increase security by preventing the copying of software to a floppy disk from a workstation. This control not only protects the company's interests in its data and proprietary programs but also guards against theft of software licensed to the company by vendors.

        e) To shorten the installation time for revised software in a network, a company can implement **electronic software distribution (ESD)**, which is the computer-to-computer installation of software on workstations. Instead of weeks, software distribution can be accomplished in hours or days and can be controlled centrally. Another advantage of ESD is that it permits tracking or metering of PC program licenses.

4) **Integrated packages** include two or more applications, e.g., spreadsheets, word processing, database management, graphics, and e-mail. The advantage is that the package does not require redundant data entry and maintenance. However, the individual applications in an integrated package tend not to be as powerful as the stand-alone versions. A **software suite** differs from an integrated package because the applications have all the features of the stand-alone versions.

5) A **browser** is software that permits a computer to retrieve and recognize HTML files. Web browsers allow the user to display the textual and graphical information that makes up much of the World Wide Web. It can also provide audio and video presentations and the ability to use e-mail, bulletin boards, discussion groups, etc.

6) **Electronic mail** permits transfer, receipt, and storage of messages within or between computer systems. The "mail" consists of electronically transmitted messages. A user's "mailbox" is the storage area allocated for messages. The advantages of electronic mail are high-speed transmission, reduction of message preparation costs, and the possibility of sending or reading messages at a convenient time. Moreover, electronic mail can be read wherever the recipient may be, provided (s)he has access to a terminal. Electronic mail can also be sent to remote offices via modem.

   a) A typical system permits a user to answer messages, compose or delete messages, edit, file, forward messages to other users, move items among files, read, retrieve from files, scan contents of files, send messages, and print.

7) **Voice mail** converts spoken messages from analog to digital form, transmits them over a network, and stores them on a disk. Messages are then converted back to analog form when the recipient desires to hear them. Afterward, they may be saved, forwarded, or deleted.

8) Conducting an electronic meeting among several parties at remote sites is **teleconferencing**. It can be accomplished by telephone or electronic mail group communication software. **Videoconferencing** permits the conferees to see each other on video screens. These practices have grown in recent years as companies have attempted to cut their travel costs.

9) A **fax machine** can scan a document, convert its text and graphics to digital form, and then transmit the result over telephone lines. The recipient's fax machine can then create a facsimile of the transmitted document.

10) An electronic **bulletin board system (BBS)** is a database into which computer users may dial to read or post messages.

c. **Basic Architectures for Desktop Computing** (Types of End-User Computing Environments)

1) **Client-server model.** A client-server system divides processing of an application between a client machine on a network and a server. This division depends on which tasks each is best suited to perform.

   a) However, **user interaction** is ordinarily restricted to the client part of the application. This portion normally consists of the user interface, data entry, queries, and receipt of reports.

   b) The **server** customarily manages peripheral hardware and controls access to shared databases. Thus, a client-server application must be designed as separate software components that run on different machines but appear to be one application.

    c)   **Security** for client-server systems may be more difficult than in a mainframe-based system because of the numerous access points. They also use distributed processing methods that result in heightened risk of unauthorized access to data and processing. New methods of accessing data and processing, such as remote procedure calls, are also available.

  2)  **Dummy terminal model.** In this architecture, desktop machines that lack stand-alone processing power have access to remote computers in a network. To run an application, programs are downloaded to the terminal. These machines are relatively inexpensive because they have no disk drives.

  3)  **Application server model.** A three-tiered or distributed network application. The middle (application) tier translates data between the database back-end server and the user's front end server. The application server also performs business logic functions, transaction management, and load balancing.

    a)   **Business logic functions** interpret transactions and determine how they will be processed, e.g., applicable discounts, shipping methods, etc. Mainly performed by the application server in contrast to the presentation logic performed by the users' front end server.

    b)   **Transaction management** keeps track of all of the steps in transaction processing to assure completion, editing, and/or deletion.

    c)   **Load balancing** is a process to distribute data and data processing among available servers, e.g., evenly to all servers or to the next available server.

  d.  **Types of Software Technology Used by Internal Auditors**

  1)  Auditors increasingly rely on software tools to accomplish virtually all auditing activities. They ordinarily use two major types of software:

    a)   Software that generates the paperwork for the audit, such as word processing, spreadsheet, and electronic working paper software

       i)   Internal auditors' use of word processing and spreadsheet software is usually limited to basic office tasks and is therefore not covered in this study unit.

    b)   Software used to analyze financial information

  2)  **Computer-assisted audit techniques (CAATs)** may be used during every phase of the audit process, from planning to reporting. CAATs may be systems-based or transaction-based, or provide automated methods for extracting and analyzing data.

    a)   The following are the most common types of CAATs:

       i)   **Generalized audit software** performs automated functions. It is useful for both tests of controls and substantive tests.

       ii)   **Utility software** performs routine processing tasks, such as sorting and merging.

       iii)   **Application software tracing and mapping** can follow an audit trail of information generated by the computer system as it processes transactions.

       iv)   **Expert systems software** automates the knowledge and logic of experts in a certain field to help an auditor with decision making and risk analysis.

b)  The leading CAAT software packages are currently Audit Command Language (ACL)® and Interactive Data Extraction and Analysis (IDEA)™ software. These software packages, designed specifically for use in auditing, perform 11 major functions.

i)  Aging. An auditor can test the aging of accounts receivable.

ii)  Duplicate identification. Duplicate data can be organized by data field and subsequently identified.

iii)  Exportation. Data can be transferred to other software.

iv)  Extraction. Data can be extracted for exception analysis.

v)  Gap identification. Gaps in information can be automatically noted.

vi)  Joining and merging. Two separate data files may be joined or merged to combine and match information.

vii)  Sampling. Samples of the data can be prepared and analyzed.

viii)  Sorting. Information can be sorted by any data field.

ix)  Stratification. Large amounts of data can be organized by specific factors, thereby facilitating analysis.

x)  Summarization. Data can be organized to identify patterns.

xi)  Total fields. Totals for numeric fields can be quickly and accurately calculated.

3)  **Other Forms of Electronic Media Used by Internal Auditors**

a)  **The Internet** is a series of networks throughout the world that facilitates information transfer among computers. Thus, it is a useful audit tool for gathering and disseminating audit-related information.

i)  The Internet carries an abundance of information useful to auditors.

- **Search engines** for the World Wide Web allow anyone to perform keyword searches.
- An auditor can research topics involving the auditee's operations.
- An auditor can verify information on the Internet as well as perform fraud investigations.
- The Internet can be used to stay informed about emerging technologies.

ii)  The majority of Internet usage by internal auditors, however, is for electronic communication. **E-mail** permits transfer, receipt, and storage of messages within or between computer systems. It can be used to

- Contact specialists
- Communicate with remote members of the audit team
- Distribute audit working papers and reports
- Correspond with management and other departments
- Transmit files

b)  An **intranet** is a network that operates like the Internet but is limited to a specific organization. Uses include

i)  Electronic communication among employees

ii)  Access to the organization's databases

iii)  Posting of daily news and reports

iv)  Development of sites to provide information on each department

c) **Image processing** is a method used to convert paper documents into electronic images. **Scanning devices** are used to perform image processing.

    i) Image processing can help internal auditors to convert audit documentation into an electronic format.

    ii) These documents can subsequently be stored, sorted, and extracted along with other electronic information.

7. Stop and review! You have completed the outline for this subunit. Study multiple-choice questions 22 through 58 beginning on page 452.

## 9.4 SYSTEMS ASSURANCE AND CONTROL (SAC)

1. SAC is a publication of **The IIA**. It updates the previous *Systems Auditability and Control* reports (1977, 1991, 1994) to reflect changes in technology and e-business models. The acronym may be written as **eSAC** to emphasize the e-business effect and the electronic orientation of the principles.

    a. The **objective of SAC** is to provide management, governance bodies, and auditors with "information to understand, monitor, assess, and mitigate technology risks" associated with "customers, competitors, regulators, community, and owners."

    b. The following are among **major IT changes**:

        1) The presence of IT in every aspect of operations

        2) Distributed computing

        3) Broadband and wireless communications

        4) Decreased costs and increased storage capacity and processing power

        5) Evolution of enterprise-wide resource planning (ERP) software, component-based software, data mining, biometrics, global positioning systems, encryption, natural language interfaces, technology standards, and open systems

    c. **New challenges** include the appearance of knowledge workers and virtual organizations, globalization, cyber warfare, and new threats to privacy. Internal auditors must consider these challenges and the related risks. They should also consider the following **ways in which doing business has changed**:

        1) In the increasingly interconnected business environment, planned change, stable technology trends, and predictable volumes of business have been replaced by continual, rapid change and uncertainty.

        2) The **organizational structure** is customer-focused because markets are no longer captive but are more **efficiently competitive**. Moreover, **reputation** has become even more important, and **brand and trademark** issues have global implications.

        3) Businesses operate in an increasingly less defined **regulatory environment** through **multiple channels**. Operations involve many **complex partnerships** and other associations. **Controls** must be oriented outward as well as inward because risks to partners and others may be risks to the organization.

        4) Businesses share data networks (e.g., the Internet), and telecommunications systems are **wireless and mobile**.

2. The following are key elements of the **technology challenges** facing organizations and internal auditors:

    a. **Open systems** are publicly accessible via the global Internet. They are subject to greater (and different) risks than closed private systems.

b. **Technology** affects all businesses and applications. **System boundaries** are becoming indistinct as interactions with suppliers, customers, partners, and associates increase.

1) Thus, internal auditors have more difficulty in giving assurance about security, control, and privacy. For example, as functions are integrated in an **ERP system** with one organization-wide database, the focus of control shifts from applications to the environment.

2) **Software development and use** have outstripped even the considerable gains in processing capacity and speed.

3) As the **Internet** has spread globally, more products, services, languages, cultures, and political systems have become involved.

a) Control over user interaction is therefore more difficult.

c. **Information security** is a technology and business issue affected by the control environment, including awareness of security issues and the tone at the top.

1) Perfect security is not possible because system access cannot be eliminated.

2) Risk assessments and cost-benefit calculations must be continually reevaluated. Changes in technology lead to different threats and risk assessments as well as better controls.

d. **Privacy** is recognized internationally as a fundamental human right.

1) The globalization of business through the Internet has resulted in legislation to protect personal information, but the requirements of different nations vary.

e. **Development and distribution processes** have changed. New products and services are brought to the market more rapidly, and systems are created as new lines of business, not just as improvements of existing operations.

1) For these reasons, the IT infrastructure is often **outsourced**, with an increase in the difficulty of assuring that controls are effective.

3. The following are elements of the **response** to technology challenges.

a. **Risk assessment** regarding e-commerce varies with the organization. One risk is that strategic planning (determining the strategy and business design needed to meet market requirements) may be inadequate.

1) Each business must

a) Identify risks,
b) Measure exposures,
c) Determine whether controls are in place and are effective,
d) Specify threats to survival, and
e) Consider the costs of mitigating risks.

2) Subunit managers must avoid the "silo attitude," that is, a narrow focus limited only to the IT risks within their areas of authority.

a) Cooperation among subunits is necessary for a complete assessment. For example, an insignificant risk for a subunit may be a greater risk at the organization level.

b. **Internal control** objectives are essentially the same although technology, risks, and control methods change.

1) Thus, many concepts of control (management's responsibility, the role of the control environment, reasonable assurance, monitoring, and cost-benefit analysis) are relevant regardless of IT changes.

c. **E-assurance services** consider "the degree to which a system deviates from industry standards or management requirements for availability."

1) **Agreed-upon criteria** should exist for measuring an assertion about the system. Moreover, an **accepted process** should exist for gathering evidence. However, assurance services must be redesigned as risks and controls change.

2) **Improvements in IT controls** include

    a) Firewalls
    b) Intelligent routers
    c) Third-party certifications
    d) Digital signatures
    e) Public-key encryption

3) Internal auditors are well placed to provide **internal assurance**, but the market may demand **external assurance** (e.g., by website seals) before the desired level of user trust is achieved.

4. The **SAC model** is a major response to the challenges posed by technology change. It is "a framework for evaluating the e-business control environment." It helps internal auditors to obtain a perspective on the technology culture. This perspective is a foundation for describing risk management strategies to management and giving assurance about systems.

a. Just as the **COSO** model (*Internal Control -- Integrated Framework*, published by the Committee of Sponsoring Organizations) created an internal control vocabulary, the SAC model is an aid to the analysis of e-business "objectives, risks, and mitigation responses."

1) For example, it may be used to address such matters as regulatory change, determination of the appropriate productive capacity, and selection of IT components.

b. The following is The IIA's **diagram of the SAC model**:

1) The **COSO control model** (objectives and risks mitigated by controls) is inherent in the SAC model.

c.   An organization

1)   Achieves its purpose (the **mission**)
2)   By stating **objectives** and
3)   Developing **strategies**

a)   In accordance with its **values** (see diagram's left-side arrow).

d.   Outcomes (see the diagram's right-side arrow) are

1)   Desired **results**
2)   Improved **reputation**, and
3)   **Learning** how to perform better.

e.   The **control environment** should keep the organization on track. The **control context** reflects COSO objectives:

1)   **Operating** effectiveness and efficiency
2)   **Reporting** of financial and other management information
3)   **Compliance** with laws and regulations
4)   **Safeguarding** of assets

f.   The **control attributes**, or **e-business assurance objectives**, in the center of the diagram are the basis for the presentations in SAC modules. The first control attribute is **availability**.

1)   **Transactions** must be received and accepted, processed, and supported so as to satisfy **customers**.
2)   In some cases (e.g., Internet access), information, processes, and services must always be available.
3)   Internal auditors should evaluate controls with respect to **business interruption**, for example,

a)   System security
b)   Storage failure
c)   Software glitches
d)   Capacity planning
e)   Recovery procedures

g.   **Capability** is the control attribute (e-business objective) that ensures the reliable and timely completion of transactions. The system should have the means to meet demand consistently even at its peak.

1)   **Bottlenecks** must be carefully managed if not identified and eliminated.
2)   **Monitoring** control over usage and service agreements with Internet and application providers are important.
3)   **Systems development and acquisition controls** should ensure that

a)   Efficient systems perform as expected.
b)   Cost overruns are avoided.
c)   Prevention is stressed in preference to error correction.
d)   Shadow systems need not be created because of an ineffective official system.
e)   Applications are designed efficiently, with inclusion of control, security, and audit features.
f)   **Cost-benefit** considerations are addressed

i)   **Optional control** does not eliminate all risk.

4) **Change or maintenance controls** ensure **business continuity** during hardware and software maintenance. They also provide for approval, confirmation, and documentation of changes. The following are typical change controls:

   a) User involvement in program changes
   b) Audit trails, including change logs
   c) IT and user approval
   d) Documentation
   e) Measures to prevent programmers from inserting unapproved code into production versions of programs

h. **Functionality** is the control attribute (e-business objective) that satisfies customers. A system must do more than merely process transactions.

1) Matters of interest to management, such as **control data**, should be recorded.
2) The system should be designed to anticipate actions of online users, e.g., hang-ups or the resubmission of the same transaction.
3) **Monitoring and feedback controls** should be in place, for example,

   a) Displays of progress indicators after user input
   b) Confirmation of transactions
   c) Monitoring of abandonment of transactions

4) Users and management should participate in **system design** to ensure that specifications suffice to produce effective applications.
5) A functional system **communicates information** relevant to the business process.

   a) Displays and reports should be adjustable to the needs of different users.
   b) Internal auditors must determine whether controls are operating to generate information that is

      i) Timely
      ii) Correct
      iii) Consistent
      iv) Usable

i. **Protectability** is the control attribute (e-business objective) that fosters protection of hardware, software, and data. Protection is rendered more difficult by **Internet access**, given the inherent flows in that network.

1) Controls should safeguard against, or at least detect, loss.
2) Many controls address the risks of catastrophic damage or internal wrongdoing.
3) Internal auditors should evaluate **general controls**.

   a) **Access controls** protect **data security and confidentiality**. The security function may

      i) Limit access on some logical basis related to user requirements.
      ii) Limit access to program libraries and data files on a need-only basis.
      iii) Establish users' **accountability** for their activities.

   b) **Program security** includes not only limiting access to program libraries and files but also

      i) Monitoring updates via library management software
      ii) Preventing programmers from accessing production programs

       c)   **Physical security** controls restrict access to processing and storage devices to personnel with a need to use them.  Other controls include

          i)   Monitoring physical access to the host server, for example, by using a card system

          ii)   Physically controlling confidential reports by restricting distribution

          iii)   Fire prevention measures

          iv)   Preventive maintenance

          v)   Insurance

          vi)   Backing up files

    4)   **Data integrity** is a protectability objective.  Data should be accurate, complete, up-to-date, and not subject to unauthorized change.

       a)   Thus, internal auditors should evaluate **application controls** in addition to general controls related to access.

       b)   The following are more specific objectives regarding data integrity:

          i)   Transactions are authorized.

          ii)   Transactions are completely recorded initially.

          iii)   Authorized transactions are accepted and completed processed.

          iv)   Duplicate transactions are not processed.

          v)   Processing is accurate.

          vi)   The proper files and records are updated.

       c)   Users as well as programmers have no access to production programs.

       d)   Access to system software is restricted.

    5)   Protectability is necessary for confidentiality and privacy.

       a)   **Confidentiality** is usually an issue with regard to trade secrets and other intellectual property, competitive strategies, or national security.

       b)   **Privacy** concerns most often apply to personal information about customers, employees, or shareholders.

          i)   The Internet has been a boon to those seeking to collect information inexpensively.

  j.   **Accountability** is the control attribute (e-business objective) that identifies the source of a transaction.  It specifies employees' roles, actions, and responsibilities.  Thus, the person who caused a transactions is identifiable.

    1)   **Fundamental concepts of accountability** are

       a)   Data ownership

       b)   Identification

       c)   Authentication

    2)   **Audit trails** should contain enough information and be preserved for a sufficient time to permit confirmation of transactions.

    3)   The principle of **nonrepudiation** prevents an authenticated system user from discovering a transaction that (s)he caused.

    4)   A difficult accountability issue arises regarding **systems administrators** and similar personnel with access to restricted data and software.  They may have the power to disable the controls monitoring their activities.

       a)   An organization must authenticate the identities of such persons.

5) An organization must reconcile **accountability and privacy**. If it holds personal information, it must authenticate those who inquire about it prior to disclosure, e.g., credit sellers seeking to identify buyers.

   a) Thus, accountability (identifying the source of a transaction) is balanced with privacy concerns (safeguarding personal information) when disclosure is made only to appropriate persons.

6) Accountability requires that sufficient, accurate, and timely **information** be available. Hence, internal auditors must evaluate processing and reporting controls.

   a) Audit (transaction) trails should give irrefutable support to the information.

   b) **Timely information** should be available when decisions must be made.

     i) Lack of timeliness is a shortcoming of financial statements issued months after year-end.

   c) Information should be consistent with relevant policies, such as accounting principles in the case of financial statements.

     i) Human error, inappropriate processing, or management override may be the cause of inconsistency.

k. **Achievement of the e-business objectives** is a function of organizational commitment, infrastructure, and other resources.

1) The **building blocks** that make achievement of the objectives feasible are shown in the middle of the diagram:

   a) People
   b) Technology
   c) Processes
   d) Investment
   e) Communication

2) The e-business environment is affected by many factors.

   a) The organization has ever greater "interaction, interconnectivity and system sharing" with **external market forces**:

     i) Customers
     ii) Competitors
     iii) Regulators
     iv) The community
     v) Owners

   b) **Velocity** is the speed of change.

   c) The following **external interdependencies** increase the environmental complexity:

     i) Providers
     ii) Alliances
     iii) Agents

    l.    The **dynamic environment** is the overall context in the SAC model, that is, the control environment or set of risks and responses.

        1)    **Monitoring and oversight** activities verify that relevant risks are identified and addressed and that controls (responses) are confirmed to be operating as intended.

            a)    These activities (the background) must be effectively designed.

            b)    Internal auditors in a paperless environment are using other methods of monitoring, e.g., logging.

        2)    In the emerging e-business environment, **business objectives** may be unclear. After-the-fact definitions and strategies may be required.

        3)    The **risks** to network security may be hard to assess in a network of networks.

        4)    The **controls** may be difficult to evaluate in a traditional way (general and application controls). Internal auditors must consider the relationship of infrastructure, business processes, and the connecting software.

    5.    Stop and review! You have completed the outline for this subunit. Study multiple-choice questions 59 through 63 beginning on page 464.

## 9.5 COBIT

    1.    COBIT (Control Objectives for Information and related Technology) is an IT control framework copyrighted by the **Information Systems Audit and Control Foundation (ISACF)**.

        a.    **Purpose**. COBIT is a set of guidelines to assist **management and business process owners** in implementing adequate controls over IT processes and resources. It is designed to be an IT governance tool that facilitates understanding and managing the risks and benefits associated with information and related IT.

            1)    **IT governance** is part of overall organizational governance. It connects IT information, resources, and processes with the organization's plans and objectives.

                a)    IT governance is a set of processes and relationships that should add value and balance risk and return. Thus, it should reflect best practices for assuring that information and technology are sufficient for achieving organizational objectives.

        b.    **Audience**. COBIT is targeted at three distinct audiences:

            1)    **Management** must balance risks and control costs in the volatile IT environment.

                a)    Management is responsible for implementing **control**, which consists of organizational structures, practices, procedures, and policies. This responsibility extends to determining whether business processes are properly supported and controls satisfy information criteria.

                    i)    A critical consideration in COBIT is the extent of IT resources needed to achieve control objectives.

            2)    **Users** need assurance about the security of, and controls over, internal or third-party IT services.

            3)    **Auditors** must be able to support their opinions conveyed to management and others about the state of internal control.

c.   The **dimensions** of the framework are information criteria, IT resources, and IT processes.

1)   Information assets should meet the **quality, fiduciary, and security requirements** that apply to other assets.  The specific **information criteria** are

   a)   Effectiveness
   b)   Efficiency
   c)   Confidentiality
   d)   Integrity
   e)   Availability
   f)   Compliance
   g)   Reliability

2)   **IT resources** must be balanced with adherence to the information criteria.  IT resources include

   a)   People
   b)   Application systems
   c)   Technology
   d)   Facilities
   e)   Data

3)   Management of IT resources is organized according to **natural groups of IT processes**.  COBIT classifies **high-level control objectives**, each corresponding to an individual IT process, into four **domains**, which approximate the main components of the systems development life cycle.

   a)   **Planning and organization**.  These objectives concern strategic planning; designing the architecture and determining the direction of IT; organizing; communicating goals; providing for compliance with external mandates; risk assessment; and managing personnel, products, quality, and the investment in technology.

   b)   **Acquisition and implementation**.  These objectives concern finding solutions to IT problems, obtaining software and infrastructure, maintenance, procedure design, installation and testing of systems, and change management.

   c)   **Delivery and support**.  These objectives concern identifying services and their levels; maintaining continuity and security of service; cost allocation; user training; customer support; and management of performance, capacity, the configuration, problems, data, facilities, and operations.

   d)   **Monitoring**.  These objectives concern process monitoring, evaluating control, and seeking independent assurance (e.g., through an external audit).

d.   **Other included resources**.  In addition to the framework outlined above, COBIT includes the following resources:

1)   The **audit guidelines** facilitate the evaluation of IT processes to determine whether COBIT's recommended detailed control objectives have been achieved.

2)   The **management guidelines** help managers to control information and related processes, determine whether organizational goals have been achieved, and monitor performance within each IT process.  These guidelines include

   a)   **Maturity models**, which are best practices and international standards

   b)   **Critical success factors**, which are the most significant guidelines for IT process control

c) **Key goal indicators**, which are post-action measures

d) **Key performance indicators**, which are measures made to determine current progress

3) The **implementation tool set** provides case studies from organizations that have successfully applied COBIT.

e. For more information, visit www.isaca.org

2. Stop and review! You have completed the outline for this subunit. Study multiple-choice questions 64 and 65 on page 465.

## 9.6 SYSTEM SECURITY

1. **Data Integrity**

   a. The difficulty of maintaining the integrity of the data is the most significant limitation of computer-based audit tools.

   b. Electronic evidence is difficult to authenticate and easy to fabricate.

   c. Internal auditors must be careful not to treat computer printouts as traditional paper evidence. The data security factors pertaining to electronic evidence must be considered.

   d. The degree of reliance on electronic evidence by the auditor depends on the effectiveness of the controls over the system from which such evidence is taken.

   e. The most important control is to install an **organization-wide network security policy**. This policy should promote the following objectives:

      1) **Availability**. The intended and authorized users should be able to access data to meet organizational goals.

      2) **Security, privacy, and confidentiality**. The secrecy of information that could adversely affect the organization if revealed to the public or competitors should be assured.

      3) **Integrity**. Unauthorized or accidental modification of data should be prevented.

2. **Access Control**

   a. Access control software protects files, programs, data dictionaries, processing, etc., from unauthorized access; restricts use of certain devices (e.g., terminals); and may provide an audit trail for both successful and unsuccessful access attempts. For example, a **firewall** separates internal from external networks.

   b. **Segregation of functions**. Many controls once performed by separate individuals may be concentrated in computer systems. Hence, an individual who has access to the computer may perform incompatible functions. As a result, other control procedures may be necessary to achieve the control objectives ordinarily accomplished by segregation of functions. Other controls may include

      1) Use of password controls to prevent incompatible functions from being performed by individuals with online access to assets and records

      2) Controls over access to equipment and data files

         a) Access controls provide assurance that only authorized individuals use the system and that usage is for authorized purposes.

            i) Such controls include physical safeguards of equipment, proper library security, and passwords.

c. **Physical security controls** limit physical access and protect against environmental risks and natural catastrophes such as fire and flood.

1) **Keypad devices** allow entry of a password or code to gain entry to a physical location or computer system.

2) **Card reader controls** are based on reading information from a magnetic strip on a credit, debit, or other access card. Controls can then be applied to information about the cardholder contained on the magnetic strip.

d. **Logical security controls** are needed because of the use of communications networks and connections to external systems. User identification and authentication, restriction of access, and the generation of audit trails are required in this environment. Thus, access controls have been developed to prevent improper use or manipulation of data files and programs. They ensure that only those persons with a bona fide purpose and authorization have access to computer systems.

1) **Passwords and ID numbers**. The use of passwords and identification numbers is an effective control in an online system to prevent unauthorized access to computer files. Lists of authorized persons are maintained in the computer. The entry of passwords or identification numbers; a prearranged set of personal questions; and the use of badges, magnetic cards, or optically scanned cards may be combined to avoid unauthorized access.

a) A **security card** may be used with a personal computer so that users must sign on with an ID and a password. The card controls the machine's operating system and records access data (date, time, duration, etc.).

b) Proper **user authentication** by means of a password requires password-generating procedures to assure that valid passwords are known only by the proper individuals. Thus, a password should not be displayed when entered at a keyboard.

c) Password security may also be compromised in other ways. For example, **log-on procedures** may be cumbersome and tedious. Thus, users often store log-on sequences on their personal computers and invoke them when they want to use mainframe facilities. A risk of this practice is that anyone with access to the personal computers could log on to the mainframe.

d) To be more effective, passwords should consist of random letters, symbols, and numbers. They should not contain words or phrases.

2) **File attributes** can be assigned to control access to and the use of files. Examples are read/write, read only, archive, and hidden.

3) A **device authorization table** restricts file access to those physical devices that should logically need access. For example, because it is illogical for anyone to access the accounts receivable file from a manufacturing terminal, the device authorization table will deny access even when a valid password is used.

a) Such tests are often called **compatibility tests** because they ascertain whether a code number is compatible with the use to be made of the information. Thus, a user may be authorized to enter only certain kinds of data, have access only to certain information, have access but not updating authority, or use the system only at certain times. The lists or tables of authorized users or devices are sometimes called **access control matrices**.

4) A **system access log** records all attempts to use the system. The date and time, codes used, mode of access, data involved, and operator interventions are recorded.

5) **Encryption** involves using a fixed algorithm to manipulate plaintext. The information is sent in its manipulated form and the receiver translates the information back into plaintext. Although data may be accessed by tapping into the transmission line, the encryption key is necessary to understand the data being sent.

   a) For example, a web server (a computer that delivers webpages to the Internet) should be secure. It should support a security protocol that encrypts messages to protect transactions from third party detection or tampering.

6) A **callback** feature requires the remote user to call the computer, give identification, hang up, and wait for the computer to call the user's authorized number. This control ensures acceptance of data transmissions only from authorized modems. However, call forwarding may thwart this control.

7) **Controlled disposal of documents**. One method of enforcing access restrictions is to destroy data when they are no longer in use. Thus, paper documents may be shredded and magnetic media may be erased.

8) **Biometric technologies**. These are automated methods of establishing an individual's identity using physiological or behavioral traits. These characteristics include fingerprints, retina patterns, hand geometry, signature dynamics, speech, and keystroke dynamics.

9) **Automatic log-off** (disconnection) of inactive data terminals may prevent the viewing of sensitive data on an unattended data terminal.

10) **Utility software restrictions**. Utility software may have privileged access and therefore be able to bypass normal security measures. Performance monitors, tape and disk management systems, job schedulers, online editors, and report management systems are examples of utility software. Management can limit the use of privileged software to security personnel and establish audit trails to document its use. The purpose is to gain assurance that its uses are necessary and authorized.

11) **Security personnel**. An organization may need to hire security specialists. For example, developing an information security policy for the organization, commenting on security controls in new applications, and monitoring and investigating unsuccessful access attempts are appropriate duties of the information security officer.

3. **Internet Security**

   a. Connection to the Internet presents security issues. Thus, the organization-wide network security policy should at the very least include

      1) A user account management system
      2) Installation of an Internet firewall
      3) Methods such as encryption to ensure that only the intended user receives the information and that the information is complete and accurate

   b. **User account management** involves installing a system to ensure that

      1) New accounts are added correctly and assigned only to authorized users.
      2) Old and unused accounts are removed promptly.
      3) Passwords are changed periodically, and employees are educated on how to choose a password that cannot be easily guessed (e.g., a password of at least six diverse characters that do not form a word should be chosen).

c.   A **firewall** separates an internal network from an external network (e.g., the Internet) and prevents passage of specific types of traffic.  It identifies names, Internet Protocol (IP) addresses, applications, etc., and compares them with programmed access rules.

1)   A firewall may have any of the following features:

a)   A **packet filtering system** examines each incoming network packet and drops (does not pass on) unauthorized packets.

b)   A **proxy server** maintains copies of Web pages to be accessed by specified users.  Outsiders are directed there, and more important information is not available from this access point.

c)   An **application gateway** limits traffic to specific applications.

d)   A **circuit-level gateway** connects an internal device, e.g., a network printer, with an outside TCP/IP port.  It can identify a valid TCP session.

e)   **Stateful inspection** stores information about the state of a transmission and uses it as background for evaluating messages from similar sources.

2)   Firewall systems ordinarily produce **reports** on organization-wide Internet use, unusual usage patterns, and system penetration attempts.  These reports are very helpful to the internal auditor as a method of continuous monitoring, or logging, of the system.

a)   Firewalls do not provide adequate protection against **computer viruses**. Thus, an organization should include one or more antivirus measures in its network security policy.

3)   The Internet site of **Certainty Solutions**, formerly Global Networking and Computer Services (GNAC), is a leading forum for discussions of firewall systems and other Internet and intranet security issues (www.certaintysolutions.com).

d.   Data traveling across the network can be encoded so that it is indecipherable to anyone except the intended recipient.

e.   **Other Controls**

1)   **Authentication** measures verify the identity of the user, thus ensuring that only the intended and authorized users gain access to the system.

a)   Most firewall systems provide authentication procedures.
b)   Access controls are the most common authentication procedures.

2)   **Checksums** help ensure the integrity of data by checking whether the file has been changed.  The system computes a value for a file and then proceeds to check whether this value equals the last known value for this file.  If the numbers are the same, the file has likely remained unchanged.

4.   **Data Storage**

a.   Storing all related data on one storage device creates security problems.

1)   If hardware or software malfunctions occur, or unauthorized access is achieved, the results could be disastrous.

2)   Greater emphasis on security is required to provide backup and restrict access to the database.

a)   For example, the system may employ **dual logging**, that is, use of two transaction logs written simultaneously on separate storage media.  It may also use a snapshot technique to capture data values before and after transaction processing.  The files that store these values can be used to reconstruct the database in the event of data loss or corruption.

3) The responsibility for creating, maintaining, securing, and restricting access to the database belongs to the **Database Administrator (DBA)**.

4) A **database management system (DBMS)** includes security features. Thus, a specified user's access may be limited to certain data fields or logical views depending on the individual's assigned duties.

5. **Encryption**

a. Encryption technology converts data into a code. A program codes data prior to transmission. Another program decodes it after transmission. Unauthorized users may still be able to access the data, but, without the encryption key, they will be unable to decode the information.

b. Encryption software uses a fixed algorithm to manipulate **plaintext** and an encryption key to introduce variation. The information is sent in its manipulated form (**cyphertext**), and the receiver translates the information back into plaintext. Although data may be accessed by tapping into the transmission line, the encryption key is necessary to understand the data being sent. The machine instructions necessary to code and decode data can constitute a 20%-to-30% increase in system overhead.

c. Encryption technology may be either hardware- or software-based. Two major types of encryption software exist.

1) **Public-key/private-key**, or asymmetric, encryption requires two keys: The public key for coding messages is widely known, but the private key for decoding messages is kept secret by the recipient. Accordingly, the parties who wish to transmit coded messages must use algorithmically-related **pairs** of public and private keys. The sender searches a directory for the recipient's public key, uses it to decode the message, and transmits the message to the recipient. The latter uses the public key and the related private (secret) key to decode the message.

a) One advantage of public-key encryption is that the message is encoded using one key and decoded using another. In contrast, private-key encryption requires both parties to know and use the secret key.

b) A second advantage is that neither party knows the other's private key. The related public key and private key pair is issued by a **certificate authority** (a third-party fiduciary, e.g., VeriSign or Thawte). However, the private key is issued only to one party.

i) Thus, **key management** in a public key/private key system is more secure than in a secret-key system because the parties do not have to agree on, transmit, and handle the one secret key.

c) **RSA**, named for its developers (Rivest, Shamir, and Adelman), is the most commonly used public-key/private-key method.

d) A public key/private key system is used to create **digital signatures (fingerprints)**.

i) A digital signature is a means of **authentication** of an electronic document, for example, of the validity of a purchase order, acceptance of a contract, or financial information.

- The sender uses its private key to encode all or part of the message, and the recipient uses the sender's public key to decode it. Hence, if that key decodes the message, the sender must have written it.

- One variation is to send the message in both plaintext and cyphertext. If the decoded version matches the plaintext version, no alteration has occurred.

ii) A **digital certificate** is another means of authentication used in e-business. The certificate authority issues a coded electronic certificate that contains the holder's name, a copy of its public key, a serial number, and an expiration date. The certificate verifies the holder's identity.

- The recipient of a coded message uses the certificate authority's public key (available on the Internet) to decode the certificate included in the message. The recipient then determines that the certificate was issued by the certificate authority. Moreover, the recipient can use the sender's public key and identification data to send a coded response.
  - Such methods might be used for transactions between sellers and buyers using credit cards.
- A certificate also may be used to provide assurance to customers that a website is genuine.
- The **public key infrastructure** permits secure monetary and information exchange over the Internet. Thus, it facilitates e-business.
- Protocols commonly used for coding and decoding functions on the Internet are **SSL** (Secure Sockets layer) and **S-HTTP** (Secure Hypertext Transport Protocol).
- **Digital time stamping services** verify the time (and possibly the place) of a transaction. For example, a document may be sent to a service, which applies its digital stamp and then forwards the document.

2) **Secret-key**, or symmetric, encryption requires only a single key for each pair of parties that want to send each other coded messages.

   a) **Data Encryption Standard (DES)**, a shared private-key method developed by the U.S. government, is the most prevalent secret-key method. It is based on numbers with 56 binary digits.

   b) The **Advanced Encryption Standard (AES)** is a recently adopted cryptographic algorithm for use by U.S. government organizations to protect sensitive information. The AES will be widely used on a voluntary basis by organizations, institutions, and individuals as well as by the U.S. government.

6. Stop and review! You have completed the outline for this subunit. Study multiple-choice questions 66 through 79 beginning on page 465.

## 9.7 CONTINGENCY PLANNING

1. **Backup and recovery policies and procedures**. A computer center should have a reconstruction and recovery plan that will allow it to regenerate important programs and database files. The center should create backup (duplicate) copies of data files, databases, programs, and documentation; store backup copies offsite; and plan for auxiliary processing on alternate systems or at another site.

2. The organization must undertake contingency planning and risk analysis. During an early stage of contingency planning for information systems, management must determine how various processing disruptions may affect the entity. **Risk analysis** identifies and prioritizes critical applications, evaluates their organizational impact, determines recovery time frames and minimum hardware platform requirements, assesses insurance coverage, identifies exposures and their implications, and develops recovery plans.

3.    It is important in any information processing environment not to lose or otherwise destroy data. Not only is the loss of data a problem, but the organization may also require continuous processing without disruptions. For these reasons, it is imperative that any system have adequate backup and recovery procedures in the event of system failure, power loss, or other potential corruption of data. The procedures implemented will normally be a function of the specific computer environment, type of processing, or storage mode.

a.    **Batch processing**. Magnetic tape and magnetic disks are used.

1)    **Checkpoint procedures** involve capturing all the values of data and program indicators at specified points and storing these values in another file. If processing is interrupted, it can be resumed at the last checkpoint rather than at the beginning of the run.

b.    **Online processing**. Magnetic disks are used for online processing.

1)    **Rollback and recovery** procedures involve the dumping of the master file's contents and associated data structures onto a backup file. In the event of a faulty run, the dump is used together with the transaction log or file to reconstruct the file.

c.    **Database management systems** use magnetic disks for online processing.

1)    **Database systems** require a more elaborate backup procedure. Normally, recovery and restart procedures must provide for continued operations during reconstruction of lost information.

2)    **Dual logging** involves the use of two transaction logs written simultaneously on two separate storage media.

3)    **Before-image/after-image** captures the data values before and after transaction processing and stores them in files. These files can be used to re-create the database in the event of data loss or corruption.

d.    **Fully protected systems** have generator or battery backup to prevent data destruction and downtime from electrical power disturbances. Loss of electrical power or voltage fluctuations need not disturb the vulnerable contents of main memory if a noninterruptible system is in place.

e.    **Fault-tolerant computer systems** have additional hardware and software as well as a backup power supply. A fault-tolerant computer has additional chips and disk storage.

f.    **Protection from malicious software and attacks**. An example of malicious software is a computer virus, a software program that infects another program or a system's primary storage (main memory) by altering its logic. Infection often results in the destruction of data. Once infected, a software program can spread the virus to other software programs. Obtaining software through a shareware network or by downloading from an electronic bulletin board is a typical cause of infection. Propagation of viruses through e-mail attachments is also common.

1)    To protect against viruses, three types of controls should be implemented.

a)    **Preventive controls** include establishing a formal security policy, using only clean and certified copies of software, not using shareware software, checking new software with antivirus software, restricting access, and educating users.

b)    **Detective controls** include making file size and date/time stamp comparisons.

c)    **Corrective controls** include ensuring that clean backup is maintained and having a documented plan for recovery from a virus.

2)    For more on malicious software and a full discussion of attacks on computer systems, see the next study unit.

g.    **Hot-site and cold-site backup facilities**.  A hot site is a service bureau.  It is a fully operational processing facility that is immediately available.  A cold site is a shell facility where the user can quickly install computer equipment.

1)   A hot site with updated software and data that can begin operations in minutes is a **flying-start site**.

4.    Stop and review!  You have completed the outline for this subunit.  Study multiple-choice questions 80 through 82 on page 470.

## QUESTIONS

### 9.1 Introduction to IT

**1.** Which of the following statements accurately describes the impact that automation has on the controls normally present in a manual system?

A.   Transaction trails are more extensive in a computer-based system than in a manual system because there is always a one-for-one correspondence between data entry and output.

B.   Responsibility for custody of information assets is more concentrated in user departments in a computer-based system than it is in a manual system.

C.   Controls must be more explicit in a computer-based system because many processing points that present opportunities for human judgment in a manual system are eliminated.

D.   The quality of documentation becomes less critical in a computer-based system than it is in a manual system because data records are stored in machine-readable files.

Answer (C) is correct.  *(CIA, adapted)*
    **REQUIRED:**  The impact that automation has on the controls normally present in a manual system.
    **DISCUSSION:**  Using a computer does not change the basic concepts and objectives of control.  However, the use of computers may modify the control techniques used.  The processing of transactions may be combined with control activities previously performed separately, or control function may be combined within the information system activity.
    Answer (A) is incorrect because the "paper trail" is less extensive in an information system.  Combining processing and controls within the system reduces documentary evidence.  Answer (B) is incorrect because information assets are more likely to be under the control of the information system function.  Answer (D) is incorrect because documentation is more important in an information system.  Information is more likely to be stored in machine-readable form than in hard copy.

**2.** The two broad groupings of information systems control activities are general controls and application controls.  General controls include controls

A.   Relating to the correction and resubmission of faulty data.

B.   For developing, modifying, and maintaining computer programs.

C.   Designed to assure that only authorized users receive output from processing.

D.   Designed to ensure that all data submitted for processing have been properly authorized.

Answer (B) is correct.  *(Publisher)*
    **REQUIRED:**  The definition of general controls.
    **DISCUSSION:**  General controls are policies and procedures that relate to many information systems application and support the effective functioning of application controls by helping to ensure the continued proper operation of information systems.  General controls include controls over (1) data center and network operations, (2) systems software acquisition and maintenance, (3) access security, and (4) application systems acquisition, development, and maintenance (AU 319).
    Answer (A) is incorrect because correction of input errors is an application control.  Answer (C) is incorrect because control over report distribution (output) is an application control.  Answer (D) is incorrect because authorization of input is an application control.

**3.** The practice of maintaining a test program library separate from the production program library is an example of

   A. An organizational control.

   B. Physical security.

   C. An input control.

   D. A concurrency control.

Answer (A) is correct.  *(CIA, adapted)*
**REQUIRED:**  The type of control represented by separating the test and production program libraries.
**DISCUSSION:**  This separation is an organizational control. Organizational controls concern the proper segregation of duties and responsibilities within the information systems department. Although proper segregation is desirable, functions that would be considered incompatible if performed by a single individual in a manual activity are often performed through the use of an information systems program or series of programs.  Thus, compensating controls may be necessary, such as library controls, effective supervisions, and rotation of personnel. Segregating test programs makes concealment of unauthorized changes in production programs more difficult.
Answer (B) is incorrect because physical security (e.g., climate control and restrictions on physical access) is another aspect of organizational control.  Answer (C) is incorrect because input controls validate the completeness, accuracy, and appropriateness of input.  Answer (D) is incorrect because concurrency controls manage situations in which two or more programs attempt to use a file or database at the same time.

**4.** In traditional information systems, computer operators are generally responsible for backing up software and data files on a regular basis.  In distributed or cooperative systems, ensuring that adequate backups are taken is the responsibility of

   A. User management.

   B. Systems programmers.

   C. Data entry clerks.

   D. Tape librarians.

Answer (A) is correct.  *(CIA, adapted)*
**REQUIRED:**  The persons responsible for ensuring that adequate backups are taken in distributed or cooperative systems.
**DISCUSSION:**  In distributed or cooperative systems, the responsibility for ensuring that adequate backups are taken is the responsibility of user management.  The systems are under the control of users, not a central information processing department.
Answer (B) is incorrect because distributed environments have no systems programmers comparable to those at central sites for traditional systems.  Answer (C) is incorrect because distributed environments may not have data entry clerks.  Users typically perform their own data entry.  Answer (D) is incorrect because, in distributed environments, there are no tape librarians.

**5.** An organization's computer help-desk function is usually a responsibility of the

   A. Applications development unit.

   B. Systems programming unit.

   C. Computer operations unit.

   D. User departments.

Answer (C) is correct.  *(CIA, adapted)*
**REQUIRED:**  The entity responsible for a computer help desk.
**DISCUSSION:**  Help desks are usually a responsibility of computer operations because of the operational nature of their functions.  A help desk logs reported problems, resolves minor problems, and forwards more difficult problems to the appropriate information systems resources, such as a technical support unit or vendor assistance.
Answer (A) is incorrect because applications development is responsible for developing systems, not providing help to end-users.  Answer (B) is incorrect because the responsibility of systems programming is to implement and maintain system-level software such as operating systems, access control software, and database systems software.  Answer (D) is incorrect because user departments usually lack the expertise to solve computer problems.

**6.** Most large-scale computer systems maintain at least three program libraries: production library (for running programs); source code library (maintains original source coding); and test library (for programs which are being changed). Which of the following statements is correct regarding the implementation of sound controls over computer program libraries?

A. Only programmers should have access to the production library.

B. Users should have access to the test library to determine whether all changes are properly made.

C. Only the program librarian should be allowed to make changes to the production library.

D. The computer operator should have access to both the production library and the source code library to assist in diagnosing computer crashes.

Answer (C) is correct. *(CIA, adapted)*
**REQUIRED:** The true statement about controls over computer program libraries.
**DISCUSSION:** The program librarian is accountable for, and has custody of, the programs in the production library.
Answer (A) is incorrect because effective control requires that programmers not be able to make undetected, unrecorded changes in data or programs. Thus, programmers should not have access to the production library. Answer (B) is incorrect because programmers should be responsible for making program changes, and users should be responsible for testing the changes. Hence, users should not have access to the test library. Accountability for changes would be diminished. Moreover, users may lack the competence to make appropriate changes. Answer (D) is incorrect because, if the operator has access to both program libraries, (s)he may be able to make unauthorized and undetected changes to the computer programs.

**7.** Which of the following would not be appropriate to consider in the physical design of a data center?

A. Evaluation of potential risks from railroad lines and highways.

B. Use of biometric access systems.

C. Design of authorization tables for operating system access.

D. Inclusion of an uninterruptible power supply system and surge protection.

Answer (C) is correct. *(CIA, adapted)*
**REQUIRED:** The inappropriate consideration in the physical design of a data center.
**DISCUSSION:** Authorization tables for operating system access address logical controls, not physical controls.
Answer (A) is incorrect because external risks should be evaluated to determine the center's location. Answer (B) is incorrect because biometric access systems control physical access to the data center. These devices identify such unique physical qualities as fingerprints, voice patterns, and retinal patterns. Answer (D) is incorrect because power supply systems and surge protection are included in data center design. Thus, two separate power lines, line conditioning equipment, and backup battery power or a generator are typical elements in the design.

**8.** What type of information system uses communications capabilities to make needed data and computing capability available to end users at separate locations?

A. Distributed processing system.

B. Time-sharing system.

C. Online processing system.

D. Personal computing system.

Answer (A) is correct. *(CIA, adapted)*
**REQUIRED:** The system that uses communications capabilities to make needed data available for end users at separate locations.
**DISCUSSION:** The advent of less expensive and smaller computers has permitted the development of a different alternative to centralization or decentralization. In a distributed data processing system, the organization's processing needs are examined in their totality. The decision is not whether an application should be done centrally or locally but, rather, which parts of the application are better performed by smaller local computers and which parts are better performed at some other, possibly centralized, site. In essence, the best distribution of processing tasks within application areas is sought. The key distinction between decentralized and distributed systems is the interconnection among the nodes (sites) in the network.
Answer (B) is incorrect because time-sharing systems are terminal-oriented systems that are connected to a central processing site. Answer (C) is incorrect because an online processing system operates under direct control of the CPU. Answer (D) is incorrect because a personal computing system is a microcomputer resource dedicated to a single user, usually in a stand-alone configuration.

**9.** Even though an organization is committed to using its mainframe for its manufacturing plant operations, it has been looking for ways to downsize other applications. The purpose of downsizing is to

A. Improve reliability.

B. Improve security.

C. Reduce complexity.

D. Decrease costs.

Answer (D) is correct. *(CIA, adapted)*
**REQUIRED:** The purpose of downsizing.
**DISCUSSION:** The purpose of downsizing is to reduce costs of applications by abandoning larger, more expensive systems in favor of smaller, less expensive systems that are more versatile. However, downsized applications are less reliable than their mainframe predecessors because they are new and have not been used extensively. Typically, downsized client-server implementations lack the monitoring and control features that permit recovery from minor processing interruptions.
Answer (A) is incorrect because client-server technology used in downsizing is less reliable. Answer (B) is incorrect because security is usually better on a mainframe. Answer (C) is incorrect because downsizing applications often increases their complexity. The data files become fragmented across multiple systems.

**10.** In distributed data processing, a ring network

A. Has all computers linked to a host computer, and each linked computer routes all data through the host computer.

B. Links all communication channels to form a loop, and each link passes communications through its neighbor to the appropriate location.

C. Attaches all channel messages along one common line with communication to the appropriate location via direct access.

D. Organizes itself along hierarchical lines of communication usually to a central host computer.

Answer (B) is correct. *(CMA, adapted)*
**REQUIRED:** The true statement about a ring network in a distributed data processing system.
**DISCUSSION:** In a distributed system, an organization's processing needs are examined in their totality. The decision is not whether an application should be done centrally or locally, but rather which parts are better performed by small local computers as intelligent terminals, and which parts are better performed at some other, possibly centralized, site. The key distinction between decentralized and distributed systems is the interconnection among the nodes in the network. A ring network links all communication channels to form a loop and each link passes communications through its neighbor to the appropriate location.
Answer (A) is incorrect because a star network routes all data through the host computer. Answer (C) is incorrect because a bus network attaches all channel messages along one common line with communication to the appropriate location via direct access. Answer (D) is incorrect because a tree configuration is organized along hierarchical lines to a host computer.

## 9.2 Operating Systems and Computer Devices

**11.** Regardless of the language in which an application program is written, its execution by a computer requires that primary memory contain

A. A utility program.

B. An operating system.

C. Compiler.

D. Assembly.

Answer (B) is correct. *(D. Payne)*
**REQUIRED:** The item necessary to execute an application program.
**DISCUSSION:** An operating system (e.g., UNIX or Windows) is required in all computerized systems to oversee the elements of the CPU and the interaction of the hardware components.
Answer (A) is incorrect because utility programs are application programs that are usually attached to larger programs. They perform various activities, such as sorting data, merging files, converting data from one medium to another, and printing. Answer (C) is incorrect because a compiler converts (compiles) a program written in a source language, such as FORTRAN, into machine language. Answer (D) is incorrect because an assembler translates an assembly language program into machine language. Assembly language uses mnemonic codes for each machine language instruction.

**12.** What type of computer processing system is characterized by data that are assembled from more than one location and records that are updated immediately?

    A. Personal computer systems.

    B. Data compression systems.

    C. Batch processing systems.

    D. Online, real-time systems.

Answer (D) is correct. *(CPA, adapted)*
    **REQUIRED:** The system allowing data entry from multiple locations and immediate updating.
    **DISCUSSION:** Real-time processing involves processing an input record and receiving the output soon enough to affect a current decision-making process. In a real-time system, the user interacts with the system to control an ongoing activity. Online indicates that the decision maker is in direct communication with the computer. Online, real-time systems usually permit access to the main computer from multiple remote terminals.
    Answer (A) is incorrect because access from multiple locations is more typical of larger computer systems than of personal computer systems. Answer (B) is incorrect because data compression systems encode data to take up less storage space. Answer (C) is incorrect because batching of transactions requires assembly of data at one place and a delay in updating.

**13.** Misstatements in a batch computer system caused by incorrect programs or data may not be detected immediately because

    A. Errors in some transactions may cause rejection of other transactions in the batch.

    B. The identification of errors in input data typically is not part of the program.

    C. There are time delays in processing transactions in a batch system.

    D. The processing of transactions in a batch system is not uniform.

Answer (C) is correct. *(CPA, adapted)*
    **REQUIRED:** The reason errors may not be detected immediately in a batch computer system.
    **DISCUSSION:** Transactions in a batch computer system are grouped together, or batched, prior to processing. Batches may be processed either daily, weekly, or even monthly. Thus, considerable time may elapse between the initiation of the transaction and the discovery of an error.
    Answer (A) is incorrect because the transactions within the batch are typically not contingent upon one another. Answer (B) is incorrect because edit checks can be incorporated into batch processing environments. However, the edit checks are used to test the transactions in batches. Answer (D) is incorrect because a batch of transactions is typically processed uniformly.

**14.** Which of the following statements most likely represents a disadvantage for an entity that keeps data files on a server rather than on a manual system?

    A. Attention is focused on the accuracy of the programming process rather than errors in individual transactions.

    B. It is usually easier for unauthorized persons to access and alter the files.

    C. Random error associated with processing similar transactions in different ways is usually greater.

    D. It is usually more difficult to compare recorded accountability with the physical count of assets.

Answer (B) is correct. *(CPA, adapted)*
    **REQUIRED:** The disadvantage of server-based data files.
    **DISCUSSION:** In a manual system, one individual is usually assigned responsibility for maintaining and safeguarding the records. However, in a server environment, the data files may be subject to change by others without documentation or an indication of who made the changes.
    Answer (A) is incorrect because the focus on programming is an advantage of using a server. A software program allows transactions to be processed uniformly. Answer (C) is incorrect because it describes a disadvantage of a manual system. Answer (D) is incorrect because the method of maintaining the files is independent of the ability to compare this information in the file with the physical count of assets.

**15.** Computers containing more than one central processing unit (CPU) are increasingly common. This feature enables a computer to execute multiple instructions from multiple programs simultaneously. This process is

A. Time sharing.

B. Multitasking.

C. Multiprocessing.

D. Batch processing.

Answer (C) is correct. *(Publisher)*
REQUIRED: The term for executing multiple programs with multiple CPUs.
DISCUSSION: Multiprocessing greatly increases system efficiency by executing multiple programs on the same computer at the same time. In systems with only one CPU, although multiple programs may be active simultaneously, program instructions can only be executed for one of these programs at a time.
Answer (A) is incorrect because, in time sharing, the CPU spends a fixed amount of time on each program. Answer (B) is incorrect because multitasking is multiprogramming on a single-user operating system. It is the process of having multiple programs active at a given time, although the CPU is executing instructions from only one program at a time. Answer (D) is incorrect because batch processing entails execution of a list of instructions from beginning to end without interruption.

**16.** Which of the following statements about personal computers, midrange computers, and mainframe computers is true?

A. Personal computers usually cost more than midrange computers but less than mainframes.

B. Because of the increased use of personal computers, there will be little need for mainframes in the near future.

C. Midrange computers must be programmed directly in machine language while mainframes use higher-level language.

D. The cost per transaction to process on each type of computer has decreased in recent years.

Answer (D) is correct. *(Publisher)*
REQUIRED: The true statement concerning personal, midrange, and mainframe computers.
DISCUSSION: Advances in technology have resulted in less expensive computers and increased computing power. The cost to process transactions on all kinds of computers has therefore decreased.
Answer (A) is incorrect because personal computers may cost less than $1,000. Relative to personal computers, midrange computers are more costly, more powerful, have more memory, and are able to interface with more peripheral equipment. Mainframes are large computers with many peripheral devices and large memories. There is virtually no upper limit on the cost of a mainframe. Answer (B) is incorrect because, although personal computers have become extremely popular, e.g., for word processing, databases, other business-related activities, and Internet use, large mainframes are still necessary for simulations and processing not possible on other smaller computers. Midrange computers fill the gap between personal and mainframe computers, and a relatively strong demand also exists for these types of processors, particularly for servers used in networks. Answer (C) is incorrect because all three computers ordinarily may be programmed in higher-level languages.

**17.** In the accounting department of a large organization, the most likely use of a CD-ROM would be to

A. Create permanent audit trails of EDI transactions.

B. Store images of documents received in the department.

C. Record the front and back of checks returned from the bank.

D. Provide a way to look up accounting standards and guidelines.

Answer (D) is correct. *(CIA, adapted)*
REQUIRED: The most likely use of a CD-ROM in an accounting department.
DISCUSSION: CD-ROM (compact disk, read-only memory) is a fixed optical medium appropriate for storage of very large quantities of unchanging information. Researching standards is the best use of CD-ROM technology for an accounting department because the data are static enough for periodic updates to remain sufficiently current. CD-ROMs commonly use indexing and searching facilities that make reference works usable. However, the use of CD-ROMs will decline as the prices of erasable optical disks become more attractive.
Answer (A) is incorrect because creating permanent audit trails of EDI transaction sequences is likely to be accomplished with write once, read many times (WORM) devices. Answer (B) is incorrect because maintaining images of documents with graphical components is likely to be done with redundant arrays of inexpensive disks (RAID). This technology is a magnetic medium that provides a primary storage method for imaging systems. Answer (C) is incorrect because recording the front and back of checks in banking applications is likely to be done with a microform such as microfilm.

**18.** Internal auditors often encounter different personal computer platforms in separate operating divisions or geographic locations. Which of the following statements is true?

I.  Most data and programs from one personal computer platform are transferable to another environment only through translation and emulation programs.

II. Neither data nor programs are transferable when the hardware is not identical.

III. Neither data nor programs are transferable when the operating systems are not identical.

IV. Most data and many programs are transferable among environments through shareware programs.

   A.  I.

   B.  I, IV.

   C.  III.

   D.  II, III.

Answer (A) is correct.  *(CIA, adapted)*
   **REQUIRED:**  The true statement(s) about personal computer platforms.
   **DISCUSSION:**  An emulator is a hardware device that permits one system to imitate another, that is, to use the same data and programs and obtain the same results as the other system.  A translator is a program that translates from one programming language into another.
   Answer (B) is incorrect because shareware does not transfer data.  Shareware is a program that can be freely copied and tested before purchase.  If the party obtaining the shareware continues to use it, there is an obligation to send payment to the author.  Shareware typically is found on bulletin boards and online information systems.  Answer (C) is incorrect because there are facilities to transfer data and programs between disparate operating systems.  Answer (D) is incorrect because there are facilities to transfer data and programs between some environments.

**19.** Response time on a local area network (LAN) was so slow that programmers working on applications kept their code on their own workstations rather than on the server.  As a result, daily backups of the server did not contain the current source code. The best approach to detect deteriorating response time is

   A.  Parallel testing.

   B.  Integrated test facility.

   C.  Performance monitoring.

   D.  Program code comparison software.

Answer (C) is correct.  *(CIA, adapted)*
   **REQUIRED:**  The best approach to detect deteriorating response time.
   **DISCUSSION:**  Performance monitoring is the systematic measurement and evaluation of operating results such as transaction rates, response times, and incidence of error conditions.  Performance monitoring will reveal trends in capacity usage so that capacity can be upgraded before response deteriorates to the point that users behave in unintended or undesirable ways.
   Answer (A) is incorrect because parallel testing is an approach to implementing a new system.  Answer (B) is incorrect because an ITF is an audit tool that uses a fictitious entity against which data transactions are processed.  Answer (D) is incorrect because program code comparison software is used to detect unauthorized changes in programs.

**20.** A manufacturer is considering using bar-code identification for recording information on parts used by the manufacturer.  A reason to use bar codes rather than other means of identification is to ensure that

   A.  The movement of all parts is recorded.

   B.  The movement of parts is easily and quickly recorded.

   C.  Vendors use the same part numbers.

   D.  Vendors use the same identification methods.

Answer (B) is correct.  *(CIA, adapted)*
   **REQUIRED:**  The reason to use bar codes.
   **DISCUSSION:**  Bar-code scanning is a form of optical character recognition.  Bar codes are a series of bars of different widths that represent critical information about the item.  They can be read and the information can be instantly recorded using a scanner.  Thus, bar coding records the movement of parts with minimal labor costs.
   Answer (A) is incorrect because any identification method may fail to record the movement of some parts.  Answer (C) is incorrect because each vendor has its own part-numbering scheme.  Answer (D) is incorrect because each vendor has its own identification method, although vendors in the same industry often cooperate to minimize the number of bar-code systems they use.

**21.** A manufacturer of complex electronic equipment such as oscilloscopes and microscopes has been shipping its products with thick paper manuals but wants to reduce the cost of producing and shipping this documentation. Of the following, the best medium for the manufacturer to use to accomplish this result is

A. Write once/read many (WORM).

B. Digital audiotape (DAT).

C. Compact disk/read-only memory (CD-ROM).

D. Computer output to microfilm (COM).

Answer (C) is correct.  *(CIA, adapted)*
**REQUIRED:** The best way to reduce the cost of producing and shipping documentation.
**DISCUSSION:** CD-ROM is cheaper to produce and ship than the existing paper, yet it permits large volumes of text and images to be reproduced. Users of the electronic equipment are likely to have access to CD-ROM readers on PCs for using such documentation.
Answer (A) is incorrect because WORM is an optical storage technique often used as an archival medium. Answer (B) is incorrect because DAT is primarily used as a backup medium in imaging systems and as a master for CD-ROM. Answer (D) is incorrect because COM is used for frequent access to archived documents, such as canceled checks in banking applications.

## 9.3 Development of Systems and Applications

**22.** The process of monitoring, evaluating, and modifying a system as needed is referred to as systems

A. Analysis.

B. Feasibility study.

C. Maintenance.

D. Implementation.

Answer (C) is correct.  *(CMA, adapted)*
**REQUIRED:** The term for the process of monitoring, evaluating, and modifying a system.
**DISCUSSION:** Systems maintenance must be undertaken by systems analysts and applications programmers continually throughout the life of a system. Maintenance is the redesign of the system and programs to meet new needs or to correct design flaws. These changes should be part of a regular program of preventive maintenance.
Answer (A) is incorrect because systems analysis is the process of determining user problems and needs, surveying the organization's present system, and analyzing the facts. Answer (B) is incorrect because a feasibility study determines whether a proposed system is technically, operationally, and economically feasible. Answer (D) is incorrect because implementation involves training and educating users, testing, conversion, and follow-up.

**23.** Effective internal control for application development should provide for which of the following?

I. A project steering committee to initiate and oversee the system

II. A technical systems programmer to evaluate systems software

III. Feasibility studies to evaluate existing systems

IV. The establishment of standards for systems design and programming

A. I and III.

B. I, II, and IV.

C. I, III, and IV.

D. II, III, and IV.

Answer (C) is correct.  *(CISA, adapted)*
**REQUIRED:** The components of effective internal control for application development.
**DISCUSSION:** Effective systems development requires participation by top management. This can be achieved through a steering committee composed of higher-level representatives of system users. The committee approves or recommends projects and reviews their progress. Studies of the economic, operational, and technical feasibility of new applications necessarily entail evaluations of existing systems. Another necessary control is the establishment of standards for system design and programming. Standards represent user and system requirements determined during systems analysis.
Answer (A) is incorrect because standards must be established. Answer (B) is incorrect because a technical systems programmer has a role in the development and modification of the operating system but not necessarily in applications development. The technical support in this area would be provided by systems analysts rather than programmers. Answer (D) is incorrect because a technical systems programmer has a role in the development and modification of the operating system but not necessarily in applications development.

**24.** Which of the following should be emphasized before designing any system elements in a top-down approach to new systems development?

    A. Types of processing systems being used by competitors.

    B. Computer equipment to be used by the system.

    C. Information needs of managers for planning and control.

    D. Controls in place over the current system.

Answer (C) is correct. *(CIA, adapted)*

**REQUIRED:** The matter to be emphasized before designing a new system.

**DISCUSSION:** The top-down method begins with analysis of broad organizational goals, objectives, and policies as a basis for the design process. This step requires an understanding of the entity's environment and significant activities. The next step is to determine the decisions made by managers and the information required to make them. The necessary reports, databases, inputs, processing methods, and equipment specifications can then be defined. The weakness of the top-down approach is that it tends to concentrate on managers' information needs at the expense of the design of efficient transaction processing at the operational level.

Answer (A) is incorrect because the needs of the organization should be the overriding factor in systems development. Answer (B) is incorrect because the equipment selection should be a function of the processing needs, not vice versa. Answer (D) is incorrect because functional controls should be designed for the new system.

**25.** A benefit of using computer-aided software engineering (CASE) technology is that it can ensure that

    A. No obsolete data fields occur in files.

    B. Users become committed to new systems.

    C. All programs are optimized for efficiency.

    D. Data integrity rules are applied consistently.

Answer (D) is correct. *(CIA, adapted)*

**REQUIRED:** The benefit of CASE.

**DISCUSSION:** CASE is an automated technology (at least in part) for developing and maintaining software and managing projects. A benefit of using CASE technology is that it can ensure that data integrity rules, including those for validation and access, are applied consistently across all files.

Answer (A) is incorrect because obsolete data fields must be recognized by developers or users. Once recognized, obsolete data fields can be treated consistently in CASE procedures. Answer (B) is incorrect because using CASE will not ensure user commitment to new systems if they are poorly designed or otherwise do not meet users' needs. Answer (C) is incorrect because, although it has the potential to accelerate system development, CASE cannot ensure that all programs are optimized for efficiency. In fact, some CASE-developed modules may need to be optimized by hand to achieve acceptable performance.

**26.** CASE (computer-aided software engineering) is the use of the computer to aid in the development of computer-based information systems. Which of the following could not be automatically generated with CASE tools and techniques?

    A. Information requirements determination.

    B. Program logic design.

    C. Computer program code.

    D. Program documentation.

Answer (A) is correct. *(CIA, adapted)*

**REQUIRED:** The item not automatically generated by CASE.

**DISCUSSION:** CASE applies the computer to software design and development. It maintains on the computer a library of standard program modules and all of the system documentation, e.g., data flow diagrams, data dictionaries, and pseudocode (structured English); permits development of executable input and output screens; and generates program code in at least skeletal form. Thus, CASE facilitates the creation, organization, and maintenance of documentation and permits some automation of the coding process. However, information requirements must be determined prior to using CASE.

**27.** Object technology is likely to become more important in companies' strategic use of information systems because of its potential to

    A. Permit quicker and more reliable development of systems.

    B. Maintain programs written in procedural languages.

    C. Minimize data integrity violations in hierarchical databases.

    D. Streamline the traditional "waterfall" systems development methodology.

Answer (A) is correct. *(CIA, adapted)*

**REQUIRED:** The reason object technology is likely to become more important in companies' strategic use of information systems.

**DISCUSSION:** An object-oriented approach is intended to produce reusable code. Because code segments can be reused in other programs, the time and cost of writing software should be reduced.

Answer (B) is incorrect because object technology has the potential to support faster maintenance of programs written in object-oriented, but not procedural, languages. Answer (C) is incorrect because object technology is being applied to relational, but not hierarchical, databases. Answer (D) is incorrect because object technology is typically implemented in a prototyping environment.

**28.** User acceptance testing is more important in an object-oriented development process than in a traditional environment because of the implications of the

A. Absence of traditional design documents.

B. Lack of a tracking system for changes.

C. Potential for continuous monitoring.

D. Inheritance of properties in hierarchies.

Answer (D) is correct. *(CIA, adapted)*
**REQUIRED:** The reason user acceptance testing is more important in an object-oriented development process.
**DISCUSSION:** In object-oriented development, all objects in a class inherit the properties of higher classes in the hierarchy. Thus, changes in one object may affect many other objects, and the extent and effects of errors significantly increase. Testing one object provides no assurance that the objects are properly coordinated. Accordingly, user acceptance testing to verify correct functioning of the whole system becomes more important.
Answer (A) is incorrect because, instead of traditional design documents, items such as the business model, narratives of process functions, iterative development screens, computer processes and reports, and product descriptions guides are produced in object-oriented development. Answer (B) is incorrect because, in general, object-oriented development systems include tracking systems for changes made in objects and hierarchies. Answer (C) is incorrect because object-oriented systems are usually developed in client-server environments, so the potential exists for continuous monitoring of system use. However, continuous monitoring typically occurs during system operation, not during development.

**29.** A systems development approach used to quickly produce a model of user interfaces, user interactions with the system, and process logic is called

A. Neural networking.

B. Prototyping.

C. Reengineering.

D. Application generation.

Answer (B) is correct. *(CIA, adapted)*
**REQUIRED:** The approach used to produce a model of user interfaces, user interactions with the system, and process logic.
**DISCUSSION:** Prototyping produces the first model(s) of a new system. This technique usually employs a software tool for quick development of a model of the user interface (such as by report or screen), interaction of users with the system (for example, a menu-screen approach or data entry), and processing logic (the executable module). Prototyping stimulates user participation because the model allows quick exploration of concepts and development of solutions with quick results.
Answer (A) is incorrect because neural networking involves hardware or software that imitates the processing activities of the human brain. Answer (C) is incorrect because reengineering salvages reusable components of existing systems and restructures them to develop new systems or to improve the old systems. Answer (D) is incorrect because an application generator is software that can be used to develop an application simply by describing its requirements to the computer rather than by writing a procedural program.

**30.** An MIS manager has only enough resources to install either a new payroll system or a new data security system, but not both. Which of the following actions is most appropriate?

A. Giving priority to the security system.

B. Leaving the decision to the MIS manager.

C. Increasing MIS staff output in order for both systems to be installed.

D. Having the information systems steering committee set the priority.

Answer (D) is correct. *(CISA, adapted)*
**REQUIRED:** The appropriate action given inadequate resources.
**DISCUSSION:** The needs assessment and cost-benefit analysis should be conducted by those responsible for making the decision. In this case, the information systems steering committee is the appropriate decision maker.
Answer (A) is incorrect because not enough information is given to conclude that priority should be given to the security system. Answer (B) is incorrect because the MIS manager should not be the only decision maker. Answer (C) is incorrect because the question indicates that development of both systems is not possible.

**31.** Which of the following is the most appropriate activity for an internal auditor to perform during a review of systems development activity?

    A. Serve on the MIS steering committee that determines what new systems are to be developed.

    B. Review the methodology used to monitor and control the system development function.

    C. Recommend specific automated procedures to be incorporated into new systems that will provide reasonable assurance that all data submitted to an application are converted to machine-readable form.

    D. Recommend specific operational procedures that will ensure that all data submitted for processing are converted to machine-readable form.

Answer (B) is correct. *(CIA, adapted)*
    **REQUIRED:** The procedure to perform during a review of systems development activity.
    **DISCUSSION:** Auditor objectivity is not impaired when (s)he recommends standards of control for systems or reviews procedures before implementation. However, drafting procedures for systems and designing, installing, and operating systems are not audit functions. Thus, reviewing the methodology used by an organization is an appropriate activity that enables the internal auditor to determine whether (s)he can rely on the systems development activity to design and implement appropriate automated controls within applications.
    Answer (A) is incorrect because service on a management decision-making committee is an operating responsibility and would impair audit objectivity. Answer (C) is incorrect because making recommendations for automated procedures is an operating responsibility. Answer (D) is incorrect because recommending operational procedures is an operating responsibility.

**32.** The purpose of input controls is to ensure the

    A. Authorization of access to data files.

    B. Authorization of access to program files.

    C. Completeness, accuracy, and validity of updating.

    D. Completeness, accuracy, and validity of input.

Answer (D) is correct. *(CIA, adapted)*
    **REQUIRED:** The purpose of input controls.
    **DISCUSSION:** Input controls provide reasonable assurance that data received for computer processing have been properly authorized and are in a form suitable for processing, i.e., complete, accurate, and valid. Input controls also relate to rejection, correction, and resubmission of data that were initially incorrect.
    Answer (A) is incorrect because access controls authorize access to data files. Answer (B) is incorrect because access controls authorize access to program files. Answer (C) is incorrect because processing controls ensure the completeness, accuracy, and validity of updating.

**33.** A mail-order retailer of low-cost novelty items is receiving an increasing number of complaints from customers about the wrong merchandise being shipped. The order code for items has the format *wwxxyyzz*. The major category is *ww*, *xx* is the minor category, *yy* identifies the item, and *zz* identifies the catalog. In many cases, the wrong merchandise was sent because adjacent characters in the order code had been transposed. The best control for decreasing the number of orders with the wrong merchandise is to

    A. Require customers to specify the name for each item they order.

    B. Add check-digits to the order codes and verify them for each order.

    C. Separate the parts of the order code with hyphens to make the characters easier to read.

    D. Use a master file reference for all order codes to verify the existence of items.

Answer (B) is correct. *(CIA, adapted)*
    **REQUIRED:** The control that prevents erroneous input.
    **DISCUSSION:** Self-checking digits may be used to detect incorrect codes. The digit is generated by applying an algorithm to the code. During the input process, the check digit is recomputed by applying the same algorithm to the code actually entered.
    Answer (A) is incorrect because having customers specify the name for each item they order would let the company correct erroneous order codes once they had been detected, but would not, in general, detect erroneous codes. Answer (C) is incorrect because separating the parts of the order code with hyphens would make the characters easier to read, but would not cure the problem of transposed characters. Answer (D) is incorrect because using a master file reference for all order codes would verify the existence of items, but would not detect erroneous order codes in which transposed characters in an order code match other items.

**34.** Which of the following computerized control procedures would be most effective in ensuring that data uploaded from personal computers to a mainframe are complete and that no additional data are added?

  A. Self-checking digits to ensure that only authorized part numbers are added to the database.

  B. Batch control totals, including control totals and hash totals.

  C. Passwords that effectively limit access to only those authorized to upload the data to the mainframe computer.

  D. Field-level edit controls that test each field for alphanumerical integrity.

Answer (B) is correct.  *(CIA, adapted)*
  **REQUIRED:** The control over completeness of data uploaded from personal computers.
  **DISCUSSION:** Batch control totals for the data transferred can be reconciled with the batch control totals in the existing file. This comparison provides information on the completion of the data transfer. Batch totals may include record counts, totals of certain critical amounts, or hash totals. A hash total is a control total without a defined meaning, such as the total of employee numbers or invoice numbers, that is used to verify the completeness of data. Thus, the hash total for the employee listing by the personnel department could be compared with the total generated during the payroll run.
  Answer (A) is incorrect because self-checking digits detect inaccurate identification numbers. They are an effective control to ensure that the appropriate part has been identified. However, the control objective is to ensure that data transfer is complete. Answer (C) is incorrect because passwords help ensure that only authorized personnel make the transfer, not that data transfer is complete. Answer (D) is incorrect because field checks are effective input controls, but they do not ensure completeness of data transfer.

**35.** When assessing application controls, which one of the following input controls or edit checks is most likely to be used to detect a data input error in the customer account number field?

  A. Limit check.

  B. Validity check.

  C. Control total.

  D. Hash total.

Answer (B) is correct.  *(CIA, adapted)*
  **REQUIRED:** The input control or edit check most likely to be used to detect a data input error in the customer account number field.
  **DISCUSSION:** Validity checks are tests of identification numbers or transaction codes for validity by comparison with items already known to be correct or authorized. For example, Social Security numbers on payroll input records can be compared with Social Security numbers authorized by the personnel department.
  Answer (A) is incorrect because reasonableness, limit, and range checks are based upon known limits for given information. For example, the hours worked per week is not likely to be greater than 45. Answer (C) is incorrect because a record count is a control total of the number of records processed during the operation of a program. Financial totals summarize dollar amounts in an information field in a group of records. Answer (D) is incorrect because a hash total is the number obtained from totaling the same field value for each transaction in a batch. The total has no meaning or value other than as a comparison with another hash total.

**36.** Payroll master file updates are sent from a remote terminal to a mainframe program on a real-time system. A control that works to ensure accuracy of the transmission is a(n)

  A. Echo check.

  B. Protection ring.

  C. Hash total.

  D. Integrated test facility.

Answer (A) is correct.  *(CIA, adapted)*
  **REQUIRED:** The control that works to ensure accuracy of the transmission.
  **DISCUSSION:** An echo check is a hardware control that provides for a peripheral device to return (echo) a signal sent by the CPU. For example, the CPU sends a signal to the printer, and the printer, just prior to printing, sends a signal back to the CPU verifying that the proper print position has been activated.
  Answer (B) is incorrect because a protection ring prevents accidental writing on a tape file. A real-time system would not use tape files. Answer (C) is incorrect because hash totals are used to control data sent to a batch system, not a real-time system. Answer (D) is incorrect because integrated test facilities are useful in testing real-time systems but cannot be used to ensure completeness of data transmissions.

**37.** Detecting errors in real memory is a function of

- A. Memory protection.
- B. Parity checking.
- C. Validity checking.
- D. Range checking.

Answer (B) is correct. *(CIA, adapted)*
**REQUIRED:** The control that detects errors in real memory.
**DISCUSSION:** A parity check adds the bits in a character or message and checks the sum to determine if it is odd or even, depending on whether the computer has odd or even parity. This check verifies that all data have been transferred without loss. For example, if the computer has even parity, a bit will be added to a binary coded character or message that contains an odd number of bits. No bit is added if a character or message in binary form has an even number of bits.
Answer (A) is incorrect because memory protection prohibits programs from accessing memory outside their designated ranges. Answer (C) is incorrect because for hardware, validity checking verifies that a machine-level instruction is a valid instruction; for applications, validity checking verifies that transaction data are complete, authorized, and reasonable. Answer (D) is incorrect because range checking verifies that input data values are within pre-determined ranges.

**38.** Omen Company is a manufacturer of men's shirts. It distributes weekly sales reports to each sales manager. The quantity 2R5 appeared in the quantity sold column for one of the items on the weekly sales report for one of the sales managers. The most likely explanation for what has occurred is that

- A. The output quantity has been stated in hexadecimal numbers.
- B. The computer has malfunctioned during execution.
- C. The printer has malfunctioned and the "R" should have been a decimal point.
- D. The program did not contain a data checking routine for input data.

Answer (D) is correct. *(CMA, adapted)*
**REQUIRED:** The probable reason for reporting a quantity item using an alphabetic character.
**DISCUSSION:** The probable explanation for reporting a quantity using a character other than a digit is that the data were incorrectly encoded and the computer program did not perform a field check, which would have detected the error. A field check tests whether a field consists of the proper characters, whether alphabetic, numeric, special, or combinations thereof.
Answer (A) is incorrect because R is not a hexadecimal character. Hexadecimal characters are 0-9 and A-F representing 0 to 15 in decimal. Answer (B) is incorrect because the probability of a computer malfunction's resulting in the printing of an R is slight. Answer (C) is incorrect because 2.5 would not be appropriate for a quantity of shirts sold.

**39.** The online data entry control called preformatting is

- A. A program initiated prior to regular input to discover errors in data before entry so that the errors can be corrected.
- B. A check to determine if all data items for a transaction have been entered by the terminal operator.
- C. A series of requests for required input data that requires an acceptable response to each request before a subsequent request is made.
- D. The display of a document with blanks for data items to be entered by the terminal operator.

Answer (D) is correct. *(CMA, adapted)*
**REQUIRED:** The definition of preformatting.
**DISCUSSION:** To avoid data entry errors in online systems, a preformatted screen approach may be used. It is a screen prompting approach that involves the display on a monitor of a set of boxes for entry of specified data items. The format may even be in the form of a copy of a transaction document. This technique is best suited to conversion of data from a source document.
Answer (A) is incorrect because an edit routine is a program initiated prior to regular input to discover errors in data before entry so that the errors can be corrected. Answer (B) is incorrect because a completeness check tests whether all data items for a transaction have been entered by the terminal operator. Answer (C) is incorrect because the dialogue approach is another screen prompting method for data entry. It is most appropriate when information is received orally, e.g., by phone.

**40.** A catalog company has been experiencing an increasing incidence of problems in which the wrong products have been shipped to the customer. Most of the customer orders come in over the telephone, and an operator enters the data into the order system immediately. Which of the following control procedures, if properly implemented, would address the problem?

I.  Have the computer automatically assign a sequential order number to each customer order.

II.  Implement a self-checking digit algorithm for each product number and request entries by product number.

III.  Request entries by product number, have the computer program identify the product and price, and require the operator to orally verify the product description with the customer.

    A.  II only.

    B.  I, II, and III.

    C.  II and III.

    D.  I and II.

Answer (C) is correct.  *(CIA, adapted)*
**REQUIRED:** The procedure(s) to prevent incorrect shipments.
**DISCUSSION:** A self-checking digit detects incorrect codes. The digit is generated by applying an algorithm to the code. During input, the digit is recomputed by applying the algorithm to the code actually entered. Oral verification also addresses the problem of incorrectly identifying the product number. Assigning a sequential number to the customer's order helps build an audit trail but does not address the product identification issue.

**41.** Which one of the following input controls or edit checks would catch certain types of errors within the payment amount field of a transaction?

    A.  Record count.

    B.  Echo check.

    C.  Check digit.

    D.  Limit check.

Answer (D) is correct.  *(CIA, adapted)*
**REQUIRED:** The input control or edit check that detects errors within the payment amount field of a transaction.
**DISCUSSION:** A limit, reasonableness, or range test determines whether an amount is within a predetermined limit for given information. It can only detect certain errors (i.e., those that exceed the acceptable limit).
Answer (A) is incorrect because a record count determines the number of documents entered into a process. Answer (B) is incorrect because an echo check tests the reliability of computer hardware. For example, the CPU sends a signal to a printer that is echoed just prior to printing. The signal verifies that the proper print position has been activated. Answer (C) is incorrect because a self-checking number is generated by applying an algorithm to an identification number.

**42.** The key verification process associated with keying computer records for input to a computer system is

    A.  Effectively used to detect the erroneous recording of data on source documents.

    B.  Inexpensive and therefore widely used.

    C.  Used to detect errors introduced by the keying process.

    D.  Ordinarily used with a computer program written to check the data.

Answer (C) is correct.  *(CIA, adapted)*
**REQUIRED:** The purpose of key verification.
**DISCUSSION:** Key verification is a procedure to determine if the keying process was performed properly. Information from source documents is rekeyed on a special keyboard by another operator and compared with that previously recorded.
Answer (A) is incorrect because key verification does not detect errors in the source documents. Answer (B) is incorrect because, although widely used, key verification effectively doubles the work and is expensive. Answer (D) is incorrect because key verification is a manual process.

**43.** Output controls ensure that the results of computer processing are accurate, complete, and properly distributed. Which of the following is not a typical output control?

    A. Reviewing the computer processing logs to determine that all of the correct computer jobs executed properly.

    B. Matching input data with information on master files and placing unmatched items in a suspense file.

    C. Periodically reconciling output reports to make sure that totals, formats, and critical details are correct and agree with input.

    D. Maintaining formal procedures and documentation specifying authorized recipients of output reports, checks, or other critical documents.

**Answer (B) is correct.** *(CIA, adapted)*
    **REQUIRED:** The procedure not a typical output control.
    **DISCUSSION:** Output controls often include comparing output totals with input and processing totals; reviewing computer logs; auditing output reports to ensure that totals, formats, and details are accurate and reconcilable; and specifying authorized recipients by formal means. The data control group also performs important output control functions. Matching the input data with information held on master or suspense files is a processing control, not an output control. It ensures that data are complete and accurate during updating.
    Answer (A) is incorrect because reviewing the computer processing logs is an output control. Answer (C) is incorrect because periodically reconciling output reports is an output control. Answer (D) is incorrect because maintaining formal procedures and documentation specifying authorized recipients is an output control.

**44.** The marketing department's proposal was finally accepted, and the marketing employees attended a class in using the mainframe report writer. Soon, the marketing analysts found that it was easier to download the data and manipulate it on their own microcomputers than to perform all the data manipulation with the mainframe report writer directly. One analyst became highly skilled at downloading and wrote downloading command sequences for the other employees. When the analyst left the company for a better job, the department had problems making modifications to these command sequences. The department's problems are most likely due to inadequate

    A. Documentation.

    B. Data backup.

    C. Program testing.

    D. Anti-virus software.

**Answer (A) is correct.** *(CIA, adapted)*
    **REQUIRED:** The reason for difficulties in modifying the command sequences.
    **DISCUSSION:** One risk of end-user computing is that documentation may be poor and that important knowledge may be limited to one person. The command sequences should have been documented so that other analysts could use and modify them readily.
    Answer (B) is incorrect because the inability of other analysts to understand the command sequences is not a function of inadequate data backup procedures. Answer (C) is incorrect because the inability of other analysts to understand the command sequences is not a function of inadequate testing. Answer (D) is incorrect because the inability of other analysts to understand the command sequences is not a function of inadequate use of anti-virus software.

**45.** After using the mainframe report writer for several months, the marketing analysts gained confidence in using it, but the marketing department manager became concerned. Whenever analysts revised reports they had written earlier, the coding errors kept reappearing in their command sequences. The manager was sure that all the analysts knew what the errors were and how to avoid them. The most likely cause of the reappearance of the same coding errors is inadequate

    A. Backups.

    B. Change control.

    C. Access control.

    D. Testing.

**Answer (B) is correct.** *(CIA, adapted)*
    **REQUIRED:** The most likely cause of the reappearance of coding errors.
    **DISCUSSION:** Change control manages changes in information system resources and procedures. It includes a formal change request procedure; assessments of change requests on technical and business grounds; scheduling changes; testing, installing, and monitoring changes; and reporting the status of recorded changes. The analysts were reusing erroneous code that should have been but was not corrected.
    Answer (A) is incorrect because inadequate backups are not the cause of reuse of erroneous code. Answer (C) is incorrect because inadequate access control is not the cause of reuse of erroneous code. Answer (D) is incorrect because inadequate testing is not the cause of reuse of erroneous code.

**46.** A control for ensuring that the source code and the executable code for a program match is

   A. Verifying that the program move request is authorized.

   B. Requiring program, system, and parallel testing of the code.

   C. Authorizing programmer access to test libraries only.

   D. Recompiling source code into the production load library.

Answer (D) is correct.  *(CIA, adapted)*
   **REQUIRED:** The control for ensuring that the source code and the executable code for a program match.
   **DISCUSSION:** Recompiling source code into the production load library ensures that the source and executable codes match because the executable code is created from the source code.
   Answer (A) is incorrect because verifying that the program move request is authorized ensures that a change was authorized, not that the source and executable code match. Answer (B) is incorrect because requiring program, system, and parallel testing of the code ensures that the code meets test specifications, not that the source and executable code match. Answer (C) is incorrect because authorizing programmer access to test libraries only ensures that programmers do not have access to production libraries, not that the source and executable code match.

**47.** Traditional information systems development procedures that ensure proper consideration of controls may not be followed by users developing end-user computing (EUC) applications. Which of the following is a prevalent risk in the development of EUC applications?

   A. Management decision making may be impaired due to diminished responsiveness to management's requests for computerized information.

   B. Management may be less capable of reacting quickly to competitive pressures due to increased application development time.

   C. Management may place the same degree of reliance on reports produced by EUC applications as it does on reports produced under traditional systems development procedures.

   D. Management may incur increased application development and maintenance costs for EUC systems, compared with traditional (mainframe) systems.

Answer (C) is correct.  *(CIA, adapted)*
   **REQUIRED:** The risk in development of EUC applications.
   **DISCUSSION:** End-user developed applications may not be subject to an independent outside review by systems analysts and are not created in the context of a formal development methodology. These applications may lack appropriate standards, controls, quality assurance procedures, and documentation. A risk of end-user applications is that management may rely on them as much as traditional applications.
   Answer (A) is incorrect because EUC systems typically increase flexibility and responsiveness to management's information requests. Such systems are more easily modified. Answer (B) is incorrect because EUC systems typically reduce application development cycle time. Answer (D) is incorrect because EUC systems typically result in reduced application development and maintenance costs.

**48.** Traditional information systems development and operational procedures typically involve four functional areas. The systems analysis function focuses on identifying and designing systems to satisfy organizational requirements. The programming function is responsible for the design, coding, testing, and debugging of computer programs necessary to implement the systems designed by the analysis function. The computer operations function is responsible for data preparation, program/job execution, and system maintenance. The user function provides the input and receives the output of the system. Which of these four functions is often poorly implemented or improperly omitted in the development of a new end-user computing (EUC) application?

   A. Systems analysis function.

   B. Programming function.

   C. Computer operations function.

   D. User function.

Answer (A) is correct.  *(CIA, adapted)*
   **REQUIRED:** The function often omitted in development of a new EUC application.
   **DISCUSSION:** Systems analysis is one step that is not absolutely required in the development of a system. The desire to produce a system quickly may result in this step being eliminated or poorly implemented. A system is often produced and then analyzed to see if it will satisfy the needs of the organization. In an EUC application, the systems analysis is often incomplete or omitted.
   Answer (B) is incorrect because, without programming, there would be no system. Answer (C) is incorrect because, without computer operations, the system would not be able to do anything. Answer (D) is incorrect because, without users, there would be no need for the system.

**49.** Responsibility for the control of end-user computing exists at the organizational, departmental, and individual user level. Which of the following should be a direct responsibility of the individual users?

A. Acquisition of hardware and software.

B. Taking equipment inventories.

C. Strategic planning of end-user computing.

D. Physical security of equipment.

Answer (D) is correct. *(CIA, adapted)*
**REQUIRED:** The direct responsibility of an individual user.
**DISCUSSION:** End-user computing involves user-created or -acquired systems that are maintained and operated outside of traditional information systems controls. In this environment, an individual user is ordinarily responsible for the physical security of the equipment (s)he uses.
Answer (A) is incorrect because the acquisition of hardware and software is an organizational- and departmental-level responsibility. Answer (B) is incorrect because taking equipment inventories is an organizational-level responsibility. Answer (C) is incorrect because strategic planning is an organizational- and departmental-level responsibility.

**50.** Which of the following represents a limitation on the use of generalized audit software (GAS)?

A. It requires lengthy detailed instructions in order to accomplish specific tasks.

B. It has limited application without significant modification.

C. It requires significant programming knowledge to be used effectively.

D. It can only be used on hardware with compatible operating systems.

Answer (D) is correct. *(CIA, adapted)*
**REQUIRED:** The disadvantage of using GAS.
**DISCUSSION:** Diversity of programming languages, computers, systems designs, and differing data structures makes generalized audit software impossible to apply in certain situations.
Answer (A) is incorrect because the use of GAS is normally more efficient. Less time is required to write instructions to accomplish a function than to manually select and examine items. Answer (B) is incorrect because the program is generalized, i.e., designed to be used on a variety of systems without significant modifications. Answer (C) is incorrect because an advantage is that GAS requires minimal knowledge of computer technology.

**51.** Specialized audit software

A. Is written to interface with many different client systems.

B. May be written while its purposes and users are being defined.

C. Requires the auditor to have less computer expertise than generalized audit software.

D. May be written in a procedure-oriented language.

Answer (D) is correct. *(Publisher)*
**REQUIRED:** The true statement regarding specialized audit software.
**DISCUSSION:** Specialized audit software is written in a procedure- or problem-oriented language to fulfill a specific set of audit tasks. The purposes and users of the software are well defined before the software is written. Auditors develop specialized audit software for the following reasons:

1. Unavailability of alternative software
2. Functional limitations of alternative software
3. Efficiency considerations
4. Increased understanding of systems
5. Opportunity for easy implementation
6. Increased auditor independence and prestige

Answer (A) is incorrect because generalized audit software is written to interface with many different client systems. Answer (B) is incorrect because the purposes and users of this software must be defined before it is written. Answer (C) is incorrect because generalized audit software purchased "off the shelf" requires less computer expertise than specialized software created by the auditor.

**52.** The two requirements crucial to achieving audit efficiency and effectiveness with a personal computer are selecting

A. The appropriate audit tasks for personal computer applications and the appropriate software to perform the selected audit tasks.

B. The appropriate software to perform the selected audit tasks and data that can be accessed by the auditor's personal computer.

C. Company data that can be accessed by the auditor's personal computer and the appropriate audit tasks for personal computer applications.

D. The appropriate sample of company data to test with the auditor's personal computer and the appropriate software to perform the selected audit tasks.

Answer (A) is correct.   *(CPA, adapted)*
**REQUIRED:** The two requirements for audit efficiency and effectiveness using a personal computer.
**DISCUSSION:** The question relates to using the computer as an audit tool. To use a personal computer for this purpose effectively and efficiently, the auditor must have the appropriate hardware and software.
Answer (B) is incorrect because access to data does not relate directly to the efficient and effective use of a personal computer. Answer (C) is incorrect because access to data does not relate directly to the efficient and effective use of a personal computer. Answer (D) is incorrect because the selection of the appropriate sample size does not apply when using software applications because the entire population can be tested.

**53.** An auditor is least likely to use computer software to

A. Construct parallel simulations.

B. Access client data files.

C. Prepare spreadsheets.

D. Assess computer control risk.

Answer (D) is correct.   *(CPA, adapted)*
**REQUIRED:** The task least likely to be done with computer software.
**DISCUSSION:** The auditor is required to evaluate the adequacy and effectiveness of the system of internal control and to assess risk to plan the audit. This assessment is a matter of professional judgment that cannot be accomplished with a computer.
Answer (A) is incorrect because parallel simulation involves using an auditor's program to reproduce the logic of management's program. Answer (B) is incorrect because computer software makes accessing company files much faster and easier. Answer (C) is incorrect because many audit spreadsheet programs are available.

**54.** When an auditor performs tests on a computerized inventory file containing over 20,000 line items, that auditor can maintain independence and perform most efficiently by

A. Asking the console operator to print every item that cost more than $100.

B. Using a generalized audit software package.

C. Obtaining a printout of the entire file and then selecting each nth item.

D. Using the systems department's programmer to write an extraction program.

Answer (B) is correct.   *(CIA, adapted)*
**REQUIRED:** The method to maintain independence and perform efficiently in testing an inventory file.
**DISCUSSION:** Independence can be preserved when the auditor acquires general audit software (GAS) from an external source rather than relying on auditee-developed audit software. Also, efficiency is enhanced to the extent GAS can be used (as compared to manual auditing or writing special audit programs).
Answer (A) is incorrect because independence is jeopardized when an operator is involved in the process. Answer (C) is incorrect because printing out the entire file is both unnecessary and inefficient. Answer (D) is incorrect because overreliance on an auditee's programmer impairs independence.

**55.** Which of the following cannot be performed by an auditor using computer-assisted audit techniques (CAATs) software?

A. Identifying missing check numbers.

B. Extracting data files containing only a two-digit year date field and changing it to hold four digits.

C. Matching identical product information in separate data files.

D. Aging accounts receivable.

Answer (B) is correct.   *(Publisher)*
**REQUIRED:** The task CAATs software cannot perform.
**DISCUSSION:** CAATs software has the ability to extract data files containing specified criteria, such as the size of a data field, but it does not enable the auditor to change the format of this information within management's computer system. However, the auditor can specify the format of data fields in CAATs software-produced reports.
Answer (A) is incorrect because identifying gaps is a function of major CAATs software packages. Answer (C) is incorrect because merging files is a function of major CAATs software packages. Answer (D) is incorrect because aging is a function of major CAATs software packages.

**56.** Which of the following is not true about audit use of the Internet?

    A. It is a useful research tool for gathering audit-related information.

    B. It provides a secure medium to transmit confidential information.

    C. Electronic communication is the major use of the Internet by internal auditors.

    D. An electronic record of a user's web browsing activities is created.

Answer (B) is correct. *(Publisher)*
    **REQUIRED:** The false statement concerning audit use of the Internet.
    **DISCUSSION:** Users transmitting sensitive information across the Internet must understand the threats that arise that could compromise the confidentiality of the data. Security measures, such as encryption technology, need to be taken to ensure that the information is viewed only by those authorized to view it.
    Answer (A) is incorrect because the Internet is a useful audit tool for gathering and disseminating audit-related information. Answer (C) is incorrect because the major use of the Internet by internal auditors is electronic communication. Answer (D) is incorrect because web browsing leaves an electronic record of the user's search path.

**57.** A company has a very large, widely dispersed internal auditing department. Management wants to implement a computerized system to facilitate communications among auditors. The specifications require that each auditor have the ability to send, file, and answer messages at his/her convenience. Transmission of messages must be quick and the preparation of messages must not be costly. Which type of system would best meet these specifications?

    A. Utility program.

    B. Electronic bulletin board system (BBS).

    C. Electronic mail system.

    D. Private branch exchange (PBX).

Answer (C) is correct. *(CIA, adapted)*
    **REQUIRED:** The best system to facilitate communications among auditors.
    **DISCUSSION:** Electronic mail permits transfer, receipt, and storage of messages within or between computer systems. The "mail" consists of electronically transmitted messages. A user's "mailbox" is the storage area allocated for messages. The advantages of electronic mail are high-speed transmission, reduction of message preparation costs, and the possibility of sending or reading messages at a convenient time.
    Answer (A) is incorrect because utility programs are provided by manufacturers of equipment to perform routine processing tasks. Answer (B) is incorrect because an electronic bulletin board system is a centralized information source and message switching system and therefore does not provide a repository to store messages for each auditor. Answer (D) is incorrect because a PBX is a telecommunications system that routes calls to particular extensions within an organization.

**58.** Image processing can be used to convert paper documents into electronic images. Which of the following concepts distinguishes the retention of computerized audit documents from the traditional hard copy form?

    A. Analyses, conclusions, and recommendations are filed on electronic media and are therefore subject to computer system controls and security procedures.

    B. Evidential support for all findings is copied and provided to local management during the closing conference and to each person receiving the final report.

    C. Computerized data files can be used in computer audit procedures.

    D. Audit programs can be standardized to eliminate the need for a preliminary survey at each location.

Answer (A) is correct. *(CIA, adapted)*
    **REQUIRED:** The distinction between computerized audit working papers and the traditional hard copy.
    **DISCUSSION:** The only difference between the computerized and hard copy form is how the working papers are stored. Electronic working papers are saved on either disks or hard drive, whereas hard copies are stored in a file cabinet. Unlike computerized working papers, hard copies are not subject to computer controls and security procedures.
    Answer (B) is incorrect because evidential support is retained and provided on the basis of the nature of the finding and not the media used for storing working papers. Answer (C) is incorrect because this capability is not an exclusive function of computerized working papers. Answer (D) is incorrect because, though the nature of the preliminary survey may change in some cases, the requirement for this phase of the audit is not eliminated by computerized working papers.

## 9.4 Systems Assurance and Control (SAC)

**59.** Which new issues, associated with rapidly advancing computer technology, create new risk exposures for organizations?

    A. Changes in organizational reporting requirements and controls over computer abuse.

    B. Controls over library tape procedures.

    C. Complexity of operating systems and controls over privacy of data.

    D. Changes in organizational behavior.

Answer (C) is correct. *(CIA, adapted)*
**REQUIRED:** Computer technology issues that create risk exposure.
**DISCUSSION:** Advancing computer technology presents more complex audit environments. With the advent of systems that permit remote access, the risk that unauthorized parties may obtain or tamper with important information is increased.
Answer (A) is incorrect because changes in organizational reporting requirements are not new issues related to advancing computer technology. Answer (B) is incorrect because controls over library tape procedures have not been materially changed by advancing computer technology. Answer (D) is incorrect because changes in organizational behavior are not directly associated with auditor responsibilities in advancing technology.

**60.** Which of the following is an important senior management responsibility with regard to information systems security?

    A. Assessing exposures.

    B. Assigning access privileges.

    C. Identifying ownership of data.

    D. Training employees in security matters.

Answer (A) is correct. *(CIA, adapted)*
**REQUIRED:** The senior management reasonability regarding information system security.
**DISCUSSION:** Senior management is responsible for risk assessment, including identification of risks and consideration of their significance, the likelihood of their occurrence, and how they should be managed. Senior management is also responsible for establishing organizational policies regarding computer security and implementing a compliance structure. Thus, senior management should assess the risks to the integrity, confidentiality, and availability of information systems data and resources.
Answer (B) is incorrect because assignment of access privileges is the responsibility of security management. Answer (C) is incorrect because determining ownership of data is the responsibility of security management. In this context, ownership of data or resources mean responsibility for ultimate use or disposition. Answer (D) is incorrect because training employees in security matters is the responsibility of security management.

**61.** Which of the following is a true statement with regard to technology challenges as outlined by The IIA's SAC?

    A. Privacy is recognized internationally as a fundamental human right.

    B. Gains in computer processing and speed have outstripped software development and use.

    C. Open systems are subject to less risk than closed private systems.

    D. Technology has helped system boundaries to remain relatively discrete.

Answer (A) is correct. *(Publisher)*
**REQUIRED:** The true statement regarding IIA SAC technology challenges.
**DISCUSSION:** According to The IIA's SAC, one of the key elements of technology challenges is the issue of privacy. Privacy is recognized internationally as a fundamental human right. The globalization of business through the Internet has resulted in legislation to protect personal information, but the requirements of different nations vary.
Answer (B) is incorrect because the use and development of software has outstripped the gains in computer processing and speed. Answer (C) is incorrect because open systems are subject to more risk than closed, private systems. Answer (D) is incorrect because, with the advancement of technology, system boundaries are becoming indistinct as interactions with suppliers, customers, partners, and associates increases.

**62.** According to The IIA's SAC, all of the following are responses to technology challenges except:

    A. Risk assessment.

    B. Internal control.

    C. Change minimization.

    D. E-assurance services.

Answer (C) is correct. *(Publisher)*
**REQUIRED:** The statement that does not respond to technology challenges, according to The IIA's SAC.
**DISCUSSION:** SAC outlines a series of responses to technology challenges. These responses include risk assessment of e-commerce, internal control objectives, and e-assurance services. While businesses must respond to technology challenges, the response does not necessarily require the minimization of changes.

**63.** According the The IIA's SAC, accountability is

A. Usually an issue with regard to trade secrets and other intellectual property.

B. The control attribute that identifies the source of a transaction.

C. The restriction of access to processing and storage devices.

D. Most often applicable to personal information about employees and customers.

Answer (B) is correct. *(Publisher)*
**REQUIRED:** The definition of accountability according to The IIA's SAC.
**DISCUSSION:** Accountability is the control attribute that identifies the source of a transaction. It specifies employees' roles, actions, and responsibilities. Thus, the person who caused a transaction is identifiable. Fundamental concepts of accountability are data ownership, identification, and authentication.
Answer (A) is incorrect because it refers to confidentiality. Answer (C) is incorrect because it refers to physical security. Answer (D) is incorrect because it refers to privacy.

## 9.5 COBIT

**64.** COBIT is

A. A set of guidelines to assist in implementing adequate controls over IT processes.

B. A set of risks and responses to technology challenges.

C. The update of the previous *Systems Auditability and Control* reports.

D. Published by the Committee of Sponsoring Organizations.

Answer (A) is correct. *(Publisher)*
**REQUIRED:** The definition of COBIT.
**DISCUSSION:** COBIT (Control Objectives for Information and related Technology) is an IT control framework copyrighted by the Information Systems Audit and Control Foundation (ISACF). COBIT is a set of guidelines to assist management and business process owners in implementing adequate controls over IT processes and resources. It is designed to be an IT governance tool that facilitates understanding and managing the risks and benefits associated with information and related IT.
Answer (B) is incorrect because it refers to the SAC model. Answer (C) is incorrect because Systems Assurance and Control (SAC) is the update of the previous Systems Auditability and Control. Answer (D) is incorrect because COBIT is copyrighted by ISACF. The Committee of Sponsoring Organizations published COSO.

**65.** COBIT is targeted at all of the following except:

A. Management.

B. Users.

C. Shareholders.

D. Auditors.

Answer (C) is correct. *(Publisher)*
**REQUIRED:** The item not targeted by COBIT.
**DISCUSSION:** COBIT is targeted at three distinct audiences: management, users, and auditors. Management must balance risks and control costs in the volatile IT environment. Users need assurance about the security of, and controls over, internal or third-party IT services. Auditors must be able to support their opinions conveyed to management and others about the state of internal control. Because shareholders are not directly involved with IT services used in the day-to-day management of an organization, they are not a targeted audience of COBIT.
Answer (A) is incorrect because management is a distinct audience of COBIT. Answer (B) is incorrect because users are a distinct audience of COBIT. Answer (D) is incorrect because auditors are a distinct audience of COBIT.

## 9.6 System Security

**66.** Which of the following issues would be of most concern to an auditor relating to an organization's Internet security policy?

A. Auditor documentation.

B. System efficiency.

C. Data integrity.

D. Rejected and suspense item controls.

Answer (C) is correct. *(Publisher)*
**REQUIRED:** The item of most concern to the auditor relating to Internet security.
**DISCUSSION:** Controls are intended to ensure the integrity, confidentiality, and availability of information. An auditor relies on the integrity of the system's data and programs in making critical decisions throughout the audit process.
Answer (A) is incorrect because auditor documentation is not as crucial as data integrity. Answer (B) is incorrect because efficiency does not affect the basis for critical auditor decisions using information provided by the system. Answer (D) is incorrect because rejected and suspense item controls represent a portion of the techniques used to ensure data integrity.

**67.** Management's enthusiasm for computer security seems to vary with changes in the environment, particularly the occurrence of other computer disasters. Which of the following concepts should be addressed when making a comprehensive recommendation regarding the costs and benefits of computer security?

I. Potential loss if security is not implemented

II. Probability of occurrences

III. Cost and effectiveness of the implementation and operation of computer security

    A. I only.

    B. I and II only.

    C. III only.

    D. I, II, and III.

Answer (D) is correct. *(CIA, adapted)*
    **REQUIRED:** The concept(s) that should be addressed in an analysis of cost-benefit considerations.
    **DISCUSSION:** Potential loss is the amount of dollar damages associated with a security problem or loss of assets. Potential loss times the probability of occurrence is an estimate (expected value) of the exposure associated with lack of security. It represents a potential benefit associated with the implementation of security measures. To perform a cost-benefit analysis, the costs should be considered. Thus, all three items need to be addressed.

**68.** As organizations become more computer integrated, management is becoming increasingly concerned with the quality of access controls to the computer system. Which of the following provides the most accountability?

| | Option I | Option II | Option III | Option IV |
|---|---|---|---|---|
| Restrict access by: | Individuals | Groups | Individuals | Departments |
| Identify computer data at: | Field level | Workstation | Workstation | Individual record level |
| Restrict access: | Need to know | Right to know | Normal processing by employee type | Items identified as processed by department |
| Identify users by: | Password | Password | Key access to workstation, or password on workstation | Departmental password |
| Limit ability to: | Delete, add, or modify data | Add or delete files | Add, delete, or modify data stored at workstation | Add, delete, or modify data normally processed by department |

    A. Option I.

    B. Option II.

    C. Option III.

    D. Option IV.

Answer (A) is correct. *(CIA, adapted)*
    **REQUIRED:** The access control option providing the most accountability.
    **DISCUSSION:** Access should be limited to those whose activities necessitate access to the computer system. Moreover, the degree of access allowed should be consistent with an individual's responsibilities. Restricting access to particular individuals rather than groups or departments clearly establishes specific accountability. Not everyone in a group will need access or the same degree of access. Thus, passwords assigned to individuals should be required for identification of users by the system. Furthermore, data should be restricted at the field level, not the workstation level. It may be possible to limit access to a workstation, but most workstations are connected to larger mainframe or network databases. Thus, the security at the workstation level only would be insufficient.

**69.** An equipment manufacturer maintains dial-up ports into its order-entry system for the convenience of its customers worldwide so they may order parts as they need them. The manufacturer promises 48-hour delivery anywhere in the world for 95% of these parts orders. Because of the cost and sensitive nature of certain electronic parts, the manufacturer needs to maintain secure access to its order-entry system. The best technique for monitoring the security of access is

A. Integrated test facility for the order-entry system.

B. Tracing of transactions through the order-entry system.

C. Transaction selection of order-entry transactions.

D. Logging of unsuccessful access attempts.

Answer (D) is correct. *(CIA, adapted)*
REQUIRED: The best technique for monitoring the security of access.
DISCUSSION: An access log should be used to record all attempts to use the system. The date and time, codes used, mode of access, and data involved are recorded. The system should monitor unsuccessful attempts because repeated attempts could suggest that someone is trying random or patterned character sequences in order to identify a password.
Answer (A) is incorrect because use of an integrated test facility (ITF) is a technique by which an auditor selects transactions and processing functions and applies the transactions to a fictitious entity during a normal processing cycle along with regular transactions. This technique cannot determine whether the data themselves are legitimate. Answer (B) is incorrect because tracing follows the path of a transaction during processing but is inadequate to determine whether a transaction is legitimate. Answer (C) is incorrect because transaction selection uses an independent computer program to monitor and select transactions for internal audit review. Like tracing, it fails to determine whether a transaction is legitimate. It would be an appropriate technique to apply to transactions suspected to be illegitimate.

**70.** Data access security related to applications may be enforced through all the following except

A. User identification and authentication functions incorporated in the application.

B. Utility software functions.

C. User identification and authentication functions in access control software.

D. Security functions provided by a database management system.

Answer (B) is correct. *(CIA, adapted)*
REQUIRED: The functions through which data access security cannot be enforced.
DISCUSSION: Utility programs perform routine functions (e.g., sorting and copying), are available to all users, and are promptly available for many different applications. Utility programs are one of the more serious weaknesses in data access security because some can bypass normal access controls.
Answer (A) is incorrect because although there is a migration of control of this type away from applications to other software, the large bulk of these controls still reside in application software. Answer (C) is incorrect because access control software has as one of its primary objectives improving data access security for all data on the system. Answer (D) is incorrect because most database management systems provide for improved data access security while they are running.

**71.** Most organizations are concerned about the potential compromise of passwords. Which of the following procedures would be the most effective in controlling against a perpetrator obtaining someone else's password?

A. Allow only the users to change their passwords and encourage them to change passwords frequently.

B. Implement a computer program that tests to see that the password is not easily guessed.

C. Implement the use of "see-through" authentication techniques whereby the user uses a card to generate a password and verifies both the key and the generated password to the system.

D. Limit password authorization to time of day and location.

Answer (C) is correct. *(CIA, adapted)*
REQUIRED: The most effective procedure for protecting passwords.
DISCUSSION: See-through authentication techniques, such as the one described, require the user to have two of the three important elements to authenticate oneself to the system, i.e., a possession (the card used to generate the password), knowledge (the new password), or a personal characteristic (e.g., fingerprints).
Answer (A) is incorrect because users often choose passwords that are easily guessed. Answer (B) is incorrect because a program to test passwords is useful but less effective than see-through authentication. Answer (D) is incorrect because limiting access to times and locations is helpful in certain environments but not when the system allows dial-up access.

**72.** Which of the following is a control that will prevent accessing the accounts receivable files from a hardwired terminal located in a manufacturing department?

A. An echo check.

B. A device authorization table.

C. Providing only dial-up terminals.

D. Using data encryption.

Answer (B) is correct. *(J. Brooks)*
**REQUIRED:** The control that will prevent access via a hardwired terminal.
**DISCUSSION:** A device authorization table restricts file access to those physical devices that logically need access. Because it is illogical for anyone to access the accounts receivable file from a manufacturing terminal, the device authorization table will deny access even when a valid password is used.
Answer (A) is incorrect because an echo check relates to the accuracy of signals sent from or to a terminal. Answer (C) is incorrect because dial-up terminals provide less security than hardwired terminals. Any terminal may dial into the communications port using public telephones. Answer (D) is incorrect because although data encryption (transmitting data in code form) might make the data unusable, it would not prevent access.

**73.** The primary objective of security software is to

A. Control access to information system resources.

B. Restrict access to prevent installation of unauthorized utility software.

C. Detect the presence of viruses.

D. Monitor the separation of duties within applications.

Answer (A) is correct. *(CIA, adapted)*
**REQUIRED:** The primary objective of security software.
**DISCUSSION:** The objective of security software is to control access to information system resources, such as program libraries, data files, and proprietary software. Security software identifies and authenticates users, controls access to information, and records and investigates security related events and data.
Answer (B) is incorrect because security software will control the use of utilities, not their installation. Answer (C) is incorrect because antivirus software detects the presence of viruses. Answer (D) is incorrect because security software may be a tool to establish, but does not monitor, separation of duties.

**74.** A controller became aware that a competitor appeared to have access to the company's pricing information. The internal auditor determined that the leak of information was occurring during the electronic transmission of data from branch offices to the head office. Which of the following controls would be most effective in preventing the leak of information?

A. Asynchronous transmission.

B. Encryption.

C. Use of fiber-optic transmission lines.

D. Use of passwords.

Answer (B) is correct. *(CIA, adapted)*
**REQUIRED:** The most effective control over electronic transmission of data.
**DISCUSSION:** Encryption software uses a fixed algorithm to manipulate plain text and an encryption key (a set of random data bits used as a starting point for application of the algorithm) to introduce variation. Although data may be accessed by tapping into the transmission line, the encryption key is necessary to understand the data being sent.
Answer (A) is incorrect because asynchronous transmission is a method of data transmission, not a means of safeguarding data. It is used for slow, irregular transmissions, such as from a keyboard terminal. Each character is marked by a start and stop code. Answer (C) is incorrect because although fiber-optic transmission lines are difficult to tap, their use will not prevent theft of unencrypted data by someone who has access to them. Answer (D) is incorrect because use of passwords will control access at the sending location and the head-office computer. However, passwords will not prevent someone from tapping the transmission line.

**75.** The use of message encryption software

A. Guarantees the secrecy of data.

B. Requires manual distribution of keys.

C. Increases system overhead.

D. Reduces the need for periodic password changes.

Answer (C) is correct. *(CIA, adapted)*
**REQUIRED:** The effect of message encryption software.
**DISCUSSION:** Encryption software uses a fixed algorithm to manipulate plain text and an encryption key (a set of random data bits used as a starting point for application of the algorithm) to introduce variation. The machine instructions necessary to encrypt and decrypt data constitute system overhead. As a result, processing speed may be slowed.
Answer (A) is incorrect because no encryption approach absolutely guarantees the secrecy of data. Answer (B) is incorrect because keys may also be distributed electronically via secure key transporters. Answer (D) is incorrect because periodic password changes are needed. Passwords are the typical means of validating users' access to unencrypted data.

**76.** All administrative and professional staff in a corporate legal department prepare documents on terminals connected to a host LAN file server. The best control over unauthorized access to sensitive documents in the system is

A. Required entry of passwords for access to the system.

B. Physical security for all disks containing document files.

C. Periodic server backup and storage in a secure area.

D. Required entry of passwords for access to individual documents.

Answer (D) is correct. *(CIA, adapted)*
**REQUIRED:** The best control over unauthorized access to sensitive documents in a local area network.
**DISCUSSION:** Different passwords may be required to access the system, to read certain files, and to perform certain other functions. Required entry of passwords for access to individual documents is the best single control over unauthorized access to sensitive documents.
Answer (A) is incorrect because password security for access to the system permits all departmental employees access to all documents in the system. Answer (B) is incorrect because this system uses no floppy disks. Answer (C) is incorrect because periodic server backup and storage in a secure area is a good security/backup procedure, but it would not prevent access to sensitive documents online.

**77.** An auditor has just completed a physical security audit of a data center. Because the center engages in top-secret defense contract work, the auditor has chosen to recommend biometric authentication for workers entering the building. The recommendation might include devices that verify all of the following except

A. Fingerprints.

B. Retina patterns.

C. Speech patterns.

D. Password patterns.

Answer (D) is correct. *(CIA, adapted)*
**REQUIRED:** The method that does not provide biometric authentication.
**DISCUSSION:** Biometric technologies are automated methods of establishing an individual's identity using physiological or behavioral traits. These characteristics include fingerprints, retina patterns, hand geometry, signature dynamics, speech, and keystroke dynamics.

**78.** An Internet firewall is designed to provide adequate protection against which of the following?

A. A computer virus.

B. Unauthenticated logins from outside users.

C. Insider leaking of confidential information.

D. A Trojan horse application.

Answer (B) is correct. *(Publisher)*
**REQUIRED:** The protection provided by an Internet firewall.
**DISCUSSION:** A firewall is a device that separates two networks and prevents passage of specific types of network traffic while maintaining a connection between the networks. Generally, an Internet firewall is designed to protect a system from unauthenticated logins from outside users, although it may provide several other features as well.
Answer (A) is incorrect because a firewall cannot adequately protect a system against computer viruses. Answer (C) is incorrect because industrial spies need not leak information through the firewall. A telephone or floppy disk are much more common means of sharing confidential information. Answer (D) is incorrect because a firewall cannot adequately protect against a Trojan horse (a program, such as a game, that appears friendly but that actually contains applications destructive to the computer system) or any other program that can be executed in the system by an internal user.

**79.** An organization installed antivirus software on all its personal computers. The software was designed to prevent initial infections, stop replication attempts, detect infections after their occurrence, mark affected system components, and remove viruses from infected components. The major risk in relying on antivirus software is that antivirus software may

A. Not detect certain viruses.

B. Make software installation overly complex.

C. Interfere with system operations.

D. Consume too many system resources.

Answer (A) is correct. *(CIA, adapted)*
**REQUIRED:** The major risk in relying on antivirus software.
**DISCUSSION:** Antivirus software designed to identify and remove known viruses is sometimes known as a vaccine. A vaccine works only for known viruses and may not be completely effective for variants of those viruses.
Answer (B) is incorrect because having antivirus software is unlikely to make software installation overly complex.
Answer (C) is incorrect because antivirus software need not interfere with system operations. Its execution can be scheduled in advance so as not to interfere with running programs.
Answer (D) is incorrect because antivirus software can be set to execute at times when it would not consume too many system resources, e.g., at startup.

## 9.7 Contingency Planning

**80.** Each day, after all processing is finished, a bank performs a backup of its online deposit files and retains it for 7 days. Copies of each day's transaction files are not retained. This approach is

    A. Valid, in that having a week's worth of backups permits recovery even if one backup is unreadable.

    B. Risky, in that restoring from the most recent backup file would omit subsequent transactions.

    C. Valid, in that it minimizes the complexity of backup/recovery procedures if the online file has to be restored.

    D. Risky, in that no checkpoint/restart information is kept with the backup files.

**Answer (B) is correct.** *(CIA, adapted)*
    **REQUIRED:** The true statement about retention of backup files but not each day's transaction files.
    **DISCUSSION:** At appropriate intervals, the disk files should be copied on magnetic tape so that restart procedures can begin at those points if data are lost or destroyed. However, not retaining each day's transaction files is risky because information processed since the last backup file was created will be lost.
    Answer (A) is incorrect because the practice of not retaining daily transaction data is unsound in that the bank loses a day's transactions for each backup that is unreadable. Answer (C) is incorrect because the practice of not retaining daily transaction data certainly minimizes complexity but at the expense of losing transaction data if the online file must be restored from the backup. Answer (D) is incorrect because checkpoint/restart information is not needed. The backups are created after all processing is finished for the day.

**81.** A company updates its accounts receivable master file weekly and retains the master files and corresponding update transactions for the most recent 2-week period. The purpose of this practice is to

    A. Verify run-to-run control totals for receivables.

    B. Match internal labels to avoid writing on the wrong volume.

    C. Permit reconstruction of the master file if needed.

    D. Validate groups of update transactions for each version.

**Answer (C) is correct.** *(CIA, adapted)*
    **REQUIRED:** The purpose of periodic retention of master files and transaction data.
    **DISCUSSION:** The grandfather-father-son approach normally employs magnetic tapes to furnish backup in a batch processing system. The procedure involves creation and retention of three generations of master files so that lost or destroyed data may be regenerated from the remaining master files and transaction data. In this case, a master file (the grandfather) and the first week's transactions are used to generate a second master file (the father). This file and the second week's transactions are the basis for the current master file (the son). Online systems employ rollback and recovery procedures; i.e., the master file is periodically dumped onto a storage medium. Reconstruction is then possible using the backup copy and the transactions log.
    Answer (A) is incorrect because comparison of batch totals is a control over the completeness of processing, not a recovery procedure. Answer (B) is incorrect because internal labels may avoid destruction of data but do not aid in recovery. Answer (D) is incorrect because validation may avoid destruction of data but does not aid in recovery.

**82.** Good planning will help an organization restore computer operations after a processing outage. Good recovery planning should ensure that

    A. Backup/restart procedures have been built into job streams and programs.

    B. Change control procedures cannot be bypassed by operating personnel.

    C. Planned changes in equipment capacities are compatible with projected workloads.

    D. Service level agreements with owners of applications are documented.

**Answer (A) is correct.** *(CIA, adapted)*
    **REQUIRED:** The condition ensured by good recovery planning.
    **DISCUSSION:** The disaster plan should embrace data center recovery, critical application recovery, and network recovery. It should be updated and current with regard to recent test results and new applications, equipment, and network configurations. The plan should also ensure that backup facilities are still able to process critical applications and that end-user responsibility is established. Another essential component of a disaster recovery plan is that backup/restart procedures have been anticipated and provided for in the application systems.
    Answer (B) is incorrect because whether change control procedures can be bypassed is not usually a consideration in disaster recovery planning. Answer (C) is incorrect because planned rather than actual changes in equipment capacities are not relevant in disaster recovery planning. Answer (D) is incorrect because ensuring that service level agreements with owners of critical applications are adequate is not a function of disaster recovery planning.

# STUDY UNIT TEN
# INFORMATION TECHNOLOGY II

(28 pages of outline)

This study unit begins with a consideration of communications, with a primary emphasis on computer networks, including the Internet. It then addresses how an information system permits efficient storage, access to, and updating of data through the development of databases. The evolution of computer networks and databases is vital to the rapid growth of e-business. Electronic data interchange (EDI) and its offshoot, electronic funds transfer (EFT) are likewise major elements in the e-business explosion. The direct and indirect costs of information technology investments are also considered. The next subunit considers the development of systems that connect all of an enterprise's applications. The study unit concludes with coverage of the severe threats posed by viruses and other malicious software and by other means used to assault the computer systems of businesses.

## 10.1 DATA, NETWORK, AND VOICE COMMUNICATIONS

1. **Data Communications**

   a. The movement of data among CPUs and remote devices requires special telecommunications technology.

      1) **Communications processors** are the hardware devices that facilitate data transmission and reception in a network.

         a) **Front-end processors** perform message switching, move data to primary storage, correct errors, format data, and otherwise relieve the CPU of certain input-output control functions.

            i) They are located between the computer and the modem in the network.

            ii) Nonprogrammable units are known as communications **controllers**.

         b) **Multiplexors** are switching devices that route or channel the flow of data. They intermix the flow of data so that multiple data streams may flow over one line. A multiplexor channel permits sending more than one message on a communication line (**interleaving**). Thus, multiple devices may be able to share a communication line to a CPU.

         c) A **concentrator** is a programmable device that collects messages until it has recorded enough to be transmitted in a burst of signals to the host computer.

d) **Modem (modulator-demodulator)** is a hardware device that converts **digital signals** from terminals and the CPU into **analog signals** for transmission across data (usually telephone) lines. The receiving modem converts the analog signal back to digital form for use by the receiving terminal or CPU.

   i) If **digital transmission** facilities are available, a modem is not required. Instead, the user employs a digital interface or data service unit (DSU) as a connection with the digital transmission service. Digital transmission is less prone to error because it is less sensitive to electrical interference.

   ii) One way in which modems and other telecommunications devices may differ is in their **bit rates**, not to be confused with **baud rates**. The bit rate, usually measured in bits per second, is a measurement of the transmission speed. The baud rate is the number of signal changes or cycles per period of time. It cannot exceed the bandwidth of the communication channel.

   - At high speeds, more than one bit may be transmitted by a signal change. Hence, the bit rate may be greater than the baud rate.
   - A telecommunications medium's transmission capacity depends on its frequency, i.e., the number of signal changes or cycles per second that can be sent through the medium as measured in **hertz**. The **bandwidth** is the range of frequencies from highest to lowest that a given telecommunications channel can accommodate. As the bandwidth increases, the capacity of the medium also increases.

e) **Communications channels** differ from the data channels connecting the CPU and peripheral equipment. They are the communications media for transmitting data and are classified according to their capacity.

   i) **Narrowband** (baseband), e.g., telegraph lines
   ii) **Voiceband**, e.g., telephone lines
   iii) **Broadband** technology provides multiple paths and therefore permits simultaneous transmission of different kinds of data. Examples are fiber-optic cable, microwave circuits, and satellite channels.
   iv) **Baseband** network is a type of LAN used solely for data communications.

f) **Other hardware items** used to connect computers in a network include:

   i) A **hub** is a central connecting device in a network that joins communications lines together in a star configuration.

   - Passive hubs are just connecting units that add nothing to the data passing through them.
   - Active hubs, also called multiport repeaters, regenerate the data bits in order to maintain a strong signal.
   - Intelligent hubs provide added functionality, such as network management, bridging, routing, and switching.

   ii) **Switches** are another type of connecting device. Each port on a switch can give full bandwidth to a single server, client, or hub.

iii) **Bridges** connect two or more LAN segments together. The segments can be of similar or dissimilar types. Bridges improve network performance by keeping traffic contained within smaller segments.

iv) **Routers** are devices that route data packets from one local area network (LAN) or wide area network (WAN) to another. Routers read the network address in each transmitted frame and make a decision on how to send it based on the most expedient route.

2) The most common types of **transmission media** include the following:

a) **Twisted copper wire** is used for analog communication by telephone. It is a slow medium for data transmission, but new software and hardware have improved its capacity.

b) **Coaxial cable** is used for cable television, high-speed modem connections, and LANS. It consists of thickly insulated copper wire that is faster and more interference free than twisted wire.

c) **Fiber optic cable** is made of clear glass fibers bound into a cable. Data is transmitted by pulses of light emitted by a laser. Fiber optics are faster, lighter, and more durable than the wire media and are difficult to tap, but they are also more expensive.

d) **Wireless** transmission media use the **electromagnetic spectrum**. For example, **microwave systems** use high-frequency radio signals transmitted through the atmosphere. Satellites may serve as relay points. They may be the conventional high, stationary orbit variety or the cheaper low-orbit satellites that require less powerful ground transmitters. Two-way digital data transmission via cell phone is made possible by the transmission standard **CDPD (Cellular Digital Packet Data)**. Moreover, networks (**mobile data networks**) have been established expressly for two-way data transmission between handheld computers. A **personal digital assistant (PDA)** is a handheld computer designed for wireless telecommunications with pen-based input. It may, for example, have e-mail, fax, and document data transmission capabilities.

3) **Transmission modes** may be asynchronous or synchronous.

a) **Asynchronous** or **start-stop transmission** is used for slow, irregular transmissions, such as from a keyboard terminal. Each character is marked by a start and stop bit.

b) **Synchronous transmission** is used when rapid, continuous transmission is desired. It transfers blocks of characters without start and stop bits but requires that the sending and receiving modems be synchronized.

4) The following are the types of **transmission circuits**:

a) **Simplex** transmission is in one direction only, such as for display purposes.

b) **Half-duplex** transmission is in both directions but not at the same time. It is appropriate when processing is online but a response is not required.

c) **Full-duplex** transmission is in both directions at once, which is a necessity for real-time processing.

5) **Teleprocessing** is computer processing via remote terminals. Communications software for teleprocessing is necessarily complex because of the multiple tasks to be performed when many terminals are in simultaneous use.

a) The CPU, the front-end processor, and the concentrator may all have communications software.

b) **Communications software** performs, among other things, the following functions:

    i) Receives input, locates the appropriate program, loads it into memory, transmits the input to the program, and passes the output to the user

    ii) Identifies and corrects errors and provides for security. Encryption is a typical security measure.

    iii) Maintains passwords and authorization procedures, monitors usage and logons, and updates the log of network activity

    iv) Manages buffers (special storage areas) that hold input before processing

    v) Manages the sequencing and proper routing of messages, polls terminals, and sets transmission priorities and speed

c) A **protocol** is a set of rules for message transmission among the devices in the network. Each device should adhere to the same protocol.

d) **Snapshot** copies of files are created at time intervals so that the files will be available on the mainframe. A risk of snapshot files is that they could be obsolete by the time they are downloaded.

2. **Types of Networks**

  a. **Private networks** are dedicated facilities, e.g., satellites, microwave transmitters, or telephone lines, leased from a common carrier. Hence, no dial-up access is required, and security is enhanced.

    1) A **private branch exchange (PBX)** is a special computer at a company facility used to store, transfer, and redial telephone calls. It can carry both audio and data and can switch digital data among computers and office equipment, e.g., printers, copiers, and fax machines. A PBX uses telephone lines, so its data transmission capacity is limited.

  b. **Public-switched networks** use public telephone lines. This arrangement may be the most economical, but data transmission may be of lower quality, no connection may be available, and security measures may be ineffective.

  c. **Value-added networks (VANs)** are mailbox-type services in which the sender's and receiver's computers are never directly connected to each other. Instead, the third-party VAN receives, logs, stores, and forwards EDI documents to the parties, thus eliminating the need for dedicated computers waiting for incoming messages. Although VANs also provide for communication compatibility across a variety of user systems, each user must purchase its own software to translate data to a standard EDI protocol, either ANSI X.12 in the U.S. or EDIFACT in the rest of the world. Once the data are in the standard format, the VAN handles all aspects of the communication.

  d. A **local area network (LAN)** is a local distributed computer system, e.g., within a single office. Computers, communication devices, and other equipment are linked by dedicated channels. Special software facilitates efficient data communication among the hardware devices. The channel technology may be baseband or broadband. **Baseband** allows one path for transmission of video, voice, text, or graphics, and only one data type may be transmitted. **Broadband** provides multiple paths.

    1) The LAN's hardware consists of several computers either attached to a host computer, linked as part of several LANs that may or may not communicate with a host computer, or connected together but not connected to a host computer.

      a) A **peer-to-peer network** operates without a mainframe or server.

2) The LAN may also use **wireless spread spectrum broadcasting** rather than a direct cable link. However, a wireless LAN is likely to have slower response times.

3) A **network interface card** links personal computers and printers in a LAN. The card creates an address for each message, determines the data transmission rate and the size of message units, and specifies the topology (how the components are connected).

4) A **server** is a computer in a network that stores programs and files for users and determines access rights. It also contains the **network operating system**.

5) A **gateway** is a means of connecting otherwise incompatible networks, nodes, or devices. It converts one set of communication protocols to another.

6) **Ethernet** is a set of LAN standards that allows networking products from different vendors to communicate with each other. It is the most widely used LAN technology.

7) A **baseband network** is a type of LAN used solely for data communications.

e. **Wide area networks (WAN)** provide data communication and file sharing among remote offices. A WAN may combine switched and dedicated lines, microwave transmission, and satellite communication. Common carriers determine rates and connections between lines. Content and management (routing of messages, editing, protocols, etc.) are the responsibility of the customer.

1) **Packet switching** divides text from many users into small groups of data (packets) and continuously transmits them independently along available communications channels.

a) **Frame relay** is faster and less expensive but, unlike packet switching, does not involve correction of errors. Frames are similar to packets. They are best used for data transmission rather than voice and video communications.

b) **Asynchronous transfer mode (ATM)** is a technology that avoids the need for separate networks. It switches audio, video, graphics, and data among users at whatever speed the network can operate and regardless of whether the computers are from different vendors. It also eliminates protocol conversion by dividing information into cells, each containing 53 groups of 8 bytes.

f. **Virtual private networks (VPNs)**

1) Businesses have traditionally relied on private leased lines to link offices so that workers could share information over a WAN. However, while providing a high degree of privacy, leased lines are expensive to set up and maintain. For many companies, a leased line may be impractical, providing more bandwidth than is needed at too high a price.

2) VPN emerged as a relatively inexpensive way to solve this problem. Rather than maintain a point-to-point leased line, a company connects each office or LAN to a local Internet service provider and routes data through the Internet, using shared, low-cost public bandwidth as the communications backbone.

3) However, the major concern in using a public network for electronic data exchange is security. Unprotected data sent across the Internet is susceptible to being viewed, copied, or modified by unauthorized persons. The success of VPNs will depend on the development of secure encryption products that protect data while in transit on the Internet.

g.   Given the worldwide proliferation of computer networks, **connectivity** has become a major issue.  The desire for greater connectivity favors open systems.

1)   **Open systems** are those for which suppliers provide components whose interfaces are defined by public standards.  For example, the U.S. government specifies that its suppliers adhere to the **Unix operating system** and the telecommunications protocols developed for the Internet.  In contrast, a closed system's components are built to proprietary standards so that the equipment made by other suppliers cannot interface with the existing system.  Accordingly, converting to open systems increases the number of vendors from which substitutable components can be acquired, which increases price competition for equipment.

2)   Although uniform standards for telecommunications, networking, operating systems, and user interfaces have not yet emerged, some standards have been created by governments, industry associations, and international organizations.

3)   **Open Systems Interconnect (OSI)** has been developed by the International Organization for Standardization.  It is a seven-layer reference model that allows different types of computers and networks to communicate.

4)   **Integrated Services Digital Network (ISDN)** provides international standards for voice, video, and data communications over telephone lines.

3.   **Network Configurations (Topologies)**

a.   **Point-to-point** networks provide a separate, direct link between each remote terminal and the CPU.

b.   **Multidrop** (or **BUS**) networks provide links for each device to a single communications line.  No host computer controls the network, and signals are transmitted in both directions to all devices.  Software determines which device receives a given communication.  **Ethernet** is an example of a network technology that uses a bus topology.

c.   **Ring networks** have no central computer.  Each computer can communicate with every other computer, but their connection forms a closed loop in which data pass from one device to another and always in one direction.  In a **token ring network**, a packet of data (the token) passes along the network.  Each computer reads it and either accepts data from it, loads data onto the token, or allows it to pass without change.

d.   **Completely connected networks**, also known as modified ring networks, have direct links among all computer locations.

e.   **Star networks** are most often used in mainframe environments.  They permit each remote computer a direct link to the central location but not to other remote computers.

4.   **Voice Communications**

a.   **Voice communications channels** differ from the data channels connecting the CPU and peripheral equipment.  They are the communications media for transmitting voice data and are classified according to their capacity.

1)   An example of a voiceband channel is a telephone line.

b.   **Voice recognition** input devices are still another alternative to keyboard input.  These systems compare the speaker's voice patterns with prerecorded patterns.  Advanced systems now have large vocabularies and shorter training periods.  They allow for dictation and are not limited to simple commands.

c.   A **voice output device** converts digital data into speech using prerecorded sounds.

d.   **Pagers** have long been used to alert the recipient of a message, but newer systems now permit transmission of brief text messages.

e. A **cell phone** uses radio waves to transmit voice and data through antennas in a succession of cells or defined geographic areas.

f. **Personal communications services (PCS)** is a cellular technology based on lower-power, higher-frequency radio waves. Cells must be smaller and more numerous, but the phones should be smaller and less expensive and be able to operate where other such devices cannot.

5. **Web Infrastructure**

a. **The Internet** is a series of networks throughout the world that facilitates information transfer among computers. Gateways allow mainframe computers to interface with personal computers. The graphics-rich environment of the **World Wide Web (web)** has been largely responsible for bringing the Internet out of the static realm of e-mail and text-only documents. The web continues to grow faster than any other segment of the Internet. Businesses, schools, government, and nonprofit organizations (in addition to millions of individuals) are flocking to the Internet to promote themselves and their products to an audience spanning the entire planet.

1) The three main parts of the World Wide Web are the **server** that holds the information, the **client** that is viewing the information, and **protocols** (Transmission Control Protocol and Internet Protocol, or TCP/IP) that connect the two.

2) The web is accessed via programs called **browsers**. A browser is software that permits a computer to retrieve and recognize HTML files. Web browsers allow the user to display the textual and graphical information that makes up much of the World Wide Web. It can also provide audio and video presentations and the ability to use e-mail, bulletin boards, discussion groups, etc. They allow text, graphics, audio, and video to be integrated for the user.

3) **Intranets and extranets** are defined by who has access.

a) An **intranet** is an internal network that applies Internet connectivity standards and web software. An intranet addresses the connectivity problems of an organization with many types of computers. Although an intranet is a network based on the same technology as the Internet, access is limited to an organization or those with specific authorization.

b) An **extranet** is an intranet to which specified parties, such as suppliers and customers, have limited access. An extranet provides web access for existing customers or specific users rather than the general public. It typically uses the public Internet as its transmission system but requires a password to gain access.

b. Languages

1) **Hypertext markup language (HTML)** is the authoring software language used to create and link pages on the web.

2) **XML (extensible markup language)** was developed by an international consortium and released in 1998 as an open standard usable with many programs and platforms. XML codes all information in such a way that a user can determine not only how it should be presented but also what it is, i.e., all computerized data may be tagged with identifiers. Unlike HTML, XML uses codes that are extensible, not fixed. Thus, if an industry can agree on a set of codes, software for that industry can be written that incorporates those codes.

6. Stop and review! You have completed the outline for this subunit. Study multiple-choice questions 1 through 9 beginning on page 499.

## 10.2 DATABASES

1.   A **database** is a series of related files combined to eliminate unnecessary redundancy of data items.  A single integrated information system allows for increased data accessibility.  When systems within the organization are not integrated, they may contain different data and may define and update data in inconsistent ways.  Thus, determining the location and consistency of data is more difficult.

   a.   **EXAMPLE**:  The various files related to personnel in the conventional record systems of most organizations include payroll, work history, and permanent personnel data.

      1)   An employee's name must appear in each of these files when they are stored and processed separately.  The result is redundancy.

      2)   When data are combined in a database, each item is usually stored only once.

   b.   The data are stored physically on **direct-access** (e.g., magnetic disk) devices.  They are also stored for efficient access.

      1)   The most frequently accessed items are placed in the **physical locations** permitting the fastest access.

      2)   When these items were stored in separate files in conventional systems, the physical locations were usually similar to the logical structure of the data.  Items that logically belonged together were stored in physical proximity to one another.

      3)   A **logical data model** is a user view.  It is the way a user describes the data and defines interrelationships based on the user's needs, without regard to how the data is physically stored.

   c.   The logical structure of a database may be of various kinds.

      1)   A **tree** or **hierarchical structure** arranges data in a one-to-many relationship in which each record has one antecedent but may have an unlimited number of subsequent records.

         a)   Because all paths, directories, and indexes must be predefined, a hierarchical structure is inflexible and does not support ad hoc queries.

      2)   A **network structure** reduces redundancy by arranging data through development of many-to-many relationships; that is, each item may have multiple antecedent as well as successive relationships.

      3)   A **relational structure** organizes data in conceptual tables.  Each column in a table is a field, and each row (tuple) is a specific record.  One relation (table or file) can be joined together or related to another by the database management system without pointers or linked lists if each contains one or more of the same fields (also known as columns or attributes).  The relational structure is the most popular because it is relatively easy to construct and is useful for unplanned, ad hoc queries.  However, its processing efficiency is relatively low because many accesses may be necessary to execute the select, join, and project commands.

         a)   A **field** is an item in a record.  It consists of a group of related characters (bytes) providing a unit of data about some entity (e.g., a customer or employee).

         b)   A **record** is a collection of related fields pertaining to some entity.

            i)   **Keys** are attributes of logical records that permit them to be sorted.  A primary key is the field that is the principal identifier, e.g., a vendor number in a file of vendors' invoices.  A secondary key is an alternative identifier used either for sorting or special processing, e.g., the payment date on a vendor's invoice.

ii) **Logical records** are defined in terms of the information they contain. A logical record contains a number of fields relating to that record; e.g., a payroll record might include the Social Security number, the employee's name, the rate of pay, etc.

iii) The attributes of the **physical record** vary according to the physical storage device. Thus, a logical record may be divided among a number of physical records either on a magnetic tape or on a disk. A physical record may also contain one logical record.

iv) In addition, the various fields constituting a record may be distributed within a database and linked via pointers to maintain the relationship.

v) **Fixed-length computer records** facilitate the handling of data on both disk and tape. They allow data to be blocked, moved, and stored in a standard-size format, thus permitting simpler treatment in programs. To handle variable-sized records, the program would have to modify itself while data are being read and processed.

vi) **Variable-length records** use space more efficiently because the storage size can vary with the record size. Data transmission is more efficient with variable-length records because they require less space.

vii) **Blocking** means putting a number of logical records into a physical record, i.e., to place a block of logical records between two interblock gaps, allowing the computer to read more data at one time.

viii) A **record layout** is used to describe the fields in each logical record of each file used in input, output, and storage. Layout sheets are preprinted forms used as documentation for record layouts.

ix) A **pointer** is an identifier that specifies the location of a data item.

x) An **index** is a list of contents of a file or document together with references to their locations, for example, an index of keys and their related addresses.

c) A **file** is a logical collection of records, such as those for customer accounts.

i) A **master file** is relatively permanent. A **transaction file** contains temporary records processed together with a master file for updating purposes in a batch processing environment.

ii) File organization

- A **flat file** contains only fixed-length files of equal length.

- A **linked list** is a file organization in which each data record has a pointer field containing the address of the next record in the list.

- In a **direct file** organization, a randomizing formula or hashing scheme (**a transform algorithm**) converts a record key into a storage address. This method permits direct access without an index.

- The **indexed-sequential-access method (ISAM)** is a system in which records are stored sequentially in a direct-access file and organized by a primary key stored in an index record. It does not use pointers. The virtue of an ISAM system is that it permits sequential processing of many records while providing for occasional direct access.

iii)   File management concerns creating, maintaining, retrieving information from, updating, and establishing control over data files. Updating totals, storing them in a record, comparing them periodically with record contents, and correcting discrepancies is an example of a file management control.

d)   **Volatility** is a commonly used measure of the relative frequency of adds, deletes, and changes to a master file during a specified time period.

e)   **Normalization** is the term for determining how groups of data items in a relational structure are arranged in records in a database. This process relies on **normal forms**, that is, conceptual definitions of data records and specified design rules. Normalization is intended to prevent inconsistent deletion, insertion, and updating of data items.

f)   The three basic operations in the relational model are selecting, joining, and projecting.

i)    **Selecting** creates a subset of records that meet certain criteria.

ii)   **Joining** is the combining of relational tables based on a common data element.

iii)  **Projecting** is the basic operation in a relational database that results in a subset consisting of columns (fields) in a table. This operation creates a new table containing only the required information.

d.   The data in a database are subject to the constraint of **referential integrity**. If data are collected about something, e.g., a payment voucher, all reference conditions must be met; thus, for a voucher to exist, a vendor must also exist.

e.   A **distributed database** is stored in two or more physical sites using either replication or partitioning.

1)   The **replication** or **snapshot** technique makes duplicates to be stored at multiple locations. Changes are periodically copied and sent to each location. If a database is small, storing multiple copies may be cheaper than retrieving records from a central site.

2)   **Fragmentation** or **partitioning** stores specific records where they are most needed. For example, a financial institution may store a particular customer's data at the branch where (s)he usually transacts his/her business. If the customer executes a transaction at another branch, the pertinent data is retrieved via communications lines. One variation is the **central index**. A query to this index obtains the location in a remote database where the complete record is to be found. Still another variation is the ask-the-network distributed database. In this system, no central index exists. Instead, the remote databases are polled to locate the desired record.

3)   Updating data in a distributed system may require special protocols. Thus, a **two-phase commit disk-writing protocol** is used. If data is to be updated in two places, databases in both locations are cleared for updating before either one performs (commits) the update. In the first phase, both locations agree to the update. In the second phase, both perform the update.

f.   A **deadly embrace** occurs when each of two transactions has a lock on a data resource that the other transaction needs to run to completion. When deadly embraces occur, the database system must have an algorithm for undoing the effects of one of the transactions and releasing the data resources it controls so that the other transaction can run to completion. Then, the other transaction is restarted and permitted to run to completion. If deadly embraces are not resolved, response time worsens or the system eventually fails.

2.   In a tree or network database, the logical relationship among items is achieved through the use of **pointers** (the disk address of a related item).

    a.   **EXAMPLE**: Consider the item EMPLOYEE #. For employee # 123462, pointers are stored with the employee # indicating the location on the disk of other items logically related to this employee, e.g., the employee's name.

3.   A **database management system (DBMS)** is an integrated set of computer programs that create the database, maintain the elements, safeguard the data from loss or destruction, and make the data available to applications, programs, and inquiries.

    a.   The DBMS allows programmers and designers to work independently of the physical structure of the database.

    b.   When programmers and systems designers need to know the physical structure of the database, creation of new applications and maintenance of existing applications are extremely time-consuming and therefore expensive.

    c.   The **schema** is a description of the overall logical structure of the database using **data-definition language**, which is the connection between the logical and physical structures of the database. A **subschema** describes a particular user's (application's) view of a part of the database using data-definition language.

    d.   A fundamental characteristic of databases is that applications are independent of the database structure; writing programs or designing applications to use the database requires only the name of the desired data item, not its location.

    e.   A data item is identified using the **data-manipulation language**, after which the DBMS locates and retrieves the desired item. The data-manipulation language is used to add, delete, retrieve, or modify data or relationships. An example is **SQL**, which is used with relational DBMSs.

    f.   The physical structure of the database can be completely altered without having to change any of the programs using the data items. Thus, different users may define different views of the data (subschemas).

    g.   In **desktop database** systems, the database application and the underlying data is usually both stored on the same PC. DBMSs commonly used in desktop applications are Access, FoxPro, dBASE, and Paradox. In **client-server** applications, the data is stored on a server that can be accessed concurrently from a "front-end" application, which may be running on multiple workstations. DBMSs commonly used in client-server systems are Oracle, Microsoft SQL, and Interbase.

4.   **Other Database Definitions**

    a.   The **database administrator** (DBA) is the individual who has overall responsibility for developing and maintaining the database and for establishing controls to protect its integrity. Thus, only the DBA should be able to update data dictionaries. In small systems, the DBA may perform some functions of a DBMS. In larger applications, the DBA uses a DBMS as a primary tool.

    b.   The **data dictionary** is a file that describes the use of data from the database in applications. It provides a mapping from the database to applications and vice versa. Thus, the data dictionary states not only the meaning of a data element but also its ownership (who is responsible for its maintenance), size, format, and usage. Moreover, it states what persons, programs, reports, and functions use the data element.

        1)   In an advanced data dictionary, a change in a data element automatically changes related programs.

    c.   The **data control language** specifies the privileges and security rules governing database users.

5.  Databases and the associated DBMS permit efficient storage and retrieval of data for formal system applications. They also permit increased ad hoc accessing of data (e.g., to answer inquiries for data not contained in formal system outputs) as well as updating of files by transaction processing. These capabilities require fast direct-access devices, sophisticated software, highly trained technical personnel (DBA, staff), and strict controls.

6.  An **object-oriented database** is a response to the need to store not only numbers and characters but also graphics and multimedia applications. Translating these data into tables and rows is difficult. However, they can be stored in an object-oriented database, along with the procedures acting on them, within an object.

7.  In a **hypermedia database**, blocks of data are organized into nodes that are linked in a pattern determined by the user so that an information search need not be restricted to the predefined organizational scheme. A node may contain text, graphics, audio, video, or programs.

    a.  Hybrid systems containing object-oriented and relational database capabilities have also been developed.

8.  Advanced database systems provide for **online analytical processing** (multidimensional data analysis), or the ability to analyze large amounts of data from numerous perspectives.

9.  A **data warehouse** contains not only current operating data but also historical information from throughout the organization. Thus, data from all operational systems is integrated, consolidated, and standardized into an organization-wide database into which data is copied periodically. This data is maintained on one platform and can be read but not changed. Graphics and query software and analytical tools assist users. Accordingly, **data mining** is facilitated by a data warehouse.

10. Stop and review! You have completed the outline for this subunit. Study multiple-choice questions 10 through 27 beginning on page 501.

## 10.3 E-COMMERCE, EDI, AND EFT

1.  **E-commerce (EC)** is the purchase and sale of goods and services by electronic means. **E-business** is a more comprehensive term defined as all methods of conducting business electronically.

    a.  EC may occur via online transactions on public networks, electronic data interchange (EDI), and e-mail.

2.  **Security issues** for EC include

    a.  The correct identification of the transacting parties **(authentication)**
    b.  Determination of who may rightfully make decisions, such as entering into contracts or setting prices **(authorization)**
    c.  Methods for protecting the confidentiality and integrity of information, providing evidence of the transmission and receipt of documents, and guarding against repudiation by the sender or recipient
    d.  The trustworthiness of listed **prices** and the confidentiality of **discounts**
    e.  The confidentiality and integrity of orders, payments, delivery addresses, and confirmations
    f.  The proper extent of **verification** of payment data
    g.  The best **method of payment** to avoid wrongdoing or disagreements
    h.  Lost or duplicated transactions
    i.  Determining who bears the risk of fraud

3. **Responses to security issues** include

    a. Encryption and the associated authentication methods discussed earlier in this study unit

    b. Adherence to legal requirements, such as privacy statutes

    c. Documenting trading agreements, especially the terms of trade and methods of authorization and authentication

    d. Agreements for end-to-end security and availability with providers of information services and VANs

    e. Disclosure by public trading systems of their terms of business

    f. The capacity of the host computer to avoid downtime and repel attacks

4. **Electronic Data Interchange (EDI)** is the communication of electronic documents directly from a computer in one entity to a computer in another entity, for example, to order goods from a supplier or to transfer funds. EDI was the first step in the evolution of e-business.

    a. EDI was developed to enhance JIT (just-in-time) inventory management.

    b. **Advantages of EDI** include reduction of clerical errors, speed of transactions, and elimination of repetitive clerical tasks. EDI also eliminates document preparation, processing, and mailing costs.

    c. **Risks of EDI** include

        1) Security of information

            a) End-to-end data encryption is a security procedure that protects data during transmission.

        2) Loss of data

    d. An extension of EDI is computer-stored records, which can be less expensive than traditional physical file storage.

5. **EDI Terms and Components**

    a. **Standards** concern procedures to convert written documents into a standard electronic document-messaging format to facilitate EDI.

        1) In the U.S., the American National Standards Institute's Accredited Standards Committee X 12 provides standards.

        2) Many international entities use **UN/EDIFACT** (United Nations EDI for Administration, Commerce, and Transport).

    b. **Conventions** are the procedures for arranging data elements in specified formats for various accounting transactions, e.g., invoices, materials releases, and advance shipment notices.

    c. A **data dictionary** prescribes the meaning of data elements, including specification of each transaction structure.

    d. **Transmission protocols** are rules to determine how each electronic envelope is structured and processed by the communications devices.

        1) Normally, a group of transactions is combined in an electronic envelope and transmitted into a communications network.

        2) Rules are required for transmission and the separation of envelopes.

    e. Because EDI formats and elements vary, a large entity may gain a competitive advantage by forcing trading partners to adopt its standards. Other entities will need to negotiate EDI standards.

6.   **Methods of Communication among Computers** (Telephone lines and modems are typically used.)

a.   **Point-to-point** is the most traditional EDI connection. Both parties have fixed computer connections, and the computers are used solely for EDI. The direct connection that is created forces all the computers to be compatible with each other. A point-to-point arrangement is very similar to networks within one entity.

b.   **Value-added networks** (VANs) are private mailbox-type services in which the sender's and receiver's computers are never directly connected to each other. Instead, both parties to the EDI arrangement subscribe to a third-party VAN provider. Because of the third-party buffer, the VAN users are not required to conform to the same standards, conventions, and protocols. Also, VANs can store messages (in a mailbox), so the parties can batch outgoing and incoming messages.

1)   Encryption, preferably by physically secure hardware rather than software, is a critical control.

c.   The **Internet** is a means of conducting business directly with a trading partner. It can be used in a more open environment in which one firm transmits documents to another. This approach is based on less formal agreements between the trading partners than in EDI and requires the sending firm to format the documents into the format of the receiving firm.

7.   **Electronic funds transfer (EFT)** is a service provided by financial institutions worldwide that is based on electronic data interchange (EDI) technology. EFT transaction costs are lower than for manual systems because documents and human intervention are eliminated from the transaction process.

a.   A typical application of EFT is the direct deposit of payroll checks in employees' accounts or the automatic withdrawal of payments for cable and telephone bills, mortgages, etc.

8.   **Implications for Internal Auditors**

a.   EDI eliminates the paper documents, both internal and external, that are the traditional basis for many procedures performed in substantive testing and in tests of controls.

1)   An organization that has **reengineered** its procedures and processes to take full advantage of EDI may have eliminated even the electronic equivalents of paper documents. For example, the buyer's **point-of-sale (POS) system** may directly transmit information to the seller, which delivers on a JIT basis. Purchase orders, invoices, and receiving reports are eliminated and replaced with

a)   A long-term contract establishing quantities, prices, and delivery schedules;

b)   Production schedules;

c)   Advance ship notices;

d)   Evaluated receipts settlements (periodic payment authorizations transmitted to the trading partner with no need for matching purchase orders, invoices, and receiving reports); and

e)   Payments by EFT.

     2)   Internal auditors must seek new forms of evidence to support assertions about EDI transactions, whether the evidence exists at the client organization, the trading partner, or a third party, such as a VAN. Examples of such evidence are

        a)   The authorized paper purchase contract,

        b)   An electronic completed production schedule image, and

        c)   Internal and external evidence of evaluated receipts settlements sent to the trading partner.

     3)   Internal auditors must evaluate digital signatures and reviews when testing controls.

     4)   Internal auditors may need to consider other subsystems when testing a particular subsystem. For example, production cycle evidence may be needed to test the expenditure cycle.

9.   **XML** (extensible markup language) was developed by an international consortium and released in 1998 as an open standard usable with many programs and platforms. XML is a variation of HTML (hypertext markup language), which uses fixed codes (tags) to describe how webpages and other hypermedia documents should be presented. XML codes all information in such a way that a user can also determine what it is. Thus, all computerized data may be tagged with identifiers. Also, unlike HTML, XML uses tags that are extensible, not fixed. Accordingly, if an industry can agree on a set of codes, software for that industry can be written that incorporates those codes. For example, XML allows the user to label the Uniform Product Code (UPC), price, color, size, etc., of goods so that other systems will know exactly what the tag references mean. In contrast, HTML tags would only describe how items are placed on a page and provide links to other pages and objects.

    a.   Standard setters and other entities are attempting to find ways to incorporate XML with EDI.

    b.   **XBRL** (extensible business reporting language) for Financial Statements is the specification developed by an AICPA-led consortium for commercial and industrial entities that report in accordance with U.S. GAAP. It is a variation of XML that is expected to decrease the costs of generating financial reports, reformulating information for different uses, and sharing business information using electronic media.

10.   **EDI controls** will vary with the organization's objectives and applications.

    a.   Authorized users with independent access may include

     1)   The people initiating transactions
     2)   The people authorizing transactions
     3)   Other authorizing parties
     4)   Senders for exceptional transactions

    b.   **Message authentication** may be accomplished using smart cards and other hardware and software techniques. Protection of message integrity by authentication is especially important for such EDI applications as EFT and ordering.

    c.   Messages also must be protected from interception or tampering while in transit. Controls include

     1)   Encryption
     2)   Numerical **sequencing** to identify missing or false messages
     3)   **Nonrepudiation** methods

        a)   **Digital certificates** are used to prove origination and delivery so that parties cannot disclaim responsibility for sending or receiving a message.

        b)    EC sellers and buyers routinely provide acknowledgments and confirmations, respectively, in a website dialogue to avoid later disputes.

        c)    In an EDI application, control over nonrepudiation is achieved by sequencing, encryption, and authentication.

11.   **Secure Electronic Transaction (SET)** is a trademarked protocol that provides a common security standard, especially with regard to Internet card (credit, debit, or chip) purchases. It is supported by Visa and MasterCard through an organization called **SETCo**.

   a.   SET encrypts the details of payment transactions at all times so as to ensure privacy and data integrity. It also ensures that the identities of sellers and buyers are authenticated using digital signatures (DSs) and certificates (DCs).

   b.   SET is based on a hierarchy of **certificate authorities (CAs)** that parallels financial relationships outside cyberspace.

       1)   SETCo issues DCs to **payment brands**.

       2)   A SET DC allows a payment brand to become a CA and issue DCs to its **member-banks**.

       3)   A SET DC then allows a member bank to become a CA and issue DCs to **merchants** and **cardholders**.

          a)    Thus, a merchant obtains the backing of a payment brand when it receives a DC authenticating its identity from its "acquirer" bank.

          b)    The cardholder's DC is equivalent to a plastic card used in a physical transaction. It is kept in a SET-enabled **electronic wallet** stored on the holder's computer or on the card issuer's server.

             i)    The wallet also contains such other data as the customer's payment brand account number and the expiration date.

             ii)    The customer obtains the wallet from an authorized financial institution.

          c)    The payment transaction data in the wallet are **encrypted** until decoded by the seller-merchant's acquirer bank. The information must be decoded so that the customer's bank can authorize the transaction. The information is recoded for purposes of notice of approval to the customer and seller.

          d)    In the SET system, the interface between the seller-merchant and its acquirer bank is the **payment gateway**. It serves to authorize payment for multiple types of cards. The gateway

             i)    Decodes the SET messages

             ii)    Authenticates all parties involved

             iii)    Reformats the message so that it is compatible with the merchant's point-of-sale system

       4)   All CAs must confirm the identities of those seeking DCs so as to ensure their authenticity.

12.   E-mail is a quick, informal, but often insecure method of business communication.

   a.   **E-mail risks** that need to be controlled include

       1)   Unauthorized access or modification

       2)   Unreliability or denial of service

       3)   Inaccurate addressing or misdirection

       4)   The effects of change to more rapid communication and of transmitting messages person to person

        5)    Legal issues, such as nonrepudiation

        6)    Remote user access to e-mail

        7)    External access to employee lists

    b.    The organization should have an **acceptable use policy** that

        1)    Limits Internet access to authorized persons

        2)    Provides for removal of unused accounts and those of departed employees

        3)    Prescribes what e-mail accounts contractors may use

        4)    Requires a disclaimer on every e-mail indicating that the message is the sender's, not the organization's

        5)    Describes what may be disclosed in e-mail

        6)    Reserves the organization's right to inspect e-mail

        7)    Explicitly permits or prohibits private use

        8)    Requires attachments to be screened by antivirus software before being opened

        9)    Provides for educating users about the dangers of malicious software, indicators of e-mail attacks, and measures for coping with suspicious items

13.    A **publicly available system**, for example, a Web server, publishers information that must be protected. If the integrity of this information is compromised, the reputation of the organization may be damaged.

    a.    The organization should implement formal policies and procedures for creating such a system.

        1)    These policies and procedures should be consistent with legal requirements where the system is located or business is conducted, for example, legislation protecting the privacy of the collection, storage, and use of personal information.

        2)    Information entry should be timely, complete, and accurate.

        3)    Access does not inadvertently allow entry to other networks.

        4)    Responsibility and accountability for (ownership of) a website should be determined so that all changes are made by the owner (a function or person).

        5)    The acceptable use policy should create an environment in which employees know their rights and responsibilities, and the organization's brand name (reputation) is safeguarded.

14.    Stop and review! You have completed the outline for this subunit. Study multiple-choice questions 28 through 39 beginning on page 506.

## 10.4 INVESTMENT IN IT

1.    Hardware and software are significant assets that require careful management. Among the decisions to be made are resource requirements, evaluation of the full costs of the investment, and choosing whether to own or lease the technology.

2.    The growth of e-business means that greater resources are needed for transactions within the organization and with outside parties, for example, as a result of hosting websites with many users.

    a.    **Capacity planning** should be undertaken by management and IT specialists. It determines whether the organization's current and future hardware resources relative to its priorities are, and will continue to be, sufficient. Among the issues are

        1)    The maximum volume of transactions that can be simultaneously processed by the system

        2)    The effect of software developments

3) Performance measures, e.g., response time

4) Changes in capacity needs resulting from business combinations, increased demand for the organization's products and services, and new applications

b. **Scalability** is the characteristic of a system that permits its capacity to be increased to meet greater demands without a system failure.

1) For example, a website should be supported by adequate processing, storage, and network assets to cope with peak demand.

3. The **costs of ownership** of IT assets include indirect as well as direct costs. Thus, rational economic decisions about hardware and software acquisition require an analysis of the true or full costs of all factors involved. Failing to consider total long-term costs may seriously underestimate the economic effects of IT decisions.

a. The **total cost of ownership (TCO) model** will vary with the organization's unique needs. The following are typical factors to be considered:

1) Capital costs of hardware, such as computers, terminals, storage devices, printers, and upgrades

2) Capital costs of software, including purchase price or licensing cost per user, with upgrades

3) Installation costs of hardware and software

4) Training costs for IT specialists and end users

5) Support costs incurred for help desks, other technical support labor, documentation, R&D, development of configuration standards, and review

6) Maintenance costs for hardware and software upgrades

7) Infrastructure costs of obtaining, supporting, and maintaining networks, back-up storage, etc.

8) Costs of unproductive time (downtime) resulting from hardware or software failure

9) Utility and real property costs of computer installations

10) Costs of nonstandard personal computer configurations

a) A standard configuration scheme for a given category of end users reduces costs by facilitating upgrades and support. However, new applications and updates of hardware may cause a loss of standardization.

11) Costs of transferring end users

a) An end user is customarily restricted to a given personal computer with needed applications and access. Hence, transfer of an end user results in incurrence of costs for reinstallation and testing.

b. **Managed systems** are less costly to maintain and administer because **hidden (indirect) costs** are understood and minimized.

1) A centralized mainframe may be cheaper than a client-server architecture despite higher initial costs because of lower network administration and support costs.

2) In large entities, centralized acquisition policies save costs because organizational subunits are not allowed to purchase incompatible or redundant hardware and software. Standardized IT resources improve operations and decrease costs of administration.

3) Management of systems should include **tracking** IT resources and configuration changes. Tracking permits measurement of the cost of a configuration change in terms of personnel, money, time, and other resources. The cost can then be compared with the benefit.

    c.    The **Systems Assurance and Control Report** provides the following framework for determining TCO for an IT installation:

        1)    Cost of the **standard configuration** times the number of **workstations**

        2)    Sum of the **technical infrastructure** costs (hardware and software costs of servers, printers, routers, bridges, cables, supplier support, utility software, help desks, taxes, shipping, and upgrades over the productive life cycle of the configuration and infrastructure)

        3)    The sum of **staff costs** for full-time equivalent positions directly involved during the productive life cycle plus **administrative costs** (e.g., for developing procedures and standards, capacity planning, and change control)

        4)    A percentage of the foregoing costs to reflect **hidden costs**, including such intangibles as end-user help provided by coworkers rather than the help desk

        5)    Costs of facilities, turnover, travel, and transportation

4.    Stop and review!  You have completed the outline for this subunit.  Study multiple-choice questions 40 and 41 on page 510.

## 10.5 ENTERPRISE-WIDE RESOURCE PLANNING (ERP)

1.    **Enterprise resource planning (ERP)** is the latest phase in the development of computerized systems for managing organizational resources.  ERP is intended to **integrate** enterprise-wide information systems by creating **one database** linked to all of an organization's applications.

    a.    ERP connects all functional subsystems (human resources, the financial accounting system, production, marketing, distribution, purchasing, receiving, order processing, shipping, etc.) and also connects the organization with its suppliers and customers.

        1)    Thus, ERP facilitates demand analysis and materials requirements planning.

        2)    By decreasing lead times, it improves just-in-time inventory management.

        3)    Even more importantly, ERP's coordination of all operating activities permits flexible responses to shifts in supply and demand.

    b.    The disadvantages of ERP are its extent and complexity, which make customization of the software difficult and costly.

    c.    The leading comprehensive product in the field is **SAP R/3**.  Other ERP products are marketed by Oracle, PeopleSoft, and J. D. Edwards.

    d.    Because ERP software is costly and complex, it is usually installed only by the largest enterprises.  However, mid-size organizations are increasingly likely to buy ERP software.

    e.    The benefits of ERP may significantly derive from the required **business process reengineering**.

        1)    Using ERP software that reflects the **best practices** forces the linked subunits in the organization not only to redesign and improve their processes but also to conform to one standard.

        2)    An organization may wish to undertake a reengineering project before choosing ERP software.  The project should indicate what best practices already exist in the organization's processes.  This approach may be preferable for a unique enterprise in a highly differentiated industry.

            a)    Carrying out a reengineering project before installing an ERP system defines what process changes are needed and which vendor software should be used.

            b)    If the organization is not especially unique, vendor software probably is already based on industry best practices.  In these circumstances, a preliminary reengineering project may not be needed.  Thus, the organization should simply conform its processes to the software.

3) The processes reflected in the ERP software may differ from the organization's. In this case, the better policy is usually to change the organization's processes. **Customizing** the ERP software is expensive and difficult, and it may result in bugs and awkwardness in adopting upgrades.

    a) Implementing an ERP system is likely to encounter significant resistance because of its comprehensiveness. Most employees will have to change ingrained habits and learn to use new technology. Hence, successful implementation requires effective **change management**.

2. **Materials requirements planning (MRP I)** was an early attempt to create an integrated computer-based information system. It was designed to plan and control materials used in a production setting.

    a. MRP was a push system. It assumed that the demand for materials is typically dependent upon some other factor, which can be programmed. Thus, the timing of deliveries is vital to avoid production delays.

    b. For example, an auto manufacturer need only tell the system how many autos of each type are to be manufactured. The MRP system then generates a complete list of every part and component needed. MRP, in effect creates schedules of when items on inventory will be needed in the production departments.

        1) If parts are not in stock, the system will automatically generate a purchase order on the proper date (considering lead times) so that deliveries will arrive on time. Hence, effective application of MRP necessitates the generation of accurate data about costs and amounts of inventory, set-up costs, and costs of downtime.

3. **Manufacturing resource planning (MRP-II)** continued the evolution begun with MRP I. It is a closed-loop manufacturing system that integrates all facets of a manufacturing business, including production, sales, inventories, schedules, and cash flows. The same system is used for the accounting, finance, and directing functions, which use the same transactions and numbers.

    a. MRP-II includes forecasting and planning capacities for generating cash and other budgets.

    b. MRP-II uses an MPS (master production schedule), a statement of the anticipated manufacturing schedule for selected items for selected periods. MRP also uses the MPS. Thus, MRP is a component of an MRP-II system.

4. The **traditional ERP system** is one in which subsystems share data and coordinate their activities.

    a. Thus, if marketing receives an order, it can quickly verify that inventory is sufficient to notify shipping to process the order.

        1) Otherwise, production is notified to manufacture more of the product, with a consequent automatic adjustment of output schedules.

        2) If materials are inadequate for this purpose, the system will issue a purchase order.

        3) If more labor is needed, human resources will be instructed to reassign or hire employees.

        4) The foregoing business processes (and others) should interact seamlessly in an ERP system. Moreover, the current generation of ERP software also provides the capability for smooth (and instant) interaction with the business processes of external parties.

    b. The subsystems in a traditional ERP system are internal to the organization. Hence, they are often called **back-office** functions. The information produced is principally (but not exclusively) intended for internal use by the organization's managers.

5.   The current generation of ERP software (**ERP II**) has added **front-office** functions. These connect the organization with customers, suppliers, shareholders or other owners, creditors, and strategic allies (e.g., the members of a trading community or other business association). Accordingly, an ERP II system has the following interfaces with its back-office functions:

   a.   **Supply-chain management** applications for an organization focus on relationships extending from its suppliers to its final customers. Issues addressed include distribution channels, warehousing and other logistical matters, routing of shipments, and sales forecasting.

      1)   In turn, one organization's supply chain is part of a **linked chain** of multiple organizations. This chain stretches from the producers of raw materials, to processors of those materials, to entities that make intermediate goods, to assemblers of final products, to wholesalers, to retailers, and lastly to ultimate consumers.

      2)   Supply chain management involves a **two-way exchange of information**. For example, a customer may be able to track the progress of its order, and the supplier may be able to monitor the customer's inventory. Thus, the customer has better information about order availability, and the supplier knows when the customer's inventory needs replenishment.

      3)   An **advanced planning and scheduling system** may be an element of a supply chain management application for a manufacturer. It controls the flow of material and components within the chain. Schedules are created given projected costs, lead times, and inventories.

   b.   **Customer relationship management** applications extend to customer service, finance-related matters, sales, and database creation and maintenance.

      1)   Integrated data is helpful in better understanding customer needs, such as product preference or location of retail outlets. Thus, the organization may be able to optimize its sales forecasts, product line, and inventory levels.

         a)   **Business intelligence** software is used to analyze customer data.

   c.   **Partner relationship management** applications connect the organization not only with such partners as customers and suppliers but also with owners, creditors, and strategic allies (for example, other members of a joint venture).

      1)   **Collaborative business partnerships** may arise between competitors or arise between different types of organizations, such as a manufacturer partnering with an environmental group. Special software may be helpful to the partners in sharing information, developing a common strategy, and measuring performance.

6.   The following are the main elements of the **architecture** of an ERP:

   a.   Current ERP systems have a **client-server configuration** with, possibly, scores or hundreds of client (user) computers.

      1)   So-called **thin clients** have little processing ability, but **fat clients** may have substantial processing power.

      2)   The system may have multiple servers to run applications and contain databases.

      3)   The network architecture may be in the form of a **local area network** or **wide-area network**, or users may connect with the server(s) via the **Internet**.

      4)   An ERP system may use almost any of the available **operating systems** and **database management systems**.

b.   An advantage of an ERP system is the elimination of data redundancy through the use of a **central database**.  In principle, information about an item of data is stored once, and all functions have access to it.

    1)   Thus, when the item (such as a price) is updated, the change is effectively made for all functions.  The result is reliability **(data integrity)**.

        a)   If an organization has separate systems for its different functions, the item would have to be updated whenever it was stored.  Failure of even one function to update the item would cause loss of data integrity.  For example, considerable inefficiency may arise when different organizational subunits (IT, production, marketing, accounting, etc.) have different data about prices and inventory availability.

c.   An organization may not have the resources, desire, or need for an ERP system with the greatest degree of integration (e.g., SAP R/3).

    1)   An alternative to a comprehensive system is a **best-of-breed approach**.  Thus, an organization might install a traditional ERP system from one vendor and add e-commerce and other extended applications from separate niche vendors.

        a)   An organization that adopts this approach needs to use **middleware**, that is, software that permits different applications to communicate and exchange data.  This type of middleware is called an **extended application interface**.

d.   An ERP system that extends to customers, suppliers, and others uses **Internet portals**.  In this case, a portal is a website through which authorized external users may gain access to the organization's ERP.

    1)   Portals provide links to related websites and services (e.g., newsletters, e-mail, and e-commerce capabilities).

7.   **Implementation of ERP** may take years and cost millions.  Moreover, a poor implementation may cause the project to fail regardless of the quality of the software.

a.   However, more rapid and less costly implementation may be possible if no customization is done.

b.   The initial step is to do **strategic planning** and to organize a **project team** that is representative of affected employee groups.

c.   The second step is to **choose ERP software** and a **consulting firm**.

    1)   One possibility is to choose the software before the consultants because the first decision may affect the second.

    2)   Another option is to hire consultants to help with the selection of the software.

        a)   The organization may then hire other consultants to help with implementation.

d.   The third and longest step is **preimplementation**.

    1)   The length of the **process design** phase is a function of the extent of

        a)   Reengineering
        b)   Customization of the software

    2)   **Data conversion** may be delayed because of disagreements about the means of defining every data field, for example, whether codes should have independent meaning.

    3)   The ERP system and its interfaces must be **tested**.

e. **Implementation** ("going live") is not the final step. **Follow up** is necessary to monitor the activities of the numerous employees who have had to change their routines. For example, a mistake caused by reverting to the old method of entering a sales order may have pervasive consequences in a new integrated system: a credit check, rescheduling of production, and ordering of materials.

f. **Training** should be provided during implementation not only regarding technical matters but also to help employees understand the reasons for process changes. For example, the employees who enter sales orders should know what the effects will be throughout the system.

    1) Other **change management** techniques include effective communication to allay employee fears and the creation of user-friendly documents and interfaces.

8. The **costs** of an ERP system include

    a. Losses from an unsuccessful implementation, e.g., sales declines

    b. Purchasing hardware, software, and services

    c. Data conversion from legacy systems to the new integrated system (but conversion software may help)

    d. Training

    e. Design of interfaces and customization

    f. Software maintenance and upgrades

    g. Salaries of employees working on the implementation

9. The **benefits** of an ERP system may be hard to quantify. They include

    a. Lower inventory costs

    b. Better management of liquid assets

    c. Reduced labor costs and greater productivity

    d. Enhanced decision making

    e. Elimination of data redundancy and protection of data integrity

    f. Avoidance of the costs of other means of addressing needed IT changes

    g. Increased customer satisfaction

    h. More rapid and flexible responses to changed circumstances

    i. More effective supply chain management

    j. Integration of global operations

10. Stop and review! You have completed the outline for this subunit. Study multiple-choice questions 42 through 48 beginning on page 511.

## 10.6 MALICIOUS SOFTWARE AND ATTACKS

1. The business assurance objective in the SAC model that is most concerned with malicious software (MS) is **protectability**. Thus, IT assets should be protected from "unauthorized access, use, or harm."

    a. Control, e.g., over access and change management, should be in place to achieve the objective of protectability.

    b. Moreover, **security awareness** by all concerned should be heightened. Consequently, the business assurance objective of **accountability** is also pertinent. The roles, actions, and responsibilities for security should be defined.

2.  Malicious software may exploit a known hole or weakness in an application or operating system program to evade security measures. Such a vulnerability may have been caused by a programming error. It may also have been intentionally (but not maliciously) created to permit a programmer simple access (a back door) for correcting the code.

    a.  Having bypassed security controls, the intruder can do immediate damage to the system or install malicious software.

        1)  A **Trojan horse** is an apparently innocent program (e.g., a spreadsheet) that includes a hidden function that may do damage when activated.

            a)  For example, it may contain a **virus**, program code that copies itself from file to file. The virus may destroy data or programs. A common way of spreading a virus is by e-mail attachments and downloads.

            b)  A **worm** copies itself not from file to file but from computer to computer, often very rapidly. Repeated replication overloads a system by depleting memory or disk space.

            c)  A **logic bomb** is much like a Trojan horse except it activates only upon some occurrence, e.g., on a certain date.

            d)  A maliciously created **back door** can be used for subsequent high level access to data, computers, and networks.

            e)  MS may create a **denial of service** by overwhelming a system or website with more traffic than it can handle.

                i)  In other cases, MS infecting may have little or no effects noticeable by users.

3.  **Controls** to prevent or detect infection by MS are particularly significant for file servers in large networks. The following are broad control objectives:

    a.  A policy should require use only of authorized software.
    b.  A policy should require adherence to licensing agreements.
    c.  A policy should create accountability for the persons authorized to maintain software.
    d.  A policy should require safeguards when data or programs are obtained by means of external media.
    e.  Antivirus software should continuously monitor the system for viruses (or worms) and eradicate them. It should also be immediately upgraded as soon as information about new threats becomes available.
    f.  Software and data for critical systems should be regularly reviewed.
    g.  Investigation of unauthorized files or amendments should be routine.
    h.  E-mail attachments and downloads (and files on unauthorized media or from networks that are not secure) should be checked.
    i.  Procedures should be established and responsibility assigned for coping with MS.

        1)  Procedures should reflect an understanding that another organization that has transmitted MS-infected material may have done so unwittingly and may need assistance. If such events occur repeatedly, however, termination of agreements or contracts may be indicated.

        2)  Procedures and policies should be documented, and employees must understand the reasons for them.

    j.  Business continuity (recovery) plans should be drafted, e.g., data and software backup.

k. Information about MS should be verified, and appropriate alerts given.

l. Responsible personnel should be aware of the possibility of hoaxes, false messages intending to create fear of an MS attack. For example, a spurious e-mail message may be received instructing users to delete supposedly compromised files.

m. Qualified personnel should be relied upon to distinguish **hoaxes** from MS.

4. The following are **specific controls**:

a. All computer media (incoming or outgoing) may be scanned by **sheep dip** (dedicated) computers.

b. Nonscreened media should not be allowed on the organization's computers.

c. Scanning may be done of standalone computers or those on networks as another line of defense if media control fails.

d. Software may reside in memory to scan for MS communicated through a network.

e. E-mail gateways may have software to scan attachments.

f. Network servers may have software to detect and erase or store MS.

g. Scanning software on a standalone device should be upgraded when it is networked.

5. Use of external rather than internal expertise for coping with MS problems may be more costly and time consuming but less risky.

a. **External service providers** should be subject to the terms of a contract, and access and other controls should be in place.

6. Off-site computers and media of employees should be subject to MS controls, such as screening.

7. Response to threats via **covert channels** and **Trojan horse** programs include the following:

a. Purchases should be of evaluated products from trusted suppliers.

b. Purchases should be in source code so that it is verifiable. This code should be inspected and tested prior to use.

c. Access to, and changes in, code should be restricted after it is put in use.

d. The availability of security patches for bugs in programs should be monitored constantly, especially regarding such items as network operating systems, e-mail servers, routers, and firewalls. Patches should be tested and installed promptly.

e. Trusted employees should be assigned to key systems.

f. Known Trojan horses can be detected by scanning.

g. Reviewing data outflows, for example, through the firewall, may detect suspicious activity meriting investigation.

8. **Hosts** are the most common targets in a network because they furnish services to other requesting hosts.

a. Protective measures include promptly installing the most recent patches, fixes, and updates.

1) How they affect other elements of the system should be considered.
2) Updates should be tested before installation.

9. **Password attacks**.

a. A number of methods may be used.

1) A **brute-force attack** uses password cracking software to try large numbers of letter and number combinations to access a network.

a) A simple variation is the use of password cracking software that tries all the words in a dictionary.

     2)   Passwords (and user accounts) also may be discovered by Trojan horses, IP spoofing, and packet sniffers.

       a)   **Spoofing** is identity misrepresentation in cyberspace, for example, by using a false website to obtain information about visitors.

       b)   **Sniffing** is use of software to eavesdrop on information sent by a user to the host computer of a website.

  b.   Once an attacker has access, (s)he may do anything the rightful user could have done.

     1)   If that user has privileged access, the attacker may create a back door to facilitate future entry despite password and status changes.

     2)   The attacker also may be able to leverage the initial access to obtain greater privileges than the rightful user.

  c.   If a user has the same password for multiple hosts, cracking that password for one compromises all.

  d.   Expressive methods of thwarting password attacks are one-time password and cryptographic authentication.

  e.   Optimal passwords are randomly-generated 8-character or longer combinations of numbers, uppercase and lowercase letters, and special symbols.

     1)   A disadvantage is that users often write down passwords that are hard to remember. However, software has been developed that encrypts passwords to be kept on a handheld computer. Thus, the user only needs to know one password.

10.   A **man-in-the-middle attack** takes advantage of networking packet sniffing and routing and transport protocols.

  a.   These attacks may be used to

     1)   Steal data
     2)   Obtain access to the network during a rightful user's active session
     3)   Analyze the traffic on the network to learn about its operations and users
     4)   Insert new data or modify the data being transmitted
     5)   Deny service

  b.   Cryptography is the effective response to man-in-the-middle attacks. The encrypted data will be useless to the attacker unless it can be decrypted.

11.   A **denial-of-service (DOS) attack** is an attempt to overload a system (e.g., a network or Web server) with false messages so that it cannot function (a system crash).

  a.   A distributed DOS attack comes from multiple sources, for example, the machines of innocent parties infected by Trojan horses. When activated, these programs send messages to the target and leave the connection open.

  b.   A DOS may establish as many network connections as possible to exclude other users, overloading primary memory, or corrupting file systems.

  c.   **Responses**

     1)   Firewalls should not permit use of **Internet relay chat** channels or other TCP/IP ports unless for business purposes. Thus, the organization should determine what relay kits have been installed, e.g., by employees connected to virtual private networks via cable or DSL.

       a)   These methods, intrusion detection, systems, and penetration testing may prevent a system from being used to make a DOS attack.

      2)    The best protection by the target is the Internet service provider (ISP). The ISP can establish rate limits on transmissions to the target's website.

           a)    Thus, only a defined amount of message packets with certain characteristics are allowed to reach the site.

12.   **Intrusion Detection Systems (IDS)**

    a.    If an organization's computer system has external connections, an IDS is needed to respond to security breaches.

      1)    The IDS complements the computer system's firewalls. It responds to attacks on

           a)    The **network infrastructure** (protected by the network IDS component)

                  i)     Routers
                  ii)    Switches
                  iii)   Bandwidth

           b)    **Servers** (protected by the host IDS component)

                  i)     Operating systems
                  ii)    Applications

      2)    An IDS responds to an attack by

           a)    Taking action itself
           b)    Alerting the management system

    b.    A **host IDS** provides maximum protection only when the software is installed on each computer. It may operate in the following ways:

      1)    The aggressive response is to monitor every call on the operating system and application as it occurs.

      2)    A less effective method of preventing attacks is analysis of access log files.

      3)    A host IDS may also identify questionable processes and verify the security of system files.

    c.    A **network IDS** works by using sensors to examine packets traveling on the network. Each sensor monitors only the segment of the network to which it is attached. A packet is examined if it matches a **signature**.

      1)    **String signatures** (certain strings of text) are potential signs of an attack.

      2)    **Port signatures** alert the IDS that a point subject to frequent intrusion attempts may be under attack.

           a)    A **port** in this sense (as opposed to the physical serial and parallel ports on a personal computer) is a logical connection to the system.

                  i)     A **port number** included in the message header stipulates how the message will be handled. Because many port numbers are widely known, an attacker may be able to send messages to determine whether ports are open and therefore vulnerable.

      3)    A **header signature** is a suspicious combination in a packet header.

    d.    The preferable IDS combines host IDS and network IDS components.

      1)    A host IDS has greater potential for preventing a specific attack, but the network IDS provides a necessary overall perspective. Thus, a host IDS should be in place for each host, with a network IDS for the whole system.

e.  **Knowledge-based detection** is based on information about the system's weaknesses and searches for intrusions that take advantage of them.

   1)  This type of IDS depends on frequent and costly updating of information about intrusion methods. It is also specialized with respect to those methods and operating system methods.

      a)  Problems are compounded when different versions of the operating system (or different operating systems) are in place.

f.  **Behavior-based detection** presumes that an attack will cause an observable anomaly. Actual and normal system behavior (a model of expected operations) are compared. A discrepancy results in an alert.

   1)  This approach is more complete than the knowledge-based approach because every attack should be detected. However, the level of accuracy is lower. False alarms may be generated, so the model must be updated whenever operational changes are made.

   2)  The advantages of behavior-based detection are that

      a)  Knowledge of specific new intrusion techniques is not necessary.

      b)  It is less specific to particular operating systems.

g.  **Responses to detection of an intrusion** normally include an automatic component. Continuous monitoring and response by individuals may not be feasible or sufficiently rapid.

   1)  An **automatically acting IDS** provides continuous security. It responds without the presence of humans. Responses may include

      a)  Disconnecting the entire network from outside access

      b)  Locking access to all or part of the system

      c)  Slowing the system's activity to reduce injury

      d)  Validating the external user

      e)  Sending console, e-mail, pager, or phone messages to appropriate personnel

   2)  **Alarmed systems resources** are dummy files or accounts, for example, a default administrator account with a default password set. They are traps for an intruder.

      a)  Access to a dummy resource results in automatic action or notice to appropriate employees.

      b)  The advantage of this method is that it is uncomplicated and cheap.

      c)  The disadvantage is that authorized persons may inadvertently cause an alarm.

13.  Stop and review! You have completed the outline for this subunit. Study multiple-choice questions 49 through 60 beginning on page 513.

# QUESTIONS

## 10.1 Data, Network, and Voice Communications

**1.** Advantages of using fiber optic cable are that

I. The signal is attenuated.
II. Data are transmitted rapidly.
III. It is small and flexible.
IV. It is unaffected by electrical interference.

    A. I and III.

    B. I and IV.

    C. I, II, and III.

    D. II, III, and IV.

Answer (D) is correct. *(CISA, adapted)*
    **REQUIRED:** The advantages of fiber optics.
    **DISCUSSION:** A fiber optic cable uses light impulses that travel through clear flexible tubing half the size of a human hair. Fiber optic cables are not subject to electrical interference and are highly reliable. They provide for extremely flexible and fast data transmission. The signal remains strong across long distances; i.e., it does not tend to weaken (attenuate).

**2.** When two devices in a data communications system are communicating, there must be agreement as to how both data and control information are to be packaged and interpreted. Which of the following terms is commonly used to describe this type of agreement?

    A. Asynchronous communication.

    B. Synchronous communication.

    C. Communication channel.

    D. Communication protocol.

Answer (D) is correct. *(CIA, adapted)*
    **REQUIRED:** The agreement as to how both data and control information are to be packaged and interpreted.
    **DISCUSSION:** A protocol is a set of formal rules or conventions governing communication between a sending and a receiving device. It prescribes the manner by which data are transmitted between these communications devices. In essence, a protocol is the envelope within which each message is transmitted throughout a data communications network.
    Answer (A) is incorrect because asynchronous communication is a mode of transmission. Communication is in disjointed segments, typically character by character, preceded by a start code and ended by a stop code. Answer (B) is incorrect because synchronous communication is a mode of transmission in which a continuous stream of blocks of characters result in faster communications. Answer (C) is incorrect because a communication channel is a transmission link between devices in a network. The term is also used for a small processor that controls input-output devices.

**3.** A real estate brokerage firm is moving into a building that is already equipped with extensive telephone wiring. The firm is considering the installation of a digital private branch exchange (PBX) to connect computers and other office devices such as copying machines, printers, and facsimile machines. A limitation of using a PBX-based system for this network is that

    A. The firm would be dependent on others for system maintenance.

    B. The system cannot easily handle large volumes of data.

    C. Coaxial cabling would have to be installed throughout the building.

    D. Relocating devices in the office would be difficult and expensive.

Answer (B) is correct. *(CIA, adapted)*
    **REQUIRED:** The limitation of a PBX system.
    **DISCUSSION:** A PBX has the advantage of using existing telephone lines and therefore not needing special wiring. Moreover, equipment can be moved without necessitating rewiring. However, because PBX-based systems use telephone wiring (most often copper wire), they cannot easily handle large volumes of data.
    Answer (A) is incorrect because the company would be responsible for all maintenance of the equipment, although it could contract for service. Answer (C) is incorrect because PBXs use telephone wiring. LANs typically require their own coaxial cabling. Answer (D) is incorrect because PBX-based systems do not require rewiring when devices are moved.

**4.** Large organizations often have their own telecommunications networks for transmitting and receiving voice, data, and images. Very small organizations, however, are unlikely to be able to make the investment required for their own networks and are more likely to use

- A. Public switched lines.
- B. Fast-packet switches.
- C. Standard electronic mail systems.
- D. A WAN.

Answer (A) is correct.  *(CIA, adapted)*
**REQUIRED:** The telecommunications networks likely to be used by small organizations.
**DISCUSSION:** Companies can use public switched lines (phone lines) on a per-transmission basis. This option is the most cost-effective way for low-volume users to conduct telecommunications.
Answer (B) is incorrect because fast-packet switches receive transmissions from various devices, break the data into packets, and route them over a network to their destination. They are typically installed by telecommunication utility companies and other large companies that have their own networks. Answer (C) is incorrect because electronic mail systems do not allow for voice transmissions. Answer (D) is incorrect because large organizations would use a wide area network.

**5.** Using a telecommunications provider affects in-house networks. To prepare for changes resulting from enhanced external network services, management should

- A. Optimize in-house networks to avoid bottlenecks that would limit the benefits offered by the telecommunications provider.
- B. Plan for rapid implementation of new capabilities in anticipation of ready acceptance of the new technology.
- C. Downsize the company's disaster recovery plan to recognize the increasing role of the telecommunications provider.
- D. Enhance the in-house network management to minimize dependence on the telecommunications provider for network management.

Answer (A) is correct.  *(CIA, adapted)*
**REQUIRED:** The appropriate action to prepare for changes resulting from enhanced external network services.
**DISCUSSION:** To prepare the company for changes resulting from the enhanced external network services, management should take appropriate action. A number of bottlenecks may limit the benefits that can be derived from the external network. For example, conversion from analog to digital technology is necessary to achieve rapid improvements in bandwidth and speed and to improve access to telecommunications services. Furthermore, applications, systems software, and communications protocols must be able to process information in a format and in a manner acceptable to end users. Communications security also has heightened importance as greater amounts of data are transmitted from remote sites.
Answer (B) is incorrect because resistance to change, inflexible organizational structures, and skepticism about the technology should be expected and must be successfully managed if the company is to reap the benefits. Answer (C) is incorrect because a company's disaster recovery plan should be enhanced to ensure the reliability of the network. Answer (D) is incorrect because network management may now be primarily a function, yet it will become more of a partnership arrangement with the communications carrier.

**6.** A local area network (LAN) is best described as a(n)

- A. Computer system that connects computers of all sizes, workstations, terminals, and other devices within a limited proximity.
- B. System to allow computer users to meet and share ideas and information.
- C. Electronic library containing millions of items of data that can be reviewed, retrieved, and analyzed.
- D. Method to offer specialized software, hardware, and data-handling techniques that improve effectiveness and reduce costs.

Answer (A) is correct.  *(CMA, adapted)*
**REQUIRED:** The best description of a local area network (LAN).
**DISCUSSION:** A LAN is a local distributed computer system, often housed within a single building. Computers, communication devices, and other equipment are linked by cable. Special software facilitates efficient data communication among the hardware devices.
Answer (B) is incorrect because a LAN is more than a system to allow computer users to share information; it is an interconnection of a computer system. Answer (C) is incorrect because a LAN is not a library. Answer (D) is incorrect because a LAN does not require specialized hardware.

**7.** Which of the following statements about voice communications is true?

    A. Modern voice recognition input devices have large vocabularies and short training periods.

    B. A voice output device converts speech into digital data.

    C. Cell phones and PCS services use the same frequency radio waves.

    D. Pagers can alert users to the receipt of messages, but cannot transmit text.

Answer (A) is correct. *(Publisher)*
    **REQUIRED:** The true statement about voice communications.
    **DISCUSSION:** Voice recognition input devices provide an alternative to keyboard input. These systems compare the speaker's voice patterns with prerecorded patterns. Advanced systems now have large vocabularies and shorter training periods. They allow for dictation and are not limited to simple commands.
    Answer (B) is incorrect because a voice output device converts digital data into speech using prerecorded sounds. Answer (C) is incorrect because PCS services use lower-power, higher-frequency radio waves than cell phones. Answer (D) is incorrect because newer pager systems permit transmission of text messages.

**8.** The Internet consists of a series of networks that include

    A. Gateways to allow personal computers to connect to mainframe computers.

    B. Bridges to direct messages through the optimum data path.

    C. Repeaters to physically connect separate local area networks (LANs).

    D. Routers to strengthen data signals between distant computers.

Answer (A) is correct. *(CIA, adapted)*
    **REQUIRED:** The composition of the Internet.
    **DISCUSSION:** The Internet facilitates information transfer between computers. Gateways are hardware or software products that allow translation between two different protocol families. For example, a gateway can be used to exchange messages between different e-mail systems.
    Answer (B) is incorrect because routers are used to determine the best path for data. Answer (C) is incorrect because bridges connect LANs. Answer (D) is incorrect because repeaters strengthen signals.

**9.** Which of the following is true concerning HTML?

    A. The acronym stands for HyperText Material Listing.

    B. The language is among the most difficult to learn.

    C. The language is independent of hardware and software.

    D. HTML is the only language that can be used for Internet documents.

Answer (C) is correct. *(Publisher)*
    **REQUIRED:** The true statement concerning HTML.
    **DISCUSSION:** HTML is the most popular language for authoring Web pages. It is hardware and software independent, which means that it can be read by several different applications and on many different kinds of computer operating systems. HTML uses tags to mark information for proper display on Web pages.
    Answer (A) is incorrect because HTML is the acronym for HyperText Markup Language. Answer (B) is incorrect because the language is relatively easy to learn. Almost anyone can learn and use HTML, not just computer programmers. Answer (D) is incorrect because a number of other languages can be used for Internet transmissions, including JAVA and XML.

## 10.2 Databases

**10.** Of the following, the greatest advantage of a database (server) architecture is

    A. Data redundancy can be reduced.

    B. Conversion to a database system is inexpensive and can be accomplished quickly.

    C. Multiple occurrences of data items are useful for consistency checking.

    D. Backup and recovery procedures are minimized.

Answer (A) is correct. *(CIA, adapted)*
    **REQUIRED:** The greatest advantage of a database architecture.
    **DISCUSSION:** Data organized in files and used by the organization's various applications programs are collectively known as a database. In a database system, storage structures are created that render the applications programs independent of the physical or logical arrangement of the data. Each data item has a standard definition, name, and format, and related items are linked by a system of pointers. The programs therefore need only to specify data items by name, not by location. A database management system handles retrieval and storage. Because separate files for different applications programs are unnecessary, data redundancy can be substantially reduced.
    Answer (B) is incorrect because conversion to a database is often costly and time consuming. Answer (C) is incorrect because a traditional flat-file system, not a database, has multiple occurrences of data items. Answer (D) is incorrect because given the absence of data redundancy and the quick propagation of data errors throughout applications, backup and recovery procedures are just as critical in a database as in a flat-file system.

**11.** An internal auditor encounters a batch-processed payroll in which each record contains the same type of data elements, in the same order, with each data element needing the same number of storage spaces. Which file structure would most appropriately be used to support this set of records?

A. Single flat file structure.

B. Hierarchical structure.

C. Network structure.

D. Relational structure.

Answer (A) is correct. *(CIA, adapted)*
**REQUIRED:** The file structure in which each record has the same type and order of data elements and the same storage requirements.
**DISCUSSION:** In a single flat file structure, all attributes and field lengths in a record are identical to those in the other records. The structure is typically a table or spreadsheet with records for rows and attributes for columns.
Answer (B) is incorrect because a hierarchical or tree structure is used to express relationships in which one attribute or item is related to many others in layers of subordinate records. Answer (C) is incorrect because a network structure expresses complex relationships in which many attributes are related to many others. Answer (D) is incorrect because a relational structure is not unlike the flat structure but is far more sophisticated. It gives the system the ability to handle many data relationships that were not anticipated by the designers. It uses a series of tables in which each table defines a relationship.

**12.** In an inventory system on a database management system (DBMS), one stored record contains part number, part name, part color, and part weight. These individual items are called

A. Fields.

B. Stored files.

C. Bytes.

D. Occurrences.

Answer (A) is correct. *(CIA, adapted)*
**REQUIRED:** The term for the data elements in a record.
**DISCUSSION:** A record is a collection of related data items (fields). A field (data item) is a group of characters representing one unit of information.
Answer (B) is incorrect because a file is a group or set of related records ordered to facilitate processing. Answer (C) is incorrect because a byte is a group of bits (binary digits). It represents one character. Answer (D) is incorrect because occurrences is not a meaningful term in this context.

**13.** An inventory clerk, using a computer terminal, views the following on screen: part number, part description, quantity on-hand, quantity on-order, order quantity and reorder point for a particular inventory item. Collectively, these data make up a

A. Field.

B. File.

C. Database.

D. Record.

Answer (D) is correct. *(CIA, adapted)*
**REQUIRED:** The term for the collection of data described.
**DISCUSSION:** A record is a collection of related data items (fields). A field (data item) is a group of characters representing one unit of information. The part number, part description, etc., are represented by fields.
Answer (A) is incorrect because field refers to a single data item. Answer (B) is incorrect because file refers to multiple records. Answer (C) is incorrect because database refers to multiple files.

**14.** An entity has the following invoices in a batch:

| Invoice Number | Product | Quantity | Unit Price |
|---|---|---|---|
| 201 | F10 | 150 | $ 5.00 |
| 202 | G15 | 200 | $10.00 |
| 203 | H20 | 250 | $25.00 |
| 204 | K35 | 300 | $30.00 |

Which of the following numbers represents the record count?

A. 1

B. 4

C. 810

D. 900

Answer (B) is correct. *(CPA, adapted)*
**REQUIRED:** The record count.
**DISCUSSION:** Input controls in batch computer systems are used to determine that no data are lost or added to the batch. Depending on the sophistication of a particular system, control may be accomplished by using record counts, batch totals, or hash totals. A record count establishes the number of source documents and reconciles it to the number of output records. The total number of invoices processed is an example of a record count. In this case, the record count is 4.
Answer (A) is incorrect because 1 is the number of batches. Answer (C) is incorrect because 810 is a hash total of the invoice numbers. Answer (D) is incorrect because 900 is the total quantity of items.

**15.** Which of the following is the elementary unit of data storage used to represent individual attributes of an entity?

A. Database.

B. Data field.

C. File.

D. Record.

Answer (B) is correct. *(CIA, adapted)*
**REQUIRED:** The elementary unit of data storage that is used to represent individual attributes of an entity.
**DISCUSSION:** A data item (or field) is a group of characters.. It is used to represent individual attributes of an entity, such as an employee's address. A field is an item in a record.
Answer (A) is incorrect because a database is an organized collection of files. Answer (C) is incorrect because a file is a collection of records. Answer (D) is incorrect because a record is a collection of data items.

**16.** A file-oriented approach to data storage requires a primary record key for each file. Which of the following is a primary record key?

A. The vendor number in an accounts payable master file.

B. The vendor number in a closed purchase order transaction file.

C. The vendor number in an open purchase order master file.

D. All of the answers are correct.

Answer (A) is correct. *(CIA, adapted)*
**REQUIRED:** The item(s) used as a primary record key.
**DISCUSSION:** The primary record key uniquely identifies each record in a file. Because there is only one record for each vendor in an accounts payable master file, the vendor number would be the appropriate key.
Answer (B) is incorrect because purchase order files can have multiple purchase orders made out to the same vendor. The primary key in purchase order files would be the purchase order number because it is the only unique identifier for the record. Answer (C) is incorrect because purchase order files can have multiple purchase orders made out to the same vendor. The primary key in purchase order files would be the purchase order number because it is the only unique identifier for the record. Answer (D) is incorrect because not all of the answer choices are correct.

**17.** When required to read customer data, the operating system finds the primary key value in a file whose records contain key values and their corresponding physical addresses. In this situation, the most likely file organization for customer data is

A. A direct-access file.

B. An indexed sequential file.

C. A sequential file.

D. A text file.

Answer (B) is correct. *(CIA, adapted)*
**REQUIRED:** The organization of a file whose records contain key values and corresponding physical addresses.
**DISCUSSION:** If records are stored sequentially on a direct-access storage device, the records can be accessed directly using the indexed-sequential-access method. An index of key fields is maintained that lists the physical location of the record corresponding to each key field.
Answer (A) is incorrect because a direct-access file has no index file. Answer (C) is incorrect because a sequential file has no index file. Answer (D) is incorrect because a text file would probably not be used in this situation.

**18.** A business has decided to use magnetic disks to store accounts receivable information. What data file concepts should be used to provide the ability to answer customer inquiries as they are received?

A. Sequential storage and chains.

B. Sequential storage and indexes.

C. Record keys, indexes, and pointers.

D. Inverted file structure, indexes, and internal labels.

Answer (C) is correct. *(CIA, adapted)*
**REQUIRED:** The data file concepts needed to answer customer inquiries as they are received.
**DISCUSSION:** A record key is an attribute that uniquely identifies or distinguishes each record from the others. An index is a table listing storage locations for attributes, often including those other than the unique record key attribute. A pointer is a data item that indicates the physical address of the next logically related record.
Answer (A) is incorrect because the ability to respond immediately to customers requires direct access. Answer (B) is incorrect because the ability to respond immediately to customers requires direct access. Answer (D) is incorrect because internal labels are used to indicate various things to the computer, such as the contents of various types of data storage media, the beginning of each file (with identification information), and the end of each file. However, they do not provide information for locating specific records in a file. An inverted file structure (inverted list) is an index based on a secondary key, for example, years of experience rather than an employee number (the primary key).

**19.** Auditors making database queries often need to combine several tables to get the information they want. One approach to combining tables is known as

- A. Extraction.
- B. Joining.
- C. Sorting.
- D. Summarization.

Answer (B) is correct. *(CIA, adapted)*

**REQUIRED:** The approach to combining tables when making database queries.

**DISCUSSION:** In CAAT software packages, joining is the combining of data files based on a common data element. For example, if rows in a table containing information about specified parts have been selected, the result can be joined with a table that contains information about suppliers. The join operation may combine the two tables using the supplier number (assuming both tables contained this element) to provide information about the suppliers of particular parts.

Answer (A) is incorrect because extraction selects data containing specified criteria from a data file; it does not combine tables. Answer (C) is incorrect because sorting allows the auditor to organize data by any data field, not combine tables. Answer (D) is incorrect because summarization reports on the information contained in several tables but does not combine the tables.

**20.** Users making database queries often need to combine several tables to get the information they want. One approach to combining tables is

- A. Joining.
- B. Merging.
- C. Projecting.
- D. Pointing.

Answer (A) is correct. *(CIA, adapted)*

**REQUIRED:** The approach to combining tables when making database queries.

**DISCUSSION:** Joining is the combining of two or more relational tables based on a common data element. For example, if a supplier table contains information about suppliers and a parts table contains information about parts, the two tables can be joined using the supplier number (assuming both tables contain this attribute) to give information about the supplier of particular parts.

Answer (B) is incorrect because the three basic operations in a relational database are selecting, joining, and projecting. Answer (C) is incorrect because projecting is the basic operation in a relational database that results in a subset consisting of columns (fields) in a table. This operation creates a new table containing only the required information. Answer (D) is incorrect because a pointer is a data element attached to a record that gives the address of another record.

**21.** All of the following are methods for distributing a relational database across multiple servers except

- A. Snapshot (making a copy of the database for distribution).
- B. Replication (creating and maintaining replica copies at multiple locations).
- C. Normalization (separating the database into logical tables for easier user processing).
- D. Fragmentation (separating the database into parts and distributing where they are needed).

Answer (C) is correct. *(CIA, adapted)*

**REQUIRED:** The item not a method for distributing a relational database across multiple servers.

**DISCUSSION:** A distributed database is stored in two or more physical sites. The two basic methods of distributing a database are partitioning and replication. However, normalization is a process of database design, not distribution. Normalization is the term for determining how groups of data items in a relational structure are arranged in records in a database. This process relies on "normal forms," that is, conceptual definitions of data records and specified design rules. Normalization is intended to prevent inconsistent updating of data items. It is a process of breaking down a complex data structure by creating smaller, more efficient relations, thereby minimizing or eliminating the repeating groups in each relation.

Answer (A) is incorrect because the snapshot technique makes duplicates to be stored at multiple locations. Answer (B) is incorrect because the replication technique makes duplicates to be stored at multiple locations. Changes are periodically copied and sent to each location. If a database is small, storing multiple copies may be cheaper than retrieving records from a central site. Answer (D) is incorrect because fragmentation or partitioning stores specific records where they are most needed. For example, a financial institution may store a particular customer's data at the branch where (s)he usually transacts his/her business. If the customer executes a transaction at another branch, the pertinent data is retrieved via communications lines.

**22.** In a database system, locking of data helps preserve data integrity by permitting transactions to have control of all the data needed to complete the transactions. However, implementing a locking procedure could lead to

    A. Inconsistent processing.

    B. Rollback failures.

    C. Unrecoverable transactions.

    D. Deadly embraces (retrieval contention).

Answer (D) is correct. *(CIA, adapted)*
    **REQUIRED:** The potential disadvantage of a locking procedure.
    **DISCUSSION:** In a distributed processing system, the data and resources a transaction may update or use should be held in their current status until the transaction is complete. A deadly embrace occurs when two transactions need the same resource at the same time. If the system does not have a method to cope with the problem efficiently, response time worsens or the system eventually fails. The system should have an algorithm for undoing the effects of one transaction and releasing the resources it controls so that the other transaction can run to completion.
    Answer (A) is incorrect because inconsistent processing occurs when a transaction has different effects depending on when it is processed. Data locking ensures consistent processing. Answer (B) is incorrect because rollback failure is the inability of the software to undo the effects of a transaction that could not be run to completion. A rollback failure is not caused by data locking. However, data locking may lead to situations in which rollback is required. Answer (C) is incorrect because unrecoverable transactions are not a typical symptom of locking procedures.

**23.** One advantage of a database management system (DBMS) is

    A. That each organizational unit takes responsibility and control for its own data.

    B. The cost of the data processing department decreases as users are now responsible for establishing their own data handing techniques.

    C. A decreased vulnerability as the database management system has numerous security controls to prevent disasters.

    D. The independence of the data from the application programs, which allows the programs to be developed for the user's specific needs without concern for data capture problems.

Answer (D) is correct. *(CMA, adapted)*
    **REQUIRED:** The advantage of a DBMS.
    **DISCUSSION:** A fundamental characteristic of databases is that applications are independent of the database structure; when writing programs or designing applications to use the database, only the name of the desired item is necessary. Programs can be developed for the user's specific needs without concern for data capture problems. Reference can be made to the items using the data manipulation language, after which the DBMS takes care of locating and retrieving the desired items. The physical or logical structure of the database can be completely altered without having to change any of the programs using the data items; only the schema requires alteration.
    Answer (A) is incorrect because each organizational unit develops programs to make use of elements of a broad database. Answer (B) is incorrect because data handling techniques are still the responsibility of the data processing department; it is the use of the data that is departmentalized. Answer (C) is incorrect because the DBMS is no safer than any other database system.

**24.** Which of the following is a false statement about a database management system application environment?

    A. Data are used concurrently by multiple users.

    B. Data are shared by passing files between programs or systems.

    C. The physical structure of the data is independent of user needs.

    D. Data definition is independent of any one program.

Answer (B) is correct. *(CISA, adapted)*
    **REQUIRED:** The false statement about data in a DBMS environment.
    **DISCUSSION:** In this kind of system, applications use the same database. There is no need to pass files between applications.
    Answer (A) is incorrect because the advantage of a DBMS is that data can be used concurrently by multiple users. Answer (C) is incorrect because when a DBMS is used, the physical structure of the data is independent of user needs. Answer (D) is incorrect because when a DBMS is used, the data are defined independently of the needs of any one program.

**25.** Which of the following should not be the responsibility of a database administrator?

   A. Design the content and organization of the database.

   B. Develop applications to access the database.

   C. Protect the database and its software.

   D. Monitor and improve the efficiency of the database.

Answer (B) is correct. *(CIA, adapted)*
   **REQUIRED:** The item not the responsibility of a database administrator.
   **DISCUSSION:** The database administrator (DBA) is the person who has overall responsibility for developing and maintaining the database. One primary responsibility is for designing the content of the database. Another responsibility of the DBA is to protect and control the database. A third responsibility is to monitor and improve the efficiency of the database. The responsibility of developing applications to access the database belongs to systems analysts and programmers.
   Answer (A) is incorrect because designing the content and organization of the database is a responsibility of the database administrator. Answer (C) is incorrect because protecting the database and its software is a responsibility of the database administrator. Answer (D) is incorrect because monitoring and improving the efficiency of the database is a responsibility of the database administrator.

**26.** The responsibilities of a data administrator (DA) include monitoring

   A. The database industry.

   B. The performance of the database.

   C. Database security.

   D. Backup of the system.

Answer (A) is correct. *(Publisher)*
   **REQUIRED:** The responsibilities of a data administrator.
   **DISCUSSION:** The DA handles administrative issues that arise regarding the database. The DA acts as an advocate by suggesting new applications and standards. One of the DA's responsibilities is to monitor the database industry for new developments. In contrast, the database administrator (DBA) deals with the technical aspects of the database.

**27.** To trace data through several application programs, an auditor needs to know what programs use the data, which files contain the data, and which printed reports display the data. If data exist only in a database system, the auditor could probably find all of this information in a

   A. Data dictionary.

   B. Database schema.

   C. Data encryptor.

   D. Decision table.

Answer (A) is correct. *(CIA, adapted)*
   **REQUIRED:** The information source in a database needed to trace data through several application programs.
   **DISCUSSION:** The data dictionary is a file (possibly manual but usually computerized) in which the records relate to specified data items. It contains definitions of data items, the list of programs used to process them, and the reports in which data are found. Only certain persons or entities are permitted to retrieve data or to modify data items. Accordingly, these access limitations are also found in the data dictionary.
   Answer (B) is incorrect because the schema describes the structure of the database. Answer (C) is incorrect because an encryptor encodes data. Answer (D) is incorrect because a decision table is a type of logic diagram that presents in matrix form the decision points and related actions reflected in a computer program.

## 10.3 E-Commerce, EDI, and EFT

**28.** All of the following are potential security issues for e-commerce except:

   A. Correct identification of transacting parties.

   B. Proliferation of computer viruses.

   C. Determining who may rightfully make transaction decisions.

   D. Verification of payment data.

Answer (B) is correct. *(Publisher)*
   **REQUIRED:** The process that is not a potential security issue for e-commerce.
   **DISCUSSION:** E-commerce is the purchase and sale of goods and services by electronic means. E-commerce may occur via online transactions on public networks, electronic data interchange (EDI), and e-mail. Security for e-commerce issues include the correct identification of transacting parties (authentication), determining who may rightfully make decisions (authorization), and verification of payment data. While proliferation of computer viruses is a general security issue with regard to information systems, it is not a specific risk associated with e-commerce.
   Answer (A) is incorrect because authentication is a security issue related to e-commerce. Answer (C) is incorrect because authorization is a security issue related to e-commerce. Answer (D) is incorrect because verification of payment data is a security issue related to e-commerce.

**29.** Companies now can use electronic transfers to conduct regular business transactions. Which of the following terms best describes a system in which an agreement is made between two or more parties to electronically transfer purchase orders, sales orders, invoices, and/or other financial documents?

- A. Electronic mail (E-mail).
- B. Electronic funds transfer (EFT).
- C. Electronic data interchange (EDI).
- D. Electronic data processing (EDP).

Answer (C) is correct.   *(CIA, adapted)*
**REQUIRED:** The term best describing electronic transfer of documents.
**DISCUSSION:** Electronic data interchange is the electronic transfer of documents between businesses. EDI was developed to enhance just-in-time (JIT) inventory management. Advantages include speed, reduction of clerical errors, and elimination of repetitive clerical tasks and their costs.
Answer (A) is incorrect because e-mail can send text or document files, but the term encompasses a wide range of transfers. EDI specifically applies to the system described in the question. Answer (B) is incorrect because electronic funds transfer (EFT) refers to the transfer of money. Answer (D) is incorrect because electronic data processing (EDP) is a generic term for computerized processing of transaction data within organizations.

**30.** Which of the following is usually a benefit of transmitting transactions in an electronic data interchange (EDI) environment?

- A. A compressed business cycle with lower year-end receivables balances.
- B. A reduced need to test computer controls related to sales and collections transactions.
- C. An increased opportunity to apply statistical sampling techniques to account balances.
- D. No need to rely on third-party service providers to ensure security.

Answer (A) is correct.   *(CPA, adapted)*
**REQUIRED:** The benefit of EDI.
**DISCUSSION:** EDI transactions are typically transmitted and processed in real time. Thus, EDI compresses the business cycle by eliminating delays. The time required to receive and process an order, ship goods, and receive payment is greatly reduced compared with that of a typical manual system. Accordingly, more rapid receipt of payment minimizes receivables and improves cash flow.
Answer (B) is incorrect because use of a sophisticated processing system would increase the need to test computer controls. Answer (C) is incorrect because computer technology allows all transactions to be tested rather than just a sample. Answer (D) is incorrect because EDI often uses a VAN (value-added network) as a third-party service provider, and reliance on controls provided by the VAN may be critical.

Questions 31 and 32 are based on the following information. A multinational company has an agreement with a value-added network (VAN) that provides the encoding and communications transfer for the company's electronic data interchange (EDI) and electronic funds transfer (EFT) transactions. Before transfer of data to the VAN, the company performs online preprocessing of the transactions. The internal auditor is responsible for assessing preprocessing controls. In addition, the agreement between the company and the VAN states that the internal auditor is allowed to examine and report on the controls in place at the VAN on an annual basis. The contract specifies that access to the VAN can occur on a surprise basis during the second or third quarter of the company's fiscal year. This period was chosen so it would not interfere with processing during the VAN's peak transaction periods. This provision was not reviewed with internal auditing. The annual audit plan approved by the board of directors specifies that a full audit would be done during the current year.

**31.** Which one of the following would not be included as a reason for the company to use EFT with the EDI system?

- A. To take advantage of the time lag associated with negotiable instruments.
- B. To allow the company to negotiate discounts with EDI vendors based upon prompt payment.
- C. To improve its cash management program.
- D. To reduce input time and input errors.

Answer (A) is correct.   *(CIA, adapted)*
**REQUIRED:** The item not a reason for using EFT.
**DISCUSSION:** The float period is the time lag between transmittal of a regular check (a negotiable instrument) and its clearance through regular banking channels. Float is eliminated by EFT.
Answer (B) is incorrect because payment schedules may be based on the time required to process invoices, prepare checks, and transmit checks. Using EFT, payment is instantaneous, and payment schedules can be based on other criteria, e.g., discounts for prompt payment. Answer (C) is incorrect because EFT allows for more effective control of payments and transfers among accounts. Answer (D) is incorrect because integration of EDI and EFT eliminates manual input of transaction data, a process that introduces errors into the accounting system.

**32.** Refer to the information preceding question 31. Which one of the following is least likely to be recommended by the auditor when an EDI-EFT system is being designed?

    A.  The identity of the individual approving an electronic document should be stored as a data field.

    B.  Disaster recovery plans should be established.

    C.  Data security procedures should be written to prevent changes to data by unauthorized individuals.

    D.  Remote access to electronic data should be denied.

Answer (D) is correct.  *(CIA, adapted)*
    **REQUIRED:**  The least likely audit recommendation when an EDI-EFT system is being designed.
    **DISCUSSION:**  One of the benefits of an EDI-EFT system is that it can provide remote access at any time from any place if telecommunications links are available.  However, appropriate controls should prevent unauthorized access.
    Answer (A) is incorrect because approval information is needed to provide an audit trail.  Answer (B) is incorrect because disaster recovery plans are needed to ensure that the company can continue to function if the system crashes.  Answer (C) is incorrect because individuals should not be able to update data without proper identification and authentication.

**33.** The emergence of electronic data interchange (EDI) as standard operating practice increases the risk of

    A.  Unauthorized third-party access to systems.

    B.  Systematic programming errors.

    C.  Inadequate knowledge bases.

    D.  Unsuccessful system use.

Answer (A) is correct.  *(CIA, adapted)*
    **REQUIRED:**  The risk increased by the emergence of EDI as standard operating practice.
    **DISCUSSION:**  EDI is the communication of electronic documents directly from a computer in one entity to a computer in another entity.  EDI for business documents between unrelated parties has the potential to increase the risk of unauthorized third-party access to systems because more outsiders will have access to internal systems.
    Answer (B) is incorrect because systematic programming errors are the result of misspecification of requirements or lack of correspondence between specifications and programs. Answer (C) is incorrect because inadequate knowledge bases are a function of lack of care in building them.  Answer (D) is incorrect because a benefit of EDI is to improve the efficiency and effectiveness of system use.

**34.** Which of the following risks is not greater in an electronic funds transfer (EFT) environment than in a manual system using paper transactions?

    A.  Unauthorized access and activity.

    B.  Duplicate transaction processing.

    C.  Higher cost per transaction.

    D.  Inadequate backup and recovery capabilities.

Answer (C) is correct.  *(CIA, adapted)*
    **REQUIRED:**  The risk not greater in an EFT environment than in a manual system using paper transactions.
    **DISCUSSION:**  EFT is a service provided by financial institutions worldwide that is based on EDI technology.  EFT transaction costs are lower than for manual systems because documents and human intervention are eliminated from the transactions process.
    Answer (A) is incorrect because unauthorized access and activity is a risk specific to EFT.  Answer (B) is incorrect because inaccurate transaction processing (including duplication) is a risk specific to EFT.  Answer (D) is incorrect because inadequate backup and recovery capabilities is a risk specific to EFT.

**35.** Which of the following are essential elements of the audit trail in an electronic data interchange (EDI) system?

    A.  Network and sender/recipient acknowledgments.

    B.  Message directories and header segments.

    C.  Contingency and disaster recovery plans.

    D.  Trading partner security and mailbox codes.

Answer (A) is correct.  *(CPA, adapted)*
    **REQUIRED:**  The essential element in an EDI audit trail.
    **DISCUSSION:**  An audit trail allows for the tracing of a transaction from initiation to conclusion.  Network and sender/recipient acknowledgments relate to the transaction flow and provide for the tracking of transactions.
    Answer (B) is incorrect because message directories and header segments provide information controlling the message, such as originating and destination stations, message type and priority level, which are part of the message and not the audit trail.  Answer (C) is incorrect because, although contingency and disaster recovery plans are important controls, they do not relate to the audit trail.  Answer (D) is incorrect because, although maintaining control over security and mailbox codes is an important control, it does not relate to the audit trail.

**36.** Which of the following is a false statement about XBRL?

    A. XBRL is freely licensed.

    B. XBRL facilitates the automatic exchange of information.

    C. XBRL is used primarily in the U.S.

    D. XBRL is designed to work with a variety of software applications.

Answer (C) is correct. *(Publisher)*
    **REQUIRED:** The false statement about XBRL.
    **DISCUSSION:** XBRL stands for eXtensible Business Reporting Language. It is being developed for business and accounting applications. It is an XML-based application used to create, exchange, and analyze financial reporting information and is being developed for worldwide use.
    Answer (A) is incorrect because the AICPA-led consortium that developed XBRL has promoted the application as a freely licensed product. Answer (B) is incorrect because XBRL will facilitate the exchange of information, for example, for reporting to the SEC. Answer (D) is incorrect because XBRL will allow exchange of data across many platforms and will soon be integrated into accounting software applications and products.

**37.** Which of the following statements is true concerning internal control in an electronic data interchange (EDI) system?

    A. Preventive controls generally are more important than detective controls in EDI systems.

    B. Control objectives for EDI systems generally are different from the objectives for other information systems.

    C. Internal controls in EDI systems rarely permit control risk to be assessed at below the maximum.

    D. Internal controls related to the segregation of duties generally are the most important controls in EDI systems.

Answer (A) is correct. *(CPA, adapted)*
    **REQUIRED:** The true statement about EDI controls.
    **DISCUSSION:** In general, preventive controls are more important than detective controls because the benefits typically outweigh the costs. In electronic processing, once a transaction is accepted, there is often little opportunity to apply detective controls. Thus, it is important to prevent errors or frauds before they happen.
    Answer (B) is incorrect because the basic control objectives are the same regardless of the nature of the processing: to ensure the integrity of the information and to safeguard the assets. Answer (C) is incorrect because to gather sufficient evidence in a sophisticated computer system it is often necessary to rely on the controls. Control risk may be assessed at below the maximum if relevant controls are identified and tested and if the resulting evidential matter provides the degree of assurance necessary to support the assessed level of control risk. Answer (D) is incorrect because the level of segregation of duties achieved in a manual system is usually not feasible in a computer system.

**38.** A control that a company can use to detect forged EDI messages is to

    A. Acknowledge all messages initiated externally with confirming messages.

    B. Permit only authorized employees to have access to transmission facilities.

    C. Delay action on orders until a second order is received for the same goods.

    D. Write all incoming messages to a write-once/read-many device for archiving.

Answer (A) is correct. *(CIA, adapted)*
    **REQUIRED:** The control to detect forged EDI messages.
    **DISCUSSION:** If the company acknowledges messages initiated externally, the alleged sender will have the opportunity to recognize that it had not sent the message and will then be able to notify the company of the potential forgery. Then corrective action can be taken by the company.
    Answer (B) is incorrect because permitting only authorized employees to have access to transmission facilities controls for unauthorized access to the facilities but would not detect forged EDI messages. Answer (C) is incorrect because delaying action on orders until a second order is received for the same goods defeats the purpose of using EDI, namely, rapid communication followed by rapid response. Answer (D) is incorrect because writing all incoming messages to a write-once/read-many device is a good practice, but it will not detect forgeries.

**39.** Which of the following statements about SET (Secured Electronic Transaction) is false?

A. SET is a trademarked protocol that provides individualized security standards.

B. SET is based on a hierarchy of certificate authorities.

C. SET authenticates users with digital certificates and digital signatures.

D. SET is supported through an organization called SETCo.

Answer (A) is correct.   *(Publisher)*
**REQUIRED:** The false statement about SET.
**DISCUSSION:** SET (Secured Electronic Transaction) is a trademarked protocol that provides a common security standards, especially with regard to Internet card purchases. It is supported by Visa and MasterCard through an organization called SETCo. SET encrypts the details of payment transactions at all times so as to ensure privacy and data integrity. It also ensures that the identities of buyers and sellers are authenticated using digital signatures and digital certificates. SET is based on a hierarchy of certificate authorities that parallels financial relationships outside cyberspace.

Answer (B) is incorrect because SET is based in a hierarchy of certificate authorities that parallels financial relationships outside cyberspace. Answer (C) is incorrect because SET authenticates sellers and buyers using digital signatures and certificates. Answer (D) is incorrect because SET is supported by Visa and Mastercard through an organization called SETCo.

## 10.4 Investment in IT

**40.** Inefficient use of excess computer equipment can be controlled by

A. Contingency planning.

B. System feasibility studies.

C. Capacity planning.

D. Exception reporting.

Answer (C) is correct.   *(CIA, adapted)*
**REQUIRED:** The control over inefficient use of excess computer equipment.
**DISCUSSION:** Planning is as important for the information systems function as for any other part of the organization. The master plan for this function should be consistent with the strategic plan for the organization and include goals and objectives, an inventory of current capacity, and a forecast of future needs. The plan is the basis for determining hardware needs.

Answer (A) is incorrect because contingency planning concerns the arrangements for alternative processing facilities in the event of equipment failure. Answer (B) is incorrect because feasibility study is one of the phases in the systems development life cycle. Answer (D) is incorrect because exception reports are meant to list errata and bring them to the attention of management.

**41.** The best plan for responding to quickly changing information requirements is to foster

A. Greater online access to information systems.

B. Competitive pressures for enhanced functions in systems.

C. Closer linkage between organizational strategy and information.

D. More widespread use of automated controls.

Answer (C) is correct.   *(CIA, adapted)*
**REQUIRED:** The best plan for responding to quickly changing information requirements.
**DISCUSSION:** An important management challenge is to integrate the planning, design, and implementation of complex application systems with the strategy of the organization, which will permit the best possible response to quickly changing information requirements.

Answer (A) is incorrect because greater online access may or may not be helpful, depending on the user organization's needs. Answer (B) is incorrect because marketplace creates competitive pressures for enhanced functions in systems. Answer (D) is incorrect because more pervasive use of automated controls may be independent of responding quickly to changing information requirements.

## 10.5 Enterprise-Wide Resource Planning (ERP)

**42.** An enterprise resource planning (ERP) system integrates the organization's computerized subsystems and may also provide links to external parties. An advantage of ERP is that

A. The reengineering needed for its implementation should improve business processes.

B. Customizing the software to suit the unique needs of the organization will facilitate upgrades.

C. It can be installed by organizations of all sizes.

D. The comprehensiveness of the system reduces resistance to change.

Answer (A) is correct. *(Publisher)*
**REQUIRED:** The advantage of ERP.
**DISCUSSION:** The benefits of ERP may significantly derive from the business process reengineering that is needed for its implementation. Using ERP software that reflects the best practices forces the linked subunits in the organization not only to redesign and improve their processes but also to conform to one standard.
Answer (B) is incorrect because the disadvantages of ERP are its extent and complexity, which make customization of the software difficult and costly. Answer (C) is incorrect because ERP software is costly and complex. It is usually installed only by the largest enterprises. Answer (D) is incorrect because implementing an ERP system is likely to encounter significant resistance because of its comprehensiveness.

**43.** A manufacturing resource planning (MRP II) system

A. Performs the same back-office functions for a manufacturer as an ERP system.

B. Uses a master production schedule.

C. Lacks the forecasting and budgeting capabilities typical of an ERP system.

D. Performs the same front-office functions for a manufacturer as an ERP system.

Answer (B) is correct. *(Publisher)*
**REQUIRED:** The true statement about MRP II.
**DISCUSSION:** Manufacturing resource planning (MRP II) continued the evolution begun with MRP I. It is a closed-loop manufacturing system that integrates all facets of manufacturing, including production, sales, inventories, schedules, and cash flows. The same system is used for accounting and finance functions, which use the same transactions and numbers. MRP II uses an MPS (master production schedule), a statement of the anticipated manufacturing schedule for selected items for selected periods. MRP also uses the MPS. Thus, MRP is a component of an MRP II system.
Answer (A) is incorrect because an MRP II system does not integrate all the subsystems internal to the organization (back-office functions), such as human resources and customer service. Answer (C) is incorrect because MRP II includes forecasting and planning capacities for generating cash and other budgets. Answer (D) is incorrect because MRP, MRP II and traditional ERP do not provide for front-office functions, that is, connections with customers, suppliers, owners, creditors, and strategic allies.

**44.** In a traditional ERP system, the receipt of a customer order may result in

I. Customer tracking of the order's progress

II. Automatic replenishment of inventory by a supplier

III. Hiring or reassigning of employees

IV. Automatic adjustment of output schedules

A. I, II, and IV only.

B. I and III only.

C. III and IV only.

D. I, II, III, and IV.

Answer (C) is correct. *(Publisher)*
**REQUIRED:** The possible effects of receipt of a customer order by a traditional ERP system.
**DISCUSSION:** The traditional ERP system is one in which subsystems share data and coordinate their activities. Thus, if marketing receives an order, it can quickly verify that inventory is sufficient to notify shipping to process the order. Otherwise, production is notified to manufacture more of the product, with a consequent automatic adjustment of output schedules. If materials are inadequate for this purpose, the system will issue a purchase order. If more labor is needed, human resources will be instructed to reassign or hire employees. However, the subsystems in a traditional ERP system are internal to the organization. Hence, they are often called back-office functions. The information produced is principally (but not exclusively) intended for internal use by the organization's managers.
The current generation of ERP software (ERP II) has added front-office functions. Consequently, ERP II but not traditional ERP is capable of customer tracking of the order's progress and automatic replenishment of inventory by a supplier.

**45.** What are the possible characteristics of a client-server configuration in a current ERP system?

I.   Thin clients, local area network, single server

II.  Fat clients, wide area network, multiple servers

III. Fat clients, connection via Internet, and single server

   A.   I, II, and III.

   B.   II and III only.

   C.   II only.

   D.   I only.

Answer (A) is correct.   *(Publisher)*
**REQUIRED:** The elements of a client-server configuration in a current ERP system.
**DISCUSSION:** Current ERP systems have a client-server configuration with, possibly, scores or hundreds of client (user) computers. Clients may be thin or fat. So-called thin clients have little processing ability, but fat clients may have substantial processing power. The system may have multiple servers to run applications and contain databases. The network architecture may be in the form of a local area network (LAN) or wide area network (WAN), or users may connect with the server(s) via the Internet. An ERP system may use almost any of the available operating systems and database management systems.
Answer (B) is incorrect because an ERP system also may have thin clients connected via a LAN. Answer (C) is incorrect because an ERP system also may have thin clients connected via a LAN or the Internet with one server. Answer (D) is incorrect because an ERP system also may have fat clients connected via a WAN or the Internet to multiple servers.

**46.** A principal advantage of an ERP system is

   A.   Program-data dependence.

   B.   Data redundancy.

   C.   Separate data updating for different functions.

   D.   Centralization of data.

Answer (D) is correct.   *(Publisher)*
**REQUIRED:** The principal advantage of an ERP system.
**DISCUSSION:** An advantage of an ERP system is the elimination of data redundancy through the use of a central database. In principle, information about an item of data is stored once, and all functions have access to it. Thus, when the item (such as a price) is updated, the change is effectively made for all functions. The result is reliability (data integrity).
Answer (A) is incorrect because an ERP system uses a central database and a database management system. A fundamental characteristic of a database is that applications are independent of the physical structure of the database. Writing programs or designing applications to use the database requires only the names of desired data items, not their locations. Answer (B) is incorrect because an ERP system eliminates data redundancy. Answer (C) is incorrect because an ERP system is characterized by one-time data updating for all organizational functions.

**47.** The current generation of ERP software (ERP II) has added front-office functions like

   A.   Inventory control.

   B.   Human resources.

   C.   Purchasing.

   D.   Customer service.

Answer (D) is correct.   *(Publisher)*
**REQUIRED:** The front-office function addressed by ERP II.
**DISCUSSION:** The current generation of ERP software (ERP II) has added front-office functions. Customer relationship management applications in ERP II extend to customer service, finance-related matters, sales, and database creation and maintenance. Integrated data are helpful in better understanding customer needs, such as product preference or location of retail outlets. Thus, the organization may be able to optimize its sales forecasts, product line, and inventory levels.
Answer (A) is incorrect because inventory control is a back-office function. Answer (B) is incorrect because human resources is a back-office function. Answer (C) is incorrect because purchasing is a back-office function.

**48.** The current generation of ERP software (ERP II) may include an advanced planning and scheduling system that

    A. Determining the location of retail outlets.

    B. Connecting the organization with other members of a joint venture.

    C. Controls the flow of a manufacturer's materials and components through the supply chain.

    D. Permits tracking of orders by customers.

Answer (C) is correct. *(Publisher)*
**REQUIRED:** The function of an advanced planning and scheduling system.
**DISCUSSION:** An advanced planning and scheduling system may be an element of a supply chain management application for a manufacturer. It controls the flow of materials and components within the chain. Schedules are created given projected costs, lead times, and inventories.
    Answer (A) is incorrect because customer relationship management applications in ERP II extend to customer service, finance-related matters, sales, and database creation and maintenance. Integrated data are helpful in better understanding customer needs, such as product preference or location of retail outlets. Answer (B) is incorrect because partner relationship management applications connect the organization not only with such partners as customers and suppliers but also with owners, creditors, and strategic allies (for example, other members of a joint venture). Answer (D) is incorrect because an advanced planning scheduling system is used by a manufacturer to control flows through the supply chain. Other software permits customers to obtain information about order availability.

## 10.6 Malicious Software and Attacks

**49.** Which of the following is a computer program that appears to be legitimate but performs some illicit activity when it is run?

    A. Hoax virus.

    B. Web crawler.

    C. Trojan horse.

    D. Killer application.

Answer (C) is correct. *(CPA, adapted)*
**REQUIRED:** The apparently legitimate computer program that performs an illicit activity.
**DISCUSSION:** A Trojan horse is a computer program that appears friendly, for example, a game, but that actually contains an application destructive to the computer system.
    Answer (A) is incorrect because a hoax virus is a false notice about the existence of a computer virus. It is usually disseminated through use of distribution lists and is sent by e-mail or via an internal network. Answer (B) is incorrect because a web crawler (a spider or bot) is a computer program created to access and read information on websites. The results are included as entries in the index of a search engine. Answer (D) is incorrect because a killer application is one that is so useful that it may justify widespread adoption of a new technology.

**50.** The best preventive measure against a computer virus is to

    A. Compare software in use with authorized versions of the software.

    B. Execute virus exterminator programs periodically on the system.

    C. Allow only authorized software from known sources to be used on the system.

    D. Prepare and test a plan for recovering from the incidence of a virus.

Answer (C) is correct. *(CIA, adapted)*
**REQUIRED:** The best preventative measure against a computer virus.
**DISCUSSION:** Preventive controls are designed to prevent errors before they occur. Detective and corrective controls attempt to identify and correct errors. Preventive controls are usually more cost beneficial than detective or corrective controls. Allowing only authorized software from known sources to be used on the system is a preventive measure. The authorized software from known sources is expected to be free of viruses.
    Answer (A) is incorrect because comparing software with authorized versions is a detective control used to determine whether only authorized versions of the software are being used on the system. Answer (B) is incorrect because executing virus exterminator programs is a corrective control against a computer virus. Answer (D) is incorrect because preparing and testing a plan for virus recovery is a corrective control against a computer virus.

**51.** Managers at a consumer products company purchased personal computer software from only recognized vendors, and prohibited employees from installing nonauthorized software on their personal computers. To minimize the likelihood of computer viruses infecting any of its systems, the company should also

    A. Restore infected systems with authorized versions.

    B. Recompile infected programs from source code backups.

    C. Institute program change control procedures.

    D. Test all new software on a stand-alone personal computer.

Answer (D) is correct. *(CIA, adapted)*
    **REQUIRED:** The best protection against viruses.
    **DISCUSSION:** Software from recognized sources should be tested in quarantine (for example, in a test/development machine or a stand-alone personal computer) because even vendor-supplied software may be infected with viruses. The software should be run with a vaccine program and tested for the existence of logic bombs, etc.
    Answer (A) is incorrect because, if viruses infect a system, the company should restore the system with authorized software, but this procedure does not minimize the likelihood of initial infection. Answer (B) is incorrect because, if viruses infect programs that the company created, it should recompile the programs from source code backups, but this procedure does not minimize the likelihood of initial infection. Answer (C) is incorrect because instituting program change control procedures is good practice but does not minimize the likelihood of the system's being infected initially.

**52.** Which of the following is an indication that a computer virus is present?

    A. Frequent power surges that harm computer equipment.

    B. Unexplainable losses of or changes to data.

    C. Inadequate backup, recovery, and contingency plans.

    D. Numerous copyright violations due to unauthorized use of purchased software.

Answer (B) is correct. *(CIA, adapted)*
    **REQUIRED:** The indicator of a computer virus.
    **DISCUSSION:** The effects of computer viruses range from harmless messages to complete destruction of all data within the system. A symptom of a virus would be the unexplained loss of or change to data.
    Answer (A) is incorrect because power surges are caused by hardware or power supply problems. Answer (C) is incorrect because inadequate back-up, recovery, and contingency plans are operating policy weaknesses. Answer (D) is incorrect because copyright violations represent policy or compliance problems.

**53.** Which of the following operating procedures increases an organization's exposure to computer viruses?

    A. Encryption of data files.

    B. Frequent backup of files.

    C. Downloading public-domain software from websites.

    D. Installing original copies of purchased software on hard disk drives.

Answer (C) is correct. *(CIA, adapted)*
    **REQUIRED:** The procedure that increases exposure to viruses.
    **DISCUSSION:** Viruses are spread through shared data. Downloading public-domain software carries a risk that contaminated data may enter the computer.
    Answer (A) is incorrect because viruses are spread through the distribution of contaminated programs. Answer (B) is incorrect because backing up files does not increase the chances of a virus entering the computer system. Answer (D) is incorrect because original copies of purchased software on hard disk drives should be free of viruses.

**54.** An organization installed antivirus software on all its personal computers. The software was designed to prevent initial infections, stop replication attempts, detect infections after their occurrence, mark affected system components, and remove viruses from infected components. The major risk in relying on antivirus software is that antivirus software may

    A. Not detect certain viruses.

    B. Make software installation overly complex.

    C. Interfere with system operations.

    D. Consume too many system resources.

Answer (A) is correct. *(CIA, adapted)*
    **REQUIRED:** The major risk in relying on antivirus software.
    **DISCUSSION:** Antivirus software designed to identify and remove known viruses is sometimes known as a vaccine. A vaccine works only for known viruses and may not be effective for variants of those viruses or new viruses.
    Answer (B) is incorrect because having antivirus software is unlikely to make software installation overly complex. Answer (C) is incorrect because antivirus software need not interfere with system operations. Its execution can be scheduled in advance so as not to interfere with running programs. Answer (D) is incorrect because antivirus software can be set to execute at times when it would not consume too many system resources, e.g., at startup.

**55.** What is the best course of action to take if a program takes longer than usual to load or execute?

A. Test the system by running a different application program.

B. Reboot the system.

C. Run antivirus software.

D. Back up the hard disk files to floppies.

Answer (C) is correct.   *(CIA, adapted)*
**REQUIRED:** The best thing a microcomputer user should do if a program takes longer than usual to load or execute.
**DISCUSSION:** The described condition is a symptom of a virus. Many viruses will spread and cause additional damage. Use of an appropriate antivirus program may identify and even eliminate a viral infection. Ways to minimize computer virus risk in a networked system include restricted access, regularly updated passwords, periodic testing of systems with virus detection software, and the use of anti-virus software on all shareware prior to introducing it into the network.
Answer (A) is incorrect because running a different program as a test may cause the virus to spread and do additional damage. Answer (B) is incorrect because rebooting the system may cause the virus to spread and do additional damage. Answer (D) is incorrect because backing up hard disk files may cause the virus to spread and do additional damage.

**56.** Six months after a disgruntled systems programmer was fired and passwords disabled, the company's mainframe computer was brought to a halt when it suddenly erased all of its own files and software. The most likely way the programmer accomplished this was by

A. Returning to the computer center after 6 months.

B. Planting a computer virus through the use of telephone access.

C. Having an accomplice in the computer center.

D. Implanting a virus in the operating system and executing it via a back door.

Answer (D) is correct.   *(CIA, adapted)*
**REQUIRED:** The most likely way the programmer caused the files and software to be erased.
**DISCUSSION:** Viruses are a form of computer sabotage. They are programs hidden within other programs that have the capacity to duplicate themselves and infect other systems. Sharing of storage media or participation in computer networks creates exposure to viruses. Viruses may result in actions ranging from harmless pranks to erasure of files and programs. A back door is a shortcut created in an operating system that permits a programmer simple access to the system.
Answer (A) is incorrect because the programmer would most likely be denied access to the center. Answer (B) is incorrect because the programmer would not know the necessary passwords. Answer (C) is incorrect because collusion is less likely than individual wrongdoing.

**57.** Because of competitive pressures to be more responsive to their customers, some organizations have connected their internal personal computer networks through a host computer to outside networks. A risk of this practice is that

A. Viruses may gain entry to one or more company systems.

B. Uploaded files may not be properly edited and validated.

C. Data downloaded to the personal computers may not be sufficiently timely.

D. Software maintenance on the personal computers may become more costly.

Answer (A) is correct.   *(CIA, adapted)*
**REQUIRED:** The risk of connecting internal computer networks to outside networks.
**DISCUSSION:** Viruses are harmful programs that disrupt memory and processing functions and may destroy data. They spread from network to network, from infected diskettes, or from infected machines. Hence, connecting all networked personal computers through a host computer to outside networks increases the exposure of all of a company's computers to viruses.
Answer (B) is incorrect because whether uploaded files are properly edited and validated is independent of whether external links to other networks exist. Answer (C) is incorrect because whether data downloaded to the personal computers is sufficiently timely is independent of whether external links to other networks exist. Answer (D) is incorrect because whether software maintenance on the personal computers becomes more costly is independent of whether external links to other networks exist.

**58.** Attacks on computer networks may take many forms. Which of the following uses the computers of innocent parties infected with Trojan horse programs?

A. A distributed denial-of-service attack.

B. A man-in-the-middle attack.

C. A brute-force attack.

D. A password-cracking attack.

Answer (A) is correct.   *(Publisher)*
**REQUIRED:** The type of attack on a computer network that uses the computers of innocent parties infected with Trojan horse programs.
**DISCUSSION:** A denial-of-service (DOS) attack is an attempt to overload a system (e.g., a network or Web server) with false messages so that it cannot function (a system crash). A distributed DOS attack comes from multiple sources, for example, the machines of innocent parties infected by Trojan horses. When activated, these programs send messages to the target and leave the connection open. A DOS may establish as many network connections as possible to exclude other users, overload primary memory, or corrupt file systems.
Answer (B) is incorrect because a man-in-the-middle attack takes advantage of network packet sniffing and routing and transport protocols to access packets flowing through a network. Answer (C) is incorrect because a brute-force attack uses password cracking software to try large numbers of letter and number combinations to access a network. Answer (D) is incorrect because password-cracking software is used to access a network by using a large number of letter and number combinations.

**59.** Spoofing is one type of online activity used to launch malicious attacks. Spoofing is

A. Trying large numbers of letter and number combinations to access a network.

B. Eavesdropping on information sent by a user to the host computer of a website.

C. Accessing packets flowing through a network.

D. Identity misrepresentation in cyberspace.

Answer (D) is correct.   *(Publisher)*
**REQUIRED:** The nature of spoofing.
**DISCUSSION:** Passwords, user account numbers, and other information may be stolen using techniques such as Trojan horses, IP spoofing, and packet sniffers. Spoofing is identity misrepresentation in cyberspace, for example, by using a false website to obtain information about visitors.
Answer (A) is incorrect because a brute-force attack uses password cracking software to try large numbers of letter and number combinations to access a network. Answer (B) is incorrect because sniffing is use of software to eavesdrop on information sent by a user to the host computer of a website. Answer (C) is incorrect because a man-in-the-middle attack takes advantage of network packet sniffing and routing and transport protocols to access packets flowing through a network.

**60.** An organization's computer system should have an intrusion detection system (IDS) if it has external connections. An IDS

A. Must monitor every call on the system as it occurs.

B. May examine only packets with certain signatures.

C. Uses only knowledge-based detection.

D. Uses only behavior-based detection.

Answer (B) is correct.   *(Publisher)*
**REQUIRED:** The way in which an IDS functions.
**DISCUSSION:** A network IDS works by using sensors to examine packets traveling on the network. Each sensor monitors only the segment of the network to which it is attached. A packet is examined if it matches a signature. String signatures (certain strings of text) are potential signs of attack. Port signatures alert the IDS that a point subject to frequent intrusion attempts may be under attack. A header signature is a suspicious combination in a packet header.
Answer (A) is incorrect because a host IDS provides maximum protection only when the software is installed on each computer. It may operate in the following ways: The aggressive response is to monitor every call on the operating system and application as it occurs. A less effective method of preventing attacks is analysis of access log files. A host IDS may also identify questionable processes and verify the security of system files. Answer (C) is incorrect because an IDS is not limited to knowledge-based detection. Knowledge-based detection is based on information about the system's weaknesses and searches for intrusions that take advantage of them. Answer (D) is incorrect because an IDS is not limited to behavior-based detection. Behavior-based detection presumes that an attack will cause an observable anomaly. Actual and normal system behavior (a model of expected operations) are compared. A discrepancy results in an alert.

# APPENDIX A
# THE IIA CONTENT SPECIFICATION OUTLINES (CSOs)

We have reproduced The IIA's Content Specification Outlines (CSOs) verbatim from their website (www.theiia.org) for your convenience. Please visit The IIA's website for updates and more information about the exam. Rely on the Gleim book and software to pass each part of the exam. We have researched and studied The IIA's CSOs as well as questions from prior exams to provide you with an excellent review program.

### PART I – THE INTERNAL AUDIT ACTIVITY'S ROLE IN GOVERNANCE, RISK, AND CONTROL

A.   **COMPLY WITH THE IIA'S ATTRIBUTE STANDARDS (15 - 25%)** (proficiency level)

1.   Define purpose, authority, and responsibility of the internal audit activity.

   a.   Determine if purpose, authority, and responsibility of internal audit activity are clearly documented/approved.

   b.   Determine if purpose, authority, and responsibility of internal audit activity are communicated to engagement clients.

   c.   Demonstrate an understanding of the purpose, authority, and responsibility of the internal audit activity.

2.   Maintain independence and objectivity.

   a.   Foster independence.

      1)   Understand organizational independence.
      2)   Recognize the importance of organizational independence.
      3)   Determine if the internal audit activity is properly aligned to achieve organizational independence.

   b.   Foster objectivity.

      1)   Establish policies to promote objectivity.
      2)   Assess individual objectivity.
      3)   Maintain individual objectivity.
      4)   Recognize and mitigate impairments to independence and objectivity.

3.   Determine if the required knowledge, skills, and competencies are available.

   a.   Understand the knowledge, skills, and competencies that an internal auditor needs to possess.

   b.   Identify the knowledge, skills, and competencies required to fulfill the responsibilities of the internal audit activity.

4.   Develop and/or procure necessary knowledge, skills, and competencies collectively required by internal audit activity.

5.   Exercise due professional care.

6.   Promote continuing professional development.

   a.   Develop and implement a plan for continuing professional development for internal audit staff.
   b.   Enhance individual competency through continuing professional development.

7.   Promote quality assurance and improvement of the internal audit activity.

   a.   Establish and maintain a quality assurance and improvement program.

   b.   Monitor the effectiveness of the quality assurance and improvement program.

   c.   Report the results of the quality assurance and improvement program to the board or other governing body.

   d.   Conduct quality assurance procedures and recommend improvements to the performance of the internal audit activity.

8.   Abide by and promote compliance with The IIA Code of Ethics.

B.  **ESTABLISH A RISK-BASED PLAN TO DETERMINE THE PRIORITIES OF THE INTERNAL AUDIT ACTIVITY (15 - 25%)** (proficiency level)

    1.   Establish a framework for assessing risk.
    2.   Use the framework to:

        a.   Identify sources of potential engagements (e.g., audit universe, management request, regulatory mandate)
        b.   Assess organization-wide risk
        c.   Solicit potential engagement topics from various sources
        d.   Collect and analyze data on proposed engagements
        e.   Rank and validate risk priorities

    3.   Identify internal audit resource requirements.
    4.   Coordinate the internal audit activity's efforts with:

        a.   External auditor
        b.   Regulatory oversight bodies
        c.   Other internal assurance functions (e.g., health and safety department)

    5.   Select engagements.

        a.   Participate in the engagement selection process.
        b.   Select engagements.
        c.   Communicate and obtain approval of the engagement plan from board.

C.  **UNDERSTAND THE INTERNAL AUDIT ACTIVITY'S ROLE IN ORGANIZATIONAL GOVERNANCE (10 - 20%)** (proficiency level)

    1.   Obtain board's approval of audit charter.
    2.   Communicate plan of engagements.
    3.   Report significant audit issues.
    4.   Communicate key performance indicators to board on a regular basis.
    5.   Discuss areas of significant risk.
    6.   Support board in enterprise-wide risk assessment.
    7.   Review positioning of the internal audit function within the risk management framework within the organization.
    8.   Monitor compliance with the corporate code of conduct/business practices.
    9.   Report on the effectiveness of the control framework.
    10.  Assist board in assessing the independence of the external auditor.
    11.  Assess ethical climate of the board.
    12.  Assess ethical climate of the organization.
    13.  Assess compliance with policies in specific areas (e.g., derivatives).
    14.  Assess organization's reporting mechanism to the board.
    15.  Conduct follow-up and report on management response to regulatory body reviews.
    16.  Conduct follow-up and report on management response to external audit.
    17.  Assess the adequacy of the performance measurement system, achievement of corporate objective.
    18.  Support a culture of fraud awareness and encourage the reporting of improprieties.

D.  **PERFORM OTHER INTERNAL AUDIT ROLES AND RESPONSIBILITIES (0 - 10%)** (proficiency level)

    1.   Ethics/compliance

        a.   Investigate and recommend resolution for ethics/compliance complaints.
        b.   Determine disposition of ethics violations.
        c.   Foster healthy ethical climate.
        d.   Maintain and administer business conduct policy (e.g., conflict of interest).
        e.   Report on compliance.

    2.   Risk management

        a.   Develop and implement an organization-wide risk and control framework.
        b.   Coordinate enterprise-wide risk assessment.
        c.   Report corporate risk assessment to board.
        d.   Review business continuity planning process.

    3.   Privacy

        a.   Determine privacy vulnerabilities.
        b.   Report on compliance.

    4.   Information or physical security

        a.   Determine security vulnerabilities.
        b.   Determine disposition of security violations.
        c.   Report on compliance.

E.   **GOVERNANCE, RISK, AND CONTROL KNOWLEDGE ELEMENTS (15 - 25%)**

1.   Corporate governance principles (awareness level)
2.   Alternative control frameworks (awareness level)
3.   Risk vocabulary and concepts (proficiency level)
4.   Risk management techniques (proficiency level)
5.   Risk/control implications of different organizational structures (proficiency level)
6.   Risk/control implications of different leadership styles (awareness level)
7.   Change management (awareness level)
8.   Conflict management (awareness level)
9.   Management control techniques (proficiency level)
10.  Types of control (preventive, detective, input, output) (proficiency level)

F.   **PLAN ENGAGEMENTS (15 - 25%)** (proficiency level)

1.   Initiate preliminary communication with engagement client.
2.   Conduct a preliminary survey of the area of engagement.

     a.   Obtain input from engagement client.
     b.   Perform analytical reviews.
     c.   Perform benchmarking.
     d.   Conduct interviews.
     e.   Review prior audit reports and other relevant documentation.
     f.   Map processes.
     g.   Develop checklists.

3.   Complete a detailed risk assessment of the area (prioritize or evaluate risk/control factors).
4.   Coordinate audit engagement efforts with

     a.   External auditor
     b.   Regulatory oversight bodies

5.   Establish/refine engagement objectives and identify/finalize the scope of engagement.
6.   Identify or develop criteria for assurance engagements (criteria against which to audit).
7.   Consider the potential for fraud when planning an engagement.

     a.   Be knowledgeable of the risk factors and red flags of fraud.
     b.   Identify common types of fraud associated with the engagement area.
     c.   Determine if risk of fraud requires special consideration when conducting an engagement.

8.   Determine engagement procedures.
9.   Determine the level of staff and resources needed for the engagement.
10.  Establish adequate planning and supervision of the engagement.
11.  Prepare engagement work program.

FORMAT:  125 Multiple-choice questions

## PART II – CONDUCTING THE INTERNAL AUDIT ENGAGEMENT

A.   **CONDUCT ENGAGEMENTS (25 - 35%)** (proficiency level)

1.   Research and apply appropriate standards:

     a.   IIA Professional Practices Framework (Code of Ethics, Standards, and Practice Advisories)
     b.   Other professional, legal, and regulatory standards

2.   Maintain an awareness of potential for fraud when conducting an engagement.

     a.   Notice indicators or symptoms of fraud.
     b.   Design appropriate engagement steps to address significant risk of fraud.
     c.   Employ audit tests to detect fraud.
     d.   Determine if any suspected fraud merits investigation.

3.   Collect data.
4.   Evaluate the relevance, sufficiency, and competence of evidence.
5.   Analyze and interpret data.
6.   Develop workpapers.
7.   Review workpapers.
8.   Communicate interim progress.
9.   Draw conclusions.
10.  Develop recommendations when appropriate.

11.    Report engagement results.

    a.    Conduct exit conference.
    b.    Prepare report or other communication.
    c.    Approve engagement report.
    d.    Determine distribution of report.
    e.    Obtain management response to report.

12.    Conduct client satisfaction survey.
13.    Complete performance appraisals of engagement staff.

**B.    CONDUCT SPECIFIC ENGAGEMENTS (25 - 35%)** (proficiency level)

1.    Conduct assurance engagements.

    a.    Fraud investigation

        1)    Determine appropriate parties to be involved with investigation.
        2)    Establish facts and extent of fraud (e.g., interviews, interrogations, and data analysis).
        3)    Report outcomes to appropriate parties.
        4)    Complete a process review to improve controls to prevent fraud and recommend changes.

    b.    Risk and control self-assessment

        1)    Facilitated approach

            a)    Client-facilitated
            b)    Audit-facilitated

        2)    Questionnaire approach
        3)    Self-certification approach

    c.    Audits of third parties and contract auditing
    d.    Quality audit engagements
    e.    Due diligence audit engagements
    f.    Security audit engagements
    g.    Privacy audit engagements
    h.    Performance (key performance indicators) audit engagements
    i.    Operational (efficiency and effectiveness) audit engagements
    j.    Financial audit engagements
    k.    Information technology (IT) audit engagements

        1)    Operating systems

            a)    Mainframe
            b)    Workstations
            c)    Server

        2)    Application development

            a)    Application authentication
            b)    Systems development methodology
            c)    Change control
            d)    End user computing

        3)    Data and network communications/connections (e.g., LAN, VAN, and WAN)
        4)    Voice communications
        5)    System security (e.g., firewalls, access control)
        6)    Contingency planning
        7)    Databases
        8)    Functional areas of IT operations (e.g., data center operations)
        9)    Web infrastructure
        10)    Software licensing
        11)    Electronic Funds Transfer (EFT)/Electronic Data Interchange (EDI)
        12)    E-Commerce
        13)    Information protection/viruses
        14)    Encryption
        15)    Enterprise-wide resource planning (ERP) software (e.g., SAP R/3)

    l.    Compliance audit engagements

2.    Conduct consulting engagements.

    a.    Internal control training
    b.    Business process review
    c.    Benchmarking
    d.    Information technology (IT) and systems development
    e.    Design of performance measurement systems

C. **MONITOR ENGAGEMENT OUTCOMES (5 - 15%)** (proficiency level)

    1. Determine appropriate follow-up activity by the internal audit activity
    2. Identify appropriate method to monitor engagement outcomes
    3. Conduct follow-up activity
    4. Communicate monitoring plan and results

D. **FRAUD KNOWLEDGE ELEMENTS (5 - 15%)**

    1. Discovery sampling (awareness level)
    2. Interrogation techniques (awareness level)
    3. Forensic auditing (awareness level)
    4. Use of computers in analyzing data (awareness level)
    5. Red flag (proficiency level)
    6. Types of fraud (proficiency level)

E. **ENGAGEMENT TOOLS (15 - 25%)**

    1. Sampling (awareness level)

        a. Nonstatistical (judgmental)
        b. Statistical

    2. Statistical analyses (process control techniques) (awareness level)
    3. Data gathering tools (proficiency level)

        a. Interviewing
        b. Questionnaires
        c. Checklists

    4. Analytical review techniques (proficiency level)

        a. Ratio estimation
        b. Variance analysis (e.g., budget vs. actual)
        c. Other reasonableness tests

    5. Observation (proficiency level)
    6. Problem solving (proficiency level)
    7. Risk and control self-assessment (CSA) (awareness level)
    8. Computerized audit tools and techniques (proficiency level)

        a. Embedded audit modules
        b. Data extraction techniques
        c. Generalized audit software (e.g., ACL, IDEA)
        d. Spreadsheet analysis
        e. Automated workpapers (e.g., Lotus Notes, Auditor Assistant)

    9. Process mapping including flowcharting (proficiency level)

FORMAT: 125 multiple-choice questions

## PART III – BUSINESS ANALYSIS AND INFORMATION TECHNOLOGY

A. **BUSINESS PROCESSES (15 - 25%)**

    1. Quality management (e.g., TQM) (awareness level)
    2. The International Organization for Standardization (ISO) framework (awareness level)
    3. Forecasting (awareness level)
    4. Project management techniques (proficiency level)
    5. Business process analysis (e.g., workflow analysis and bottleneck management, theory of constraints) (proficiency level)
    6. Inventory management techniques and concepts (proficiency level)
    7. Marketing- pricing objectives and policies (awareness level)
    8. Marketing- supply chain management (awareness level)
    9. Human Resources (individual performance management and measurement, supervision, environmental factors that affect performance, facilitation techniques, personnel sourcing/staffing, training and development, and safety) (proficiency level)
    10. Balanced Scorecard (awareness level)

B. **FINANCIAL ACCOUNTING AND FINANCE (15 - 25%)**

    1. Basic concepts and underlying principles of financial accounting (statements, terminology, relationships) (proficiency level)
    2. Intermediate concepts of financial accounting (e.g., bonds, leases, pensions, intangible assets, R&D) (awareness level)
    3. Advanced concepts of financial accounting (e.g., consolidation, partnerships, foreign currency transactions) (awareness level)

4.    Financial statement analysis (proficiency level)
5.    Cost of capital evaluation (awareness level)
6.    Types of debt and equity (awareness level)
7.    Financial instruments (e.g., derivatives) (awareness level)
8.    Cash management (treasury functions) (awareness level)
9.    Valuation models (awareness level)

   a.    Inventory valuation
   b.    Business valuation

10.    Business development life cycles (awareness level)

C.    **MANAGERIAL ACCOUNTING (10 - 20%)**

1.    Cost concepts (e.g., absorption, variable, fixed) (proficiency level)
2.    Capital budgeting (awareness level)
3.    Operating budget (proficiency level)
4.    Transfer pricing (awareness level)
5.    Cost-volume-profit analysis (awareness level)
6.    Relevant cost (awareness level)
7.    Costing systems (e.g., activity-based, standard) (awareness level)
8.    Responsibility accounting (awareness level)

D.    **REGULATORY, LEGAL, AND ECONOMICS (5 - 15%)** (awareness level)

1.    Impact of government legislation and regulation on business
2.    Trade legislation and regulations
3.    Taxation schemes
4.    Contracts
5.    Nature and rules of legal evidence
6.    Key economic indicators

E.    **INFORMATION TECHNOLOGY (IT) (30 - 40%)** (awareness level)

1.    Control frameworks (e.g., SAC, COBIT)
2.    Data and network communications/connections (e.g., LAN, VAN, and WAN)
3.    Electronic funds transfer (EFT)
4.    E-Commerce
5.    Electronic data interchange (EDI)
6.    Functional areas of IT operations (e.g., data center operations)
7.    Encryption
8.    Viruses
9.    Information protection
10.    Evaluate investment in IT (cost of ownership)
11.    Enterprise-wide resource planning (ERP) software (e.g., SAP R/3, Peoplesoft)
12.    Operating systems
13.    Application development
14.    Voice communications
15.    Contingency planning
16.    Systems security (e.g., firewalls, access control)
17.    Databases
18.    Software licensing
19.    Web infrastructure

FORMAT:  125 multiple-choice questions

**PART IV – BUSINESS MANAGEMENT SKILLS**

A.    **STRATEGIC MANAGEMENT (20 - 30%)** (awareness level)

1.    Global analytical techniques

   a.    Structural analysis of industries
   b.    Competitive strategies (e.g., Porter's model)
   c.    Competitive analysis
   d.    Market signals
   e.    Industry evolution

2.    Industry environments

   a.    Competitive strategies related to:

      1)    Fragmented industries
      2)    Emerging industries
      3)    Declining industries

        b.    Competition in global industries

           1)    Sources/impediments
           2)    Evolution of global markets
           3)    Strategic alternatives
           4)    Trends affecting competition

    3.    Strategic decisions

        a.    Analysis of integration strategies
        b.    Capacity expansion
        c.    Entry into new businesses

    4.    Portfolio techniques of competitive analysis
    5.    Product life cycles

B.  **GLOBAL BUSINESS ENVIRONMENTS (15 - 25%)** (awareness level)

    1.    Cultural/legal/political environments

        a.    Balancing global requirements and local imperatives
        b.    Global mindsets (personal characteristics/competencies)
        c.    Sources and methods for managing complexities and contradictions
        d.    Managing multicultural teams

    2.    Economic/financial environments

        a.    Global, multinational, international, and multilocal compared and contrasted
        b.    Requirements for entering the global market place
        c.    Creating organizational adaptability
        d.    Managing training and development

C.  **ORGANIZATIONAL BAHAVIOR (20 - 30%)** (awareness level)

    1.    Motivation

        a.    Relevance and implication of various theories
        b.    Impact of job design, rewards, work schedules, etc.

    2.    Communication

        a.    The process
        b.    Organizational dynamics
        c.    Impact of computerization

    3.    Performance

        a.    Productivity
        b.    Effectiveness

    4.    Structure

        a.    Centralized/decentralized
        b.    Departmentalization
        c.    New configurations (e.g., hourglass, cluster, network)

D.  **MANAGEMENT SKILLS (20 - 30%)** (awareness level)

    1.    Group dynamics

        a.    Traits (cohesiveness, roles, norms, groupthink, etc.)
        b.    Stages of group development
        c.    Organizational politics
        d.    Criteria and determinants of effectiveness

    2.    Team building

        a.    Methods used in team building
        b.    Assessing team performance

    3.    Leadership skills

        a.    Theories compared/contrasted
        b.    Leadership grid (topology of leadership styles)
        c.    Mentoring

    4.    Personal time management

E.　**NEGOTIATING (5 - 15%)** (awareness level)

　　1.　Conflict resolution

　　　　a.　Competitive/cooperative
　　　　b.　Compromise, forcing, smoothing, etc.

　　2.　Added-value negotiating

　　　　a.　Description
　　　　b.　Specific steps

FORMAT:　125 multiple-choice questions

# APPENDIX B
# THE IIA EXAMINATION BIBLIOGRAPHY

The Institute has prepared a listing of references for the CIA exam, reproduced beginning below. These publications have been chosen by the Board of Regents as reasonably representative of the common body of knowledge for internal auditors. However, all of the information in these texts will not be tested. When possible, questions will be written based on the information contained in the suggested reference list. This bibliography is reorganized in an alphabetical listing by part to give you an overview of the scope of each part. The IIA also indicates that the examination scope includes

1. Articles from *Internal Auditor* (The IIA periodical)
2. IIA research reports
3. IIA pronouncements, e.g., The IIA Code of Ethics and SIASs
4. Past published CIA examinations

The IIA bibliography is reproduced for your information only. The texts you will need to acquire (use) to prepare for the CIA exam will depend on many factors, including

1. Innate ability
2. Length of time out of school
3. Thoroughness of your undergraduate education
4. Familiarity with internal auditing due to relevant experience

## SUGGESTED REFERENCES FOR THE CIA EXAM

### PART I: THE INTERNAL AUDIT ACTIVITY'S ROLE IN GOVERNANCE, RISK, AND CONTROL

Sawyer, et al, *Sawyer's Internal Auditing*, 5th Ed., The Institute of Internal Auditors.

OR Sears, *Internal Auditing Manual*, WG&L Financial Reporting & Management.

The American Institute of Certified Public Accountants, *Internal Control - Integrated Framework*, 1994.

The Institute of Internal Auditors, Inc., *Professional Practices Framework*, 2002.

OR *Other Control and Governance Frameworks*.

Supplemental:

Albrecht, Wernz, and Williams, *Fraud: Bringing Light to the Dark Side of Business*, Irwin Professional Publishing.

Murphy and Parker, *Handbook of IT Auditing*, Warren, Gorham & Lamont.

Reider, *Complete Guide to Operational Auditing*, John Wiley & Sons, Inc.

### PART II: CONDUCTING THE INTERNAL AUDIT ENGAGEMENT

Sawyer, et al, *Sawyer's Internal Auditing*, 5th Ed., The Institute of Internal Auditors.

OR Sears, *Internal Auditing Manual*, WG&L Financial Reporting & Management.

The Institute of Internal Auditors, Inc., *Professional Practices Framework*, 2002.

Supplemental:

Kreitner, *Management*, 9th Ed., Houghton Mifflin Co., 2004.

### PART III: BUSINESS ANALYSIS AND INFORMATION TECHNOLOGY

Information Systems and Control Foundation, *Cobit: Governance, Control, and Audit for Information and Related Technology*, 3rd Ed., 2000.

International Accounting Standards Committee, *International Accounting Standards*, 2002.

Kieso, Warfield, and Weygandt, *Intermediate Accounting*, 11th Ed., John Wiley & Sons, Inc., 2004.

Kreitner, *Management*, 9th Ed., Houghton Mifflin Co., 2004.

Sawyer, et al, *Sawyer's Internal Auditing*, 5th Ed., The Institute of Internal Auditors.

OR Sears, *Internal Auditing Manual*, WG&L Financial Reporting & Management.

The Institute of Internal Auditors Research Foundation, *Systems Assurance and Control*, 2003.

Weber, *Information Systems Control and Audit*, Prentice Hall, 1998.

## PART IV: BUSINESS MANAGEMENT SKILLS

Bruner, Eaker, Freeman, Spelkman, Teisberg, and Venkataraman, *The Portable MBA*, 4th Ed., John Wiley & Sons, 2002.

Fisher, Ury, and Patton, *Getting to Yes, Negotiating Agreement Without Giving In*, Penguin USA.

Hill, *International Business with Global Resource CD, Powerweb and World Map*, 4th Ed., McGraw-Hill/Irwin, 2002.

Kreitner, *Management*, 9th Ed., Houghton Mifflin Co., 2004.

Kotler, *Marketing Management*, 11th Ed., Prentice Hall, 2002.

## PUBLICATIONS AVAILABLE FROM THE IIA

The listing on the previous pages presents only some of the current technical literature available. Quantity discounts are provided. Inquiries should be sent to

Customer Service
Institute of Internal Auditors          Request a current catalog by mail or call
249 Maitland Avenue                           (407) 830-7600, ext. 1
Altamonte Springs, FL 32701-4201

Book orders can be placed directly by calling (877) 867-4957 (toll-free) or (770) 442-8633, extension 275.

## ORDERING TEXTUAL MATERIAL

The IIA does not carry all of the reference books. Write directly to the publisher if you cannot obtain the desired texts from your local bookstore. Begin your study program with *CIA Review*, Parts I through IV, which most candidates find sufficient. If you need additional reference material, borrow books from colleagues, professors, or a library.

Addison-Wesley Publishing Company
One Jacob Way
Reading, MA 01867

Basic Books, Inc.
Harper & Row Publishers
10 East 53rd Street
New York, NY 10022

Business Publications, Inc.
1700 Alma, Suite 390
Plano, TX 75075

The Dryden Press
One Salt Creek Lane
Hinsdale, IL 60521-2902

Harcourt Brace Jovanovich
1250 Sixth Avenue
San Diego, CA 92101

Harper & Row
10 East 53rd Street
New York, NY 10022

Holt, Rinehart, Winston
383 Madison Avenue
New York, NY 10017

Houghton Mifflin Company
One Beacon Street
Boston, MA 02108

Richard D. Irwin, Inc.
1818 Ridge Road
Homewood, IL 60430

Kent Publishing Company
20 Park Plaza
Boston, MA 02116

McGraw-Hill Book Company
1221 Avenue of the Americas
New York, NY 10020

Mitchell Publishing, Inc.
915 River Street
Santa Cruz, CA 95060

Prentice-Hall, Inc.
145 South Mt. Zion Road
Lebanon, TN 46052

Reston Publishing Company
11480 Sunset Hills Road
Reston, VA 22090

South-Western Publishing
Company
5101 Madison Road
Cincinnati, OH 45227

West Publishing Company
P.O. Box 55165
St. Paul, MN 55101

John Wiley & Sons, Inc.
605 Third Avenue
New York, NY 10016

# INDEX

## COMPLETE GLEIM CPA SYSTEM with REVIEW ONLINE

All 4 parts, including 5 books, 4 audios, CPA Test Prep software, **Review Online**[1], plus bonus book bag.

☐ $924.95   $_____

Also available by exam part
(Does not include book bag.)

| | | | | |
|---|---|---|---|---|
| Auditing ☐ $256.95 | | Business ☐ $256.95 | | |
| Financial ☐ $256.95 | | Regulation ☐ $256.95 | | $_____ |

## GLEIM CPA SET

All 4 parts, including 5 books, 4 audios, CPA Test Prep software, plus bonus book bag.

☐ $539.95   $_____

### CPA REVIEW

| | Online Simulations (included in Review Online) | Book/Software/ Audio Package Save 18% | Book/Software Package Save 16% | Audio Reviews | Software | Books | |
|---|---|---|---|---|---|---|---|
| Auditing | ☐ @$99.95 | ☐ @$143.95 | ☐ @$74.95 | ☐ @$89.95 | ☐ @$49.95 | ☐ @$39.95 | $_____ |
| Business | ☐ @$99.95 | ☐ @$143.95 | ☐ @$74.95 | ☐ @$89.95 | ☐ @$49.95 | ☐ @$39.95 | |
| Regulation | ☐ @$99.95 | ☐ @$143.95 | ☐ @$74.95 | ☐ @$89.95 | ☐ @$49.95 | ☐ @$39.95 | |
| Financial | ☐ @$99.95 | ☐ @$143.95 | ☐ @$74.95 | ☐ @$89.95 | ☐ @$49.95 | ☐ @$39.95 | |
| A System for Success | | ☐ @$19.95 (FREE with the purchase of any Gleim CPA Review book.) | | | | | _____ |

## COMPLETE GLEIM CMA/CFM SYSTEM

Includes: 5-part set (book, software, and audio), plus bonus book bag.

☐ $566.95   $_____

## GLEIM 4-Part Set

Includes: 4-part set (book, software, and audio), plus bonus book bag.   ☐ CMA@$453.95    ☐ CFM@$453.95   $_____

### CMA/CFM REVIEW

| | Book/Software/ Audio Package Save 15% | Book/Software Package Save 10% | Audio Reviews | Software | Books | |
|---|---|---|---|---|---|---|
| Part 1 Eco., Fin., & Mgmt. | ☐ @$120.95 | ☐ @$64.95 | ☐ @$69.95 | ☐ @$44.95 | ☐ @$26.95 | $_____ |
| Part 2CMA Fin. Acc. & Rep. | ☐ @$120.95 | ☐ @$64.95 | ☐ @$69.95 | ☐ @$44.95 | ☐ @$26.95 | |
| Part 2CFM Corp. Fin. Mgmt. | ☐ @$120.95 | ☐ @$64.95 | ☐ @$69.95 | ☐ @$44.95 | ☐ @$26.95 | |
| Part 3 Mgmt. Rep./Behav. Iss. | ☐ @$120.95 | ☐ @$64.95 | ☐ @$69.95 | ☐ @$44.95 | ☐ @$26.95 | |
| Part 4 Dec. Anal. & Info. Sys. | ☐ @$120.95 | ☐ @$64.95 | ☐ @$69.95 | ☐ @$44.95 | ☐ @$26.95 | |

### CIA REVIEW

| | Book/Software Package Save 10% | Software | Books | |
|---|---|---|---|---|
| All 4 Parts | ☐ @$279.80 | ☐ @$199.80 | ☐ @$119.80 | $_____ |
| Part I Internal Audit Role in Governance, Risk, & Control | ☐ @$69.95 | ☐ @$49.95 | ☐ @$29.95 | _____ |
| Part II Conducting the Internal Audit Engagement | ☐ @$69.95 | ☐ @$49.95 | ☐ @$29.95 | _____ |
| Part III Business Analysis and Information Technology | ☐ @$69.95 | ☐ @$49.95 | ☐ @$29.95 | _____ |
| Part IV Business Management Skills | ☐ @$69.95 | ☐ @$49.95 | ☐ @$29.95 | _____ |

### EA REVIEW

| | Book/Software Package Save 10% | Software | Books | |
|---|---|---|---|---|
| All 4 Parts | ☐ @$279.80 | ☐ @$199.80 | ☐ @$119.95 | $_____ |
| Part 1 Individuals | ☐ @$69.95 | ☐ @$49.95 | ☐ @$29.95 | _____ |
| Part 2 Sole Prop. & Partnerships | ☐ @$69.95 | ☐ @$49.95 | ☐ @$29.95 | _____ |
| Part 3 Corp./Fid./Est. & Gift Tax | ☐ @$69.95 | ☐ @$49.95 | ☐ @$29.95 | _____ |
| Part 4 IRS Adm/Other Topics | ☐ @$69.95 | ☐ @$49.95 | ☐ @$29.95 | _____ |

## "THE GLEIM SERIES" EXAM QUESTIONS AND EXPANATIONS BOOKS, SOFTWARE, AND CPE[2]

| | Book/Software Package (Save 25%) | Software | Books | Books & CPE | |
|---|---|---|---|---|---|
| Auditing & Systems | ☐ @$29.95 | ☐ @$20.00 | ☐ @$19.95 | ☐ @200.00 | $_____ |
| Business Law/Legal Studies | ☐ @$29.95 | ☐ @$20.00 | ☐ @$19.95 | | _____ |
| Federal Tax | ☐ @$29.95 | ☐ @$20.00 | ☐ @$19.95 | ☐ @200.00 | _____ |
| Financial Accounting | ☐ @$29.95 | ☐ @$20.00 | ☐ @$19.95 | ☐ @200.00 | _____ |
| Cost/Managerial Accounting | ☐ @$29.95 | ☐ @$20.00 | ☐ @$19.95 | | _____ |

[1]For more information on our **CPA Review Online,** please visit **www.gleim.com/CPAOL/**

[2]For our online **CPE** courses and course catalog, please visit **www.gleim.com/CPE/**

**SUBTOTAL**   $_____

Complete your order
on the next page.

# GLEIM Publications, Inc.

## P. O. Box 12848    Gainesville, FL 32604

TOLL FREE:    (888) 87-GLEIM

LOCAL:    (352) 375-0772

FAX:    (888) 375 -6940 (toll free)

INTERNET    www.gleim.com

E-MAIL:    sales@gleim.com

Customer service is available (Eastern Time):

8:00 a.m. - 7:00 p.m., Mon. - Fri.

9:00 a.m. - 2:00 p.m., Saturday

Please have your credit card ready,

or save time by ordering online!

**For audio purchases, please select:** ☐ CD    ☐ Cassette

**SUBTOTAL** (from previous page)    $_____

Add applicable sales tax for shipments within Florida.    _____

Shipping (nonrefundable): **First Item\* = $5; each additional item = $1**

\*Sets and package deals contain multiple items. Each book, audio, and software counts as 1 item; online courses have no shipping charges.

**TOTAL** $_____

Fax or write for prices/instructions on shipments outside the 48 contiguous states, or simply order online.

NAME (please print) _____

ADDRESS _____ Apt. _____
(street address required for UPS)

CITY _____ STATE _____ ZIP _____

____ MC/VISA/DISC    ____ Check/M.O.    Daytime Telephone (____) _____

Credit Card No. _____ - _____ - _____ - _____

Exp. _____ / _____    Signature _____
       Month / Year

E-mail address _____

1. We process and ship orders daily, within one business day over 98.8% of the time. Call by noon for same day service.
2. Please PHOTOCOPY this order form for others.
3. No CODs. Orders from individuals must be prepaid. Library and company orders may be purchased on account.
4. Gleim Publications, Inc. guarantees the immediate refund of all resalable texts and unopened software and audios if returned within 30 days. Applies only to items purchased direct from Gleim Publications, Inc. Our shipping charge is nonrefundable.
5. Components of specially priced package deals are nonrefundable.

Printed 11/03. Prices subject to change without notice.

For updates and other important information, visit our website.

**GLEIM**
KNOWLEDGE
TRANSFER
SYSTEMS

# www.gleim.com

Please forward your suggestions, corrections, and comments concerning typographical errors, etc., to **Irvin N. Gleim • c/o Gleim Publications, Inc. • P.O. Box 12848 • University Station • Gainesville, Florida • 32604.** Please include your name and address so we can properly thank you for your interest.

1. _____

2. _____

3. _____

4. _____

5. _____

6. _____

7. _____

8. _____

9. _____

10. _____

11. _____

12. _____

13. _____

14. _____

15. _____

16. _____

17. _____

18. _____

**Remember for superior service:**  Mail, e-mail, or fax questions about our books or software.
Telephone questions about orders, prices, shipments, or payments.

Name: _____

Address: _____

City/State/Zip: _____

Telephone:   Home: _____   Work: _____   Fax: _____

E-mail: _____